To the unwavering grace and faithfulness of God

and

To the family that He gifted me,
who make up the best parts of this story,
and without whom none of this was possible.

For my children and theirs to come.

WHAT OTHERS THOUGHT

endorsements for Jason T Smith and UNLIKELY

"Jason's memoir is both inspiring and informative. It is a peak under the hood of an authentic entrepreneur, exposing both his successes and failures. It is a gripping read – his honest and humble insights will motivate and equip anyone on their own entrepreneurial journey. Having also built a health franchise, I find the parallels uncanny. Enjoy the unexpected surprises in Jason's story, as I'm confident they will help you navigate your own."

Jack Gance
Co-Founder and Global Chairman, *Chemist Warehouse Franchise Group*
Australian Entrepreneur of the Year 2023

"It's hard to put this book down. It lifts from the page as you read it and takes you on a journey with a man intent on making his life count. What strikes me is Jason Smith's honesty, drive and integrity. I love the way his faith undergirds his business decision-making, even when the pressure is enormous. A must-read if you want to make your life, your work and your business thrive with an impact that matters."

Rev Tim Costello AO
Director, *Ethical Voice*
Former CEO, *World Vision Australia*
Rated Top 100 in Australia's National Living Treasures, *National Trust poll 2014*
Victorian of the Year 2004
Australian Peace Prize 2008

"Jason is a daring and authentic entrepreneur. And his story, as told in *UNLIKELY,* is a riveting expose on his enthralling breakthroughs and misadventures in life and business. Few people are willing to reveal this much, but Jason tells a relatable story by putting it all out there, creating a motivational guide for everyone with a dream and passion."

John Sikkema
Entrepreneur, Author, Coach, Speaker
National Director, *Halftime Australia*
Former Franchisor, *Garrisons Financial Services*

"Jason Smith's remarkable book should be compulsory reading for those who, not only have an entrepreneurial gene, but appreciate the higher purpose in all that we do. Indeed, it has gems in it for anyone exploring a call to create a better world. Jason could have simply recounted a story of the extraordinary growth of Back In Motion, but he elected instead to share with vivid candour the struggles and challenges that he experienced, underpinned by the constant themes of God's purpose and the centrality of family, especially his wife, Paulina. *UNLIKELY* will be addictive for many who read it. It is a wild ride, which at times can be exhausting, but I know that many will ultimately thank Jason for his intimate shares and for the impact this book will have on their lives."

Simon McKeon AO
Lawyer, Businessman, Philanthropist, Sportsman
Chancellor, *Monash University*
Director, *Rio Tinto* and *National Australia Bank*
Former Executive Chairman, *Macquarie Bank*
Australian of the Year 2011

"*UNLIKELY* is an authentic and accessible leadership story for those looking to integrate purpose and vocation. Jason never gave up on his mission to improve the lives of the poorest children. Inspired by this deep conviction he worked to build, what in time, became a world class physiotherapy franchise. There were many seemingly insurmountable challenges that would have derailed most leaders, but not Jason. His purpose was rooted in a faithful resolve and uncompromising determination, something we can all now read and learn from."

George Savvides
Chairman, *SBS (Special Broadcasting Service) Australia*
Chairman, *World Vision Australia*
Former Managing Director, *Medibank*
Former Chairman, *Macquarie University Hospital*

"In *UNLIKELY*, Jason dares to crack open the shiny facade that tends to surround successful businesses, and has the courage to reveal the chest-tightening reality of risking everything… again and again. If you want to believe the fairy tale of the business person living a carefree resort life, rolling in wealth, don't read this book!"

Craig Winkler
Entrepreneur, Investor, Portfolio Director, Philanthropist
Non-Executive Director, *Xero*
Co-Founder and Former CEO, *MYOB*

"Jason questioned the traditional physiotherapy practice model, and implemented strategies of health reform that we all see as normal practice today. His battle scars have made him street wise, future-focused, business-hardened, and visionary, while maintaining humility and being true to his origins and faith. I have watched his journey with interest and commend him... he has ensured that the profession continues to evolve and be sustainable into the future."
Scott Willis
National President, *Australian Physiotherapy Association*

"It has been my privilege to witness Jason's journey firsthand and see his reluctance in business become a formidable strength in channelling a truly unique entrepreneurial vision. Compelled by his heart for impact, Jason built an organizational framework that enabled other "unlikely" business owners to start their practices in a safe and scalable way. He challenged the effectiveness of title-based hierarchy, he empowered independent wealth creation, he fostered a professional values-driven community, and he equipped hundreds of physiotherapists to change their career arc from practitioner to owner. Jason's story inspires, because in the face of significant opposition and adverse circumstances, he kept people and purpose at the centre of his vision."
Dan Daniels
Founder and Global CEO, *Daniels Health USA, Canada, UK, Australia*

"*UNLIKELY* offers readers a window into the soul of a man who is trying to do God's will, but wrestling with what that should look like. Jason has lived an amazing story, from his desire to be a medical missionary to feeling called to a different path: to found and lead Back in Motion, one of Australia's largest physiotherapy businesses. Jason shares openly about his successes as well as his challenges and failures. This book will not just help the Christian business person, but anyone who desires to have a positive impact in the world, understanding that living a life of impact and significance is not easy. The journey is not always smooth, but always worth taking."
Warwick Fairfax
Executive Coach, Author
Founder, *Beyond the Crucible*
Of the *Fairfax Media* family dynasty

"*UNLIKELY* is an open and honest account of Jason's life and journey from humble beginnings to becoming a leader of leaders. What an adventure of ups and downs, showing a spirit of tenacity that didn't compromise his core values. Reading the book reminded me of the proverb: 'Don't despise the day of small beginnings'. A great story, now a great book."

Jeff Lestz
Entrepreneur, Author, Speaker
Co-CEO, *Genistar Limited UK*

"I'm a mum of four young kids; not a physio; don't run a business; and frankly, would never have *chosen* to read Jason's book. However, when *begged* to review the raw manuscript, I was instantly gripped. Much like the romance novels I usually prefer, the opening pages caught my breath, and kept me engaged to the very end. Feel free to skip over the technical details of Jason's commercial achievements, but revel in the personal drama that unfolds like a fictional thriller. I felt privileged to peek 'behind the curtain' of the polished façade so often presented in public settings. Each page felt like a glimpse into the intimate diary of a complex entrepreneur – talented, courageous, and passionate, yet deeply conflicted and personally flawed. Jason held his nerve when others folded; kept up the poker face when his soul faded; and eventually made it to the top – albeit not how he planned. My verdict: this book transcends boundaries. It's a captivating read for anyone who appreciates a plot twist!"

Kristy Echeverria
A reluctant proof-reader
The wife of the brother of the wife of Jason

UNLIKELY

The surprising personal story behind the garage
startup that became a $100m national health brand

JASON T SMITH

Ark House Press
Arkhousepress.com

© Jason T. Smith 2024
jasontsmith.com.au

The moral rights of the author have been asserted.

No part of this book may be reproduced, stored in a retrieval system, communicated, or transmitted in any form or by any means without prior written permission from the author, except for the use of brief quotations in a book review. All rights reserved.

Ordering Information
Quantity sales – Special discounts available on quantity purchases by corporations, associations, and others. For details, contact the author at info@jasontsmith.com.au.
Individual sales – Ark House Press publications are available online and at select bookstores. They can also be ordered directly from the author's website at jasontsmith.com.au.
Orders for university textbook/course adoption use – For orders of this nature, please contact the author at info@jasontsmith.com.au.

Cataloguing In Publication Data:
Title: Unlikely
ISBN: 978-1-7635303-4-8 (pbk)
Subjects: BIO026000   BIOGRAPHY & AUTOBIOGRAPHY / Memoirs; BIO018000   BIOGRAPHY & AUTOBIOGRAPHY / Religious; BIO017000 BIOGRAPHY & AUTOBIOGRAPHY / Medical;

Internal Design by Ark House Press
Cover Design by Wallace Creative
Cover Photography by Fotografi Group

All Scriptural quotations, unless otherwise indicated, are taken from The Message: The Bible in Contemporary Language © 1993, 2002, 2018 by Eugene H. Peterson. All rights reserved.

PUBLISHER'S NOTE

The author has shown great care in the writing of this memoir to avoid causing anyone else harm. Whilst the stories throughout the book are factually accurate, some names, companies, locations, and other identifying details have been eliminated or changed to protect the privacy of individuals and to fulfil the author's moral and legal obligations to confidentiality and non-disparagement as they relate to sensitive circumstances. Therefore, in such instances, any identifying resemblance to actual individuals is merely coincidental.

AUTHOR'S NOTE

Throughout my life, I've come to learn that the same event is often experienced differently by each person. Whether directly involved, observing from the sidelines, or reflecting afterward, everyone brings their own unique perspective. This book recounts my journey of building Back In Motion—told through my eyes, as I remember it. Given the complexity and subjectivity of memory, I acknowledge that others may recall certain moments differently or offer alternative viewpoints.

CONTENT WARNING

Some content may be emotionally challenging, containing references to sexual assault, abuse, and suicide. The decision to include such material is not taken lightly, and highly sensitive details have been omitted to avoid unnecessary harm.

Apostle Paul:

"God can do anything, you know – far more than you could ever imagine or guess or request in your wildest dreams! He does it not by pushing us around but by working within us, his Spirit deeply and gently within us."

Ephesians 3:20

FLASH-FORWARD
page 1

THE WONDER YEARS
1975-1999
page 5

BOOTSTRAPPING
2000-2008
page 105

THE UGLY MIDDLE
2009-2015
page 245

CRESCENDO
2016-2022
page 371

FLASH-BACK
page 567

FLASH-FORWARD

24th August 2018

Twelve metres below the water line…
Nine and a half…
Five metres with a safety stop for three minutes…
and then eight strong kicks toward the sun.

BREAKING THROUGH THE surface of the gently rolling swell of the Malolo Lailai Strait, I let the regulator fall out of my mouth as I glided my scuba mask up past my hairline. After 43-minutes of submersion that first gulp of natural air felt like a rebirth – a fresh beginning after being engulfed in serene weightlessness. I exercised my lock jaw, spat out the warm brine, and gracefully rolled over into the comforting support of my buoyancy vest.

While I waited for the other divers, I lay there basking in the radiant heat of the Fijian sun with the unfettered joy reminiscent of our family pup anticipating her belly rub. As my companions surfaced one at a time, we clambered up the side of the small timber runabout, each awkwardly juggling our cumbersome gear.

With the air tanks properly secured and the final head count confirming our diving party was all present, Jone, our Fijian dive master and boat captain, reached for the starter cord of the 75cc Honda four-stroke outboard motor. Two sharp pulls awoke the sluggish engine as we lazily reclined on our wooden seats for the short commute to the resort jetty.

The Mamanuca Islands of Fiji is my favourite vacation spot in the world. Paulina and I celebrated our honeymoon on one of them at Mana Island, and have returned five more times to the region, taking our children and friends. The secluded sandy beaches and turquoise bays hold a special place in our family's memory vault, where laughter echoes through the years and stories are shared with a nostalgic twinkle in our eyes. It's the hallowed ground where inside jokes were born, not enough sunscreen was ever applied, and unforgettable moments unfolded. It's more than a destination; these Fijian atolls have become honorary members of our family now, forever etched in our genealogy.

This time, we were staying at the Plantation Resort on Malolo, one of the larger islands making up the volcanic archipelago that lies to the west of Nadi and to the south of the Yasawa Islands.

I felt invigorated that morning after my two-dive excursion – one being a tidal drift along Wilke's Wall, the other a 21-metre plunge into Gotham City where schools of batfish darted through the shadows. Like an astronaut returning from another world with spellbinding stories to tell, I sauntered up the beach toward Paulina and the kids with an undisguisable look of awe and wonderment.

I described in voluminous adjectives the two-metre Grey Nurse shark now tagged in my dive log, the beloved sea turtle that we stalked while it fed on the coral floor, and the inquisitive blue-spotted ribbontail ray that followed our dive path for much of our crawl along the bombe wall. True encounters of another kind; experiences I never tire of.

But Paulina didn't look engaged in any of my underwater adventures. Seemingly irritated by my verbose ramble, she impatiently waited until I took a breath before calmly explaining her ill-ease.

"I don't want you to freak out, but something has happened."

When you hear a deliberately vague and unmistakably macabre warning like this, your mind splinters in different directions. Every one of my thought trajectories landed in an equally disturbing place – one of loss, pain, disappointment, horror, or despair. I didn't know which tragedy to hope for, which imagination to entertain.

"What?", I cautiously ventured.

The kids seemed okay. They were consumed with their metropolis of sand, a cityscape of bridges, tunnels, castles, and rivers on the shore edge, blissfully unaware of any crisis. Nobody looked injured, sick, or missing. Paulina was, until this doom-filled statement, appearing to be comfortably reclined in a hammock strung between two palms, engrossed in her latest page-turner. There were no police, nurses, or resort management attending to our needs or even within sight.

How bad can it be? I silently rationalised.

Paulina handed me my phone.

Tapping the screen, I read the headline in that day's *Sydney Morning Herald*, Australia's number one masthead with a cross-platform audience of over eight million people. In big, black, and offensive letters, the headline bellowed, "Hell on Earth: Back In Motion physio franchisees bullied and trapped".

Beneath the banner hung the photo of a long-time friend staring back at me with a grave and wrathful glint in his eyes. My stomach clenched. I drew in a long breath as I prepared myself for the story that followed.

I felt excoriated.

It didn't matter that the claims in the article were libellous fiction, reading them in a reputable newspaper gave them credibility.

The article was syndicated across more than 18 different Fairfax publications, including the popular print rag where I lived in Melbourne, *The Age*. Presumably, that morning, my story was getting the attention of everyone who knew and loved me, and especially those who didn't.

During my three-hour dive trip, my phone registered 24 missed calls. Four from my second-in-charge, and one from my lawyer. My mum was even among them.

So, I thought, *this was how my "great adventure" would end!*

After nearly two decades of tirelessly investing myself into the brand of Back In Motion, my untimely demise would come through death by public criticism and parliamentary inquiry.

I don't remember being warned about these risks in 1999 when we first launched our humble physiotherapy practice in the carport at home. Nor did I expect to face such an existential crisis while imbibing the tranquillity of our Fijian paradise.

Blind-sided! *Again.*

Despite being back on solid ground, I immediately began to feel queasy. Unmoored and adrift in a swirling current of fear and disorientation, my stomach lurched with relentless motion and my legs started to give way. Grasping for the seasickness tablets stashed in my dive bag, I dry swallowed a handful, desperate for the world to stop spinning.

THE WONDER YEARS

1975-1999

*the formative years of childhood and adolescence
marked by awe, curiosity, and possibility*

God:
*"I know what I'm doing. I have it all planned out – plans to take care
of you, not abandon you, plans to give you the future you hope for."*
Jeremiah 29:11

THE WONDER YEARS

1	fraud alert	9
2	leap of faith	13
3	side hustles	20
4	school heroes	27
5	secret brothers	36
6	panic attacks	39
7	fail	44
8	Kampuchea	51
9	vomitus	59
10	get MAD, not even	67
11	landmines	69
12	rules of engagement	71
13	hitched	77
14	code brown	83
15	bow ties	90
16	pretty as a picture	94
17	amway	98
18	hypothetical	102

fraud alert

IMPOSTER SYNDROME IS a real thing. It's the self-doubt that tempts you to believe your achievements in life are underserving or illegitimate.

Despite success at different times in my life, I have suffered from a chronic sense of intellectual inadequacy that bred deep-seated inferiority. I could play the game with everyone watching, no doubt. I recited the buzzwords, wore a tailored suit, and gave a firm handshake when it counted. I effectively chaired controversial meetings, managed the tactical workflow of multiple portfolios, and even addressed corporate audiences of unknown thousands with seeming ease. I spoke to colleagues with confidence about the principles of business and leading teams, and mentored countless other professionals, sometimes for exorbitant fees. But behind the veil of these literal interactions, I frequently felt detached from my own body.

It was as though I viewed my life from a virtual balcony, overlooking the speeches, conversations, negotiations, and high-stakes decisions I made from one day to the next. The imaginary version of me was an irreverent heckler. I criticised myself – and sometimes out loud – for being stupid, naïve, impatient, clumsy, impetuous, self-focused, too emotional, unrealistic, and unreasonably demanding. But most of all, I murmured "fraud". My inner bully knew I was a reluctant CEO running an accidental business with a flimsy strategy, no formal credentials, and an abject sense of incompetence.

But of course, that's not what was embossed on my business card.

Group Director of the *Back In Motion Health Group*. The largest and fastest-growing franchise of physiotherapy services in Australia and New Zealand.

"Imposter!", I thought I heard somebody squawk from the shadows.

I didn't think I deserved to be in this position, leading and advising others in business success. I hadn't planned for it; didn't want it; and I felt no good at it. But here I was, nonetheless.

Nobody was more surprised than me.

Maybe my doubts came from my lineage – a family tree that branched out in many honourable directions, just not this one. To my knowledge, no one on either side of my extended family had ever been to university, let alone run a large business of their own. Was I fooling myself that I could?

I descended from a long line of successful blue-collar labourers and armed service personnel. Fitters-and-turners, technicians, motor mechanics, plumbers, shipbuilders, utility workers, maintenance foremen, and clerical workers. There is no shame in this. They were all hardworking, intelligent, and fulfilled in their career choices. Some civilian, some military – and I love them all for their enduring commitment to the important work they do.

My father learned his trade while serving in the Navy. His brother, the Army. And their father, my Pop, was in the Air Force. The defence service's dream recruitment poster family. The men of our family epitomised a line from Churchill's famous war-time monologue when he vowed to fight the monstrous enemies on *land, sea, and air*. It seemed the Smiths had the symmetry of all three services covered.

But I didn't carry on the generational legacy.

I couldn't really swing a hammer, and I had no aspiration for the lifestyle of the corps or the rigors of combat. It turned out I was a terrible sailor anyway, which as a young teen I discovered while attempting to navigate a small catamaran on a solo voyage off the windy foreshore of Phillip Island. The lineal distance covered was a mere fourteen nautical kilometres, but when I finally hit landfall (after numerous failed attempts to turn the watercraft), what should have been a short trip had turned into a two-hour ordeal.

I felt like a failure at just about everything I started.

WEEKENDS WERE GROUNDHOG Day in our household during my childhood – a predictable repetition. Mum worked in the house and Dad worked outside. This division of duties didn't appear to create tensions; it was just a pattern that worked. Of course, today, we live in a different era – no such delineation exists in my marriage. I push my share of the weight behind the vacuum and clean up at the kitchen sink, and Paulina is adept at cutting the grass and washing the cars. But the delegation of chores in my childhood flowed along the lines of traditional gender roles. My older sister, Leanne, generally helped Mum in the kitchen and around the house, while I mowed the lawns, swept the leaves, and was expected to help Dad in the garage.

Problem: I wasn't any good in the garage.

I knew it. Dad knew it. But this was a truth not spoken aloud by either of us.

Dad would don his overalls early on a Saturday morning and beaver away at his workbench all day on a variety of jobs – fixing the toaster, tuning the car engine, and constructing things out of timber. Incredibly, my dad built an entire extension on our family home over a two-year period. He expertly completed the stumping, framing, flooring, brickwork, plastering, roof-tiling, and even ran his own electrical cables and plumbing pipes, with all appropriate checks and compliance. He was a man's man!

There was nothing my dad couldn't make, repair, or improve. So much, that Mum regularly "loaned" him out to the neighbours and friends long before *Hire-a-Hubby* was a franchise. Dad's resourcefulness did have a downside, however. He often complained about his list of unfinished jobs to do, as the people around him could write their wants and needs much quicker than he could fulfill their requests.

Dad seemed to love the manual work. It gave him purpose and satisfaction. And I expect he envisioned sharing these skills and talents with his son. But sadly, I was a poor apprentice. Not through lack of trying or interest, it's just the "handyman" DNA seemed to have leaked out or sunk to the bottom of the ancestral gene pool when I was conceived.

In short, I wasn't – and still aren't – mechanically minded. I was never destined to pull a trailer of power tools or earn a trade certificate, and profoundly, this reality dinted my self-worth and identity. My feelings of inadequacy compounded over time when many of my sister's boyfriends and her eventual first husband were tradespeople. So too was my long-time friend and best man at our wedding, a competent carpenter and home builder. And my eventual wife's father and brothers would even be cut from the same cloth too – university trained in engineering, robotics, and electronics – they could build or fix almost anything. I would sit across the table at family gatherings and often feel the odd one out. Uninformed. Confounded by their topics. Tempted to believe I was a *lesser* man.

Imagine spending all those formative years feeling like a misfit. If there is a list of risk factors for the Imposter Syndrome, this must be one of them.

Grappling to fit in with the men of my life, I was oblivious to the divergent paths that awaited me. It's ironic now, that my eventual passion for physiotherapy demanded a strong grasp of human biomechanics and the deft handiwork of manual therapy, later affirming that the apple rarely falls far from the tree. But it was a long and arduous journey before I could make peace with this truth.

My emerging dream at the time was to become a medical doctor. I quickly became obsessed. All my favourite TV shows had medical themes – *A Country Practice*, *Doogie Howser*, and even *M.A.S.H.* The autobiography of Ben Carson, *Gifted Hands*, which was an account of his early medical career long before his presidential campaign against rival Donald Trump in 2020, was an early inspiration. A true-life story of a boy who went from "class dummy" to brilliant world-renowned paediatric neurosurgeon gave me hope in the seemingly impossible.

My teachers and friends at school were in the loop. If any one of them was placed under a bright light in a damp, dark room suffering prolonged hunger and sleep deprivation, and questioned "What does Jason want to do when he grows up?", their answers would consistently reassure the most suspicious interrogator. I was committed to a career in healthcare. Doctor, if I could; nurse, as my next choice; and open minded to the broad spectrum of roles and opportunities between those two classic bookends.

What eventually became a rapid ascent in my clinical achievements, soon catapulted me into the unfamiliar realms of business dealings long before I was prepared. Unready, ill-equipped, and un-enthused for the commercial world – the haunting childhood fears of being an unwelcomed misfit quickly returned. It seemed obvious that people knew I didn't belong. I wasn't an entrepreneur. I didn't know how to lead and manage people. I couldn't grow a business.

I felt like an imposter in a grown-up marketplace, and the silent shame and burden fell on me like a weighted blanket, near up to the very end.

2
leap of faith

BLOOD WILL TELL. Like begets like.
We are clearly a creation of our early context, moulded by our milieu. The shape of my imagination and achievements can be traced to so many early childhood impressions, and I owe most of that to my parents. Their unwavering love and commitment to our family gave me a strong footing to launch from.

But of course, they reflected their upbringing too.

Dad was a straight-up, respectable, shirt-tucked-in, shoes-polished, and grammatically correct Navy man. He didn't have a woman-in-every-port, nor took advantage of the weekend furloughs from the ship to indulge in drunken binges and other reckless behaviour. He was loyal to his wife and lived a clean life. No smoking. No booze. No gambling. He worked hard, kept the house in order, and provided fully for our family without Mum needing to find employment if she didn't want to.

Whilst Mum might have preferred short mini-skirts and chasing boys around the docks in her early years – as revealed by her own admissions – this gauche adolescent behaviour belied her strong values toward family and hard work. Mum made many sacrifices to provide a house and home for the four of us, putting herself a distant last anytime we couldn't all have what we wanted. She shape-shifted to become the emotional support needed for whatever was missing in the relational geometry of our family. And importantly, despite her willingness to serve others' interests first, this didn't suppress her effervescent personality. She often broke the tension in our home with noise and laughter, playing practical jokes, hosting countless friends for dinners, and was always available for a board game or excursion together.

It's possible that the very trait my children mock me most for, is something I inherited from my mother: I shamelessly laugh at my own jokes. I defend this self-deprecating habit by justifying that there's no fun in entertaining everybody else if you can't enjoy your own humour. Subsequently, my kids laugh *at* and *about* me, but rarely *with* me. I've earned the charmless description in our household as the family "kettle", because apparently its exactly how I sound when I chortle and choke back my own amusement enroute to the punchline. I build up a head of steam and then boil over before anyone can make out what I just said.

Mum does something remarkably similar, reminding me that our starting points in life have a considerable effect on our eventual trajectory.

MY PARENTS WERE not devout Christians when they met and married. Nor were they by the time they chose to start a family. Mum had some nominal church exposure as a child, but it certainly wasn't a dedicated lifestyle. And it had never been Dad's experience. In fact, true to colloquial disparagements about Australia being settled by convicts, one of my earliest ancestors on my mother's side was a convicted criminal. Peter Bassett was tried in Stafford, England, for stealing a pair of shoes on 12th March 1846, and transported to Australia for seven years' incarceration. He eventually received his Certificate of Freedom in November 1853, requesting to be sent to Tasmania to start a new life.

Sometime around my eighth birthday though, my parents placed a genuine faith in God. Mum first, and Dad sometime later. As such, I concede on every practical level that I was raised in a Christian home on a foundation of strong traditional Biblical values – because for most of my living memory this was true.

Amongst many wonderful insights and experiences, the greatest gift my parents gave me was the confidence to find God in my own searching. Rather than lay out all the "dos and don'ts" and hope I swallow the pill of religion, there was space and encouragement for me to explore my own journey toward Jesus Christ.

Our family prayed together, attended church on a regular basis, discussed the stories and lessons in the Bible, and explored how we could live what we were learning. But it was up to me to decide *who* I was going to follow, *what* I was going to live for, and the price I was willing to pay to remain committed to these two things!

While I was otherwise preoccupied with riding skateboards and playing *Space Invaders* on the Atari Commodore 64, my life irrevocably changed. At ten years of age, I chose to follow Jesus and His teachings. It was the most important decision I ever made – a transformative moment leading to a profound personal awakening that I have continued to cherish and pursue to this day.

God became the centre of my life. Experiencing His love was like stepping into a world suffused with vibrant colours, transcending my human understanding, evoking a sense of awe, reverence and overwhelming acceptance. A veil was lifted, revealing a reality beyond the confines of the physical world – a realm of divine peace, joy and infinite compassion.

Typified by the Hollywood blockbuster *The Matrix*, I "unplugged". The landscape around me immediately looked different. It was now more spiritual than physical. I sensed a bigger, more diverse, and much more powerful world behind the natural circumstances obvious to everyone.

God didn't become part of my life that day, I became part of His – and nothing could dissuade me from my newfound faith.

WE OFTEN CAMPED on the Murray River with my parents – a beautiful spot with sandy beaches on the river bends, flat bushland clearings for pitching a tent, abundant native wildlife, and veritable peace and quiet. Leanne and I would sometimes convince Dad to drive us half-an-hour up track, bumping along in the back of the four-wheel-drive, before we would spill out of the car, wave goodbye, and send our chauffeur back to camp. We would then wade into the water with our inflatable mattresses and float down the fast-flowing river that formed the border between Victoria and New South Wales. If we planned it right, the current would deliver us right to the floormats of our tents just in time for the damper to be taken out of the coals.

On one such trip in my early teens, I was swimming with my cousins in the river when my uncle noticed what appeared to be a stick floating upstream. It warranted closer inspection and, as you could guess, it was no stick at all.

It was a thick, two-metre long, Eastern Brown snake, slithering its way at great pace toward where we were bathing. The snake was native to those parts of the bush, and highly venomous, so nobody took unnecessary chances. After we all hurriedly cleared the water, I heard two sharp cracks followed by a deafening boom. I looked up the bank to see Dad having fired off a couple of rounds of his .22-calibre rifle, and my uncle soothing a bruised shoulder from the kick of his shotgun. I'm not sure who claimed the kill-shot, but we retrieved the dead snake from the river and cooked it over the fire. I sat there for most of the night mesmerised by this reptile crackling in the coals. Unbeknownst to me, the experience cemented in my subconscious a fear of snakes reminiscent of Indiana Jones.

Later that evening in the obsidian darkness, I had zero chance of falling asleep alone. I was on guard and alert. My mind anticipated all the entry points a snake might breach my tent: through the zipper; under the fly; over the ground sheet and between a possible tear in my canvas. I wondered if maybe a snake had already slithered into bed before me and was curled up below my feet waiting for its moment to strike!

My mind raced, the fear brewed, and I broke into a night sweat.

Then it occurred to me to *pray*.

If God was real, then these were the times it really counted. It wasn't a memorised catechism or sophisticated appeal; I simply asked God to protect me from snakes and give me a peaceful sleep.

In a flash of unnatural light, I was startled into an upright position. I clearly observed that my tent's zipper was firmly closed, the fly was secure, the ground sheet was in place, and there were no tears in the tent wall. I happened to also see the foot of my sleeping bag was flat and empty of any unwelcome intruders. I immediately felt divinely protected from both real and imagined Eastern Browns.

I often reflect on this experience, not with any lingering fear of snakebites, but because it reminds me of God's comforting presence during times of vulnerability. His reassurance to never abandon me became a cornerstone of my faith, a confidence I would lean on in countless moments to come.

SINCE CHOOSING TO follow Jesus, I wondered deeply what vocation I should pursue in my adulthood. While conventional paths such as becoming an ordained minister, lay pastor, charity worker, or missionary initially occupied my thoughts, I always harboured a curiosity for less obvious and more creative opportunities.

What initially fuelled my childhood passion for a career in healthcare was the distressing sickness and poverty in the world beyond my reach. I knew this wasn't God's plan. These overwhelming problems were a result of war, corruption, different climates, natural disasters, crime – and in some cases – poor individual choices or plain bad luck. But, as a child, I wasn't smart enough to analyse the causal effects to over half of our globe being considered third-rate and, thus, unworthy of the basic needs we take for granted.

My great awakening to the plight of the needy in the developing world happened in the most unlikely of circumstances.

It was a Saturday morning in 1985. With the rest of the household still adrift in their dreams, enjoying a lie-in after a hard-fought week, I arose with the birds. I was immediately spellbound by loveable cartoon heroes and villains screeching, dancing, and flitting their way across the family television set. With my brown vinyl bean bag moulded just right to my boyish shape, all I needed to complete the ensemble were two pieces of toast smothered in thick creamy peanut butter.

Bugs Bunny, Daffy Duck and Road Runner – familiar childhood companions to many – staged the opportunity for one of my most defining moments. It wasn't their animated antics that set my course, but rather the seemingly benign commercials that interrupted their episodes.

One captured my attention – or, more accurately, broke my heart.

World Vision was popular for airing iconic television campaigns to raise awareness and funding to help the plight of impoverished Ethiopians. I watched in horror as images of young dying children flashed in front of me. My screen filled with distended bellies, frail limbs, and tear-stained faces. A mother gestured her lifeless baby toward the cameraman, wailing in distress, begging for a miracle. A quick pan of grass hut villages with malnourished cows and dogs roaming the dirt then zoomed in on more children looking aimlessly into the distance, covered in flies, exhausted to move, looking hopeless. And then predictably, toward the end of the visual assault, a celebrity ambassador went full-face-to-camera and challenged me with a guilt-laden pitch that only a dollar a day could save a life. A long phone number I couldn't memorise scrolled along the bottom of the screen in a flashing banner, and I was left feeling nearly as hopeless as those being campaigned for.

Ten minutes later the advert was recycled in more cartoon breaks. And then again, for weeks on end.

I was almost numb from the trauma.

At such a young age, how was I supposed to respond? I could do *nothing*. I felt helpless.

Nearly forty years later, it still eludes me at times to know what is the right *something* I should do to help those trapped in the cycle of inter-generational poverty. It's a difficult problem to solve, but it's also part of our collective moral obligation to try. It's important to pursue restoration of these communities to a humane standard of safe and healthy living.

In my youthful naïveté, I followed my intuition. In that moment, I did what I could with what I had.

I *prayed*.

I asked God to save the little children. I requested food, clothing, and money to be sent to them. I specifically begged God to not let the *mummies* and *daddies* die too, as I was saddened by the idea that these children would be orphaned. On top of being sick, naked, and hungry, they wouldn't have their parents to comfort and love them.

Who would hug them at night when they were sad and afraid, I worried.

I didn't tell my parents anything about this, but on more than one morning while watching the cartoons I shed a tear over those dreadful scenes. I was deeply impacted, forever changed. My innocence and good fortune had been confronted. The big world suddenly appeared cruel, unfair, and frightening, catching me by surprise.

Was it clever advertising gambits used by a creative agency to strategically hook me in? Had they captured just the right angles and cast the perfect kids to tension the heart strings? Did they superbly walk the thin line that balances guilt with a call to action? Or was I just a gullible child, sensitive at heart?

I don't think any of these things matter, even if some are true.

I believe God was at work in me. He was stirring my compassion, empathy, and planting a seed for my life assignment.

In addition to praying, one morning I made a pledge. An irrevocable promise. As a pre-teen, without a sophisticated vocabulary, I confided in God that I was willing to become a doctor, travel to Ethiopia, and help the people in trouble. Whatever it took, I was willing, even if not yet able.

With this calling, I was drafted into my own kind of war effort. Not like my elders who joined the armed services, but I enlisted in a meaningful global cause nonetheless: medical missionary to the poorest of the poor, bringing practical help and spiritual hope.

All I had to do now was work hard, get good grades, earn a place in medical school, make some money and book a plane ticket. It didn't sound too hard. It shouldn't matter that my family weren't medically minded – if God was in it, then so was I.

I figured I had eight to ten years to be ready. I put myself on the clock, and every year counted given the needless suffering on the other side of the world. I just hoped the hungry children could hang on long enough until I got there.

3
side hustles

"**WORK SMARTER, NOT** harder!", people told me. It's a populism that belies the significance of a disciplined work ethic.

I wasn't the smartest kid in class, but I might have been the hardest working one.

Even now, after two decades of growing our business, winning awards, and being credited with scaled success, I'm still not the smartest "kid" in the room. One of my greatest discoveries was that I didn't have to be.

I'm proof, however, that the harder you work, the "luckier" you get.

Dad taught me this. He was a hard worker. And a selfless one too. In his seventies, he's still quick to pull on his overalls and repair a tap, paint a room, or replace a taillight for someone in need – family member, neighbour or just a friend-of-a-friend.

What Dad lacked in diplomas and credentials after his name, he more than made up for in sweat and persistence. If hard work was a qualification, my father would be a professor with a double-degree and a PhD. This was one of his pedigree traits that did manage to float through the gene pool to me – one that I'm forever grateful for.

These days, I'm often introduced before a keynote address as an "entrepreneur" (despite it sounding more like a life-threatening diagnosis than a personal quality). If it's meant to be a compliment, thank you! For the record though, I barely know how to pronounce the word, and so I'm not quite sure how I've earned the title. It's true, I've started lots of businesses, failed at some, and made others work. And, if that makes me an entrepreneur, it's a by-product, not an intention.

More than an entrepreneur though, I'm a work horse. I had over a dozen sources of income by the time I was 18 years old.

SIDE HUSTLES

In primary school I took on regular home gigs for pocket money. These included sweeping the leaves in the driveway, mowing lawns, washing cars, and other outside chores. Occasionally, Mum would sneak the inside jobs onto my list. I admit that I spent more time trying to get out of those than it would have taken to just complete them – a phenomenon I find common to my children too. They are inclined to argue longer over the illegitimacy of a task than it would have taken them to just complete it in the first place. (But when you're young, you have so much time in front of you that I guess using your time this way seems like an effective strategy.)

I was especially devious with washing the dishes. Rather than do a good job that would demonstrate to Mum a dependable capability, I purposely left food stains on plates and pots to prove that I was not cut out for the work. I hoped she would become worried that her continued requests for me to wash up after dinner were going to put the family at risk of domestic health and safety standards. Of course, she was not that gullible.

Beyond the division of labour within the home, I was creative. Long before garage sales were a popular thing in our neighbourhoods, I hosted card-table sales on the footpath of the busy road where we lived. I'd gather the obsolete toys I'd outgrown and collect them in a box. I often extended the invitation to my sister also, selling her items on consignment with a fair commission for my efforts. We spread out matchbox cars, swap cards, marbles, skateboards, sporting equipment, Barbie dolls, and other knick-knacks for discerning passers-by. I arranged items in price categories and was always up for trading with neighbouring kids, sometimes resulting in no money exchange but just a better mix of toys to sell the following weekend.

Often, I sat on the front lawn of my "store", bored and restless, hoping strangers would stop out of curiosity or sympathy. When they did, I would spruik and tout with vigour, sometimes making as much as $15 a day. One afternoon, I haggled with an older man over 10 Star Wars figurines and an X-wing fighter, and eventually emerged the victor with $30 in my back pocket. I was so excited, I offered to shout the whole family fish and chips for dinner that night. You could imagine my disappointment to learn that Mum had already put the vegetables in the pot.

I even promoted guinea pigs for sale from my backyard breeding stud. These randy critters could yield a litter of up to six offspring each gestation term, approximately 8-10 weeks after their late-night rendezvous. This made for a steady stream of product that was in high demand from my neighbourhood peers and school friends.

The most lucrative of all my childhood ventures was the gardening business I launched at 14 years of age. Surprisingly, Dad let me wheel his lawn mower around the block one day with a can of fuel by my side. I doorknocked random neighbours, offering to cut their grass for a discounted fee. Given Dad was far too generous to charge me a fixed equipment fee, I figured I could build "time and fuel" into my prices and the whole amount would fall to my bottom line as profit.

The first round of the block was a wild success – or maybe just a lucky start! Two different homes, both strangers to our family, accepted the offer for lawns mowed at $5 each. When I whistled down the driveway with an empty can of petrol and a pocket full of coins, Dad couldn't hide his surprise.

This was the beginning of many profitable weekends. I even expanded my services to pulling weeds and general garden maintenance at the very affordable price of $7 per hour. This was a boon, until I discovered how backbreaking the work was for 60 minutes straight. I almost wished I had just stuck to pushing a mower, but the weeding money was too good to pass up. So, I innovated.

One evening, after a hard morning on all fours in some older lady's vegetable patch, I slipped through the side gate to the back door of my neighbour and long-time play buddy, Emma. She was a flame-haired sprite with infectious energy, her round cheeks often playing host to a mischievous grin that could outshine the Sun. That day, I offered her "the opportunity of a lifetime": to partner with me in my gardening enterprise. She accepted without obtaining any independent legal advice, which I'd come to learn later would cost both of us our future together.

Emma became chief-weeder, and I exclusively mowed lawns. At $3 per hour, it was great income for Emma, and better for me. I retained $4 per hour as my margin for bootstrapping the idea, finding the work, overseeing quality control, and taking personal responsibility for the finished work. If you think this all sounds like corporate lingo for reaping the rewards off the sweat labour of an oppressed minor, you might be right. It wasn't long before Emma's mother caught wind of the inequities in our arrangement, and quickly dissolved our partnership.

Not many kids can boast an industrial legal dispute and failed business before they have finished puberty.

SO OPPORTUNISTIC WAS I to earn a buck in my younger years that I looked for every seasonal advantage.

A solitary pine tree stood as a centurion near our letterbox at the front of the houseblock. With its growing height, the tree's root system spread deep and wide. Eventually its underground network became a nuisance, causing the driveway to crack, move and lift. Dad took to that tree with a chainsaw to preserve order in his front yard. As he lopped the branches from atop, I was delegated the task of rounding them up and stacking them on the trailer. After hauling a dozen or more, I noticed that each branch resembled the perfect shape and form of a classic Christmas tree, all in different sizes, like sequential festive Babushka dolls.

An idea was born.

It seemed entirely believable that these branches were saleable assets to the same sympathetic neighbours who had already funded numerous of my other half-baked, but entirely adorable, ventures. So rather than load the trailer, I started sorting the harvest of my newly defined Christmas farm into a product range of small, medium, and large trees. I priced them from $3 up to $8 based on size and quality, because every salesman knows it's important to cater to different customers' budgets and preferences. I even gathered a basket full of what can only be described as scraps and offcuts, really nothing more than fronds of pine needles with some occasional pinecones still attached. They were to be my ultra-low budget options for the very cost-sensitive pool of buyers, or simply a range of add-ons and up-sells for those with cash to burn.

I convinced my sister to accompany me on our first promotional lap of the block, despite her initial objections about how lame the idea was – but someone had to carry the larger trees, I couldn't do everything. I don't recall this being my highest yielding concept, but I still moved a few $8 trees and a handful of the smaller ones. I even sold two of the single dollar decorations to Mrs. Goode, our hairdresser who lived fifteen houses away. It probably rates a mention that any proceeds I received from these transactions should not have been taken for granted, as the pine was felled in October and none of these home-grown Christmas trees were ever going to last to the first of December, let alone Christmas Day. I've since learned, a good marketer appreciates the importance of timing.

When I wasn't exploiting Emma, or relying on my sister's reluctant participation in hare-brained schemes, I was busy repacking sets of Lego into their original boxes, complete with instructions, and selling to "cheap" parents in the month before Christmas. Or I was looking for bargains in the Trading Post (my generation's version of eBay and Craig's List), flipping anything from fish tanks to boxed toy sets, taking more and more pride as the margins grew bigger with each new trade. I even bred guppies by the net-full, tropical fish that I would rear to four weeks of age and then sell for 50 cents each to the local pet shop, or simply barter for a different selection of other tropical species to add to my growing aquarium.

For those wondering, my business ventures weren't all start-ups. I also pursued more traditional forms of income in my early asset portfolio. That of bona fide legitimate employment. In fact, I held more positions of formal employment before I finished university than I have occupied in the three decades since.

I cleaned, catalogued, and sold prestigious cars after school on Friday nights – model diecast cars, that is. A family friend was a world-renowned model car collector, and he needed a young helper to clean the storeroom, pack mail-orders, and serve customers in his shop. Paying $3 an hour, I sometimes wondered whether I should return to mowing lawns.

I was also a drug dealer at the age of 14 – a purely legal one. I delivered prescription medicine on behalf of a local pharmacy to its elderly customers who couldn't attend the store.

In my latter teens, I morphed into a personal care attendant for a quadriplegic father of three kids. I prepared his meals, wheeled him to the shops, and generally kept him company. The most distinct recollection of this time was squeezing as many as 40 lemons for my client on each visit. He went through a phase where he had an insatiable appetite for citric juice. Lemon tea, lemon tart, lemon on his fish, lemon basting for his lamb. I was tempted to make him a lemon sandwich at one point to get him over this addiction, but I resisted. One day he just didn't want lemons anymore – *souring* on the whole idea.

I even took a job working at the local bottle shop. It was not my preference, but hungry for another dollar and with time to spare in my school holidays, I floated my resume to every shop and factory warehouse in my local area. After walking the beat for four hours, cold calling every proprietor that was open, I felt the pangs of rejection directing me home. My last stop was the Woolworths supermarket near the Glen Waverley train station. The store manager said there were no packing roles or checkout positions available in the main store, but they needed help in the bottle shop. Initially I agreed, and then hesitated. I wasn't sure if a Christian should serve the "Devil's drink" for the "love of money". I quickly rationalised that I would only be stacking the beer fridge and mopping the floors, and completed my first shift the following day. So, whilst by association I might technically be considered an accomplice to someone's probable drunkenness, I anticipated a swift and merciful acquittal.

Inevitably, it wasn't long before I was needed front-of-house in the bottle shop. Someone called in sick, and the Christmas rush demanded all hands-on-deck. There I was, selling alcohol to every thirsty patron. Truth is, I'd never touched a drop of liquor in my life. I hadn't snuck a beer at a family BBQ, or even had a sip of champagne at my aunt's wedding. I'd not binged anything behind the school shed, or at a friend's birthday party. My parents had long given up alcohol in the home since becoming Christians, so the temptation wasn't even available in the cupboards or fridge.

A complete phony, I would describe to customers in descriptive terms the apparent differences between the full-bodied pleasant flavours of the sweet wines, accented by their oaky vanilla character, with the somewhat complex taste of the dry wines, lingering long on the palate with a fine balance of acidity, smoothness, and crisp edge. Clearly no sommelier, I just read off the labels and reviewed the catalogue descriptions to make myself sound half-intelligent.

Un-initiated and ill-suited to this role, I didn't even realise at first that certain types of wine were named in languages other than English. I would pronounce them phonetically, until my supervisor one day overheard and scolded me for good reason. Apparently, "cab-sav" is not said with an ocker accent, just as it's written: *Cab-er-nat sav-ig-non*.

My strategy eventually became simple: I simply asked customers what they liked to drink, found something similar on special, and boldly recommended it. People seemed happy at the register when it cost them less – another important and lasting lesson in salesmanship.

Clearly not all my work during my formative years turned out to be successful. Nonetheless, I found plenty when I needed it. And I wasn't afraid of hard work or working hard – two subtly different attributes! Along the way, I gained all-important street-smarts that propelled me further, faster. I discovered the fusion of working smart AND working hard.

Crucially, I didn't let any of these money-making capers distract me from my end game: a career in healthcare. I knew I had to apply the same principles of creativity and persistence to getting through high school with a straight-A record to meet the high bar of medical school. Whilst I might have had some people fooled, I knew my education goals were not something that would come easy for me. Compensating for my shortcomings in academic intuition and book smarts with grunt and courage, they were only going to get me so far, but I was willing to push it as hard as I could. Too much was riding on everything for me not to try.

I was convinced that God was waiting for me with a special assignment to serve the poor. This belief was like aviation fuel in my two-stroke lawn mower, pushing me at times at a near-dangerous pace. Whether it was one of my side hustles, or pounding the school books, I gave it everything, knowing the realisation of my God-sized dream was going to take extraordinary effort; and anything less was tantamount to failure.

4
school heroes

NAVIGATING SCHOOL WAS, at times, like running a marathon in lead boots. Keeping my eyes focussed on the distant finish line was a challenge, particularly amidst the frequent stumbles and setbacks typical of adolescence.

Most of my primary education was spent at a local state school in Glen Waverley. I walked the six large blocks to and from school, often with Leanne and other neighbouring kids. We only had to cross two roads to get to school, and both were relatively quiet streets – still, the journey provided a feeling of independence to seven- and eight-year-olds as we ventured out into the brave world without the protection of our overbearing parents.

In 1986, my parents transferred both Leanne and I to Waverley Christian College, a small, emerging private school. We didn't resist. I don't even remember the change being traumatic or disruptive. We had recently started attending a local independent church, and this school operated under its auspices. The transition made sense.

My new school embraced a self-paced learning model from America, which meant that even though students sat together in the same classroom, we were often working on completely different curricula. By the time I moved into secondary school at the same campus, literally all year levels were accommodated in one large bullpen, with five rows of twenty desks called "corrals". Each workspace was divided by wooden partitions that you could only see across if you stood up. I was shorter than the average bear, and needed to squat on my chair to scout the room around me.

Teachers were not assigned to specific subjects or class levels. Instead, four teachers would simply roam the room like predators stalking their prey. You could be deeply engrossed in a calculus problem, navigating your way through the sixth line of derivations, and then sense a shadow hovering across your right shoulder. Or your olfactory senses might give them away sooner when they are triggered by a whiff of Old Spice aftershave, or some "old-lady-in-a-bottle" perfume; warning of approaching authority. By any means, a teacher would suddenly appear in your personal space, cast a watchful eye over what you were doing and, without a single word, float right past you to the next unsuspecting student.

The notion of sticking up your hand was frowned upon. Not because the school begrudged questions, but because of the gross inefficiency of sitting idle with your hand in the air. Instead, we had small replicas of the Australian flag on thirty-centimetre masts, mounted to small wooden plinths. If we had a question, we simply hoisted our flag on the bulkhead of our desk. Teachers kept vigilant watch for flags of distress, and progressively made their way around the room to the students in need. A quick survey of the classroom at any time would reveal a haphazard array of flags flapping under the gentle breeze of the air conditioning. There are many days now when I wish I could simply raise a souvenir flag for someone to attend to my life and business problems, infinitely more complex than the principles of geometry I faced back then.

Two older and popular students at school made college folklore by running covert wires under the school building to facilitate a network of Morse code communications for the students inside their corrals. The school's old weatherboard building was built on stumps, providing easy access for the boys to scamper under the floorboards and execute their plan. They enjoyed tapping out their exam answers to each other, swapping weekend stories, and telling harmless jokes about the teachers. These channels of espionage remained open for at least three months before being detected by a suspicious teacher. Memories like this remind me that school is a place for learning much more than just a formal education. Any self-respecting STEM teacher at the time should have been very impressed with the boys' ingenuity, application of basic science, and appetite for risk in executing this stunt – even if they had been the butt of some of the student jokes, communicated by dots and dashes.

I knew what was happening at the time, but I was too busy to get caught up in these clandestine activities. I was on a mission of my own. I had set a lofty goal of getting to medical school. I needed to accelerate my learning through as much material as possible, to get ahead of the pack and meet the predictably high thresholds for university. So, as my head went down, my desk-mounted Australian flag when up more than most.

By the end of my first year of self-paced education I was mid-way through Year 7 mathematics and science when my peer level was still in Year 6. I was encouraged by this early progress, but felt the slim margin was hardly enough. I pushed myself further.

By the end of Year 7, I was completing elements of the Year 10 and Year 11 curricula in all my mainstream subjects. I had a voracious appetite for workbooks. I would think nothing of getting home from school, eating a light snack, then putting in three hours of study before dinner. Once the meal was over, and any obligatory chores were completed, I'd retreat again to my bedroom to close out another two to three hours of homework before bedtime. I devoured the stuff. Driven often by an unhealthy sense of volume over quality, I took pride each time another chapter or workbook was discarded. I savoured the delight in crossing off a checklist, putting a tick on my progress chart, and requesting of my long-suffering teachers yet another round of materials. I recall some Parent/Teacher interviews where those who were meant to be encouraging my education were expressing concerns about how fast I was moving through the curricula. My parents and teachers wanted me to slow down, take a breath, and do *less* homework.

But I had convinced myself I wasn't smart. I feared that if I slowed down I might lose momentum, and stray off course. No matter what they said, I knew I had to keep working if I was to compete with the unreasonably high entrance scores the universities were demanding.

What I lacked in intelligence, confidence, and common sense, I was determined to make up through insane work schedules, repetition, and volume. It was addictive. I realised that while others at school had a reputation for spunk and mischief, mine was fast developing around bookwork and academics. I didn't intend it that way, it was the consequence of my work ethic. Sure, I could rival the best jocks at lunch time in a bat tennis championship, and certainly held my own in weekend sports and interschool track and field events. But my reputation was undisputedly for academics. What irony, given half the kids in the class were more brilliant than me, and either didn't know it, or didn't care. My advantage was a heart-felt goal that drove me sometimes beyond reason, and certainly beyond my natural capabilities.

In my mind, I was destined to become a doctor. I had pledged to the all-powerful and ever-present God that I would fulfill my part in His plan to solve poverty in Ethiopia. I had promised to help because I was so moved by compassion for marginalised people I didn't know, suffering in a place I'd never been. And yet it was as real as though I had experienced it firsthand.

An American preacher, visiting our church at the time, called me out of the congregation midway through a service, making an embarrassing moment of it. He boldly declared, in front of everyone, that I would not be able to run from the mark of God on my life. I didn't know what to make of it all, but in my heart, I felt called for the second time. First, as a 10-year-old watching cartoons. And now again, at 15 years of age.

Rightly or wrongly, smashing out schoolbooks was part of my answer to serving God.

RELATIONSHIPS OFTEN MAKE or break our time at school. They shape us for good and evil. Who we hang out with defines the good days, months, decades… and most certainly, the bad ones.

During our wonder years we are wet cement. Imprints come easily. As the concrete sets, so does our willingness to trust, learn, and adapt. There is nothing like running your own business to test you on all three of these attributes. And there is nothing like close friendships to catch you when you fall.

My best friend at school was the middle brother to one of the infamous codebreakers who had run a mesh of electrical wires under the class bullpen to exchange secret messages. Ashley was medium height, stocky build, and had a mop of blond hair that could be styled into just about any creation he wanted. With a light dusting of freckles, and a perfectly round face accentuated by symmetrical dimples, everything seemed to work for him. He was sporty in all the ways a young high schooler wants to be, and could keep up with the academics when he cared to. A great all-rounder, and fun too. Always able to tell a joke, spin a yarn, and keep the teachers on edge just enough to win over their affection without collecting too many demerits.

Ashley and his brothers —there was a younger one too, making them a trilogy – struck the sweet spot of "cool" in the late eighties and early nineties. As seminal pranksters and basketball tricksters, they appealed to the boys. Their charm, cheek, and good looks meant they scored highly with the girls too. And if that wasn't enough, they could all sing. Especially the eldest who went on and built an impressive resume of amateur and professional musical career highlights.

As it happened, Ashley and I were predictably the first and second choices for many live school theatre productions. With my photographic memory and commitment to repetition, I could learn the lines easily enough, and managed the acting okay, but I was struck with paralysing fear any time my parts required me to sing. Twenty years later, when our music teacher retired from the school, I was asked to come back and give an alumni speech to honour her investment into the student body. I joked then that I was the worst candidate to speak of her success as I was a blatant musical failure. I squeaked the recorder, could only generate static from the electric guitar, and bombed with singing. To this day, the only instrument I can really play with any confidence is Spotify, and even then, my kids are appalled at the song choices in my playlist.

Ashley, on the other hand, could carry it all. Sing, act, memorise lines. He had charisma and swagger. Even now, when I sit with him and watch my kids playing with his, I can't expunge the picture in my mind of Ashley as a twelve-year-old during one of his stand-out performances. In the peak of summer, he sat on the school stage for ninety minutes inside a large blue cardboard box three times his size – with holes for arms, legs, and head – hilariously transformed into *Psalty* the human Bible, singing songs from the book of Psalms. He was a sweaty hot mess when we finally got him out of his costume later that evening, hoarse in the voice and dangerously dehydrated.

But most importantly, Ashley's family lived within walking distance from school on a large, abandoned council-owned nursery. Towering pine trees stood sentry around the boundary, giving the impression of a secluded, impenetrable fortress. Naturally, it became the default location for birthday parties, end-of-year celebrations, and any get-together we could rationalise with our parents late on a Saturday afternoon. We built rafts that never did quite float well on the dam at the bottom of the property. We smoked "barkies" out of sight of Ashley's parents which, as the name suggests, were nothing but bark and leaves hand spun and rolled into our very own smouldering cigars. When it was dark enough to hide in the shadows, the largest coordinated games of spotlight tag and forty-forty broke out – sometimes it was girls matched against the boys; other times, we split along lines of age, with the senior school against the primary. It didn't matter, as I'm not sure any of us cared enough about the rules to ever declare a winner. It was just extreme fun. Many nights I would return home with mud up my legs, t-shirt ripped or stretched beyond shape, and a bruise or cut on my head, elbow, or knee needing first aid. But never with any complaints; adventures with Ashley were a welcome break from studying so hard.

Ordinarily, I doubt my parents would have encouraged any of this reckless play and moonlit escapades, but I think they were quietly relieved to see me doing something – *anything* – other than homework. It gave the perception of balance, even if there wasn't much really.

I was content with one good mate. I enjoyed a large group of friends throughout my childhood, and could be social with everyone, but frankly I didn't feel drawn to hanging out in big groups with friends – and that has never changed. If I didn't realise it then, it's clear on reflection now, that Ashley was my "other half" through school; we were a good fit.

IF MY APPETITE for peer level connection was modest, my desire to engage with those of the older generation seemed unusually strong. Despite feeling loved and supported by my parents, I was uncommonly drawn to mentors – hungry for role models who lived with purpose. I had a radar for the adults in my world who struck that equilibrium between Godly virtue and professional excellence, probably because somewhere in my spirit I knew I was going to have to find the same balance in time to come.

Some would say you are not meant to be *friends* with your teachers, and I'm not sure I disagree. But a distinct quality of the school I attended was the genuine care and personal engagement the teachers extended to their student body. I have journalled many of the dates and times when teachers stopped, looked, and chose to make a difference in my life. They left indelible imprints on my values and experiences during those formative years of my identity, faith and education. Far beyond explaining the mystery of Pythagoras' Theorem, rules of English grammar, and the intricacies of plant biology, they cared deeply about my personal growth and future aspirations.

None more so than my school principal Mr Sheahan. A tall, wiry frame, with short-cropped hair, round-rim tortoise shell eyeglasses, and a tightly curled beard, he was adept at sports as much as he enjoyed his music. Emotionally steady, and reserved in speech, his quiet demeanour concealed a wellspring of insight and reflection, and an indomitable resolve when demanded of him. Thirty years later, as the principal now to *my* children, and having served on the school council alongside him, I'm not sure he would know that he rates amongst the top ten adult influences in my life. I admire his tenacity, resilience, conviction, and consistency. He was a significant role model who captured my attention then, and continues to inspire me, providing lessons from afar.

I will not forget Mrs Aboagye either. She was a fiercely strong and intimidating Ghanaian who pointed at her students with a long-crooked index finger when she spoke. Half the time I couldn't tell whether she was scolding or encouraging me. My favourite semester with her was for Business Studies, although she also taught me History and Geography. Regardless of the subject, what I really learned from her above all else was to love God with every fibre within me. She set a high expectation for my life. She demanded excellence in everything I did, pushing for more than I was inclined to offer. And when I got there, she challenged me to reach for just a little bit extra. At the time, I found it unfair that she would drive me harder than anyone else in the class. In hindsight, I'm grateful for it; she helped prepare me for the rigours of self-employment like nothing else at school.

One of the assignments Mrs Aboagye set for me in Year 10 was to develop a business plan for a start-up initiative. With my experiences in selling Christmas trees, and launching a mobile mowing service, I wanted to stretch myself. I set about considering all the options, and landed on the merits of establishing a canteen on the school property. Our school was small, under-resourced, and seemed to have an unwritten objection to the unhealthy food a canteen would usually be associated with. So, as students, we were deprived of an iconic school experience. I felt it was time to turn that disadvantage in my favour.

After thinking through the pragmatics and economics of a small, portable, and limited supply canteen, I wrote my business plan and aced the assignment. I challenged Mrs Aboagye that, if she really felt it deserved the A+ she had credited me, then the idea was probably worth implementation. She smiled broadly, her grin reaching the uppermost parts of her ears on both sides; her pristine white teeth perfectly contrasted against the dark hues of her cheek bones.

"No!" she said, absent of any explanation.

I asked, "Why not?".

She mounted some feeble arguments that fell away one by one when tested; so I persisted with my request. Tired of my appeals, she eventually waved me off with a flick of her curled, bony phalanx, and I promised to return tomorrow. I kept pressing Mrs Aboagye over consecutive days – after all, she was the one who encouraged me to reach high standards and exceed expectations.

I can't quite recall how many cycles of the same argument took place, or when she finally obtained approval from the school council, but the light eventually turned green. At the start of the next term, I launched my makeshift canteen during lunch breaks, and enjoyed a healthy margin doing so. I would transit my supplies back and forth in insulated cold boxes. Mum was my chocolate mule, moving what would ordinarily be considered school contraband from the car to the storage room in the library. It all worked wonderfully, until kids started spending more than their parent-set quotas. Others complained when my limited supply couldn't meet demand, and fights started breaking out amongst the younger students pushing in line. The final straw was when a concerned mother accused me of exploiting her children with unreasonable prices.

Have you never heard of margin percentages, mark-ups, or price spread, lady?

So as quickly as it started, my canteen project was over. Another business failure, all adding weight to my speckled history as an apparent entrepreneur.

In time, my own kids undertook something similar. In 2017 they birthed a small snack food service for the National Support Office of the Back In Motion Health Group. Complete with their own logo and respective designations as CEO, Treasurer, and Operations Manager, the three boys quickly took to the idea. I would run them to the nuts and chocolate wholesaler on weekends. We spent our evenings making up small bag mixes, and then we priced them between $2 to $5 a pop. Displayed in a little plastic box, I put them in the staff room at work to take advantage of the impulse buy. Normally, the inventory was all gone by the end of the second or third day. The procedure became rinse-and-repeat. When I finally conceded that I was buying more than my fair share of the product in the office, and the kids got distracted with other interests, the company soon folded. But the whole affair reminded me again that we reproduce after our own kind.

IN RETROSPECT, IT'S clear my strike rate for business start-ups was rather underwhelming. Full *mea culpa* here – the failures were on me. I was learning the ease with which to come up with ideas and get them off the ground, but wasn't so competent with keeping them going. I was bound to be a commercial wash-up before even finishing high school if something didn't change. Although, I did wonder if my pattern of failure implied good long-term odds, as on a purely statistical basis, I was due a success soon.

Missteps, disappointments, frustration, embarrassment – I chalked up all these early setbacks as a necessary part of the hard-won lessons in learning what *not* to do when it counts, which would only sweeten the victory when greater opportunities followed.

But frankly, it seemed logical at the time for me to tune down, or even abandon my entrepreneurial spirit, as it was a distraction I couldn't afford. I needed to keep my eyes on the grand prize: study hard, get accepted into medical school, and become a missionary. It was a simple three-step algorithm and there wasn't going to be any time or need to invest into further business ventures when I was working in the developing world.

Or so I thought.

5
secret brothers

SISTERS CAN TEACH you so much – it's just hard to realise this when you're young.

Three years my senior, and light years ahead of me in terms of personal experience, Leanne jammed a lifetime into her teenage epoch. Competitive netball, weekend work at the same pharmacy for whom I delivered prescriptions on my BMX, aerobic classes, hanging out with friends, and church youth group activities – her schedule was overloaded. Yet, she always managed her fair share of homework in there too. And boys. Yes, there was often a male suitor on the scene, trying to get her attention. Given she was tall, intelligent, attractive, and full of energy – nobody was surprised.

Leanne is a powerhouse of optimism and joy. Her vivacious personality overflows with boundless enthusiasm and an irrepressible zest for life. She vaults though most days with an effervescent charm, her laughter ringing out like chimes on a breezy day, drawing others into her orbit with warm magnetism.

I am blessed to have a sister like Leanne. However, it's no secret I always wanted a brother – preferably, an older one who might look out for me. Not in place of my sister, but in addition to her.

Knowing that what I longed for was impossible, it seemed apparent the best way to achieve my wish was to latch onto Leanne's boyfriends. As new romances blossomed for my sister, I saw an opportunity to adopt another brother. Then, when Leanne's relationships grew tired and deteriorated, I, too, had to let them go.

The attaching and detaching got progressively more difficult. There were times I found the breakups harder than either Leanne or the departing love interest. Mum had to remind me at one point that I wasn't the focus of these dating relationships, and that it would be better for me to step back and not be the third wheel.

But Adrian was a keeper. My pick, for sure! I wasn't going to let this one go, even if Leanne might. I instantly adopted him as my "forever" big brother.

During the years they dated, Leanne and Adrian graciously let me tag along to the movies and took me to McDonald's after church. We played Monopoly together on the lounge room floor some weekends, and shot hoops in the driveway after school. Adrian would even come camping with us to the Murray River, floating on an inflatable mattress right alongside me, always alert for snakes in our peripheral vision.

Adrian eventually recruited me as a mower for his own gardening business, which was somewhat more developed than my childhood start-up. He had weekend contracts with schools, churches, and local industrial parks, and occasionally needed a second hand on the big jobs. I could spend a few hours with him on a Saturday afternoon and earn as much then as any month that my previous ventures ever afforded me.

And most notably, Adrian was studying civil engineering. He was an academic who did maths all day long at university – difficult arithmetic. I was so relieved to finally have a guy in my world I could relate to without having to pretend I liked power tools and dirty overalls.

When Leanne's relationship with Adrian concluded, I feared the worst. A break-up for her had always been a break-up for me. When my "big brother" left town – living abroad to work, clear his head, and reset – I felt a palpable vacuum in his absence. It was devastating – for me, not Leanne.

A surge of apprehension gripped me upon learning of Adrian's return to Melbourne four months or so later, uncertain if our bond could withstand the test of time and distance. Yet, when we finally reconnected, it was if no time had passed at all. Leanne might no longer have been part of the relationship, but Adrian and I seamlessly slipped back into our old rhythms, reaffirming that true brotherhood knows no bounds.

I was thrilled when Adrian eventually married – years later, visiting them in hospital or at home shortly after all three of their beautiful children were born. When it was my turn, Adrian stood beside me as a groomsman in my wedding and held each of my babies as we welcomed them into the world.

I HAD ANOTHER secret brother, affectively nick-named Crofty.

Fifteen years my senior, a leader in the youth group I attended in my early teens, Crofty was a rugged man. A bricklayer by trade, and dairy farmer by choice, he had a stocky build that made him almost wider than he was tall. His sport of choice was Australian Rules football, and he was fanatical for his beloved Geelong Cats.

At 14 years of age, I spent two weeks working with Crofty – mixing cement, loading pallets of bricks, barrowing mud from front to back, as he directed. He picked me up at the letterbox before the Sun rose and dropped me home well after dark. They were long and gruelling days, cold in winter, but reinforced to me again that hard work matters. After working in the wet trenches of the building site together, a bond formed, as strong as the cement we poured and groomed.

For years after, Crofty picked me up for church, surfed the sandy breaks at Smith's beach together, hit the movies, and grabbed burgers. So many evenings we just sat in the car outside my house for hours talking about God, life, parents, and girls. As a single guy well into his thirties, admittedly, he didn't have a lot to teach me about the opposite sex – but he sure had everything else on that list covered.

WHEN I LOOK back at my teenage years, I feel privileged I wasn't alone. I have been blessed with loving parents, a devoted sister, invested teachers, one close school peer, and two big brothers. All these relationships have endured the tests of time, grounding me in the necessary values that I've come to cherish.

It's true that our successes are not solely our own. They are rightfully shared with all those who have played a role in shaping the individuals we have become. In this sense, it's clear that my achievements are not solitary feats but rather a collaborative masterpiece, woven from the diverse influences and collective efforts of those who have supported and guided me along the way.

As for my many imperfections, and the challenges that eventually arose, they were uniquely mine. They represented the loose threads and frayed edges of my personal tapestry - all contributing to the richness and complexity of my story, as you are about to discover.

6
panic attacks

I RAN THE 10th grade corridors for the last time in 1991, the highest level of education then provided at Waverley Christian College. Each year culminated in Presentation Evening – the marque night following weeks of rehearsals and preparations. Parents and grandparents filled the seating of our local church (which doubled as the school auditorium), and the stage was set for an evening of riveting entertainment or flat-out boredom – the former, if you were the one paying the school fees and the latter, if you happened to be the one attending the college.

With the musical talent of a deaf walrus, my student contributions were limited to either dramatic monologues or house captain speeches – never *a cappella* solos. One year, I provided an interlude between performances when I spoke to the parents for five continuous minutes about "absolutely nothing".

Placing an empty cardboard box on a stool, I proceeded to describe to my audience the significance of what was inside. I hinted that the mysterious contents included what my grandfather had given me for Christmas the year before, what I had retained from my French class during first semester, the value of political debate on specific topics, and various other things. I finished with the notion that my obscure and curious box also contained the price of kindness – the cost of being invested in others' lives and showing generosity and compassion.

With my monologue nearly complete, I readied for the big reveal. As I flipped over the lid of my box, and showed the audience it was completely empty, I took childish delight in de-mystifying my statements. I got *nothing* for Christmas from my grandfather, I learned *nothing* in French class, the politicians of the day were going around in circles and adding *nothing* to the crucial debate, and… for the big finale, it costs us *nothing* to use words of kindness to encourage and invest into others. With the irony resting over the room, I concluded with the punchline "...and you have let me ramble on here for five minutes without a breath, literally talking about *absolutely nothing*?".

Whilst people applauded on the night, on reflection, it was likely out of awkward sympathy. Some of my underlying messages were a bit altruistic, if not entirely flawed. For one thing, having lived a few decades since, I now realise it costs a lot to invest into others. The price may not be in hard cold cash (although, I have learned that plenty of times it is that too), but it certainly exacts a high price in other ways. Nonetheless, parents are unduly kind and supportive when children take the stage.

Cheesy performances aside, the night always finished with student awards. Apart from individual class and subject achievements, the Heads of School reserved a few acknowledgements for special accolades. In the days leading up to Presentation Night the students would jest the odds on who would take out the big prizes. My name was always in the mix because, in successive junior years, I had proven myself in the academic stakes. That said, any genuine contender never wanted to underestimate their competition, so I would defer the attention that started to mount as the student bookies spruiked their favourites.

In the final hour of the final day of my final year at the college (noting the school only went to Year 10), I was awarded three of the four special prizes. The trifecta was the Headmasters' Award, the Pastor's Award, and the penultimate, Dux of the College. The only one I missed was the Courtesy Award, and it's possible I'm still working on that quality. It was an awkward sight as I tried to hold three trophies, shake the hand of our school council chairman, and then navigate the half-dozen steps off stage. If only medical schools deployed academic talent scouts like football and baseball teams, I just might have been discovered that night, recruited to a development squad, fast-tracked with a scholarship to a medical degree, and then spared the pain of having to go through two more gruelling years of high school.

The school trophies stood proud on a shelf for a year or two, adjacent to various others from tennis championships, school athletic carnivals, and prior year academic achievements. Sometime after, during university, they were placed in a box. The box lived in the garage of my parents' house. When I got married, they were moved to the garage of our first house. And then one day, like all boxes that haven't been touched in over a decade, they got moved for the last time to the trailer heading for the refuse depot. Not an unsurprising circle of life, but a little sad, nonetheless, given what I went through to earn them.

It's a harsh reality that today's achievements can quickly become tomorrow's forgotten memories. And anyone who builds their self-worth on what they do – rather than who they are – put themselves at great risk of mistaken identity. I hadn't learned this lesson yet, as the scaffolding for my belief system was still under construction. Hard work, academic success, the acknowledgement of others, and competitive edge were all cornerstones being laid in the foundations of my life. It was going to be a long time later until God could renovate a healthier and more virtuous base on which to frame my life.

TO BECOME A doctor, and move into Phase Two of my life plan, the most important years of my schooling were Years 11 and 12. My performance in core subjects would be used to calculate the score of my Victorian Certificate of Education (VCE), from which doors would either open or be slammed shut in my face.

Syndal Secondary College was home and host to those crucial two years. As I moved into a new and larger school community, the only person who came with me from my previous school was Ashley. There is nobody I would have preferred more, but within a few months, partly due to different subject choices, we drifted apart. There was no upset, rather our lives started to track in different directions.

I was focussed – working hard in every class, maximising my opportunities, and driven for success. I knew exactly what I wanted, and where I was heading. My new running mates were academic sparring partners. Chris, who would go on to become a successful audiologist. Philip, with an IQ off the charts, an aspiring aeronautical engineer who would eventually settle for something a little more mundane – accounting. And Jonathan, a whiz at chemistry and physics, but completely unaware of where it all might lead him.

So excessive was the pressure I put myself under during VCE, that I had a mini panic attack on my first afternoon on campus. I spent the day meeting new faces, navigating the map of the school grounds, reconciling my class timetable, and trying to remain calm and controlled. At four o'clock that afternoon, after returning home, I fell apart. With tears and deep breaths, I persuaded Mum to drive me back to school that same evening so I could trace out my class itinerary for the next day, stack my locker with whatever essentials I needed, and check the student noticeboard in case I'd missed important announcements. Mostly, I think, I just wanted to reorientate myself to the place my future depended on, without all the chaos that had assaulted me earlier that day.

Whilst never diagnosed, I experienced disproportionate anxiety as a child. A "worry wart" was the unattractive description Mum gave me. There were nights as an 11- and 12-year-old that I would lay in bed awake, unable to rest for fear of oversleeping the next day and missing school. Sometimes my parents would invite me to sit up later than my normal bedtime to watch a family movie, and I'd refuse the privilege, putting myself to bed for fear of being too tired the next day and then unable to concentrate on my work.

We were camping one Easter weekend with my extended family and, having such a great time, my parents offered me to stay another week with my cousins while they returned home for work. I was so distressed about the notion I'd miss classes, and potentially fall behind my peers, I outright rejected the idea. It took my parents to phone the school in my earshot and get the teacher's expressed consent (or as it turned out to be, *"strong preference"*) for me to concede to the invitation. I was, after all, doing mathematics two years ahead of my age grade at this point, and any concern about losing my lead was simply unbridled fear. I suffered conscientiousness to such an extreme that it became a fault – now testing my sanity again in the first few moments of the most important years of my schooling life.

Thankfully, my VCE years morphed into a great season. I navigated my way back into a traditional classroom again with fondness for the model of a teacher-at-the-blackboard. The self-pacing system of my previous school had lost its appeal when I realised how lonely it can be working on material in isolation from your friends. I made a meal out of biology, physics, physical education, and all levels of mathematics. Chemistry had its challenges, but I soon came to terms with the obtuse Periodic Table.

My nemesis, surprisingly, turned out to be English. Mostly, I think, because I didn't gel with the teacher. But also, as the cliché defence goes for any student who falls behind in their humanities, the grading was so "subjective". I could write three different essays on the same topic, and my scores wouldn't budge. I could write the same essay and give it to three different teachers, and take my pick of the grade I preferred, as this approach always drew a predictable spread. It seemed to me Ms Holloway marked the student, not the papers – and, for whatever reason, she didn't seem to like me. As it turned out, the feeling was mutual.

Wanting to make every possible preparation for life as a medico, during these years I sought out personal introductions to the doctors and surgeons we knew. Colin was memorable. Completing his final year of medical school at Monash University, he worked part-time as a tutor in anatomy and would spend countless hours on weekends dissecting the cadavers in the wet specimen laboratory. It was a perfect learning opportunity for me. Worried I would be turned off by the smell of formaldehyde, let alone the sight of dead bodies, I braced myself.

As it happened, I was a natural. Totally transfixed by the layered dissections, I saw every muscle, joint, nerve and organ as a marvel. Suited up with white coat, facemask, and gloves, I ended up elbow deep into chest cavities and the tissues of the lumbar region, building my confidence with each probe, cut, and separation that all my hard work was worth it, and a medical career was going to be the perfect choice for me.

LIFE AT SYNDAL became a crucible for testing, refining, and ultimately proving my faith in God. Having been schooled through my formative years in the nurturing environment of a Christian community, it was a shock to hear teachers swearing at the students, boldly touting the merits of Evolution, smoking in the carpark, and laughing at the lewd jokes they overheard students whispering at the back of the class.

But it was good for me. It caused me to distil further what I believed, and why. I searched the Scriptures to better understand the Biblical perspective around what I was learning, and with this my confidence grew. I read up on apologetics and the great debates of science so I could give compelling, well-informed answers for my growing faith. And I closed out high school with stronger convictions than those I held when I first started.

All these experiences brought me to the last few weeks of November 1993. As the clock started in my final exam, I bowed in prayer, asking for God to make a way for me to achieve the requisite standard to be accepted into the medical programs with either the University of Melbourne or Monash University. I was very specific – this goal had been the focus of my last eight years.

God couldn't plead ignorance.

7
fail

IT DIDN'T WORK out like I dreamed.
An otherwise unblemished record of straight A+'s across all my final year results was marred by one C grade – in English, of course. Specifically, I was marked down for my lack of understanding of the texts we read that year and for my inability to present "…a substantiated and organised response to the topic, using language accurately and appropriately". Given I can't even recall what the texts were, maybe the assessment was fair.

On the 9th of December 1993 the Victorian Tertiary Admissions Centre posted the final Scaled Study Scores to each student's household. I received a perfect score in all sciences and mathematics, but I dropped seven points in English. I immediately feared the worst; this was going to cost me a place in medical school.

I was right, damn it!

I did not receive any first round offers for medicine, falling below the cutoff score by only a few points. What happened over the next few weeks of my summer break is a blur. My head was in a fog and my heart felt drained of all its blood. I skipped all five stages of grief and went straight to numbness.

I could have my pick of almost any other course in any faculty of the best universities in Australia – law, engineering, political science, economics. None of them equipped me for medical missions though, even if they promised a fulfilling and well-paid career. The secondary preferences on my tertiary application forms really mattered at this point. I was immediately offered a place in the School of Physiotherapy at the University of Melbourne.

Truthfully, I didn't really know what a physiotherapist did.

The notion of sports massage came to mind, but with such a high bar entrance score it had to encompass more than this. I had spent nearly a decade projecting my life as a doctor that I hadn't scoped out any of the allied health professions in much detail. I had never been to a physiotherapist as a patient, I didn't know any physiotherapists, and so I was tentative when the time came to accept the invitation.

I was well advised to at least reserve my seat in the physiotherapy course on a placeholder basis, and then push hard on every door into any possible medical school in the southern hemisphere. I wrote letters to the different medical faculties of multiple institutions, sought recommendations from my teachers, and enquired about my probabilities of receiving a second-round offer if other *smarter* students turned down their place in favour of an alternative.

The only invitation I received was from the medical faculty at Monash University. I was scheduled for an interview a week from Tuesday to "explore the options" with them.

As I sat in front of a panel of selectors, my forehead beaded with sweat as I suppressed a growing nausea. My right leg gently bounced uncontrollably like a nervous tic before I had even taken my seat. When I opened my mouth to answer the first few questions, I was shocked to have lost the ability to make a sound. Panicking, I pushed air harder through my vocal cords, creating a run of mid-pubescent voice cracks that betrayed just how nervous I really was. The sympathetic jurors smiled, encouraged me to relax, and proceeded with questions that slowly eased me into a rhythm of more natural conversation.

They were initially interested in that dreaded English score that cost me an automatic *token to play*. They asked me some technical science questions around compounds, solutions, and suspensions – absurd detail that has never left me. They queried my choice of VCE subjects and wanted to know why I chose chemistry and biology over physics. I was given the opportunity to explain the role of sports and physical activity in my childhood. And most importantly, they were curious as to why I wanted to become a doctor.

I shared the abbreviated events of my coming to faith, the pledge I made in front of the cartoons to serve the poorest nations, of my fanatical drive to be a medical missionary, and that for nearly a decade I had given close to every waking moment committed to the cause. I thought I presented a compelling and emotive case with noble intentions. The panellists wound up the interview just before the hour, thanking me for my application and advising any offers resulting from this process would be made after thirty days.

As I stood to leave, feeling very optimistic that God was opening a backdoor into medical school, the selector on the far left rose and met me at the exit. He was a tall, middle-aged, slightly balding, friendly man. He also happened to be a physiotherapist, employed by the faculty of Medicine, serving as an independent assessor for tertiary placements. As he leaned across me to open the door on my behalf, he encouraged me to look further into physiotherapy. He believed the motivations that attracted me to medicine could be equally fulfilled through physiotherapy, and to keep my options open.

I couldn't tell whether he was letting me down gently, inferring I had just bombed the interview. Or whether this was a sign that God was preparing another way for me to stay on mission.

I wasn't left in suspense for very long. I bombed!

No second-round offer came from Monash University Medical School. With their rejection letter in my left hand, my right hand signed final acceptance to take up a course in physiotherapy at the University of Melbourne. Enrolment was scheduled for Thursday, the 3rd of February 1994.

It was official: I wasn't going to be a doc. I was to become a physio instead. I consoled myself that regardless, the dream to be a "medical missionary" was not dead.

LIVING IN THE outer eastern suburbs of Melbourne, my daily commute to university started with a five o'clock rise, rushed breakfast, 15-minute drive to the train line, usually a cold and dark 45-minute express ride into Flinders Street Station if the connecting city loop wasn't running, and then a 30-minute walk due north to the Berkeley Street off-campus School of Physiotherapy. Of course, it was the reverse at the end of the day, which meant I spent at least three hours a day in transit.

Having not been previously reliant on public transport, this was a new experience. I enjoyed the sub-culture of those who regularly travelled by train. Given most people had work routines around consistent start and finish times, familiar people seemed to get on the third carriage of the same train most days. Before long, a few of us became "travel-buddies".

There was the rotund businessman, always dressed in a three-piece suit, who meticulously unwrapped his hand-delivered, plastic-sealed newspaper as soon as he sat down. As we pulled into each successive station, he synchronised a head nod, acknowledging those who embarked, with an exaggerated unfolding of the broadsheet he was reading, flipping to the articles on the reverse side. We would lose him again for four minutes, as he buried his head in the increasingly dishevelled papers, until the train slowed for another stop.

There were the two ladies who seemed to work together. They, too, were well dressed, chatty, normally with a latte in hand. Characteristically, they wore sneakers, despite clashing with their formal attire. I could see that they carried their high heels in a shoulder bag, presumably to change into after footing it to their destinations at the other end of their rail journey.

I routinely saw a long-bearded, thirty-something hipster who must have been part of a tech lab or skunkworks. He would get on and off the train, effortlessly traversing the gap, with his laptop open, tethered to earphones.

There was a hospital worker who sat at the other end of the carriage, clearly observable by the scrubs she wore under her long jacket. And there were lots of other students, just like me, who lamented in unison that we couldn't afford to live on campus, or even pay for car parking in the city, and were thus destined to endure the long commutes together as our lot in life.

Before long, I was reputed for my snoozing superpower, as within minutes of taking my seat I was asleep. It was a combination of chronic sleep deprivation, the rhythmic rocking of the carriage, and the boredom associated with the monotonous scenery. My body clock became well-honed and would reliably wake me up at Richmond station, two stops from my destination. If my biology failed me, Suzanne, an older woman who typically sat three seats away, knew to reach around and nudge me. I would stir, recognise the cue, instinctively wipe my face in case I'd dribbled in my slumber, and politely thank her... again.

So comfortably did I sleep on the metro, that one day travelling to an end-of-semester exam, I dozed right through my stop, went full circle through the city loop, and started heading home again. I woke somewhere mid-way back along the return route, confused and disoriented, as everything outside the window seemed back to front. In a panic, I changed trains, reversed direction, sprinted to the lecture theatre, and only just made it in time before they closed the auditorium doors.

MY FIRST DAYS on university campus were as disorienting as my new start at Syndal Secondary College had been. Another mild panic attack reminded me there were uncertainties in life I couldn't control.

In one of my first anatomy lectures I was feeling incredibly intimidated by the whole experience. I was shy, nervous, trying to make new friends, still orienting to the campus modus operandi, and anxious about not fitting in.

An opinionated professor took to the lectern five minutes late. Without any introductions or context, he boomed to the mixed audience of medical and physiotherapy students a tirade of mockery toward anyone who can be so "stupid and unintelligent" to think a god could have created "everything" out of "nothing".

When he finally took a breath, the typically chatty lecture hall had fallen silent. He invited every undergraduate who believed in Creation to stand in our seats (as though his unmistakable disparagement gave us any sense of safety). I froze. Paranoid that the slightest muscle twitch might blow my cover, I didn't dare breathe. Watching a handful of people scattered across the room awkwardly rise to their feet, my core temperature quickly ascended with them – but not my body. I slipped further down in my seat. I felt like everyone was watching me, when, of course, they weren't.

I was such a coward.

My first opportunity at university to literally stand up for my faith, and I hid. Momentarily – when it counted – I was ashamed of Jesus Christ and everything I believed in. All I would have potentially suffered that day was perhaps some inconsequential humiliation - criticism from a man I'd rarely see again – and yet I was intimidated.

On the long train home that day, I thought of the countless men, women, and children who, over centuries, were willing to be martyred for their faith. Me, I couldn't even get out of my chair in a lecture theatre. I have few true regrets in life, but that choice is a grave one that I carry with me to this day. Turning my shame to good, I resolved in the weeks that followed, a determination to live my faith with conviction and pride. I went on to start a prayer group with other members of our undergraduate cohort, supported on-campus evangelistic activities, and would often take the lectern myself in years to come to share with peers my personal testimony of the forgiveness and love God extends to all those who seek Him.

THE UNIVERSITY OF Melbourne is a proud institution. They have enjoyed a long association with the physiotherapy profession in Victoria, beginning in the 1890s when Miss Eliza McCauley first undertook anatomy studies at the university, and then clinical studies at the Melbourne Hospital. In 1906 the forerunner of the Australian Physiotherapy Association (APA) was established, and the first formal training course for physiotherapists commenced in connection with the University of Melbourne. Eventually government approval was given for the formation of a modern, progressive School of Physiotherapy within the medical faculty. This opened in 1991, with the first intake being only 40 undergraduate students. By the time I finished my degree, the school boasted an enrolment of over 340 students across all four years of learning, and a postgraduate cohort of approximately 60 students.

I worked hard during high school, but took it to a whole other level at university. I was now surrounded by the *creme de la creme*. Literally, some of the smartest people in the state measured by academic record. I knew I had to keep putting in the hours if I were to keep pace with these brilliant peers. I hoped the strategy that got me there would keep me there.

The spread of subjects in my first year included medical biology, anatomy, applied kinesiology, behavioural science, physiology, human development, and applied practice. It was a tough first year, worsened by the pressure I put myself under to excel with a chance of then transferring from physiotherapy into a medical degree program. I had approached the Head of the School of Physiotherapy, and the Dean of the Faculty, to garner their support to endorse my transfer into medicine if I aced the first year. I bolstered my argument, acknowledging that given most of my lectures were shared with medical undergraduates, the credits and exemptions I'd earn for subjects already completed would not cost the place of another first-year year medical student in the following enrolment.

Whilst they were non-committal, both suggested I come back at the end of the year with my academic transcript when hypothetical scenarios could be superimposed with actual results.

Every December, after exams were finished, the faculty published the Dean's Honour List to formally recognise the achievements of the most outstanding students. Only a small number of undergraduates with high distinctions across all subjects were considered. At the end of my first year in 1994, I sat on top of that list. Accordingly, having proven myself, the two program heads approved my transition into medicine.

And then, with my dream of becoming a doctor within reach – I didn't want it anymore.

8
Kampuchea

AFTER A YEAR immersed in the study of physiotherapy, which had clearly been my second choice after medicine, something shifted in me. I'm not sure when or how it happened, but I fell in love with physiotherapy.

My vision was no longer focussed on being a doctor. Instead, I made plans to travel abroad and use physiotherapy to serve the needs of the poor. Throughout the year, I had confided this vision in Gillian, one of my senior lecturers. This struck a chord with her, a child of missionary parents herself. She encouraged me to keep an open mind while exploring the possibilities physiotherapy might offer, affirming in me the need for allied health care workers in the developing world.

As though to punctuate this desire, one morning while walking up the back streets of Melbourne city, I passed a lifeless human form curled up in a sleeping bag in the alcove of a warehouse roller door. The stash of tattered calico bags, wet cardboard matting from the night's rain, and some empty take-away food containers made it obvious the person was alive, at least twelve hours earlier. Uncharacteristically, I felt compelled to wake the man and ask if he needed help. This action began a fleeting seven-week friendship with Steven, homeless through a series of bad luck and misadventures.

Then aged in his early forties, Steven was divorced at 37 due to a problem with gambling. Soon after, he lost his job as a salesman for one of the leading soft drink brands based in Sydney (also costing him his company car). After numerous other setbacks, he moved to Melbourne for a fresh start. He now found himself without money, friends, or opportunity in the middle of a harsh winter, sleeping rough.

I got in the habit of bringing Steven a packed lunch most mornings as I'd stop to talk for a few minutes. Surprising to me, he carried a small

Gideon's New Testament Bible in his pocket, and regularly highlighted passages in the Good Book. He was courteous, grateful, and an engaging conversationalist. Steven took interest in my physiotherapy studies, and often retold stories of past sporting injuries and the back pain he then suffered from sleeping on hard surfaces.

One morning, as I pre-empted our catch up, he wasn't in his makeshift sleeping cove as usual. Nor the next day. Regrettably, I never saw Steven again.

I still think of him from time to time because of the impact he had on me. Steven was my first living example of a relatable human being facing real poverty and personal disadvantage. He wasn't a stranger on a television commercial, or someone I read about in a fundraising brochure. His friendship, however brief, challenged me to do more for people like him.

The world was full of *Stevens*. I wanted to help, but grappled with uncertainty about how I could be personally effective. Gillian kept pushing me to think outside of the box.

MY FIRST MISSION experience came in January 1996; a short adventure to Cambodia – otherwise known as the Republic of Kampuchea. I had prayed for Cambodia over many years and donated small amounts of money to support causes our church was facilitating. Now, I was visiting the people I had heard so much about.

Jill (physiotherapist and, fun-fact, the first employee we would take on when Back In Motion eventually started) led our team of seven. With Jill having been to Cambodia only once before, and the rest of us first-time travellers, there was plenty of nervous excitement, unanswered questions, and apprehension toward what lay ahead.

The experience was a trip of many firsts for me.

First time in another country. First time on a mission trip. First time even on a plane. At 21 years of age, I had never flown interstate, let alone travelled internationally. Pleading my case to one of the hospitable flight attendants, I managed to score a quick visit to the cockpit to see what happens in the pointy end of the plane, meet the pilots, and share the purpose of our trip. I was so excited to be taking the first cross-cultural step toward my missionary life, it was hard not to spread the news with everyone I met – whether they were interested or not.

During the months of preparation, I immersed myself in Cambodia's history, customs and culture. I watched documentaries and read international news reports to keep up to date on current affairs. I learned a few conversational phrases and pleasantries in the national language, Mon-Khmer.

I even read the book, *From Phnom Penh to Paradise: Escape from Cambodia* written by Var Hong Ashe. This amazing and inspirational story detailed one family fleeing from the Khmer Rouge for refuge in Thailand. This opened my eyes to the terror-filled reign of Pol Pot, a communist revolutionary who inflicted unthinkable suffering on his own people between 1975 and 1979. Seeking to create an agrarian socialist society, Pot was the driving force behind a genocide that saw the systemic persecution and killing of nearly two million people. Decimating approximately a quarter of Cambodia's population, the infamous Killing Fields remain a potent reminder today of the dangers of any totalitarian dictatorship.

Some 20 years later, on our visit, it was apparent that the country hadn't recovered. I was especially sensitive to the realisation that anyone older than me had lived through the massacres and had seen – and likely suffered – firsthand atrocities. There was no doubt they were a people in need. I just couldn't be sure what seven green Aussies could do to help in a brief three-week exposure.

A nation of abject poverty groaned in the wake of horrific injustice. Health care, education, food, housing, electricity, employment – all things I took for granted at home – were in short supply. I saw the deep spiritual void created by the fracturing of human trust and solidarity. Everywhere we turned, there was pollution, sickness and disease, fear, amputees from landmines, a corrupt and divided government, cities littered with monuments to the dead, human loss, and despair. There was no end to the misery.

It was obvious to me that Cambodia needed more than a physio or two – their only hope was Jesus.

As it was, I nearly didn't even make it to the boarding gate. The cost of the trip was $1,800. That was a lot of money for a third-year university student, especially given how few successes I had enjoyed in my earlier business ventures. I was able to scramble together the $300 deposit through savings, some contribution from my parents, and a split of some fundraising events we had hosted as a team. But $1,500 was still a big gap to close, and I stayed awake many nights pondering ways to earn my passage.

Jill kept encouraging me that if God wanted me on the team, He would provide a way. I learned how to pray fervently when there was only three days left before final payment was due. That night, stepping off the train from university, I was anxious about the looming deadline. Driving home, a light rain mixed with the dust and dirt made the roads more slippery than normal. Whilst I braked carefully with enough time to pull up safely at the red-light intersection, the driver behind me didn't. They locked their brakes, slid two metres, and collided with my car's rear end.

My first thought was "#$!!%#".

My second thought was far more serious.

Knowing I'd now have insurance payments and repair bills to cover, I conceded my trip to Cambodia was over before it had even begun. I started wondering when Jill might lead her third trip so I could reserve my seat, with defeat this time a foregone conclusion.

I limped my car home feeling distressed, although uninjured. I was only nursing a dented rear quarter panel, busted taillight, and crooked rear bumper bar. The following day I diligently chased numerous panel beaters for the obligatory three quotes to present to the insurance company. The cheapest repair estimate came in at just under $3,000. My heart sank as I did the math. My parents had bought me the car the year before, paying only $1,700, and the capped replacement value under my insurance policy was even lower. The claim manager immediately declared my car a financial write-off.

It was horrible news. Not only could I not afford to go on the trip, but I also now didn't have a car.

He then explained apologetically, "A cheque will arrive in the mail for the sum of $1,500 in the next few days. Given we are paying you out, it is your responsibility to dispose of the car. This payment will settle your claim and close your policy with us immediately."

Dispose of the car? There was barely anything wrong with it. And as for the $1,500, *thank you very much for making up the exact difference I needed to confirm my trip.*

Dad was confident we could do a home-repair job. Of course, he could – there wasn't anything he couldn't fix.

After an impromptu trip to the wreckers, we found a matching taillight and bumper bar for less than $50. As for the panel damage,

Dad had a solution for that too. We screwed a towing hook into the centre of the indentation, connected a thick heavy-duty strap between the hook and the back of his four-wheel drive. As I kept my foot heavily planted on the brake pedal of my car, he took off suddenly in his. The panel popped out like an ice cube from a freezer tray! We bogged up the edges, sanded it all back, and spray painted the patch, feathering in the colour to match as best one could without colour charts and computerised tint compositions.

It didn't look new, but I didn't care. I was going to Kampuchea.

The cheque arrived, the money cleared, and I bought a ticket almost entirely paid for by my insurance company. Or at least, by the God who seems to pull the strings behind their operation.

OUR ITINERARY HAD us flying into Pochentong Airport, near the capital Phnom Penh. There, we met our local handlers on the ground, connected through our church.

Eric Dooley was the man with the vision; New Life Foundation was his established mission work in Cambodia. He had coordinated the arrival of expatriates from the USA, England, Philippines, and Singapore to converge for the important work we had arrived to contribute to. We engaged in university and street evangelism, and Bible distribution. Our group taught English classes to help those on the poverty fringe improve their chances of some paid employment. We worked with the children in orphanages and rescue shelters, and were quick to share our stories and testimonies of how God had sent us. And we volunteered in their makeshift medical clinics with limited supplies, doing the best we could for those who came for help.

Admittedly, it all seemed a feeble effort at the time, like holding up a paper umbrella in a hailstorm. Regardless, people were consistently thankful.

It was eye-opening to walk the streets of Cambodia and be surrounded by beggars. Desperate mothers sent children to do their bidding, because who could deny a hungry toddler the last coins in your pocket? Old men dragged themselves through the dirt in front of us, having to avoid being trampled by rickshaws, but hoping for a compassionate donation. As we rode mopeds to central temples and observed the King's Palace, the stark contrast between the opulence of the few and the misery of the many was impossible to reconcile.

Poverty breeds crime, and there was plenty of both everywhere I looked. Walking with some Buddhist monks along a high bank of the mighty Mekong River in a rural area two hours from the city centre, we were rushed upon by two boys no older than 12 or 13 years. One of them fired a pistol in our general direction. I felt rooted to the spot.

What was going on?

I had been around rifles most of my childhood, enjoying weekends of target practice and occasional rabbit hunting with Dad on farms and in the outback, but this was different. Nobody even knew where we were. We stood motionless, vulnerable and afraid. I could tell Jill and others were sizing up the situation fast. It became clear, soon enough, that the kids looked neither aggressive nor agitated – they were simply running through the village firing live ammunition as some disturbing form of entertainment. *Why?* Presumably, just because they could.

Another time I felt genuinely concerned for my life was when we took a public bus along the well-worn tourist route from Phnom Penh to the popular town of Siem Reap. The coach was stopped by an unofficial roadblock of masked men with machine guns. We were ordered off the bus, told to stand to one side in a line, and pay 100,000 Cambodia Riel each (which translated roughly to only A$33). As soon as we paid the non-negotiable sum, the men herded us back onto the bus with the barrel tips of their rifles. The driver seemed completely unfazed, as though this was a routine stop on his schedule when transporting foreigners to the recommended tourist hotspots.

Visiting Tuol Sleng was another sobering experience. Formerly a secondary school, it was converted into Security Prison S-21 by the Khmer Rouge during their bloody reign, and now stood as a graphic museum of the genocide. An estimated 20,000 people were imprisoned and tortured there before the fall of the regime in 1979. The prison's chief, Kang Kek Lew, was eventually convicted for Crimes Against Humanity in July 2010, dying a decade later in 2020 while serving a life sentence.

Most prisoners taken to S-21 were the academic elites, government officials, teachers, students, and monks who resisted the communist ideal. Arrested on fabricated charges of "espionage", the walls of their cells today are plastered with photographs taken of people literally moments before their interrogation and execution. There were still blood stains on the floors, chairs, and tables where we walked, making it almost impossible to look where you were going without being abhorred at the evidence of inhumane violence all around you.

The only experience worse than all of these was a walk through Choeng Ek, one of the so-called Killing Fields, which changed my life forever. The atrocities of the Khmer Rouge regime were all too real at this site, where pieces of clothing, human bone, teeth, and buttons still heavily littered the dirt. A bad day for me in Australia was incomparable with the tragedies faced then – and still now – by almost every Cambodian national. My childhood had been peppered with love, fun, and family adventures, while my peers in Cambodia were watching their parents and older siblings being tortured and murdered in cold blood.

I wondered what God was teaching me.

Why did I need to see this? Why had He revealed himself to me as a young boy in front of the television, when most of these beautiful people had never heard of the love of Jesus?

We spread out as a team as we walked the fields, keeping our thoughts and emotions private. Nobody spoke; respectful silence consumed us. I desperately prayed under my breath for God to show me how my life could help.

Returning to Melbourne to continue physiotherapy studies didn't seem a proportionate response to everything I had experienced on my trip. One of our team members, shortly thereafter, enrolled in a six-month training school with a popular para-church group called Youth With A Mission (YWAM), expecting to make repeated trips in the near future to help in developing countries. Another trip participant returned to Cambodia shortly thereafter with his wife, devoting many years as full-time workers in the ministries of New Life Foundation, the same organisation we had partnered with.

What was I going to do? Keep learning the Latin names of the 406 muscles of the body and their specific nerve supply in some vain hope that this medical knowledge was going to somehow heal a broken nation more than 7,000 kilometres from my lecture hall?

"RE-ENTRY" INTO TYPICAL suburban life after a confronting three-week exposure is one of the hardest parts of short-term humanitarian work. You embark on the trip, full of hope and enthusiasm to change the world, only to return disillusioned by the acknowledgement that the only one needing to change is you.

Coming home via Singapore was certainly not helpful to this end. In contrast to Cambodia, Singapore is Asia's richest country. It is a centre for finance and advanced technology, full of incredibly wealthy, ambitious, motivated, hard-working people living in high-rise apartments amongst glitzy shopping centres. It is a mecca for the Asian elite, and a hub for so much international transport. The culture shock of coming to Singapore from Cambodia was extreme.

It's clear to me now that it was part of Jill's devious plan, using the contrasts of both countries to reveal the condition of our own hearts. I didn't like what I saw in mine – selfish greed and an overdeveloped sense of entitlement!

When I did return home, I was utterly disgusted with the waste, frivolity, and ungratefulness in those around me. My family had to put up with a lot of huffing and puffing and self-righteous indignation, when they welcomed this weary traveller home. But slowly, and sadly, the sting wore off during my immersion back into our materialistic western culture!

But not before I intercepted Gillian, my lecturer, in the corridors of the university. With an upcoming summer elective where students could choose to work in any clinical setting they preferred, I campaigned her to let me return to Cambodia and work amongst the amputees as a final year physiotherapy student.

She didn't say no.

9
vomitus

ONLY WEEKS BACK from my first experience in Cambodia, I felt something stirring in my heart, knotting my stomach, and making me weak in the knees.

The source of my angst was a girl.

I first met Paulina in Grade 5 at Waverley Christian College where we shared a class together. A year apart, me being the older – as she would enjoy asserting for the remainder of our lives together – we had not seen each other since I left the school in Year 10. But I was looking at her now, five years later, and saw something I had previously overlooked!

Noticeably shorter than most of her peers, Paulina stood tall on personality. And beautiful beyond description. She was famed in our friendship group for her captivating round eyes, charming dimples, and warm, inviting smile. From Chilean descent, born in Brazil, she immigrated to Australia as a ten-year-old. She didn't know a single word of English at the time she arrived and had already overcome a lot. And yet, she had succeeded at almost everything she tried. Gregarious in all the ways I wasn't, Paulina drew me into her forcefield of laughter, energy, and conversation – and I didn't resist.

In the month before travelling to Cambodia, 20 friends gathered for the weekend to celebrate the New Year. Paulina had only recently started attending our youth group after years of being part of a Spanish-speaking church in a distant suburb. Carloads of young adults, compacted by tents and eskies filled with food, rendezvoused at picturesque Cowes at Phillip Island on the south coast of Victoria. It's one of my favourite local spots, occupying 100 square kilometres of koalas, wallabies, penguins, and some of the nicest beaches in Australia. Accessible by only a single vehicle bridge, the one downside was that it turned into a carpark on hot summer days. As 1995 closed out with obligatory fireworks and toasts of new year's resolutions, I found myself giving Paulina far more attention than anyone else.

Earlier in the day, the boys in the group decided to go surfing, and the girls chose shopping and cafés along the main street. Accepting the agreed plan, we all split in our different directions. I was sitting out on my surfboard behind the breaks of Smiths Beach, taking a breath between sets, when I noticed some of the guys shouting and waving to two girls swimming out.

As I looked around, I was startled by a sudden emergence from the water. Paulina and a friend had duck-dived under the breaker that I had just rolled over, bobbing up a metre from where I was floating. Having clearly abandoned her shopping trip at the last minute, Paulina confidently asked to have a turn on my surfboard. Equally shocked and excited to see her there, I quickly slipped off my leg rope in her readiness for the next inbound wave.

With no wetsuit in the chilly waters, or much surfing experience (as it was soon apparent), Paulina showed raw courage and determination. She persisted with the five-foot unbroken waves despite swallowing mouthfuls of seawater with each successive dumping. Undeterred by the difficulty, and seemingly enjoying herself, I bobbed in the swell, mesmerised by her spunk. With my pending departure for the three-week mission, I admit the timing wasn't ideal, but I felt compelled to let her know that day just how impressed I really was.

IN THE WAKE of my eye-opening travels in Cambodia – while still suffering the re-entry blues – I casually bumped into Paulina as we were both walking out of church. We joined up with a small group of mutual friends for an impromptu dinner somewhere and, as I drove home that night, my soul danced to a symphony of unfamiliar emotions. I was completely smitten.

During the next week the same friends decided to catch a movie. Contrary to my usual self, I made the bold move of offering Paulina a lift on my way, discreetly omitting any reference to this being a "date", considering the group dynamic. Inwardly, I hoped she would perceive my gesture as an obvious sign of my interest in her.

Evidently, I was too vague with my approach.

On arriving at Paulina's house, I was met by Paulina *plus* a friend she had invited to tag along with us. Ximena jumped into the front seat, making for only platonic conversations in the car that evening, while I tried to determine where our signals had so clearly crossed.

I plotted my recovery strategy: make sure I sit next to Paulina at the cinema. Carefully watching which row she entered, I opted for the gentleman's approach and went the long way round to meet her at the other side, expecting to sit in the adjacent chair. Sadly, one of the other guys in our group irreverently climbed over the seats and took my spot seconds before I arrived.

It seemed good guys *do* finish last!

The only solace that evening was that my intruding friend had no romantic intentions – just bad timing – thus preserving my confidence to keep pursuing Paulina's attention.

I wasn't prepared to leave things to chance any longer. A few weeks later I phoned Paulina and unambiguously asked her out to dinner. I was clear, just the two of us. No uninvited girlfriends. It was to be an official first date.

She agreed.

Hearing what I had hoped for, I immediately felt unprepared. I asked my friends the next day at university which restaurant I should take Paulina to. Bernie, the consummate networker and dealmaker of our undergraduate cohort, said there was no choice – it had to be *The Stokehouse* in St Kilda. Accepting his recommendation with blind faith, I made reservations for two for Wednesday night.

Come Tuesday, I was worried I had *nothing* to wear! Racing to the train station after clinical rotations at the student hospital, I detoured via a men's store and purchased a new shirt. As I was paying at the counter, I momentarily felt nauseous. The squeamishness passed as quickly as it came, and I tore off to catch the 5:55pm train to Glen Waverley, thinking nothing more of it.

I woke the next day – the morning of our date – feeling waves of nausea roll over me again and again. I put it down to nerves, completed my classes for the day, purchased a bunch of roses, and was parked outside Paulina's house a few minutes early. Taking a deep breath, I bounded out of the car and confidently skipped up the driveway, only to splash into a mud-filled puddle, wetting my socks right through. Unbeknownst to me, Paulina's younger brothers, Cristian and Carlos, were watching television in the loungeroom and saw me pull up. They knew me from school and couldn't understand why I was at their house, until they saw the bunch of flowers in my arms. They put the unfolding events together very quickly. As Paulina tried to race out the front door before I could hear anything, the boys taunted her with whoops and hollers and the sounds of mock kissing as they smacked their lips against the inside of their elbows. I pretended not to hear, while Paulina pretended not to notice that I most definitely had. She whisked the flowers from my grip before I even had the chance to hand them off, throwing them on the credenza inside the front door as she slammed it shut hard and fast.

Arriving at the restaurant, surprised that my nerves hadn't abated yet, I parked my 1977 canary yellow Toyota Corolla (nicked the "chick-mobile", despite Paulina denying it was the first thing that attracted her to me) between a midnight blue 7 series BMW on the left and a black Porsche 911 to my right. Feeling incredibly emasculated by my vehicle inadequacy, Paulina couldn't have cared less.

We walked into the lobby and a dishevelled, over-worked waitress impatiently guided us to a crowded long table with bench seats by the window. She hurriedly explained our menu options off a cheap laminated card, and directed us to the bar when we were ready to order. I looked at Paulina, dressed so elegantly, and me in my new shirt, and paused.

There wasn't anything classy about this venue. Thanks Bernie, for the bum steer!

Embarrassed, I scanned the room again before excusing myself from the table and confirming with a different waitress that we had a private booking. After a quizzical look, she recognised the problem. Sounding sincerely apologetic for the oversight, she presumed we must be expected *upstairs*. I quickly agreed with her, not knowing what "upstairs" was, but anything had to be better than the rowdy bar and bistro on the ground floor.

As we ascended to the second floor, it was like passing through the magical wardrobe in one of C.S. Lewis's novels; we entered another world. We were greeted formally by waitstaff dressed all in black and shown to a table for two, formally set with silverware and a tablecloth. Classical music played gently in the background, accompanied by the hushed sounds of other couples delicately chinking their glasses while exchanging intimate conversations. The ambience was superbly elegant.

Ok, Bernie, you came through after all!

As we turned our attention to the menu, I was disoriented to find it all in French, and therefore completely unintelligible. The exorbitant prices needed no translation though. On my meagre part-time salary, I hoped Paulina didn't mind if we skipped dessert. Thoughts of the credit card debt I'd be paying off over the next few months churned my upset stomach even more.

I kept puzzling why I still felt nervous given we were past the precarious first impressions, and Paulina was her predictably warm and chatty self. No sooner had I ordered something off the menu, my stomach made it clear it would not tolerate being ignored any longer.

Va aux toilettes rapidement. Translation: The toilet beckoned.

When I stood from the table, little did I know that was the last time I'd be seated with Paulina that evening. I only just made it to the bathroom stalls before dropping to my knees and vomiting into the toilet bowl. And so, this repeated for the next 45 minutes.

I had poorly judged a 24-hour bout of gastritis for first-date jitters, leaving Paulina to literally eat our first dinner together, all on her own. She told me later that the food was delicious, the company average, and the noise of my retching from behind the rear partition wall, absolutely horrendous.

When I finally emerged from the back room to settle the bill – for a meal I hadn't touched and ironically, could barely afford – I got a sudden flush of confidence. Rather than escort Paulina straight to the car and call it a night, I believed I could salvage the evening with a romantic walk along St Kilda pier.

Despite Paulina's protests, I assured her the fresh air would do me good. Apparently, it wasn't enough. After three further episodes of vomiting over the rail, feeding the grateful fish their own meal of fine French cuisine, Paulina insisted on driving *me* home.

There I was, chauffeured home by my date while I sat in the front passenger seat with a paper bag feeling like the night couldn't have gone any worse. I didn't dare contemplate a kiss of any sort to wrap up the evening, not with what was almost certain barf-breath. The only positive memory of the occasion were the flowers that greeted Paulina as she returned home that evening. An arrangement, I knew, that would only last three to four days, at best.

Our night at The Stokehouse is reminiscent of a popular scene in *Wayne's World*, a 1992 Paramount Pictures comedy. The eponymous character Wayne Campbell is giving dating advice to his half-witted side kick Garth Algar and postulates: "I say hurl. If you blow chunks and she comes back, she's yours. If you spew and she bolts, then it was never meant to be."

Well, with that immutable relationship principle applied and tested, time would tell. I certainly "hurled" enough times for Paulina to bolt – in a week or so I would learn whether she was mine.

IT DIDN'T TAKE that long.

A few days later, Paulina rang to enquire how I was doing. I asked for a do-over, and she graciously accepted. Without flowers, new shirts, or foreign menus, our second date was everything our first one should have been.

We had a casual dinner at *The Keg*, a simple family restaurant five minutes from home. I ordered a foot-long chicken pastry with gravy. I'd had this dish before, but it had never tasted so good – the flavours enhanced this time by the beautiful company I shared it with. We talked for nearly four hours about Paulina growing up in Brazil, the experiences that led her to move to Australia, and some of our shared memories of school. More importantly, we swapped dreams for the future. Conversation flowed so naturally, it felt like we had been friends forever.

Toward the end of the evening, I was determined to share my heartfelt conviction about life on the mission field. I wasn't smart enough to realise it could be a romance-killer to tell a would-be partner that my ideal job was living in a grass hut while learning an unknown dialect. That my family vision excluded the fantasy of a house in the "burbs" with a white picket fence, two kids and a dog.

I emphatically started to describe my ambition, but before I got past the story of my God-pledge given during the Saturday morning cartoon routine, Paulina stopped me.

This couldn't be good, I thought.

She said very gently, but full of compassion, "I believe God is calling me to a life of serving the poor." She described the abject poverty she had observed in Brazil, an awareness of how fortunate her life had been, and her confidence that God wanted to mobilise her to make a difference in the lives of others.

My jaw dropped, my heart went into asystole, and my eyeballs popped. If I had a ring in my pocket that evening, I would have dropped to one knee and presented it to her. I barely felt the need to finish my own sentences because Paulina and I were so aligned in all the things that mattered. With her studying nursing, and me committed to physiotherapy, it didn't take a genius to see that together we made a great package to any mission agency that needed medical skills on their team.

Call it presumption, but I was confident at that point she really was *mine*. At the very least, from that night forward, I decided I'd happily be *hers*.

AND THEN ALL the normal things happened.

We told our families we were officially dating; we had lots more dinners and movies together; and we occasionally caught the same train to university when our schedules aligned, making those early morning commutes far more tolerable. And Paulina's brothers continued to tease, torment, harass, annoy, irritate, provoke, bait, and goad us for the whirlwind romance we had been swept up in. Things moved so fast that, by the end of the same year, we were talking about engagement.

As poor students we often joked (not so carefree, on my part) that the best ring we could afford would be one of the plastic varieties that fall out of the $2 slot machines near the trolley bay at the supermarket. But as we casually walked through the shopping centres at different times, we gazed in the windows at various jewellery stores. Paulina progressively educated me on the ones she liked and, more strenuously, on the designs she didn't. I took detailed mental notes, although I tried to act nonplussed and indifferent.

Things really got serious when she saw the one that suited her perfectly. We had it pulled from the locked drawer, plucked from the tray, and fitted to her ring finger before I could finish my double chocolate milkshake. And I'll admit, it looked fantastic. Partly because it was a central brilliant cut diamond in an 18-carat yellow gold rub setting, flanked by two shoulder diamonds. But more so because it signalled our imminent wedding and an enduring life together.

Movies and pop culture constantly depict men's fear of commitment, and comical delay tactics to avoid settling down and getting married. I'm not sure if that's real for most men, or just media hype that makes for entertaining sitcoms and raucous stand-ups. For me, at least, it was never a problem. I couldn't wait to be married to Paulina, even if at times I played it as cool as the waters off Phillip Island that day she first got my attention.

We agreed it was the right ring, at the right price, but I was going to have to earn it off. We put it on lay-by and swore ourselves to secrecy. I gave Paulina my commitment I would work hard over the coming year to pay it off before we graduated. I then went to the bank the next day and withdrew my covert savings that had been squirrelled away for such an occasion.

I rushed to the store, paid for the ring in full, and hurried home to hide the blue velvet box until I was ready to reveal it. I felt quite smug when I saw Paulina later that day, knowing I could pick my preferred timing for the proposal, and would use the element of surprise to my full advantage.

10
get MAD, not even

DURING THESE FRENZIED years of university, dating, and young adulthood, I took on the shared responsibility to lead a youth group of 13 to 15 year olds at our local church. Together, with a fellow school alumni, we dedicated every Wednesday night, Friday night, and however many hours it demanded of us in between, to help this wonderful, but sometimes unruly, mid-adolescent gang of teens journey through puberty, faith, and school. We aptly called ourselves MAD, an acronym for *Making a Difference*.

I facilitated Bible studies, worship services, mission fundraisers, and games nights. We were also especially creative with wild debates on moral issues, inciting leaders-versus-kids shaving cream fights, music concerts, and weekend camps.

One unforgettable event was a two-day retreat to Delhuntie Park, an adventure camp that caters to disadvantaged kids. The facility is fully equipped with flying foxes, water sports, rope courses, and other physical activities – the risks of which we were soon to discover. Within 15 minutes of unloading the kids from the buses at the campsite, two boys suffered compound fractures of their left arms from separate unsanctioned activities. Before we had even assigned them cabins or unpacked their bags from the trailer, the injured youths were immediately ferried in cars to the nearest hospital, never to return to the campground that weekend. What a tragic start to a hopeful weekend.

At my peak, I was coordinating more than 30 adult leaders (many much older than myself) to care for about 150 youth. It was incredibly fulfilling to observe these children grow into men and women of strength, integrity, and faith in God. I have watched some of them graduate, buy and sell businesses, marry, have children, work for the church, and go abroad themselves on their own mission adventures.

It's helpful for me to remember that sometimes our best fruit grows on other people's trees.

DURING A TIME when I was investing hours of my limited availability into children I barely knew, it was especially poignant that one couple chose to invest themselves into Paulina and me.

Michael and Marion had two sweet girls, and the eldest of them participated in our MAD program. At an information evening we hosted for parents at the beginning of term, they thanked us for the positive input we were having in their daughter's life, and reciprocated with a genuine offer of help. They gestured if we ever needed advice or encouragement in our relationship or leadership, they would be honoured to serve.

Only a few years later, we seized the opportunity.

As Paulina and I transitioned out of youth leadership and into other voluntary roles within the church, Michael and Marion became important friends. With genuine interest, they carefully coached us in our marriage, the business we were soon to start, and our spiritual journeys.

It was clear to me then: God enables us to reap when we sow. His rewards are disproportionately greater than what we ever offer up in the first place. I was willing to give some discretionary time to a room full of youth a few nights a week and, in return, I was blessed with mentors for a lifetime.

11

Landmines

BY DECEMBER OF 1996, only eleven months after my first trip, I packed my bags for a return to Cambodia. Most people never get to visit this incredible country once in their lifetime; I was going to land at Pochentong airport twice in the same year. This time, I was a co-leader of the trip, Paulina was part of the team, and our mission was specifically medically orientated.

My trip included a four-week clinical placement sanctioned by the University of Melbourne. The intention was to work with an international team of Japanese and English prosthetists and orthotists from Calmette Hospital on a string of amputee limb projects in central and regional Phnom Penh. A Christian friend from university, Kate, agreed to accompany me on this placement, as the work was too demanding for one physiotherapist. Kate and Paulina formed such a strong bond during this trip, and on subsequent occasions, that Kate was in our bridal party less than two years later.

The prosthetists and orthotists measured, manufactured, and fit the artificial limbs; and we, as physios, were tasked with teaching the patients how to walk on them. It all sounded relatively straightforward, but the language barrier proved excruciatingly frustrating, especially without the benefit of a translator. Teaching wound care, the biomechanics of gait, and exercises to strengthen the core muscles around the hip and knees proved a complex task when we were reduced to charades, *Pictionary*, sign language, and universal facial grimaces as our only means of educating. But it was a rewarding experience, amidst an otherwise fatiguing and confronting month.

Giving the Khmer people their legs back meant more than just being able to walk again; they could work again too – a necessary precursor for any form of financial independence and societal restoration. Soldiers, farmers, mechanics, bus drivers, bakers, chefs, and road builders. We watched many of our new friends stand tall in their custom prostheses, mirroring the same transformation that was happening to them as a nation. Despite their frightening hardships, each patient learned to lift their heads high and take another brave step.

The work we were doing in Cambodia was made popular by Princess Diana and her tireless campaigning for the safe removal of landmines from the countryside of war-torn nations. Left over from the reign of the Khmer Rouge, mines were exploding every day in farmlands and rice fields, robbing countless lives of innocent civilians nearly two decades after the official genocide ended.

Only a month after my trip, in January 1997, Princess Diana displayed her signature determination and global appeal. In the Huambo province of Angola, she walked through a cleared lane in one of the active minefields, wearing protective armour and headgear, while escorted by mine-clearance experts. Images from her tour immediately circulated across international media, and raised awareness in the average household to the importance of this cause in a humanitarian context. Nobody could have imagined the media storm that would eclipse this issue by her own premature and tragic death in August of that same year.

It was a profound and disturbing observation that I saw very few children in our rehabilitation program. The shrapnel of a landmine blast typically reached about a metre off the ground, taking out the legs and lower torso of a fully grown adult, but fatally wounding a child. Never had I hoped to encounter more amputee children, because the grim alternative was knowing an even larger number of them did not survive the explosions.

As Paulina and I talked on the flight home that Christmas, we agreed this was a life worth living; God had purposed us for this mission. We recommitted again to the plan of studying hard, finishing our degrees, getting married, and then returning with fervour to give our life for the cause of Christ – feeding the hungry, clothing the naked, teaching the lame to walk, and sharing the Good News.

There was nobody I would rather do it with than Paulina.

12
rules of engagement

I LOOKED FOR an opportune time in early 1997 to speak about sensitive matters with Paulina's father, Raul, but hoping not to raise suspicions with either Paulina or her mother, Nelly.

Arriving one day with a feigned look of annoyance, I burst through their front door complaining that my car wasn't running well. Raul took the bait exactly as I knew he would. Never shy to throw his weight behind an engineering dilemma, he followed me out to the street where I already had my bonnet open, fully committed to the ruse. After speaking for a few minutes under the hood, I made it obvious he needed to "hear" the problem himself by taking the car for a drive. Once he was securely strapped into the front passenger seat, I dropped all pretence and confessed I wanted to speak about a serious topic.

Naïvely, I chose an open table at McDonalds for the second-most significant question I planned to ask that month. I bought Raul a coffee and, with a level of nervousness and nausea on par with the day I had taken Paulina to The Stokehouse, I requested his blessing to marry his daughter.

Raul was generous and gracious in his response, quickly granting his approval. Relieved how well the conversation was going, I asked him to teach me a few lines in Spanish to surprise Paulina with my proposal. Strangely, in hindsight, we sat at a fast-food restaurant, exchanging lines of Spanglish, as I practised asking Raul to *marry me*. I've thought since then, if there were any Latinos casually sitting nearby, this scene would have struck them as disturbingly odd.

ANZAC DAY COMMEMORATES and honours the service and sacrifice of Australian and New Zealand military personnel who served in wars, conflicts, and peacekeeping missions, often giving their lives for the good of their countries. It falls on the 25th of April every year. In 1997, it was also the day I planned to propose to Paulina. But, like so many other actions I've taken in life, I didn't follow the easy path.

To make best use of our public holiday, I planned a day hike through the Cathedral Ranges, a part of the Great Dividing Range in Victoria. The trail – if you can call it that – is dominated by a 7km jagged ridge with outcrops of upturned sedimentary rock. The objective was the South Jawbone Peak from Sugarloaf Saddle carpark, traversing the best parts of the Razorback Track. I covertly placed the blue velvet ring box in a redundant pair of socks in my backpack, hoping to avoid detection until the choice moment *on top of the world.*

As we laced our boots at the back of the car, Paulina noticed the spare socks sitting on top of the pack and went to grab them for an additional layer of comfort. I rudely snatched them and said, "You can't use those. They are too big for you." I pretended not to notice her offended glare, hoping she would forgive my abruptness when my full intentions were later made known.

Without any further explanation, I grabbed my pack and headed for the trail head, completely panicked by the near miss. My sharp response didn't help the mood for the first 30 minutes of our walk, nor did the fact that I got us completely lost. What should have been a half-day trek turned into a six-hour off-road bush-bashing ordeal that left Paulina frustrated with my misdirection and sore from cuts and bruises down her legs. With the Sun fading, so was my confidence we would make it to the summit for my big reveal. And, even if we did, whether Paulina would now say "yes", given what I had put her through.

We eventually reached the peak and enjoyed a *very late* lunch together. I then plucked up the courage to do what I had gone up the mountain to achieve that day.

In the traditional pose, down on one knee, I presented Paulina with a spare pair of socks for the homeward descent. Of course, amidst her giggles, I made sure she knew that securely placed inside was her hand-picked engagement ring. I also managed to stutter through a paragraph of Spanish poetry to convey the important question I had prepared weeks earlier.

"Quiero pasar el resto de mi vida contigo. ¿Quieres casarte conmigo?"

Paulina threw her arms around me. Without any hesitation she accepted my proposal through a curtain of tears, accompanied by jesting slaps for having made her earn every bit of this special occasion by the gruelling scramble over boulders. She was also suspiciously curious how I raised the money to pay for the ring that only weeks prior I supposedly couldn't afford.

Our wedding date was set for the month after we were due to finish our university degrees, neither of us wanting to delay the exciting beginning of the rest of our lives together.

WITH A WEDDING to plan, a youth group to lead, and the pressure to build a small savings balance through my various jobs, it was hard to concentrate on my final years of study. I pushed through pharmacology, neuroscience, electrotherapy, pathology, community health, integrated physiology, and research methods. The course of study was demanding, requiring 35 contact hours each week, plus clinical experience in the major teaching hospitals.

I spent six weeks as a live-in resident at Geelong Hospital, and then St. Vincent's Hospital, the Ballarat Base Hospital, and the Royal Melbourne Hospital. During these placements, I rotated through the specialties of cardiothoracic inpatients, musculoskeletal outpatients, neurosurgery, gerontology, and paediatrics. The Melbourne University School of Physiotherapy was world renowned for its comprehensive curricula and high standards; we were regularly encouraged that any hospital of the world would welcome us based on the pedigree of our learning.

Summoning all my energy to remain focussed on my schedule, I was wrong-footed by an unexpected and confusing proposition in my final year of study.

Paulina and I were still volunteer leaders of the MAD youth group in our local church at the time, and our senior leaders called us for a private meeting. Despite knowing something of the trajectory my study and missions were taking us, they invited me to consider a full-time role as Youth Leader, accepting responsibilities for the 13 to 18 year-old age group, some 600 children. The opportunity was to start immediately.

Flattered by the offer – and willing to go anywhere God was sending me – I flinched. Momentarily, I was ready to give up my near-complete physiotherapy degree and accept the position on the spot. Nudged back to reality by Paulina's interjection, she thanked them for their confidence in me, and said we would pray and sleep on it.

This proved to be the first of many flashpoints that Paulina and I had to wrestle together. Whilst we were not married, we were committed to one another. It was naïve to think this decision wouldn't have profound impact on both of us.

After a strained week of indecision, mounting pressure, and many high stakes conversations, I was grateful for both Paulina's gentle counsel and my parents' encouragement to remain with physiotherapy. I was so close to the end; it didn't make sense to abandon the course now. We agreed I would reassess the direction God was leading me shortly thereafter and, if this opportunity felt right, then we would trust it would still be available after I graduated.

Grateful for the offer, I declined the invitation to work for the church, and turned my undivided attention to the last big push through my final semester.

This choice was a powerful lesson for me to never let circumstances dictate my decisions, especially when doubts loom large.

I ENDURED WHAT seemed unending hours of study, and I topped the Deans Honour List every year of my degree with the highest weighted average performance. After four arduous years, I was relieved and exhausted to finally reach the end.

At our graduation ceremony on the 6th of December 1997, I was honoured to give one of the two valedictorian addresses. I told three stories that day to encourage and prepare the graduating cohort for life after university; I remember at least one of them clearly.

Knowing nothing about greyhound racing, I repeated what someone else had taught me.

I explained that professional race stewards were known to wave a fake rabbit in front of the dogs immediately before the starting traps opened, agitating the animals, making them eager to race. This preamble assured a competitive spectacle. When the gates flung wide and the race began, the dogs instinctively chased the mechanical lure with unbridled madness, rounding track corners like they were at Talladega. As the first animals crossed the finish line, and the "rabbit" suddenly disappeared, predictably the dogs would pull off the chase, ending the race.

I told the audience that week after week, this routine is repeated at greyhound tracks all over the country. The dogs line up again, the "rabbit" makes another appearance, and the race is run like the last.

At this point, I turned to my student peers and empathised with them how easy it would be to criticise the stupidity of the dogs. *Why don't they learn? Isn't it obvious to them the event is rigged?* We collectively agreed that the canines would never catch the "rabbit".

With my story finished, I used a dramatic pause to setup the application. I asked my audience – faculty members, family, and students alike – to take a step back and look at the frenetic pace we all ran every day. I challenged them to be honest about what drives them – and about how fiercely they chase unattainable or counterfeit pleasures. I reflected with them: "If someone was watching our lives from afar, like we just imagined the dog race, would they see some similarities?"

I spent another few minutes breaking down the parable, getting people to reflect on their motivations in life. I extended the story and explained to them that any greyhound that catches the lure, and chews into the plastic moulding, will quickly realise they have been duped. These dogs are ruined for racing.

I postulated: "What happens when we buy the dream car, move into the house by the beach, and finally outplay the competition for the promotion to the corner office? Will we too quickly find life's momentary pleasures are not what they promised – often empty and unfulfilled?"

I took a risk in my closing comments, many knowing my strong convictions. My final words of encouragement to the 80 people with whom I had spent four long and gruelling years, shoulder-to-shoulder in lectures, practicals, tutorials, and clinical placements, was to not chase the fleeting trappings of a temporary life. I encouraged them to look higher, look deeper, look wider. Discover if there is a God and, if so, what He might be planning for their life. To be a healthcare practitioner who doesn't just treat the body but also cares for the soul of their patients.

Regardless of whether people agreed with me, I think they liked my sincerity.

Reminiscent of my final year at Waverley Christian College, I went on to scoop nine of the 25 subject awards, including the coveted Josephine Jennings and Edith Pratt Memorial Award for equal dux of the graduating year. Paulina was there to witness my celebratory toss of the mortar board, just as I was with her a year later when she graduated from the School of Nursing at Latrobe University.

We both stood on the threshold of an exciting life together; soon to be married, working in our chosen professions, and expecting to be deployed into the developing world on a mission to help those who needed it most. We were dizzy with hope and ideas; cautious to not let the "lures" in our peripheral vision run us off course.

13
hitched

IT WAS THIRTY-SIX degrees Celsius outside, and not much cooler inside the church. Clearly the evaporative air conditioning was no match for the penetrating heat of our midsummer January Sun in Melbourne. I was regretting my choice of attire; a three-piece black wedding suit. But that's where the regrets stopped.

It had been 13 intense months getting to the altar – nearly a year to the day since we had been haggling in the dusty markets of Cambodia. Since then, we celebrated our engagement, transitioned the youth group to new leadership, both graduated from university, landed (but not yet started) our first professional jobs, joined a church-planting team, and planned a wedding ceremony for 250 guests.

On 11th January 1998 Paulina and I exchanged rings with the words "no back doors" etched on the inside of our wedding bands. This inscription was shorthand for a mutual commitment that, with God's help, we would never back out on each other. We promised to always face each other, talk it out, work it out. We were entering marriage through the "front door", and it was for life!

Paulina looked radiant in her brilliantly white, sequined gown, contrasted perfectly against her smooth bronzed skin. The whole ensemble was set ablaze by her gorgeous smile and electric eyes. We held each other, *for better, for worse; for richer, for poorer; in sickness and in health.*

Hundreds of people witnessed our exchange of vows that day including hordes of teenagers from our MAD youth group, friends from both of our universities, and past participants from our mission trips. Teachers from Waverley Christian College turned up to congratulate us, and our previous school principal and mentor, Mr Sheahan, presided over our wedding reception. I was joined by my closest friends: Aaron, my Best Man; and Adrian, the "big brother" I never had. Paulina and

I felt loved and valued by all those who mattered, proving to be an essential platform on which to springboard into married life together.

OUR HONEYMOON PROVED magical. We spent our first night together in the quiet hills of the Dandenong Ranges in an exquisite suite. The next day we escaped to the "spa country" of Daylesford in the northwestern region of outer Melbourne, famous for its natural mineral springs. We were deeply tired on reaching the secluded cottage on the outskirts of town and slept most of the five days. It was as though the ten years of school, university, and work had all accumulated into an enormous sleep debt, and our bodies were making a margin call. It was refreshing to have no demands placed on us and, for that week, simply enjoy each other's company as we talked, planned, dreamed, and snored on the couch with a B-grade movie softly muted in the background.

Married for one week, we then embarked on a trip abroad to Mana Island, a four-star resort in an idyllic sanctuary at the epicentre of Fiji's breathtaking Mamanuca chain of islands. Surrounded by postcard perfect turquoise seas, coral reefs, and white sandy beaches, we fell deeply in love with the people and paradise, vowing to return many more times in the years to come.

Lazing together in the afternoon breeze by one of the many pools, books in hand, we were approached by a Fijian concierge. He carried a handwritten message, penned in the form of a question, with a return phone number to whom I should provide the answer. The note was from the Human Resources manager at my new employer, the Royal Melbourne Hospital (RMH).

Paulina and I had both successfully won our first graduate roles at the same hospital, and agreed with them to a common starting date in mid-February. We figured this would give us time to enjoy our honeymoon and set up house before our commitments to the new roles commenced.

That plan quickly evaporated.

The memo carried by our tropical courier advised me that the RMH physiotherapy department was so short-staffed that summer that they tracked me down on our remote island honeymoon to ask me to start "…immediately".

The concierge concisely replied by email, on my reluctant behalf, with two-words: "One week!"

PAULINA'S FATHER, RAUL, was a qualified electrical engineer from Chile – who escaped the Pinochet regime in the 1970s – and worked in complex and well-paid professional roles as an expatriate in Brazil. A proud and accomplished man who achieved excellence in his field, Raul set his sights on a long and fulfilling career. But plans changed! To be close to extended family, he and Nelly landed in Melbourne in 1986 with Paulina and her two brothers, all under the ages of ten.

If crossing continents was not disorienting enough, the fact that Raul's university qualifications were never to be recognised in his newly adopted home "Down Under" had devastating effects on both his income and identity. Never afraid of hard work, however, and always exercising an innate entrepreneurial sense, Raul initially worked long hours hauling plasterboard on a manufacturing line, before buying – with the help of some friends – an old six-tonne truck and freelancing as a furniture removalist.

We often laugh that Raul never bothered to get the necessary endorsement on his driving licence to legally operate the truck. Typical of his pragmatism and bravado – if not, an indifference to rules – Raul saw an opportunity and went for it.

He needed a truck; he bought a truck; he drove a truck.

It was a simple formula, and he made it work. Both sons jockeyed in the truck for Raul over the years at some point, casually labouring when the jobs were too big for one man, or when they simply needed to earn extra money.

I was invited into the removalist crew at times. Working for Raul was a rite of passage in the Echeverria household, along with stomaching avocado milkshakes and swallowing a heaped serving of their favoured rice and beans dish, *feijoada*.

One time, Raul and I shifted the contents of an entire house from the outer suburbs of Melbourne to the coastal town of Merimbula in southern New South Wales. We packed not only the truck, but also a four-tonne trailer, and headed off together late in the evening after a full day's work.

As Raul drove the truck, I could barely stay awake in the passenger seat. Like an ancient form of interrogation torture, he kept talking loudly and clapping whenever I dozed, needing me awake to keep him alert. What should have been a seven-hour drive through the night took over ten-hours for reasons neither of us could explain, except to notice the truck really struggled up the hills. It wasn't until we reached our destination and started to unload the furniture, the cause was immediately apparent; we had driven the 580 kilometres with the hand brake on the hired trailer.

In that very same truck, fully loaded with the few pieces of second-hand furniture we had collected in recent months, Paulina's parents picked us up from Melbourne airport. The honeymoon was over, but I was convinced the best was yet to come.

WE MOVED INTO a small, two-bedroom unit in a block of ordinary, outdated, and unremarkable flats in Coburg. When surveying the options on where to live, Paulina only had one condition: "No horrid 1980's orange benchtops, please" – as though it was framed as a request, and not the demand I knew it to be.

Like a Nostradamic self-fulfilling prophecy, you can probably guess the décor of our first kitchen – gaudy, bright orange laminate on every wet surface in the kitchen, bathroom, and laundry!

We chose the location because it was about all we could afford close to RMH, despite feeling a little unnerved that our new home was situated between a drug and rehabilitation clinic on one end of our street and a train station notorious for disorder and crime at the other.

The shift from our respective family homes in the outer eastern suburbs of Melbourne to the less familiar, less affluent, and more ethnic inner northern suburbs was a cross-cultural experience. I was surprised we didn't need our passports stamped when we moved into the neighbourhood. It was our first place together, and we loved the promise of adventure.

We had not completed our first 24 hours in the neighbourhood before becoming a victim of local crime. Raul parked the removal truck in the driveway of the block of units, lowered the tailgate, and swung open the two rear doors. As he progressively moved items toward the rear of the truck, the rest of us took turns running up and down the two flights of stairs to our flat with armloads of goods. In the coming and going, Raul didn't notice that an unidentified person simply helped themselves to our television on the tailgate. It wasn't until the end of the day that we had even discovered our loss by the brazen thief.

Months later we also had our bikes stolen from the bottom of our stairs. In the short time it took for us to park them, run inside for a drink, and then return to pack them away, they disappeared. We quickly learned this new community had a different idea of sharing and borrowing.

So used to these sorts of disturbing occurrences, we learned to laugh at them. Like the time I went to borrow some ingredients for dinner from a neighbour and, after some repeated knocking, she greeted me with a knife at the door for her own protection. Or when plain clothes AFP detectives showed us photos of two criminals who had escaped the nearby rehab centre, questioning us if we had seen their whereabouts nearby, and cautioning us of danger.

Or the morning after Paulina had returned from night shift at the hospital and was startled by a loud banging on the front door of the flat above. Curious as to the commotion, and wary of our neighbour above in potential danger, Paulina walked onto the small brick balcony to investigate. Within minutes, she saw a large man bounding down the external staircase carrying a television across the lawn. So paranoid that every suspicious encounter was someone taking advantage of us, Paulina convinced herself she was witnessing another robbery in progress. Reckless toward her own safety, Paulina shrieked from the vantage point of the first floor, "Stop. You're caught! I saw your face. Put that television down. I'm calling the police right now!"

As adrenaline put her sympathetic nervous system on high alert, Paulina was somewhat subdued on hearing a quiet but determined voice appealing to her from the balcony above: "It's OK Paulina, thank you. Really! I just sold that man my TV." The poor gentlemen, nearly stumbling under the awkward weight of his recent purchase and disoriented by all the yelling, made a B-line for his car without a word of defence or explanation.

Life in Coburg was a series of humorous anecdotes that, one day, we agreed might make an entertaining book (*and here it is!*).

Not because of these events alone, but in hindsight our first year of marriage was certainly our toughest. Starting new jobs, moving churches, living in a new neighbourhood, learning how to share a house and, most significantly, dealing with the distorted rhythms created by Paulina's oscillating day and night shifts, all contributed to early challenges.

For many consecutive weeks we savoured brief moments of crossover when Paulina wearily stumbled up the stairs from a night shift, and I carried my bike down on the way to work. We weren't sure how long we could sustain this asynchronous pattern, reminding ourselves it was only a temporary arrangement.

Our saving grace in that first year was the heartfelt encounters we shared over a plate of home-baked, cheese-laden nachos in front of a new episode of *Seinfeld*. We would sit and talk those evenings – in the glow of the orange light reflecting off our very bright kitchen benches – about how excited we were to eventually travel overseas and join a medical mission project. "It's only a matter of time", we consoled each other.

We were convinced of our calling, and determined to do God's work, which kept us motivated throughout the mundane. Our suitcases were kept close at hand; and our travel documents were in order. To my reckoning, an invitation or opportunity to join a missionary team overseas was imminent, and we just had to tread water a few months longer.

14

code brown

MY HOLD-OVER STRATEGTY was to work in the Intensive Care Unit (ICU) at RMH until the right missionary opportunity presented itself. It was an important job, being responsible for intubated patients recovering from life-threatening accidents or life-saving surgery.

My shift typically started the same way most mornings, with a ward round. A gaggle of over-worked yet indefatigable medicos would hover around the end of each bed in the ICU, conversations led by the intensivist masquerading at times like a game show host. Using dramatic flair, and the art of theatrics, the senior doctor would ask questions of the registrars and support team they already knew the answers to. With an air of arrogance and superiority, only the more gracious consultants would sometimes offer multiple choice options to the quizzical scenarios presented, throwing a bone to the sleep-deprived "contestants" who were trying to win favour with their medical overlords.

I found it somewhat ironic that I was a junior member of this team, yet usually spared the humiliation and intimidation from above. The senior doctors made the registrars and residents their primary targets, given RMH was, after all, a teaching hospital. And despite the IQ of any one of these student doctors exceeding that of all the combined scores of everyone else attending the round, they were often made to feel stupid and incompetent. I did not understand the strategy, but observed this to be a common, albeit regrettable, culture of the hospital system everywhere I worked.

My graduate rotation was under the lead of George, a highly credentialed cardiothoracic therapist. He was accompanied by Jonathan, who would go on to have a career in health policy and peak body management, eventually becoming CEO of World Physiotherapy, representing more than 125 countries. As both men were highly intelligent, quick witted, and openly gay, they took great pleasure in not only holding me to task for my medical knowledge, but also testing my conservative Christian views.

The banter would ebb and flow across the different shifts we shared. Nobody took offence, but equally nobody gave up much ground. We swapped stories of their trips to the Sydney Mardi Gras with my weekend church services, somehow all ending up in mischievous laughter together, enjoying the camaraderie. I certainly learned much more than just physiotherapy from these mentors, and reflect on this being a great start to my professional network.

My first patient was the most memorable – for all the wrong reasons. On my first day in the ICU I was assigned the care of Chris, a 17-year-old apprentice plumber who had fallen off his trail bike while riding without a helmet on a family property. He had broken his mid-cervical spine in three places, leaving him paralysed below the chest, and suffering irreversible brain damage from a subdural haemorrhage.

With Chris suspended in a medically induced coma, my primary role was to stabilise his head as his rigid neck collar was changed every day for skin hygiene and wound care. I also had to mechanically suction and posturally drain his lungs to ensure Chris didn't develop any infectious pneumonia or pulmonary complications from the prolonged intubation.

For six consecutive days, right through the weekend, Chris was my highest priority. I watched as his parents and older brother came and went, carrying a burden of grief and deep sadness that can only be truly known from direct experience. As I diligently worked on Chris, I tried to strike gentle and sensitive conversation with his mother. She was more open and engaging than the father, looking for ways to physically connect with her son and get involved in his treatment. I taught her how to assist me in positioning Chris for relative comfort, and to optimise his airways. She assisted with the collar changes by handing me gauze and towelling when I needed it.

I sensed their deep loss long before Chris even passed; but he inevitably did. It was confronting to lose my first patient. Debriefing with Paulina in the days that followed, I was determined to be more attentive to life and its many opportunities, not wanting to take any day for granted.

A less profound, but equally memorable moment came when I assisted a stroke patient up from lying to facilitate limb exercises over the side of his bed. With a colleague supporting his paralysed legs in front, we had Harry recline against me as I kneeled up behind him on the hospital bed.

Not atypical of some patients with neurological disorders, the movement caused Harry to completely lose control of his bowels midway through the therapy session. My uniform shirt and dress pants were irreplaceably soiled. To the humour of the staff around me, this event triggered what we called in the industry a "code brown"! I spent the rest of the day doing my rounds in theatre scrubs generously offered by one of the orderlies, disposing of my uniform without any interest in attempting to launder them.

I always kept a spare change of clothes in my locker after that day.

PAULINA WAS STATIONED as a neurosurgical nurse on the fourth floor of RMH. Two of my supervising physios on that ward regularly reminded me how lucky I was to have married Paulina. They liked to announce loudly in staff meetings, and as we passed in the busy corridors, that I was "batting well above my average", as is often said of young men in my fortunate situation.

The only sympathisers who would sometimes come to my defence were the elderly female patients on the ward who thought I reminded them of their grandsons. The *yayas* always thought I looked Greek. The *nonnas* claimed me as Italian. It seemed I could pass for most west European heritage, even though my genes are only one part Italian for every thirty-two parts Anglo Saxon. It's an example of people seeing what they want to see.

There were occasions where Paulina and I worked the same shift on the same ward, and shared patients in common. I enjoyed spreading cheeky scandals amongst the patients during their rehab sessions, pointing out how pretty I thought the nurse was. Some would mock-reprimand me, but most couldn't help but agree. Within minutes, I felt compelled to tell them the whole story, sharing accounts of our recent wedding and being called up by the hospital during our Fijian honeymoon to start work earlier than planned. When I freely admitted to them that Paulina was way out of my league (as it's always better to jump than be pushed), occasionally one of the dear older ladies (with failing eyesight and severe neurological deficits), would encourage me that we both looked a "beautiful match".

From the ICU, I moved through various other hospital rotations including aged care, infectious diseases, inpatient orthopaedics, neurology, and neuro-spinal surgery, before landing in what was to become my sweet spot: outpatient orthopaedics. Working in this area, I saw a mix of limb fractures, soft tissue sporting injuries, major joint (mostly hip and knee) replacements, post-operative hand and wrist injuries, and chronic spinal pain. As the name suggests, whilst these patients had presumably been in hospital at some point, they were well enough to be discharged home and attended the hospital by appointment as a day patient.

Operating under the distant supervision of the senior physiotherapist of the outpatient clinic, I essentially managed my own patient caseload and appointment schedule. The people attending the clinic had fewer complex conditions than inpatients, and I could be far more adventurous and creative in the design of treatment programs to progress them through to full recovery.

It was extremely fulfilling to see people at the tail end of their rehabilitation return to full function after often extended periods of hospital stay. I was able to watch them resume their ordinary lifestyle activities, including a return to work and, in some cases, facilitate their competing in high level sport again. I came alive; this was an area in which I felt I could invest my career.

I also noted that the risks of any future "code browns" were dramatically lower in this specialty!

AS I WAS starting to find my stride in the outpatient department, sadly Paulina was losing hers. In the same way that I was led by senior clinicians in my rotating placements, Paulina received oversight from Nurse Unit Managers and Clinical Educators in the different fields of expertise that made up her first-year program.

Whilst some of her supervisors were wonderful people, there was a notable exception: Matron X. Having already been warned about this senior nurse by friends who had rotated through the ward, Paulina approached the situation with care to avoid any provocation.

From her first shift though, trouble began; and within weeks it was unbearable. Paulina was not surprised, but deeply disappointed. The verbal abuse, intimidation, aggression, and gaslighting terrorised the junior nurses. Paulina came home crying many nights, reluctant to go to work the next day. She counted the weeks on the calendar, marking time before the end of her rotation. I repeatedly begged her to report the behaviour, as too many people before her had experienced the same, and it was now the worst-kept secret in the hospital café. I relied on false hope and empty platitudes just to get her out of the house some mornings, knowing she would have to endure the same abuse all over again.

So bad at one point, Paulina broke down. On a weekend when we were riding our bikes through the streets of Brunswick, she got her tyre caught in a tram track and flew over the handlebars. She just laid on the asphalt sobbing. Fearing she had hurt herself badly and aware that we had traffic approaching from both directions, I quickly bent down to help her up. She resisted; preferring just to lie there, completely still, and in no hurry to get up. She was not especially hurt from the bike accident, but completely exhausted by the continuous taunting from her supervisor. She knew that if she got up it meant she would have to go to her next shift and face more emotional battering. So, for just a moment, she allowed herself to pretend she didn't have to move. She could just lay there and weep for a few minutes in an artificial bubble of denial.

Eventually, Paulina and a colleague courageously reported the continuous verbal abuse everyone had suffered. The supervisor was confronted by senior management and Matron X was removed. All this happened just as Paulina was readying to transition through her next ward rotation, so the timing was too late for her direct benefit; but she had spared some pain for those who followed. For months to come there was palpable relief spoken amongst the graduates that the ward on the fourth floor was safe again.

It was our first real encounter with how dangerous and hurtful the workplace can be. Little did we know how many times we were going to face similar and worse challenges in the future.

FOR MOST OF our first year of marriage, we worked opposite shifts. Paulina was stumbling into bed while I was hopping out of the shower most mornings. Or in the evenings, I was staying up late to catch her after an afternoon shift, which would have her home little before 11pm.

We were burning the candle at both ends as we tried to savour some time together in the matrix of our conflicting schedules.

When I didn't ride my bike to work, I would sleep my way on Tram Route 19. Even though the commute was a short 14 minutes from our apartment to the front door of the hospital, because of perpetual sleep deprivation, I managed to reach stage two REM most times – where my eyes fluttered behind heavy eyelids and my heart rate sped up under the spell of vivid dreams of the mission field.

On one tram ride, I remember conceding that I no longer wanted to continue at the hospital. I was growing increasingly impatient about being stuck in Australia and not already living and working in the developing world. And I felt my impact on the wards was limited with the constraints of the public health model. Both frustrations made the status quo unbearable.

Paulina was supportive of me exploring all my options; this included me seeking approval from my department supervisor to take up some special projects at RMH to broaden my experience and stimulate other interests. I took on a raft of administrative responsibilities in addition to my clinical caseload, including Department Inservice Coordinator, New Graduate Representative on the Northwestern Health Care Network Physiotherapy Board of Studies (what a mouthful!), and Coordinator of Second Year Melbourne University Student Clinical Program.

Later, I added to this portfolio the Clinical Supervisor role for third- and fourth-year Student Clinical Placements at RMH, which required me to prepare tutorials, teach practical skills, provide continual clinical assessments of student performance, and then supervise their final examinations. This latter opportunity was an especially big responsibility as the students' graduation and future careers were somewhat determined by my judgement. I felt the pressure to be well prepared every day, often working well into the evening the night before to ensure I was ready.

As I succeeded in these responsibilities, I was also asked to tutor the first- and second-year physiotherapy students on campus at the University of Melbourne and, in addition, take on a supervisor role for third-year Melbourne University Inpatient Orthopaedic Student Placements at the affiliated Austin Repatriation Hospital in Heidelberg West. This meant I was now working across three different locations in any given week: the RMH, the university, and the Austin. I felt busy as

I tried to keep all my rising tensions in balance. It was a lot to handle in only my second year of professional life.

To top this off, I was offered to undertake a PhD in osteoarthritis of the knee. Whilst I wasn't compelled toward research, all this diversity provided me broader experiences and revealed my love for mentorship and teaching. And whilst I doubted I would enjoy a career in academics, I certainly was grateful for the mix-up in responsibilities, as it provided a welcomed break from monotonous ward rotations and distracted me from one poignant fact: I still wasn't a missionary yet.

15

bow ties

MIDWAY THROUGH MY second year as a graduate, I resigned from the hospital and, along with it, all my other extracurricular responsibilities, never to return to public health. Of course, at the time, it didn't feel like a big loss, as I expected to be working overseas before the year was through.

There was insufficient staff and resources at the hospital to deliver evidence-based, quality *health*care, and so I felt reduced more often to delivering its poor substitute; *sick*care. This is less of a criticism of the great work my peers were doing, and more a reflection of my then-emerging philosophy of what true holistic health should look like.

I wanted to be a therapist at the top of the proverbial cliff, preventing people from falling off, rather than standing at the bottom and fixing them when they inevitably did. I was attracted to preventative medicine, integrated services that empowered people to live in optimal health. Rather than just treating the sick, injured, and unwell, I wanted to explore how I could coach people to live at their physical best. The hospital was never going to offer these opportunities; I had to cross to the *dark side* and join the private sector to pursue these ideals further.

I accepted a junior associate role at a small obscure practice in the eastern suburbs of Melbourne. This private business was owned by a veteran Olympic physiotherapist, Mark. In the year to follow I humorously told him that he reminded me of the *Monopoly* man, minus the monocle. Mark was short but strong, had thinning hair atop a small round face that was framed by wire-rim glasses and a permanent smile, and was rarely seen without sporting one of his many colourful bow ties. Even when he was down at the football club treating dirty, sweating players, the bow tie remained; it was his signature accessory. Others in the profession may not have known his name, but when I referenced the "bow tie", they knew exactly who I was working for.

I enthusiastically returned from my first interview with Mark confident I had landed the job, but more eager to report to Paulina how amused I was to see a physio wearing such ridiculous attire. Paulina taunted, "You know that he is going to expect you to wear a bow tie, too!". I laughed away her mocking prediction, confident that wouldn't be the case. I boldly declared that I would refuse to work there if that were the case.

It was certainly a humbling, if not infuriating, experience, to turn up on my first day of work in a crisp professional shirt, only to have Mark refuse me treating my first patient until I donned one of his bow ties. To this day, one of my most embarrassing media articles (and there have been quite a few!) is a full-page advertorial Mark paid to run in the local newspaper announcing my arrival to the practice, showcasing our mugshots complete with matching bow ties. One of us wasn't smiling for the camera, although Paulina milked the humour of this at every opportunity.

After about three months of complying with the bow tie rule, I raised the issue with Mark in our "staff meeting" of four people. There was Mark and me as the physiotherapists, his wife the receptionist, and his father, who was something of a drop-in casual handyman. At my earnest suggestion that I could wear a necktie instead of a bow tie, Mark flatly refused. I tried on every plausible argument – orthopaedic surgeons weren't going to refer their patients to a pretentious 23-year-old dressed for a gala ball; patients thought it was laughable; I was diminishing his iconic trademark and identity brand. I went as far as citing research that the restricted blood flow might even impair my clinical reasoning and professional judgment. Every defence fell flat. I persisted for week after week with my appeals, hoping to wear him down.

Eventually, Mark's wife spoke up and agreed with me. She admitted to Mark, possibly for the first time, that we both looked ridiculous in the bow ties, and that neither of us should wear them. From that day, at least I gained my freedom and have barely worn one since. All these years later, whenever I see Mark, true to his convictions, he can be found proudly boasting one from his latest collection!

MARK WAS RELIABLY upbeat and optimistic. He was passionate, intelligent, hard-working, and ambitious. He was a wonderful mentor in many ways, helping me adjust to life in a private practice after being what he called "institutionalised" by university and the teaching hospitals. He helped me understand that patients were also "customers"; that we needed to "sell" our benefits; and that we must differentiate ourselves from the various "competitors" around every corner.

Mark also exposed me to a wide variety of clinical techniques. He put a huge emphasis on differential diagnosis, manual therapy, adjunctive electrotherapy, and the importance of quality aftercare with our patients. And he especially liked to school me in the way temporo-mandibular joints (TMJ) of the jaw should be treated. He never waited for an invitation to don his gloves and dive into my mouth when he heard me clicking my way on every bite through a sandwich at lunchtime. He was convinced there was an enormous market to reach through referrals from oro-facial surgeons and orthodontists if he published his techniques, establishing them as mainstream.

Mark was so well loved by his clients that it was hard for me to build a personal caseload in his practice. His name was on the door as the principal practitioner, and for 20 years everybody only saw him. I was now the first associate to join the practice and it was hard to convince clients to take a risk on the "new guy".

For those first few weeks I did more vacuuming and sorting of the mail than seeing any clients. I remember putting together a two-page proposal for another one of Mark's "staff meetings" in the kitchen, asking him to invest $1,000 into a coordinated marketing campaign to promote my services and kick-start a client list. I had conservatively budgeted for mail drops, sporting club sponsorships, local newspaper adverts, fridge magnets, and a brochure with embedded discount vouchers. Mark agreed with the concept but was stuck on the money. He ducked, weaved, and deflected the conversation for three weeks, hoping my enthusiasm for the ideas would wane. But I kept pressing, eventually forcing from Mark a definitive "No". He told me the best way to establish my name in the area was to patiently let word-of-mouth reputation build. I silently acknowledged that, in his case, momentum had taken two decades, and I wasn't going to wait that long.

I knew, in that moment, I wouldn't stay long in the job.

I'm grateful that during my short stay with Mark, he introduced me to the world of professional weightlifting. I served at several national championships, including the 1999 Telstra Australian Open. I will never forget both the size of the male and female competitors I had to work on (often unable to get my small hands around the biceps and thighs of these giants), but also the chess-like strategy that played out in the athlete's "green room" behind the scenes as they tactically determined what weights to attempt to gain psychological advantage over each other.

I look back now and realise Mark was a shamelessly unique blend of clinician and businessman. A centaur – half-man, half-beast – who was comfortable to talk about evidenced-based clinical practice in one sentence, and then cite popular business principles in the next. He was the one who first put a copy of the well-known book, *The E-Myth*, into my hands, prompting me to read it through multiple times and mark up the sections that gained my attention.

To this point, our industry hadn't put much emphasis on business training, shunning it as being "beneath us" as a profession. Mark, however, opened my eyes to the noble cause of holding both dimensions of clinical and commercial practice in positive tension, even if I had a tumultuous journey yet to travel in coming to any convictions of my own.

Mark and I regularly disagreed on some of his approaches to life and practice, but I marvelled at his determination to take on the world with his mildly eccentric views. I watched as he willingly stirred some good-natured controversy within the profession to defend his opinions. Unknowingly, he taught me a lot about resilience, passion, work ethic, and clinical excellence. I'm very grateful to Mark for taking me on as a young and unproven associate and then graciously releasing me only a year later when I felt it was time to move on. He had arguably invested more into me than any return he had benefited from, as is often the case for small business employers.

Sitting with Mark at a café only a few years ago, I enjoyed reminding him that if it weren't for the bow tie and his denial to do some local marketing to build my referral base, I just may never have left his employ, and everything I went on to achieve through Back In Motion could have been realised under his banner.

He laughed, and in characteristic fashion, disagreed!

16

pretty as a picture

PAULINA AND I became house-hunters during my time working for Mark. We were determined to move closer to our parents in the outer south-eastern suburbs of Melbourne, where houses were considerably cheaper than the runaway prices in the inner-city suburbs.

These were the days when you looked at house adverts in a newspaper, registered your interest with as many available real estate agents in the area, and then ruled off full weekends to drive around in the back seats of their cars as they toured you through the options. It was tiring, mind-numbing, and demoralising, as you traipsed through other people's kitchens, garages, and walk-in closets – trying not to look too nosey.

But houses cost money – lots of it – and we didn't have any!

During our early years of marriage, Paulina and I learned fast that we had different philosophies when it came to money. Put simply, I was cheap! I was excited if I could get a quarter of the quality for half the price. I typically started my selections at the low end of the market, and reluctantly moved upwards when I had no choice. Paulina was the exact opposite: she started at the top, and reluctantly came down to somewhere just above the mid-range, but only when necessary.

We laugh now, but she had a *gift*: I could blindfold and spin Paulina around three times in a store, and she could point to the most expensive item every time. It wasn't that Paulina was materialistic; she just valued quality and was prepared to pay a premium for it. She believed in the axiom "You get what you pay for" – so spend more upfront, and your purchase will last longer.

Can you see the tension brewing?

We were set on a collision course time and again when it came to opening our purses and wallets. Paulina was from Venus, and I was from Mars. And buying a house together only made these differences more apparent.

The one thing we had in common with regards to finance was a mutual hatred for debt. We had borrowed $5,000 from my parents to cover some wedding expenses and the start-up living costs of setting up our first rental home. We were so determined to pay that off as quickly as possible that we set up a budget from the first week of marriage. Literally every cent was tracked and logged in an Excel spreadsheet, ensuring we remained accountable to targets on a monthly reconciliation. We were so disciplined about our spending that we relied heavily on a steady source of discount vouchers for meals and entertainment, otherwise we refused to eat out. We got into the habit of getting receipts for every purchase, right down to a Slurpee at 7-Eleven. So ingrained was this behaviour that, even today, despite electronic bank statements and in-app purchases, I still find it hard to resist taking a paper receipt as a record of my spending.

We thought if we stuck to our plan, we could pay off our debts by the end of the first year and have just enough surplus to buy ourselves a mountain bike each to commute to work. You can imagine our elation when, at month five, we settled the monies owed to our parents and were able to purchase two new Shogun Metro hybrid road bikes for $230 each – one of which, incidentally, is still going strong after 25 years (such is the value of paying for "quality"!).

Our pleasant success in paying down our first debt quickly reinforced to us the power of living within our means, and being disciplined with our money. A problem remained; house prices were going up with every month that passed, and the quality of what we were seeing was going down.

WE EVENTUALLY AGREED the upper budget limit for buying a house was $150,000. My sister had recently bought her property a little below this price, so it seemed reasonable. (Secretly, I was hoping to spend less, but I didn't share that idea with my wife.)

One property really caught Paulina's attention. It was more spacious and modern than many of the others, aptly headlined in the advertisement "Pretty as a Picture". But despite its appeal, it was so far beyond what we could afford, we walked away from it. All I could offer Paulina was the flimsy hope that if God intended us to have it, He could perform a miracle.

A pattern quickly became obvious: most of the houses available exceeded our budget by a significant margin. Not only was my frugal wish of spending less than our threshold completely obliterated, I figured we'd have to increase our limit by another $50,000 to get something that was remotely acceptable.

We prayed regularly for God to guide such a big purchase; and otherwise continued trawling through the real estate guides, inspecting houses outside our reach, and progressively becoming more despondent.

Months later, I took a phone call from an agent suggesting to us a "renovator's delight" in Scoresby. It was a three-bedroom home with a unique blue brick facade, set on a generous 800 square metres block, shadowed by numerous large silver gum trees. The home hadn't been advertised yet, not scheduled for listing for another two weeks. The agent encouraged us to take an early look to try and beat the market interest.

The price expectations were around $160,000, so Paulina and I made the time to inspect the property that evening, and quickly agreed it had lots of potential. I immediately placed an offer of $145,000 to the agent and nervously sat in his pokey office as he phoned the vendor.

It turned out we weren't the only people to inspect the house that day; another offer had been put forward through a different agent and was marginally higher than ours. We were told that a bump to $150,000 should secure the purchase.

I don't know why I didn't simply concede the extra $5,000 – it seems now a very modest increase to pay given the circumstances. Maybe I was hesitant to over-pay, sceptical of the legitimacy of the "other offer". Whatever it was, unflinchingly, I countered with a firm and final offer of $147,000, convincing the agent that it was as high as we could go. He looked surprised, as did Paulina, but dutifully relayed the revised price down the phone.

Disappointed, I felt the opportunity slipping through our hands. Paulina and I held each other and quietly prayed that God would open the "right doors" and close the "wrong ones"; we only wanted this house if it was meant to be.

After some anxious waiting, the agent walked out with an outstretched hand ready to shake. He admitted triumphantly, "That's the easiest $3,000 I've ever seen someone make." With that, he produced the contracts for sale, and we excitedly paid the deposit on our first home.

Some weeks later, thumbing through the real estate guide out of habit, we spotted our new house with it's now obsolete advertisement that had obviously been scheduled for publishing prior to sale. Above the blurb, boasting the quiet street, large block, and polished floorboards, was an attention-grabbing headline, "Pretty as a Picture".

It seems we received our miracle home after all.

17
amway

HAVING EXPERIENCED THE limitations of working in a small practice for a single owner, I swung my career pendulum to the other end of town. Living now in our new home in Scoresby, I searched for the biggest and most respected practices within a 20-minute drive.

There were a few attractive options, but one stood out. Located nearby was a double-story, purpose-built, sports medicine clinic. It boasted a team of eight physiotherapists and other sessional staff, including a podiatrist, psychologist, nutritionist, and exercise physiologist. The facility was well equipped with state-of-the-art rehabilitation equipment, the principal was well connected with elite sport, and the job offered an immediate start.

I didn't hesitate.

First impressions were amazing! The place buzzed. There were people everywhere being treated in an open-format studio; we were associated with state and national sporting teams; referring to integrated services was easy; computerised terminals made it efficient for me to take clinical histories; and I had a full client list from day one, thanks to the sudden departure of my predecessor. I immediately started hosting my own rehabilitation classes, meeting local surgeons, and participating in the multi-disciplinary in-service program. This practice had everything my last job didn't.

The shine didn't last long though. By the end of the first week, I came to learn that three more of the physio team had resigned and there was a significant cultural rift between the principal owner and his staff. The back-room talk was toxic, and two people warned me to get out before I was caught up in it too.

Before long, the dysfunction within the team was even obvious to my clients. I had patients confess I was the fourth clinician they had seen in as many months, and that the turnover of staff was affecting their treatment. Cliques formed between different employees, receptionists started favouring certain physios for receiving new patient referrals, and further resignations followed. At my 100-day milestone, I was the longest serving staff member on the team at the time. For the most part, I was able to keep my head down and plead ignorance as the "new guy", but two events brought things to an unavoidable head.

FIRSTLY, A DINNER to remember.

With what initially appeared to be a sincere effort on the owner's part to build some personal connection, he invited Paulina and I to dinner with his wife at their luxurious home in Brighton. It started well with cordial conversation, and then took a turn neither of us were expecting.

Our host started pitching Amway products to us with full brochures and catalogues. He went on to explain that he made most of his wealth through multilevel marketing, not physiotherapy, and that if I were to subscribe under his hierarchy of resellers, I too could benefit.

With awkward naïvete, Paulina and I politely deflected the offer, hoping the evening could resume its otherwise expected trajectory of light social conversation.

It didn't!

My boss didn't like hearing "No", and thought Paulina was the hesitant one. He invited me outside to the patio and continued to assert all the ways he could help me if I signed onto his program. By the time the ambush was over, Paulina and I were emotionally exhausted at defending ourselves from the persistent sales pitch. The evening never recovered after that, and on the drive home, Paulina, understandably, expressed her concerns about me continuing to work there.

THE SECOND STRIKE in my short tenure at this practice came shortly after the scandalous dinner date.

Our upcoming wedding anniversary prompted me to request a weekend off, one month in advance. I ordinarily worked Saturdays in the seven-day-a-week practice, and offered to pick up Sundays as well on the weekends either side of our anniversary to offset the one shift I planned to miss. Anticipating the helpful solution, I tentatively made these arrangements with two colleagues who were willing to help.

With the hard work done, I approached my Amway boss with confidence, believing there wasn't anything sensitive or inconvenient about my request. In fact, my preparation made it easy for him to approve the leave.

I don't know if I caught the owner on a bad day, whether he was still smarting over my refusal to join Amway, or whether this was his normal demeanour. Regardless, he exploded!

He was offended that, after less than three months working at the practice, I was asking for time off. He raised his voice and challenged my priorities. He said my career should come before celebrating anniversaries, and it was irrelevant whether other staff were prepared to adjust their schedules.

I was shocked at his outrage and immediate refusal to even consider my request.

In that moment, I felt an unusual courage to stand my ground. Indifferent to the consequences, I cited reservations about the culture in the practice, to which he questioned my loyalty and abruptly ended the meeting.

Resting at home, I was annoyed that I didn't take the opportunity to resign. Still feeling bold out of indignance for his outburst, I left a phone message to speak with him urgently. On his return call after 10pm that night, I advised of my immediate resignation, offering the obligatory one week's notice as outlined in my contract. He angrily said one week wasn't long enough, pleading for a month.

When I walked into the lunchroom the next day he berated me in front of other staff, who were unsuccessfully trying to be inconspicuous. He demanded I leave the practice immediately and not return. Holding a sandwich in one hand, I picked up my belongings from the pigeonhole in the staff room, and literally walked out the door three minutes later for what was to be, unknowingly at the time, my final day as an employee for anyone ever again.

My hands trembled on the steering wheel all the way home. I was only 24 years old, newly married, recently burdened by a mortgage bigger than I wanted, and now unemployed.

The last words I heard being yelled by my now-former-boss as I said a few casual goodbyes to the receptionists were, "You will never work as a physio again. I will finish you!".

I cried as many tears as I could before I got home so Paulina wouldn't think I was scared and weak.

As I've shared already, I was a born worrier. By the time I reached home and debriefed with Paulina, I had catastrophised this event into being the end of my career. I believed the man could do what he said, and totally ruin me. I accepted that I would never be able to get a job as a physio again – and by extension, never work as a medical missionary – as his influence and reach would be enough to destroy my reputation.

I sought advice from a trusted senior lecturer from Melbourne University. Bruce always made time for me during my undergraduate years as I was an enthusiastic student. We shared a common faith in Jesus and I loved that he volunteered his time to worthy social causes. Over the course of a long phone call I explained the last three months, and especially the last three hours. Bruce effortlessly de-escalated my emotions, reminding me the world is bigger than one principal in a suburban private practice, and assured me the Sun would rise again the next day.

Over the coming weeks I investigated the background of my prior employer. Others shared reports of this person having been brought before the physiotherapy registration board with accusations made against him for the alleged selling of Amway to patients during their consultations. Some also said he had a reputation amongst peers for being bullish and aggressive, and was believed to be disliked by a few in the profession.

The news gave me confidence that I might survive the ordeal, even though I was still unemployed. One obvious thought crossed my mind: it seemed a perfect segue for me to move to the mission field. I just hoped God agreed.

18
hypothetical

I WAS DISCOURAGED that my short career in private practice had been so unfulfilling. Although relieved to have left a toxic workplace, I didn't know what to do next. I lay on the couch for six weeks, pondering my options, wondering which third-world country needed a physio and a nurse.

Jesus is famously quoted, when teaching his disciples about reaching lost people in the world, that "the harvest is plentiful, but the workers are few" (Matthew 9:35-38 NKJV).

Paulina and I were willing to be two of those *workers* deployed for the *harvest*. But we were stuck in Scoresby – me, without a job, and Paulina working 12-hour shifts in the ICU. Our asynchronous schedules meant we passed like ships in the night, trapped in suburbia, heading nowhere we wanted, and running out of time.

I couldn't understand why God didn't want us.

MY FATHER-IN-LAW RAUL was visibly frustrated with my situation too. I'm sure he was wondering how I was going to provide for his daughter when I had changed jobs three times in our first two years of marriage. Graduating dux of my year meant nothing if I couldn't earn a living and put food on the table.

Raul repeatedly challenged me to start my own practice. I had been seeing a few friends and family from a makeshift consulting room in our carport at home during my recent employment, and Raul wanted me to make something more of that. He was confident I could build a strong client following in the local area and, with that, enjoy a reliable income.

I was convinced he underestimated the situation.

Starting my own practice would be risky and hard, two things that didn't motivate me at the time. If I couldn't make it as an employee for someone else, how could I do it by myself?

Furthermore, I kept reminding everyone, working a normal job was not what my life was about. We were committed to God's work in medical missions on the other side of the globe. Starting our own business would only distract us from that. In numerous conversations while dating Paulina, I had assured her that I had no intention of ever owning my own practice. This wasn't in the blueprint for my life.

But, on every visit to my in-laws over the next few weeks, Raul persisted.

As the idea percolated in my head, I could feel my heart race and temperature rise. I found myself playing different mind games, entertaining all sorts of hypothetical scenarios.

I envisioned the necessary renovations to convert our carport into more serviceable facilities. Thoughts darted between where I would advertise my services, and which referrers in the local area might send their patients to me. I rehearsed, in my mind, conversations with patients explaining the humble set-up to mask my embarrassment. I even caught myself running through a creative list of possible business names while I was chewing breakfast one morning. Few of these mental exercises were intentional, but the seeds that Raul and others had sown over the recent period were starting to sprout in my subconscious.

Most importantly, I started crystallising a unique and distinct philosophy of clinical care that could serve as an operational framework if I ever launched my own practice. Having had three very different formational experiences in such a short time – RMH, Mark's small practice, and the large sports medicine centre – the combination provided a crucible of insights to forge my preferred approach.

I didn't want to be a reactive practitioner, who only managed pain and symptoms after it was too late – that's how I felt working in the public health system. I wanted to get onto the front foot with clients, and help coach them in lifestyle health and fitness to prevent disease and injury.

My time with Mark in his practice taught me that there was no substitute to forming a strong alloy of sound clinical excellence with proven business practice. I couldn't expect to succeed with one and not the other. I had to merge the two worlds of healthcare and commerce if I was to make a sustainable living.

I also learned from my year with Mark that I didn't want to have a practice that relied entirely on me and took ten years to establish. I would have to do things differently to grow fast and build a team.

It was also obvious I eventually needed the look and scale of the larger and more modern sports medicine practice – where I had regrettably lasted less than four months – minus the hardship and trauma.

All three jobs helped shape and inform a possible future. The time spent in each had taught me that every experience is worthwhile, even the heartbreaking ones. I was able to cherry pick what I liked from each of the different models, and selectively bring forward the best of all worlds to form my own opportunity.

I concluded that, if one day, I was to run my own show, I would invest in a wholesome culture, develop strong team relationships, ensure it hung together on a viable ethical business model, and was all underpinned by Godly values.

Hypothetically, of course.

Like an unsuspecting frog being slowly and imperceptibly boiled in the proverbial pot, I felt myself conceding little parts of my will to the inevitable notion that my next project would be to run a small practice from home. It felt less of a choice, and more like God was using my circumstances to rail-road me into it – clearly with some help from Raul.

There was no euphoria. No grand vision. No declaration of world domination. I just morphed over the course of a few months into accepting my reality; I needed to earn a living, and I could do that from home.

Besides, the developing world didn't appear in any rush to have me.

BOOTSTRAPPING

1999-2008

*building something from the ground up with
nothing but personal savings, a little luck,
and a whole lot of grit and attitude*

Job:
*"Do you think I have nerves of steel? Do you think I'm made of iron?
Do you think I can pull myself up by my bootstraps?
Why, I don't even have any boots!"*
Job 6:12-13

BOOTSTRAPPING

19	pizzapreneur	109
20	homefront hustle	112
21	leaving the nest	120
22	a sporting chance	125
23	maiden team	128
24	ransacked	134
25	quarter life crisis	137
26	dear diary	141
27	God does math	148
28	jump	154
29	questioneering	156
30	triple threat	160
31	stretched	164
32	manifesto	166
33	Kakinada	168
34	industry debut	170
35	last hurrah	176
36	first born of franchising	182
37	mini-MBA	185
38	the gift	190
39	infertility	196
40	resentful retainers	200
41	dirty "F" word	205
42	meningitis	210
43	gouged	217
44	iceberglets	222
45	media darling	224
46	border crossing	228
47	board-om	231
48	breakthrough	235
49	feined litigation	239
50	double crash	242

19
pizzapreneur

THE SINGLE MASTERMIND who first suggested the name "Back In Motion" is disputed; but we agonised over various alternatives for weeks, convinced that the right logo would set up the business for early success. I've come to believe this is hardly true, as the name is often the least important contributor to brand value.

Take the likes of McDonalds and Apple – there is nothing clever or strategic with those name choices. It's less about the words, and more about the incredible effort someone put into defining the value and experience behind those names that have turned them into household brands. So, we probably could have launched with *any* name, and still succeed.

Nonetheless, back then, I wanted something clever, catchy, and unique. I couldn't afford to have my suburb location or surname embedded into the brand, as that would prove too restrictive if I moved the practice or wanted to sell the business. I needed a clear theme that conveyed movement and activity, as I wanted to offer a service that focussed more on health than injury. I was also drawn to a bright colour scheme for the logo to differentiate us from our traditionally beige peers.

My best recollection of this iconic moment was an evening where Paulina and I sat with my sister and her husband in their lounge room. We had ploughed through some local pizzas and were about to put on a movie, when we started brainstorming possible names for the umpteenth time. I shared my starting list, which included *Premier Physio*, *Complete Physio*, *Motion Physio*, *Back In Action*, and *Active Physio*. None of them were especially creative, but it was the best I could imagine at the time; and I still needed to check the state register of business names to see if they were even available.

We noodled on different iterations for half an hour. It was either Paulina or Leanne who offered "Back In Motion" as an alternative configuration – they can share the bragging rights - but nobody voted it the standout winner on the night. The name appealed for its quirky play on words, and was merely added to the short list scribbled on a crumpled serviette next to a pepperoni stain.

Excluding the names I subsequently found out were unavailable, we narrowed down the choices and officially registered *Back In Motion Physiotherapy* on 28th October 1999. Our figurative *first born* had been christened.

STARTING THE BUSINESS provoked hundreds of conversations, and many more personal reflections, as Paulina and I thought deeply about what we were embarking on. One of the lifelong disciplines that came from this process was my annual recording of life goals, personal vision statements, and submission to accountability partners. For more than 25 years now I have been devoting several days every January to documenting my reflections from the year just complete, and prayerfully casting forward hope and intentions for the one to come. It's a detailed process that typically results in 40 or more pages of journaling and goal setting that helps set my posture for each new year.

As Back In Motion was birthed, I penned my first set of values to kick-start the vision quest.

First, I sought for Back In Motion to become synonymous with Christian care, esteemed for its compassion and clinical excellence in equal portions, and leading the way in industry best practice.

Secondly, I hoped to become debt-free and financially secure as quickly as possible. I reasoned that the sooner we were free of any obligations to others, I could distribute our money as God directed.

Both goals were intended to be the means to achieve our third and ultimate priority: to preserve our missionary focus, ensuring all our efforts would one-day converge to providing medical care to those in desperate need, and share the Gospel of Jesus with those who were ready to hear. We expected to travel abroad as we were able, provide extensive financial support when we weren't, and equip and train others to leverage the impact.

I dreamed it out, wrote it down, and nailed my declarations to the wooden castle doors of my heart, just as Martin Luther had done centuries before when igniting the Great Reformation.

Whilst I was inexperienced in marriage, and green in business, the strength of my spiritual life was a great foundation on which to build both these things – triggering the beginnings of my own personal renaissance.

20
homefront hustle

MY BUSINESS START couldn't have been more humble or ignoble.

My attentions first turned to converting an unfinished makeshift detached room that filled one half of our double carport into a professional physiotherapy consulting suite. My Best Man, Aaron, assisted me, building a timber framework to hang external fibrocement sheeting that enclosed and waterproofed the space. We laid second-hand carpet on the floor, put architraves around a tiny window facing into the backyard, and removed the roller door to expose sufficient frontage to affix our first sign.

Given this was before the days of readily accessible online stock images, or websites like Fiverr to generate budget logos, I borrowed a computer disk of 1,000 clip-art files from our neighbour. I searched through a limited selection of relevant options and eventually conceded the only suitable choice was one depicting a man illustrating the throwing action in six sequential stages - beginning with a fully recoiled shoulder and concluding with the eventual release and follow-through of the ball. The progressive movements were silhouetted against a dark jade green background, which I thought looked elegant.

When I mocked up the image on the word processor to show Paulina, she immediately pointed out to me the figure was an American gridiron player that nobody in Australia would relate to. I dismissed her concerns, confident the picture looked generic, and convinced that the likely resolution of the image planned for uniforms and signage would not be very high quality anyway. (I then spent the next four years fielding the repeated question from friends, clients, and referrers about the story behind the *American footballer*, and whether I was from the USA. I should have listened to my wife.)

It was an exciting day when we hung our first sign, boldly advertising *Back In Motion Physiotherapy* to the nonplussed neighbourhood. To accompany our great unveiling, I ordered some custom vehicle licence plates to match: "FIZZEO" – a creative spelling of "physio" for those who could decrypt the code.

Next was my inaugural stationary with the name "Jason Smith & Associates" boasted on the letterhead when, of course, there were no other employees than me. Listing the predictable physiotherapy services, such as sports, spinal, and manipulative therapies, I courageously added massage, hydrotherapy, mobility assessments, exercise prescription, and home visits – even though I wasn't sure how I was going to meet all those demands yet. I reluctantly advertised my home phone number, as I didn't have a mobile phone for an alternative; and there was no email or website to add at that point either.

(To put life in perspective in the year 2000, Amazon was still struggling to make a profit; Wikipedia wasn't yet active; we were grateful to go from dial-up to DSL internet access; and the advent of the iPhone was still seven years in the future.)

I opened the carport practice with no receptionist, no waiting room, and no available toilet. It was a small suite with a portable massage bed, a miniature desk, and a second-hand ultrasound unit I had bought from a local sports club through the Trading Post.

I hadn't thought through all the logistics when my first few patients started attending. I quickly realised we needed somewhere for the waiting clients to sit, so I hastily located two green plastic garden chairs from the garage and set them in the driveway. To those who preferred, I offered they simply remain in their car until I was ready to usher them in for their session. This was an especially better option on wet days, as there was little protection from the rain and the wind near the entrance to our consulting room.

The set up was… *unique* – but it was ours, and patients didn't seem to mind.

Our road was a narrow, quiet suburban street, not much of a thoroughfare in our local neighbourhood. It was obvious when cars started parking on the nature strip that our little practice was going to arouse objections. I hadn't arranged any permits to operate the business from home, and hoped nearby residents didn't complain to local council.

Where possible, I asked patients to park up our driveway to avoid a nuisance. Of course, this option created all sorts of awkward manoeuvring as some people arrived while others were leaving. I discovered that treating complex injuries was the easy part; the dual roles of parking attendant and crowd control proved far more challenging.

On more than one occasion, I experienced sensitive moments as our house doubled as our practice. Such as when patients needed to use our bathroom inside, and Paulina wasn't expecting company. Or when I had patients arriving for appointments while Paulina was up a ladder painting the gutters of our carport. And when our little cocker spaniel puppy, Jessie, escaped the backyard and entered the consulting room uninvited, barking, jumping, and occasionally leaving behind a little deposit of her excitement.

Most times these moments created wonderful conversation-points with my patients; they seemed to enjoy the casual approach of our start-up enterprise, along with the more affordable prices that accompanied it.

FINDING NEW CLIENTS took creative energy. I was certainly grateful for family and close friends who actively supported our initiative, but I couldn't run a profitable business with only a dozen patients. I had to think bigger.

In that first month, I wrote 20 letters to the surrounding doctors and surgeons promoting my services. I offered to visit their practices and run education sessions on topics of interest, such as the latest research on ACL knee rehabilitation or management of herniated spinal discs.

I received a referral from one notable neurosurgeon in my third week, asking me to design a rehabilitation program for one of his patients following their fractured vertebrae. The first session was positive, and the patient continued for six weeks as they progressed through different stages of flexibility, strengthening, and core stability. Towards the end of the patient's recovery, I received a call from the surgeon, thanking me for the great results, but noting he had just learned I was working from home. He didn't realise from my promotional activity that I was operating in what he diplomatically referenced to be a "temporary setup". I assured him there was nothing amateur about my service, and that his patients would continue to receive the best care available, regardless from where I practiced. He seemed satisfied with my assurances and continued to send referrals, albeit I suspect, with a bit more explanation to his patients of what to expect.

I also offered to treat the medicos and – often with greater success – their family members at no cost so they could make referrals from first-hand experience. Often the wives of some busy GPs took up this offer, even if just for a massage. They would later speak well of the service to their spouse, yielding subsequent referrals. It was the principle of reciprocity working in my favour.

I learned it was especially valuable to establish rapport with the practice managers of local medical centres. They were the gatekeepers to the flow of patients in and out of their busy facilities, and often had more influence over physiotherapy referrals than the GP. I would offer the managers discounted services or free information brochures, reaping the rewards when their patients sought recommendations for a local physio and my name topped the list.

Undoubtedly, our local church was a great place to attract clients too. Word of mouth spread at the speed of sound. Before long, I was looking after several people from the large congregation, including many senior leaders, as well as teachers and families from the associated school where Paulina and I previously attended.

I ran inside our home one afternoon, in my third month of trade, proudly announcing I had just seen my 100th client. I had all their clinical records handwritten in manila folders, stacked alphabetically in a filing cabinet, filling the first of its three drawers and eager to spill into the remaining two in coming months.

Most memorable was Michelle, a good friend of my parents, and the 13th client of Back In Motion. Well into her fifties, with a gregarious personality, Michelle talked and laughed more than she listened, making it difficult to have a serious conversation with her.

But I needed to.

Michelle was suffering ongoing back and neck pain from her recent diagnosis of terminal bone cancer. I tried so many times to be sensitive and serious with her about what she was going through, but she turned every moment into a joke. I'm sure this was part of her coping strategy, but Michelle was genuinely a joyful and grateful person who believed God had her future in His hands. One day, this slightly overweight lady opted to *jump* onto my portable old treatment table, rather than use the step I provided. Michelle lost her balance and the table half-folded on itself. In my attempts to support her in free-fall, we both ended up on the floor. I felt utterly mortified and deeply embarrassed, but Michelle laughed so hard, I couldn't get her off the floor until she stopped.

Michelle came for treatment every week for the first year of our practice before she lost her battle with cancer. Hers was a sad yet funny funeral, as many people recounted the comical stories that made up her life. It's a shame Michelle is not still around to see what became of Back In Motion from the time she first showed confidence in us.

THE HARDEST THING I faced during those first months of business was asking for payment after each consultation. As I think about it now, it's illogical, given every time I bought bread and milk, or filled my car with petrol, I expected to pay for it. Strangely, it was an awkward confrontation that left me dry in the mouth, repeating itself every 30 minutes as the next patient arrived.

I just desperately wanted to avoid the *money* conversation.

Near the end of the treatments, I would dread the inevitable moment that approached. I'd stutter and fidget as I wrote up my clinical notes, made the patient's next appointment, and then sat silently hoping they would offer payment without me having to ask. On more than one occasion I knowingly let people walk away without paying rather than confront the topic. This, of course, made it very hard to meet our monthly mortgage commitments, let alone allow me to look Paulina in the eye at dinner when I knew I wasn't man-enough to ensure we got paid.

Eventually, I accepted it was part of my responsibility to initiate the payment conversations, but it took courage. And a lot of prompting from Paulina. I played with different scripts until I was comfortable with speaking about fees, insurance rebates, and payment plans. Of course, I was the only one with the hang-ups; everyone else knew my services were not for free. I imagine those who occasionally were permitted to leave without paying were confused by the missing step, if not grateful for their unexpected gain.

My first price schedule pegged physiotherapy rates at $30 per half-hour session. This equated to a billable rate of $60 per hour when I was fully booked. Cancellations or no-shows obviously halved my earnings. On my best and longest days, I would treat more than 20 patients. This was physically exhausting, but a great boost to the income of my young practice (when I was brave enough to charge them!). I would see patients as early as 7am, people getting in early before work, and occasionally some as late as 10pm, when my limited availability provided few other options.

Generally, I kept consulting hours between 8am and 6pm, Monday through Friday. I would however, open the practice on Saturday mornings for select patients who needed emergency treatment. I averaged about 12 patients per day over the course of the whole week.

I experienced the snowball effect quickly. Word of mouth was powerful. New patients rang almost every day, and existing patients kept returning – although obviously not because of our stellar premises or modern equipment. As I started to press what it was that gave them confidence in my treatment, the consistent feedback was my personalised holistic approach. Many were frustrated by previous therapists who either misdiagnosed their problems or simply treated the symptoms.

I made it my habit to undertake a very systematic and comprehensive review of all body systems, posture, sleep patterns, movement disorders, past injuries, lifestyle risk factors and precipitating events. This led me to educating clients about causative factors and long-term strategies, rather than just masking the pain.

I typically offered longer courses of treatment with each of my patients, this approach achieving more sustainable results and empowering them in effective self-management strategies. This was all part of my integrative philosophy that eventually became the bedrock of our franchised network – a treatment framework called Results4Life®.

I spent my evenings writing up my clinical notes, responding to referral letters, devising local promotional campaigns, visiting the club rooms of sporting teams on their training nights, and learning basic bookkeeping and administration for a small business. Paulina assisted with all these activities, and was a master at detail and organisation.

We made a pact to always consult each other before making any financial decisions for the business. This commitment led to countless nights pouring over supplier catalogues together, meticulously comparing prices before finalising orders. Most supply representatives realised immediately that I was a small practice, with a low ordering volume, that barely met their minimum threshold. This meant few people were willing to make the effort with me. I eventually placed a minuscule order with a friendly medical sales rep called John, one of the first people to take me seriously. He always treated me well, even though I was likely his smallest customer.

My first order was for creams, gels and resistance exercise bands totalling only $360.11, but it felt like we were risking the farm. Paulina and I wondered if we would ever see a return on this money. Fortunately for John, over time he would go on to sell us full practice set-ups for most of our network. His sincerity and risk certainly paid off over the long term, when we became the biggest customer on his database, spending millions of dollars every year for over two decades.

DURING THOSE FIRST months working from home, I earned less than $3,000, which I invested entirely back into the business. I upgraded some equipment, advertised more services, purchased further supplies, and tried to stay ahead of the negative cashflow cycle.

Paulina had been promoted to team leader of her neurosurgical ward. We agreed that we needed to fund our lifestyle on her wages alone, and not be dependent on any proceeds from the practice for at least a couple of years. Paulina was effectively my angel investor, or seed funder, in the business. All her work during those 12-hour shifts at the hospital paid our way to set the business up on a firm financial footing.

Our plan wasn't just to keep up with the mortgage and put food on the table either. We were trying to make good on our "renovator's delight" – hoping the house we had purchased might one day look *pretty as a picture*. It took us nearly three years to work through the lengthy repairs list for each room, finally achieving the desired result.

Like most first-time home buyers, we had lots to learn in the DIY space. As you may recall, I was less than competent with the typical tools that adorn most men's garages, and YouTube videos had yet to enlighten people like me. So we achieved our dream home through the painstaking process of trial and error, with lots of help from both sets of parents. We painted the inside and outside of the house, updated our bathrooms and toilets, installed a spa bath, put down new carpets, changed all the curtains, installed downlights throughout, felled some of the large gum trees, relocated a four-car galvanised shed from one side of the block to the other, concreted the back half of our driveway, and sowed new lawn. Every weekend commenced with a trip to Bunnings, followed by tedious hours of hard work and determination.

Our master bedroom was the last frontier. After we had disassembled our bed, and moved the furniture into the shed to prepare the walls for painting, we hit the *wall*. We placed our mattress on the floor in a spare room and slept there for nearly nine weeks, exhausted from the unending renovations and depleted of any motivation to continue. It wasn't until winter that year when we eventually caught our second wind and finished the master bedroom. We reassembled the bed and collapsed onto it with exhaustion, heaving a big sigh of relief that our project list was complete.

Timing was perfect. Most of our clients were now unknown referrals from the public – rather than familiar faces within the community – and Paulina was increasingly less comfortable with patients attending the house. There was no separation between work and home, so Paulina firmly gave the ultimatum one afternoon: shut down the practice and go work for someone else, or relocate the business into rented premises so we could regain some privacy.

The choice wasn't obvious to me.

I was still hopeful that the business was a mere stepping stone to moving overseas and working in communities of need. Relocating the business would cost more money, necessitate more risk, and bind me to longer obligations – three new obstacles between me and the developing world. The alternative wasn't appealing though. Prematurely shutting down early momentum that was building in my client list seemed irrational, especially if God continued to linger in opening doors to the mission field.

I felt anxious and indecisive.

It was a surprise to me that three weeks later I was searching through real estate guides for commercial medical premises.

21

leaving the nest

I SIGNED A 12-month sublease in May 2000. It was for a single room at a medical and specialist centre in Scoresby, a premium location in an otherwise obscure suburb. Mind you, shortly afterwards, Scoresby achieved cartographical glory by making it to the nightly news weather map as the iconic identifier for the south-eastern suburbs of Melbourne. I hoped, at the time, a sign of great things to come for Back In Motion also.

So nervous to commit to a full year's term, Paulina and I mulled over the decision for weeks. The total cost was nearly $12,000, and I worried the expense was too heavy to carry for our fledging business. The meagre three-page leasing contract was our biggest commercial risk to date. I literally lost sleep throughout the week prior to, and the week after, signing the document. Looking back, we laugh at the concern then, given at our peak many years later, we would carry an indirect contingent liability of over $15 million for occupancy leases alone.

Our new commercial landlord was Vikram, a very serious, conscientious, and intimidating Indian Sikh. He not only owned the premises but worked in the adjacent building as a busy sole medical practitioner.

Vikram ran notoriously late with every patient. Any time I wanted to meet him to discuss a matter relating to the sub-lease, I had to wait in line with the rest of his frustrated patients. When I was finally ushered into his medical suite, he dispensed with any pleasantries and demanded to know what I needed. He would barely make eye contact as he shuffled papers from one dishevelled stack on the left of his desk to a new unbalanced pile on the right side. I rarely felt like I had his full attention, which only added to my nerves when I needed to raise matters of jammed door locks, a disconnected phone line, or the possibility of getting more client referrals from him.

After a few months, I came to enjoy my short but frequent encounters with Vikram, as I turned them into my own little game. My objective was simple: get him to smile or laugh at least once in the conversation. Most times I was about ready to leave – feeling an inevitable loss in the secret score I was recording – before delivering a well-timed quip, interesting patient anecdote, relevant joke, or sincere compliment that would cause the corners of his stern mouth to round upwards ever so slightly. By the end of the first year, my smile strike rate was well over 70%, which made negotiating with my landlord far more bearable.

WITHOUT DELAY, PAULINA and I set about making our new location ready for business.

Transitioning from a single, makeshift consulting room in the carport of our driveway to the expansive medical centre initially overwhelmed us. There was so much space, we doubted we would ever fill it.

The building was an old three-bedroom house that Vikram had recently obtained medical permits for. He had barely done any conversions or renovations, which meant most of the floor plan was awkward and clumsy for what we needed. For instance, patients entered our building through a side door into a fully intact domestic kitchen; hallways and laundries were unusable obstacles; some of the floors were carpeted, while others were tiled or covered in linoleum.

The bedrooms were obvious choices for consulting suites, but most of those were already taken by other subtenants, including a dentist and psychologist.

The L-shaped lounge room belonged to our subtenancy. We divided the space with curtains, creating two treatment cubicles, a small reception area, and a little space for some rehabilitation equipment. When I look back at photos, the condition of the room was hideous, but it felt like the Taj Mahal compared with our carport facilities.

Patients could now park their cars with ease, go to a bathroom whenever they wanted, and even had chairs to sit and wait in until I was ready – all the modern conveniences one can easily take for granted unless you started your enterprise in a garage.

THE EXTRA SPACE added overheads, pressuring me to tip the scales with more income by growing my caseload. I pressed harder on the local medical practitioners for more referrals, distributed more letterbox advertising, contacted the local paper for advertorials and special interest features, sponsored council awards, dropped into local chemists and footwear stores to give them business cards and coupons, and started the predictable tour of local sporting clubs at training nights to triage injuries and offer full-service treatment the next day back at the practice.

I was driven to succeed. I craved marketing opportunities that other physio owners seemed to overlook. I paid for small runs of cinema advertising at a local independent theatre, and did consecutive months of shop-a-dockets with two supermarkets. I also paid to have business cards placed at the Subway outlet and service station across the road from our practice, expecting one to be slipped in with most receipts for customer purchases.

I even booked casual leasing space at a large shopping complex for a pop-up physiotherapy display. I carved out limited availability from my full work schedule to stand all-day at a mobile booth I created. I positioned a full-length articulated model skeleton at the front of the display to spark curiosity and offered interested shoppers their choice of free postural assessments, injury advice, and vouchers for physio ball classes, or treatment back at our clinic. At the very least, I collected their phone numbers and emails so I could follow them up with further information.

It was a horrible first experience, leaving me feeling very conspicuous and unprepared. Although I was confident in my expertise, I couldn't shake the impression that I was pitching snake oil in a den of charlatans. My opinion shifted when I finished the day with 12 new referrals, and a list of over 50 names added to my database. The $350 booking fee was indeed a worthwhile investment.

ONE OF MY first media pieces was titled "Physiotherapy Day a PR winner for Jason" (*Waverley Gazette*, September 2000). The story described my promotional activities to help celebrate International Physio Day. I provided free neck and shoulder massages, taping and strapping of knees and ankles, and spruiked the benefits of exercise and early injury intervention. The article credited me for my creative marketing approach that didn't feel like a "hard sell". The caption beneath the single photo read, "Jason promotes Back In Motion physio to a shopper with the help of his bony assistant." The assistant was Max, my model skeleton (short for *Maxilla*, the jawbone). The random shopper was my mum, incognito, whom I had enlisted as part of my rent-a-crowd strategy.

Some of my best and early referrers were a married couple who owned a foot-care practice in Wantirna South. The team of podiatrists and orthotists often relied on external physiotherapy assessments to help diagnose injuries related to the lower limbs and spine, and considered what I did therefore as complementary and non-competitive.

We eventually joined forces to develop a premier professional education event called the South-Eastern Medical Forum. Our goals were to inform medical practitioners on the latest research and advanced integration of physiotherapy and prosthetic/orthotic interventions, hosting high-profile speakers in their various fields of expertise. It was clear to me, even way back then, that our adjunctive health philosophy was a compelling point of difference. Patients needed a collaborative medical approach to achieve their total health and fitness goals; and so the best thing we could all do in the sector was build strong links between primary medicine and allied health to offer a co-operative care model.

My inexperienced marketing mind kept spinning with unproven ideas.

A lucrative opportunity was discovered when I cold-door-knocked a new aged care residential facility that was being developed near us. Rod and Maggie were the husband-and-wife proprietors. They explained to me that in a few months they would open their doors to 60 residents who would need weekly physio attention.

I talked about all the ways I could assist them, including the design of the recreation room, mobility assessments of the residents as they likely deteriorate over time, and integration with their care rounds each day. I even offered to run complimentary inductions for their new staff on safe lifting and patient handling.

Without any formal documentation – just a handshake of agreement – we began what became more than four years of wonderful partnership – eventually extending to three more facilities of similar size.

The unlikely success with this novel approach inspired me to ensure every practice we ever launched searched out and secured strong connections with their local aged care providers, eventually forming an entirely new speciality sub-brand of our group, Revita.

Some years later when Rod would seek to open his fourth aged care facility, and was looking for investors, I chose to get involved. Our business by the mid-2000s had started to render modest profits, and the opportunity to diversify appealed to our accountant. Combining our meagre savings with some bank borrowings, we secured a $100,000 stake in a development syndicate that was to build and own the new aged care facility.

It was a sad and expensive lesson when we learned that, five months later, Rod had skipped the country leaving the investors with an unfinished building, construction debts exceeding our equity, and a bank foreclosing on our first mortgage. We lost every cent I had injected, and never heard from Rod again despite my best efforts to chase him down through every available lead, some taking me as far as Ireland, where he was rumoured to be raising money for a new aged care initiative.

At a generous estimate of $15 profit per consultation, I had to personally treat nearly 6,700 patients to recover my losses – effectively a full year's caseload. It was a costly blunder during my formative years, instilling in me the importance of calculated risk-taking in future decisions.

22
a sporting chance

DESPITE A FORMER boss railing against me, promising he would finish me in the profession, the Victorian Soccer Federation (VSF) approached me in early 2000 to assist with their campaign to win a junior national championship. Limited in my availability, as I was wedded to my emerging business every waking moment, I welcomed the players to attend the practice at subsidised rates, so I could monitor their progress and ensure they were ready to compete.

In July, as the team medical officer, I accompanied the under-16 male squad to Sydney for the National Talent Championships.

It was a tiring week of repetitive warm-ups, cool-downs, ankle strapping, rubdowns, and injury management to an 18-member squad who were playing up to three games of soccer a day for a whole week. My schedule started at 6am, I'd work all day, then finish with a medical briefing to the coach and team manager at 10pm. There wasn't a lot of downtime in between, as I either sat pitch-side on the bench to assist the rotating players, or I was in the locker room helping someone who was previously injured. I remember thinking that whilst the pay for the week was only a modest stipend, the experience was priceless. Little did I know that I would return to these very same national championships more than 15 years later to watch my own boys enthusiastically compete.

I enjoyed my time with the VSF so much that I said they could count on me the following year. With my practice starting to build up steam, a week away with the team was a sacrifice on Paulina's part, as she forwent a holiday we could have shared together. Still, she supported me.

It was in the infamous month of September 2001 when I accompanied the under-15 female squad to Coffs Harbour for their National Talent Championships. After escorting a player with a dislocated kneecap to the local hospital for x-rays, I watched in horror and disbelief at the small television mounted in the corner of the waiting room as the twin towers of the World Trade Centres in New York City collapsed in plumes of smoke and horrendous screams. It's true that most of us remember where we were and what we were doing at that critical moment.

THE FUSION OF sport and physiotherapy was a natural alloy. I was grateful to have discovered a means to indulge in both passions during the nascent stages of my practice's expansion.

Apart from supporting national athletes in soccer and weightlifting, I also managed patients in wheelchair tennis, body building, Australian-rules football, netball, basketball, marathon-running, and many others. The walls of the unrenovated kitchen and cumbersome hallways of our newly rented medical facility were increasingly adorned with striking photographs and sincere letters of thanks autographed by local, state, and national sporting heroes.

Jeff was one of those appreciative athletes. He lost part of his left leg in a motorbike accident, having been struck by a taxi that failed to stop at a red light. Despite attempted grafts and multiple operations to save his left leg, Jeff eventually underwent a below-knee amputation. His personalised number plate, STMPY, was his way of irreverently acknowledging the stump he was left with.

Jeff's sense of humour and competitive nature instilled him with confidence to take up wheelchair tennis. He excelled in the sport, ranking number ten in Australia at the time, and was aiming for the top!

To stay competitive Jeff needed regular physiotherapy. In those early years I prepared him for the Australian Wheelchair Tennis Open where some good performances resulted in a rise in his ranking, eventually opening doors for him to compete in the Far East and South Pacific Games for the Disabled in South Korea.

I TOOK OFF only one other week in the first year of starting our new practice.

This was to complete a Bible course called *Keys of Knowledge,* facilitated by internationally recognised theologian, Kevin Conner. I was still convinced that I would eventually end up on the mission field, and knew I had very little time to study any formal degrees in religious doctrine. I decided a week-long intensive course in self-study techniques of the Bible was a strategic investment, as it promised to equip me with insights to continue my theological learning independently.

Travelling with the soccer teams, and attending this course, forced me to temporarily close the business on each occasion. During my absence, there was obviously nobody available to treat my patients or even answer the phone, resulting in a complete halt to our income. It was quickly obvious to me that if I ever fell ill and couldn't work for one day, we faced the same issue.

I felt vulnerable. Our financial stability was precariously linked to my personal efforts. Essentially, it was a "no work, no eat" dilemma. Paulina and I recognised this risk early in our ownership, and agreed we needed to mitigate it swiftly if I were ever to be liberated from the daily obligations of the practice.

Employing staff became inevitable, as did the anxiety that would accompany it.

23

maiden team

BECOMING A FIRST-TIME employer is a daunting proposition. Many people warned us against the idea, emphasising that with a larger team, problems would be magnified.

Before I brought on any physios, and risked being unable to afford them, I decided on a receptionist to enable me to treat more patients at maximum capacity, creating optimum revenue.

It was a good plan and, to play it safe, we offered the part-time job to my mum. She shared the reception duties with Paulina, who was still juggling full time shifts at the hospital. Whilst the perils of working with family are well-documented, the arrangement suited everyone, and we kept it going for many years.

Mum was a natural lover of people, and quickly built rapport with patients of all ages. She might have struggled at first with the computer system, and some of the medical report writing, but what she lacked in practice management expertise, she more than made up for in customer service and client relationships. To this day, Mum is still personal friends with some of the clients she met at the front desk. Watching Mum work cemented my view that often it didn't matter what I did (or didn't do) in the consulting room. If my patients' first and last impressions at the reception desk weren't positive, they were unlikely to come back. For decades to follow, I reinforced to my franchisees the essential impact of an effective support team in building a practice culture of excellence.

Progressively, our practice grew busier. Patients continued to refer family and friends, on top of the many active sources of direct referral I had established. The various innovative marketing strategies had created compounding demand, necessitating a waiting list for already over-subscribed 12-hour clinical shifts that stretched from 8am to 8pm each day. Clearly, patients were loving our health philosophy, despite being surrounded by alternative options for their care.

Over the next 12 months, I employed physiotherapists to assist me in meeting the relentless demand. Jill (my team leader from Cambodia) and Natalie (introduced by Kate, who accompanied me on my second trip to Cambodia) were the first two. Both excellent practitioners, strong women with Christian convictions, and determined to combine their faith and profession in ways to honour God. A perfect fit to Paulina, Mum, and myself, ensuring our values were not diluted in our formational years.

Jill was ten years my senior and much more clinically experienced. Returning to work after having started a family, Jill worked part-time only, accommodating the various pregnancies and other commitments motherhood necessitated. Clients loved her. She was especially passionate about women's health and pregnancy-related services, and nobody could argue she lacked recent first-hand experiences to draw on. This meant we offered a range of services that I otherwise wasn't experienced in, or comfortable delivering, serving a whole new demographic of clients. Through Jill's creativity, we started running Mums-In-Motion peri- and postnatal classes, leveraging off the play in brand name.

Natalie graduated in the same year as me, but from Latrobe University. Despite our good-natured banter over the Melbourne-versus-Latrobe prowess, Natalie was a strong, all-round musculoskeletal therapist, and very committed to her caseload. She worked full-time, and quickly established herself as my right hand in the practice.

That said, I admit to being frustrated with Natalie early in her probationary period. She was always reluctant to meet doctors, engage in the promotional activities of the practice, and look for new clients. I was the one left holding that awkward burden of pseudo-marketing officer, despite not feeling gifted or comfortable with it myself.

I raised my annoyance to Paulina one evening. She smiled and patiently reassured me, saying, "The team dynamic thrives on each of you contributing different strengths." With gentle wisdom, she continued, "Natalie might not feel confident to promote the practice, but she excels in retaining every patient we send her way."

Encouraged by the insights, I decided to devote more time to growing the business, even if it meant having less availability to treat new patients myself. Sometime later, I came to better understand the difference in sales approaches that had initially upset me. I realised I was a "finder"; Natalie was a "minder". I was a "hunter"; she was a "farmer". Both were important elements of servicing our clientele, even if we played different roles.

Moving forwards, I intentionally sought careful proportions of both attributes in my various team members, to ensure we struck the right balance.

WHILST WE WERE a great maiden team, the burdens of small-business ownership and employment were mounting. For some months, the money going out exceeded what was coming in. School holidays and the Christmas periods were especially tough, as I still had to pay staff and rent when client visits ebbed into unsustainable seasonal lows.

My marketing experiments were also costing more money, and it was hard to know whether I was wise spending a bit extra to try and reach new audiences.

One time, I ordered 2,000 full-colour brochures at a cost of over $600. When I excitedly opened the box, I realised my horrible mistake: I had put one digit wrong on the phone number and I couldn't afford a re-print. Rather than binning the collateral, I contacted the supplier and begged for a solution. Experienced in these mishaps, as a cheap fix they sent me 2,000 stickers with the correct details. It was up to Paulina and me, along with my school friend Ashley and his wife, to bear the arduous task of replacing the incorrect phone number with new stickers during three consecutive movies on a lazy Friday night. I discovered there is always a solution to every problem, no matter how tedious or compromising.

We encountered one fresh challenge after another – dealing with fickle medical referrers, balancing the monthly books, complying with employment contract law, and managing the various payment compensation schemes (such as the Victorian Workcover Authority and the Transport Accident Commission). We dealt with demanding clients who expected after-hours consultations, friendly clients who simply wouldn't pay their overdue accounts, and staff who wanted holidays despite having just taken a week off last month. Computers didn't work; tax laws were changing; professional indemnity insurers were difficult; and toilets would not flush properly.

To top it all, we were running out of space!

That's right. Despite all this hardship and trouble, our practice kept growing and I could barely keep up with the demand. Every four months, I found myself sitting in Vikram's waiting room for 45 minutes to be granted an audience with a peevish landlord whose assistance I needed in solving our capacity issues.

We moved the reception desk out of the "lounge room" to create a third treatment cubicle. This meant, Mum and Paulina were sitting in a "kitchen" between a fridge cavity and the double sink, a desk jammed into position to form a physical barrier between them and the waiting patients. When we needed more space, I negotiated taking on one of the other "bedrooms", relocating the sessional psychologist to the adjacent building. Eventually, we took over every room in the house, including the "laundry" for storage of our medical supplies.

With every new square metre of space we occupied, our rent (understandably) went up. Whilst growth in patient referrals yielded higher revenues, our costs rose at the same, or sometimes faster, rate. We needed more treatment beds, ultrasounds, and computers. I extended our opening hours to accommodate more people when all of the treatment cubicles were filled. I contracted our physios for longer sessions, paying higher commissions and retaining less margin. There was no end to our costs.

The classic irony of a fledgling small business is that many run out of cash in their high growth phase. This was our problem. I still wasn't taking a wage, and working harder than anyone I knew. Paulina was pulling three 12-hour nursing shifts every week and then putting in additional time at our practice and behind the scenes. This little adventure was starting to devour us.

At this point, I recognised I needed help.

Only 25 years old, I was way out of my depth running a fast-growing physiotherapy practice without any experience. I reached out to the Australian Physiotherapy Association (APA), inquiring if they could connect me with suitable mentors or provide other resources to support me in these challenging aspects of professional practice. I found no sympathy on the end of the phone line. Worse, the APA representative rebuked me for launching into private practice at such a young age, explaining nobody should own a practice without a requisite ten years' experience. When I gently advised that my *horse* had already *bolted*, they were indifferent and pitiless, advising me to close the business. Their solution was to simply return to employment under a more tenured principal until such time I gained sufficient confidence to revisit my own enterprise.

I was numb when I hung up the phone. The problem was, I believed them! Launching Back In Motion felt like a serious mistake. I immediately regretted stepping out into the risky endeavour, simultaneously knowing it would be difficult now to retreat.

Desperate, I sent five letters to the neighbouring practice owners in my locality. Some I had met, others I only knew by reputation. My letter was less than a page long: it introduced me, spoke briefly about our new practice; and queried their interest in monthly meetings to solve common problems we faced in private practice ownership. I was candid about my interest in mentorship and building camaraderie with peers in similar situations.

Most letters went unanswered, with only a single reply received. Declining the invitation, the one colleague who rang cited the track record of every individual who had attempted to run a physiotherapy practice from Vikram's rooms, sharing they all faltered within a year or two. It was apparently known in our small local profession as the "physio graveyard". To reinforce the metaphor, she wished me well in my "coffin" as she hung up the phone.

I was in trouble, and it was seemingly my own naïve fault.

In a last-ditch effort to engage with other practice owners, I joined the Victorian chapter committee of Physiotherapy Business Australia (PBA). It was a small special interest group operating under the auspices of the APA, but felt like the black sheep of the physio fraternity. Doing so immediately put me on a first name basis with a handful of seasoned practice owners, and so began a slow journey of learning the less-often taught *business* of physiotherapy through our monthly schedule of meetings.

Sadly, it also added another night out every month, on top of an already unmanageable workload, accelerating my decline in enthusiasm and optimism.

AMIDST ALL THIS rejection and despondency, it became apparent that the gridiron player that formed the keystone of our Back In Motion logo didn't capture the sentiment of our practice very well. This was apparently obvious to everyone, except me.

At various times, Paulina and different members of the staff suggested a do-over. When patients started making the same overtures, I conceded that my cheap clipart had served its purpose, and we needed to professionalise our image.

I engaged a brilliant designer to create a new logo. Dressed in chic attire, Dion was a tall, slender figure with an artistic aura, exuding confidence and style – everything we wanted in our new practice look. I asked Dion to create a personalised trademark that couldn't be easily replicated, nor could we be found guilty of having copied it from elsewhere.

The words I suggested in the creative briefing to help inspire his designs were "movement", "health", "life", and "freedom". I didn't prescribe any preferred colour schemes, tag lines, or geometric dimensions. I left all those entirely to the pro, expecting to be thoroughly pleased with his creative insights.

Oh, and I asked for this excellence to be delivered within a budget of only $1,000.

After reviewing different versions, we reached a major milestone in the development of our brand identity. Dion provided us with our official final logo and colour matching guide, the foundation for all future promotional material, and the icon on which we would later become recognised nationally.

Originally hand sketched, the final image was a striking depiction of a nude masculine torso seen from the back, stepping forward with outstretched arms. The man's head was postured slightly downward and to the right, inferring focus and determination. The typography, split by the image of the human form, was a sleek and modern, burgundy-coloured text, adding a touch of warmth and sophistication to the overall design. The sense of strength, vitality and forward motion perfectly encapsulated the essence of our commitment to promoting physical well-being and mobility.

Whilst our logo would go through numerous iterations over the next 20 years with different words, colours, proportionality, and trademarks, the centrality of what we affectionately referred to as the "naked man" was created that day, and remained our one branding constant.

All these experiences created a lot of transition in a short amount of time. We had changed practice address, changed our team composition, changed our pace of growth, and now changed our defining brand image.

Regrettably, I also couldn't deny the nagging *change* of heart I felt toward running my own business.

24

ransacked

PAULINA RESIGNED FROM her role as neurosurgical nurse at RMH toward the end of 2001 to take up her dream job: a post graduate opportunity as an ICU nurse in the trauma centre at the world-renowned Alfred Hospital.

As the workload at Back In Motion intensified and Paulina's responsibilities at the hospital grew increasingly demanding, she suffered a prolapsed vertebral disc in her lumbar spine. While she persevered through several weeks of excruciating pain during her shifts, it became evident that Paulina required intensive physiotherapy treatment of her own, along with some much-needed time off to recuperate. Balancing her care amidst numerous competing responsibilities was challenging, especially knowing that the survival of the practice was at risk.

Paulina suffered intense pain every day, the sporadic spasms twisting her into a human pretzel without warning. Breathing was difficult, moving was unbearable, and sleeping was impossible. Her exceptional pain tolerance, and remarkable resilience, could have warranted its own square on the Periodic Table. The radioactive chemical depicted by the shorthand *Pa* and atomic number 91, commonly known as protactinium – a malleable material that doesn't tarnish easily – may well be such an element, named in Paulina's honour.

I watched her closely, with both the worry of a concerned husband and the unavoidable knowledge of a seasoned physiotherapist. Her prognosis was poor if the disc herniation wasn't managed quickly and rehabilitation completed thoroughly, especially in her line of work. I treated her injury morning and night for an extended period, as she slowly recovered strength and mobility.

The distress was just about more than we could handle. My brain was fried from nearly two years of small-business start-up challenges, and Paulina's ill-health seemed the lowest point in the series of stacked hardships.

The doubts about our future were constant topics of conversation as we lamented how we got sucked into running a business when we wanted to be living abroad and part of an international mission. The stitching of our sensible intentions was quickly fraying in the turbulent wash of reality. And I feared things would continue to unravel.

AS IF TO punctuate this point, Paulina was first to arrive one morning and was startled to find the front door of our practice ajar. She didn't have to venture past the lintel to see why.

We had been ransacked.

The reception desk drawers were pulled out and upturned in the waiting room. All the medical supplies from our storage cupboards were strewn down the hallway. Our computers were gone, as was our recently purchased interferential machine and our clinical ultrasound unit.

The place wasn't just burgled; we had been vandalised. Windows were broken, the sliding door to the treatment area had been smashed, and it was clear an axe had been used to slice through one of the report writing desks.

I turned up an hour later, after facilitating a hydrotherapy class at a nearby pool, to find a detective fingerprinting the door handles and various hot spots around the practice. He was not very optimistic about finding the criminals, suggesting that our medical equipment was probably long gone. He suspected it had already been shipped across state borders overnight and sold to an unsuspecting purchaser through the second-hand medical equipment on the black market. After he took our official statements, we began the heart wrenching clean-up.

The first patient scheduled for treatment that morning was Julia, who battled the challenges of multiple sclerosis. Her presence brought immediate relief to both of us, Paulina tearfully leaning into her embrace, grateful for the solace.

A team-favourite, Julia had won our hearts quickly with her cheerful disposition, love for a tale, and optimism in the face of her own dire circumstances. Suffering reduced mobility due to her condition, Julia had been referred to me from the outpatient department of a local hospital.

Unable to receive from them the continuity of regular care needed, she was squeezed from the public system into the expensive private sector.

In her first few weeks of treatment, I outlined the intensity and frequency with which I would need to see Julia and her husband, to assist them both in getting ready for her likely deterioration in health. Julia was embarrassed to explain her financial limitations. Unable to afford more than one treatment a week, I agreed with her that I would treat her as often as she needed for as long as it helped – I didn't like asking for payment anyway, so money wasn't an issue.

I'm pleased to report that right up until 12 months before penning these words, Julia remained mobile and engaged in her local community. For nearly 20 years she received physiotherapy from one of our loyal therapists at the Wantirna South practice, until her eventual passing. She learned to self-manage her condition exceptionally well, and kept up with many of her beloved activities, including painting, choir and bell-ringing.

Hanging in my study above where I am writing this paragraph, I have one of Julia's works – a beautiful painting of a terracotta bowl of burgundy flowers. The morning after we were ransacked, Julia went home and pulled out a fresh canvas to paint something that would remind Paulina and me that new life can spring from difficult situations. Her own story proved to be a great testament of this, a radiant smile never fading right to the end.

Whilst facing far less ordeal than my adored patient Julia, it was challenging for me to summon a genuine smile throughout those days. My expression was more often plastered with a semi-permanent grimace, betraying the anguish within.

25
quarter life crisis

I HAD REACHED my breaking point. Disillusioned, exhausted, frustrated – I feared the proverbial light at the end of the tunnel shone from a freight train headed my way.

Whilst the practice continued to grow in referrals and income, and our staff seemed relatively stable, I felt like I was trapped in a prison of my own making. Strangely though, I blamed God for my situation, bitter toward His perpetual denials of all my pleas to be sent somewhere – *anywhere* – as a missionary.

I suffered an existential, quarter-life crisis.

I lost my identity; I didn't know what life was about. My vision for everything that I had planned to do, and hoped for, through my teenage years had evaporated. Paulina also felt like I was working too hard, seeing too few friends, and heading for a mild breakdown, or worse.

I needed to change something. I needed time out of the business before it consumed what little sanity I had left.

In July 2001 we started planning a three-month trip around Australia to rediscover our passion for God, and the purpose in life He was leading us toward. Upon sharing our intentions with close friends and family, we were met with immediate caution against abandoning the practice. People warned us that the business, still in its infancy, might not withstand such a prolonged absence. Our parents posed sensible questions about the possibility of financial strain if our bank accounts were to run dry; concerned staff raised worries about who would handle difficult decisions in our absence; and apprehensive patients voiced concerns about the continuity of their treatment.

To just about everyone, our decision seemed a bad idea; but to Paulina and me it sounded wonderful.

I was at peace with the possibility of the business failing while we were away, accepting I might return to nothing. The notion of being free of the burden was an attractive thought, giving me a second chance at medical missions without having to resolve a going concern.

The biggest heartbreak we faced was putting our puppy up for adoption. Paulina interviewed candidates like they were taking her only child, putting them through a rigorous battery of tests and questions, triangulating their answers for any inconsistencies. Stopping just short of Interpol checks and full-scope psychological profiling, she was thrilled to eventually find a single older woman who had a daughter with another dog of the same breed, excited to welcome Jessie into their home.

With heaving sobs, we stood in the centre of the road as Jessie was driven away. The last thing we saw was her fluffy head, with droopy ears and brown curly eyebrows, turned back toward us, wearing an expression of puzzled disbelief.

PREPARING FOR OUR three-month holiday was half the fun. We wanted to travel by campervan and, with my ever-present frugal qualities on show, I unpleasantly surprised Paulina with an impulse purchase of a Volkswagen combi van, bargained down to only $1,800.

Paulina's heart sank immediately. Admittedly, it had high kilometres, looked well-used, and did not have air-conditioning or a kitchenette. However, I excitedly defended my choice by showcasing what it did have: ample storage under the makeshift bed; and "free" plates, cutlery, and cooking gear in one of the compartments.

When we took the van to my brother-in-law for the obligatory roadworthy inspection, he emphatically declared it a write-off. The chassis was nearly rusted through, the steering was gone, all the tyres needed replacing, and he hadn't even started assessing the mechanical aspects of the engine or brakes. When I advised the vendor that his vehicle had not passed the inspection and I expected a full refund, he flatly refused – muttering something about "buyer beware".

After numerous failed attempts at sensible negotiation, I filed a complaint with the Victoria Civil Claims Tribunal (VCAT). One month later, Paulina and I represented ourselves in the kangaroo court that VCAT appears to be, and "Judge Judy" ruled in our favour. Within 24-hours we had our money returned, and were back where we started.

Round two: Paulina ensured we went vehicle shopping together. She led the strategy, and we ended up spending $12,000 on a Mazda E2000, nearly seven times the *bargain* I had found. But true to Paulina's spending style, her decision was value-for-money. It was a fully converted campervan with air conditioning, five-speed auto gearbox, microwave, sink, gas stove, twin battery backup, fridge, portable toilet, and a kitchen table that converted into a double bed. It was amazing, and worth every cent.

Nicknamed *Ollie*, we spent the next three weekends building extra storage compartments under the bed, installing overhead cupboards, and working out how we could carry our two bikes without a rear tow ball. We started packing all the necessities, excited to hit the road on the 1st of November 2001.

My brother-in-law gave it a full service, and opted to change every pipe fitting to avoid any problems on the long trip round. Whilst seemingly diligent at the time, after 1,000 kilometres into the trip, we discovered he had forgotten to tighten up the circular clamps on both ends of all seven hoses he fitted. We left a trail of radiator fluid or water everywhere we went, necessitating numerous checks with different roadside mechanics to find the next offending leak. Eventually, someone properly pressure-tested the whole system and found the remaining clamps that needed securing.

A good lesson for all of us is that sometimes our diligence can be overly zealous.

FUNDING OUR TRIP was certainly a challenge. The practice was only generating notional profit at this stage; my employed staff, including receptionists, receiving higher salaries than me.

My commitment to the team was that I would employ another therapist in my absence to help absorb the displaced workload. The only application I received was a three-year experienced physiotherapist from Napier in New Zealand – Marcus Pain. (I know, an unfortunate surname for a physiotherapist. It sparked dread in the heart of every new patient until they met him and realised he was a gentle soul.)

Marcus was willing to relocate to Australia to further his career in private practice, an industry far less established in New Zealand at the time. We met over a series of video conferences, both eventually agreeing on the role, sight unseen.

When Marcus first arrived, I offered him the use of our second car – a bile green Ford Cortina affectionately dubbed *Kermit*. Unfortunately, Kermit was a gift with unintended consequences. The car broke down on Marcus multiple times before we even left for our trip. One night, I had to retrieve it with a tow truck because the car wouldn't start for him.

Marcus ended up buying his own car shortly afterwards – but, strangely, chose another green Ford Cortina. Supposedly, his vehicle was superior to mine, as it was a *station wagon* as opposed to a simple sedan. Without any originality, he nicknamed his vehicle *The Frog*, and together we became the "Cortina Muppets".

I left Marcus a 12-page procedural guide for managing the practice in my absence. Handing him a fistful of keys and, giving assurances that I would process the payroll from the road, I left a mobile phone number for unavoidable emergencies only.

As it happened, we were not yet 300 kilometres from home before Mum rang the *bat phone*. Opening that morning's mail, she read me a letter from the Physiotherapy Registration Board, citing they had received complaints against me for aggressive marketing and unlawful advertising. Apparently, I was to be investigated for using testimonials from patients, which was illegal under the Australian Health Act. The penalty, if found guilty, was a $10,000 fine – money, I didn't have.

Somewhere in that first week of our road trip, I carved out the time to write my defence and the claim against me was withdrawn before we even made it out of the state – but the stress of it all convinced me that running away from the business was the right move.

I WANTED THINGS to change.

The night before leaving for our Australian odyssey, I convinced the neighbour across the road to bleach my hair with hydrogen peroxide and then run a buzz cut all over. I was starting on a journey of self-discovery, and it seemed a great visual reminder that my whole identity needed to be re-imagined.

I walked in the front door and announced to a frightened Paulina that I was ready to go. She worried my mental breakdown was too far progressed for a *holiday* to fix.

The new blonde skinhead remained hopeful.

26
dear diary

LIKE JONAH OF old, running from what God had asked him to do, I set off northeast to get as far away from the practice I could. We spent our first night at Eden, just across the state border. We then meandered through Mimosa Rocks National Park, pausing briefly at the Blue Rock Pool in Bermagui, before arriving in Sydney a few days later. Every stop for fuel or meals, I worried about how much we were spending and whether our credit cards would last the distance.

Our first extended rest was Coffs Harbour, where we completed a five-day PADI scuba dive course. After being led through classroom theory and training exercises in the swimming pool, Paulina and I undertook our first open water dives in the national marine park.

It was like stepping into a whole new time and space dimension. As I nervously submerged below the water surface, the familiar sounds of the world above faded away, replaced by the gentle hum of my solitary breath and the muffled echoes of the ocean. It was surreal not to be bound by the constraints of gravity or the limits of the terrestrial world. I could move in any direction, weaving through the intricate coral formations, or simply hover in mid-water, suspended like an astronaut taking in the awe-inspiring sights of a cosmic wonderland. Colours popped in the clear, filtered light, and marine life of all shapes and sizes danced around me. Every nook and cranny harboured hidden wonders waiting to be discovered. The whole experience left an indelible mark on my soul, igniting a passion for more exploration that I expected would endure for a lifetime.

Paulina's first experience was also breathtaking – but not in the same way. She breezed through the theory segments to qualify as a certified diver, but struggled with the practical assessment. Paulina had difficulty equalising her ear pressure on the deeper dives, felt horribly seasick in the underwater swell, and panicked when she vomited through her regulator. Understandably, she lost confidence with the mouth-only breathing technique – fearful of swallowing water or her own regurgitated fluids – and, as a result, was encouraged to gain more experience as we travelled farther north before diving independently.

Paulina ended up completing her qualification in Byron Bay, having some of the best underwater experiences of her life, including observing from below a cormorant plunge into the shallows, swiftly snatching a fish from the shoal, before ascending back through the surface into the open sky. That memory alone warranted the trauma she endured in mastering the unnatural instincts to breathe calmly underwater.

THROUGHOUT OUR TRIP, I made various entries into a personal journal, revealing a clear insight into my disturbed state of mind and heart at this low point in my life.

I was down on myself for having let the busyness of the practice overwhelm me, displacing the spiritual disciplines I had previously been committed to. I was surprised with how far I had slipped, and how quickly it happened.

Like a wayfaring vessel with a damaged keel and a snapped mast, I found myself adrift, utterly devoid of direction.

My journal entry on the 13th of November 2001 read, in part:

> *I feel lost … It is now two weeks since I left my busy work schedule and regimented lifestyle to go on holidays and discover God again. But it hasn't happened – oh, I AM LOST.*
>
> *How did I get here so fast and why hadn't I read or followed the road signs along the way?*
>
> *I can remember a day not that long ago when my future in God was as reliable as tomorrow's Sun; the joy of His presence was like three square meals a day feeding my soul.*
>
> *At one point, I felt like I knew God – I was probably only 15 years old then. Today, I am 26 years old, but a shell of that boy; a hastily disappearing shadow of him, or at least my memory of that person.*

I closed that day's journal entry with the dreary conclusion:

> *Whilst I really don't know what to believe, I can't ignore that for the last two years I've been going to sleep at night and waking the next*

morning with the nagging, grievous thought that somewhere along the line I've missed it.

By that I mean, I've turned a wrong corner, ignored a clear sign, failed to take a right step, or obviously chosen a wrong path that has led to my loss of direction. I am indeed LOST.

My only hope is that God hasn't lost me yet – that is my thread to hang onto at this point.

OVER THE NEXT 30 days, I went in earnest search of myself.

Paulina and I experienced the incremental rejuvenation that comes from connecting with each other, engaging with nature, and resting in God.

We did some off-road camping on Fraser Island, jet skied around Keppel Island, snorkelled off the Mollo catamaran as we cruised through the Whitsundays, and sun-baked on the famous silica sands of Whitehaven Beach.

My journal entries reveal my ongoing search for significance:

In the last three weeks I've tried to "suck the life" out of everything – bleeding my waking hours dry with fun holiday activities and thrill-seeking adventure. But there is still an all-too-familiar feeling of emptiness at the day's end.

I admit I am more "God-conscious" – a term referring to those fleeting moments throughout my day when my attention is drawn to an awareness of God. It's like that first break of daylight penetrating the long dark night of the soul – a fragile but definite rendering of promise. It's the first stage to my recovery. It's the strand of hope to which I cling, proving I haven't completely lost my faith. It's the weak little flag I wave in the air to remind everyone, "I am still here!".

Days later, as my heart kept bleeding through my pen, I scribbled:

Unfortunately (or not), I can't fool myself into believing that this is the existence God has planned for me. This truth – a profound personal realisation – is a baby step on a gruelling pathway of restoration, along which I should be bounding and leaping with youthful energy. But somewhere I tripped; my countenance fell, and the stumble laid me out for three or four years.

Maybe I tried to run too quickly, or didn't take the time to properly prepare myself for the great "race" of life. It wasn't through lack of

Godly friendship and mentors though, as I feel I've had the best of those.

It proves one thing for sure — my relationship with God is exactly that: MINE! Nobody else can bridge the distance and intercede on my behalf or create for me the intimacy with God that I am longing for.

ARLIE BEACH WAS our launching dock for a five-day diving adventure in early December 2001 aboard the *Stella Maris* – a ship that would take us nine hours to the outer reaches of the Great Barrier Reef (GBR).

A rookie mistake we made before boarding the boat was spending an idle day ashore wandering through Vic Hislop's shark museum. Whilst entirely engaging for casual visitors, with their feet firmly planted on dry ground, it did occur to us halfway through the tour that we would soon be swimming in the depths of the South Coral Sea, fully vulnerable to the very predators we were being warned about through one gruesome picture after another.

While we intended to thoroughly enjoy the wonders of the reef, our primary goal was to obtain further certification in some specialised diving skills. Over the week that followed, the advanced scuba qualifications demanded we complete multiple night dives, navigation dives, drifting in strong underwater currents, and cave diving down to depths of 40 metres. We both successfully passed these rigorous tests; Paulina having resolved the previous challenges with her breathing technique.

With every new adventurous day at sea, I continued to curate my negative and defeated thoughts that raged at the core of my inner world. My mind and soul were at war with each other as I sought to reconcile the pain of missed opportunity. I had expected my life to look differently; I wanted to be working on the mission field, and instead was stuck in a small business in middle class Australia. I felt I had failed God – and Paulina – which meant I had failed myself.

Reclining on the foredeck of the catamaran at dusk, serenaded by the enchanting sounds of numerous turtles gulping the humid surface air, I reflected again in my journal:

Looking back over the recent years, I can trace the beginnings of my imperceptible decline to the second half of 1997. It was a difficult year, full of excessive university and church commitments. I was out five nights a week with youth groups and related meetings, sitting for my final physio exams, and preparing for a new-year wedding. I started my days at 5:30am and would generally crawl into bed in the early hours of the following morning after a gruelling study session.

By October of that year, I had resigned my volunteer position in our church, and joined an outreach team to pioneer a city church an hour from home. In the January that followed, my wife and I returned from our honeymoon to an inner city flat in an unfamiliar neighbourhood, 45 minutes' drive from anyone we knew.

We started high-pressure jobs at a major metropolitan hospital, and embarked on the mammoth task of learning to live with each other. Our good moments were GREAT, and our bad days were TERRIBLE. Cultural incongruities, and differences born out from our families-of-origin, revealed that conflict resolution was a weak point in our marriage.

We rarely saw old friends. Shift work took its toll on our energy levels and job satisfaction. Church life was unfulfilling. And the dream of becoming a missionary seemed to evaporate in front of me.

Welcome to the beginning of my end…

As I continued to trace the events and emotions that contributed to my downfall, distilling the truths from myths about who God had created me to be, my journal entries subtly began to pivot and trend more upbeat.

By the last day of our time at sea, now feeling I just might have a bit of navy-DNA in me from Dad after all, I wrote these more hopeful words:

I have fooled myself for months into thinking the world is against me; and presumed that on its side has been God himself. I have let self-pity guide me into a valley of spiritual barrenness, dragging my soulmate and wife into the downward spiral with me.

Today, all that stops. I see it for the lie that it is.

With every chance God gives me from this day forwards, I'll try to make up for my wasted years so that a time will come when I can lift my head again.

LIKE JACK AND Elwood Blues in the 1980 cult-classic movie the *Blues Brothers*, I felt I was on a "mission from God" to clarify my purpose in life. With each new town we travelled through, and the conversations with Paulina and others we met on the road, the message became ever so much clearer.

After the GBR, we moved to the croc country of Cape Tribulation in far north Queensland, swimming in the freshwater Mossman Gorge. We celebrated Christmas amidst the luxuries of Port Douglas, splurging on ourselves a night at a swanky beachside resort, rather than having to wake Christmas morning in the back of a cramped, over-heated campervan. With no family to celebrate the holiday with, Paulina and I phoned home to send our love, and later enjoyed a prawn cocktail lunch with two UK backpackers we had previously sailed through the Whitsundays with.

As our trip continued, it was clear God was restoring me. I wrote a few days after Christmas:

> *I'm a blessed man. I've met a lot of people in my already short life – partly because of the line of work I'm in – and most of their stories remind me how fortunate I am. I really do appreciate all I have.*
>
> *As I sit in an arid emotional climate, my wife and I still have enough perspective to count our blessings. Most nights, we* lose *count because of how many on our list!*
>
> *It seems strange to write at times how miserable I feel – being so distant from the God to whom I belong – when there is so much obvious evidence that He has never left me.*
>
> *I am choosing to reach for His outstretched hand; open the door to his persistent and patient knocking; invite Him once again into the home of my heart, rendering all the rooms and dark hidden corners His domain.*
>
> *I surrender.*

AFTER OUR NON-TRADITIONAL Christmas celebration, we headed inland to the Northern Territory. With every new truck stop, logged dive, and conversation with strangers in exotic places, Paulina and I became more confident that we had found what we had left home to discover: God was with us and answering some of the longings of our hearts.

But that wasn't going to pay our fuel bills. Almost every day I had the fleeting fear that our money was going to run out and leave us stranded in the vast outback. We could eat simply, sleep anywhere, and forego expensive tourist attractions. But we needed petrol, and it was expensive.

Each time we swerved Ollie into the service station to fill-up, I held my breath as I swiped the credit card, expecting it to be declined.

But it never happened.

Our bank account remained afloat; the money kept flowing; and the mobile phone sat idle in the glove box as the team at home rarely rang it. So, I kept logging my bumbling thoughts and the murmurings of a broken heart in my tattered journal; and the campervan wheels kept rolling forwards.

27
God does math

AFTER THREE THOUSAND kilometres, cutting inland through the remote areas of northwestern Queensland and the Northern Territory, we eventually made it to the Top End.

We were spoiled by breathtaking waterfalls everywhere we went, swimming in as many as it was safe to do so without risk of a nip from a hungry salt-water crocodile. We visited Edith Falls near the Cutta Cutta caves, somewhere between Katherine and Darwin; got wet underneath the Florence, Tolmer, and Wangi Falls in the serene Litchfield National Park; and saw the spectacular Jim Jim and Twin Falls in Kakadu from the vantage point of a four-seater Cessna as we navigated our way around brewing storm clouds in the notorious wet season. We were mesmerised by the millions of litres of water cascading over the different escarpments throughout Arnhem Land, reverent at the sheer force of nature on display, reminded of the smallness of our own humanity.

This was clearly God's country – as we were about to discover in more ways than one – but not before we endured the worst diving experience of our lives.

FELLOW TOURISTS, SOJOURNING from the opposite direction, raved about the opportunity to dive the many World War II wrecks that lay submerged in Darwin Harbour. The city had been bombed by the Japanese Imperial Navy the morning of the 19th of February 1942. Four Japanese aircraft carriers launched 188 aircraft, with the HMAS *Gunbar* being the first ship to be attacked, strafed by several Zero fighters.

With the town's air raid sirens triggered far too late, the local residents were not ready when the Japanese dive-bombed the remaining ships in Darwin Harbour and its nearby port facilities. The attacks lasted for 30 minutes, resulting in the sinking of three warships and six merchant vessels and damaging countless others.

Despite extensive salvage operations throughout the early 1960s, the remaining wreckages have created a playground for marine life and divers alike. Understandably, we couldn't wait to get wet and explore the submerged history everybody was talking about.

It was apparent on the morning of our two-dive adventure that timing was against us. Monsoon rains and strong tidal flows had created an underwater sandstorm, turning the seabed into a raging tornado, and reducing visibility to almost zero. The bay looked like a caramel latte.

As the only two brave (or foolish!) enough to carry on with the excursion, Paulina and I were briefed by the dive master to be especially careful of box jellyfish, as it was their peak season. Named for the rectangular body shape, their tentacles are covered in biological booby traps, known as nematocysts – tiny darts loaded with poison. People and animals unfortunate enough to be injected with this poison experience paralysis, cardiac arrest, and even death – all typically within a few minutes of being stung, as made famous by Will Smith's character in the film, *7 Pounds*. On the outbound boat trip, the fair warnings were avidly punctuated by the counting of dozens of the jellyfish seen floating in the placid waters of the harbour.

The customary cautions to avoid the many crocodiles and sharks that were also known to frequent the waters, set in motion a harrowing imagination before we even broke the surface of the water.

Despite being equipped with underwater torches to improve our chances of visibility, I could barely see my submerged hand at the end of my outstretched arm. We were told to stay strictly within one body's length of each diver to avoid separation and disorientation in the opaque sea.

I'm pleased to say that on our first dive I managed to miss the nearby stonefish and put a hand on the hull of one of the sunken ships. Frankly, I couldn't tell you if it was the HMAS *Gunbar* or some local fishing boat, or whether we were at the stern or bow of the vessel. It just felt metallic and sharp, and with that, we returned to the boat, thankful to have not suffered any tragic mishap.

So distressing and meaningless was the whole diving experience for Paulina, she opted to stay on the boat and forego the second dive; I returned to the water with only the tour lead.

Somehow, during this subsequent dive, I went adrift in an invisible current, losing my physical grip with the divemaster. As I kicked frantically while trying to recover my bearings, I lost one of my fins in the blind distress, making underwater mobility incredibly difficult. Panicked, I ascended to the surface far sooner than my air tanks necessitated – and far quicker than is recommended – but I had no idea where I was in the pea-soup bay.

When I returned to the boat, there was no hiding my relief to be out of the ocean. I collapsed on the deck and admitted to Paulina that she had chosen wisely to remain on board. Having been unable to see anything on the mustard sea floor, and without any replacement dive equipment, there was no value in any further attempts.

Paulina and I agreed that, moving forwards, we would stick to recreational dives in tropical, clear waters with shallow reefs and colourful marine life that we could see and appreciate from a safe distance only.

GRATEFUL TO BE on dry land, Paulina and I walked along the Darwin foreshore, holding hands loosely as the soft sand slid between and caressed our toes with every step. It was a peaceful, pleasant evening. The orange glow of the sunset was starting to disappear over the horizon, giving way to the dark canvas of the night sky. An electrical storm brewed in the distance over Kakadu, creating a celestial kaleidoscope of coloured patterns amidst the first dusting of stars. Whilst there was lots we could talk about, neither of us said much; myself, lost in the thoughts of why I had run from home.

My inner voice began to agitate. The frustration of the recent years bubbled up again. The exhaustion of running a small practice I never wanted, combined with the disappointment that we had not been able to secure a volunteer position in a medical mission or community development project, compelled me to ventilate.

God was the target of my anger and resentment.

"Why am I stuck doing this, God?" I lamented. "I thought the agreed plan was we would move overseas and help the poorest of the poor? It's your fault I'm now trapped in a physio business with obligations that I can't manoeuvre out of. Paulina and I are willing and ready to be missionaries, but you won't send us!"

I droned on; complaint after criticism, protesting with misery. I didn't speak any of this to Paulina but, instead, I contained the dialogue between me and my Maker, an intense exchange of the heart. With each cycle of the grieved rhetoric, my inner world winced and contorted with pain and disappointment, until I sensed God finally breaking His silence.

"OK, Jason!" I sensed him conceding in a gentle tone.

"OK, what?" I replied, without moving my lips.

"OK! You have my blessing. If you want to be a medical missionary and go overseas and become part of a community that serves the poor and reaches the lost, I'll open the door."

I caught my breath. *Open the door?*

In that moment, I felt the weight of the last four years of failure and disappointment begin to dissipate. My persistent prayers and fervent pleas had broken through the brass heavens, convincing God that I was ready. He had finally acknowledged what I thought I had always known: that this was the right path for my life. God conceded; my time to work overseas had arrived. We would be cross-cultural missionaries, *salt and light* to a dying world, as Jesus metaphorically explains in His famous first sermon on the Mount of Beatitudes (Matthew 5:13-16 NKJV).

As my mind started racing ahead with all the preparations that now were necessary, and before I had even opened my mouth to share the exciting breakthrough with Paulina, God interrupted my thoughts again.

"Or..."

"Or? Or what?" I wondered. "There is no 'Or...'."

God said we were going; I didn't want to consider any alternatives. I secretly hoped He wasn't about to retract His offer or put unreasonable conditions or unbearable timeframes around His approval for us to travel.

I held my breath again as I repeated, ever so quietly, "...or, what?"

God continued, "Or... you could remain home, intentionally invest yourself into the business of physiotherapy that I have gifted you with, grow it into an ethically profitable, scaled network of practices that will become an economic engine to send more than just the two of you to do My work. In time, the business could support ten more, even hundreds, maybe thousands of pairs of hands committed to the work of feeding the orphans, clothing the widows, and sharing My love." (James 1:27 NKJV)

I imagined a cosmic "mic drop".

My heart stopped beating for what seemed like minutes. I felt captured in a suspended state, as though my eyes were opening for the first time to a vista of meaningful opportunity and significance that presumably had always been there, but not visible. My life seemed to fast-forward at a million frames per second, revealing what could become of our lives under God's careful direction to build the business as He was proposing. The film reel then snapped back to my present day, before setting off again in an accelerated projection of what our lives might become, should we instead stick with our original intention of joining a medical mission team straight away.

Possessed with what seemed limitless capabilities to compare and contrast the different trajectories of both potential lives, and simultaneously immobilised by the profound choice God seemed to be offering, my knees buckled as all rational faculties shut down.

Words fail to describe what happened next.

It was as if a sudden flip of a light switch transformed me; I was *off*, and then *on*.

For most of my life, I had imagined leaving the comforts of suburbia to live long-term amongst disadvantaged people groups. That night, my perspective pivoted 180 degrees. Having spent years appealing my case and finally winning a favourable ruling from the Celestial Judge – granted freedom to pursue my childhood dream – I suddenly found myself wanting something entirely different.

In a flash, I understood that all the seemingly disconnected and random experiences in my young adulthood, early professional career, and accidental business ventures, were converging to reveal part of God's architectural genius. My life resembled the disorganised and chaotic web of differently coloured woven threads, hidden behind the façade of the tapestry; but when God turned it over, for the first time I caught a glimpse of the picture that was emerging.

I could not argue with God's mathematics. While I was focussed on *addition*, God was proposing *multiplication*. I saw only *linear* progression; He envisioned an *exponential* effect.

If impact and long-term change were the lofty ideals, then any strategy that served to scale the effort, mobilise more people, and sustain greater longevity couldn't be argued against. And it wasn't lost on me that if I were to take the option of volunteering my time now in an overseas assignment, then I'd be forever dependent on faithful others who stayed home to generate the funds I'd rely on being donated –

something I previously seemed unwilling to do myself. God's blueprint framed a far superior approach to the long game.

Instantly, my life reset.

This was what I had been searching for, the very reason I had embarked on the trip around Australia in the first place. I was running away from the pain of an unwanted business, and running toward fresh purpose and meaning. God showed me they were inextricably linked; He was the Creator of both.

I resolved on that warm January night in 2002 that God's second option was the better choice. I willingly embraced my newly imagined role as a compassionate capitalist, forgoing the life of a typical missionary, and agreeing to remain at home to build an enterprise that would serve the same important purpose.

The *means* was different, but the *end* hadn't changed.

The self-doubt, looming fear of failure, and the profound sense of abject rejection stemming from my perceived shortcomings in fulfilling what I believed to be God's intentions for my life, began to dissolve. Whilst I continued to wrestle with the push-and-pull of these tensions on my heart for years to come, in that moment, I felt assured that God had marked our lives to play this part as He had revealed. Of this, I was immediately confident.

In the hours and days that followed, I shared with Paulina what God had shown me. It was hard to put it all into words, but she recognised the immediate shift in my attitude and energy.

Unable to pinpoint a specific moment of her own divine confirmation, Paulina reflected on her awakening as a gradual evolution in the weeks and months leading up to and following that pivotal night. Throughout this journey, she carried a profound sense of peace, recognising that we were entrusted with a mission to return home with revitalised aspirations to build our business for the greater purpose of God. Central to this vison was an unwavering commitment to remain faithful to those in need, serving them wholeheartedly with our utmost dedication.

United, I steered Ollie homeward.

28
jump

THE DIRECT ROUTE home took us through the Red Centre of Australia – named after the iconic hue of crimson dirt that fills almost a million square kilometres at our nation's centre of gravity, the high levels of oxidising iron in the soil responsible for the rust-coloured pigmentation.

Despite the new enthusiasm for our refreshed life mission, we made the most of a rare opportunity while in the pristine outback of our sun-burned country. Detouring to explore the vast desert landscapes outside of Alice Springs, Paulina and I spent a week at Ayers Rock – an isolated giant formation of weathered sandstone, regarded by many as the largest monolith in the world – revered by the Aborigines, calling it *Uluru*. We rode camels around this significant cultural and natural landmark, took in the natural wonders of the granite rocks of *Karlu Karlu* (humorously known as the Devil's Marbles) and hiked the sandstone formations that make up *Kata Tjuta* (or more commonly referred to as the Olgas). We also thoroughly enjoyed participating in a heli-muster of wild camels at King's Station in the Watarrka National Park, giving us a high-speed aerial perspective of how far and fast these beasts can move.

These spectacular experiences were only matched by floating in a hot air balloon over the 72-kilometre span of the rugged MacDonnell Ranges. Our pilot's precise timing coincided with the dawning Sun showering its golden light over the horizon, highlighting the untouched natural beauty of the vast landscape below. As I watched the unfolding of this scene with my natural eyes, I sensed an inward mirroring of divine hope welling up in me for our promising future.

Paulina took the wheel for most of our homeward journey south along the Sturt Highway, revelling in the freedom of being unlimited by any speed restraints, but regularly intimidated by the long road trains that would overtake her with their six trailers swaying wildly by her side. As Paulina played chicken with long haulers coming the other way, I often retreated to the bed in the campervan to scribble notes, ideas, and plans in my journal. Having thoroughly disconnected from the practice for the previous 12 weeks, I now found my imagination racing with fresh vision and excitement. I filled those pages with random thoughts, disconnected strategies, and high-risk actions for our business, my pen rarely able to keep up with my next insight. To any reader at the time, it would have looked like the ramblings of a mad man; but to me, these notes were the beginnings of an unlikely road map to transition Back In Motion from a small single practice into a national footprint.

WE ARRIVED HOME on an overcast afternoon in late January 2002. Ollie had clocked more than 12,000 kilometres as we parked her weary chassis in the driveway of our renovated house in Scoresby. As I looked up and noticed the discoloured outline on our carport fascia of where the original Back In Motion sign had first hung, it reminded me why I was back.

I had run away from a life and business I couldn't reconcile; I had sought input from a God I knew and loved, but didn't understand. He had taken us halfway around Australia, and met us in our desperation. He affirmed who we were, and redefined what we were to do.

As though I was standing on the clifftop of our next great adventure, my toes excitedly dangled over the edge, anticipating the jump.

29
questioneering

THE PRACTICE EXPANDED during my absence, suggesting I could – and maybe *should* – have gone on holidays sooner and more often. The difference now was that Paulina and I were both motivated, with full tanks of rocket fuel, ready to invest ourselves into accelerated business growth. We wanted to see how close to the moon we could reach, knowing God controlled the launch.

One of the first things I read on business was the *E-Myth,* by Michael E. Gerber. "Bow-tie Mark", who gave me my start in private practice, swore by this book. Regarded as a true legend of entrepreneurship, Gerber's subtitle promised answers: *Why most small businesses don't work and what to do about it.*

In this invigorating read, Gerber warns that 80% of the millions of new businesses that start every year, fail within the next five. His recommendation is to approach your business like a franchise, systematising your processes so that everyday tasks don't ultimately rely on you.

Gerber goes on to differentiate the three primary roles within an organisation: the entrepreneur who creates the vision; the manager who creates the systems; and the technician who does the work. I realised in that moment I had been working as the technician in my practice, and would inevitably fail if I predominantly relied on only my skills and competencies as a physiotherapist.

Gerber predicted that I was likely to keep doing what I loved and was good at – which, in my case, was treating patient injuries and training other therapists. It would only be a matter of time before the volume of my work exceeded my capacity to get it all done, and my exhaustion and neglect of staff and other responsibilities would eventually render me ineffective and unsuccessful.

I closed *E-Myth*, realising I had to think, feel, and act differently to most of my peers in physiotherapy if I were to beat the odds. The seed of franchising was planted in my consciousness but, greater than this, I heeded Gerber's sober warning: do myself *out of a job* or the practice will forever *own me*.

I WENT ON to consume two or three books a month that year, devouring their lessons and warnings, ruminating on their anecdotes and metaphors, and putting into action their recommendations and strategies for everyday practice.

Favourites included *How to Win Friends and Influence People* (Dale Carnegie), *Rich Dad Poor Dad* and *Rich Dad's CASHFLOW Quadrant* (both by Robert Kiyosaki), *The Purpose Driven Life* (Rick Warren), *The 7 Habits of Highly Effective People* (Stephen Covey) and the *One Minute Manager* series (Ken Blanchard).

I also formed a penchant for biographies of successful businesspeople, and the brands they had built. I was impressed and inspired by the early ventures of Phil Knight, selling his Nike running shoes out of the boot of his Plymouth Valiant at track meets in the US. I learned that the McDonald brothers experimented with repeatable quality drive-up service at their original "Golden Arches", and then it was Ray Croc who went on to create the global phenomenon we know the hamburger chain to be today. Other impactful stories included Andrew Carnegie as the steel and rail baron of the 1800s, Richard Branson in losing his business "Virginity", and a young Donald Trump living out his real estate madness in New York City.

As it's often said, *leaders are readers*; we become voracious learners when we exercise the discipline of systematic reading. I began to take interest in the business section of the daily newspaper, and special periodicals such as *Business Review Weekly* and the *Australian Financial Review*. I paid more attention to Alan Koehler's *Finance Update* at the end of the nightly ABC news program, when previously I took that as my cue to flip channels.

And it was in these formative months that I developed the habit of buying more books than I could keep up with – a habit that continues to frustrate Paulina to this day. Every time someone mentioned a favourite title, I would rush out and buy it, adding to the queue of waiting literature. Paulina commented more than once during those years that the tower of books on my bedside table was approaching the toppling threshold. Fortunately, I have now switched to Kindle and other e-reader formats, enabling me to catalogue my reading (and hide my addictive literary tendencies) more effectively.

ALONG WITH MY passion for reading, a boldness to ask questions grew. This would develop another lifelong leadership habit I've come to call *questioneering* – the engineering of insightful questions to learn what other people know or think.

Undoubtedly, smart people learn from their mistakes. But I figured the real game was to learn from *other* people's mistakes, not just my own. I turned on my business radar wherever I went – at church, professional events, weekend parties, and summer BBQs.

Surprisingly, maybe, the greatest source of talent and wisdom bubbled up from my very own patient database. Every 20 minutes, for ten hours a day, I would usher a new patient into my consultation room – many of them happy to share their experiences in life and business as I pushed, poked, rubbed, and contorted them for therapeutic benefit.

If my antennae tweaked in the presence of another small business owner, corporate manager, or executive professional, I could barely contain my curiosity. I wanted to know how they picked the right staff, what advertising strategies worked, the growing pains they had faced, and what kept them up at night. Whilst some were put off by my somewhat aggressive approach, most were all too obliging to share with a fellow soldier the war stories of their latest victories or defeat, whichever was more recent. It was almost like they recognised in me the hunger and determination to go further, faster – and it reminded them of themselves.

In all my discussions, Michael Magyar epitomised the learned businessman that I wanted to become. The same father who offered his help when Paulina and I were leading the MAD youth group in our late teens, he was faith-led, values-driven, experienced in the real world, and yet still idealistic. Michael had a background in engineering but had spent ten years of his early married life as a youth and adult pastor in a fast-growing church in the Western suburbs of Melbourne. After some changes in direction, he now boasted 20 years in corporate business, driving sales for an Australian healthcare company across the US, the UK, and into South Africa.

Michael had the balance of both wings – commercial insights and Christian ministry. He had reconciled how the two work together for optimal effectiveness. And it just so happened that Michael, and his wife Marion, were the assigned support coaches to Paulina and I in our new roles as Young Adult leaders at our local church.

I now had motive, means, and opportunity to get up close to Michael; the three prerequisites to winning the case I passionately argued for him to mentor me. By mid-2002, he finally acquiesced, becoming my first official business coach.

30
triple threat

ONLY WEEKS AFTER returning home from the Red Centre, I was greeted by our no-nonsense, all-business landlord requesting a meeting. I lingered in the reception area far longer than I could spare, seated among Vikram's long-suffering patients, until he finally summoned me to his office. After dispensing with a cursory "welcome home", he proceeded to advise that he had unilaterally chosen to triple our rent. *Triple*!

Over the 18 months we had been a subtenant, Back In Motion progressively occupied increasing space in the two buildings on site – now officially with more square metreage than any other practitioner, including Vikram.

Naturally, as we took on more space, our rent increased proportionately - that much was expected. Applying a three-fold multiple to the market rate was not. More so, it was entirely unaffordable.

I feared the worst. What value was there in working tirelessly to build my practice, only for all the proceeds to evaporate in the form of extortionist rent? I begged Vikram to reconsider. When that failed, I threatened to take it up with the Ombudsman at the Small Business Commission responsible for commercial property leasing disputes in Victoria. When his vacant stare showed no interest in negotiation and no intimidation from my feeble threats, I realised my fate. I left Vikram's room convinced I needed to find alternative premises if I was to survive.

In my desperation and vulnerability, I reacted badly. I felt agitated, fearful, overwhelmed, and strained. I had barely returned home from our trip up north, with a passionate mandate to build a scaled practice, and it seemed I couldn't even get passed *Go* square on the Monopoly board.

Somewhere in those tense but quiet moments, God whispered to me, "Surrender it, and trust Me". Michael encouraged the same, reminding me it was God's idea to build our practice, not my own. He alone can make good on His promise.

With a growing peace, I felt the tangled emotions slowly unravel. I set about exploring a new address for the future home of Back In Motion's flagship practice, resting in the confidence of God's unseen hand at work.

A POPULAR PIZZA shop on a major thoroughfare transecting the middle-class suburb of Wantirna South, reportedly burned down in a suspicious kitchen fire. And in the classic version of one man's tragedy turning into another person's good fortune, the opportunity for a new tenant to refit the space to their custom specifications was on offer.

The most direct route from our existing site was 3.7 kilometres and took just under six minutes, with the assumption of one red traffic light. The location also happened to be equidistant from where I lived.

The shop totalled 178 square metres at the cost of $40,000 per annum. It was more space than we needed, but gave us room to grow; and the cost was less than what our rent was about to triple into. We rationalised that the exposure to drive-by traffic alone could be worth thousands of additional revenue dollars every month.

The big hurdle to climb was the five-year lease term – this was a big test of our commitment to God's plan. I hadn't even been a physio for five years, so it was a time horizon that I couldn't imagine or evaluate. But I signed my personal guarantee as though I understood the risks I was taking, even though I likely didn't.

Paulina and I then very quickly learned about the processes and challenges of commercial construction. We engaged town planners, surveyors, architects, disability access consultants, local council representatives, builders, equipment suppliers, signwriters, painters, specialist plumbers, carpet-layers, audio-visual technicians, telephony and computer specialists, cabinet makers, concrete cutters, body corporate representatives, and so on. We earned an honorary degree in shopfitting, relying very heavily on good friends – and friends-of-*their*-friends when needed – to help us navigate the unavoidable complexities and provide mate's rates where possible.

The estimate to build our state-of-the-art design exceeded a quarter-of-a-million dollars – a lot of money now, let alone then. Added to this picture of financial burden was a large mortgage on our first home, severely dwindled savings in the bank due to our holiday around the eastern half of Australia, minimal business earnings in our two-year start-up history, and no other assets for security.

Our saving grace in those days was that banks took confidence from the perceived low risk of D.I.N.K.s (Double Income, No Kids), especially those on professional healthcare salaries. Their reasoning was that our professional salaries were secured by safe jobs, and so we could always earn our way back from whatever debt we fell into. I qualified to be one of the first "test" borrowers for an innovative new lending product being trialled by the Bendigo Bank specifically for healthcare workers. They loaned me $200,000 on a cash flow basis, with no security required other than my personal guarantee.

Upon advice of a local accountant who helped set up our initial business structure, we shifted ownership of our home into Paulina's name and hoped, if everything went belly up, we would at least keep a roof over our heads. Our business loans meant we needed to clear a minimum of $100,000 profit annually for five consecutive years to meet the obligations to both our landlord and bank. That was a lot of patients to find, given that to date our small team averaged much less.

After four months of planning and construction – and hurdling one obstacle after another – Back In Motion moved into its stunning new premises in mid-2002. There was no cutting of a red ribbon or formal opening, just an email to our client base to attend for their next treatment at the new location. We hoped the unexpected pleasure in what they found would be a welcome surprise. For most, it was.

Our large entrance boasted a long timber reception desk and ample couches for waiting patients. We had five private treatment spaces accessible off the corridor, and the back third of the premises ballooned into a fully equipped rehabilitation studio, complete with Pilates apparatus and cardio and strength training equipment, accompanied by a fleet of electrotherapy machines. Adjacent to the open plan studio, we designed a staff retreat with a private office shared by Paulina and I. The decor and upholstery were predictably burgundy and cream to match our new-brand colour palette, complemented with rich warm timber finishes. We even installed computers in every consultation room to commence our crossover to paper-light administration and electronic clinical records – a shift that felt a little ahead of its time.

And we had Max – our mascot skeleton – hanging in the corner of the waiting room for the appeal of both the kids and adults alike. Predictably, their curiosity inevitably led them to tickling a rib, pulling a finger, or examining the funny bone of the elbow, great to the amusement (if not, encouragement) of my mum, who still worked behind our reception desk.

Martin, a serious-minded physiotherapist from Sweden who had recently joined our team, and would go on to earn a doctorate on and be ranked in the top 1% worldwide for soccer expertise, remarked as he walked into the new practice for the first time: "This is the nicest physiotherapy practice I've ever seen. I don't think there is anything like it in Melbourne."

He probably wasn't correct, but I appreciated the flattery.

31
stretched

AS I WAS launching our team into their new purpose-built premises, Paulina was immersed in a demanding objective of her own. Having completed her graduate years as a nurse, and all her rotations through neurosurgery and ICU, she decided to commence a postgraduate degree in Intensive Care. Paulina had already taken on a new role at the Alfred Hospital – renowned as one of Australia's busiest emergency and trauma centres – and was perfectly placed to gain the right experience with the promise of early promotion.

She was pulling three 12-hour shifts a week as part of her full-time roster – a mix of days and nights – occasionally filling other vacancies as she drew the short straw. At the same time, she slavishly completed online postgraduate study units, and filled in the gaps where I needed help at the practice. I don't know how Paulina had the stamina to endure it all, but I'm guessing that radioactive protactinium in her DNA might account for some of it!

The two of us worked unsustainably long hours and, even when Paulina attended the practice, we barely connected. I was taking patients in 20-minute intervals, delivering as many as 25 appointments a day. Whenever I emerged from my consultation room, Paulina was usually engaged with other clients and our staff, or had a telephone glued to her ear. It was manic, with very little downtime to enjoy together in the fast-paced chaos of the growth.

The pattern forming bode poorly for a vibrant and enriching relationship together, especially so early in our marriage. It seemed our only times of regular crossover were after 9:30pm. Out of necessity, we agreed "our time" would be reserved over a late evening meal, when we could engage in meaningful conversation without the threat of interruption. Whilst eating a large bowl of carbohydrates just before bed is not recommended for digestion, it was critical for our hearts.

IF BUSINESS AND study wasn't stretching us enough, we compounded our commitments with additional responsibilities at church.

We accepted the leadership of a small cohort of other young professional couples in what was called a "Life Group". We met every alternate Wednesday night in our home to study the previous week's sermon, explore new topics in the Bible, and debate contemporary issues. What started as a gathering of four or five couples we knew well, eventually grew into a small crowd of more than 40 people. Friends brought friends, which was wonderful, but our small house couldn't accommodate the growth. Most nights we had to push the couches aside, remove the coffee table, and bring in extra chairs. Even then, people had to sit on bean bags or the floor, perch on the kitchen table in the other room, or stand somewhat awkwardly in the doorways.

We met inspiring couples through this Life Group – some becoming life-long friends. Despite the constant exhaustion we felt, it was exhilarating to see God working in other peoples' lives at different paces, and in unique ways. Some weeks we would be crying over a couple's difficulty to fall pregnant, or one person having lost their dream job; other times, we would be celebrating a parent healed from an intractable sickness, or another experiencing a breakthrough in their career.

Paulina and I savoured the opportunity to share with these couples our own tumultuous journey of being redirected into business as part of our mission, relying at different moments on their prayers and encouragement to keep moving forwards.

Life Group was friendship and community at its best. But it wasn't just the meetings that required our time. Leadership required that we follow up with each member during the week, a workload that soon became more than we could handle.

Through the support of Michael and Marion, we deputised three mature couples from within the group to step up and take a third of the members each, forming new and separate meetings. We thought of it less as a *splitting* of friendships, and more as a *multiplication* of opportunities. The change was difficult for some, but it provided room for new people to be invited, and certainly relieved us from an escalating burden that was soon to overwhelm us.

In some ways, I now deem these Life Groups our first three successful franchises.

32
manifesto

I DRAFTED MY mini manifesto in 2002; one thousand, three hundred and eighty-four words foreshadowing my best life. Built on an earlier rudimentary vision statement, I went further and deeper. I penned the things I wanted to achieve for our marriage and in our business, and how I wanted to be remembered.

I wrote it for an audience of one: *Me*. As such, I have chosen not to overshare the details of it here, but some highlights are relevant.

Specifically, I dreamed of building Australia's leading physiotherapy network. I defined the criteria for a successful private practice as modelled on our first business in Wantirna South. I forecast the development of 12 more locations over the ensuing 15 years. I described in detail the patient experience I wanted to deliver; the career pathway for future colleagues who joined me; and the Godly values I was committed to.

My manifesto explicitly detailed the financial milestones and thresholds I sought to achieve, the competencies that would be demanded of me, and the impact I hoped I would have on our profession.

A large portion of my private proclamation was devoted to how our business would serve the poor, orphans, and widows. In some detail, I connected the dots of commercial opportunism with social cause, mapping the pathways that would achieve these ends in mind. Our business was to become a means to serve those abroad in greatest need. We wanted to deliver better healthcare, provide safe drinking water and sanitation, improve education, help service microenterprise loans to those with start-up business ideas, and we wanted to share the Gospel.

In short, my aspiration was to know Jesus more, and make Him more known.

I concluded the paper with profound pledges to my family. I put myself on the hook, colourfully describing the culture and values

I wanted to lead in our home, devoting myself to the needs of those closest to me. I clearly wanted to be a better husband and father (when the time came) than I ever dreamed of being as a physiotherapist or entrepreneur.

The details of my manifesto have remained private, even to this day, and I certainly haven't yet fulfilled everything I wrote down. I may not ever. But the process of auditing my heart, asking the tough questions, and putting it down in ink was a powerful and sobering exercise.

I have returned to those pages countless times over the years. When I felt discouraged and beaten, I reflected on the key phrases and promises I'd dreamed, reminding myself of where my hope comes from. Inevitably, doing this inspired in me the strength to push a little harder, the endurance to go a little further, and the patience to try one more time.

33
Kakinada

DESPITE HAVING LAID to rest our hopes of becoming medical missionaries, Paulina and I were asked to lead a three-week medical mission to southern India in the latter months of 2002. It was a small team of only two nurses (including Paulina), one physiotherapist (me), an assistant, and a photographer.

We flew into Chennai International Airport and embarked on an arduous overnight train journey to Kakinada. The experience was marked by overcrowded carriages, onboard curries with generous portions of infectious gastro, and mysterious individuals keeping a suspiciously close watch on our expensive medical equipment and luggage. The sixth largest city of the Indian state of Andhra Pradesh, Kakinada lies on the coast of the Bay of Bengal. We met with local pastors and translators on arrival, then drove four-wheel drives and motorbikes to small, remote villages to set up a string of single-day medical campsites.

The nurses worked hardest of all, providing vaccinations, primary wound care, and general education. I treated patients with chronic pain and limb deformities as best I could in the primitive conditions. I also helped coordinate the logistics, support the nurses, and manage the crowds as word spread through the community of our free medical services.

The local pastors who facilitated our itinerary reached out to the villagers, connecting their families to schools or food services, and following up other needs as they arose. Our evenings were spent telling stories to the children and giving short Bible messages to the locals who continued to hang around long after the clinic was closed.

The next day, we repeated the pattern in another village.

Most communities we visited were extremely poor. People lived in shanty structures, on dirt floors, with no electricity, plumbing, or sanitation services. They relied on basic sustenance farming, which meant a very plain, lean diet – and that only happened when the weather conditions were right for a humble harvest.

When we needed the toilet, we were directed to a designated area about 200 metres from the village centre where a thatched roof with no walls denoted the drop zone. We had to literally tiptoe in sandals through piles of human excrement to find the least offensive patch to squat – often in full sight of anyone who chose to look. It quickly became motivation to plan our bathroom runs before and just after leaving our overnight accommodation every day.

We spent our last day of the trip at an orphanage where 80 children had been gathered from numerous districts and were being fed, schooled, and cared for by a Christian family and their team. It was moving to see how well adjusted many of these children were from the loving support provided.

We participated in one of the school graduation ceremonies and were entertained by the kids as they sang and danced in traditional costumes. To the casual observer, their lives seemed *normal*. It was only afterwards that we learned the trauma and hardship many had endured.

We departed that day with a generous gift of cashews, hand-picked and processed in the plantations around the orphanage. I devoured my bag on the long train ride back to the airport, each glutenous handful prompting another reason to ponder how I could help these people, and others just like them, all over the world.

My lasting memory of Chennai was the sky opening, unloading torrential rain as we made our way to the airport. So flooded were the streets that we left our suitcases inside the rickshaw and pushed it from behind, assisting the driver, in knee-deep water. Upon reaching the airport terminal, we were drenched through all our clothes and eagerly anticipating a warm shower before our departure. Above all, we were deeply grateful for the experiences we shared amongst these beautiful people, and were contemplating when we could schedule our return.

34

industry debut

NOT LONG BACK from India and our practice exploded with opportunity. Yet again, the business seemed to do better when I wasn't there.

Any fears that we might be unable to afford the increased rent of our new premises and pay back the expensive fit out faded into nonsense. We closed out the fiscal year of 2002 with sales just short of $1 million, representing substantive growth on the previous period. Each quarter, our accountant explained the figures, unable to hide his enthusiasm for the success we were experiencing. Paulina and I were delighted, and a little bit surprised, to see the hard work paying off.

The Back In Motion team was growing, as were our expansion opportunities. A barrage of marketing initiatives to dragnet referrals from doctors, sporting clubs, schools, and gymnasiums had unearthed an opportunity for us to sublet a second location, leasing the first aid room at a fitness and aquatic centre in nearby Boronia. We were already using their pool on a weekly basis for hydrotherapy classes, and referring Workcover patients to personal trainers for extended rehabilitation memberships, so it was a natural progression to provide an onsite physiotherapy triage service at the same location. I bought more equipment, painted the room to our preferred colour scheme, hung promotional posters on every available wall, plugged in a laptop and EFTPOS machine, and officially launched our second practice.

The client demand at these premises would only ever be modest, but I gained lots of relevant experience in replicating our business model for a second time, transferring our learnings to a new environment. In the years to come, these experiences proved our tentative expansion to be very worthwhile.

CONTRARY TO MY negative experiences with the APA, the editor of their members' magazine approached me in late 2002 for a feature story to celebrate my early success. Having previously chided my start-up attempts as being irresponsible, now they were curious how we went from zero to $1 million in only three years. They were confident their readers wanted to know too. I relished the irony.

The profile was a favourable, two-page spread that told of my quarter-life crisis, reluctant start in business, and newfound drive to make money to be significant in the lives of those more needy. Naïvely, maybe, I outlined the broad brushstroke of our business plan, shared some of our marketing wins, and encouraged people to invest in a valuable team. I even disclosed in the interview our intentions of soon opening a third practice, although I'm not sure it was any more than a vague idea at that stage.

In fact, almost as a premonition, I'm quoted in the article as expecting to take 20 years to achieve my goals. Whilst I'm sure it was a throw-away line then, the estimation proved to be eerily accurate. Almost exactly two decades after the date of publication, we celebrated a fabulous milestone exceeding all my projections.

This article marked my debut on the industry's radar. The APA portrayed me somewhat as an ambassador of the emerging generation of physiotherapists, distinguishing me from a previous era that frowned upon discussion of business, finances, and patients as "customers". I staunchly asserted that, without additional skills beyond our clinical training, physiotherapists like me would fail as business owners. I provocatively argued that our undergraduate education moulded us as altruistic clinicians, but failed to provide competencies to endure and thrive in the competitive marketplace. I identified that we, who chose a career in private enterprise, had a duty of care to be excellent and ethical in business. We needed to excel in the commercial realities of recruiting staff, managing finance, building a brand, and dealing with patient complaints. If we were expected to just learn this all on the run – hoping the noble objective of making people healthy would otherwise be enough – then we were inevitably going to struggle. And every failed physiotherapy business would become another reason to deter the next person from trying.

My cautions and challenges clearly struck a chord with the editor and readers alike, as I received questions and comments from many colleagues who wanted to continue the conversation. Invitations followed to speak at state-based industry events, host in-services at other people's practices, and sit on opinion panels for different healthcare forums.

Of course, I wasn't a model for others to emulate. At the age of 27, I was still a novice, learning as I went along.

My day in the practice typically started at 6:30am. I spent an hour at my computer before any of the team arrived, planning the day, load-balancing the clinical roster, clearing emails, reviewing payroll, or attending to other administrative tasks. My first patient arrived at 7:30am, and my whole demeanour changed; it became a blur of bones, joints, and muscles.

New patient appointments were scheduled for 40 minutes, and repeat consultations happened in 20-minute intervals. I consulted to at least ten patients before midday, with no breaks in between, and squeezed in new clients with urgent needs as required.

I swapped exhausted smiles with my team as we collided in the corridors, calling our next patient through or looking for the mobile ultrasound trolley that was usually passed between us like a baton in a relay race. The pace was frenetic and energising, and I revelled in the camaraderie with staff and patients.

It was important to me that we all got to know each other's clients. I wanted to take interest in the progress others were making in their recovery, even if I wasn't the primary therapist. Patients even engaged in conversation and humour with each other as we tortured them in the exercise studio or conducted gait assessments up and down the passageway, navigating around the crowds coming and going.

I typically stopped for an hour in the middle of the day to review case files, host a staff meeting or education session, run an errand or two, and occasionally eat lunch.

The afternoon then became a repeat of the morning. Back-to-back client appointments with a 20-minute break only when a patient cancelled or I had a scheduled visit from a supplier representative. Receptionists started to wind-up about 6:30 in the evening, but I kept seeing patients until 8pm.

Of course, this wasn't the end of my day. The next hour or two was consumed with cleaning down the treatment rooms, stripping the beds of linen, and replacing all the equipment and consumables as was required. I'd then sit at the computer to complete all my unfinished clinical notes, write letters back to referring doctors updating them on their patient's progress, filling in Workcover certificates, and reviewing subpoenas for medico-legal opinions required for upcoming compensation claims.

Typically, by about 9:30pm I was turning off the final bank of lights, arming the security system, and relieved to be heading home for another late-night dinner with Paulina.

The only times I wasn't in the practice was when I was consulting offsite at aged care facilities or some of my corporate clients. Given the large volume of Workcover injuries I saw in our practice, it was prudent for me to get ahead of the problem and offer preventative and educational services to employers to keep their people safe. I serviced enduring contracts with Nubrik Quarries, Unilever, Amcor, Cadbury Schweppes, Paul's Dairy, and many others – making for a very diverse caseload.

I carved out two afternoons every week to rotate onsite to these various work sites. There I conducted risk assessments of their picking and manufacturing lines, wrote recommendations for improvement to health and safety, designed exercise routines bespoke to workers of different roles and responsibilities, did physical pre-employment assessments, triaged injuries as they occurred, and wrote return-to-work plans for people during their recovery.

Inconveniently, for many years in a row, I was asked to attend some factories from 2am to 4am to provide a range of similar services to the night shift; otherwise, they progressively became more neglected and were at greater risk of mishap or injury. Fortunately, hard work was never my problem, and I still made it back to the practice for my first patient at 7:30am later that same morning.

Of course, the APA journalist failed to mention the daily grind that underpinned the sheen of our achievements. Some people prefer not to see how the sausage is made, savouring the dish without ever getting a glimpse into the kitchen.

THIS ROUTINE CONTINUED month after month. I was young, and felt invincible, so I kept saying "yes" to every opportunity that presented, burning the candle at both ends, and setting it alight in the middle if I needed to.

My weeks became so full of clinical work, my business and managerial responsibilities spilled into weeknights and weekends. It was during these times I considered new marketing strategies, proofed copy for brochures we were producing, conducted desktop research of other people's websites, analysed the service and price cards of my competitors, posted recruitment advertisements, reviewed résumés, prepared performance reviews of existing team members, bug-fixed computer issues, ordered new equipment, kept track of our finances, and mused and noodled on complaints from both patients and staff.

I also dreamed about further expansion possibilities; not just how to harness the organic opportunities of new referring doctors or sporting clubs, but where to develop our third and subsequent practice locations. I attentively researched every practice for sale in the APA classifieds, kept my ear close to the ground on any new leasing opportunities that might emerge in nearby shopping strips or medical precincts, and ran the numbers of what it all might cost.

I frequently quipped that I held the title of the lowest-paid employee in the practice due to the extensive hours I put in, although Paulina was a strong contender too. When we crunched the numbers, it turned out that I was making a meagre 72 cents an hour in the first few years. I was cheating myself to keep sufficient cash in the business to invest into *new* staff, *new* equipment, *new* marketing endeavours, to achieve *new* growth. I hoped the investment would pay off one day, reminding myself of God's promises.

AT THE END of 2002, I invited the Back In Motion team for a weekend to the surfside town of Anglesea. It was the first of many staff retreats to come.

We hired a large beach house, paired up the staff in share rooms like a dormitory arrangement from our school camp days, and arranged a mix of activities; a round of golf, sea kayaking tours, and dinner out on the Saturday night. There was no agenda for most of the weekend, until we woke to what many hoped would be a lazy Sunday morning.

Having stoked the open fire in the lounge room, just after breakfast I ceremoniously mounted a portable whiteboard onto an easel in full view of everyone. I politely asked for 30 minutes of their attention before we commenced our final day together.

As I stood with my black marker, I drew three concentric circles, mimicking a dartboard. The bullseye represented everyone in the room – the core team who were central to the business. I explained that if we pulled together and took some risks, we could significantly leverage ourselves into numerous other locations and services, depicted by the progressive rings I continued to draw around the epicentre.

As I cast my inaugural vision to them, my enthusiasm grew; my kettle built up a head of steam. My big crescendo was an invitation to participate in a... *wait for it...* "40-year plan to launch ten practices" in the immediate and surrounding areas of Melbourne.

I waxed lyrical about the unprecedented size and scale a network of ten practices would represent and how much impact we could have on the profession and communities we served. I linked the significance of achieving commercial success on one hand with the potential for meaningful mission opportunities on the other, reinforcing the unbreakable nexus. Channelling my best version of William Wallace of *Braveheart* I became unnecessarily animated, spitting as I preached, waving my arms with sweeping gestures of conviction and determination. When I eventually stopped, I had no clever strategy or dramatic close. No blistering finale or mic-drop moment. I simply ran out of words with nothing more to say. It was all over in less than 15 minutes.

Most people just sat silently and listened to me rant. A few politely thanked me for the weekend, as they gathered their belongings for the return trip home. Some obvious naysayers settled for quizzical looks to express their disinterest or disbelief.

I had bared my soul in front of the team, and I couldn't *un*say things now, despite my ambitious plan having more chance of failure than success. If the only person I had motivated that day was me, it was going to have to be enough.

35
last hurrah

OUR NEXT ADDITION came without the laborious planning that had gone into every other expansion decision.

We decided to blow off some steam one Friday evening by taking the team go-karting. As we lapped the track at increasing speeds, jostling for the perfect position in the tight corners, everyone drove with an unquenchable thirst for victory. On the way home, when Paulina complained of abdominal cramping, we both just assumed she had taken some hard bumps against the tyre walls in the heat of competition. As the pain worsened, we ended up in the emergency department near midnight. The registrar took an ultrasound of Paulina's abdominal region to inspect for internal injuries and found an entirely other explanation for her symptoms: Pregnancy.

The surprise and elation quickly turned to despair and disappointment when the doctor couldn't find a heartbeat. Having started our day completely unaware that new life had been seeded together, we were now ending it with the shock of having lost our first child within an hour of its discovery. I had a fitful night's sleep as we cried and blamed ourselves for being so irresponsible in the go-kart, despite there being no way we could have known of the potential danger at the time.

Attending a follow up appointment the next day, to our great astonishment, the sonographer detected a vibrant, healthy beating heart – our baby seemingly just needing a good night's sleep after the rigorous track work the night before. Our 12-hour ordeal had been a cruel test of our resilience and fortitude, but we were ecstatic that little baby Smith was on his way.

BECOMING A FATHER was a sobering contemplation. Whilst we both looked forward to being parents and had always loved interacting with the young children of friends and family, the burden of the business was real. I harboured genuine concerns about how I was going to balance parenting with the competing time priorities necessitated by the long, grinding hours in the practice.

My preparation didn't instil a lot of confidence. I had failed as a father to our fur-baby, Jessie. After less than two years, we offered up our playful Cocker Spaniel for adoption because our work schedule was so inflexible and all-consuming. Sadly, I also bombed out with Tommy, our long-necked turtle. Occasionally taking him out of the aquarium for a wander in the backyard, one day I turned my back for only a few minutes and lost him under the bark chips of the garden bed. He went missing in February, and then in December I saw a poster on a shopfront window declaring a family had found him. Tommy had travelled more than nine large residential blocks in about as many months. (I wonder the stories he could tell!)

Despite my abject failures in these regards, another little life was about to be thrust upon me, and I had to be ready.

AS PAULINA'S BELLY kept expanding, so were our practices.

The building in Wantirna South needed constant renovations and adjustment to its floor plan to accommodate our rapid growth. We split one of the larger consultation rooms into two smaller ones; rearranged the waiting room to fit more chairs; and the back office and staff retreat were reconfigured to accommodate extra workstations for the additional staff we hired.

To prioritise the floor space in the practice for more patients, we moved all non-core administration back home. The original makeshift consultation room in the carport, now sitting idle, was fitted with two desks and a battery of filing cabinets. We employed my mother-in-law, Nelly, to oversee the bookkeeping, payroll, and administration duties, allowing Paulina to focus on policy manuals, supplier relationships, and the management of our receptionists. If you are keeping count, that's both mothers on the team now!

It was a pokey office providing barely enough space for two adults, let alone Paulina occupying one and a half seats as she advanced into each new trimester. The room became more crowded when suppliers arrived to present their latest product lines, accountants met to review the finances, or I dropped in for a meeting of the minds. Paulina made it work though, finding comfort in working from home, establishing a rhythm that she hoped to maintain with a newborn.

Unknowingly then, the offsite administration systems we designed for home became the predecessor of our more sophisticated Network Support Office (NSO) – later transforming into the parent company that licensed our intellectual property through a national franchise. Necessity really is the mother of invention; and not a single experience is wasted learning.

With our practices operating separately from the administration hub, I needed technology on my side. My solution was found in a young patient who hurt his back changing the differential on his Commodore. At seventeen years of age, Dan was a self-taught technical whiz, having already cut his teeth networking hundreds of computers at his local school. With his nose pressed hard into the face hole of the treatment bed one day, I asked him to connect the carport office with the high-speed internet connection attached to the house. Following his advice, I bought a reconditioned laptop and a handful of desktop terminals for the practices, and have never bought a computer from anyone else since.

That quarter, our accountant made his routine visit to the home office and walked us through our performance. We were comfortably covering payroll, meeting our debt repayments, and growing in sales every month. Most relevantly, he endorsed my intentions to expand to a third location.

IN A FINAL act of freedom before the onset of full-term parenthood, Paulina and I made a whirlwind dash around western Europe. Our "last hurrah", people called it.

With tickets completely paid for using loyalty points accrued courtesy of our Back In Motion credit card, we started in London. Failing to anticipate the debilitating impact of jet lag, we made the rookie mistake of attending a live performance of *Les Misérables* at West End within hours of arriving. Last minute cheap tickets landed us in budget seats, perched high in the nosebleed section. The discomfort was exacerbated by the searing temperatures brought on by a freak heat wave sweeping through the UK at the time. We both limped through the performance, dozing and, at times, Paulina outright snoring, through the energetic refrains of Jean Valjean and Cosette. I took special delight in nudging

Paulina each time her head involuntarily bobbed under the hypnotic effects of the heat-induced coma inside the theatre oven, and the sleep deprivation of the long-haul flight.

Things improved after that first night, and Europe was spectacular. The Trafalgar bus zipped through a full itinerary; 14 days packed with tourist hotspots and must-see destinations like an overstuffed suitcase. Our tour took us to the windmills of Holland and the sparkling blue seas in the Bay of Naples. We experienced life on the Cote d'Azur and soaked up the beautiful mountain scenery in Tyrolean, Innsbruck. We cruised the Rhine in Germany, climbed Mt Pilates in Lucerne of Switzerland, enjoyed the canals and cafés in Venice, crawled the catacombs of Rome, prayed in the Vatican, disappeared beneath the false floors of the Colosseum, suffered neck strain starring at the ceilings of St Peter's Basilica, lunched at the Leaning Tower of Pisa, swam in the French Riviera, and rolled the dice at Monte Carlo Casino. I even kissed my wife at the top of the Eiffel Tower. Thousands of years' history across nine countries in only two weeks!

ANTICIPATING SOME DOWNTIME during my holiday, Michael handed me a thin book to read: *Halftime* by Bob Buford. I initially thought it was suited to someone approaching their mid-forties and possibly a plateau in their career, neither of which were my circumstances. In hasty judgement, I deemed the content irrelevant.

Turns out, Michael knew best.

Buford was a cable-television pioneer in America, social entrepreneur, and venture philanthropist. He was the first to differentiate for me the attributes of *success* and *significance*: the former being the benefits you enjoy from your achievement of personal and career goals; and the latter being the meaningful and positive impact you can have in the lives of others. Whilst one can almost certainly lead to the other, they often don't.

He writes: "In the first half of life, there is barely enough time to [get everything done]. We are hunter-gatherers, doing our best to provide for our families, to advance our careers, and to pass our beliefs and values on to our children." Buford described the first half of life being focused on *achieving, gaining, learning,* and *earning.* It's a mad race! We tend to be self-focused during this period, mostly trying to achieve whatever we define as *success* in our personal and professional lives.

This was certainly true for me. I was clearly still in the first half, and running as hard as my legs could keep up! As I sat on the tour bus, occasionally looking up from the book to take in the beautiful surrounds, I conceded my second half needed to look different to my first.

"The second half is riskier because it has to do with living beyond the immediate," Buford continues. "It is about releasing the seed of creativity and energy that has been implanted within us, watering and cultivating it so that we may be abundantly fruitful. It involves investing our gifts in service to others."

The important link between the first and second halves is predictably what he calls *halftime*. Just as a football team retreats to the locker room in the middle of the game, regroups and adjusts their gameplan to ensure a winning strategy, so we need to take an intentional break in our busy schedules and make necessary adjustments. It could be quarter time, half time, or ten minutes before the final whistle. Metaphorically, I realised I needed to stop as often as it's required in the game of life to reassess my plan and tactics: at any age and every stage of my life and business.

The concept caught my breath. Buford's writings compelled me to pause and reflect on the first four years of my career. I silently wondered again: *"Who am I? What do I want to achieve with my life?"*

On some backroads of Italy, I pulled out a copy of my personal manifesto, and pressure-tested my beliefs and intentions. I wasn't interested in waiting until I was 40 years old to work all this out. I had already lived through one life crisis; I didn't want to endure another one unnecessarily. Buford promised that the second half of my life can be better than my first if I found a way to synthesise my *time, treasure,* and *talents* effectively. My eagerness to learn how to do this was almost palpable.

Jim Collins eloquently writes in the foreword to the second edition of Buford's book (2008): "We only get one life, and the urgency of getting on with what we are meant to do increases every day". In a strange way, while only in my late twenties at that time,, I felt urgency to make a difference. Still a long way from achieving maturity in the business, I resolved that day to serve the needs of others in real time as we built the business. With every new practice, I wanted to make an impact along the way, and not wait until the end to do some good.

As we toured the highlights of Europe, I reflected on the many lessons of *Halftime*, and was grateful for Michael's timely gift. My conviction for a missional business was solidified. More growth equated to greater impact; the formula seeming more obvious than ever before.

As my immigration card was stamped, and I cleared the customs line coming back into Australia, I brimmed with confidence, newfound energy, and a determination for explosive growth.

36
first born of franchising

I NEGOTIATED THE purchase of a small, underperforming physiotherapy practice in the northern suburbs of Coburg in late November 2003. Having never bought a business before, it was confronting to evaluate the true value of a client list and room full of equipment, when there were no guarantees that I would fare any better than the failing vendor who was exiting.

Appraising someone else's goodwill is a dark art. Despite negotiating more than 143 separate practice transactions in the decade that followed, I was never quite sure whether I struck a fair price for either party.

Marcus, my next most senior therapist on the team, had seriously contemplated relocating abroad or pursuing employment closer to home. When I presented him the opportunity to become a part-owner in the new practice only five minutes from where he lived, he nervously accepted the offer, cautious to step up to the challenge as the principal of his own Back In Motion practice.

It was not an easy decision for Marcus, as the risks were substantive. He had little money to invest, and I was still up to my eyeballs in debt with our first two practices. Back In Motion was hardly a household brand, and I was far from an experienced business owner myself. To add to complexity, I was proposing to structure the arrangement as a franchise relationship, which to this point was either unprecedented, or at least very uncommon, in the physiotherapy industry. There were so many uncertainties and hesitancies for both of our liking, and we needed help.

I randomly called a general lawyer from a list generated through an unsophisticated online search, to learn what documentation we needed to substantiate a franchise agreement. The news wasn't great.

Franchising, as I was fast discovering, was a complex area of regulatory compliance and legal risk. Apparently, I needed to provide Marcus with a long list of documents, including a complete history of our business, a detailed franchise agreement, and numerous certificates and guarantees. My jaw dropped when my newly appointed legal counsel estimated a fee of around $20,000 for a first draft of the paperwork – the business we were buying wasn't even worth that much.

With youthful cheek, I asked the lawyer what I needed to do to get the costs under $5,000. Other than conning a desperate junior lawyer into that price bracket, he suggested I read the Franchise Code of Regulations and draft the documents myself, after which he would sense-check them for any obvious inconsistencies and serious legal irregularities, editing accordingly. I agreed to the latter approach and spent three weeks getting an honorary degree in the basics of franchise law, cutting and pasting clauses from templates I found online, and reconstructing a version of documents nuanced for healthcare rather than the typical retail context. It was a painful process, and not a very pretty result. But true to the offer, the lawyer then tidied up my drafts into a presentable format, most likely spending more time than he had anticipated for the lowball price he graciously honoured.

Paulina spent a significant amount of time enhancing our 12-page procedures document into a formal set of franchise systems. Every repeatable task, routine, and "secret" to our success was drafted into a comprehensive manual of standard operating procedures – instructing Marcus how to open and close the practice, market and promote the brand, deliver various clinical services, manage his finance, troubleshoot IT problems, and every other detail we could think of. We aimed to eliminate any room for the new team to guess, speculate, misunderstand, misinterpret, or improvise, if we could help it.

What resulted was two hefty folders complete with over 800 pages of tools, templates, flowcharts, diagrams, and proformas – a roadmap to guide any "wannabe" into a successful practice operator. I walked into our kitchen one day to find Paulina spreading the pages of the manual over every available square centimetre of floorspace, accurately sequencing the order of different chapters with their corresponding appendices to finalise her table of contents and index. Of course, some years later, all this information was converted to an online format, but there was something compelling about holding the heavy-laden manuals in both hands and acknowledging the weightiness of their content.

To de-risk the opportunity for Marcus, I agreed to fund half of the new practice. I facilitated the sale in December 2003 by incorporating a new entity with both of us as directors. On the same day, I formally issued our inaugural set of franchise documents to Marcus. He sensibly requested the Christmas break to review the mountain of complex contract law in front of him.

The proposed time frame of the franchise agreement was five years, with an option for renewal. The joining fee was $4,500, with an additional $1,000 for the manuals and associated training. I set the royalty at 11% of the professional fees earned by the practice, with an additional advertising levy payable each month. To protect his investment from internal competition, Marcus was granted a three-kilometre territory, inside of which I agreed not to launch any other practices.

Naturally, Marcus was personally liable for only half of these costs, given he only owned 50% of the practice; I subsidised the other half of the expenses. That aside, I recall Marcus sitting at the table ready to execute the documents, genuinely concerned that $2,750 was still too much money to pay for what he argued was an unproven business model. He would later learn it was possibly the best commercial investment of his life.

As the year closed, we had two babies incubating in tandem: Paulina was well advanced in her third trimester, flourishing in her pregnancy, and our first franchise was primed for launch after a similar period of gestation. I joked at the time that we should have a child for every new practice we launched. Paulina didn't see the humour in it then, or any time after, especially when our network expanded into double digits.

37
mini-MBA

PAULINA ENJOYED A dream pregnancy – except for some third trimester reflux, dosed with an ever-present supply of Mylanta. She suffered no complications. In fact, all her medical assessments affirmed she was tracking above the mean. Sadly, this didn't continue into the birth.

On New Year's Eve, amidst a joyous gathering with friends, we found ourselves immersed in a fiercely competitive game of Pictionary, pitched as a battle of the sexes. However, despite the high stakes rivalry, Paulina could barely remain seated due to severe contractions she assumed was false labour. Adding to the evening's drama, when lighting celebratory sparklers to welcome in the midnight count, Paulina set fire to the curtains above the kitchen sink. Thankfully, quick action prevented significant damage, but the chaos triggered further cycles of Braxton-Hicks.

By the time I helped Paulina into bed in the early hours of New Year's Day, she was feeling more settled and convinced the baby would not arrive until due, some ten days later. Her prediction quickly proved premature, just like our baby. We were in the birthing suite that same afternoon, with one very impatient little boy.

What followed was one of Paulina's most challenging physical experiences; a failed epidural, excruciating pain, and a forceps delivery that led to a protracted and debilitating recovery that lasted almost 12 months. It was horrible to watch, and undoubtedly more traumatic for Paulina to endure. The only salve for her horrendous sacrifice was the birth of a beautiful, healthy child.

Lachlan joined our family on New Year's Day, and the world celebrated this new beginning with us, filling the night's sky with fireworks all over the globe. He was perfect, and we have thanked God for rescuing our precious gift every day since, reminding Lachlan at times that he was racing go-karts before he was even born.

IN THE SAME month, Back In Motion Coburg was born; making me simultaneously a father and a franchisor. Both deliveries were traumatic for different reasons.

The Coburg practice was scheduled for official launch in January 2004, with new patients steadily building for the auspicious first day. A light fit-out of the facilities was completed, new signage was hung, a marketing campaign was on foot, and Marcus felt a mixture of excitement and apprehension. Fortunately for him, there was no forceps required.

What neither of us could plan for was Marcus contracting acute appendicitis the weekend prior to him seeing his first patients at the new location. As he recovered from emergency surgery, I had to drive the hour every day of the first week to and from the new practice, carrying Marcus' caseload myself – all of which displaced my new fatherhood responsibilities at home, and caused me to neglect staff and patients at Wantirna South.

It was a testing start on both the home and work fronts, but Marcus recovered quickly, and I salvaged the remaining weeks of self-approved paternity leave by cultivating precious bonding moments with my heir.

TOWARD THE END of February, I signed up for a business coaching program with Geoff. It was clear that Michael was more of a personal and spiritual mentor, but I needed help with managing the tactics of my business. With approximately 20 staff spread across three locations, an emerging franchise opportunity, accumulating debt, and a raft of obvious commercial and leadership deficiencies, I was hungry for formal training.

I agreed to the gold level package, committing to 18 modules over a six-month period, with the promise that my work with Geoff would culminate in a comprehensive business plan to scale our fledgling practice group into a national network. It was a lot of time and money to risk, especially when you include the indirect cost in lost revenue when I could have been treating patients. But this was my mini-MBA – and I owe a lot to Geoff for his equal measures of patience and discipline as he guided me through the extensive materials.

We set a five-year plan together with lofty but attainable goals:

- Five practices with five different principals (or managers);
- 25 physiotherapists;
- Up to eight support staff;
- $2 million aggregate annual revenue; and
- 15% sustainable margin, facilitated by centralised management.

The kicker off the back of these commercial objectives was the personal goal to eventually work only two days a week as a billable clinician, and also be available to travel overseas into the developing world for weeks at a time as God opened the doors. This was how I understood my *success* and *significance* would work together.

Geoff made me aware that most people overestimate what they can achieve in one year, but grossly underestimate what is possible in ten. So, I accelerated my 40-year ambition for ten practices and set the expectation to achieve this in a single decade: forming my "10-in-10" plan! Ten practices in ten years – four company-owned and six franchised.

As I contemplated these possibilities, it struck me that achieving a high level of automation and independence in my business would truly render me free and flexible to invest in missional work anywhere, anytime. I would not be a slave any longer to the business; it would serve me.

The coaching process taught me that the difference between a fast-growing business and one that just bumbles along is the owner's willingness to make courageous decisions every day. That it was better to make the *wrong* decisions, fast, than not make any at all, as at least I would learn from my mistakes and develop experience. I accepted my practices would never outperform ordinary expectations if there was a culture of apathy and indolence. A continual process of taking action, reviewing results, and refining direction proved to be the essential elements to advancing my opportunities.

Very quickly, I learned to design and rely on the spreadsheets of Key Performance Indicators (KPIs) measuring client inquiries, conversion averages, active clients, average value of sale, appointment visit averages, profit margins, injury cycles, service costs per client, and performance appraisals for each clinician. These numbers were eye-opening; without them, I was driving blind. When I understood them, I could navigate the corners and chicanes like a precision race-car driver.

Over the course of the business coaching program, I worked through different focus areas – employee culture, lead generation, competitor analysis, products and services design, financial literacy, and myriad legal considerations.

Geoff explained the importance of differentiating our practice from all the other physiotherapy competitors. Most physios earned the *same* degree, relied on the *same* clinical diagnostic tests, applied the *same* treatment approaches, charged the *same* amount of money, and achieved the *same* ordinary results with their patients. So, on what basis would someone choose me over a more convenient practice? Where was our high-value distinction?

Emerging from my study, I curated our first Unique Selling Proposition (USP), a clearly defined brand message to attract clients to Back In Motion and separate us from the rest.

We came up with eight solid reasons for a patient to choose us:

1. Extra time on their first visit to get to know them.
2. A free, initial assessment; no cost, no obligation.
3. A "no help, no charge" guarantee, meaning patients didn't pay for treatment if for any reason they didn't feel better afterwards.
4. Affordable services by offering treatment packages to suit every budget.
5. Self-help strategies to progress a patient's recovery at home; saving them time and money.
6. Personal monitoring with follow-up calls after treatment to ensure every patient made objective measurable progress.
7. Convenience of longer opening hours, including early morning and late evening appointments to suit people's schedules.
8. 24-hour free injury support line, available whenever people needed us most, and especially when everybody else was closed.

I put a lot of energy into the little touches to ensure Back In Motion stood out head and shoulders above the rest. For instance, I struck an arrangement with a local bakery to bring in fresh cookies every morning. We set them on the waiting room table, so even if clients didn't choose to eat one, a sweet and homely aroma filled the front half of the practice, tempering the otherwise pungent odours of our anti-inflammatory creams.

Whilst many of our gambits attracted criticisms from peers in the industry, we embraced the confidence that we were striving for exceptional growth that could not be achieved through ordinary behaviour.

Geoff was energetic and persistent with me each week of the program. He was like a deep southern preacher with ADHD, talking loudly, emphatically, and unable to sit still. Occasionally, I would unleash him on the team in a lunchtime workshop, to rally their ideas about how we move forward, or to make his own assessments of the culture and skills mix we were forming. There were moments where his almost abrasive style and exaggerated enthusiasm tired me, but by the end of that year, I had extracted every ounce of value from the experience.

Geoff's parting gift at the end of the program was a hardcover, rigidly bound business plan, hundreds of pages thick, complete with every worksheet, spider graph, matrix table, position description, financial forecast, and marketing strategy we had created, debated, and curated together in the months prior. It was my battleplan; the strategic blueprint I was to follow in executing my ambitious plan for ten practices.

AT THE CLOSE of the 2004 financial year, I put in place a more robust corporate structure to support the new growth I hoped was coming.

I established an investment trust to hold all the intangible copyright, trademarks, and other assets I was creating, protecting them from litigation and misuse. I also registered a new head company to separate my franchise licensing activities from my trading practices. In all the corporate restructuring, I remained the sole director and sole shareholder of every entity, preserving absolute control and full beneficial ownership.

Whilst we only had one genuine franchisee at the time, the precedent was set. As the network grew – and with it, the associated sales of what I expected would become thousands of patient-visits every year – the business was primed to earn a substantial income in perpetuity to fund the essential mission work we first set out to accomplish.

The stage was set for greatness.

38
the gift

OUR NEWBORN LACHLAN was recruited early to the business as an infant apprentice, helping his mother and abeulita (his grandmother) in the home-based support office. He would cheerfully bounce in his bassinet, supervising Nelly as she wrestled the growing payroll and burdensome bookkeeping. And, of course, he had plenty to giggle and burp at Paulina as she continuously refined our practice procedures for the network expansion I assured everyone was coming.

By October of that year, I found location four.

Driving through the sleepy suburb of Seaford, I noticed an understated physiotherapy practice operating out of a badly-weathered home, marked by a conspicuous "For Sale" sign. With curiosity piqued, I ventured in and met Mary, the sole therapist of the business who had served the local community since 1991. On inquiry, Mary confided in me her ongoing struggle with progressive hand pain, a common problem for manual therapists after years of practice. She had made the difficult decision to accept a new role as a corporate ergonomist for the Ford Motor Company in Broadmeadows, necessitating an urgent sale of her cherished practice.

I eagerly shared the news with Paulina, who tempered my enthusiasm with a cool response. She was concerned about the added load to my already busy schedule, adding a 40-minute drive from home, and in the opposite direction from the newest site in Coburg. She also pointed out that the facility needed an enormous amount of restorative work, the patient list was minimal, and the socioeconomics of the area were subpar.

Paulina was right on all accounts; the business case was weak.

Over the next six weeks, unable to put the opportunity out of my mind, I prayed about the acquisition. With time, I felt peace from God that this opportunity presented a low-cost entry into what will likely become a thriving practice with our new systems and emerging brand.

By the time I reconnected with Mary nearly two months later, she had closed her practice, issued redundancies to the two part-time receptionists, and pro-actively referred her patients to the nearest competitors in the area. In short, there was no longer a business to buy.

Not about to give up, I perceived an opportunity to seize. At the end of November, I signed an agreement with Mary to acquire the rights to her practice – including hard copies of her patient files, electronic database, and the contact details of her referrers – in exchange for a long-term lease of the premises she still owned. I paid no upfront sum, just a weekly occupancy fee that included the use of all her existing equipment that she no longer needed. It was a gift to both of us!

With formalities in place, Paulina and I loaded Lachlan into his baby capsule and spent two consecutive weekends demolishing the kitchen to open more space in the waiting room, cleaning the premises from top to bottom, applying a fresh coat of paint to all the treatment rooms, building new IKEA furniture, and finalising our permits for new street-front signage. Lachlan more than pulled his weight in his first practice renovation.

The following Monday, I contracted the two recently unemployed receptionists to ring every client on the database and let them know that the practice was open again under the name Back In Motion. Patients were invited to a complimentary session with a senior physiotherapist to counter the inconvenience they had suffered (and to hopefully win back some loyalty in return). I offered $10 to the receptionists for every client they re-booked. After 13 days of flogging the phones from dawn until dusk, I had a full appointment schedule and the beginnings of a thriving business. And the receptionists both made more money that fortnight than ever before.

MY NEW PROBLEM was that I now had to be in four places at once: Wantirna South, Boronia, Coburg and Seaford. There wasn't enough hours in the day, nor were there enough clinicians to spread across the demanding timetable at different sites.

Out of necessity, I offered to prematurely promote Bao Hoang to supervisor of the Seaford practice. He was a Vietnamese-Australian new graduate who had recently joined us, accepting the role before he was even a fully registered physiotherapist. With no experience, but truckloads of personality and ambition, he seemed the best choice at the time to lead our newest venture.

It proved the right decision.

Bao thrived in his independence, a natural-born promoter, with boyish charisma and sincere warmth. Whatever he lacked in leadership competencies, he more than compensated for with engaging customer service and youthful grit. He doubled down every month, soon showing himself more than capable to not only lead the practice, but take up ownership.

Bao wanted to become our second franchisee, submitting his formal application for partial equity in March 2005. His business case for success focussed on hitting the local schools with workshops on safe schoolbag use, postural advice, and strengthening for growing bodies. He even outlined his ideas to host a colouring competition in the area, expecting that children would proudly display to their parents the "prizes" that he intended every child to win – a low-cost postural assessment thinly veiling his shameless promotion of the practice.

Bao was as much opportunistic, as he was strategic. The new Medicare initiative, called Enhanced Primary Care, was just emerging after a recent federal government policy change. The program allowed qualified patients up to five physiotherapy visits at heavily subsidised rates. Bao immediately leveraged this opportunity to loosen up referrals from local doctors, given the cost-sensitivity to private health care in the Seaford demographic.

I was convinced that Bao was ready for equity. We sat with his family in his parents' home one evening, enjoying Momma Hoang's home-cooked Vietnamese pho, Goi, lobster tails and rice paper rolls, Paulina raving how good all the food tasted. As I raised my glass in a celebratory toast, officially acknowledging Bao's purchase of 50% of the franchise, Paulina boldly declared that Momma Hoang should open her own restaurant, sharing her exotic flavours with the world.

It was a wonderful beginning to an even better partnership than I could imagine. Bao leap-frogged every year, to eventually owning a portfolio of five practices with substantial interests in our speciality sub-brands catering to aged care and occupational health. Over the years that followed, we attended his wedding, took part in the christening of his children, and even holidayed in Fiji together as family friends.

Bao sold most of his holdings in Back In Motion about ten years later to launch his own successful franchise, *Roll'd* – the runaway retail food sensation based on Momma Hoang's inherited recipes, tried-and-tasted over generations. I am very proud of everything Bao has achieved, his success another initiative that Paulina secretly deserves some credit for seeding.

THE LAUNCH AND subsequent franchising of the Seaford practice was a stark reminder that God carried us in His capable and gracious hands. With deep gratitude for the opportunities He was weaving into our path, I felt compelled to record every miracle, breakthrough, and achievement in my journal to never forget the "secret" behind our success.

In reflection of this, I penned a simple agreement in April 2005 declaring that all dividends earned from the Seaford practice be dedicated to serving the poor. I recognised this practice as a pure gift from God and felt to steward the resources responsibly and faithfully as He directed. Our family wasn't to touch the spoils for our own benefit, and I vowed not to invest the gain into other business interests.

I signed my hand-written deal with God and slid the paperwork into the back of the filing cabinet.

Shamefully, I failed to disclose this pledge to Paulina. My self-imposed obligations became inconveniently relevant some years later when we profited substantially from this business. It was an awkward moment when I had to hesitantly confess to my wife and accountant my side deal with the Creator of the Universe, and that I couldn't use even one dollar of the proceeds to pay off any of our accumulating debts.

FOUR LOCATIONS PRESENTED many new challenges to overcome, but none more so than our lack of a secure and efficient means to share real-time patient and administrative information between the different teams. We needed a more powerful technology platform that connected all our sites, and automated our increasingly more complex processes.

When we first switched to electronic clinical records, I adopted a basic industry program that was initially developed by a local practitioner for a small user base. Some years later, the software was acquired by a more commercially minded individual who saw the opportunity in the primitive code to commercialise it into a robust, ubiquitous product for our profession. However, there were few multi-site physiotherapy groups at that time, and so the functionality to network different locations still didn't exist, and the cloud-based flexibility we have all come to rely on was still years away.

I spent months working with the new software vendor trying to get synchronisation between our various practices to allow seamless data transfer, only to find the links would continuously break when we needed them most. It was eventually obvious to everyone that Back In Motion's demands exceeded the scope of general industry requirements, and I needed an alternative.

With a sudden and unexpected leap of faith, I ventured into the mysterious and disturbing vortex of custom software development. I engaged a local development house to build a bespoke patient management system, dubbed BIMLogic™. The modular application was designed to manage bookings, clinical records, product inventory, analytical reports and, most importantly, deliver interoperability across all practice locations.

I signed the contract in August 2005 for what was estimated to be a four-month build. I then spent weeks collaborating with the development team on a 200-plus page specification that included wire frame drawings to capture the intended workflow, taking into consideration the graphic interface and the end-user experience I imagined. Everybody warned me technology projects run over time and over budget. They were right. I ended up spending almost double the money for just a beta version of the first desktop application, and that didn't go live in practice until mid-2006.

And so commenced my love-hate relationship with all things IT-related. Back In Motion was forever a technology business from that day forward, not because it was our core service or product, but because it became the essential enabler to delivering scaled, effective healthcare across a growing footprint of practices with optimal efficiency. I reluctantly learned the language of bits and bytes to bring fair contest in the project management meetings that determined our future technology roadmap, ultimately resting in the expertise and recommendations of trusted advisors, now an essential part of my team.

MY COMMITMENT TO remaining in front of evolving technology was explained in a 2008 editorial I wrote for *Business in Practice*, titled: "Physios hamstrung without the byte of a good IT system". I spoke of the IT revolution impacting healthcare services, from which physiotherapy was not exempt.

I outlined the series of projects that led to our custom application which, after two years of ongoing development, then enabled live data transfer between practices via VPN connections, and innovatively gave clients the autonomy to schedule bookings, submit queries, pay their accounts, and view their visit history and loyalty reward points online via secure credentials. We also built a fully interactive and secure intranet (BIMnet™) for the 170 employees at the time, hosting a repository of over 3,000 discrete templates, documents, procedures, forms, and publications for their use.

I even developed a Clinical Wiki, modelled on the familiar approach of Wikipedia, providing detailed guidelines and education for the assessment, diagnosis and treatment of different regions and conditions of the body. It was an industry-first, an online library complete with video analysis, evidence-based literature reviews, case studies, and anatomical diagrams.

The two years of software development cost more than half a million dollars. I persisted through 43 code revisions and subsequent updates. Whilst an unfathomable expense and workload at the time, little did I know how infinitesimal this investment would be in contrast with the whole-of-life cost of our technology requirements in the decade that followed.

My one big regret in this whole undertaking was failing to secure ownership of the source code from the small development house at the very beginning. I had only negotiated a perpetual royalty-free licence to use the custom application within our business, and locked down our essential intellectual property that underpinned many of the industry-specific features we embedded in the functionality. But I was to be forever limited from commercialising our technology for wider industry usage because of my naïvete in those days of what *source code* even was, let alone how valuable it would later become.

It was a mistake I vowed never to repeat.

39
infertility

I HAD ENDURED a hectic 18 months – one newborn baby, four newborn practices, and numerous newborn staff. Paulina and I compared our scars and stretch marks – literal and otherwise – noting their similarities and accepting their differences.

We needed a break, and booked a five-week circumnavigation of the North and South Islands of New Zealand in a large family RV. We flew into Auckland in early May 2005, picked up our home-on-wheels, and strapped Lachlan in for his first overseas adventure.

It was a different rhythm to our travels around Australia. Adding a one-year-old to the mix has a way of bringing newfound joy and excitement, along with notable limitations and challenges.

For one, Lachlan needed to sleep during the day, and so we aligned our large stretches of driving with his routine nap schedule. Another thing, Paulina and I couldn't do any adventure activities *together*. One of us had to stay with Lachlan while the other embarked on the many daring experiences New Zealand has to offer.

Paulina went for the adrenaline rush of the Canyon Swing in Queenstown, screaming all the way through the heart-pounding 60-metre free fall, while I navigated the intricate black-water labyrinths in the Waitomo Caves by inflatable raft. Paulina conquered ice walls and trekked the Franz Josef glacier one day, and I followed suit the next.

This occasional inconvenience of holiday tag-team had its frustrating moments, but it provided a welcome relief from the relentless pressures of the burgeoning practices that awaited us on the other side of the Tasman.

ON MY RETURN, it was evident the small carport office could no longer accommodate the necessary people and voluminous administrative workflow demanded of it. For one, I had now joined the cramped space, requiring a desk away from the practice to manage the clinical workforce across the emerging practice group, and to spearhead our franchising opportunities.

I moved the small administration team into a commercial tenancy on the first floor above an accounting office in Boronia. Not an elegant location by any definition, but cheap rent with ample space for a boardroom, numerous offices, and storage space for the fast-accumulating marketing collateral and clinical supplies we were buying in bulk.

I sat at my desk in those first few months of our new Network Support Office (NSO), watching one storefront opposite me turn over three times. It shape-shifted from being a tobacconist to a kebab store, before settling on a candle shop. Presumably, that meant three different owners in less than a year – a stark reminder of the high failure rates of small businesses in suburban Australia. As consistent research reveals, whilst the economic costs of these losses are substantial, it's the human costs that matter most.

Every time I watched a retailer displaced from their tenancy, it reminded me of the risks we faced when we launched a new practice. Once again, my trust was in God's promises that He would enable our success against whatever odds we faced.

MY TIME WAS now unevenly split across multiple practices and the NSO, and I couldn't keep up with the growing demand. My solution was to deputise a senior therapist, Persi, as my replacement in the original Wantirna South practice.

Persi was a great fit for the role, having worked in private practice previously and demonstrating a vibrant mix of clinical knowledge and commercial common sense. I handed over my entire clinical caseload to him, introducing Persi to staff and clients as the new Principal. He was quickly well-liked for his humorous wit, good looks (earning him the nickname, the *Black Prince)* and endearing Italian mannerisms.

Among my many routines, every Wednesday I scoured the classifieds in the trade journals looking for equipment to buy, new suppliers to engage, watching recruitment cycles for new staff and, most importantly, seeking practices to buy.

It was there I found our fifth gem – a small opportunity in Hillside on the remote outskirts of the city of Brimbank, northwest of Melbourne.

For a very affordable sum, I acquired the goodwill and equipment of a single clinician practice that had been struggling throughout its three years of operation.

My latest acquisition was not good news to Paulina. Once again, she pointed out that the location was an hour's drive from home, in a separate direction from most of our other sites. To her it meant I would be leaving home earlier most mornings, and getting back later, compressing further our already limited time together at home.

To overcome some of these concerns, I employed an experienced physio from Queensland who had worked in a multi-disciplinary environment with physiotherapists, chiropractors, and masseurs. Nathan embraced the idea of joining an integrated health group, and preferred a salary to manage the business on my behalf, declaring an early disinterest in owning a franchise.

One early setback at Hillside was when one of Nathan's first recruits, a newly married female therapist, was caught using the practice for late night rendezvous with a much younger male patient. Repurposing our treatment beds for activities they were never designed for, she immediately lost her job, the patient was referred elsewhere, and I found myself comforting a distraught husband having learned of his wife's sordid affair. Nathan quickly recovered our lost momentum, achieving a revenue in that first year equivalent to the aggregate of its former three.

WHILST ALL THIS was happening, Paulina and I wanted to grow our family too. We were joyful parents and had our hearts set on three children, despite our small house being completely out of room for even one more occupant.

So, with more kids in mind, we bought a block of land in a new housing estate in Ferntree Gully – a picturesque family-friendly neighbourhood complete with open grasslands, a nearby golf course, and bike paths around a central lake. We broke ground in December of that year, in expectation we might fall pregnant around the same time.

But things didn't go as we planned.

The first pregnancy with Lachlan happened quickly and unexpectedly, so we assumed number two would follow suit. It didn't, to our great frustration, leading to many tears throughout the summer of early 2006.

Paulina had resumed one shift a week at the ICU in Box Hill Hospital, a university teaching facility over 65 years old. She was also busy caring for an active toddler, working in the NSO on scattered half-days, and generally filling all the gaps at home that I was creating by my extended absences. The load Paulina carried was possibly so heavy that her body refused to take on anymore.

I didn't think making babies was meant to be this hard.

One Sunday at church, an acquaintance approached Paulina with some hesitation and apparent trepidation. She shared a series of unusual dreams she had received over three consecutive nights, revealing that Paulina was having difficulty conceiving. After praying together for some further insights into the cause behind our troubles, God reminded Paulina that during her traumatic labour and protracted recovery with Lachlan, she had said: "I'll never do this again". Whether the result of intense pain or rational choice, this declaration now mattered.

Paulina sat with God and asked those spoken words to no longer have a hold on her.

As a testament to the power of prayer, the next month we fell pregnant after nearly a year of failed attempts. Our second child was due in November, perfectly aligned with the scheduled completion of our new home.

40
resentful retainers

THE HARD-WORKING, HIGHLY engaged, fun-loving, open-minded physio enthusiasts that worked for me in those first five years were *family*. My "dream team". I was about the same age as most of them, sparking plenty of self-doubts about how to lead my peers, but it never got much better in terms of camaraderie, cultural unity, and shared focus.

We worked hard, but we also played hard. Our team spent weekends in the snow during winter, and escaped to the beach when the season warmed up. We celebrated birthdays, had Friday night drinks, and put on special events and Christmas parties each year for the families to attend together. We also supported our people in times of hardship, one of them sleeping on our couch at home for an extended stint when she found herself in the middle of a personal crisis.

There was even love in the air at Back In Motion. One night, about 9pm, I answered a knock at the front door to find one of my senior physios standing there nervously, wearing an anxious grin. Moments later, a second colleague slowly stepped out of the shadows, as they both hesitantly shared their decision to date each other, hoping for my blessing. In a rare workplace romance that turned into a fairytale ending, they eventually moved to London and were married sometime later.

But life wasn't perfect. There were also some tensions in our team when I pushed the envelope with controversial and risky business initiatives. For the most part, my people understood what I was trying to achieve and learned to try new things, but this didn't always make life at Back In Motion a pleasant or comfortable place to work.

ONE NOTABLE EXAMPLE of team strain emerged shortly after my introduction of an innovative payroll scheme I called the Retainer Deficit.

For the 100 years our profession existed, physiotherapists in Victorian private practices were traditionally engaged as contractors rather than bona fide employees. As such, the business owner only paid the contractor for their billable work – a percentage commission of their consulting fees rather than a salary or hourly rate – and didn't have to cover costs for leave, superannuation, or insurance. In return, the contracted therapist earned a higher gross income than what might otherwise have been offered with fulltime employment, and could choose when and how hard they worked.

The arrangement seemed a win-win; except it generally wasn't legal. The early advice I received when setting up our health group was that, according to tax and commercial law, few of our clinicians qualified as true contractors and were likely deemed legitimate employees. This meant, regardless of common practice, I felt obligated to pay the minimum conditions of state-based workplace awards, providing salaries, meal breaks, personal and annual leave, the Superannuation Guarantee, uniform allowances, leave loading, and various other statutory benefits. The effect of all these on-costs was a much higher gross remuneration package than most of my competitors, limiting my ability to afford, on top of this, the attractive commissions that were otherwise expected.

During school holidays and Christmas breaks, when patient numbers predictably dropped, I still paid our physios their higher-than-average salaries while their peers in other practices suffered a substantial loss in earnings. But when our therapists were billing at the peak of the season, they complained they were earning much less compared to their colleagues elsewhere, who were receiving a percentage commission of their total fees. Whilst there were swings-and-roundabouts that offset the overall cost of wages between both models of payment, it quickly became a point of contention within our workforce because I did things differently to the industry at large.

To solve this perceived imbalance, I created the Retainer Deficit. I pitched it as the best of both worlds; the upside of contracting where therapists earned commissions on patient fees, whilst simultaneously enjoying the safety net of a fixed salary (retainer) with all the award conditions of a secure employee. But there was a catch. For as long as someone's payroll record showed a *deficit* (that is, the retainer I paid them was higher than the commissions they would have otherwise earned as a contractor), the business accrued the shortfall in entitlements and offset them against future commissions. If our physios were patient, in time they could consistently exceed the remuneration and rewards of any other industry offering.

Enthusiastic staff who built strong, consistent caseloads cleared their *deficit* within three to four months of their starting date. Others took much longer and, in some cases, never quite got there.

The crossover point – when the retainer deficit was exceeded and commissions were paid – became a celebratory milestone for every physio. It was a big moment, signalling a coming-of-age for the new team member, and rendering them a significantly higher pay cheque in the months that followed. However, for those it seemed that day might never arrive, our payroll model was a source of constant criticism and discontent. I lost many team members in those early years over this arrangement, as some felt it was a bar too high to clear.

Mischievous competitors and poorly informed university lecturers didn't help the cause. Some knowingly, and others naïvely, created bad will in the industry with language that inflamed suspicions of unfairness around my creative payroll scheme. Job applicants shared distorted rumours they had heard that Back In Motion made their staff "pay back their salaries" if their patient lists were too low. This was, of course, a blatant lie; it was neither legal nor practical to claw back salaries in almost any circumstance. But that didn't stop the sinister gossip spreading through the grapevine, creating one of our first major brand crises.

Eventually, enough positive stories were shared by our growing workforce, showing increasing confidence in our approach and helping to shut down the rumour mill. I also wised up over time to using more positive language, and referred to this payroll feature as a retainer *offset* rather than a *deficit*, proving again the power of words.

Despite the cultural unrest caused initially by my maverick payroll model, within a decade we were considered an employer-of-choice, deploying the largest private workforce of physiotherapists in the Australasian region – and our unique commission model was considered a national benchmark for remuneration.

THE OTHER HIGHLY contentious initiative I launched in those early years was a patient approach, inelegantly called "BIM Solutions".

Later known as Results4Life, the novel idea was to provide every client with written advice regarding their personalised diagnosis, tailored recommendation of services, and a likely prognosis based on a range of presenting symptoms and conditions.

This innovation should have been received as a positive and progressive tool in practice, but I quickly learned that professionals didn't want to be told what to do. Every attempt to systematise our collective approach was met with resistance from my staff. Their hesitation stemmed from a somewhat-misplaced entitlement to *clinical sovereignty* – the belief that each therapist is empowered to make individual and independent clinical choices using evidence-based information and clinical tests at their discretion. They did not want to follow a template I had researched and prepared for their use, passionately arguing that the company should not dictate the form or substance of any clinical intervention.

With a seemingly insurmountable barrier to group-wide uniformity in our services, I felt restrained. How could I market our services across different communities if every physio was going to approach an acutely prolapsed lumbar disc or torn shoulder rotator cuff differently? For the same reasons, McDonalds didn't allow their franchisees to creatively change the core ingredients of the Big Mac at their individual whim.

I needed a model of clinical care that didn't offend highly intelligent, superiorly opinionated, and ego-driven health professionals. I spent years working with university specialists and clinical advisory groups to develop the right solution. Fourteen iterations later, having put all my leadership capital at risk, I eventually got there.

Results4Life ultimately became our defining clinical philosophy for the group, and foundational to our brand promise across all our locations. The system we built offered every client consistency in experience, confidence with outcomes, clarity of expectations, and shored up the value they received for our high-priced services.

As a franchisor, Results4Life assured that our practitioners were following a proven system that delivered benefits to every customer. For our franchisees, it was one of the prized toys in their showbag when they bought a licence from us.

For Results4Life to become the benchmark standard however, people had to trust me at times when they couldn't see it working. Such blind faith tested our relationships throughout these formative years, as we all wrestled with the delicate balance of independent critical thinking and towing the party line for the benefit of the brand.

BY THE END of 2005, at 30 years of age and with six years' experience under my belt, I boasted seven locations, a dedicated support office with my wife and two mothers on the payroll, a range of blue-chip high-value corporate contracts, and the beginnings of a successful franchise brand. I registered the name *Back In Motion Health Group*, dropping the word *physiotherapy* from our original trademark, with a clear expectation that, in time, I would introduce broader allied health services into our mix.

Amidst all this heady growth, my heart could still not be deterred from missions. God had set our course, and we were walking through each door as He opened it. The positive groundswell was noticeable, as was the earliest whiff of the rancid breath of a wolf lurking at the door.

41
dirty "F" word

OUR FIRST FRANCHISE dispute emerged in early 2006. Marcus and Bao formed a convenient coalition and challenged the affordability of my 11% royalty. They wanted better business support, reduced marketing payments, and an overall re-balance in commercial terms to align value and cost. In an obvious contest of two against one, I was outnumbered; and had everything to lose.

It dawned on me, for the first time, that the larger our group became, the more I stacked franchisees against me to align their forces and push views, opinions, and negotiations. There was never going to be a balanced argument or a fair fight again. Either I would overcome this predictable opposition with authentic leadership and gritty resolve, or I'd become a pitiless victim of my own success. This was franchising.

As a newly minted member of the Franchise Council of Australia (FCA), I engaged an advisory firm with the strap line: "do it right, do it once". I reasoned they could help me build the right framework of franchise terms for fairness and sustainability so I would never again have to deal with another franchisee dispute.

The consultants reviewed my self-drawn franchise agreements, amateur business model, and lengthy procedures manual. They prepared a feasibility study of costs, scale, risks, and benefits as we modelled growth in the network over the coming ten years. We did a sensitivity analysis to ensure there was enough reward and margin for the hard-working franchisee, while continuing to provide financial run-off into our mission trust.

After months of exhaustive, in-depth work, Paulina and I accepted this firm's recommendations to increase the initial franchise fee to $25,000 (up from only $11,000 at the time), but reduce the monthly royalty from the contentious 11% to a mere 7%. Furthermore, I substituted the recurring marketing fee of $2,000 per calendar month to a flat 2% of sales, and introduced a software levy for the bespoke technology platform we had recently built and deployed.

On the numbers we projected, I needed 30 franchised practices to break even on the capital I had invested and to start turning a notional profit as a franchisor. It seemed like an overwhelmingly high target, given I had initially aimed for a network of only ten practices.

To draw up all these changes officially, I chose Chris of Gadens Lawyers, a franchising veteran who had acted for numerous credible national brands over many decades. He was an older, softly spoken Austrian gentleman who took his work very seriously. He reviewed the franchise agreements I had co-authored years before and was unguarded in his opinion; whilst he thought I made a half-decent lawyer for a physio, Chris was worried I'd end up in jail if I continued to use them. He advised to bin them all immediately and, with no change from $50,000, I commissioned Chris to write a new set of compliant documentation including a formal disclosure statement, franchise agreement, and software agreement.

The new terms and paperwork weren't a total hit with Marcus and Bao. I engaged a mediator to facilitate some of the formal discussions to keep our conversations objective and constructive. Whilst, naturally, the reduction in royalties was well received, their advisors felt the overall rigour of Chris' new agreements had stepped up the franchisees' obligations by many levels.

And they were right.

In the spirit of "being careful what you wish for", our thorough review of the franchisee terms caused me to fill all the gaps I had neglected in my first version. I paid more attention to warranties and guarantors, exclusivities and restraints, terms of renewal, tripartite lease authorities, fit-out specifications for the practice, supplier rebates, assignment fees in the event the franchise was transferred to an approved buyer, and protections around the client list and other data embedded in our custom software. I instructed Chris to leave very little to chance.

Further discussions between respective lawyers afforded the necessary tweaks and edits to shift the nuances of our agreements closer to a middle ground that everybody could live with. All existing franchise agreements were surrendered and, by July 2006, I issued new documents to every practice location to ensure consistency for all.

This timely overhaul of our legal terms proved Providential as, shortly thereafter, I ushered in a fresh wave of new franchisees into the network and, with each deal, attracted more sceptics who were gunning for my failure.

FRANCHISING WAS REGARDED as the dirty "F" word in physiotherapy. A few had tried it before us but had either failed, or worse, soiled its name. I initially did everything I could to distance myself from its disreputable past.

At Back In Motion, we referred to those who bought a franchise licence as *Practice Directors* rather than "franchisees", and our business as a *Health Group* rather than a "franchise network". I chose to be known as the *Group Director*, not the "franchisor". I didn't charge "franchise royalties," but called them *Health Group Fees* instead. This custom parlance was all to avoid the distasteful stigma associated with the unwanted commercialisation associated with franchising. It was a charade I kept up for many years until we reached a threshold of success that it didn't matter so much what others thought.

My earliest encounter with a physio franchise was an exercise class format designed and supervised by physiotherapists to prepare women for pregnancy, labour, and optimal recovery. The founders first pitched the franchising opportunity through the entertaining TV show, *Shark Tank*, where high net worth individuals give budding entrepreneurs the chance (but rarely the eventuality) of securing capital investment and partnership deals to hopefully become millionaires themselves. I don't recall them having any success on the show, and the brand fell away into obscurity shortly after.

Denis Boyd launched a far more promising attempt at franchising physiotherapy just before the turn of the millennium. By 1999, just as Back In Motion was starting in my Scoresby carport, physiotherapist Denis partnered with his highly successful multi-millionaire accountant son, Michael, and built a group of 24 company-owned and franchised physiotherapy centres in Perth, under the name LifeCare. The company reportedly owned 1.5% market share at the time, and set their sights on achieving growth to an unprecedented 20% of the assessable physiotherapy industry.

Arguably ahead of their time, LifeCare floated 50% of the company on the Australian Securities Exchange (ASX) in December 1999, with a promise to build a "franchise network involving physiotherapists, sports medicine, and podiatry" across Australia. They made an impressive share market debut, raising $8.5 million through the issue of 24 million new shares at $0.25 each. It's possible this transaction made the Boyd family the wealthiest beneficiaries of the physiotherapy sector in the history of our profession to that point (although I'm not sure the value moved the dial for Michael, who reportedly held a $176.5 million stake in Sonic Healthcare Ltd at the time).

During the two years following this launch, LifeCare dabbled in dentistry, occupational health, and medical computer software, while they expanded into Victoria, New South Wales, and Queensland. It moved its headquarters from Perth to Sydney, eventually forming an alliance with Foundation Medical Centres, Sonic Healthcare, and Sigma Pharmacies, to augment their commercial opportunities through shared patient referrals and common administrative services.

Sadly, for those involved, LifeCare's profits did not live up to their forecasts. By the middle of 2001, LifeCare was operating at a loss. The shares plummeted from their notional listing price in late 1999 to only $0.07, before slightly rebounding to $0.13 by the end of 2001. LifeCare was heavily criticised in the media and industry for poor management, allowing clinical decisions to be dictated by suits in the boardrooms rather than by health practitioners. In April 2002, the share price languished at $0.11, before a raft of corporate takeover manoeuvres ensued.

To recover lost momentum, Michael successfully merged a general medical group with LifeCare in a reverse takeover. The company was renamed the Independent Practitioner Network (IPN) by late 2002. Eventually IPN became a wholly owned subsidiary of Sonic Healthcare in 2005, before undergoing a raft of other corporate restructures, changes in institutional and private ownership, ASX listings and de-listings. In January 2022, IPN fell under the unlikely custody of ASX-listed APM, a large provider of employment services.

Despite how one recounts the LifeCare brand story, with its contortions and reincarnations, they clearly never really succeeded with a franchise model. This highly public failure made what I was attempting at Back In Motion, all the harder. I faced an uphill battle as we tried to separate who we were, and what we did, from the unfortunate bad will resulting after this corporate fiasco.

It's not that I couldn't build a watertight case for franchising in healthcare. In fact, I could point to numerous Australian success stories in radiology, pathology, and optometry. And if I wanted to cast a wider net, I could confidently cite large and credible franchised physiotherapy and chiropractic networks in the US and Canada especially. The obstacle arose from the fact that my profession lacked vision. Our leaders and influencers were conservative by nature, breeding scepticism for anything new, risk-laden, and seemingly commercial. Once bitten, twice shy.

All this negative sentiment prevailed, despite the franchising sector in Australia enjoying booming success in the mid-2000s. It was widely reported that new franchises grew by 15%, with total sales exceeding $130 billion. This industry juggernaut represented just under 4% of all small businesses in Australia, creating over 400,000 jobs. Supposedly, less than 2% of all franchisees resulted in disputes, which is a surprisingly optimistic low number given the negative perception so many people had formed.

It was my job to meet or beat these statistics in my own network, building confidence that physiotherapy could be successfully franchised, even though it hadn't been done properly yet. I reflected on the historical tendency for people to view certain obstacles as insurmountable, until someone shattered that perception.

In the early days of aviation, many believed that it was impossible for an aircraft to travel faster than the speed of sound due to the extreme aerodynamic challenges, and the belief that the forces involved would tear the aircraft apart. However, on October 14, 1947, American pilot Chuck Yeager broke this barrier in the experimental Bell X-1 aircraft, demonstrating that what was once considered an insurmountable limitation, could indeed be surpassed with the right technology, innovation, and determination.

It dawned on me that all I needed to do was push myself a little beyond the perceived boundaries of those who came before me to demonstrate the feasibility and believability of my concept.

42
meningitis

BECOMING A FRANCHISOR was an exhaustive and daunting journey. I diligently sought guidance from industry stalwarts, actively participated in franchise networking and educational events, and joined an executive roundtable alongside fellow franchise owners. I immersed myself in reading industry journals and online blogs, analysed financial and other metrics using publicly available data, and closely examined the trends and achievements of well-established brands.

It was a sluggish grind, akin to trudging through a swamp of molasses. With the pressure to keep my head above the sludge, I did what I knew best: I worked *harder*. Longer hours, more practice visits, late nights, weekends. What I lacked in intelligence, I made up with effort.

But it all came at a price.

I was perpetually tired, sleeping only four or five hours a night, compressed between a late evening of emails and an early rise to beat the traffic to the other side of town for a team meeting. If people asked to meet with me for an hour, I'd offer them only half. Where possible, I'd see two people at once if I thought their questions or issues were even remotely aligned. I started scheduling my diary in 15-minute increments to ensure that every available space was optimally utilised.

My habit, when I walked in the front door at home, was to immediately set up my laptop in the study for what would become another long evening of inevitable work. I would just make it to the dinner table most nights, physically present but emotionally absent. Paulina was incredibly patient with me, but frequently felt like a single parent.

We agreed I needed more balance. Gradually, I adjusted my schedule to pause work from dinner until 8pm, dedicating that time to the bath and bedtime routine with Lachlan, relishing those precious moments together. However, once the house fell silent, I would bid Paulina an early goodnight with a kiss and return to my laptop, toiling away until the early hours of the morning.

These months and years wore me down. More than once, I lost sight of what God had assigned us to do. Instead of being fuelled by His intentions to build the business for missional purposes, too often I got sucked into a version of the *Matrix* – a illusionary vortex of *more* work, to build *more* practices, to make *more* money, and forgetting why.

I regularly met with Michael to centre myself again and again. It must have felt like Groundhog Day for him, although he rarely showed impatience.

In the middle of 2006, to help me see the end from the beginning, Michael encouraged me to accompany him on a mission trip to his homeland in Hungary. We shared our stories, and prayed with business owners and church ministers there who were seeking God to bring revival to their communities. Typical of such experiences, I came away with more than I gave.

Two weeks abroad marked the longest stretch I'd been apart from Lachlan. Days before my return, I confided in Paulina a genuine concern that my toddler might have forgotten me during my absence. Yet, as I stepped through the international arrival gates at my home airport, all apprehensions dissolved in an instant. At the mere sight of me, Lachlan's face ignited with joy, and he dashed into my waiting arms, embracing me with the fierce affection of a passionate two-year old.

If only I could run toward and hang onto my Heavenly Father with the same level of faith, abandon, and confidence. The trip with Michael, and the many conversations we exchanged, helped me remember who Back In Motion really belonged to, and why I had been called to lead it.

MY FAITH AND business journeys intersected and traversed four distinct phases during these first seven years.

Initially, I had erroneously decided that I must choose business *OR* ministry. The two were mutually exclusive – if I was to be a physio practice owner then I couldn't be a medical missionary. Instinctively, the former was dirty and evil, and the latter was good and holy – so, having chosen the lesser of the two, it left me feeling shameful and guilty. As I realised God's purpose for my life incorporated owning and operating a business, I slowly accepted I must have this dichotomy wrong.

Sometime after, I came to believe that I could do both – business *AND* ministry. I was relieved to learn that the two could co-exist, even if in parallel worlds with little in common. I reasoned that I could be an ethical businessman by day, and a church-going, Bible-believing, Christian vigilante at night and on weekends. It worked for Bruce Wayne, although not without some complications.

After conversations with Michael and others who had lived decades balancing their ministry and marketplace expressions, it was obvious there was more to this intentional life than simple co-habitation, or a marriage of conveniences. As our profitability in business grew, I came to understand that my business was *FOR* ministry. As I earned more money, it could be invested into the church and other missional programs to help those in greater need. This perspective made perfect sense, as charitable work all over the world required funding.

After a year or two thinking my mission was to make as much money as possible and give it all away, it dawned on me that the Bible says God "owns the cattle on a thousand hills" (Psalm 50:10-12 NKJV) and Jesus fed more than 5,000 people with a little boy's packed lunch of just two fish and five loaves (Matthew 14:13-21). He didn't need my meagre offering, as He knew how to miraculously multiply His resources whenever required.

I was momentarily deflated, as I felt my efforts in business were, at best, redundant, and worse, possibly an illusion in self-grandeur and false righteousness. Fortunately, God had more to teach me.

I eventually landed where I presume He always intended, with the conviction that business *IS* ministry. My time, effort and finance were a means to an end; what really mattered was that my work became a form of worship to Him. My greatest gift on any altar of sacrifice was that of complete obedience to the God who entrusted us with a business to serve His purposes. The people in our marketplace community – our team, suppliers, patients, and other industry stakeholders – were my mission field. I met different ones every day who might never otherwise hear the Good News of Jesus, and learn about His love and sacrifice for them. If all I did was become a worthy ambassador for Christ in the workplace, I wouldn't need any other ministry assignment. This was the highest calling, to be a missionary right where I was, doing what I knew and was good at, and feeling completely satisfied with the opportunity.

With this revelation, Paulina and I resolved that should we never again set foot outside our country and work directly with the poorest of the poor, we were going to completely devote ourselves to the work of Back In Motion with the understanding it was God's sacred business. That despite how monotonous and dull running physio practices might seem in comparison to the life of a cross-cultural pioneer, what we were doing was equally significant in the eyes of God, and mattered for all the same reasons.

GOD REINFORNCED HIS heart for people late one evening, when I was working hard at my desk in the NSO. Feeling the strain of little sleep, physically worn down and emotionally weak, the cadence of my keystrokes on the laptop became irregular and slow. Paulina had already rung twice to ask when I was coming home. And then, seemingly without warning, I momentarily lost my vision; literally blinded.

Fear gripped me. I couldn't see anything – not the screen of text in front of me, my outstretched hand as I waved it about, or even the lights hanging from the ceiling. Just the black of dark. I panicked. It was a strange sensation – not dissimilar to the slow descent we made on the outer reef as we completed our many night dives on our trip around Australia. Then, as we slipped below the water level into the inky underworld, I felt weightless and fully exposed. This was the same feeling.

I groped at the surface of my desk for the phone to ring home.

As I attempted dialling the number, most of my sight returned; like I was peering through the frosted glass of a chalet window, my field of view was obscured and speckled. I had black and white dots flickering and floating through my periphery, and I couldn't focus on anything specific. Intense pain started to develop on the right side of my head and, although seated in the chair, vertiginous hallucinations made me reach for the assurance of the ground. As I slowly knelt to the floor and lay supine with my legs at full stretch under the desk, I willed the strangeness away. It slowly abated after five or six minutes, but it felt closer to an hour.

I landed in the emergency department later that evening, undergoing a battery of tests. The eventual diagnosis was viral meningitis, exacerbated by overwork and stress. I was kept in hospital overnight for further investigations and observation, and then recommended two weeks of bed rest – a completely impractical suggestion, given how many problems I had to deal with on any given day.

Paulina, as both nurse and wife, was unimpressed when she found me the next day lying flat in bed (as sitting up would cause intolerable headaches and extreme visual disturbances), my laptop resting precariously on my chest, my neck craning into extreme flexion as I tried to type and view the screen from its obtuse angle. While I waited for the neurological registrar, I was making a list of everything I had to do. There were new staff to recruit, existing team members to review, marketing collateral to proof, franchise agreements to be disclosed to prospective new interests, suppliers to negotiate new terms, doctors to liaise with, sporting clubs to sign off on sponsorship agreements, software updates to review and release… and it all needed to be done *yesterday*. Tomorrow would have its own new list of overwhelming demands.

I careened into a black hole of despair and exhaustion, hating my role and wishing again that this was not my life, when I felt the gentle whisper of God. He reminded me that money didn't matter, business didn't matter, tasks didn't matter… only *people* matter. People matter!

At the very heart of His gospel is a desire to connect with and love people. It's the one-word summary of the whole Bible. He craves a wholesome and restored relationship with each one of us, and he deputises Christians to go and represent Him to people around them. The greatest two commandments are to (1) love God with all our heart, mind, and strength; and then to (2) love others as we would like to be loved (Matthew 22:37-40 NKJV).

God knew I had drifted from this truth. I had become so consumed with the never-ending busyness of Back In Motion that I had forgotten whom I was doing it for, and that relationships mattered above all else. He wanted me to know that business was not just *for* ministry, it *was* ministry, and I couldn't do it in my strength or vanity. It was His business and needed to be done His way.

While I recovered from that episode of meningitis relatively quickly, I continued to have small relapses every year for the next decade, characterised by two- to three-hour bouts of visual distortion and disabling migraines, for which there was no obvious treatment. And whilst I would rather it didn't happen, I learned to use each one of those occasions as a crucial reminder that God values people above all other things and, if I was to become more like Him, then I should value them too.

WITHOUT AN ADOPTED charity to get behind or any social cause to advocate, I boldly announced to the group that we needed one. The first welfare initiative was the H.E.L.P. Crisis Support Program, an acronym for *Helping Employees through Life's Problems*. I designed a basic brochure with the headline "Because People Matter", extending an open invitation to our teams to approach Paulina and me for financial help at any time if they or their family faced personal hardship.

We set up a specialised email domain for inbound requests, and appointed HELP representatives as the first points of contact – volunteers from each practice, making up a a cross-section of our workforce. The momentum built very slowly, but we were eventually engaged in all sorts of support, including subsidising the rent for a team member's parents whose uninsured house burned down, covering medical costs for various ones falling ill, and even using our time to equip one young physio with training to escape a cycle of crippling and destructive personal debt.

Paulina and I also took up the cause of Southern Cross Kids Camp (SCKC), an initiative founded by the late Carolyn Boyd to interrupt the downward spiral of abuse, neglect, and abandonment in primary school-aged children who were in the foster system, and suffered various forms of significant trauma.

Based on an outstanding five-day camp program, SCKC gives a week of happy memories for the kids who need it most. Apart from donating funds, I also provided basic administrative support and strategic input to their emerging board. We even co-located SCKC in our NSO for a short period, eventually buying and fitting out a dedicated office space for them. In 2021, despite the disruption of COVID-19, they engaged more than 500 kids with the support of 700 volunteers. They hosted 16 different camps in the six states and territories of Australia. The children who attended these camps were so positively transformed by the experience that many have returned as camp volunteers in their young adulthood, perpetuating a cycle of hope and restoration.

None of what we were doing was very sophisticated, or necessarily even sustainable in its current form. In fact, most of the time it added work to my already busy schedule. Home was hectic; the business was demanding, and the charitable projects at times threated to tip me over the edge. But it was totally right to have it all in the mix, as it was God's plan I was working towards and not my own.

And anytime I forgot this, my brain would go fuzzy, the lights would go out, black dots flashed across my visual horizon… and I would remember, *people matter*!

43
gouged

IN LATE NOVEMBER our second beautiful son, Sebastian, was born, weighing in at 3.3 kilograms.

A caesarean delivery had been scheduled because of Paulina's difficulties during her first birth. I confess, knowing Sebastian's planned arrival almost to the hour, suited me. It meant I was able to plan my day for optimal productivity, working right up to the deadline with little fear that Paulina might go into labour sooner. (Yes, my name is Jason and I'm a workaholic!) It also allowed me to arrange self-appointed paternity leave, allowing Lachlan and I to venture together on daily trips to the hospital, checking on Paulina's recovery, and getting our fill of cuddles from *Froggy*, the name Lachlan petitioned his new baby brother be called.

It was the beginning of a new chapter in our lives; seismic shifts took place in the tectonic plates that lay beneath our family and business. We had so many competing priorities to contend with, and Paulina and I were rarely aligned in what needed to be attended to first.

With two youngsters under three years of age, and having moved into our new house and neighbourhood in Ferntree Gully, Paulina decided it was time to devote herself to being a full-time mum. She handed off all her responsibilities at the NSO, and no longer worked her roster as a nurse. I was overwhelmed with the pressure to grow our fledging franchise business, accepting the goalposts had shifted from ten locations to 40 practices to make all the risk worth it.

The challenge of balancing my time and energy between the increasingly irreconcilable responsibilities at home and work, exuded an aura of impossibility. I feared that when I inevitably got my priorities "wrong", a formidable gap would open an uncrossable chasm between

Paulina and I, its sheer walls and yawning depths plunging me into the unknowns.

I was living on the precarious edge some days. I walked through the front door of our new home one evening, exhausted from work and yet fully aware I needed to clock in for my *second job* – doting father and sensitive husband. The first thing I noticed was a cluster of deep gouges in the newly polished jarrah hardwood floors of our hallway entrance. Suffice to say, I did not react well.

Paulina rushed to calm me down and explained that an elderly lady had come over to assist with some cleaning and, unknowingly, trapped a small stone under the vacuum head as she dragged it back and forth. Surges of anger and frustration washed over me, as I wondered how she failed to notice the irreparable damage she was doing from the staircase all the way to the front door. Apparently, her eyesight wasn't very good, even if her heart was in the right place. It took all of Paulina's persuasive negotiation to keep me from calling this well-meaning lady and demanding recompense. I'm embarrassed to say it took me hours to calm down and regain some logical perspective – I'm sure God was as equally unimpressed with my childish behaviour as was Paulina.

Ironically, I was due to give a keynote presentation the next morning to a Christian school faculty on the topic of success and significance, encouraging teachers that their influence every day makes a profound difference in the lives of their students. I wanted them to understand that, above all else, relationships trump academic or athletic performance; and less than twelve hours earlier, I failed my own test. With unveiled hypocrisy, I was more concerned with my floors than the relationship Paulina was developing with the elderly housecleaner – who inadvertently needed the work and was grateful for the minimum-wage opportunity.

Once again, God took (and maybe even created) the opportunity to reinforce another teaching moment with me, a frustratingly slow learner: *things* don't matter, *people* do.

Weeks later, when the insurance company wrote me a cheque to have the floors repaired, I felt it was better to leave the timber scars untouched to serve as a daily memorial of what really matters. Instead, we assigned the cheque to Southern Cross Kids Camps, and thanked God that a few little imperfections under our feet would soon help one or more children in experiencing stability under their own.

BUSINESS CONTINUED TO boom despite all my inadequacies; 2007 became our biggest year yet. I prepared numerous more Back In Motion practices for launch even before the start of the new year.

I was approached by a large medical centre to set up a practice within their facility. I negotiated the space we needed, including shared reception, suitable signage, and the rental terms, in the few hours just before Sebastian's birth.

I also secured a new practice facility adjacent to the world-renowned Monash Medical Hospital. The practice was surrounded by specialist consulting suites and other allied health services – a premium destination for our growing physiotherapy brand. We committed to a full renovation and upgrade of the premises, believing this to become a marque site for us.

I did not have any staff yet, let alone franchisees, to operate the new practices in either location, but hoped I could channel Kevin Costner's magic from *Field of Dreams*: "if I built them, *someone* would come".

Gabriella eventually did – a Latrobe alumnus who graduated a few years ahead of me, with private practise experience and clear commercial interests. She was also a highly disciplined athlete who had enrolled into an MBA to start soon.

Gabriella wasn't your average physio – she knew it, and so did I. As such, she wanted to work at the NSO to oversee the growth of the *whole* network, and not be confined to just a single location, let alone a tiny consulting room treating patients in twenty-minute intervals. I appreciated her ambition.

Eager to prove to me she could build and lead a team, Gabriella proposed that instead of going on the payroll, she would take up half ownership in two new practices I had recently launched. We agreed that if she accelerated their performance to break even in the first 12 months, I would provide her a structured pathway into management. On this basis, her franchise agreements were settled before the close of the first quarter of 2007.

I had also secured a new franchisee for the coveted suburb of Camberwell. I met Quinn at a professional weekend course we both attended in Melbourne, riding the lift together to the carpark after a long Sunday session. With my radar always tuned to young and energetic hopefuls, my antennae tweaked when he said he was thinking of moving on from his current employment. I gave him a literal *elevator pitch*, explaining who Back In Motion was, and what we did, inviting him to visit the NSO to learn more if he was interested.

Entrenched in levels of detail, matched only by his cautious disposition, Quinn engaged in an extensive back-and-forth on commercial and franchise terms, before agreeing to proceed with a franchise on a fifty-fifty ownership basis. Preparing the small, elongated shop front in Camberwell for its February launch turned into a collaborative family effort. Quinn convinced a friend to build the internal partitions, his dad painted the premises inside and out, and I called in a favour from a mate to produce and hang the signs. Meanwhile, Quinn, three-year old Lachlan, and I laboured the weekend, wheelbarrowing loads of mulch and decorative stones from front-to-back to create a simple tasteful landscaping effect.

Welcoming Quinn into ownership of a practice was something of a watershed moment for me. Marcus had simply taken a path of least resistance; Bao probably would have started his own business if I didn't have one on offer; and Gabriella took up the franchise offer with an ulterior motive for a career in management. But Quinn represented everything *difficult* about our industry. He was risk-averse, prohibitively conservative, super intellectual – often confident he knew better than everybody else and, in some cases, may well have – and was sceptical of anything he didn't understand. When Quinn eventually said "yes" to a franchise, I was infused with confidence that we might just make this work.

The fact Quinn went on to become one of our top ten profit generators vindicated my original decision to franchise in the first place. He was our physio equivalent of the *canary in the coal mine*, demonstrating that our business model had integrity and substance. His experience certainly went some of the way to quieting the critics and drowning out some naysayers; there was a long queue of both at times who otherwise refused to be dissuaded.

With this percolating boldness, I also chose to welcome Persi and Bao into minority shareholding of our fast-growing Corporate Health business. I built a team which specialised in industrial ergonomics and workplace injuries, coining the phrase "industrial athlete" to argue that the philosophical approach and principles of clinical care we applied to elite level sport, was a good fit for factory and sedentary office-bound workers too.

This innovative segment was winning new work every month across a broad range of industries. In the two years that followed, I sold various other minority equity holdings of this emerging revenue stream, to form an intimate syndicate of five owners, causing a never-ending flurry of new share sale and subsequent shareholder agreements. Many hands made for light work, even with a few of us already wearing multiple hats - but somehow it worked.

44

iceberglets

PAULINA HADN'T BEEN back to South America since her late teens. With two children now, she was keen to introduce her *abuelos* to their great-grandchildren. Because I was overwhelmed with work, we agreed Paulina would fly to Chile with the children in late April 2007, and I would join them two weeks later for the last half of their visit.

The trip was a major undertaking for Paulina, with a three-year-old and a newborn. It certainly didn't help when mix-ups with the plane seating arrangements sought to have Lachlan sitting three rows apart from her. It seems ludicrous to have to explain to anyone why this isn't appropriate but, nonetheless, Paulina repeatedly made her argument with multiple flight attendants before they conceded to rearranging other passengers.

The family endured more than 24 hours of flight time and transit, passing through New Zealand, Dubai, Santiago and, eventually, a domestic flight to Temuco, in the mid-south of Chile, ironically on almost the same latitude to that of Melbourne. All three were exhausted when they arrived. In hindsight, it may not have been the wisest decision for me to gloat two weeks later, that when I arrived at the airport, my flight had been considerably more enjoyable because of an unexpected upgrade to business class, resulting from a similar seat mix up – this one, of course, in my favour. It was only fair that I was delegated sleep patrol for the next few nights when Sebastian woke for a feed or nappy change.

Not that I expected any sympathy – nor would I have received any – but I did spend most of the flight to Chile, and a good portion of my downtime over there, putting the finishing touches on a unique leadership development curriculum I was writing. The biggest limitation to the quality and rate of our network growth was finding the right people. My solution was to equip the ones I had, designing the program to train our staff for emerging responsibilities, building teams from the ground up.

I curated my favourite leadership material from the plethora of books and articles I had been reading since 2003, and merged that with what I was being taught in the sermons and discipleship courses at church. I thoughtfully compiled the topics into a 12-month program, where attendees participated in a monthly tutorial with homework before and after each session.

I called it the Iceberg Leadership Development Program, only partly inspired by the geography of the south of Chile where I was visiting at the time. The original reason for this namesake was my foundational thesis that effective leadership had less to do with titles, qualifications, and obvious features of workplace authority (the iconic *tip* of the iceberg), and was more determined by the character attributes that lay beneath one's superficial actions and behaviours (the *substance* of the iceberg).

I had long lamented that our industry was starved for compelling leadership. People had titles, qualifications, job experience, and technical skills, but these were no substitute for a person impassioned with a vision for positive change, who could influence and inspire others to strive for greatness. As soon as I returned to the office, I promoted the opportunity to my staff as a program to strengthen the connection between their clinical knowledge and their leadership potential, with the promise of a richer career within Back In Motion, and presumably more broadly.

Only 13 people completed the first intake in 2007, including all seven of my Practice Directors (franchisees) and a handful of their practice managers. The interest built quickly thereafter, with the second course immediately oversubscribed.

Without planning to add to my already-full dance card, hosting the Iceberg Leadership Development Program became another time-intensive responsibility in a very time-poor schedule.

45
media darling

MY FIRST AND only appearance as a cover model was in the July 2007 edition of our profession's leading publication, *In Motion*. (Not to be confused with *Back In Motion*, although some believed this magazine was underwritten by me as a brand promotional strategy.) Unfortunately, I was sporting the awkward phase of regrowth after a clean-shaven buzz cut suffered only eight weeks prior for the Shave-For-A-Cure campaign we hosted in our practices.

I had been asked numerous times to present at various industry events, the rising success of our group gaining attention across an increasingly interested subgroup of peers. My talks typically polarised the audience because of my shameless enthusiasm that physios should be stronger advocates for their important role in community health, and how we needed to run businesses more effectively to be sustainable long term.

My zeal attracted a conspicuous following, with more and more invitations to share my story. It seems the APA finally conceded and accepted that Back In Motion was here to stay – leading to a three-page feature article on us. Headlined, *From clinician to businessman*, the article reported me employing 75 staff with revenue in the many millions – facts, I conceded, surprised me more than anybody else. The article disclosed my young aspirations to be a medical missionary, accentuated the humble beginnings of our carport start-up, and shared some funny anecdotes of the mishaps along the way.

The publication changed tone halfway through, and acknowledged that over 60% of Australian physio practices were struggling to be commercially viable because they lacked the size and leverage to be profitable. They also noted the high level of workforce attrition due to private practice offering little or no career path, or adequate earning potential. The fact physiotherapists lacked the training in the fundamentals of small business was a glaring handicap threatening the future of our profession.

The cover story boasted our 16 flagship practices, another ten satellite locations, and our Corporate Health service. I promised to keep expanding and welcomed interest from those who wanted to learn more. The article closed on my reflections about success and significance, challenging people to reflect how they can have a profound positive impact on the world around them through their influence and affluence.

Surprisingly, my phone rang off the hook for a month or two after the issue's release – momentarily a physiotherapy celebrity, enjoying my 15 minutes of fame. I seized the tempting opportunity this article provided to showcase the benefits of franchising to overcome many of our industry challenges. I shared the evidence that we were enjoying high rates of growth and improved profitability through higher-than-usual retention of staff. I referred to the structured, six-stage career pathways I had developed, the automated technology, our Iceberg Leadership Development Program, and our comprehensive administrative systems – all which gave therapists the freedom to focus primarily on what they love and were good at, which is treating their patients.

Invitations flowed to speak at more events, including guest lectures at various universities and graduating physiotherapy classes. This, in turn, led to further articles in other industry publications, all of which built a virtuous cycle of franchise interest (along with some healthy scepticism), resulting in further network growth.

In response to the growing demand, I launched the *Allied Health Biz Blog*, a resource library and discussion forum for allied health professionals around the world. The website published materials I created on best practice for private health care. I covered themes such as profitability, workplace reform, legislative changes, recruitment issues, the power of technology, and the ethical debate around the commercialisation of healthcare. It was the only blog of its kind at the time; of course, since then there are thousands of them, now that it's safe and popular to talk about the business of health.

Amidst all this fanfare, I was also invited to contribute a chapter in a mainstream book titled *Top Franchise CEO's – Secrets Revealed* (Global Publishing Group, 2007). Alongside Australian business superstars Janine Allis of Boost Juice, Michael Sherlock of Brumby's

Bakeries, Tony Lattouf of Hairhouse Warehouse, and Sara Pantaleo of La Porchetta – I got to tell some of my story, warts and all, of what it was like to kick-start a franchise concept in an altogether-unfriendly profession that shunned commercial success. I also was invited to share some of my faith journey, as I morphed from a discouraged graduate to a God-driven entrepreneur, despite the uncharacteristic narrative it portrayed when compared with some of the other profiles in the book.

All this publicity positioned me as a thought leader in the emerging commercial healthcare space, propelling our brand saturation, and cementing our credibility with accelerating momentum.

IT WAS AN especially proud moment when Back In Motion was featured in the prestigious *Business Review Weekly* (BRW) as a star performer, ranked as the eighth fastest growing franchise by outlet, and the eleventh fastest growing franchise by revenue for 2007. Two notable brands that beat us that year were Sumo Salad and Healthy Habits – both food retailers with a focus on health and wellbeing. Proudly, we ranked well above many household brands, including Nandos, the Coffee Club, Gloria Jeans Coffees, and Mortgage Choice.

Because of our sensational debut in that year's result, the BRW included a comprehensive profile of our business success in their magazine. The reporter noted the rise of franchise companies in home and personal services, and celebrated our contribution to aged-care, which accounted for a substantial 20% of my annual $2.5 million annual royalties – a message not lost on many wannabe franchisees.

Physiotherapist Anthony recounts the story of first hearing me speak in late 2005 at the Abbotsford home of the APA. He was drawn to my lecture that night because a friend of his had shared the urban myth of a Melbourne physio who was starting lots of practices and could afford to "…just travel around Australia whenever he wanted to". Obviously, the legend was not true (as you are reading the real story here), but it became compelling fiction nonetheless. (It amuses – and at times, frustrates – me to think how distorted my story became when people filled in the white spaces between the half-truths they heard.) My reported experiences especially appealed to Anthony, as he was more interested in learning business and building wealth than being a clinician. He had already considered leaving the profession for greener, more lucrative, pastures when his interest was again piqued by the various media promoting Back In Motion.

Anthony had been initially deterred from joining our group because, up to that point, the APA warned a minimum of three years' experience was necessary before anyone took up a role in the private sector. I clearly thought differently. Bao was a classic example of the risks I was prepared to take for the right people, our youngest serving physio quickly jumping the queue into ownership before the first anniversary of graduating from university. Anthony harboured a similar hope for himself.

By mid-2007, Anthony joined the Directorship by taking on the Hillside franchise, buying a second larger practice in the area, and merging the two into a sizable enterprise. At just 24 years of age, after buying the businesses, refitting the practices with new equipment, and paying his initial franchise fees, Anthony was in the hole for a little over half a million dollars – quite likely the largest investment made by any franchisee to this point. The pressure was on both of us for him to succeed; me feeling almost a kindred bond with Anthony, given he was risking everything at the same age I had done so only eight years earlier.

Grateful for the little bit of stardust that settled on me and our brand that year, it was the APA that had promoted our message to the world, albeit somewhat unwittingly.

46

border crossing

EVERY PRESS REPORT and news story that added to our media coverage set up more opportunities for me within the industry.

I first met Jared, the principal owner of a reputable practice in Adelaide, at a weekend physiotherapy course hosted by the APA. We got talking over the lunch buffet, lamenting together the difficulty of finding quality staff to grow our respective clinical teams. I briefly mentioned the success of our Iceberg Leadership Development Program, toward which he immediately showed interest.

Soon after, Jared asked me to fly to Adelaide and mentor his team in some of my leadership content. It was the first time I shared the training outside the Back In Motion sphere. I remember boarding a plane and feeling surprised at myself for being willing to equip another team, with whom I had no commercial interests, especially when I was drowning in work and family commitments at home.

After delivering 12 manic tutorials in a compressed two-day program, I went back to my hotel room, mentally exhausted, and then preoccupied with the unyielding schedule that awaited me on my return to the office the next day.

The hotel phone rang, and the concierge asked permission to patch a call through from Jared. I felt groggy from my physical depletion, and really didn't want to talk. After some undisguisable clearings of the throat, I greeted Jared, who immediately declared he wanted to join the group, becoming the first interstate practice of Back In Motion.

It was a short dialogue, lasting no longer than a few minutes. No details were exchanged, no commercial terms were considered, and no timelines were proposed. It was just an idea being floated as a test balloon, so I was nonchalant and promised to call back during the week to explore the matter further. After ending the call, I enthusiastically pumped my fists in the air as I pondered the prospect of expanding to Adelaide.

Things moved quickly from there. I did a full due diligence on Jared's current operations, team structure, financial performance, and service model across his two locations. He too had his key advisor give Back In Motion a comprehensive once-over to ensure we were a bona fide business.

Whilst there were more reasons to unite than go our separate ways, the biggest sticking point in the franchise terms was the royalties. Although I hastened to point out that I had already reduced them once, down from 11% to now only 7%, Jared and his advisor still feared the costs would be too high given their small profits. I overcame the objection with an innovative work-around; I created the *Preserved Revenue Threshold* (PRT), a unique idea unheard of in all my vast research into the world of franchising. To make it attractive for an existing business to join our network, I agreed for a specified quantum of patient billings to be royalty-free for the life of the arrangement.

In Jared's situation – being my first test case – I agreed to only earn royalties on those sales that exceeded his existing turnover, or on the billings of only *new clients* who attended after his joining our franchise, whichever was the greater sum. It was my way of recognising and honouring the goodwill Jared had already built up in his client list – drawing a line in the sand – and not expecting to financially benefit from his historical hard work.

The quid pro quo in this generous concession was that Jared needed to commit to a Minimum Performance Requirement (MPR) of 10% growth year-on-year, providing assurance that, over time, I would at least be partially compensated for the many support services I was committing to.

Chris, my franchise lawyer, hadn't seen this gesture before, didn't like it, and was immediately sceptical. It seemed to me a fair approach for both parties, so I didn't budge.

With the trade-off agreeable, Jared and I signed agreements for the first two franchises in South Australia, effective October 2007. The impact of becoming an interstate business was almost immediate, relocating Paulina and our young family to the beachside suburb of Glenelg for two weeks so I could train our two newest teams in the preliminary operations of our burgeoning franchise system.

IT WAS QUICKLY apparent that Jared wanted more.

Before the ink was even dry on his franchise agreements, he opened conversations about the likelihood of a master franchise. To be fair, it was obvious to both of us that the combination of his local contacts and commercial ambition positioned him to be a real influencer in South Australia.

In consultation with Chris, I shied away from the traditional master licensing arrangement, which had become somewhat outdated, and agreed to the more novel approach called Area Development. The spirit of the agreement was similar, but the technical differences were substantial.

Notably, as our inaugural Area Developer, Jared had no direct legal and commercial exposure to the downstream franchisees. Instead, he functioned more like an agent; Jared promoted the franchise opportunity, met with prospects, screened them for suitability, and eventually introduced them to me as the franchisor for formal negotiation, approval, and signing of binding franchise agreements. The risk of failure was squarely on me if the eventual relationship with franchisees broke down.

In return for these services, Jared was offered half of the initial franchise fee and half of the future royalties in perpetuity. By any standards, it was an extremely generous deal in Jared's favour – one I would have happily taken up if someone else was willing to carry all the risk for what amounted to an equal financial return. He had few direct overheads, as it was mostly an investment of his time, didn't have to build or invest into any network systems or infrastructure, didn't employ staff, and could earn the same amount as me for every practice he introduced. The offer amounted to sharing the spoils right down the middle.

Proposing only a modest price for exclusivity to all South Australia, Jared didn't hesitate – leaving only five states and two territories left for someone else to conquer.

47

board-om

I **CLOSED OUT** 2007 with a long overdue conversation with our accountant about our cashflow position. He finally conceded the business was ready to pay Paulina and I a fair ongoing wage commensurate with our responsibilities. My meagre drawings, up to that point, was lower than the salary of most junior graduates, even though I boasted the largest private workforce of physiotherapists within our profession; such is the slow crawl to the summit. By Christmas though, Back In Motion could afford to pay me a $100,000 salary for the first time – not a fortune, but welcome news nonetheless.

The cash boost arrived just in time, given Paulina and I were about to add another mouth to feed at home. Whilst we had anxiously waited more than 18 months before experiencing the miracle breakthrough of falling pregnant with Sebastian, our third conception happened significantly faster than we expected.

When the time came, all four of us were so excited to meet our third son, Morgan – who got bundled into our arms in February 2008.

SIZE DEMANDS STRUCTURE. The bigger our business got, the more organised I needed to become. I was so dependent on my friend and mentor, Michael, to help keep me sane amidst all the swirling pressure and contention that we agreed to set up an advisory board to offer more formal support to my demanding role.

Between the two of us, we made a laundry list of nine names for potential board members, progressively interviewing them over the months that followed. I was looking for commercial edge, Godly values, and a compatible chemistry. It was easier to say "no" to most than "yes". After a lot of consideration, there was only one person who stood out as the right fit: John.

John was an accomplished businessman, having built and sold a large international publishing business many years earlier. He now busied himself as a non-executive portfolio director in various companies – including the franchising giant Gloria Jean's Coffees – and otherwise spent his days overseeing his investments and leading local and national church initiatives.

I didn't know John personally but had heard him speak a year ago at a Christian business event. He described eternity as an imaginary line stretching from one side of the room to the other, with our lives represented by an imperceptible dot on the expanse. His challenge that morning was to ensure we used our limited time and talents to make a difference, and to keep our eyes firmly fixed on the everlasting reward of Heaven. It was another great reminder to me that business, money, and tasks don't matter nearly as much as people and relationships.

I wasn't offering him much in terms of financial compensation, but John enthusiastically accepted the opportunity to join with Michael and I to what became our first Strategic Advisory Board (SAB), with Michael as inaugural chairman. Given we were only three, we agreed to invite professionals for input on an as-needed basis. At different times, we included financial advisors, tax accountants, a business law specialist, franchise consultant, HR/IR consultant, patent and trademark attorney, business development mentor, insurance and risk management consultant, and a marketing director. As we faced strategic challenges in different areas of the business, I would *phone-a-friend* to bolster our intelligence, keeping the core board otherwise a nimble and simple trio.

People were, and still are, sometimes confused by my decision to put the SAB in place. As a sole director, and the only shareholder, peers wondered how the dynamic worked. Given we weren't a formally ASIC-registered, fiduciary board, and Michael and John were not bona fide directors, both knew I carried the final decision on all matters, and could choose to ignore their input; but doing so too many times over would quickly disengage their commitment. It was an important discipline that I build strong and compelling business cases for my intended decisions, submitting them to the SAB monthly, somewhat like an employed executive. I learned to value the objective and independent thinking of people who were seasoned in business. The rigour of the advisors' external accountability protected the interests of all stakeholders – mine, and those of the franchisees.

More than anything, I needed their prayer support, spiritual wisdom, and Biblical counsel. Michael and John understood the importance of using business as a mission to serve God above all else. They kept me grounded, focussed, and motivated. And when I needed a hug there were plenty of those on offer too.

WITH THE NSO team and SAB around me, I felt one voice was missing; a representative group of franchisees with perspective and feedback from the ground level. Often known as a Franchise Advisory Council, I called our first iteration the Group Advisory Panel (GAP). Partly because we still weren't comfortable with the dirty "F" word infiltrating our lexicon, but also because I liked the imagery that these elected franchisee representatives bridged the *gap* between the clinical coal face and the ivory tower of the NSO.

Once formed, I charged the GAP to give input to state and national growth strategy, clinical protocols, marketing spend, and operational improvements. Whilst I valued unity between all our members, I put huge emphasis on the importance of constructive debate, even if at times lively disagreements ensued. In the true form of any contest, I hoped for the best ideas to win every time, and my job as chair of this forum was to create the right balance between safety and candour.

The members of the GAP were nominated, and then elected, by peer franchisees. Each member served a term of 24 months, unless there were grounds for removal – which happened only once. I hosted GAP meetings four times a year, flying all delegates into the boardroom for a full-day meeting. Twice a year, I also hosted all-in Director Forums where every franchisee was invited to hear the GAP's progress, participate in polls, and answer questions on anything unclear or controversial.

The SAB and the GAP became the bookends that helped me chisel and shape the growing network into a high-performance business, keeping me both accountable and motivated in equal measures when there was no shortage of distractions that could have otherwise taken me off course.

PAULINA AND I also felt convicted at this time to put in place dedicated prayer covering for ourselves and the business. Whilst this ebbed and flowed in its formality and consistency over the years, our good friend Liesl took the initial lead on this initiative. She regularly asked for both prayer requests and praise reports from us, distributing the information to a small discrete group of faithful prayer warriors, interceding on our behalf, and otherwise remaining anonymous in the background.

To this day, I am convinced there have been countless times when guardian angels and the unseen hand of God went ahead and protected me, intercepting threats that were meant to harm me, and showing me favour even when I didn't deserve it.

OF COURSE, THE NSO team kept expanding in proportion to the growth in our network. By June of 2008, I had a full composition of senior management and support staff, making a headcount of 15 professionals.

As Group Director, who was also the *face* of the brand, I spent inordinate hours as an industry advocate with peak bodies, and in the media, serving on committees, and contributing to working groups to generally improve healthcare in Australia. As such, I relied heavily on the team around me for daily operational compliance.

By this stage Back In Motion comprised 23 flagship practices and an additional 21 satellites, making a total footprint of 44 locations. We had one interstate expansion into Adelaide, a pending agreement to move into New South Wales, and three more franchisee applications under review in Victoria. The only practice I now owned outright was the original business in Wantirna South; I had either sold my holdings in all the other locations to new franchisees, or retained, at most, only nominal equity.

New franchises at the time now paid $30,000 to join our group, and another $120,000 on average to fit out their new practice. These were numbers that were unfathomable when I first ventured into franchising, but somehow seemed entirely normal now.

In the moment, I felt there was no stopping us.

48

breakthrough

OUR COMBINED ACHIEVEMENTS through 2007 and 2008 afforded Back In Motion one of the most celebrated industry honours at the FCA's black-tie awards: Victorian Emerging Franchise of the Year.

Judged on seven key criteria considered essential to franchising, our category was open to any business that had been in operation for at least three years and was currently operating in at least two states with a minimum of 20 outlets. We not only qualified, but were recognised as the most trusted brand with a credible system for success – which wasn't bad for an inexperienced and disillusioned physio, who was first dismissed when he dared approach the concept less than ten years earlier.

As health professionals in a cottage industry, where approximately 64% of Australian physiotherapy businesses were reported as being staffed by a solo practitioner (IBIS Physiotherapy Report 2006), the threats of practice failure were unacceptably high. This was due, in part, to therapist isolation, low clinical accountability and peer stimulation, personal fatigue and burnout, poor business planning and financial control, and ultimately a lack of resources applied to effective business management. Revenues, and therefore margins, were typically so low in physiotherapy practices that owners suffered a negligible (if any) return on their investment. In many cases, practitioners were simply "buying" themselves a high-pressure job rather than operating a well leveraged business. For all these reasons – and many others – practice owners lamented very few exit options when they wanted to sell their practice. The goodwill of these businesses was usually inextricably linked to the personality and competency of the outgoing practitioners, and prospective buyers were reluctant to pay too much for a revenue stream with such inherent vulnerabilities.

We built our franchised brand on a different appeal; we combined the experience of the local, boutique practice where clients received personalised attention from physios they came to know and trust, with the benefits of a corporate model that improved resources for staff and clients. Due to this hybrid approach, our franchisees enjoyed financial stability and certainty, as they gained capital appreciation in their businesses. With time, it was evident that our training in skills and systems enabled Directors to successfully grow several practices at the same time, multiplying their opportunities.

Our real competitive advantage lay in the relationships we formed between the NSO and Practice Directors; we were *partners* in the true sense of the word. Advocating for aligned culture and sincere relationship, Paulina and I often hosted informal dinners with franchise applicants, meeting their spouses and families, before any licences were granted. We ran a program to recognise and celebrate key milestones and special achievements in the practices, gifting them with food hampers, dinner and movie vouchers, flowers, and even weekend stays at the Sofitel to celebrate their incremental achievements. We hosted fun social days and staff retreats, invited people to regular leadership forums and clinical education sessions, and promoted individuals in the press to acknowledge their personal contributions.

Back In Motion overcame all the various industry curses by bringing together the best of both worlds – a molten alloy of clinical excellence, relational integrity, and commercial competence – achieved through the power of franchising. It was incredibly rewarding to be formally recognised for taking so many risks, and not folding when the opposition mounted against us. It was fitting we share the limelight and accolades with all our franchisees – as any success was all of ours.

FRESH OFF OUR win, I invited the Directorship and their families to our first franchise conference scheduled for October 2008. It was not an elegant affair, just a two-day gathering featuring some amateur keynote sessions, and a casual Saturday night dinner at La Porchetta. There were no sponsors or exhibitors, no top-level entertainment, and it was not an expensive event.

I set the theme as *Purposeful Profitability*. We spent most of the time helping franchisees make their peace with profit statements, cost control, balance sheets, cash flow statements, and Kaplan and Norton's famed *Balanced Scorecard*.

Somehow, I even managed to convince Paulina to run a session. She gave insightful perspectives on how to balance a demanding home life when a slavish, all-consuming franchise jealously stole her husband, and the kids' father, for unreasonable lengths of time. The session was well received by everyone present, but especially the spouses who could relate to the competitive tension between work and family. Encores were requested for years to come, as franchisees hungered for more of Paulina's wisdom and encouragement into how to achieve sustainable rhythm and equilibrium in their personal lives.

The highlight, however, was an energetic, heart-pounding, sweat-producing, personal development workshop to help us push through self-set limitations and psychological barriers. A martial arts instructor spent 30 minutes physically and mentally preparing us to karate-chop a timber board into two. With each of us inscribing our individual challenges in bold black marker on the face of our boards, we arranged ourselves, poised to literally break through the obstacles.

Typical of such occasions, I was expected to go first.

I felt paralysed. Standing in front of 20 or so people, leader of the group, I was terrified I wouldn't be able to break my board. I envisioned images of me breaking my wrist instead, wailing in distress, instead of mastering the challenge and setting an example for everyone else to follow.

I went through the preliminary routine as I was instructed: I performed five deep breathing exercises; practiced my intentional weight shifting, smoothly rocking from rear foot to front foot; and I rehearsed the shadow thrust of my dominant palm. I visualised the heel of my hand driving forcefully through to the chest of the instructor holding the board outstretched in front of me.

Apparently this was the key: "Don't try to break the board by snapping it at the point of impact. Push all the way through the board to an imaginary target far beyond the centre of contact, and be pleasantly surprised when the board crumples like paper on the way through."

No more practicing; no more stalling. I put my ego on the line and went for it!

Snap!

It was such a relief to punch my hand forward, and hear the timber splinter in front of me. Literal and metaphorical success; I broke through the barrier, hoping this to be true in all my business ventures that lay ahead.

Paulina went second and broke her board. So did Bao, Jared, and some of our newest franchisees.

It still surprises me that the strongest and most athletic person present in the room that day couldn't break her board. Gabriella, a disciplined athlete who trained daily, had no success despite multiple attempts. We cheered Gabriella on, as we watched in some disbelief, her repeated failures in front of the team morphing into desperate frustration and personal humiliation.

The approach taught to us that day was less about strength and more about technique. Breakthrough was an exercise in mind over matter; but the harder Gabriella tried, the less confidence she felt. In the end, she retired from the exercise with an ego more bruised than her hand – a foreshadowing of an even bigger demise ahead.

49
feined litigation

WITH ART IMITATING life, Gabriella's difficulties at our conference started to manifest in other concerning ways; subtle fracture lines beginning to emerge as her disciplined life unravelled.

Having experienced some disappointing performances at a recent international competition, Gabriella was trying to work out her future as an elite athlete. She also explained to me in October that she had been hurt badly by investment losses, caused by the Global Financial Crisis (GFC).

Adding to her woes, the four practices we now co-owned together began under-performing as Gabriella wasn't in practice as often to monitor and coach the relatively young teams in person. This meant some of the businesses demanded monthly cash top-ups from us as co-shareholders, risking insolvency.

Gabriella couldn't afford to continue, so I was having to singularly shoulder the cash flow shortages. The inevitable solution was to buy Gabriella out of her various equity holdings, but every attempt to fairly value the practices was thwarted, as a business not making money (and worse, requiring capital injection to survive) was difficult to price.

We were caught between a rock and a hard place.

A reasonable compromise was a deferred payment arrangement, which we struck in December 2008, shortly before she left my employ. Gabriella was assured the repayment of her previous capital investments into the businesses, and a half share of any future profits, if the practices hit certain performance thresholds or I could sell them above their aggregate debt value. There were no guarantees, but we agreed to a ten-year time horizon on the deal to give us both sufficient time to hopefully achieve a mutual win.

This solution was bittersweet; resolving one problem created more.

I EVENTUALLY MANAGED to save all four practices, but only after many years of persistence and several further cash injections.

I had a calendar reminder set every anniversary to review my obligations under the contractual agreements with Gabriella, knowing the terms survived a decade. In December 2013, more than five years later, the first of some conditions for two practices were fulfilled, entitling Gabriella to a large cash settlement that she was grateful to receive.

After radio silence for the next ensuing five years, Gabriella wrote to me in September 2018, requesting payment of another tranche. Unfortunately for both of us, the last two practices to which her entitlements related, hadn't triggered any of the conditions for further payments. Suspecting foul play, Gabriella referred the matter to a lawyer, commencing a frustrating game of legal ping-pong for a 25-month marathon.

Gabriella's accusations were fierce and unsubstantiated, provoking her lawyer to demand an unreasonable payment beyond the scope of our agreed terms, threatening legal proceedings and a cost order against me. We continued to push and shove through to February 2019, when Gabriella's lawyer presented a foolhardy analysis of various misinterpretations of tax law, notional holding interest rates, and the bookend dates on which such calculations were applied. With both of their eyes set on an undeserving, massive payout, a frivolous lawsuit seemed inevitable.

As I sat idle, waiting for the bomb to drop, nothing happened for the rest of the year until the sound of Christmas carols playing on the radio must have cued Gabriella to call her lawyer again. More than a year after their first contact, in December 2019, I received another demand for full and final payment of a large baseless claim.

This time, her lawyer eloquently crafted prose elucidating fraudulent misrepresentation, financial advantage by deception, and other improper commercial practices – all for which there was no evidence. He tried to persuade me of the economic loss his client had suffered, spruiking numerous incomplete and erroneous calculations in her favour. In closing, the lawyer demanded all my financial records relevant to their case for the purpose of assessing the veracity of my relentless defence, ungraciously allowing only 30 days to comply after they sat dormant on the claim for ten months prior.

My legal team didn't even bother with the matter, dismissing its importance as a shameful overreach. To their reckoning, Gabriella was a nuisance claimant, exhibiting opportunistic behaviour as the timeframe of her agreement neared its end. They had seen this before; people in similar circumstances manipulating the facts and fabricating false claims before the statute of limitations closed them out. In their opinion, this was a classic case of the opposing attorney exploiting vulnerabilities within the legal system, exaggerating or entirely inventing grievances to suit their agenda. They believed the pattern of deceitful actions, delay tactics, carefully-timed ambushes, and empty threats – all while knowingly perpetrating falsehoods with baseless allegations – didn't deserve their time to construct a fulsome response. They recommended I simply make a notional offer to settle the dispute, ridding me of the annoying distraction.

Despite extending a heartfelt gesture to Gabriella, an email from her attorney in February 2020 confirmed his client still intended to issue proceedings, using powers of subpoena to obtain necessary documents to indict me. Nothing followed; and since Gabriella had an unwinnable case then, and our agreement has long since expired, I presume her spurious complaints and nebulous arguments are even less claim-worthy now.

50
double crash

BY THE END of 2008, having just released Gabriella from her role within our group, more stitching started coming undone. Loose threads, when pulled, revealed sketchy workmanship in many of our business systems. Nowhere was this unravelling felt more than in my IT set up.

Despite having spent more than half a million dollars on our own bespoke software platform by this stage, the technology clearly had not kept up with our accelerated growth. Data flow was slow, new features weren't streamlined, bugs were crawling, links were breaking, and tempers were rising.

And then it all blew up.

Paulina and I were sitting in the cinema late one evening, six-month-old Morgan asleep on my lap, when my phone vibrated. I let it go to voicemail four times before Paulina nudged me, concluding it must be important.

Almost relieved to be spared the boredom of the disappointing film, I stepped into the foyer and rang my Operation's Manager. She apologised for the late call, but advised the main patient database server in the NSO had failed. All connections with the practice network were lost, and our franchisees were ringing constantly to report downstream problems. Some forensic IT contractors were first at the scene, and the early prognosis wasn't good.

I returned to my seat in the theatre and calmly whispered to Paulina that I needed to go to the office after dropping her home, purposely understating the issue I feared.

As it turned out, I didn't see Paulina for the next 41 hours.

I walked into the NSO server room just before 9pm to see racks of servers being dismantled, computer componentry sprawled over the floor, and four technicians trying to put Humpty Dumpty back together again. People were obviously anxious – me, chief amongst them – but I could offer no meaningful support other than do food and drink runs to keep the nerds hard at it.

Frustrated by the lack of progress – resulting in a severe lack of confidence – I called Dan. He had fitted out every practice we ever launched with computers, telephony and other hardware, but I had given the central network maintenance contract to what I thought was a more credible outfit. When it counted though, I only trusted Dan. He called in every favour from anyone he knew who might be able to help us, scrambling to recover our lost data and get our machines up and running again.

With little to contribute, I slept on the floor in my office waiting for good news.

After nearly two days of around-the-clock work, a $100,000 priority shipment of componentry overnight from Sydney, and a hack-team of cybernauts performing microsurgery on our hardware, Dan had the jigsaw finished. Our data was restored, we had a functioning network, and my franchisees were happy and trading again.

It was a near-death experience. I felt shell-shocked for days later, realising how vulnerable the business was when everything that was valuable was encoded in zeros and ones. I agreed to spend whatever it cost to ensure we were never exposed like that again. Dan and I invested the next three weeks reworking the design and architecture of our IT infrastructure. We improved performance, secured faster speeds, and extended our redundancy options to prevent future downtime. I had spent an additional $140,000 on new hardware by the end of that month and, to Dan's credit, we never experienced another tech crisis on that scale again.

IT WAS A shame Dan couldn't do much about the second crisis brewing.

It began with whispers, murmurs of instability lurking within the financial markets. Subprime mortgages, bundled into complex securities, formed the shaky foundation upon which the crisis was built. As housing prices plummeted, and defaults surged, cracks appeared in the façade of economic prosperity.

One fateful morning in September 2008, trillions of dollars of personal investments were wiped out overnight by a stock market crash ignited by the bankruptcy filed by Lehman Brothers in the US. Panic gripped the markets as investors scrambled to salvage what remained of their assets. The GFC became a seismic event.

The provision of credit dried up around the world, and business confidence plunged. The Australian economy, whilst it performed better than most other advanced economies at the time, was still hit hard by the global recession. To hold things together, the Reserve Bank of Australia (RBA) immediately cut interest rates by 100 basis points to 6%, and the Australian government announced it would guarantee all Australian bank deposits – the first time such actions had been taken in Australia's history.

The government shortly thereafter also announced a $10+ billion stimulus package to spike consumer activity, around 1% of our Gross Domestic Product (GDP). Not long after that, in early 2009, a second stimulus package was released worth $42 billion. Titled the *National Building and Jobs Plan*, the funds were established to stave off rising unemployment, depreciating house prices, and recession panic.

I wasn't going to be able to just fall asleep on the office floor this time and wake up to the crisis magically being over in 41 hours.

The first impact we felt at Back In Motion was the loss of our NSW opportunity. We had been carefully preparing a physiotherapist in the Sutherland shire of Sydney to be our first flagship practice in his state, with mutual hopes he might then take up an Area Development opportunity like that we had secured for Adelaide. Over nine months of due diligence, pre-emptive training, trips there and back, and time spent even hosting his family for a weekend in Melbourne, all of it evaporated in front of me. In one short phone call, the deal was off. The counterparty had no confidence to proceed, given banking glaciers were melting around the world.

I wondered what would be next.

Could patients keep affording treatment? Will we need to make staff redundant? Will franchisees, like Anthony at Hillside, lose his house? Will our charitable projects stop? Will all the time and money Paulina and I have invested into this business for God's sake, dry up and come to naught?

I slumped into my chair and said to nobody in particular: "What good is it to be crowned the Emerging Franchise of the Year if the world collapses around me?"

THE UGLY MIDDLE

2009-2015

*the messy space between the thrill of a
dream and its ultimate fulfilment*

God:

"When you're in over your head, I'll be there with you. When you're in rough waters, you will not go down. When you're between a rock and a hard place, it won't be a dead end... So don't be afraid, I'm with you... Be alert, be present... I'm making a road through the desert, rivers in the Badlands.'

Isaiah 43:2,5,19

THE UGLY MIDDLE

51	aftershock	249
52	philanthro-nomics	254
53	milestones	258
54	the Yolngus	261
55	BackU	263
56	new digs	266
57	live on air	268
58	pint-sized philosophy	273
59	the buy-back	278
60	serious felony	281
61	gullible	285
62	destined to fail	290
63	mistaken identity	295
64	the west goes south	299
65	reality check	304
66	sabbatical	308
67	best-seller	315
68	top gear	321
69	and the winner is…	324
70	her sacrifice	328
71	ONEteam	331
72	room for one more	338
73	location, location, location	342
74	unforgiving servant	346
75	metamorphosis	354
76	foreign affairs	358
77	civil uprising	364

51
aftershock

IN THE TURBULENT wake of the GFC the world teetered on the precipice of economic collapse. Australia, its shores seemingly distant from the epicentre, found herself ensnared in this tumultuous upheaval. Waves of financial devastation crashed upon our nation as businesses shut their doors, a multitude faced the bitter bite of unemployment, and the housing market trembled under the weight of mortgage defaults. Families, once buoyed by prosperity, now grappled with the stark reality of shrinking savings and uncertain futures. A long shadow was cast over the collective psyche of our country that was unaccustomed to this type of instability. Some commentators were prophesying the end of the capitalist system – if not literally, at least as we knew it.

I was momentarily disorientated by the turmoil.

My instinct was to hunker down, stop spending, and try to ride out the financial tempest. The alternative, of course, was to courageously stretch ourselves into new opportunities, and pursue any advantage that could be found in the changing times. "Spend money to make money", they say. "*Offence* is the best form of *defence*."

I chose to back myself.

To pull through the economic downturn, in early January 2009 Back In Motion spent hundreds of thousands of dollars that we scarcely had and launched our first ever national marketing campaign. Themed *Feeling Fine in '09*, we deployed a tactical mix of radio advertising, digital marketing strategies, point of sale materials, direct mail and email to targeted demographics, and we published a refreshed website with a range of new services that were designed, and priced, to appeal to the middle band of everyday consumers. Every month that year we rolled out a different promotional offer against the backdrop of coordinated activities in each state to harness the group's collective presence, and hopefully drive more interest toward the local practices.

I didn't leave anything to chance and, fortunately, our calculated bold risk paid off. Group revenues soared during some of the toughest economic months our country had faced in my lifetime, growing over 50% from just over $6 million in 2008 to past $9 million in 2009. We continued to launch numerous new practices in Victoria and South Australia throughout this period, not at all discouraged by the cautious prevailing sentiment.

Such was our growth in this period, we were listed in the BRW *Top 5 Fast Franchise* list for a second consecutive year.

GROSS REVENUES ONLY told part of the story. Whilst the group continued an exciting upward trajectory, some individual practices struggled to make payroll during the leanest months, random supplier bills went unpaid, and franchisees weren't always able to take an income for themselves.

I needed to give more support.

With real-world ICU experience from our hospital context, Paulina and I decided to launch our own Intensive Care Program during the challenging times of the GFC, delivering a tailored approach to helping franchisees who found themselves in hard times. For those who needed it, we upped the site visits by our business coaches, conducted internal deep dives into performance blockages, put them on payment plans for their royalties, and advocated with financiers on their behalf to ease cashflow strain.

As a franchise organisation, we innately recognised that our chain was only as strong as the weakest link, and the brand grew better when everyone within it flourished. Our ethos favoured transparency and candour over keeping up appearances. We encouraged the team to share their distress early, so we could work out a proactive strategy together.

This renewed attention to our business model led to the refinement and upgrading of our franchise system. After months of examining the needs of our practices, I revised and republished our original operations manual – a comprehensive thousand-page document with new insights into the optimisation of our practice performance.

Our scrutiny also resulted in upgrading the online toolbox with an expanded array of forms and tools, bolstering the clinical protocols that governed our service model. We released new IT manuals, practice fit-out guides, site selection criteria, staff induction handbooks, and even created a suite of new industrial instruments approved by Fair Work Australia. This included individual workplace agreement templates, collective bargaining agreements, and common law employment contracts to suit the different corporate structures each local franchise employed. We compiled and distributed these materials to everyone as quickly as we finished them, adding more support than ever before.

One of the most important interventions at the time was the introduction of our Accelerate Internship and Graduate Program. As a services-based business, Back In Motion depended heavily on a supply of new, skilled physiotherapists every year to accommodate the fast-paced organic growth most sites were experiencing. A critical benefit our national brand offered franchisees was access to motivated and enthusiastic final year physiotherapy students from all Australian universities to join our expanding and highly respected health group.

The Accelerate Internship was an innovative mentoring program for physiotherapy students in their penultimate year of their study, equipping them to be more work-ready for their first employers. This internship segued into our Accelerate Graduate Program, a highly supportive initiative for physiotherapy graduates entering the workforce for the first time. Aimed at fostering excellence in clinical and professional development, our Accelerate graduates were offered a salaried three-month induction with formal clinical mentorship and enrolment in the fully subsidised Iceberg Leadership Development Program.

It's hard to quantify the direct impact these initiatives had on our ability to successfully navigate the GFC, but our workforce doubled in each of the next two consecutive years, compounding the burgundy army of physiotherapists proudly representing our brand. A ready pipeline of promising new clinical talent has been one of the hallmarks of our ongoing success since then.

THE STRAIN WE all felt during these months of uncertainty reinforced the truism taught by Greg Nathan, one of the foremost international experts on people issues in franchising. Author of the bestseller, *Profitable Partnerships,* and a business psychologist, Greg drilled into me that franchising is a partnership; it needs to be win:win!

Whilst our Practice Directors were in business *for* themselves, they were not *by* themselves. My primary role was to keep them united, motivated, supported, and encouraged. Our group's survival relied on the smallest, youngest, weakest and most troubled team member pulling through. This was the spirit of *our* partnership.

Greg outlines the six emotional stages that franchisees go through during their business journey. This became a favoured module I taught all new franchisees on their first day of training, and was especially tested during times of crisis.

Denoted the *Glee-Fee-Me-Free-See-We* continuum, franchisees typically paid their initial franchise fee with *glee* as they expected all their problems to be solved after they became part of our established brand. Soon after though, the high costs distracted their attention. As the royalties added up, they wondered if the value they were receiving was a fair exchange for the *fees* they were paying. By the time they slipped into the *Me* and *Free* stages, they had convinced themselves that all the success they enjoyed was a result of *their* hard work alone, and they didn't need to be part of the franchise anymore. The imposed restrictions, compliance, and rules we placed on them only served to frustrate and annoy them, and their minds drifted toward breaking ranks. The uptick in mood didn't return until the *See* and *We* stages, when the partnership dynamic was resurrected by both parties. People recognised, at this point, that the real secret relied on both the systems and support services made available by the franchisor, combined with their sweat equity and grunt work. Franchisees, who made it through the whole cycle, ended up accepting that working together was a stronger business model than risking isolation, and typically become an enduring and successful member of the team.

I always found it interesting to note that it wasn't just the franchisees who went on this journey. The whole NSO team – me included – bounced along the same emotional path as a wayward yo-yo, reacting at times in very negative ways to the new franchisees joining us. There were multiple times where we wanted to release people early because we feared they were the wrong fit, high maintenance, ungrateful, or simply unintelligent. But time seemed to resolve most premature judgements, and a return to the commitment of partnership underpinned our longevity.

The crash of 2008 was a cautionary tale of the price of hubris in the pursuit of wealth. As the dust settled on the GFC, the world emerged irrevocably changed. Lessons were learned, regulations tightened, and economies rebuilt; but the human cost was immeasurable, leaving scars that would linger for years to come. It was because of this – and our commitment to culture and partnership – that I was so grateful we stuck together as a team. We were undoubtedly stronger in a network, no matter how many times people tried to pull us apart.

52
philanthro-nomics

DESPITE THE GLOBAL economic crisis – or because of it – Paulina and I agreed to double down on our charitable activities in 2008. If we were about to lose everything, we were going down swinging for the things that mattered most to us. We rationalised that if we didn't step up now, when people needed us most, then when would we?

Having recently shifted all our group's tax and compliance work from our loyal but overworked solo accountant to a mid-tier firm, our new advisors immediately set about restructuring our organisation to protect any financial downsides that might be exposed during the GFC, and to enhance our ability to give to meaningful causes.

Subsequently, we established the SOS Health Foundation (SOS) – a non-profit public benevolent institution – with Paulina and I as the founding members.

Whilst we operated the charity under the auspices of the Back In Motion Health Group, law and best practice required SOS to have its own legal governance structure. This formal registration meant we enjoyed the benefits of income tax exemptions and the coveted status of becoming a Deductible Gift Recipient (DGR) – all amounting to the trappings of a formal charity that demanded far more complexity on my part than first expected.

The inspiration for the name was obviously a wordplay on the international signal of extreme distress (which traditionally was used by ships at sea, but related closely to what many individuals were feeling during the GFC in their personal lives). The acronym conveniently carried the dual meaning of *Success Or Significance*, providing a cryptic reference to the Halftime message I had been so hugely impacted by some five years earlier. I openly embraced our namesake, purposefully infusing it with a provocative challenge for those receptive to it: *Will you strive solely for personal success, or dare to pursue something far grander?*

The sentiment caught on.

Across our Group, the franchisees and staff began to ponder and repeat the question. Accepting our mission behind the business was to help those in need, SOS became synonymous with the idea of working for the good of others, for lasting significance and impact. With time, I was able to mobilise hundreds of practitioners, from both within and outside our group, into a virtual medical missionary force-for-change, adding to our credibility and deepening our collective impact.

THE BROAD OBJECTIVES of SOS were to create a long-term difference in the lives of those less fortunate. We wanted to harvest the fruits of our growing *success* – increased financial reserves, learning experiences, skills diversity, and availability – and find creative and meaningful ways to support those in need with long lasting effects. *Significance*, as we defined it, came from the way we built relationships with people, the encouragement we offered, the food we gave, the shelters we built, the children we educated, the money we donated, the training and health services we delivered, and through the kindness we showed.

In addition to supporting at-risk children through SCKC, and subsidising financial and medical needs for staff and their families with our internal HELP Crisis Support Program, we invested into a mix of other social initiatives and varied communities.

SOS sponsored the services of more than 20 physios around-the-clock for a continuous 24-hour period to provide injury support to participants who were pushing their physical limits to raise money for the Oxfam Trailwalker – a mission to end the injustice of poverty and advocate for a fairer world. I went bald more than once to fund blood cancer research as part of the World's Greatest Shave, and the men of our group grew a wide variety of obscene facial hair during Movember to raise money and awareness for mental health and suicide prevention. We got behind the Uniting Care Pancake Day every year, made lunches for the homeless at Ozanam House, operated pro bono pop-up physio clinics in partnership with the Salvation Army, and reflexively jumped in as needed when natural disasters hit, like the Black Saturday bushfires of 2009, ravaging more than a million acres of native forest.

Things escalated quickly. Leading SOS could have easily displaced all my work at Back In Motion, but instead became a *second* full-time job. Desperate to keep up, I enlisted the efforts of a small team to further the work of the foundation. Extending the reach of our efforts into every practice, I nominated SOS Advocates in every local team to identify the right opportunities, ring the bell, and recruit local volunteers. Before the first year was complete, I had 19 volunteer regional leaders.

Our most significant campaign – which was to become an annual marque theme – was dubbed *Work4Significance* (W4S) and was modelled on the likes of the Red Nose Day and other iconic appeals. On a nominated day in September 2009, 100% of every dollar spent by clients in more than 40 Back In Motion practices across Australia was donated to our first outreach mission; providing medical and allied health support to disadvantaged Indigenous communities in Arnhem Land and surrounding remote areas. Practices were issued promotional kits, branded t-shirts, coin tins, and information packs for clients to learn more about the causes we supported. Every September, from that year onwards, our typical burgundy practices turned *Papa Smurf Blue* as Back In Motion faithfuls got behind the SOS Health Foundation.

Our first attempt raised over $47,000 in direct donations and pledges through over 200 franchisees and staff who forfeited all or part of a day's salary toward W4S. Our people clearly heard the heart of our mission, and were all in.

LATER THAT YEAR, I combined a short family holiday with some business development opportunities in Perth. Our trip also conveniently coincided with the FCA's annual gala event, making it three birds with one stone.

Swimming in the hotel pool with the kids, I realised far too late that I had missed the opening of the award's black-tie function. Arriving to the big occasion shamefully tardy, I settled at a table in the far back nook of the dark room with people I barely knew. I was almost ready to get up and leave, when I heard my name announced for an award. For most of the long walk from the obscure corner of the room, amidst the crowd's rapturous applause and the roving lights of the stage master, I had no idea what I had just won.

Despite not seeking any recognition for what SOS had achieved in our short tenure, the Back In Motion Health Group was jointly awarded the 2009 Franchisor Social Responsibility Award. We shared the honour with Baker's Delight for their support of the Breast Cancer Network, who over nine consecutive years raised an accumulative $3.7 million in cash and donated an estimated $143 million in bread to charities. I couldn't see the comparison.

I was speechless at the microphone, having been completely surprised by the acknowledgement. I quickly gathered my thoughts and recounted an abbreviated version of my quarter-life crisis, leading to what motivated our group to be significant in the lives of others, before the clapping resumed.

I didn't even sit down after I exited the stage. I walked past all the tables, engaging in a few congratulatory handshakes and a hug from one or two I knew, right through the rear doors of the reception hall, out into the humid night air, and straight to my rental car. I drove the thirty minutes back to the hotel, still stunned by what had happened, but eager to share the news with Paulina. This was as much her award as anyone else's – probably, more so.

When I finally reached my room, the lights were out and everyone was asleep. I slipped into bed without disturbing the kids or announcing our win. I simply placed the trophy and award certificate on Paulina's bedside table, pleased that she'd wake to the deserving surprise in the morning.

53
milestones

BUILDING ON OUR momentum from one celebration to the next, shortly after returning from Perth, Paulina and I marked our tenth wedding anniversary at our favourite holiday destination in the remote islands of Fiji. When I returned from this brief escape, it was time to crank up the Back In Motion engine again.

Most businesses tend to follow a pattern of growth, plateau (or consolidation), and then notional decline, unless fresh innovation and motivation spurs further growth again. I watched this pattern repeat itself in numerous examples around me, like clothes in a tumble dryer.

At this time the mean age of our workforce across the entire network was only 32 years – my own age setting something of a glass ceiling on the demographic of staff I could attract. Nonetheless, our staff survey in 2009 rated us an 8.34, 8.36, and 8.23 out of 10 for staff culture, clinical service delivery, and credible leadership, respectively. Just under 92% of the workforce felt their role was valued and acknowledged, with 68% anticipating a career promotion within the next 12 months.

Practice Directors ranked the three most valuable services we offered at the NSO being national and local marketing, HR/recruitment services, and business development coaching. And we scored an impressive 8.9 out of 10 on the Net Promoter Score in response to the question whether franchisees would recommend others joining our group.

It was clear we certainly hadn't plateaued yet, but the rate of Back In Motion's growth was beginning to slow after our heady years of steep success. And because I had conditioned myself to expect ever-increasing performance, no matter how unrealistic the textbooks and common sense cautioned me, I became worried when I couldn't see it continuing.

WITH NEWLY MINTED executives comprising a full team at the NSO, and with the confidence of our franchisees, I immediately added more practices in the field.

In July 2009, I launched our first Western Australian location in a picturesque northern coastal suburb, four new franchises in Victoria, and four more to the growing cohort in South Australia. Significantly, I also signed our first practice in Queensland, welcoming an existing team of physiotherapists on the Gold Coast into the fold after the local owner had completed one of my four-day Iceberg Leadership Programs.

If all this new growth wasn't enough, I also relocated a handful of existing practices to new sites with upgraded facilities and larger space. One of my favourite strategies to leap-frog local market share was to acquire, and then consolidate, two or more nearby practices into a single flagship location to bolster our foothold in the adjacent community.

As our practices carved out their niche for sports and spinal injuries, it seemed obvious to spin off our corporate health business into a specialty sub brand. Actif® Workplace Health was born in this same frantic year, officially launching at the Safety In Action trade show at the Melbourne Exhibition Centre, where incidentally, we won *Best Stand* amongst an array of blue-chip sponsors.

Actif boldly occupied its own competitive brand space, and presented a compelling commercial proposition for employers to subscribe to our onsite workplace solutions. The workflow increased over 300% that year through various industrial contracts, and was primed to expand its reach into the new states Back In Motion had recently forged into.

I definitely wasn't allowing myself to be talked into any "plateau" or "consolidation"; the only conversations I was interested in were about "innovation" and "growth".

OUR SECOND DIRECTOR'S conference – themed *Loyalty, the Final Frontier* – took place on the crest of this wave of new opportunities. Our success afforded us a significantly upgraded experience from the humble event we hosted the year prior at La Porchetta.

I brought on seven corporate sponsors, partially subsidising the four-day residential event at The Grange Cleveland Winery in regional Victoria. The program featured guest author Mark Dobson, and a specialist customer loyalty consultant who unpacked the four-dimensional attributes of loyalty in the context of our teams, clients, franchisees and families. We offered high ropes and obstacle courses, and our own version of the Amazing Race, stretching our minds and deepening our friendships. Forty-three delegates attended and, to better accommodate the expanded participation, we even catered for the 14 children belonging to our franchisees with a lively and creative kids' program including clowns, craft and physical games.

Underscoring the occasion, I took a moment to celebrate Back In Motion's tenth birthday – finally reaching double figures. A decade had passed, almost to the day, since Paulina and I crookedly hung our embarrassing bile-green sign of an American gridiron player over freshly painted cement sheeting, converting our single carport into our first consulting room. By almost any standard you cared to measure, our foray into business had been a success.

By Christmas we confidently boasted Australia's largest physiotherapy footprint, spread over four key states, despite losing NSW because of the GFC disruption. Across our network, we delivered nearly 190,000 consultations in that year alone, averaging 428 patients a day. Our biggest driver of new clients was the holy grail of word-of-mouth referrals from loyal customers. In an industry hugely reliant on low-fee-paying compensable schemes - such as Workcover, Veterans Affairs, and the Transport Accident Commission - I was ecstatic that 68% percent of our revenue was privately funded through the discretionary payments of individual consumers. We boasted one of the most progressive remuneration models in the industry for our well-deserving team, and had achieved full endorsement of our collective employment agreement by Fair Work Australia. I had even completed one of the first scaled accreditation processes within the physiotherapy private sector, adding to our credibility and professionalism.

There was so much to love about the year that everyone else predicted to be end of the world.

54
the Yolngus

SPONSORED BY THE SOS Health Foundation, in February 2010 I led a team of seven Back In Motion staff on our first official outreach mission. We touched down in Nhulunbuy, the front door to ancient Arnhem Land of the Northern Territory; there to support the work of Mission Aviation Fellowship (MAF) in the township of Yirrkala and the remote community of Gapuwiyak.

Nhulunbuy sits at the northeastern tip of Australia's Gove Peninsula. The land has been the home of the Yolngu Aboriginal people for thousands of years. In 1963, the Australian Government excised part of the land for a bauxite mine and alumina refinery, which was strongly opposed by the Yolngus. To serve the mine, the town of Nhulunbuy (Gove) was established, housing the workers and their families employed there. All this industrialisation led to a disruptive, and at times destructive, interface between the white man and local first peoples. Social and political unrest has continued to this day, manifesting in challenges with housing, education, employment, preservation of culture, and delivery of healthcare, to name just a few.

Arnhem Land is a hot, humid, and remote area, defined by rugged coastlines, rocky escarpments, rivers, swamps, and waterfalls – roughly twice the size of Switzerland, and bigger than Hungary, Portugal and Austria combined. Unpaved roads and long distances between the communities make land travel a dangerous, time-consuming, and arduous task. During the wet season these roads flood, becoming impassable for months at a time. MAF flights enable passengers to overcome these barriers and help them reach their destination safely and efficiently; and connect otherwise inaccessible communities to the mainland.

MAF has been operating in Arnhem Land since 1973 at the invitation of the Church Missionary Society and the Methodist Overseas

Mission. In the early days, MAF was the only airline serving the widespread, remote homeland and Aboriginal communities in the area, primarily facilitating health and education services. They have earned the appreciation, trust and respect of the Indigenous Yolngu people, and are a welcomed part of their community.

Our week in Nhulunbuy felt longer than seven days, with the incessant 36-degree heat, 93% humidity, and red-staining dust. The only entertainment in town was an IGA supermarket and public swimming pool. They did have a surf club, but it wasn't much use – there was no surf and, even if there had been, the crocodiles on the water's fringe dissuaded you from going in.

But the place and the people were unforgettable for all the right reasons. We made ourselves available for whatever help the local community needed; painting houses, building decks, clearing rubbish, demolishing derelict shelters, treating locals who suffered from chronic, neglected injuries and lifestyle diseases, teaching health awareness in local schools, organising sport and games with the Aboriginal children, and giving preventative health education to teachers and parents. Our evenings were spent debriefing with the team on what we had seen and experienced, many feeling personally confronted by the exposure.

Our Back In Motion team went to Nhulunbuy with the expectation of helping others; but just as with my first trip to Cambodia all those years ago, they left admitting to themselves they had each been more impacted by those they went to serve.

For the next decade, right through to the eve of the COVID-19 pandemic, we sent at least one team every year, sometimes more, to Arnhem Land to work with the Yolngu people. We flew in women's health specialists, hand therapists, orthopaedic and neurological surgeons, dieticians, occupational therapists, podiatrists, and hundreds of physiotherapists to serve where they were needed most. And the work was meaningful – for both those we visited, and those who went.

It seemed I could call myself a medical missionary afterall. As God had foretold, if I built a noble business that produced ethical profits and scaled nationally, then it would serve as an economic engine to send many more people than just Paulina and me.

His promise and our dream were being realised.

55
BackU

A CASCADE OF good news kept flowing, seamlessly weaving its way into our 2010 Annual Report.

Whilst the year just completed was to be remembered by some for other reasons – the FIFA World Cup in South Africa, the Deepwater Horizon oil spill in the Gulf of Mexico, the Haiti earthquake, the release of the first-generation iPad, the election of the first African American president in the US and, closer to home, the horrific Black Saturday bushfires in Victoria – for us, it was another year of unexpected excessive growth.

The Health and Community Services Sector in Australia enjoyed an optimistic performance of 3% growth in 2010 but, by contrast, we catapulted with a 45% explosion in revenue. With group sales surpassing $13 million, our growth trajectory surged even more sharply than the preceding year. There were no surprises when we made the BRW *Top 10 Fast Franchise* list for the third consecutive year.

Actif was smashing it, too – adding Inghams, Bluescope Steel, Tip Top Bakeries, DHL, Volgren and KR Castlemaine to their stable of blue-chip clients. Such was my confidence in our model that I kept rolling out new practices with fervour in all states.

Ensuring hubris (especially my own) did not become our undoing, the NSO hosted a special one-day Directors Retreat themed around *sticking to fundamentals* and *getting back to basics*. Despite our runaway success, I didn't want people distracted with bright and shiny opportunities, and neglect the core of our business model. We drilled the franchisees on financial analysis, budget planning, staff optimisation, and customer service. We reinforced over and again the importance of clinical best practice and evidence-based care. And I never let them think one member of the group was more important than the whole; we were stronger because we remained united and aligned.

One franchisee, who studied his Key Performance Indicators (KPIs) and applied what we were teaching, managed to increase his monthly turnover from $28,000 to $87,000 within five months of our Director's Retreat – a staggering 309% growth!

Michael, still my personal mentor and chair of the SAB, was especially determined to drive more retail sales through our practices. Having sat on other boards where products were a big contributor to the revenue mix, he was frustrated every month to learn that Back In Motion averaged only between 1 to 2%. It became a personal mission for him to turn this around.

What Michael didn't know was, retail sales was a massive lost opportunity right across our sector. Physiotherapists had a natural aversion to selling ice packs, anti-inflammatory creams, and ankle braces. It was like the entire profession suffered a missing strand of DNA carrying the gene for commercial common sense. They simply felt it was beneath them to peddle products, and preferred to refer patients to the local chemist, forfeiting the mutual benefits to staff and patients of a full-service experience. In doing so, the client suffered the inconvenience of another stop on the way home, paid inflated shop prices, and often got the wrong advice from a junior retail assistant.

Following Michael's impassioned advocacy, and my subsequent agitation of the issue with the GAP, I led a new initiative dubbed *Retail10%*. My objective was to teach ethical sales processes to our support and clinical staff to achieve a five-to-ten-fold increase in our retail revenue, such that it made up at least 10% of our total sales. It was *Mission Impossible*, if anyone chose to accept it.

Astonishingly, with almost no effort other than some basic awareness training, we halved that gap in our first year by achieving an average of 5.5% retail sales. Some practices exceeded double figures almost immediately, demonstrating that the barrier was unlikely a training issue, and mostly a function of attitude and motivation.

As it turned out, the first 5% of increased sales was the low-hanging fruit, and it took many years to progressively crawl to, and exceed, the 10% threshold; but Michael was ecstatic when we finally got there.

The Operations and Training teams were not to be outdone with some of these innovations and new initiatives. Success in the top line made us wary of the bottom line. Whilst we had various induction programs and detailed manuals to train our new franchisees and their staff, we lacked a highly coordinated immersion in the culture, experience, expectations, and growth strategies of our group. Growing frustrations from both the field and NSO eventually spurred us to initiate a full-week, residential Back In Motion Franchise University – or *BackU* for short.

The five-day event featured different presenters on key topics, starting with a history lesson from me that always turned to vision-casting. We then adeptly maneuvered the new franchisees through every pivotal facet that propelled our business model, delving into marketing strategies, cost management, team leadership, hiring practices, technological advances, and clinical protocols. They engaged with each of our key executives, tapping into their specialised domains of expertise and responsibility, discovering our "11 herbs and spices" to shore up their hopeful success.

The final day of BackU always consisted of in-practice observations and experience, where the new franchisees walked through a full operational fit out, spent time at reception processing payments using our custom software, and observed an experienced therapist delivering our proprietary Free Initial Assessment and full Results4Life presentation in real time with a live patient. Further to this, we facilitated an opportunity for all newcomers to interview an exemplary franchisee, hoping to set a clear standard to model themselves on in the years to come.

By ushering new franchisees through BackU every few months, and ensuring their alignment with our foundational success model, I hoped there were few barriers that prevented us from continuing to shatter industry expectations year after year. After all, records were made to be broken.

56
new digs

AS MY MANAGEMENT team grew, we no longer fitted comfortably in our upstairs NSO office, despite having taken the adjoining tenancy a year beforehand. After considering our options, I eventually secured a ten-year lease at a small industrial park in Mulgrave, optimistically filling 600 square metres of abandoned showroom space (up from our previous 180 square metres in Boronia).

Matthew, my Fit Out and Supply Manager, was commissioned the task of rallying our trades – from interior designer, draughtsman, builders, cabinet makers, and signwriters – to transfer their knowledge of our practice fit out and find a suitable expression for our new NSO. It was intended to be our *forever home* – as I couldn't imagine ever growing out of it – so I set a healthy budget for its completion.

The result was fantastic, but the process nearly killed me.

Matthew failed at just about every deliverable of the agreed project plan; he ran late on deadlines, went well over budget, and well below expectations. Dan and I had to rescue the project on more than one occasion, and I personally chose to oversee the final six weeks of construction and handover to avoid our team being homeless when our former lease expired. Sadly, Matthew only enjoyed two weeks in the new premises before I released him to a "new adventure" better suited to his strengths.

We moved into our fully refurbished, state-of-the-art NSO in July 2010, celebrating our housewarming with more than 120 guests. We were joined by executives from the APA, key university lecturers, representatives of our supplier network, franchisees and staff, and a healthy presence of close friends and family. I offered a public acknowledgement to God for His faithfulness in our lives and business, as Paulina and I cut the red ribbon that spanned the front double doors into our reception.

I had appointed the new offices with a Google-esq flair, as was the fashion then, providing table tennis, a Wii games console, and dartboard in a small open plan lounge area off the training room – all designed to stimulate staff creativity and increase productivity. (I think the jury is still deliberating whether this approach is effective.) Guests wandered through the new 60-seat training room, swanky boardroom, multiple glass-partitioned private meeting rooms, and possibly wondered why I had commissioned so many workstations in the bullpen – a capacity for 38 people in total. At times, I wondered myself whether I had bitten off more than I could chew.

The inauguration of our new office symbolised a shift into a new era; a launchpad for yet another phase of growth and expansion that I was praying for and expecting. We had blitzed our way through the GFC, thrown off the limitations of our old NSO office and mindset, and I had onboarded a new robust posse of ambitious franchisees who were hungry to further our brand across the country. It seemed like the next summit beckoned us.

Regrettably, with time, I came to understand the pitfalls of my blind optimism and naïve assumptions. Just as some trees grow too swiftly, unable to bear the weight of their abundant yield, so too can certain businesses buckle under the load of their lofty dreams and achievements. Our roots were surely to be tested; just not quite yet. A storm was brewing beyond the horizon and still out of sight; the clouds building, but not yet ready to roll in and rain down on my happy parade.

57
live on air

DESPITE SOME NATURAL disasters plaguing our nation at the time, including devasting floods in Queensland and Victoria, the mood of Australians was relatively buoyant in early 2011. The mining and resources sector gave us all reason for great optimism for the future, surging ahead with double digit growth, and more than compensating for the sluggishness our country felt in retail during the aftershocks of the GFC. This contrast birthed the well-publicised "two-speed economy" Australia became famous for; Back In Motion fortunate enough to be experiencing the thrills of full throttle.

We closed the 2011 fiscal year with nearly $19 million in group revenue, representing an overall growth of 46% over the previous year. We inducted more than a hundred new staff nationally as we stocked up with new graduates and experienced clinicians for the further growth I anticipated in coming months.

Humorously, even the size and spectacle of our Christmas parties were gathering epic status and earning a reputation in the industry at large. It wasn't just that we put on amazing food with live music in funky venues for over 300 people – although that was mostly unheard of in physiotherapy circles – it was our annual video competition that really got the tongues wagging.

Practices spent weeks leading up to these end-of-year extravaganzas; planning, scripting, filming, and then submitting team videos – of humorous parodies and questionable antics – to the official NSO judging panel. The winner in 2011 was a franchisee who, shaving his head for the occasion, donned a black fishnet singlet and mimed Right Said Fred's 2007 original mix, *I'm too sexy*. As I stood in the audience next to our chairman's wife, I didn't know whether to cover my eyes in embarrassment or applaud enthusiastically for the flawless performance. I was relieved to see Marion thoroughly enjoying the innocent mayhem, albeit in future years some videos became so risqué I was compelled to ban the amateur film festival.

It was our marketing team who began to take the risks I wanted to see more of. We launched a service guarantee with every clinical treatment, promising that if patients were not thrilled with their experience, we would refund their fees and offer their next treatment free. Despite widespread fear and resistance throughout the workforce that this was going to be Jason's last decision before the business went bust – expecting my irrational policy would bring every franchisee to their knees – the gambit attracted an avalanche of newfound confidence with our patients. As a result, we welcomed hundreds of thousands of new consultations through the front doors of more than 40 locations that year, and only received five reported redemptions of the guarantee I had promised.

It didn't stop there.

Following our prior year foray into advertising on Melbourne's most popular Christian radio station, our marketing lead decided we were ready for television. Our debut appearance aired on the popular entertainment talk show, *The Circle*. We commissioned three professionally written television infomercials to promote clinical Pilates, custom orthotics produced through an innovative 3D technology, and our unique management of headaches. I was the face of the brand in each episode, although ably supported by three franchisees to demonstrate our therapeutic techniques. Our advertisements ran 32 times for 96 minutes in total across both Melbourne and Adelaide daytime audiences – our two biggest markets at the time.

At the risk of never recovering my dignity, you can still download these clips on YouTube. If you bother to search for an episode, make sure you view the one where television presenter Pat Panetta interviews me on the topic of foot pain. He is almost literally twice my size, a thin giant of a man, emphasising my below-average height. I resemble a clean-shaven hobbit in bare feet as I demonstrate use of our gait analysis technology. I'm not sure how many new patient referrals we generated from the television campaign, but the entire team enjoyed value-for-money in the entertainment of the reruns they kept playing in the office at my expense.

Despite being the punchline of some very funny jokes shared by peers in the industry because of my amateur television debut, Back In

Motion was formally announced again as an envied member of the BRW's *Fastest Growing Franchise* for a fourth consecutive year. People started to think we owned this publication. Few franchised brands could boast the speed and scale of our success, and we took every opportunity to promote the good news.

The APA commissioned me to host a series of leadership lectures to their membership in most states of Australia. As I toured the capital cities to present these lectures, I shamelessly carried with me bundles of copies of the BRW magazine to give away, each one with a custom printed special jacket screaming the headline *Four Years Running*. Inside the cover, the bold and provocative question that awaited every reader was: *Who said franchising wouldn't work in physiotherapy?* We showed evidence of now 55 locations, established in less than seven years, consistently outperforming industry benchmarks. I offered a money-back guarantee to any would-be franchisee who joined our group and didn't experience the same high-level results, demonstrating supreme confidence in my model. I was even kitted out with a promotional DVD and copies of my recently published book for interested parties; and with a pitch like this, I had plenty of takers.

IT WASN'T JUST Back In Motion enjoying fantastic success. The Iceberg Leadership Program was demanding more of my time. I hosted no less than nine separate four-day leadership weekends throughout the year, after having abandoned the less convenient format of the 12-month program that catered only to those living in Melbourne. Eventually, plumbers, accountants, and executives from completely unrelated sectors, paid to join my program because word of mouth spread, and clearly there was a hunger for mentorship.

Similar popularity followed our SOS Health Foundation. I was constantly asked to speak about our initiatives to colleagues across the industry, with the number of expressions of interest from people willing to volunteer in our programs starting to create a *demand* problem. My workload became so overwhelming with growth on all fronts that I was starting to drop some of my spinning plates. Paulina and I agreed we needed to employ someone to help administrate the foundation. Lynda joined the team and immediately took responsibility for the various programs we had on foot, including our local activities with Ozanam House, our internal HELP Crisis Support program, and the very important outreach missions in Arnhem Land that were gathering more steam.

Given our early foothold in serving the Indigenous communities of Nhulunbuy, I was introduced to Cathy Freeman. Ranked then as the ninth-fasted woman of all time, Cathy had won gold for Australia in the women's 400 metres track at the Sydney 2000 Summer Olympics – at which she also lit the Olympic flame – and was (maybe, still is) considered one of the world's most inspiring athletes.

Cathy was softly-spoken about the objectives of her eponymous charity established in 2007 to support First Nations children and their families – initially launched on Palm Island, and now more broadly operating through Queensland. She aimed for more people to recognise the power of education in achieving their dreams, providing positive relatable role models to encourage students to stay in school. Cathy wondered aloud whether SOS could partner with her, providing much-needed healthcare solutions alongside their school sponsorship programs.

I didn't know anything about the sordid history of Palm Island until I returned home and researched it.

The Aboriginal Shire of Palm Island was home to the Bwgcolman people – meaning "one people from many groups". They lived amongst an archipelago of fifteen islands with a population then of less than 2,000 people. Estimates vary, but the number of tribal groups represented by the descendants was at least 43, converging up to 57 different languages. From 1914 to 1971, Palm Island was a penal settlement for unwanted Indigenous people, some 5,000 forcibly removed from Queensland, the Torres Strait, and the Melanesian Islands.

Palm Island became known for riots, violence, and outbreaks of diseases. In 1937, it became a medical clearing station where Aboriginal people were sent for sexually transmitted diseases and admission to one of the few leprosariums still operating.

Housing shortages on the island were a serious problem, with up to 15 people living in three-bedroom dongles. Unemployment ran at unprecedented levels of 92%. The local Catholic church floundered amidst this hardship, with one priest and three nuns feeling well out of their depth. The few government services located on the island were vastly insufficient to meet the education, health, and social demands of the inter-tribal community.

Cathy asked me for help, and I didn't know where to start. But in mid-2011, I led a small team for three nights to scout the community on Palm Island, meet the locals, liaise with other service providers, and assess the possibilities. Immediately, I fell in love with the Bwgcolman people and appreciated the great need.

Everyone on the trip agreed these people deserved more. And so began our decade-long commitment to the cause of Palm Island, sending Fly-In-Fly-Out (FIFO) healthcare teams multiple times a year, and eventually establishing a permanent pro bono practice on the island.

I COULD ONLY fund our growing charitable initiatives by expanding Back In Motion.

Fortunately, we enjoyed the Midas touch in South Australia during our first two years there. Adelaide has always been a parochial town with an inferiority complex, and it was clear the local profession was responding more positively to one of their own in a leadership capacity. Jared was my point man in the role of Area Developer, and I rode shotgun. He softened up his list of prospects, and then I would fly over for the dog-and-pony show – giving formal presentations, casting the vision, answering questions from well-meaning loved ones, and placating overpaid, cautious advisors. It was an effective strategy, and one that landed us top quality people, eventually on-boarding eight new franchises.

I was grateful; every new practice meant at least one more mission trip in the future.

58
pint-sized philosophy

WE MADE BIRTHDAYS a major celebration in our household. Designing special occasions for each of our children at certain milestones, every year played host to continuing a beautiful tradition that we all looked forward to.

For example, when each of the kids turned four, I invited them on their first solo camping trip. And then at seven, I also arranged a weekend with them at the beach in Queensland. At ten years, Paulina planned a full schedule of special events in the city, culturing them with live theatre, fancy restaurants, and a two-night stay in an elegant hotel. When they reached thirteen, Paulina took them on a mission trip into regional Australia or a developing community overseas. And at fifteen years, I planned to take them on a business trip to see what happened behind the curtain of the brand they heard so much about at the dinner table most nights.

Things don't always go as planned.

The weekend I took four-year-old Lachlan away for his first camping experience, it rained non-stop, leading to a series of laughable mishaps. I left him standing in the boot of our SUV, dry and comfortable, while I hurriedly tried to set up the tent in the torrential downpour and ink darkness of the Cathedral Ranges. It took longer than I expected, and sadly for Lachlan, longer than he could hold his bladder. I couldn't hear his cries for help over the noise of the rain, and when I finally went to collect and carry him to the tent door, he was wet through, as were our sleeping bags, the cornflakes box sitting on top of the food container, and the upholstery of my car.

Things didn't improve after that. I couldn't get a fire started because the ground and kindling were so wet. I resorted to toasting marshmallows for my son inside the tent by matchstick, despite the obvious risk of naked flames setting alight the highly combustible nylon fabric of the fly-over. When we did venture out of the tent to go for a walk through the soaking bush and play *pirates*, he tripped and fell face-first in the mud, rendering his last pair of clean clothes unusable. And it was almost impossible to cook, given the inclement weather. Accepting defeat, I chose to pack up early on the final day, buy fish and chips at a nearby township, and sing the hit songs of Veggie Tales for an hour with him on the drive home until Lachlan was sound asleep.

The trip seemed to me a failure on every level, but as time has passed, the rich memories haven't. The whole family regularly enjoys the hilarious side of those experiences – and many others like them – teaching me not to take *success* so seriously at home or work.

To reinforce the same lesson, at the beginning of 2011 – just as I was launching more practices in South Australia and balancing my little available time coordinating mission trips to Palm Island – Lachlan turned seven. It was time for the long-awaited boys' trip to the Gold Coast for a weekend of age-appropriate frivolity. I planned jet-boat rides, water parks, mini-golf, and a five-hour lock-in at Timezone, intentionally scheduled to extend well past his usual bedtime for added appeal. Nothing would derail us; that is, until we attempted to check-in our fold-up push scooters aboard Tiger Airways at Melbourne airport. This proved a problem, as the crew would not allow us to take them as carry-on luggage. Following unsuccessful negotiations, I paid a small fortune for each of the scooters to be stored in oversized baggage, costing more than our tickets and, I dare say, more than the value of the scooters themselves. At my encouragement, Lachlan pledged to write an angry letter to the CEO of the budget airline for taking advantage of a young boy's vulnerability when no published terms or conditions precluded fold-up scooters as permittable carry-on items.

True to my previous point, we have laughed for hours over this debacle, quite apart from Lachlan learning to appreciate the fine print in any transaction.

It was a rare opportunity that weekend with Lachlan to thoroughly disconnect from all my work pressures for an entire 48 hours. Back In Motion was a possessive force, all-consuming if I let it; my highly tuned work ethic made finding the *off* button extremely difficult. If I wasn't careful, office emails and legal deadlines jealously stole every ounce of my energy, robbing my wife and children of the husband and father they needed, and risking the greatest adventure of all – the joy of a family that God had placed me in to love, protect, and belong.

Paulina and I agreed these weekends were an investment into our children, but like every mission trip I've ever participated in, I came away with much more than I gave. My children were like peewee professors, or pint-sized philosophers, teaching me lessons through laughter, and giving me insights from the sandbox. Wearily unpacking my suitcase after each of these trips, I couldn't suppress my excitement for the next one that followed.

Painfully, with a penchant for calamity, the trip to the Gold Coast with my seven-year-old second-born was punctuated by me fracturing my coccyx in a water slide accident. I spent the next four weeks sitting on donut pillows or lying on my side, as direct weightbearing felt like squatting on a cactus. (Beads of sweat are forming on my forehead now as I recount this story, evidence of the mild PTSD I suffer from the embarrassing episode!) Sebastian, however, thought it uproarious mayhem.

My point again; I slowly learned to laugh at every setback, misfortune, blunder and disaster. Disappointment hurts at the time (there are few things as sensitive as a displaced tailbone), but the lessons are plentiful. The most important of all: if we keep the right company through the difficult times, we can enjoy a depth of intimacy with the people we love the most.

My family equipped me every day in expected and surprising ways to face my responsibilities at work. Paulina and I started Back In Motion, but we quickly realised that, with children, it was a shared experience. We were all carried to the dizzying heights and nauseous depths of the waves that rolled through the business and, inevitably, into our home, spilling onto the loungeroom floor and across the kitchen table regardless of the breakwaters we tried to erect. I'm grateful now, more than I could appreciate then, that God placed me with the right family to endure the calling to lead our business. It has always been, without doubt, a team sport; and my wife and children make up the key players.

FROM THE MOMENT I touched down at Melbourne's Tullamarine airport, returning from a weekend with Lachlan, my resolve was tested. As I turned my phone back on, an avalanche of work swamped me. I was immediately swept up into a six-week whirlwind of frenetic decisions, threatening to distract me from the recent precious moments I'd just shared with my son.

A new franchise owner took over the Seaford practice, and we relocated it to an impressive new facility in Carrum Downs. I sold my practice at Blackburn South to an emerging franchisee. A team member at our Bayswater location peeled off to start his own franchise at Bentleigh. I sold partial equity in Actif to two investors to shore up further interstate representation in South Australia and Queensland. I even launched a new sub brand specific to aged care, called Revita®, demanding countless hours from a crowded team. These were just a few of the matters that preoccupied me on the Monday morning back at my desk.

By March, I hosted another National Directors Conference as the merry-go-round kept gathering speed year-on-year. Now in its fourth appearance, it was the most anticipated event on the Back In Motion calendar. The week-long function took more than six months of planning and a dedicated sub-team to coordinate every detail. Hundreds of creative ideas were discussed, debated, and fought over, to ensure each new experience topped the last, so we could exceed the expectations of our delegates.

Our 2011 conference intentionally provoked the conservative and cautious mindsets typical of health professionals. I headlined with the theme of *Valiance*, affirming the brave, courageous, and bold few who were prepared to stand up and be counted in an otherwise mediocre landscape of industry-wide peers. It was a dramatic battle cry to rally the fearless risk takers who were unwilling to accept the average, the status quo, or the meagre outcomes of an otherwise impotent and disillusioned profession.

Hosted in picturesque Lorne, Victoria, at the beginning of the world-renowned Great Ocean Road, I inspired the franchisees to become the most progressive and ambitious team of practice owners our country had ever seen. We wanted them not only equipped, but willing, to charge forward and usher in an entirely new season of change and opportunity for our group.

It was the best week of professional development and collegial networking I had ever experienced. Our invited speakers included Olympic swimmer and sports commentator Linley Frame, author and speaker Mark McKeon, and our board chairman, Michael. The adventurous team-building activities - such as paintball, surfing, and waterfall hiking - accentuated our push to be anything but ordinary.

Most memorably that weekend, our gala event in the 200-seat ocean-view room had one simple rule: *no* costume, *no* entrance. People were asked to dress as someone they admired for their boldness. The tables were filled with superheroes and noble characters from history, making for an evening of animated storytelling and dramatic speeches. But it was Simon who garnered the most attention. Dressed in a skin-tight lycra Spiderman suit that left nothing to the imagination, every body part that is normally hidden by modest dress was on full display for everyone to see. That image was burned into my memory forever.

From the lessons my children unknowingly taught me when I played alongside them, to the wisdom and many new experiences I was learning from the intelligent and ambitious colleagues in our network, I reflected throughout the evening on my greatest discovery that year: as we are often taught, courage is not the absence of fear, it is the willingness to proceed despite it.

As Back In Motion began to transition into the ugly middle of adolescence, it was clear I needed new measures of resolve and conviction to overcome the mounting opposition that awaited.

59
the buy-back

PROBLEMS FIRST BEGAN in late 2010 when the burden of his growing network in South Australia pushed at the seams of Jared's capacity – both time and finances. With two large businesses of his own to manage, and a large cohort of needy franchisees sprouting around him, the demands became overwhelming.

Despite earning over 200% return in franchise sign-on fees and accumulative state royalties inside the first 24 months, Jared was barely profitable in his own locations. Caught in a tortuous dilemma, Jared found himself torn between the conflicting demands of his role as the Area Developer, and the imperative to sustain solvency within his own franchises.

Over time, more and more people echoed compounding frustrations: inadequate support; disorganisation; and personal conflicts of interest. They believed Jared was favouring his own practices with the pick of new staff from centralised recruitment campaigns, and taking a disproportionate share of group patient referrals. Regardless of whether these accusations were true, frustrated franchisees, who didn't trust Jared anymore, came to rely on the Melbourne-based NSO team for direct help. As this worrisome habit cemented, Jared became increasingly irrelevant to the network in Adelaide, and animosity grew between all parties in the complex love triangle.

This created a big problem for me: I couldn't afford to add more staff in the NSO to manage the extra workload, because Jared received half of the state royalties under his exclusive contract.

Intending to preserve Jared, I invited him to brainstorm with me every possibility moving forward. Regrettably, our progress was limited. Jared believed the criticisms of his underperformance were unfair, and that my General Manager had a hidden agenda to oust him from the group. It sounded like a paranoid conspiracy theory to me, as Jared was, undeniably, a cultural pillar amongst our senior franchisees, and it didn't serve anybody's interests to lose him.

Breaking the deadlock, I put a choice to Jared: resume supporting his local state network as he was contracted and paid a generous sum to do, or sell back his half of the royalty so we could hire substitute staff to deliver the on-ground support. I secretly hoped Jared would go for the first option, as otherwise I faced the same time and financial constraints with filling the support vacuum as he had encountered. Alas, selling back his Area Development rights seemed more agreeable to Jared, except for one thing: my upper price limit was little more than half of his demand.

I went to Christmas with a heavy heart over an unsolved problem, and the risk of a broken relationship with one of my closest allies in the business.

2012 OPENED WITH a letter from Jared's advisors, urging a face-to-face meeting in Adelaide to settle the matter.

Based on an independent market valuation of the master licence, the most I was prepared to offer Jared was an approximate mid-point between our two respective opening gambits. The catch: my offer was subject to securing necessary finance, as I was not flush with cash after our big spending spree during the months post GFC. All my available money was heavily absorbed in network growth, software development, brand promotion, the growing NSO payroll, and now – because of this dispute – unaccustomed legal costs. I was going to have to borrow money to buy my way out of the jam.

Somewhere amidst attending Lachlan's first day at school, Sebastian's first day at kindergarten, and making a dozen other critical decisions demanded of me elsewhere in the business, I finalised the paperwork with Jared in March 2012 to liberate the state of South Australia. With my back against the wall on what I could afford, Jared reluctantly accepted two tranches of payment: three-quarters on settlement and the balance six months ex post facto. I sweetened the pot by offering to relinquish my quarter equity stake in a jointly owned franchise, thereby keeping all our interests separate and bringing this interminable matter to a close.

It was a promising end to a painful experience, forever etched in my memory. I deeply valued Jared's friendship, and regretted the stain it left on our record. For years, I wondered what I could have done differently, and remain baffled by the few choices available to me then. I thought contracts were for life; at least, that's how I entered them. Untying the intricate legal knots left me emotionally drained as each unravelling thread revealed the weight of a complicated relationship.

In a mere span of three years, an unsettling reality emerged: once rock-solid agreements were beginning to wobble, with one now crumbled into dissolution. This sparked new tremors that rippled beneath the bedrock of my commitments with others. Tectonic plates shifted, ever so slightly. The erosion of trust with Jared signalled a disquieting possibility – that similar fractures could surface with others, casting doubt on the reliability and unity of our group.

Jared was not a malicious person who we excised from the group. On the contrary, I was pleased he remained a franchisee for another ten years, successfully selling his two flagship practices for millions of dollars. Even as the ink dried on the deeds of sale that won me back exclusivity over South Australia, I was planning at next year's Director's Conference to honour Jared with the inaugural *Pioneer's Award* to reiterate his enormous contribution during our formative years.

As it happened, with opportunities elsewhere in new states – and even new countries – I never really circled back to South Australia to intentionally grow the network further. New franchisees came and went, and some new locations popped up and closed. But, for the most part, the core group that stood to the end – succeeding through more than a decade in Adelaide – were mostly the same people that Jared and I prospected together in those first years of a healthy partnership. Their performance and endurance stand as a fitting legacy for what Jared and I achieved together, even if we couldn't make it last.

60
serious felony

PAULINA TRIED REGULARLY to impress upon me a simple lesson that should have been self-evident by this stage of my career: answering the work phone on holidays is a bad idea. I should have known better and let the inbound call go straight to voicemail that balmy summer afternoon in January 2011.

I didn't.

"Are you sitting down?" cautioned the sombre tone on the other end.

"Yes, on the sand, with my kids, having fun. Please don't ruin that!" I responded sarcastically, knowing full well my plea would be ignored.

"I don't know how to say this..." they hesitated.

The next sentence shattered all the serenity of our Christmas holiday, like the knock of a small hammer atop a fragile disco ball, fracturing the sphere into a thousand tiny reflective pieces.

Police had apprehended one of our physiotherapists for sexual crimes.

BD, an Indian only recently registered to practice in Australia, was at the centre of the allegations. Completely unaware of his existence, the first I knew of this man was on the day of his arrest, as I sat in wet board-shorts building sandcastles with the kids on the foreshore. It was reported to me that he had inappropriately performed an unwarranted invasive vaginal examination on a female patient, causing extreme physical trauma.

The arresting officer from Adelaide CIB refused to speak with anyone other than the employing franchisee or me – and I was the only one in the country at the time!

The seriousness and sensitivity of a situation like this are beyond any preparation. It hit me like an abrupt plunge into icy water, leaving me gasping for air, my breaths shallow and inward. As I hung up the phone, all I could muster was a silent scream as Paulina tried to interpret my contorted facial gestures.

BETWEEN BRIEFING INSURERS, reporting to the APA and our registration board, and responding to police enquiries, the next 24 hours was hectic. In some ways, there was no time for my detached feelings to catch up with the frenetic pace a disaster likes this sets in motion.

BD had been escorted from the practice in handcuffs in front of a waiting room full of patients and staff watching on in disbelief. He was then released on bail the next day on the conditions that he surrender his passport and make no contact with the victim. On police direction, I immediately terminated BD, pending the outcome of his investigation.

Our franchisee in charge had been warmly adopted into our group a few years earlier as our beloved *grandfather*. At 65 years of age, he was a conservative, gentle man, short in stature but engaging and big-hearted. The news hit him like a sledgehammer at a time when he was visiting his children in Cairo that summer. He was utterly distraught. In tandem, we facilitated counselling services to the team and patients who were directly impacted by the situation, and made allowances to load-balance the needs of other patients with the limited staff available.

The most unnatural thing to do was remain distant from the patient who suffered the most. Despite all inclinations to reach out in support to the victim and her family – someone who was well known personally to our franchisee – we reluctantly heeded police instructions not to do so. Our lawyer was quick to add that if we were to contact them, we would be *obstructing justice* and likely charged with civil, if not criminal, liabilities. Our team did everything we could for everyone else, knowing we were powerless to help the most aggrieved person of all.

Presuming the physio grapevine had raced ahead of me, I penned a memo to our franchisees about the complexities. It seemed insincere to reassure people when I lacked any certainty of my own – and yet this is often demanded of those in leadership positions during such unenviable times.

BD's court date was initially set for late November, but eventually got pushed out nearly 18 months to July of 2012. That was a long time for everyone to wait, especially the victim. Understandably, given the sensitive nature of the charge, the patient gave her testimony via CCTV from a secure and safe location to avoid having to face the crowded room. The exact details of her testimony were kept private from the media and the public, but her account was harrowing for the rest of us to digest.

Day two of court proceedings opened with the replay of a lengthy interview recorded by police where BD tried to give legitimate medical rationale for his actions. His summary defence was that he was trying to determine if any of his patient's neck pain stemmed from pelvic floor tightness or soreness, and that he had gained verbal consent from the patient to proceed. Expert witness evidence by a Fellow of the Australian College of Physiotherapy destroyed the veracity of this feeble assertion. He testified without ambivalence that such technique would never be necessary, or advised, given the clinical circumstances.

The trial was a distressing experience for everyone involved, and I can only imagine how painful it was for our patient to re-live her horror over those three days. The judge found in favour of the prosecution, and ruled BD guilty of rape. Sentencing was deferred to December.

Later that afternoon, a sudden sense of grief swept over me like a colossal wave rising from nowhere. I was ashamed that this unspeakable offense was perpetrated under our brand, bearing a deep personal responsibility for the resulting verdict. A turbulent mix of emotions surged within – regret, fear, and disgrace – as if caught in a tumultuous storm of conscience. On hearing the news, Paulina too was momentarily breathless, both of us grappling with the weighty responsibility we carried. My medical oath echoes in my mind to this day – it's solemn commitment to *do no harm* – yet the suffering this lady endured was amongst the gravest harms imaginable.

I commissioned a full team to scour every policy and procedure to ensure our standards of care and compliance would prevent a repeat occurrence. Of course, our fateful conclusion was, with a network our size, we couldn't legislate "common sense" and "moral judgement". I sat with the uncomfortable realisation there was no future proofing against people who were irrational, or worse, had malicious intent.

The story broke in two second-tier news outlets the day of final judgement, both regionally and nationally. A television crew captured footage of BD leaving the courthouse, but nothing aired during the prime-time news slot later that evening.

For two years, our patient endured the agonising wait for the formalities of the charges to be settled, and for sentencing to be concluded. I wince at the thought of her never fully recovering from the compounded trauma. Her patience and strength during this time was remarkable. Long after the ordeal, we remained intent on doing all we could to support her and the family in recovering from the strain and impact. We offered help in lots of ways, always attempting to strike the right balance of sensitivity, given the negative association we presumed she would have with anything to do with our practice. Despite her suffering, she maintained a strong relationship with our franchisee for years to follow.

I was fast realising that the world of franchising was fertile ground for every conceivable mishap and tragedy – many of which were outside my control and yet could bring our business to its knees. Surprisingly, despite the seriousness of the charge, neither our franchisee, the local practice, or even our national brand was brought into disrepute through any of the court's formal proceedings. Obviously, we couldn't control the errant tendencies for some predictable people – notably, our mischievous competitors – to catastrophise the event and spread distasteful innuendo. But after their distorted facts, sensationalised mistruths, and cruel inferences did the short rounds within the industry, the story lost its sting, and had little effect on the people who really mattered. Most of all, our distraught patient.

61
gullible

SHELBY IS ONE name I will never forget. Ironically, it wasn't even his *real* name. It was obvious to me then that his story would inevitably make for an interesting chapter in someone's book – regrettably, it now features in mine.

Nearing the end of the first quarter of the calendar year of 2010, I lost one of my favourite senior physiotherapists. Paul, a gentle soul with loose blond curls and piercing blue eyes resembling a striking doppelganger of Justin Timberlake, suffered a series of setbacks, including a prolapsed disc in his lumbar spine that resulted in his necessary resignation to self-rehabilitate. I reluctantly searched for his replacement.

By March, I found Shelby – who at first presented as a worthy substitute for Paul, but soon proved to be the complete antithesis.

Shelby was a UK citizen with a compelling resume, who immediately set about completing all his induction procedures, participating in our leadership forums, and reorganising his new team with defined strategy. I received monthly reports from the executives that his early effort and decisions were positive, building confidence in those around him.

Seven months later, Shelby applied for a minority stake in one of the franchises I owned outright. He was funnelled through the same process as everyone else, completing our 30-page application, undergoing psychometric analysis, and sitting through rigorous interviews with our recruitment team designed to sort the wheat from the chaff. The final hoops to jump through were the finance, credit, and police checks to ensure no unpleasant surprises. Somehow, he ran the full gauntlet of tests without raising any alarm.

Furthermore, Shelby endeared people to himself. Such as when he promised to organise his childhood friend Jamie Oliver – the famous

Naked Chef – to speak at our conference, who apparently was filming a television show in Perth at coincidentally the same time of our planned arrival. I was ecstatic to have the renowned British restauranteur and cookbook author headline our event, and proudly announced to the group his highly anticipated guest appearance. In a magnanimous personal gesture, Shelby even promised a signed cookbook from Jamie, for which I had ghost written a personal inscription specifically for Paulina: *Jason tells me you always put your boys first and yourself last – including in the kitchen! Here's something just for you!*

I was utterly impatient for the day when I could eventually show Paulina this exquisitely unique gift, all made possible by our newest *favourite* franchisee.

THE FIRST SIGN of caution arose in late November of 2010, like a small grey cloud far off on the horizon, appearing deceitfully unthreatening. Shelby missed the payment date for his franchise deposit. He explained that he had various bank accounts and trust funds locked up in the UK that he was trying to access, lamenting that red tape and foreign exchange complications might take another month or two. It seemed completely plausible, and so I agreed to commence his franchise term in good faith.

That was my first misstep.

What should have been the beginning of a wonderful partnership like with most other newcomers to our group, quickly turned into the ghost train from Hades. In the following months, Shelby went missing-in-action for days at a time, routine compliance reports weren't completed, and money in the practice cash register rarely balanced at the end of each day's taking. A long list of other troublesome patterns started to build. For three consecutive months, NSO staff independently reported anomalies in the accounts of the practice, along with further questionable activity, that ultimately couldn't be ignored.

When I first confronted Shelby about these irregularities, he immediately gushed a waterfall of tears onto our boardroom table, confiding in me his recent diagnosis of a serious pituitary tumour that required urgent specialist attention. In an artful turnaround of the initial purpose for our meeting, he appealed for special leave to fly to Sydney for a week of medical treatments and begged for a short-term loan from the company to pay the gap on his insurance coverage. Overcome with sympathy and compassion, I didn't hesitate. He had my blessing for whatever he asked, and I chastised my management team for doubting his integrity.

Misstep number two.

During Shelby's subsequent absence, my finance team presented me the real-time bank accounts of the practice. The transaction listings were peppered with cash withdrawals and private purchases for expensive shoes, designer clothing, five-star hotel bookings, and tickets to the Gay Mardi Gras in Sydney.

All compassion quickly evaporated.

On Shelby's return to work, I presented him with irrefutable evidence of his unauthorised spending. He broke down *again*. He admitted to taking money from the business, as his grandmother was ill and needed help that he couldn't afford. Shelby said he had used the company account for private outlays in Sydney because he had left his personal credit card at the hotel, and fully intended on repaying every cent. And he explained that whilst he attended the Mardi Gras, it was between hospital visits for chemotherapy, and was grateful for the distraction.

It was as though Shelby had anticipated my legitimate concerns and arrived prepared with well-considered, sincere defences. He had documented his entire saga in explicit bullet-points in a pre-emptive four-page statutory declaration, notorised by a Justice of the Peace, sitting conspicuously on the table between us.

Intermittently weeping as I confronted his indiscretions, Shelby escalated the conversation by threatening to kill himself if circumstances got any tougher for him. Paralysed by the apparent fragility of the man, I absorbed his soap-opera of heartbreak, and felt drawn to his need.

Despite warnings from Paulina and others that Shelby should not be trusted, I believed him. His emotion was raw, his sincerity was compelling, and his pain was palpable. "Nobody would make all this up" I defended. He was just the *unluckiest* franchisee I had ever met.

I have now lost count of my missteps.

In a follow-up conversation later that week, Shelby tripled down on the misery of his plight. He disclosed that he had been savagely beaten and violently raped by seven men in a nightclub in Spain several years earlier. His recovery took more than nine months and several surgeries before being discharged from hospital. A criminal case proceeded against the perpetrators and, because of the personal risk Shelby felt in giving his testimony, he had been provided an alias under the European witness protection program. Rather than choosing to go home to the

UK, where he felt ashamed and embarrassed by what had happened, he made Australia the place for new beginnings.

When Paulina questioned the elaborate overreach of Shelby's stories, I defended his claims with the compelling evidence contained in the two thick folders he provided; medical reports and detailed surgical procedures, legal transcripts of court proceedings, victim impact statements, and witness testimonies. I even sighted a letter signed by the Honourable Julia Gillard, 27th prime minister of Australia, advocating on his behalf to the Immigration Minister to fast-track his confidential and safe passage to Australia on grounds of special circumstances.

The complex interlude became more circuitous when Shelby confided his civil partnership with new husband Frankie was becoming dangerously untenable. Behind closed doors, Frankie allegedly beat him, and had been doing so for over a year. Shelby complained that his husband controlled their bank accounts, and was unwilling to let Shelby access what he needed for medical treatment or other personal needs.

It was a downward spiralling catastrophe, a twisted tale of pain and despair. Shelby needed rescuing before suicide masqueraded as his only way of relief. He and I were both in tears one afternoon in the boardroom at the hopelessness of his situation.

Paulina grew increasingly agitated at home, convinced Shelby was lying. Our management team were divided along lines of trust and believability. Most intuited his complicated episode to be odious fiction – the whole sordid saga an obvious scam – but a few of us remained steadfast.

I swallowed the hook, line, and sinker – and most of the rod, right up to the reel.

Leading the way with embarrassing credulity, utterly spellbound by the seriousness of events and emotionally suspended in Shelby's obvious grief, I was willing to do whatever I could to help Shelby. For my troubles, I earned a PhD in naïvete and gullibility.

GIVEN THE SEVERITY of Shelby's claims, I was compelled to involve the police. This led to an internal investigation of emails, phone calls, practice records, software audits, and bank accounts. I liaised with overseas authorities, the Australian immigration department, hospitals and numerous other parties to triangulate the truth, verify timelines, and fact-check details.

I even met with Frankie – the accused husband-basher – and his mother, both for the first time, who were shocked to hear of the accusations against him. Shelby had apparently walked out of their lives over four months prior without a word, and all their attempts to contact him since had failed. Frankie was doing all he could to move on with his life after being abandoned so suddenly after their recent marriage.

By August 2011, Shelby was a ghost. His only legacy was a pile of six unpaid invoices for psychology consultations I had referred him to in desperation.

All findings confirmed the same thing: Paulina was right; I was profoundly wrong. Shelby was a professional fraudster.

I discovered in his aftermath that he had unlawfully obtained thousands of dollars via unauthorised refunds using our credit card machine, channelling the money through undiscernible small amounts onto his personal credit card. He had stolen a large sum in cash from daily receipts. His personal spend on the company credit card for clothing totalled another hefty deficit. He had defrauded health insurers by illegitimately claiming insurance rebates for bogus consultations that I had to eventually make good on. He filed purchase orders for new medical equipment worth nearly $30,000 but, instead of paying our suppliers, pocketed the money (maintaining the ruse that "the cheque was in the mail", hoping he could keep deferring inevitable consequences). And he owed me more than $160,000 in unpaid franchise fees, training costs, and share purchases.

The financial hole was so deep and wide that I could barely see the bottom of it, and teetered dangerously close to falling headlong into it myself.

Shelby's deft art of deception enabled him to mislead and subsequently evade the Department of Immigration for the entirety of his employment with us, as we later found his work visas and primary identification were all false.

To summarise – in case you haven't been able to keep up with this epic telenovela – there was no tumour, presumably no gang rape, no ministerial intervention, no sick grandmother, and no abusive husband. Shelby never paid his debts, Julia Gillard's signature wasn't authentic, and the police never located him.

And of course, Paulina never received a signed copy of Jamie Oliver's cookbook with my heartfelt inscription – I had to buy one of those for her myself.

62
destined to fail

I KNOW I'M an optimist. No matter how many times I've been shown that rose-coloured glasses tint reality, I look for the upsides in every possibility – the previous chapter a classic case in point.

I did it again with Penny.

Having previously launched a small home-based practice, and recognised as a 2008 Finalist for the Telstra Business Awards, Penny was passionate, resilient, and seemed a perfect fit for Back In Motion. After toying with the idea for nearly half a year, she triumphantly secured a franchise licence in the middle of 2010, for me only to watch all our meticulously crafted plans disintegrate in front of us.

A dire crisis erupted in Penny's household not long after signing. Literally mid-way through one of her BackU training sessions, I watched her face turn a pale green as she visibly shook from the inbound text message she received. Later that day, she confided in me something not even her boys, parents, or friends were aware of: her marriage was over. This threatened everything – her faith, personal identity, and financial security. And having just announced her welcome to the group, Penny was talking about exit strategies.

Despite being incredibly capable in her own right, Penny worried the demands of the franchise might push her and the children past their limit. I agreed, making immediate preparations to unwind the legalities of our newly formed agreement. By the time she had flown home, Penny did an about-face and was determined to proceed. She shared our conviction that Back In Motion was doing such important work to reach and impact people in need, and there were few things more important for her to be involved in. She sensed a personal calling, and asked Paulina and me to trust her in the same way she was putting her confidence in our brand.

What proved most difficult was Penny's request for me to keep the details of her personal challenges confidential from everyone on the team. In hindsight, this was a key factor in our shared undoing, as people did not have context for her situation, and thus did not show sufficient grace or understanding for Penny's eventual shortcomings, seeded by her crisis at home. I should have pushed for appropriate disclosure to protect everyone – especially Penny.

OUR FIT OUT team immediately grabbed the ball and ran for the end zone, adamant Penny's practice needed relocating from home into commercial premises. They were right, but given the recent destabilisation Penny faced, she couldn't be convinced. Regrettably, my team pushed harder than they should have, unaware of the delicate implications. This kept fanning a flame, eventually igniting a fireball of heated disagreements about what renovations were required at home, how much it would all cost, and who was responsible.

With every sharp-barbed phone call and email exchanged, trust and patience diminished on both sides, leaving the newly formed partnership between NSO and Penny, paper thin.

Early one morning, I caught a red-eye flight to meet her at home and mediate a resolution to the escalating challenges. Empathetic to her strained circumstances, but aware our business model and branding required certain imperatives, I brokered tolerance with all parties for some reasonable compromises. The silver lining during these months of delay was that the practice had grown with new patient referrals and total consultations up two-fold from its best historical month. The new revenue helped buffer some necessary costs.

Tensions continued to escalate as practice fit out and technology integrations stalled month after month. In desperation, I gestured Penny an unprecedented option that my NSO team kicked against strongly: suspend all interventions for three months. I sanctioned the "go slow" to help Penny focus on her health, and that of her family, while we backed away from enforcing any obligations under the franchise agreement. I promised nobody would chase or pressure her regarding fit out, branding, or other transitions, until she had found some stability in her chaotic world.

Grateful for the reprieve, and seemingly better for it, by mid-October Penny committed to obtaining the necessary finance to resume her fit out and other obligations to fully launch her practice under the Back In Motion brand. We all welcomed the news.

PENNY'S INTENTIONS WERE, once again, thwarted by circumstances outside her control. This time, a serious car accident left her with debilitating spinal injuries. She suffered several fractured vertebrae and was in severe pain for months, unable to work, let alone care for her boys. I visited her in hospital, and could see the unspeakable pressure she felt as a single mother, carrying the financial strain and operational burden of a half-transitioned practice, and now physically incapacitated.

We meandered through Christmas and into the first quarter of 2011 in these unworkable circumstances. With caution, our team picked up Penny's file again in February to push through the second half of her fit out, with expectations to officially launch her under the brand in May – nearly a year after joining. But with prohibitive debt, Penny couldn't raise the necessary finance.

It was a dreaded ritual, but I became accustomed to trawling through long, convoluted, late night emails in which Penny ventilated frustrations against my staff, or her challenges at home. It became increasingly difficult to know how to respond. As I shared the electronic rants with Paulina, she cautioned me to keep some distance. I now fully regretted not abandoning our partnership when the signals of its likely demise first presented. My bullish optimism revealed a soft underbelly of poor commercial judgement that hurt me more than once.

I DROPPED THE hammer in April 2011, attempting to restore order from chaos. It was untenable in a franchised system, that inherently relied on uniformity and alignment, to allow a practice to indefinitely trade unbranded and without a compliant fit out. The situation was creating confusion for staff, clients, referrers and other franchisees. I needed Penny to step up and fulfil her obligations without any further delays, or forfeit the opportunity.

Penny's reply was not hopeful. Although she was grateful for the personal concern I showed, her legal counsel sought special consideration, citing the *Doctrine of Frustration*. An obscure remnant of archaic law, the provision sought to protect a disadvantaged party by rendering a contract (in this case, our franchise agreement) as non-binding when one suffered (or was "frustrated" by) a disaster beyond their control. Our lawyers scoffed at its relevance, but I was sympathetic.

Eager to release Penny from the burdens of her franchise commitments, I couldn't ignore the commercial realities of the hundreds of thousands of dollars in sunk costs; I didn't know how to reconcile the difference. Attempting to strike an equitable balance, I proposed Penny keep the business as an independent brand, and pay down the debts as she was able over the next four or five years on an interest-free basis.

I should have realised this offer would float like a lead balloon. Penny threatened to report her case to a local politician, who had made it his public mission to bring unruly franchisors to his own definition of "overdue justice". Agitating for franchising reform, Penny's story could become an unwanted example cited by the MP through his biased lens. Under the cover of parliamentary privilege, with immunity from legal action for slander, I would not even be afforded a right of reply.

I began imagining the damaging headlines: *Heartless franchisor threatens to bankrupt poor single mother who fell down on hard luck.*

I knew it was my role to advocate for the franchisee, protect the victim, and fight for the underdog. Whenever there were misunderstandings, unmet expectations, confusion in the franchise agreement, or disagreements with suppliers, I tried to absorb the hit, make the concession, roll over, and yield. Maybe the perception was that I could afford to do so. Regardless of our balance sheet, it was evident to me that I could rarely afford *not* to do so – as failing to pick up the financial tab of other people's misfortune seemed to always result in relationship fallout. And *bad* relationships made for *bad* business. So often, I felt caught between the *rock* of being gracious to those in need, and the *hard place* of protecting myself from exploitation and my own financial distress. You could rarely slide a razor blade between how tight that space felt most days.

Regrettably, at times, I held my ground too hard and for too long, unnecessarily extending the longevity of some battles. This was my folly with Penny. The exchange of increasingly terse emails left our rapport in ruin, both of us worn down by the emotions and fatigue of our failed partnership. I felt a constant tug-of-war between empathy for Penny, and sympathy for myself.

It didn't help I was juggling other balls – fighting battles on different fronts with Jared and Shelby; onboarding a raft of new practices interstate; and managing the fast-paced growth of our emerging network in Victoria.

Hope for a mutual compromise progressively crumbled as I inevitably lost interest in what was *right* and *fair*, and conceded to whatever was demanded of me. Caught in a tornado of disorientating disputes that year, I desperately wanted the spinning to stop.

Foregoing an unnecessary stoush on contract technicalities, my lawyer encouraged me in the same manner a father mentors an adolescent son: "Settle with Penny and move on! Save the time, money, and emotional expense of an elongated fight that you will probably win in court, but lose in the public square."

I stopped the bloodletting with a swift cauterising iron, agreeing to accept just a quarter of Penny's debt. Afterward, Penny wrote Paulina and me a heartfelt letter, expressing relief that we didn't pursue our full entitlement. Her words landed softly; the sincere gratitude soothing some of our bruising.

My lesson: discern more quickly how to avoid the wounds in the first place – for everyone's benefit.

63
mistaken identity

UNABLE TO CATCH a break, another battle raged on the western front as I finalised Penny's release from our network. We only had two practices in Perth, soon to be none. Seemingly unrelated to one another in the events that brought them undone, they nonetheless lived parallel and tragic lifecycles.

The trouble started when the Insurance Commission of Western Australia (ICWA) opened an investigation into Back In Motion for fraudulent billing of undelivered services, false travel charges, and unapproved medico-legal reports issued to Workcover. They had apparently been talking with my CFO for months, describing Preston as uncooperative and evasive; they felt no choice but to escalate their concerns to a formal investigation.

All of this was an absolute mystery to me. Preston was characteristically diligent in all matters of compliance and legislation, and hadn't disclosed any warnings to me. Furthermore, he had no motive, even if there were means and opportunity, to take advantage of the compensation payment scheme in WA, as there was no personal benefit to him. Preston emphatically denied any communication with ICWA, let alone wrongdoing.

I was slowly learning that when things didn't add up, to dig a little deeper. Hope for the best, but prepare for the worst. Having been taken for a ride too many times, I was now proud of my wariness and scepticism, however late I started to exercise those survival instincts.

I commissioned a forensic audit of the NSO digital phone system, to trace all inbound and outbound calls to and from the registered ICWA phone number that allegedly occurred over the previous months. It was clear there had been a lot of two-way traffic between parties, but I couldn't find anyone on our side willing to admit to having the conversations. ICWA representatives tipped me off about a particularly incriminating conversation with who they thought was *Preston*, at a specific time and date. Using the time-stamped call logs and the accompanying handset extension number it was easy to determine the meeting room the call was conducted from. A review of our office access records, and meeting room bookings for the day in question, narrowed our likely suspects to Travis and one other; both were stringent in their denials.

The leading ICWA investigator remarked to me some time later that their dealings with *Preston* were often hostile and antagonistic. She admitted, however improper it may have been at the time, "Americans can be so hard to deal with. They are often combative and adversarial".

Americans?

I had my smoking gun.

There was only one American in our group. Clearly, *our* Preston of Asian descent was innocent; and *their* Preston was someone we all knew to be Travis – a franchisee in Western Australia.

On various interstate visits to our office, Travis had been impersonating Preston in a series of communications with ICWA to deflect the heat that was concentrating on him from their internal investigations team. Despite all his clever obfuscation and scapegoating, by December 2010 my sleuthing started to pay off; albeit only revealing the tip of the iceberg.

Unbeknownst to me, prior to him joining Back In Motion, the police had conducted a separate investigation into Travis for charges by the Insurance Commissioner of ICWA for billing services that patients had not attended for. The APA had tried to have Travis de-registered or, at the very least, receive disciplinary action, but there was insufficient evidence to convict him. Travis later confessed he had recently engaged lawyers to also defend a pending unrelated court case regarding claims made against him concerning an unlawful sale of a private property. If that wasn't enough, his property insurer was investigating him for a suspicious fire that had incinerated his family home.

I now had some reasonable explanation for all his other misdemeanours, including being six months late in franchise royalties, behind in his employee's Superannuation Guarantee payments, and defaulting with the landlord for failure to render a bank guarantee. Travis excused his delays with a collection of confusing explanations relating to company structures in the US and myriad hurdles put in front of him by the bank because of his complex property dealings.

It's amazing what you find when you go looking. I was embarrassed to share all this with Paulina for fear of undoing whatever confidence in her I had won by identifying the villain in the first place.

THE BLATANT FRAUD made it untenable to keep Travis in our group.

In the week before Christmas 2010, I met with Travis to offer him a mutual surrender of his franchise licence rather than a formal breach, seeking to wind up our relationship on a civil basis and avoid unnecessary bloodshed. It was a win for me to distance myself from Travis and his unsavoury past, letting the various investigations into his affairs continue without tainting our brand.

Travis and his wife wept through the discussion, oscillating between sadness, regret, and relief. Unfortunately, they chose to settle on belligerent denial and anger; refusing to go quietly. I made clear to Travis the only alternative would be an expensive, protracted legal process that I would not lose, but he couldn't be persuaded.

Our lawyers crafted a masterful ten-page legal letter citing 22 irrefutable breaches with such weighty evidence that any pragmatic defence attorney would concede as a fate accompli. But Travis was no ordinary man; he read the infractions as an invitation to defend himself with colourful explanations, long-winded technical responses and, at times, just plain denials. And so continued the merry-go-round of interminable negotiations for a nauseating four weeks. I feared we might be stuck with him unless we issued formal legal proceedings, and pushed the matter all the way through the courts.

Enduring an unrelenting dispute with someone who is obstinate and aggressive is a formidable challenge. My advisory board prayed often about the cultural and legal challenges we faced during these ugly middle years. Michael and John were convinced that God was "cleaning house" of the bad actors to prepare us for another season of explosive growth. It seemed I had to walk through a series of valleys before we could enjoy another mountaintop.

Month after month, the audacity of Travis' stubbornness made each step excruciating. It felt like navigating a storm in a small boat with a mutineer determined to steer me off course. I was dragged through endless loops of irrational conversations by someone who possibly felt he had nothing more to lose. As I scrambled for truth, Travis' unyielding personality perpetuated an exhausting tug-of-war, a just resolution appearing increasingly impossible.

The matter dragged to April 2011. Then, with unspeakable frustration, Travis suddenly left his family and retreated overseas to an unknown location in the Middle East. No one – not even his wife, allegedly – knew where he had gone. During his absence, the emails didn't stop. He prosecuted and debated by email every jot and tittle of his franchise agreement; death by a thousand cuts.

I don't know if Travis ever returned to Australia. Many of the investigations into his strange and suspicious circumstances were apparently never resolved. I've not seen, talked with, or even heard of him since.

It's a mystery to me what specifically compelled Travis to eventually concede, but the jostling suddenly stopped, and one day in August I received his signed surrender without having to plead my case to a jury.

If God was schooling me in patience and resilience, I might have passed the test, but I certainly didn't top the class. There was no financial upside in the win for me, just relief that I had excised a tumour before metastasising to the core of our culture. And I enjoyed a little win for my heart and sanity – one less battle to fight as I re-centred myself on the business of health to serve those in greatest need.

64
the west goes south

ON THE PERIPHERY of the furore with Penny and Travis emerged the hopeful rise of a West Australian Area Developer, Damian.

An honours graduate, Damian operated various physiotherapy and occupational health businesses over the 20 years prior to coming to Back In Motion. His entrepreneurial tendencies made him well-suited to his more recent role as a small business coach, specifically for fellow health practitioners. He spoke with many of our existing franchisees and, after nine exhausting months of protracted negotiations, Damian joined our group in November 2010. However, he didn't just want a franchise, he wanted to control all of Western Australia.

Learning from my failed attempt in South Australia, I carved out a special clause for Damian's master licence. Rather than granting exclusive geographical territory, I limited his initial rights to six practice licences that, in effect, he could on-sell or sub-licence to other physiotherapists under his own agency. We agreed, if the first tranche went well, we would do more.

Damian's first act as new Area Developer was, understandably, to assign one of the six-pack of licences to his own practice. A well-established business that had been launched more than a decade earlier, Damian employed physiotherapists, chiropractors, massage therapists, podiatrists, and Pilates instructors. He was generating nearly $1million in revenue every year, and was granted one of the highest Preserved Revenue Thresholds (PRTs) in our network – ensuring he only paid royalties on the new growth his practice experienced above the high-water mark of his historical revenue. I accepted all this was in the spirit of fairness, playing the long game, expecting my commercial return to come in time through an enduring and fruitful partnership.

THE NEXT FOUR months were not easy for anyone. Staff bickered and squabbled over just about every integration decision relating to the transition arrangements. Counterparts couldn't agree on signage specifications, fit out plans, staff orientation and training, or even the employment contracts. All I heard were problems in our management meetings, week after week.

Then, in another case of a disappearing franchisee, Damian took off to Borneo for three weeks – in the peak of the chaos when so many key decisions were demanding his attention. My team was livid, seriously questioning Damian's suitability as Area Developer.

Confidence hit a new low in June 2011 when Damian refused to pay marketing and software levies for his practice, arguing he was somehow exempt by his special circumstances. He harboured numerous grievances, much like us, but clearly stemming from entirely different motivations.

Damian then unilaterally cancelled all the trades that we had organised for his fit out and stopped paying our suppliers for the equipment and services he had commissioned. Suffering incurable buyer's remorse, he wrote me a short and poorly punctuated email expressing he had decided to leave the group, wanting a full refund of his costs.

Damian's casual (if not, careless) approach was a slap in the face to everyone who had worked for six months preparing for his launch, and a foolhardy disregard for his weighty legal obligations. A series of candid, but civil, exchanges between the two of us were not promising of a simple and amicable resolution.

The conflict created febrile tensions in the NSO. Chris – my long-suffering solicitor, now feeling sympathetic for the incessant barrage of "bad luck" I was facing – drafted a gentle legal perspective to bring gravity to Damian about what was at stake. It all seemed too little, too late. Another showdown was imminent. Regrettably, I was becoming well-rehearsed for the scenes and acts that were likely to follow in the unfolding drama.

DAMIAN'S PRACTICE GREW a staggering 50% in his first six months with us, his August performance report celebrating a run rate of over $1.5 million in revenue. We hadn't even turned on our marketing machine yet (as the practice was still unbranded), but his training alone in our proprietary system of patient care substantially improved his billable revenue.

I suspect Damian feared that his rapid growth would result in higher royalty costs than he originally anticipated, despite him retaining 96 cents of every dollar we generated together. With a scarcity mindset on full display – anxious there might not be enough to go around – his impulsive withdrawal from the agreed partnership terms set us both on a troublesome trajectory.

Damian complained he did not comprehend the fine print of his franchise agreements when he signed them – despite contemplating them for nine months. Whilst our agreements were unfortunately long to comply with extensive franchising legislation, I strived with my legal team to avoid them being confusing or opaque; I feared unnecessary disputation. In fact, I regularly tested with Chris, that unless a 12-year-old could interpret the correct meaning of each clause from a literal reading, we had to try harder.

Most difficult for me was that my team had already trained Damian's staff in our Results4Life clinical model, and rolled his entire workforce onto our exclusive employment agreements, stamped by the WA Fair Work Commission. Dissolving our partnership was as straight forward as extracting cordial out of the water; it couldn't happen.

With unveiled intimidation, Damian disclosed he had been speaking with "other franchisees" to garner their support for a potential class action against me if I didn't return his money. I was suspicious he was, at least, colluding with Penny and Travis, two sympathisers with their own axes to grind. Despite barely knowing these people, Damian astutely concluded that the enemies of his enemy were in fact, his friends.

Damian also tried to solicit Shelby into his nefarious campaign, hoping his victim story might reveal a pattern of unethical dealings on my part. When the truth about Shelby's identity theft and litany of other sins came to light, Damian quickly distanced himself from that toxic legacy.

Deep within I presumed Damian's threats were a bluff, but my nagging internal voice of doubt and insecurity made me panic-stricken. Chris was convinced that, from a legal perspective, we were beyond reproach; however, the cultural turmoil was far less predictable.

DESPERATE FOR A resolution, I cleared three days in August to fly to Perth and work things out with Damian. Discussions were heated on the Wednesday night; we both postured aggressively with needless threats about whose lawyer was bigger and meaner, and how far the other should roll over and give up. It was a shameful mix of fear and ego talking for both of us. As I walked the long way back to my hotel, I was grateful for the night air to cool my jets.

I barely slept that night. Tossing and turning in an uncomfortable bed thousands of others had found slumber in, I ruminated on our futile dispute, catastrophising the next day.

Rising to pray at 2am – a combination of the three-hour jet lag and relentless anxiety – I sought God for a way forward. He surprised me with His response. Rather than inspiring me with cunning legal strategy or negotiating tactics that would break our gridlock, God revealed my personal failings in the matter. Impatience, carelessness, self-righteousness, hasty judgements, half-truths, exaggerations, lies of omission, misdirection, obfuscation, manipulative language, gossip, anger, selfishness, and pride – an embarrassingly long laundry list. I was wracked with guilt as I counted my shortcomings in the reflection of God's holiness, melting in a puddle of shame. Like a gentle father inviting a son onto his lap for careful correction, God was firm without breaking my spirit. I felt an urgent need to expunge the vengeful instincts raging within me as the famous words of Jesus echoed in my broken heart: "He who is without sin among you, cast the first stone" (John 8:7 NKJV). In the grey hours of that early morning, it took some time to sincerely repent for the dark side that had overtaken me. But as the Sun rose, so did I, with hope of an opportunity to set things right.

I can't be sure, but it's possible Damian had a similar experience that night.

The next day, the mood between us was obviously different; conciliatory, open-minded and solutions focussed. I apologised for how I had spoken to him, and Damian agreed to reset. Neither of us were pushovers as we negotiated balanced terms, but we were determined to find common ground, giving as much as the other was willing to forfeit. When the temperature in the room began to rise on some obnoxious point, one of us would defuse it. If we couldn't resolve a certain matter, we deferred it and moved on, noting to circle back later. To onlookers at the café that day, we may have seemed old friends reminiscing passionate memories, not always in support of the same version of events, but agreeing to disagree.

After eight hours, we had meticulously outlined an acceptable solution.

Back in the boardroom, Michael was more enamoured that I had heard God speak in my hotel room when I was wound up in anxiety and frustration, than he cared for the detail of whatever terms we had reached. Never to be distracted by the loss of money, Michael was confident the business was only the context through which God would continue to shape me into the man He intended me to become. It was the same lesson repeated in different form – *people* matter to God – not winning an argument, making a profit, or building a brand.

Deeds for the dissolution of partnership were drawn and executed on the ominous ten-year anniversary of the 9/11 New York terrorist attacks. Ironically, Damian took off to the US the next day to decompress from the stressful months I had put him through – an escape I pined for also. But the rest of the business wasn't slowing down just because I hit a few speed bumps on the back roads. It needed all my attention, as new practices were launching faster than I could keep up; six steps forwards despite the painful one or two that lurched me backwards.

Four years later, Damian wrote me a sincere email, grateful for the way we resolved our differences. He offered to share a meal together next time I was in Perth. We haven't broken bread yet, but I often reflect how more satisfying it was to bury the hatchet than sharpen the blade for another blow.

65
reality check

I WAS FINALLY coming up for air, feeling the constraints of all the legal battles releasing their grip on me. But not before being yanked back from some unfinished business with Jared.

In the arrangements to release Penny from her franchise agreement, it was acknowledged that the significant financial losses incurred by me as the franchisor would be shared liabilities with Jared, the Area Developer, given his substantial compensation for her initial recruitment. He supported Penny's release and understood in principle that a claw-back of commissions and royalties were likely. It was a tough pill for both of us to swallow.

When the time came for his payment of these monies, I was not surprised that the unwelcomed news triggered a barrage of emails between our lawyers for weeks on end.

Paulina and I seized the opportunity during these unwanted troubles and visited close friends in Thailand. Our connection with them had begun years ago at church, not long after David had assumed ownership of his father's signage business. I swiftly entrusted him with the contract to fabricate and install all our branded signage as we expanded to numerous new locations; and the foundation of a lifelong friendship was formed.

Years later, at the peak of their success, David and his wife felt called by God to leave their business, family, and everything that was familiar to them, and relocate with three pre-school children to Chiang Mai in Thailand. They immersed themselves in the incredible work of rescuing trafficked children from harrowing circumstances with an internationally recognised organisation – offering shelter, education, and vocational guidance to precious little lives – hoping to set them on a new path.

It was a privilege for Paulina and I to escape our daily grind, visit the mission, and regain perspective on what hardship really looked like. We met with rescued children, toured the orphanage, and travelled remotely to see the micro enterprises we were supporting in the villages at risk. We met many generous, compassionate and determined people who served God with every breath, every day. It reminded me to live with the same conviction as I flew home and re-engaged with the business.

I HAD AUTHORISED Chris to resolve the matter with Jared on my behalf during my absence. Sadly, things hadn't gone well; they were at a stalemate. Jared was immoveable, resigning his seat on the GAP, withdrawing all support from SOS, and announcing he was selling his two practices and leaving the group. His wanted to distance himself from Back In Motion and, in particular, me.

Upon my arrival back to the office, I found waiting in my inbox a four-page email from Jared, best characterised as a personal assault than a well-considered legal argument. I was advised by one of the toughest litigators in Melbourne to serve Jared with a notice of dispute, followed by a writ with the full force of the law behind it. He reasoned that if Jared wanted good faith negotiations at that point, I could acquiesce from a position of strength.

I called on the experience of a close friend who had overcome many setbacks in his business. His story was one of incredible hardship, personal faith, and unprecedented success – a likely, albeit inconvenient, combination. In his business adventures he had faced hostile competitors, near bankruptcy more than once, and a count of over forty different court cases – including one landmark case against the Australian Competition and Consumer Commission (ACCC), which he eventually won in the Supreme Court after six years, setting a legal precedent for many to follow.

His warning: "Litigation is an ugly business, crazy expensive, and will take you off your mission."

The gentle urging aligned with the hard-won lessons I had recently been learning about putting people and relationship first.

I talked with Jared and his wife. It was another tough conversation, but to the credit of everyone involved that night, we agreed to a ceasefire. Akin to the near catastrophic nuclear conflict that was averted during the 1962 Cuban Missile Crisis, caution and diplomacy won on the day.

Not only did we resolve perilous tensions that could have reshaped the group as we knew it, but we laid the platform for another decade of rewarding business together. A real victory for both sides.

2010 AND 2011 delivered a perfect storm of unwanted relationship fallout. The buy-back of Jared's South Australian rights, the deceit of Shelby, the heart-wrenching misfortune for Penny, the fraudulent exploits of Travis, and the near miss with Damian.

The result was a hot pot of legal mess, all converging into a chaotic maelstrom, where I spent more time briefing lawyers, and crying myself to sleep, than building a health group I was once passionate to lead. My software analytics revealed I averaged 273 emails per day over that two-year period. I scored above 300 points on the Holmes-Rahe Life Stress Inventory tool, dangerously landing me in the range of likely heart attack or stroke, with 80% chance of a health breakdown within 18 months. The prognosis wasn't good. Paulina and the kids watched from the sidelines, wondering when I would turn up each day, and what shape I would be in when I finally did.

On reflection, I wished I had shown more grace to Penny, and far less to Travis. I wished I had encouraged Jared that his underperformance could be overcome with more support and patience at my end, and not rushed to buy back his exclusive rights. I wished I had allowed Damian to leave when he first wanted, and not draw out the injustice unnecessarily. As for Shelby, so much of his story remains a mystery, I just wished I hadn't been so gullible.

Hindsight, they say, is 20/20 vision. It's easy to see clearly, now.

I felt desperate at times to keep our house of cards standing amidst so much internal strife and pressure. I didn't like who I was becoming or, at least, the painful words some people said about me. My naïvete exposed me, and I could no longer afford to be trusting or optimistic. Hardened from the years of pummelling, I felt myself becoming sceptical and jaded.

I teetered on the brink of civil war for nearly two years on multiple fronts, depleting my adrenal glands of all reserves from the strategic manoeuvres, calculated risks, and tireless efforts. The relentless defence left a residue of exhaustion and doubt in its wake. As the dust settled on each hard-won conquest, the vulnerability of the battle wounds revealed themselves.

I was not well. For a long time I needed to get away. Paulina needed it too. Both of us were exhausted, in part for the same reasons, and in part for completely different ones. We had played the game intensely, ignoring the pain in face of dire costs. But as we stepped off the field, the bumps, knocks, and strikes took their toll. As the catecholamines and neurotransmitters responsible for the adrenaline rush started to evaporate, we felt dangerously fragile. The tax was high.

What I really needed was a break. More than a holiday – I needed personal respite. Despite record growth in revenue that year, I admitted that I had come as far as I wanted, allowing myself to ponder walking away from the business, if that's what God allowed.

Eight days after settling matters with Jared, our family headed abroad for long overdue leave. But not before launching two new practices and some high-value contracts for Revita – in addition to attending board meetings, facilitating Iceberg Leadership programs, and travelling across the country to build our interstate teams. It was unsustainable madness.

The plane, scheduled for Buenos Aires, left behind a year I tried to forget.

66

sabbatical

IT HAD BEEN possibly 11 years in the making, and at least five years since our last visit. Paulina and I were eager to reconnect with her abeulito and cousins to explore South America. Only two of our three children had ever visited Chile previously, and neither could remember it. We were set for a great adventure together.

The first six weeks on the road were difficult for four-year-old Morgan. He tore his anterior cruciate ligament (ACL) in his left knee just before our departure, courtesy of a treacherous double-bounce on the trampoline, perfectly synchronised by his two lively older brothers. My shoulders throbbed from bearing Morgan on my back as I carried him everywhere, because he was either too sore or too slow to keep up with the pace.

Over three months we embarked on 13 flights, four boat rides, two trains, multiple buses, countless colectivos and taxis, and even one horse-and-cart. We covered expansive territory from the east coast of Brazil, across the sugar-coated Andes, to the west coast of Chile; from the Peruvian peaks of Cuzco to the southern reaches of Patagonia. We sand-boarded in the lunar landscapes of the Atacama Desert, and licked icebergs in the glacial wonderland of Laguna San Rafael. We feasted on churrascarias, parrilladas, brigadeiros, feijoadas, alfajores, and empañadas with shameless unrestraint.

Our children were more travelled in their first decade of life than I was by my late twenties. So used to visiting other cultures and hearing different languages, many months afterwards when we passed through Adelaide airport, Sebastian wondered aloud what language they spoke in the latest exotic *country* he was visiting – innocently offering "Adelaidian" as one possibility.

Argentina was the first leg of our amazing journey, and proved an ideal haven for our weary spirits to touch down and rejuvenate. Paulina and I were so fatigued – from years of raising children, building a business, and obvious jet lag – that we slept 18 hours on the first night, waking at 3pm the following day to the sound of hotel housecleaning. Paulina was disappointed in herself for not honouring her travel dictum of never letting jet lag interrupt the normal daily routine, as ruled by the clock of your destination location.

The main attraction our three boys were set on was a live game of professional football (soccer). We managed to source expensive tourist-tickets to watch Bocca play River Plate at their home ground. We arrived with a hotel chaperone to absolute mayhem surrounding the stadium. Passing three different security checks, surrounded by armoured vehicles and hordes of police in full riot gear, the cacophony of sounds scared all of us, not just the children.

As we sat in the stands, our seats pulsed with energy at the roar of the crowds when their teams appeared on the pitch. Somehow, it reached even higher decibels when the first goal was scored. Seated beneath the flight path of the nearby international airport, I marvelled how many planes silently traversed the sky above without as much as a faint drone – completely outmatched by the roar of the passionate Argentinian soccer tragics. Five-metre-high cyclone fencing separated the fans from opposing teams to avoid milieus, so often characterised by the hooligans of the game. The whole spectacle was a delight, as the memories of Back In Motion faded into obscurity.

OUR NEXT STOP was Paulina's hometown of Suzano, just outside of Sao Paulo. We visited the hospital where she was born, tracing the roots of her story. We also strolled through the corridors of the primary school where Paulina spent her formative years until the age of ten, triggering a flood of cherished memories for her, and some first-time experiences for us.

One of the highlights of Brazil was meeting with the volunteers we supported through the international aid organisation, Compassion. We shared a meal with 40 of the children who lived in favelas – the crime-ridden and poverty-stricken slums – creating a sharp contrast for our own boys, who had only known the luxuries of suburban, middle-class Australia. That memory was conveniently pinned for future reference, often drawing on it to remind ourselves how fortunate we are whenever tempted to think otherwise.

We then drove nine hours north along the east coast of Brazil. Twice, I confused myself on the wrong side of the road because of careless lapses in concentration. I got lost and had to stop four different people for directions. Working from an itinerary that was far too tight, we arrived 30 minutes late for the last ferry of the day to take us to Ilha Grande.

Paulina loved the chaos and drama, and pretended she was a contestant on the reality television show, *The Amazing Race*. I was not as imaginative. So desperate were we to make that ferry that I drove the car right onto the pier and unloaded all five large suitcases into a nearby golf cart that we commandeered from the local security patrol. I handed the keys of my rental vehicle to a local car park attendant and asked him to store it for me. We didn't sign anything, get names or identification of any sort, and wondered how many valuables we might have left behind.

By the time we arrived at the gangplank, I realised it was only a small schooner taking us the 60-minute trip across the flat-water strait. The dozen other passengers were understandably unimpressed that we had made them wait. As Paulina and I collapsed into the few remaining seats, we seriously wondered if the car would still be there when we returned and, if so, in what condition. My mind played tricks on me, and questioned whether the person I so trustingly surrendered our car keys to was even employed by the tourist-operator. I couldn't recall him being in uniform; didn't notice a name badge; and couldn't describe his face to a police sketch artist if asked.

Did I just give our keys to a random stranger, who just happened to be walking in our direction when we arrived? Did I just make his day – gifting him a car that can't be traced by people who barely speak the language? Thoughts like these plagued me for days.

I was ashamed of my doubts when we disembarked the ferry three days later to find the port staff having acted beyond reproach, protecting all our belongings, with the car ready and waiting for our onward journey.

Uncharacteristically, I gave a large gratuity that afternoon.

WE CONTINUED THE drive to beautiful Rio de Janeiro, the kids enthralled to see *Christ the Redeemer* – the statue made popular (at least, in our family) by that year's highest rated, animated musical, *Rio*. Bouncing along to its endearing soundtrack, we enjoyed all the touristy hot spots, before flying to Foz do Iguacu to walk the perimeter of the incredible Iguazú Falls. Composed of 275 separate cascades, this natural phenomenon boasts the largest known broken waterfall, rated as one of the seven natural wonders of the world. It's often reported that, upon seeing Iguazu for the first time, First Lady Eleanor Roosevelt reportedly exclaimed "Poor Niagara!".

It was eventually time for my anticipated highlight: a flight into Cusco, a city embedded 3,500 metres above sea level in the Peruvian Andes, and once the capital of the Inca Empire.

We made it on foot that night to the central square of the old city, known for its archaeological remains and Spanish colonial architecture. We had hardly settled to order a meal at a restaurant (where my children were horrified by the offering of deep-fried guinea pigs), when I was overcome with a violent bout of altitude sickness. With an acute headache and disabling nausea – rivalled only by the symptoms I encountered on my first date with Paulina – I abandoned my wife in a foreign city with our three babies. I stumbled back to the hotel to chew on coca leaves generously provided on our arrival by the knowing concierge. Apparently, more than half of their visitors rely on these plant extracts for acclimatisation. The leaves of the coca plant contain alkaloids which, when extracted chemically, are the source for cocaine. I went straight to bed and didn't stir until the next day – seemingly an effective remedy.

We rendezvoused the next morning with Paulina's parents and her eldest brother. Our mission was to reach Machu Picchu – home to the ancient ruins of the fifteenth century citadel above the Urubamba River valley, believed to be the estate of Inca emperor Pachacuti in the period 1438-1472. Renowned for its sophisticated dry-stone walls that fuse huge blocks without the use of mortar, it proved everything that was promised, possibly more!

We scored a brilliant day of blue sky and warm sunshine, which our guide claimed only happened five times a year. The pristine beauty of the moment was unexpectedly interrupted when Sebastian dropped his pants to showcase his peeing prowess, aiming for a record-breaking distance over the stonework ledge. In his fascination with the epic 450-

metre drop, he transformed a historical sacred site into an impromptu comedic show. Ah, the unscripted joys of travelling with children!

From the great heights of Peru we flew to the northern reaches of Chile, dancing with the pink and white flamingos in the great salt lakes of Salar de Atacama. We bathed shamelessly in the 4,000-metre-high geysers of El Tatio, celebrated Christmas with Paulina's abuelito in his hometown of Temuco, wished Lachlan a happy eighth birthday against a backdrop of the snow-capped volcano in Villarrica near Pucon, and welcomed the birth of a new year as we snapped amazing photographs floating amongst icebergs down south near Puerto Chacabuco. That latter souvenir created an idyllic opening slide for my next Iceberg Leadership masterclass.

The trip left indelible impressions on all of us in different ways. Lachlan sweetly confided in Paulina during a precious mother-son moment that, when he was 35 years old, he intended to bring his future wife and children to South America and re-live the memories. Lachlan added to his bold plan a mandate that our family should visit a new continent every 15 years. As they did the maths and giggled together, Paulina helped Lachlan accept that we were going to need his help to get around Africa in our nineties.

FEELING CONFIDENT ONE afternoon during the latter part of the trip, I ventured solo into the streets of Temuco with a mission – remedy an overdue haircut. Unfazed by my broken Spanish, I trusted a mix of limited vocabulary and animated gestures would suffice. With a stammered request, "pelo corto por favor", the barber responded with a smile and a nod, setting the scissors in motion.

What a relief, he understood me, I thought.

Turns out, he didn't.

My request for *short* hair resulted in a *shaved* head. Paulina was devasted for what that meant for the remainder of our vacation photo album.

It was now the second time I found myself both bald and at my wits end, even though one did not cause the other.

The first had been when I abandoned our small practice in 2002, after a neighbour bleached my buzzcut, immediately before taking off around Australia in search of renewed purpose and meaning. God spoke to me very clearly then about investing our lives into the business of physiotherapy as a means of serving His heart for the poor and disadvantaged. I had been doing that for nearly ten years.

But now, I felt stuck again.

It's not that I hadn't made significant inroads. Back In Motion had grown, on average, between 15-40% year-on-year during our first decade. The company was not just regarded as one of the largest physiotherapy providers in Australia, we were amongst the best. I employed hundreds of professionals across more than 40 locations.

And because of all this, I was tired.

Even with my three-month sabbatical, I didn't feel like my batteries were properly recharged. The rigours of managing the business had been so overwhelming, and the complexity of legal entanglements in the prior two years, had drained the emotional fuel in my reserve tank.

I slumped in my overly zealous barber's chair, asking for God's permission to resign the business.

In the final weeks of our time away, God wooed me into quiet and wonderful spaces of retreat and reflection. It allowed me to search the deepest recesses of my heart, where the seeds of God's purpose and my personal identity had first taken root. The foundations of truth and conviction were still there, even if bruised and anaemic. I was taken back to the images I saw as a young boy of the unexplainable poverty and suffering in Ethiopia. I saw the Indigenous faces of the children I worked with in Arnhem Land. I recalled stories of how the money we had sent to a hospital in Burma had enabled them to buy blood-gas analysers to help diagnose hundreds of diseases in their community. The laughter of the children we helped fund the rescue of from Thai brothels, echoed in my memories.

God connected the dots for me, again. He showed me that He was working a perfect plan through my obvious imperfection. *People* still mattered. Hope began to rise like a helium balloon set free. Defying gravity, soaring higher with each new revelation, unburdened by the missteps and setbacks of my recent business challenges.

Fresh vision settled on me like a warm blanket. It seemed obvious to me that more growth enabled more impact. An other-worldly desire to reach 100 practices in our network began to awaken in my conscious mind. The determination grew, emboldened with plans and thoughts I didn't think were my own. God was healing my pain, restoring my strength, and rekindling a courage to go further.

I toyed in my mind with the cute acronym 7/50/100 – launching our brand in seven states, delivering $50 million in revenue, and franchising 100 locations. I was drawn to achieve this unreasonable target – an effective doubling of our network – in only three years. It was ambitious, if not irrational. If Paulina knew my thoughts at that time, she would have jammed a fistful of coca leaves down my throat, thinking I was ascending too fast again, suffering detrimental effects of unaccustomed altitude.

But my mind and heart were synchronised; they schemed in concert. Dreaming, planning, strategising for two weeks before our homeward-bound plane descended for its touchdown at Tullamarine Airport. As the tyres of the aircraft screeched and smoked in early 2013, I was ready to go back to work.

I was on a mission from God again. Ironically, the same one.

67
best-seller

FOR AN IMPRESSIVE five consecutive years, Back In Motion ranked prominently on the esteemed BRW *Fast Franchise* list! Our presence among top-performing brands became a familiar and predictable sight for many, until the final issue of the Fairfax Media group publication was printed in November 2013.

The top ten practices in our network increased by more than 40% that year, and our new conversions (existing businesses which had previously traded under their own brand) had a phenomenal uplift of 54% growth pro rata. Our group was exceeding $2 million sales every month from May of that year, and never slipped backwards. Every Back In Motion franchise grew, on average, anywhere between 3-7 times the size of their industry competitor.

Our marketing mavens capitalised on our momentum with more television advertising. Once again, I took to the couch in the cheesy advertorials that consumed daytime television. We raised brand awareness amongst fitness-conscious consumers and family-decision makers, promoting our Results4Life philosophy, free initial assessment, and money-back satisfaction guarantee. Campaign results showed a spike in website activity, and public relations efforts drove several high-profile media pieces.

After extended conversation, it was recommended to me that I publish a nationally recognised consumer guide to physiotherapy and wellness as the gold standard reference. It seemed a missing piece in our national brand strategy. I hoped I could leverage the book during my speaking engagements in the franchising and health sectors, along with the mainstream media attention I was getting on television and radio.

In February 2012, I signed a contract with Global Publishing Group. I was familiar with the publishing team as I had contributed to one of their earlier titles some years prior. But this was different; I had to write the entire book, and it was a daunting undertaking given how busy I was in the business. Their chief editor convinced me, however, that a book pitched at the right audience would be a game changer for our brand-building ambitions.

This suggestion triggered eight months of research, writing, and market preparation for the launch of *Get Yourself Back In Motion – A physiotherapist's secret to pain relief and optimal health* (GYBIM).

LIFE HAD A way of pushing the book along. Paulina put a load of washing into the machine before she left the house one day, returning hours later to a wave of soapy suds washing up at the front door. The discharge hose of the washing machine had been dislodged, dumping 45 litres of dirty water on the beautiful hardwood floors of our relatively new home – filling the gouges we never repaired. We had to move out of our home for three months as all our furniture was removed, the timber boards were sanded and repolished, and life as we knew it could be restored.

During this inconvenience of relocating our family into a three-bedroom rental unit, I drafted the 90,000-word manuscript for GYBIM. The publisher's instructions were to write in plain English for a literacy level of an average year nine student. I was strongly advised to avoid overly technical and medical language that would confuse or bore the reader. It proved an engaging challenge to distil four years of university study and 15 years of clinical practice into conversational language for a teenage layperson.

I engaged the support of a research assistant to assist in compiling the information I needed, often sending her hour-long instructions dictated into an audio file and emailed late at night. When I received her research packages a week later, I'd sort through the literature reviews and compilation of materials she had prepared on my behalf. This would typically trigger a week of furious writing on my part, before we repeated the process, chapter by chapter, 24 times.

Without the privacy of my spacious study in our home that was under repair, I only had a cramped kitchen table in the rental unit where I was readily disturbed. These circumstances gave impetus for what developed into an unwise strategy of staying up late, and getting up early, to create windows of quiet. In fact, desperate to keep my head above the drowning waters of workload, I negotiated with Paulina a leave pass on Tuesdays. Rather than returning home for dinner and bathtime with the family, I stayed in the office all night. Creating the proverbial eighth day in the week, I literally did not go to bed, but worked around the clock. The phone didn't ring, emails didn't ping, and staff didn't have questions, because the world was asleep. I got so much done in those extra ten hours, I started to look forward to my Tuesday all-nighters, stockpiling high priority and creative tasks throughout the week in a special "8th day" folder. When the office cleaner turned up the next morning at 6:30am, it was my cue to jump in the shower, put on a clean shirt, and be sitting at my desk again before the first colleague arrived for the day – appearing as though I had only beat them in by a few minutes. The irony was not lost on me as I slaved over my book manuscript, sleep-deprived in the early hours one morning, drafting a chapter on the importance of sleep. I vowed to myself that after the book went to print, I would set better habits to avoid dying young!

The book's central theme was empowering readers to take charge of their own health, saving both time and money. The text became a complement to every treatment session we offered a patient, empowering them with specific information relevant to their individual case that we couldn't cover in a single visit. Results4Life was the framework for the book, as it was the defining clinical philosophy of Back In Motion. Whilst I had been espousing this value-driven approach for nearly a decade, it was exciting to watch the support it attracted from the academia of our profession. What was once controversial and frowned upon, now found overwhelming support in recent research, with a growing evidence base to follow. The APA even pushed an agenda for physiotherapists' scope of practice to enlarge and capture the growing wellness market, congruent with our cornerstone approach, leading the CEO of the APA to write a flattering endorsement of my work in a full-page foreword.

To ensure the book didn't flop, I undertook a national tour of our practices just before its release. I used the opportunity to explain to franchisees the strategy behind the initiative as a brand-building opportunity. Many were quick to get on board, meaning our initial print run exceeded 12,000 copies, instantly placing the title on the official best-seller's list before a retail customer even bought their first copy.

The book was released in early 2013, with some pre-release copies available the Christmas prior. Sales online, in store, and through our practice network, were certainly helped by encouraging reviews generated by high profile medical professionals and sporting celebrities. The first pages of my second edition included quotes of praise and support from preventative health expert and television presenter Dr. Ross Walker, four-time Paralympic medallist Don Elgin, triple Olympic gold medallist Lydia Lassila, Olympic swimmer Cameron McEvoy, world record holding marathon swimmer Tammy van Wisse, and Mark Inglis, the only double amputee to reach the summit of Mount Everest. Every endorsement pushed sales a little further.

I engaged a public relations firm to manage the press we were enjoying off the coattails of the book release. Their efforts resulted in an incredible wave of further exposure, landing me over 70 editorial pieces in widespread media. I had radio interviews, morning television spots, print and online articles in mainstream newspapers and magazines, speaking invitations, and requests to appear on more podcasts than I could accept in my compressed work schedule.

EARLY ACCOUNTS VINDICATED the strategy and hard work behind getting GYBIM into print. The difficulty was keeping up with my responsibilities and workload in an already full schedule. In addition to my core focus on Back In Motion, Actif and Revita were growing in their demands, as was the SOS Health Foundation and the Iceberg Leadership workshops, soaking up enormous amounts of my time.

I felt deeply committed to raising leaders at every level of our organisation. It wasn't just a commercial strategy, but what I believed God had, in part, placed me in this role to do. I passionately believed that any hope of a worthwhile legacy rested in raising like-minded people who shared my vision.

Acting on this conviction, I incorporated the Iceberg Leadership Institute. With a dedicated budget, staff allocation, and strategic plan, my new formalised approach afforded greater opportunities to invest into the training and growth of our people. My team collated valuable feedback from the hundreds of alumni who had previously graduated through the masterclasses and, armed with this knowledge, I enriched the program with more relevant content and engaging formats.

Paulina raised an eyebrow at the prospect of yet another brand vying for my attention, competing with our family for my priority and affections. She regularly posed a valid question: "Was I primarily the franchisor of Back In Motion, a committed philanthropist with SOS, or the principal mentor for the Iceberg Leadership Institute?". She was adamant it couldn't be all three, but I was unable to choose between them. Balancing these demands, alongside the needs of my family, church and local community, was an intricate puzzle, risking daily tension with those I loved the most.

I struggled to distinguish between the fragile glass balls and resilient rubber ones, as cautioned in various leadership metaphors. Glass priorities irreparably shatter if dropped, while rubber ones can bounce back from neglect. Differentiating between the two was crucial. Unfortunately, on increasing occasions, I fumbled this delicate balance.

Craving the mentorship of experienced leaders who seemed to carry much greater loads with apparent ease, I regularly sent up a flare in the night sky in the form of wishful prayers. Michael and John on my advisory board were great sources of guidance and insight. I drew on others in church leadership and community roles when opportunities presented. And I attended regular roundtables with peer CEOs, crowd-sourcing their wisdom on how to stay ahead of the business curve without losing my soul.

I was surprised at my own chutzpah one afternoon, after meeting Simon McKeon at an event. Australian lawyer, businessman, philanthropist and sportsman, he had recently been announced the *Australian of the Year* – so I thought who better to seek input from than the *best* our country had to offer. Seeking his mentorship through an introduction from a friend, Simon was hesitant to commit. He juggled so many high-end roles – Macquire Bank, Rio Tinto, Monash University – he feared it was unlikely he could spare the time. I was audacious to keep pressing. Assuming he spent a lot of time in taxis and airport lounges as he travelled between his many engagements, I suggested I could send Simon three questions in advance by email that would only take ten minutes of his time while in transit. He graciously agreed to a weekly call, guiding me for over a year on managing the tensions common in our roles. He taught me about defusing conflict within my executive team, balancing personal health with corporate responsibility, threading the needle of faith and commerciality, and understanding what "success" at home and work was for him. I was incredibly grateful for Simon – and many others like him – who invested into me in ways they might underestimate, but helped shape me in the fires of my personal crucible. Sometimes the influence came from unexpected places, even the backseat of a taxi.

One of my regrets now is not always inviting Paulina into the same conversations. Her perspective was often a much-needed counter-balance to the problems I was wrestling, and she too may have benefited from some of the insights I was receiving from industry luminaries. Regardless, we hung on tightly – to each other and our respective convictions – as we trusted God to guide our steps and reconcile our tensions as we served at the "pleasure of the King".

68

top gear

I RANG IN the new year nursing two broken ribs – another temporary hurdle to juggling my various roles.

We had gathered with friends on New Year's Eve, dining outdoors on a steep sloping acreage. It wasn't long before the dads concocted a plan involving a last-minute trip to the local hardware store, buying large continuous sheets of black plastic and as much liquid soap as five grown men could carry. All of this to build the world's biggest slippery slide for the... (ahem)... *kids*.

With an inflatable kiddie pool strategically placed at the bottom of the property, we laughed and screamed our way through the afternoon as everyone took turns sliding on their stomachs, knees, and boogie boards. At one point, two of us catapulted Paulina head-first down the slide, her reaching terminal velocity just before the crash-splash at the end.

An hour before midnight, the stakes got higher. We initiated five-person races to the bottom, each run getting more physical, and competitive, as we jostled for position and sought to nudge each other off the plastic and into the thistles and weeds shouldering the slide. On what became my last run for the night, I managed to lead the race. Halfway down the hill I hit a small rock the size of a child's fist, buried beneath the plastic, and felt a crack on the right side of my ribcage. Two small fractures demanded slow, shallow painful breaths as we counted down the seconds to midnight.

Despite the unfortunate beginning, 2013 was a year full of promise.

NEW PRACTICES WERE launching in all directions as our brand credibility continued to grow. I was flying every month to most of the capital cities, and some regional centres, to meet with physiotherapists interested in becoming our next cohort of franchisees.

I was especially struck by one instance, sitting at a café in idyllic Byron Bay – a premier location known for its spectacular beaches, unique shopping and dining experiences, world-class festivals, and vibrant community spirit. Waiting for my guest to arrive, I was dressed in a Back In Motion polo shirt – my characteristic uniform for first-time meetings with new prospects. On a cool, windy Tuesday morning, as I watched shade umbrellas blow over and waiters scramble to protect their patrons, I was interrupted by a stranger sitting at the adjacent table. Having noticed the logo on my chest, she proceeded to rave about her experience as a client at her local Back In Motion practice in Adelaide.

Introducing herself as Emily, she recounted that from the moment she stepped through the door of our practice, she felt enveloped in warmth and compassion. The soothing ambiance, coupled with the genuine smiles of the staff, immediately eased her apprehensions. For her, our premises quickly became more than a clinic; it was a haven where her well-being was the top priority – something she desperately needed to be assured of. The camaraderie among patients further enriched Emily's experience. In the waiting area she found herself engaging in uplifting conversations with fellow individuals on their own paths to recovery. She described the sense of community fostered within the practice as one offering palpable hope and encouragement to many more than just herself. She was sincerely grateful for the compassionate care and holistic support she had experienced, and confessed she was never shy to tell others about it.

It was a surreal experience. 2,000 kilometres north of the garage where I had started our business, I was being thanked by a random bystander, who was 22-hours' drive from her home, and about to meet another stranger who was practically begging to pay me $70,000 to join our network.

At the heart of our business was my hope that every patient experienced profound impact that transcended their treatment I wanted our practices to be sanctuaries of healing and empowerment. This, at least, had become true for Emily. I smiled as I went to bed that night, thinking how far we had come, and how many people had been touched by the Back In Motion experience.

BY FEBRUARY I was ready to host our fifth annual Director's conference in Torquay, Victoria. Nearly $30 million in annual revenue and 26% comparative growth, our franchisees were eager to party.

I believed early in my career that leaders were built, not born. Businesses didn't happen by accident; they were created by careful design. And we didn't improve by doing the same things repeatedly, but through planned innovation and change.

This conference was the perfect occasion to remind my people of these truths. It was a breeding ground for fresh ideas, new strategies, insightful reflection, and stronger relationships. Through the inspiration of our keynote speakers, the interaction of our social activities, and the delight of gathering with like-minded friends and colleagues, we savoured the opportunity to return to our practices as more robust, intentional people.

In 2013 the conference theme was *Drive*. In a light-hearted rally cry, I had the team on their feet cheering in a frenzy of unbridled enthusiasm as I read aloud a benediction of my expectations for the year ahead. Declaring more than 40 puns linked to our theme – each one intended – I made references to *torque*, *need-for-speed*, *power output*, *high octane*, and *turbo super-chargers*, all met with a mixture of wolf-whistles, laughter, and admittedly, some eye rolls. I managed to integrate familiar quotes from films *Days of Thunder*, *Cars*, and *Top Gun*, before climaxing with the big finish it was time to get our "wheels in motion".

Double-clutching, I shifted our group into top gear.

69

and the winner is...

BACK IN MOTION won numerous industry awards over the years, landing high in the BRW franchise rankings, and our practices piling up a string of local business achievements for innovation, customer service, and community engagement. I was also formally acknowledged for white papers I prepared on industry issues, invited to present at conferences on a range of topics, and enjoyed a steady flow of positive media attention as a soft endorsement to the success of our venture.

The risk of external validation through awards and accolades is that they can often serve as distractions and, at their worst, incentivise the wrong habits and behaviours. I found that seeking such affirmation only led me to working harder and longer in pursuit of more, feeding an insecurity that what I had already achieved wasn't good enough.

It's tragic that faithful, hard-working, stay-at-home parents don't receive similar plaudits and acclaim, despite pouring their best efforts into their children and spouses year after year. This deeply meaningful work often goes unnoticed and unrewarded, inadvertently suggesting that the role at home is less significant.

This work-versus-home contest was a recurring tension that Paulina and I wrestled with over our two decades in business. I found myself pulled into an incessant cycle of striving for greater accomplishments at the office, at times leaving Paulina feeling undervalued for her unwavering dedication to anchoring our family life.

This unease percolated again when I was nominated for one of the world's most prestigious business awards – the Ernst and Young (EY) *Entrepreneur of the Year*. After two months of interviews and screening, I met my competition at a launch event in May 2013 – a humbling experience given how strong the field was. Like candidates in a pageant, we underwent scrutiny by an independent judging panel comprised of industry leaders and previous winners. Judges included Spencer Long, deputy chairman of the Ten Network; Joycelyn Morton, chair of Noni B; and Greg Roebuck, founder of carsales.com.

It was an intense day as I bounced from room to room, answering a spread of questions about my business strategy, risks and innovations, and future aspirations. I was assessed on my entrepreneurial spirit, financial performance, national and global impact, personal integrity, influence, and strategic direction. I had no idea how I was placing during such fast-paced conversations, but I felt invigorated by running the gauntlet laid by such intellectually stimulating stalwarts of business.

PAULINA AND I donned our black-tie evening attire in September, and attended the Regional Awards Dinner at the Plaza Ballroom. The evening was hosted by popular stand-up comic, Peter Berner, and we were joined by both sets of parents and my executive team. I sat in the back half of the audience, incredibly nervous throughout the proceedings, yet quite positive I was an unlikely winner.

Imagine the sheer astonishment and euphoria that swept over me as my name resonated through the hall, heralding me as the Victorian *Entrepreneur of the Year*. In a whirlwind of emotions, I hurried to the podium, exchanging a handshake with Peter, before stumbling through an impromptu interview with him. Making my way back to my seat in a haze of disbelief, I was surrounded by a sea of congratulations as people rose to back-slap and hug me.

I was especially pleased my family were part of the evening celebrations, as it reflected my heartfelt gratitude toward them for their enduring support and positive influence through many of the difficult times. I regarded the award as a shared honour with Paulina – something we had earned as a couple through the way we pulled together – at home and at work. Whilst I didn't sip an ounce of alcohol all evening, I don't remember much about what happened afterwards; it was a haze of blissful relief that extended long into the early hours of the morning.

The impressive trophy was just the beginning. More importantly, I was invited into EY's *Winner's Network* – an online community exclusively for the 27 years of previous winners from around the globe. It quickly connected me with vetted high-growth leaders in over 60 countries of my choice, providing a trusted private network to address confidential business challenges. I also gained direct access to a vault of industry insights, trends, best practices, exclusive events, and resources not previously available to me.

The PR machine kicked in quickly after that night also. EY's team generated radio interviews, newspaper articles, podcasts, and other media appearances for the winners. Our Marketing Manager received a full press kit to leverage the opportunities in every way possible. It was great for our business, as everywhere I went I told our brand story and promoted positive opportunities for every local franchisee.

Two months later, EY flew Paulina and I to Sydney for the national showdown. The Australian *Entrepreneur of the Year* flew to Monte Carlo for the penultimate honour of the International Awards. Other nominees included Dr Fiona Wood AM, a burns surgeon made famous by her work with the Bali bombing victims in 2002, who had started her own foundation to advance the development of innovative treatments for use in burns; Iwan Sunito of Crown Group Holdings, one of Sydney's largest residential property developers with $3 billion of development projects in the pipeline at the time; and Andrew Bassat, co-founder of SEEK Limited, the largest global online employment marketplace by revenue, earnings, and market capitalisation. I felt dwarfed standing in the company of these commercial giants!

We mulled around the foyer of the event venue, meeting each other for the first time as we filed through the choke point of a small media scrum which was taking photos and conducting impromptu interviews of each nominee. In an attempt at small talk with Andrew, I questioned whether he had been caught in the morning delays on the Qantas flight to Sydney. Andrew bashfully conceded he had taken his own private jet to avoid the interruptions – yet another reminder that I was not in the same league as any of my fellow contenders. As Andrew turned to face the flashing lightbulbs of the cameras, I couldn't resist reaching out and straightening his collar that was crimped under his jacket. He smiled and thanked me.

As it turned out, helping dress Andrew was my only noteworthy contribution in the formalities that evening. Some hours later, I stood in chorus with the rest of the room to applaud when Andrew deservedly won the top honour. Whilst he did not fare as well on the international stage some months later, nobody can minimise the meteoric success of his venture. SEEK Ltd was then listed on the ASX with a market capitalisation of over $7.5 billion, more than 250 times the value of Back In Motion.

Paulina and I didn't retreat to our hotel room in defeat. On the contrary, we were grateful to be welcomed into the alumnus of the EY network. Our business was not perfect, and there was so much more to achieve, but we did not let these realities displace what we had accomplished in such a short time after starting with so little. We were often told by the faceless physiotherapy industry that we were cowboys who wouldn't last, so it was especially meaningful to reflect that night on the many esteemed opinions in the entrepreneurial sector who obviously thought differently.

70
her sacrifice

BACK IN MOTION was always a joint project of our marriage; Paulina and I were partners. Whilst we continuously felt strung between the tensions of home and work, we both knew that I couldn't make my best contribution if Paulina wasn't making hers. We depended on each other, enjoyed working together, and complemented one another's attributes beautifully. Central to the adventure was a confidence that God had called us to the mission.

Whilst perpetually busy juggling our three boys in primary school, Paulina demonstrated this the time she partnered with a franchisee and team of volunteers to coordinate our inaugural Winter Gala Ball – a spectacular fundraiser for SOS. She hosted 200 guests, each paying exorbitant ticket prices for entry to the delightful Wonderland Spiegeltent under the Melbourne Star Observation Wheel.

Dutch for *mirror tent*, the Spiegeltent is a replica of the famous Belgium traveling dance halls, with its luxurious and exciting ambiance. It was a truly unique experience; an intimate mix of circus, cabaret, and theatre, in a stylish, historical European setting, complete with stained glass windows and mirrors. Apart from speeches and a charity auction, our festivities included world-class performances from magicians, comedians, aerialists, and circus performers. We enjoyed hours of music and dance late into the night, inspired by the 1920s. Paulina was elated – the event an incredible success – raising over $125,000 to extend the work of our foundation.

As a result, we hosted ten outreach missions in that one calendar year, deploying more than 80 volunteer health professionals. We opened urban pro bono clinics in Melbourne and Adelaide in partnership with the Salvation Army, and also set up a full-service practice on Palm Island.

I ALSO GREATLY valued Paulina's willingness to build meaningful connections with our suppliers and partners. Our growth and relative success were, in many ways, dependent on how agile our suppliers were in keeping pace with our needs. Paulina seemed to inherently understand this, honouring their contributions, making her an essential ambassador of our team.

In some cases, an individual supply-chain had to grow quickly to match our demand. I remember reading about a similar phenomenon with Ray Kroc and McDonalds; as the number of restaurants grew from coast to coast in America, the Golden Arches needed their suppliers to grow with them. McDonalds didn't just make millionaires out of their franchisees, they have also made multi-millionaires out of those suppliers who took up the challenge to scale proportionately to the speed and size of the hamburger chain. At Back In Motion, we noticed a similar phenomenon emerging, albeit on a smaller scale.

It took time and intentionality to bring our suppliers on the brand journey so they felt part of our story and included in our culture. Paulina was brilliant at this sensitive task. She sought them out at group and industry events to ensure their contribution was never taken for granted. Naturally drawn to meaningful relationships, Paulina did far more than just "work the room" and toss empty platitudes to sponsors and company executives. Never one to nod insincerely to shallow stories or feign interest with a polite laugh at the appropriate time, Paulina was the real deal. She learned about their families, enquired about their personal interests, asked genuine questions about their product and service ranges, and shared her perspectives on life and culture in kind.

Paulina could easily spend 30 minutes with the same small group of guests and not look bored – the only tension being my own as I wondered if she noticed the haphazard queue of others waiting for her attention. But her refusal to be rushed, and her determination to value every person in the room, stitched and glued our many suppliers into the fabric of our cultural tapestry.

Paulina was my ideal complement, not just in business but in every facet of life; together, we were a powerful alloy. Her accomplishments leave me awestruck; she is hardworking, resilient and cares deeply about the spaces she invests into. She has always had an innate sense of those glass balls that needed catching, and the rubber ones that could bounce in the high-wire circus act that had become our lives.

But the personal commitments to our family and business, and her responsibilities to SOS, left very little bandwidth for much else. Unwilling to do things in half-measures, Paulina sensed the inevitability of letting her nursing registration lapse – something she had tried to maintain to this point, keeping her career options open. It was a solemn moment when it eventually happened, unlikely to ever return to a profession she had given most of her adult life to. As Paulina let that significant part of her identity drift away, it was like watching a treasured page of her personal journal float downstream, eventually carried out of sight by the gentle current.

It is unlikely I'll ever fully know the personal cost of all Paulina's sacrifices.

71
ONEteam

ONE YEAR AFTER returning from long service leave in South America, it was time to accelerate the plan around 7/50/100 – launching Back In Motion in seven states, delivering $50 million in revenue, and franchising 100 locations.

I knew it was bold, ambitious, and unlikely to come easy, but I was determined. The team had spent over a decade building a strong foundation of effective clinical protocols and excellent business systems, overseen by talented people with a proven track record and heart-felt values. If I didn't scale now, I feared we would fall a long way short of our potential.

I reminded my team that *healthy* things grow. Healthy plants grow; healthy babies grow; and healthy economies grow. It stood to reason that healthy business should grow too. I preached to them with daily fervour that, if a brand (or person, practice, or franchise) isn't growing, it's *slowing*. I desperately didn't want to go backwards.

But I knew growth could cost us dearly if we weren't calculated. I couldn't afford to expand our business at the expense of compromising clinical excellence or integrity in the relationships we had spent so long investing into. I couldn't slow innovation in clinical practice, either. And I knew my hopeful growth must never distract me from supporting those in need.

I reassured the team that I wasn't advocating growth solely for the vanity of larger numbers. 7/50/100 encompassed far more than mere size increments; it was an initiative focussed on the evolution and expansion of our entire business ecosystem. As it thrived, it also meant our people would be enriched, our processes would be refined, and our impact would be enlarged.

Reasonable team members knew we had to make sacrifices. It was time to change some old habits, reshuffle priorities, and endure the pains of transition.

PURSUING THE FIRST year of step change, I proportionately scaled our NSO to keep pace. Investing an additional $1 million in new executive and management salaries during 2013 and 2014 to fill the key talent gaps should have set me up for accelerated success; sadly, not everyone was on board.

Catastrophically, right when I needed my most senior people the most, their resolve unravelled, morphing into a nightmarish scenario. My two general managers were at the centre of the uproar – one was in charge of Group Operations and the other, Corporate Services. As the lieutenants under whom everybody else found their place and rhythm within the organisation, they had huge influence over the culture, tone, and workflow. At a time when their loyalty and alignment was essential, increasing interpersonal clashes between them turned their previous harmonious blend into a cacophony of complaints and criticisms.

Gradually, their mutual antipathy grew, fostering animosity between the teams under their leadership. What had once been only tensions behind closed doors, and dislike masquerading as sharp humour, now devolved into open disrespect and strategic sabotage between the pair. The profound rift between them manifested as an unmistakable presence – an elephant squatting in our office, impossible to ignore.

A change-up in my executive leadership seemed inevitable.

THESE EVENTS TRIGGERED a full review of my entire team model and organisational structure. For the first time in ten years, I questioned whether our top-down hierarchy was beneficial.

Was it the right approach with just the wrong people? Or were there fundamental flaws in the leadership model?

I invested 12 months investigating the psychology of organisational design and behaviour. I burned through a packet of multi-coloured highlighters as I marked up every journal, magazine article, textbook, and bestseller that in any way contributed value to my situation. I skilled up on the principles of adaptive change, appreciative inquiry, Holacracy, strength-based leadership, and the tenets of requisite organisation. I compared the traditional hierarchical model with flat organisations, de-centralised structures, inverted pyramids, hypertext organisations, matrix management, and even virtual workplaces (long before the advent of the COVID-19 pandemic had even popularised such a thing!). Whilst there were useful lessons in everything I studied, there was no silver bullet or plug-and-play solution that perfectly fitted my needs.

My model seemed to be unintentionally suffocating talented people through hierarchy and self-limiting position descriptions. Job titles and lines of reporting had become discriminatory. Strategy and decisions were mostly formulated in a linear, top-down fashion. Too many conversations were happening in secret. Elitism and class divisions had crept into our workplace and cast a cloud of disunity. Colleagues had been artificially designated into executive, management, and support strata, implying that one's influence was driven more by seniority and position than by intelligence and merit. In short, our creativity was evaporating before me, and I was afraid we were losing our edge – all on the eve of embarking on 7/50/100.

In fact, 2014 marked the lowest rate of growth in the history of our business. Admittedly still quadruple that of the rest of our industry, it was only about half our norm. Our revenue curve was flattening, presumably in response to the internal pain and dysfunction. I suffered diluted vision, fragmented strategy, disenfranchised staff, underwhelming client service, reduced effort, and indifferent results. This was more than just growing pains; it was an outbreak of toxicity.

It was on me to clean up the mess, rebuild the team, re-engage my people, and introduce a new way of life into the office.

One morning, as I stood beneath the warm cascade of the shower, contemplating the challenges before me, a vision unfolded in my mind. It was a cross-section of the Earth, revealing its core, mantle and crust, with orbiting moons as the planet gracefully rotated around its axis, basking in the Sun's glow. In that moment, I recognised a profound connection – a parallel between the intricate workings of our natural universe and the dynamics of our franchise system.

This mental image inspired me to think beyond simply flipping or flattening our organisation chart to address our cultural ills. Instead, I envisioned shaping it into a revolutionary spherical model, reminiscent of the planetary system. I christened it ONEteam™ – a fitting moniker because I aimed to eradicate divisions and silos within our workforce, fostering a unified and collaborative effort focused on the common goal of 7/50/100.

A SUN IN any solar system has an irresistible pull on the planets within its reach. It's that big, bright, shiny thing, way up high that you can't look at directly for fear of blindness. You know it's always there, even if you can't see it. The Sun is the primary source of the planet's oxygen and food, and therefore sustains life and, with it, hope.

In the same way, our business relied on a primary source of life. Our Sun was a set of deeply held spiritual convictions which framed my calling to serve the purposes of God. As such, Back In Motion – and myself as its director – was submitted to a higher standard than just human endeavour.

I freely admit I was a reluctant businessman, and an accidental franchisor. Despite having been applauded for apparent entrepreneurship, I always expected to be a medical missionary, not a CEO. The plan for Back In Motion was never really my own, but rather a series of intense and personal encounters with God that had set my life on this course.

As I rebuilt a team around the mandate of ONEteam, I felt compelled to revisit my calling – sharing again with my colleagues the significance behind what we do and who we do it for. That *people* mattered, not just business. This was my way of ensuring the Sun remained in its rightful place, the centre of our universe.

Subservient to the Sun is its swath of planets; each with its own physics of orbit. Just as the Earth rotates around its axis every 24 hours, pivoting in perfect rhythm on a geometric centre point, ONEteam needed to be reminded of its precise focus. This came in the form of carefully re-crafted identity statements:

> Our *mission* (what we did) was to empower clients in *optimal lifelong health*.
>
> Our *purpose* (why we existed) was to be *significant in the lives of others*.
>
> Our *vision* (where we saw ourselves in the future) was to be the most *loved and trusted provider of allied health services*.
>
> Our *strategy* (how we would achieve our mission) was to *provide effective leadership and comprehensive support to become the clinical provider, workplace, and business model of choice*.

Our *values* (the beliefs we were committed to) were *excellence, leadership, loyalty, integrity,* and *significance*.

With our axis aligned, I could focus on the other attributes of the planetary cross-section.

The core of the planet became the strategic target of 7/50/100. The mantle – the layer between the core and the exterior crust – became the newly engineered management functions of our business. The crust represented the outer ring of accountability, strategy, governance, and leadership.

This model of ONEteam, imprinted in the minds and hearts of our people, became the mental map of our imperatives as we prepared to move forwards. Collectively, our team objective was to build a living ecosystem of self-led, highly collaborative, and peer-accountable colleagues in the NSO who were equally committed to the vision and mission of Back In Motion. Putting this into practice, I radically de-titled the entire office, and released everyone from their formal job descriptions. People were asked to re-think how they could best contribute to the new growth strategy, inventing different roles, debating creative strategies, and taking risks we previously would have frowned upon. The new regime gave people permission to work with an open mind, alive to new possibilities.

This was not an exercise in short term change management or cultural re-engagement. What we did in 2013 and 2014 became the most confounding experiences of my working life. I won't repeat the minutiae here, but if you are curious to study our leadership revolution – warts and all – I detail the entire sordid story in another book, *Outside In Downside Up Leadership* (2018). In it, I reveal 50 valuable insights gleaned from this painful episode of organisational transformation.

Looking back, the discomfort of discovering our spherical organisation model was undeniably worthwhile. It provided a genuine and scalable method to empowering every team member to pursue their passions and excel in their strengths, ultimately fuelling our rocket to the Moon and back. However, this achievement did not come without sacrifices.

NATURALLY, NOT EVERYONE shared my enthusiasm for ONEteam.

Overwhelmed by the extreme changes and the strain of the broken relationships that initiated the cultural revolution in the first place, one of the original warring GMs offered his resignation. In a move that caught many on his team completely off guard, I swiftly accepted his offer, looking for an opportunity to demonstrate my commitment to the new order.

Within the same year, I eventually parted company with the second GM also – effectively, my number two guy. Despite having substantial commercial aptitude and a growth mindset, he kicked against the pillars of my new ONEteam philosophy. Understandably, he took special umbrage when I obliterated his GM title and stationed him in the bullpen alongside everyone else. Agreeing his performance had gone over a cliff, neither of us were confident he could make sufficient positive changes in the direction needed.

Sometime later, I even had to let my CFO go. Having a background as a troop leader in the military, Callum took no prisoners. He had the physical stature of a mountain man and was tough, loud, and dominant in the way he engaged with the team around him. Contrary to everything we were trying to achieve through ONEteam, Callum made few friends for being this way, but he didn't care.

More acutely, it soon became obvious Callum couldn't balance his personal books, let alone the $32 million budget he was responsible for at the NSO. Regularly appealing for help with his personal cash flows, I suggested he could sparingly use his work credit card to make rent and keep food on the table if he offset the loans against his salary each month. I expected short accounts that didn't accumulate and become unruly, slipping into my old patterns of naïvete. I was too trusting and gullible to think Callum wouldn't take advantage of my kindness.

Soon after, another finance colleague tipped me off that Callum's personal line of credit to the company exceeded $36,000. Unexplainably, it included home computer equipment, accommodations in Sydney for a family stay, and fine dining restaurants he apparently deemed essential to treat his wife. I confronted him about these expenses. Callum vowed to pay it all back from progressive salary redraws, but we both knew that if his generous six-figure-salary wasn't even covering his weekly expenses, there was little chance of him being able to repay his debt.

His solution the next day was that I give him an unearned, unentitled, annual bonus of $60,000 to clear his debt and build some financial buffer. Instead, I invited Callum to a *walk-and-talk* – a meeting format

I liked to have on foot with my executive team to avoid being stuck in an office chair all day long. We commenced a five-kilometre loop of the local back streets around the NSO. At about the halfway point, our discussion moved from terse to heated; my top guy in finance was too foolish with our money to fathom why I was so upset. Almost speechless, I scrambled just enough words to suggest it was time he looked for another job. Exasperated by the saga, I turned to walk back to the office the same way we had come, inviting him to take the long way home on his own.

All these changes led to a blank canvas of talent for my newly commissioned ONEteam. It was a busy summer at the start of 2014, as I employed a slew of new executives in core financial and operational roles.

I crouched at the new starting line like a poised runner. My muscles tensed, coiled like springs, as my body leaned slightly forward, toes digging into the track. With a gaze fixed on 7/50/100, every nerve tingled with anticipation for the explosive burst of energy I felt prepped to release at the sound of the starting gun.

72
room for one more

JUST A WEEK before Paulina and I were set to co-host our 2014 annual Director's Conference on the Gold Coast, she received an unexpected phone call from a case worker at the Department of Family, Fairness and Housing (DFFH) – our state child protection agency. Initially, I didn't pay much attention, as these check-ins had become routine. However, Paulina's reaction caught my attention immediately.

Her serene expression slowly morphed into one of shock and concern. Her eyes widened as she absorbed the weight of the apparent news. I witnessed the beautiful bronze hue drain from her face as a mix of emotions became etched across her gentle features.

Hanging up the phone, Paulina sat in momentary silence.

I then learned the reason behind her reaction: our family had been matched with a vulnerable child who needed emergency care, two years earlier than we expected.

OUR JOURNEY TO this point had been a long one.

It started together on our first date back in 1996, when we both expressed an uncanny desire to adopt a child in our futures. The alignment in such uncommon intentions only accentuated our attraction to each other. We wondered aloud, during those early years, whether we would help a child from Latin America where Paulina has strong roots, or whether we would rescue someone from Asia (Cambodia, especially) because of the early mission trips we had experienced. We didn't mind, but with such a passion to help those in need, it seemed adoption was a tangible way to significantly impact at least one vulnerable life.

After we were married, our initial inquiry with the international adoption agency in Australia revealed a stipulation: we needed to have had all our biological children before being eligible for assessment. At that juncture, Paulina wasn't even pregnant with our first son. The prospect of revisiting adoption when we were much older seemed improbable, yet we held onto that dream over the years as we started our own family.

With the arrival of Morgan – our third son – our quiver felt near full of arrows, leaving space for just one more. However, new inquiries to DFFH at the time revealed another hurdle; adoption applications were only accepted after our youngest child reached a minimum age of two years, ensuring at least this much age gap between our biological children and the adoptee. It was a disheartening setback, especially considering our advancing years. The intricate requirements of the complex and changing process left us questioning our suitability at times.

God kept a flame of hope flickering within us, fuelling our desire to offer a child a second chance at life. Paulina broached the topic with our boys in a manner suitable for their ages. As she flipped through the pages of a specially purposed book, narrating the story of a child without parents seeking a safe and caring home, I caught her asking our sons what they believed a family like ours should do in response.

Lachlan said it was obvious: "Given we have room in our house, another seat in the car, and lots of food to share, we should let them live with us."

His two younger brothers agreed. They were deeply saddened that some children had no mum and dad, and regularly prayed at meal and bedtimes for whoever might become their new sibling.

As we heard the reaction of our children, tears welled up in my eyes; a silent testament to the profound work that God had been quietly weaving within all our hearts throughout this journey. It was evident that each of us had been prepared for this moment, poised and ready to embrace the next step together.

We eventually formalised an application with DFFH to become a guardian to a vulnerable child, commencing a rigorous and extensive assessment process. This included over 45 hours of formal training, along with the requisite review of our finances, education, family history, extended family composition, support network, employment history, home set up, marital rhythms, business commitments, school participation, church involvements, medical histories, stress reactions, good standing in the community, parenting style, and personal values.

Paulina and I each had to write a 30-page life story in response to a detailed questionnaire, submitting ourselves to the intimidating assessment of a panel of experts who determined our suitability and readiness for adoption.

It was an unnatural and exhausting period of scrutiny. One day, a social worker attended our home to watch our interaction with the three boys. We played a contrived game of Monopoly on the floor together for their clinical observation, and otherwise went about our usual after-school routine whilst this unwelcomed stranger ticked and crossed checklists on her private clipboard. With our permission, she also interviewed the boys, one at a time, about their thoughts and concerns regarding another child coming to join them.

Paulina and I discreetly concealed our curiosity, positioning ourselves just around the corner of the kitchen to eavesdrop. However, our attempt at stealth crumbled when an audible gasp escaped us upon hearing Lachlan's unexpected responses to the questions.

"So, Lachlan, how would you describe the general mood at home?", quizzed the awkward social worker.

"Violent!", our nine-year-old boldly declared, without any hesitation.

Paulina and I exchanged horrified glances as we imagined being struck as an adoption candidate for what the authorities were going to conclude is a home marred by accusations of child abuse and neglect. Fortunately, before we had to interject with any explanations or excuses for our son's clearly misguided response, Lachlan broke into laughter. He began posturing like a Kung-Fu fighter, playfully karate-chopping the air, diffusing the tension with his infectious joy and mischievous antics.

"Yup, home is super *violent*! Dad always wrestles me on the floor just before bed. Sebby jumps on him from the couch to protect me. We gang up on him together."

Innocently unaware of how close he came to dashing our hopes of qualifying for a child placement, we still giggle to this day about Lachlan's poor choice of words.

Despite the exhausting process, our excitement to welcome a new child into our family grew. We knew it would pose lots of adjustments, challenges and inconveniences, but all five of us were hopeful the addition would also bring into our world a wonderful new life to cherish and learn from.

We were officially advised in November 2013 that our application had been approved by DFFH, and to be patient over the next four years as we sat on the waiting list for the right child to be matched to our specific family's attributes. Mentally prepared for nothing to happen for some time, and with our youngest boy starting school in 2014, Paulina took on the corporate events portfolio at Back In Motion.

The timing of that fateful DFFH phone call, one week before our conference, couldn't have been more unexpected. It came merely four months after our official approval – years ahead of our anticipated schedule. Superhost to over 110 delegates at our premier networking and education event for the year, Paulina struggled to maintain her focus on the task at hand.

The news sent shockwaves through our home, catching us all off guard. Blindsided by the sudden turn of events, I found myself grappling with uncertainty about how to raise someone else's child.

The weeks, months and years that followed were a blend of joy and sorrow, a bittersweet transition for all of us as we navigated the tender and pivotal moments of juggling the mismatched needs of four different children now in our mix. Whilst the intricacies of this story are our family's precious moments to hold in privacy, I take comfort in knowing that God placed this special life in ours for a season, and nothing happened by accident or chance.

73
location, location, location

WITH THREE KIDS in primary school, drop-offs and pick-ups were proving a massive time sponge. The home we built in Ferntree Gully was perfect in every way for our growing family, except that it was a 40-minute round trip to and from our preferred college – WCC, the same one Paulina and I had attended. With an estimated 15 years ahead of the same daily grind, it quickly became apparent that we needed to move.

Fuelled by curiosity, and having trekked the streets on foot, Paulina logged into Google Earth, scouting for properties adjacent to the school. The satellite views were especially helpful, as she analysed the shapes of the various blocks of land, imagining the style, size, and orientation of the house that she wanted to build to suit our family.

Then one night after dark, in torrential rain, Paulina picked me up from an event and drove in the opposite direction from home. Acknowledging my obvious confusion, she explained that she had short-listed four potential properties from her satellite research. Soon after, we pulled up at the address of her top choice – a 1250-square-metre, triangular-shaped block at the apex of a shallow private cul-de-sac. As she parked in the driveway and turned off the engine, Paulina urged me to knock on the door and persuade the unsuspecting homeowners to sell to us. Blindsided by her request, I quickly verified whether she had already reached out to the owners, or confirmed if the property was officially on the market, factors that would justify my involvement. Her playful smirk, betraying her lack of prior action on either front, signalled my cue to step out of the car and take on her clandestine task.

I tentatively rapped on the front door, hoping nobody was home. Unfortunately, the outside porch light flicked on immediately, and I was caught in the crosshairs. As the owner appeared, the dimness inside the house obscured their features, leaving only a silhouette. As fate would have it, the proprietor turned out to be one of my patients. Standing in the chilly evening air, we both found ourselves in an uncomfortable moment of unexpected intrusion on my part.

After an exchange of minimal pleasantries, I took the risk and disclosed our interest to move into the area, inquiring if they might consider selling their home. Instead of being flattered by my approach, the couple promptly rebuffed my interest, firmly refusing the opportunity. Returning to the car having struck out, Paulina was mildly disappointed with my feeble negotiation, smiling as she remarked, "There are three more options on the list".

A year later, the homeowners reignited our interest in purchasing their property. Following numerous discussions, and a swift walk-through of the house, Paulina was convinced that this was the perfect site for our future family home – situated literally on the school boundary, separated only by a gently flowing urban creek with contoured bike paths and a footbridge. The objective was to knock the existing dwelling down and build a rambling home for our kids and their friends to congregate after school and local church activities.

We eventually settled on price and terms, paying modestly above market value – which tugged at my inherently stubborn and frugal nature. But I recognised that the genuine value of the lifestyle, and potential it offered, was something that one can't easily put a figure on. We signed the sale documents in mid-2014 with settlement scheduled for February 2015. The ink of our signatures dried just before Morgan and I took off to the Gold Coast to celebrate his seven-year-old milestone.

WHILST WE WERE figuring out one real estate solution, our friends in Thailand had their own to resolve. Working for the anti-human-trafficking organisation that we had visited only three years earlier, they sought to raise funds to purchase land to build a much-needed safe house for their rescued children. Paulina and I stood on the ground they planned to acquire when we visited back in 2011.

Momentarily pushing aside the rough architectural sketches we had received for our new home, I gathered the family around the blueprints sent to us for the children in Thailand. Convinced that we had been blessed with enough to share, we involved the kids in the discussion, pledging a substantial contribution towards the safe-house project.

In a heartfelt agreement between the six of us, we decided not to move into our new house until the children in Thailand moved into theirs. This became a nightly prayer with our kids, anchoring them to the belief that serving those in need sometimes took precedence over our own desires.

DESPITE THE meticulous planning, my endeavours faltered. Our business capitulated to the cultural discord I described earlier, leaving me consumed with spearheading the ONEteam leadership revolution as my strategy for navigating out of the turmoil. The result: I had my slowest year of growth since inception. This severely depleted the cash reserves I relied on to make good on our charitable pledge to Thailand, and to build our new home, making for some stressful months. Eventually, it was apparent the best way to decompress my financial pressure was to sell our existing family home in Ferntree Gully.

Our house went on the market in September 2014 and was sold and settled by early 2015. This released the necessary funds to fulfil our commitment to purchasing land in Thailand, and offered a modest buffer for the immediate needs of the business. It also created uncertainty about where we would then live.

The financial strain persisted. Over a 12-month period, I lost more than $1million, driven by factors that will unfold shortly. While we had acquired land for our dream home near the school in Wantirna South, our financial situation prohibited us from proceeding with the planned demolition and its construction there. Our options were limited.

In early 2015 we reluctantly moved into the original house on the new property, despite its near-uninhabitable condition, as we couldn't afford anything else. Many windows were cracked or broken, the doors didn't shut properly, and there was no adequate heating or cooling – except for an old, sluggish combustion heater tucked in a corner. After removing the foul-smelling carpets, we resorted to bare concrete floors. Paulina arranged for the entire house to be paint-bombed an off-white colour – walls, ceilings and floors alike – ensuring no surface was spared. And in the kitchen, we made do with antiquated and unreliable appliances. It was a sacrifice we made to stay afloat financially.

I prepared the family that we would need to endure this arrangement for a few years, until the business regained some momentum, providing the necessary cashflow to proceed with our original plans. I sold the hardship to the kids as a "great adventure" – like camping, or sleeping in a makeshift cubby or treehouse. Whilst the children embraced the make-believe, after a few especially cold nights in August, Paulina hoped it wouldn't take more than one winter to find an alternative.

Months later, we heard the exciting news that construction was underway for the safe house in Thailand; the rescued Thai children would move into their new home before we moved into ours, just as we had committed.

74

unforgiving servant

AS BACK IN Motion celebrated its 15th birthday in late 2014, we regained our mojo, prospering with double-digit growth, and a record revenue of nearly $37 million. Our franchise footprint continued to expand with several new locations in Tasmania, Western Australia, Victoria, and South Australia, progressively closing in on the goal of 100 flagship locations.

As Group Director, I considered it my primary responsibility to stay relevant and connected to the people in our practices. For this reason, I made it a priority to visit all our locations every year, to engage in individual and small group conversations with as many of our clinicians and support staff as possible.

After most of my group tours, I would return to the NSO and distil the key findings into a strategic list of group imperatives to share with our GAP and advisory board. I considered literally hundreds of data points every trip and, in many cases, had to synthesise conflicting views and opinions on what to keep, stop and start as we contemplated improvements to patient experience. The consistent themes were short-listed into a tactical framework so I could transform the best ideas into everyday practice. As often was the case, my enthusiasm outweighed practicality, and I regularly put more pressure on my people than was reasonable. But incrementally, our performance grew better, our culture grew stronger, and our group grew larger.

After one such trip to the northern states, however, it was clear that not all was well with Spencer.

SPENCER WAS INNATELY entrepreneurial, hardworking, committed to clinical excellence, and wanting to run a network of more than 100 locations – something eerily familiar to my own mission. After he learned of my story, he applied to the Iceberg Leadership Institute to experience Back In Motion first hand. Observing the scale we had already built, he chose to join us rather than compete; a reason for which I felt a stronger connection with Spencer than some others.

The precipitating event for Spencer's angst was an email about revised royalty calculations I sent to a handful of franchisees in 2012 – a sensitive topic at the best of times. I explained that a software glitch had failed to factor new patients after their joining date into the royalty assessment and, as a result, significantly understated their annual liability by tens of thousands of dollars. Although I assured them I would absorb all the historical losses – as it was my mistake in the first place – the warning was clear: prepare for a step up in royalty as I applied the correct algorithm in the future.

Spencer's reply was as swift as it was combative. Despite having tripled his practice size in the three years with us, becoming one of the largest locations in our network, he wrote that he did not want to continue with the franchise. It was clear he was concerned that the correct royalty on his explosive sales was more than he wanted to pay.

Adding to his deteriorating mood, Spencer became embroiled in some local industry controversy around the same time, worsening things for him. Members of the profession complained to the APA that Spencer behaved unethically, poaching elite athletes from surrounding practices. The matter quickly blew over, but it seemed to destabilise Spencer like a compass spinning wildly, momentarily unaware of his true north.

In December 2012, Spencer threatened to unilaterally terminate his franchise licence. Such a move was complicated because he had a business partner who didn't want to leave. They had both just launched a second location, which had a separate five-year franchise licence fully paid for. Spencer also owned a small share in our occupational brand, Actif, so there was a lot of equity at risk.

Spencer also knew that if he prematurely abandoned his responsibilities we could assume the operations of his practice, because I owned the client database and held a right of transfer over the leases to his premises – weighty provisions embedded in the franchise agreement to protect me against bad leavers.

In short, the stage had been set for another good ol' fashioned gunfight... one that was going to take years to resolve and leave us both wounded and regretful.

TENSE BUT RESPECTFUL conversations ebbed and flowed between us for many months. Accordingly, I decided to suspend all increases in the royalty calculation, recognising wisdom as the better part of valour.

But Spencer and his partner were out of sorts; they were having predictable difficulties as they spread themselves across two practices. Spencer was also simultaneously balancing his commercial responsibilities with considerations of joining the Australian Olympic Team for Rio as a supporting physiotherapist, a pathway with no certainties of success. There were enormous competing tensions.

Spencer's situation worsened with a data breach in his local practice during the intervening weeks. Ransomware temporarily crippled his local network, despite industry-grade enterprise protections. It was a brute force password attack that caught us by surprise. An international hacker infected Spencer's practice software with a virus, demanding $5,000 to unlock 8,000 patient files. The scam was linked to a recent spate of malicious cyber-attacks within the Australian small business sector and across Russia, Europe, and America.

Our IT team responded immediately, quickly confirming the data was fully encrypted and thus an impotent threat. A full system backup was restored, helping Spencer resume trade quickly. Whilst I'm sure he was grateful being part of our franchise system that day, careless alarmism and hunger for free press led him to report the activity to the mainstream media. Our brand quickly became the face of negligence throughout public social media platforms and industry chat groups. Scandalous click-bait reporters inaccurately wrote of personal health data being breached, scaremongering that our patients' privacy was at risk. Spencer even took to his own Twitter account to promote the "hacking" out of misguided appeal for sympathy, completely naïve to the backlash he (and Back In Motion) would receive.

I had to go into full-scale, brand damage-control mode – issuing statements to the franchisees, APA, and publishing a short press release to the public media myself. Whilst I assured everyone the matter was an isolated case, and the threat had been swiftly resolved, the whole affair heightened my interest to deal with the more serious underlying question of Spencer's long-term loyalty to our brand.

THE UNCERTAINTY LINGERED whilst I was in the process of launching ONEteam, changing the composition of my executive team and senior staff, finalising our guardianship application with DFFH, travelling back and forth overseas, celebrating my award for Entrepreneur of the Year, and hosting the SOS Winter Gala Ball. I certainly had more than one plate spinning, but regarding this particular issue, I was largely at the mercy of Spencer's timeline.

After a failed informal mediation, Spencer and I ended up in a marathon phone call on New Year's Eve of 2013. Our family was staying at Phillip Island, and I excused myself from the dinner table to take the call. I returned well after dark, having spent more than two hours pacing the wet sand of the beach front, locked in relentless horse trading. We eventually found middle ground, a fair compromise for both parties. The success of our peace treaty hung in the balance of Spencer securing the necessary finance to meet his financial obligations, and agreeing to terms with his business partner over their intended share swap. Regardless, I felt we had summitted the hardest peak of the mountain range. The agreed terms were captured in an email just before the stroke of midnight – marking the end of a troublesome year.

BY FEBRUARY, SPENCER had reneged. Formal mediation was slated for late March 2013. My battle-weary lawyer went for the top and secured the Chairman of the Victorian Bar, also an Honourable Justice to the Victorian Supreme Court Bench, as the independent mediator. He ran the arbitration like his court room.

Spencer pulled no punches in his opening remarks, characterising me as "opportunistic", "unscrupulous", "unreasonable", "unfair", "unconscionable", and one who "acted in bad faith". I'd heard the same accusations from anyone who didn't like my decisions – as though it was a lift out of page nine of the franchisee playbook. Otherwise, Spencer may have simply googled every unsavoury term of reference in the Franchise Code of Conduct, jamming them into one paragraph to sound convincing. His choice of words certainly didn't bode well for a constructive negotiation.

Fortunately, I had everything I needed to defeat Spencer's arguments – royalty summaries, billing reports, financial statements, performance statistics, and our franchise file notes. My compelling counter proposal to the mediator was a fair and reasonable way for Spencer to exit the group, and for his business partner to remain.

When the joint session concluded, as typical in these situations, we were ferried to private rooms as the mediator ran up and down the corridor exchanging terms and counterpunches like a mere messenger boy. It was a predictably long and tedious day but, just before 6pm, we all put our signatures on three separate, handwritten deeds, co-authored by the representative counsellors.

As we stood to leave, I walked the labyrinthine corridors of the legal firm alongside Spencer's lawyer. He privately confided his relief that it was "finally done".

Sadly, it wasn't.

THE NEXT DAY, I commissioned *Project Seiko*; the offboarding of Spencer and one of our largest flagship practices from our group – so named because *time* was of the essence. The team reluctantly took charge of unscrambling the egg.

Problem is, Spencer did not pay his debts. He didn't remove his signage and branding. He did not refit his practice like he was required. He did not return all promotional and training materials, including our systems manual and marketing collateral. He continued to enjoy all the benefits of our brand and franchise system without fulfilling his obligations under our agreed terms.

Spencer wouldn't return my calls; nor would his lawyer. Seemingly, his legal fees hadn't been paid either.

My team urged me to pursue Spencer relentlessly with every military grade weapon at my disposal. Everybody wanted the nuclear option. In mid-June, against all legal advice, I wrote to Spencer and his wife off the record, appealing to them on a personal basis to retain legal counsel again, settle their debts, and avoid the serious escalation our litigation team were otherwise hell bent on pursuing.

My concern wasn't for Spencer at this point, but rather his business partner. The younger physio was a valued franchisee who had remained loyal to me, and was at risk as a co-guarantor if Spencer's actions attracted claims from creditors under their unsettled partnership agreements.

It was a three-way standoff. I couldn't envisage a strategy that won any party their desired victory. Any one initiating legal aggression against the other was likely to trigger their own demise. At the same time, none of us were able to walk away, extricating ourselves from obligations, without suffering a commercial loss and legal exposure. We were all trapped in the same strategic tension, three mice exhausting ourselves with frantic energy in an unsolvable maze.

The drama kept driving me to prayer, hoping for an outside event or interparty dialogue to break the gridlock. I needed a miracle.

NOVEMBER 2014, THE second anniversary of our dispute, was marked by Spencer reaching out and pleading with me to accept a third of his debt as full and final payment, releasing the registered securities I held over him.

I was torn between the competing opinions of Paulina, our board, legal counsel, management staff, and Spencer's junior partner. The right strategy forward wasn't obvious. Most advised against releasing the securities without ensuring closure on all matters. Spencer had proven to be consistently untrustworthy in our dealings, and we didn't believe his intentions were honourable. But I sensed God whisper to me to pull away from conventional thinking and seek His direction.

I was in the habit those years of going on a prayer walk at lunchtime. I had the hour reserved in my diary so my Executive Assistant wouldn't sneak meetings or phone calls during that time. But this matter required more than a conversational prayer as I walked around the block; I needed to *go up the mountain.*

I took a few days to fast and pray in isolation.

God drew my attention to the parable of the *Unforgiving Servant* (Matthew 18:21-35). It tells the story of a king who was calling in the debts from his workers. One servant owed a huge amount of money (let's say $100,000) but couldn't pay it. The king ordered that the man and his family be sold into slavery to pay off the debt. After the man pleaded for mercy, begging for more time, the king showed compassion and forgave the debt. This same servant was owed a relatively small amount (let's say $100) by a fellow worker. Ironically, even though he had just been granted a pardon, the first servant demanded that the other's debt be paid immediately. When the second worker was unable to pay, the shameful debtholder sent him to prison. This *unforgiving servant's* actions were seen and reported to the king. Upon hearing that the ungrateful worker refused to forgive his fellow man, the king reneged his mercy from the first servant and sent him to be tortured until his debt was paid.

Whilst unlikely a true story, Jesus is damning of the unforgiving servant's ingratitude and hypocrisy. The story teaches us that God is like the king, willing to show mercy and forgiveness to those who are also merciful and forgiving to others. This principle is embedded in the Christian liturgy of the Lord's Prayer: "Forgive us our trespasses, as we forgive those who trespass against us" (Matthew 6:12 NKJV). The enduring profundity of this timeless message is inescapable throughout universal human culture.

The implications for me were obvious; I immediately knew which character I was in this story. I felt ashamed for my unforgiveness toward Spencer, and sensed that many blessings and breakthroughs I had been praying for over the last year may have been suffocated, hindered, or even blocked by my sin. I thought about missed business opportunities, stymied cash flow, trading losses, and the difficulties I faced with our various property dealings.

God searched my heart and revealed the anger I harboured towards Spencer for publicly criticising me, sabotaging our group culture, and disregarding his legal responsibilities. All this, yet knowing I had been forgiven such a great debt by God already.

It was a sobering conviction; I was compelled to yield. Not to Spencer, as it were, but rather to God and His purposes. I knew my behaviour was not reflecting the nature of God or bringing Him honour. It was clear I had to let go of my emotions, ego, and will.

God wanted me to learn how to forgive and love my enemies (Luke 6:27, 35), rather than seek fleeting satisfaction with revenge or payback. As Saint Augustine said: "Unforgiveness and resentment are like drinking poison and hoping the other person is going to die". Bitterness had polluted my inner world, and the only antidote was to release Spencer from his obligations to me.

My legal and management teams naturally had difficulty accepting this position, especially given the mountain of evidence we had accumulated in our defence. It was difficult to walk the line between grace and justice, clearly a tightrope on which I had lost my balance many times before.

I wrote to Spencer, accepting his reduced settlement offer and agreeing to release his securities. My only condition was that he provide the same to his business partner, thereby facilitating simultaneous, three-way relief of everybody's obligations. I hoped the concession would defuse the atomic bomb suspended in mid-air above each of our homes.

To guard our own hearts against insidious greed, Paulina and I committed every dollar we received from Spencer's payment to be sent to the children in Thailand. We yearned for a meaningful outcome from this ordeal, unable to envision anything more impactful than to invest into the young lives of those who had suffered more than we could imagine.

SPENCER PROMISED SETTLEMENT on three different occasions over the next few months and, unsurprisingly, failed to deliver each time. It's not clear whether he mistook my offer to be a sign of weakness that he could exploit, or whether he was preoccupied with other worries, but he didn't sign the revised deeds, pay his reduced sum, or release his business partner from overshadowing securities.

By October 2015, all formal communication between the three parties ceased without any formal resolution.

It had been an exhausting episode with an unsatisfying end. Spencer had seemingly won. He kept his practice, had an independent brand, didn't pay his fees, and had no legal consequences. I feared that the hurtful mess, and a vast number of practical issues, had been simply swept under the proverbial rug, praying that God would help anyone who happened to trip upon it in their travels. But my business with God was done. I moved on with renewed focus for my mission of 7/50/100, as did Spencer's business partner. He who went on to become one of our most successful and celebrated franchisees of all time.

75

metamorphosis

THE DIRECTORS' CONFERENCE in February 2015, themed *Metamorphosis*, was hosted in Mooloolaba and, once again, proved one of the highlight events of our year. We took advantage of the superb weather and atmosphere of the Sunshine Coast to treat our franchisees to industry-leading professional development, an elegant black tie masquerade ball, and a message focussed on the importance of change.

It was clear to me that healthcare in Australia was evolving. Legislators were becoming more open-minded about commercial opportunities. Public health services were being de-centralised. Service providers were looking to horizontally integrate. Insurers had commenced vertical integration, acquiring primary and allied health services under their umbrella. Compensable third parties were expecting more accountability. And clients were understandably demanding more holistic service and sustainable results. Everybody in the stakeholder chain wanted more value for their money, and I was determined Back In Motion could deliver.

My mantra that year: "Change is inevitable, progress is optional". Previous personal and business experiences had sculpted and eroded me like the crashing of waves upon the cliffs. I didn't want to let the new tide rush in without us being prepared for it. I encouraged our team to increase their tolerance for strain, enlarge their capacity for growth, and see change as an opportunity.

To achieve 7/50/100 we needed to be innovators, positive disrupters, influencers, and early-adopters. Too many people within our sector were conservative, resisting opportunities to try new things. That wasn't to be us! I wanted to ride the waves of possibility, and if we couldn't find any, create our own.

One paradigm I wanted to smash was the perceived $2 million glass ceiling everyone presumed existed in our franchises. We had dozens of businesses that had cracked the $1.5million thresholds – sometimes very quickly after launching – but, for whatever reasons, people had duped themselves into thinking that was the limit.

I joined with a handful of ambitious franchisees within the GAP to challenge this, commissioning Taskforce 2/20 – a campaign to identify creative strategies which enabled our practices to sustainably exceed $2 million annual revenue with minimum 20% profitability. As if anyone needed incentives, given the obvious financial benefit they'd enjoy from such success, I sweetened the pot and offered the first franchisee to hit the target, lunch or dinner *anywhere* in Australia at a restaurant of their choice.

In a case of poetic justice, Spencer's prior business partner was the first past the post in this challenge; a fitting salve considering the hardships he had endured in the years preceding. Like Roger Bannister breaking the four-minute mile in 1954, and then paving the way for 1,663 others who then realised it was possible, many other franchisees followed suit.

A connoisseur of fine dining, and an enthusiast for resort living, our winner and his wife elected for lunch at Pebble Beach – an exclusive waterside restaurant nestled inside the extravagant resort Qualia on the northernmost tip of Hamilton Island. Famous for being the set of the 2022 Hollywood rom-com *Ticket to Paradise* with George Clooney and Julia Roberts, Paulina and I didn't need any convincing to share a beautiful weekend with them in the Whitsundays.

Whilst the occasion was a wonderful way to cement our friendship, the greater celebration became the recognition that, despite facing unprecedented change, Back In Motion was primed for new achievements previously thought impossible.

TECHNOLOGY WAS THE future of healthcare, and our in-house software BIMLogic was fast-becoming obsolete. A rigorous review of the alternatives was necessary.

Evo™ was born in April 2015 – the first version of our newly developed super-code. This updated application endured numerous testing phases before being released to the group, providing access to faster and more advanced business and clinical reporting, positioning us for the new world of online bookings and compatibility with smartphone technology.

A further three stages later rolled out in 2016, making Evo one of the leading technology platforms in our sector, and the envy of competitors who couldn't keep up with the millions we invested every year.

Uncertainty in Australian manufacturing and production industries was another burgeoning risk. The downturn in manual labour sectors threatened many of our longstanding Actif contracts with blue-chip clients. Workcover also introduced numerous reform measures around return-to-work, leading to the strongest and most imposing legislation governing worker's compensation and injury in our country's history. Both changes demanded Actif to be innovative with our injury management and rehabilitation approaches, and to think creatively how we approached commercial opportunities.

It was obvious we needed more scale and expertise in our small occupational health team to withstand the forces against us. I went shopping for a new business to propel Actif with a different trajectory.

Rankin Occupational Safety and Health (ROSH) was established in 1990. It provided risk management consultancy services to a wide range of industries in South Australia, Victoria, and New South Wales, and was far better entrenched in the Australian industrial sector than Actif. Its team specialised in rehabilitation, return-to-work services, occupational health safety risk management consultancy, pre-placement medicals, and onsite injury management services. ROSH was a medium-sized consultancy, highly respected for their quality and expertise, and the perfect vehicle to carry us to new heights.

In August I announced our outright purchase of ROSH and its integration as a specialist division of Actif, immediately securing exciting pilot projects with insurance agents in South Australia to cement our place as a credible, national service provider. The timing proved fortuitous. Actif doubled, and then multiplied again the following 12 months. We leap-frogged competitors and won contracts that previously were out of reach. In turbulent water with unpredictable currents, our group not only floated, we made significant headway.

Not to be outdone by their smaller cousin, Revita stepped up and punched against its weight. Enjoying 100% comparative growth, it become the number one choice in allied health for many large nationalised aged care providers. We launched in Queensland, bringing on more occupational therapists and podiatrists to our growing staff of professionals to further complement the service model.

In the home stretch of our three-year strategic plan, 7/50/100 felt within reach. To ensure we didn't falter in the final months, I brought on two colleagues to specifically drive network growth; established new practices in all major capital cities; and converted many local independent brands into our group.

As the dust settled on another hectic year of growth, it was clear: new miracles had unfolded. Despite the industry-wide headwinds of change and adversity, we were on track to achieving the seemingly impossible goal I had set forth with the inception of ONEteam – doubling the group within three years. We were on the cusp of a transformative moment, poised to break free from the constraints of the past, a papillon emerging from its cocoon.

76
foreign affairs

IN EXPLORING EVERY conceivable way for our brand to expand, I entertained numerous international opportunities; some came to us, others I chased.

Whilst my network development team was hungry to unearth every possibility to push our brand into new countries, Paulina had concerns about taking our business offshore. She foresaw the unsustainable workload, extensive travel that would keep me away from home for longer stretches, the challenge posed by conflicting time zones, and the inherent complexities of managing a multinational presence.

In my folly, I was determined.

Applying for extensive trademark protections in as many countries possible, it quickly became clear that others had beaten me to the register in the United Kingdom and New Zealand. I also learned of imitators using variations of my trademark in the USA and Canada, copycats riding our coattails.

The only way forward in countries where our trademark was unavailable was to accept a variation in name, retaining only the recognisable imagery of our beloved "naked man" as the consistent thread. Obviously, we weren't the first to resort to alternate branding strategies when moving abroad. Diet Coke trades as Coca-Cola Light in Europe. Kellogg's Coco Pops in Australia are Choco Krispies in Mexico. And when Burger King expanded to Australia, the name was already taken, so franchise veteran Jack Cowin took the opportunity to christen the company after himself, Hungry Jacks – literally making a *name* for himself.

I now joined the fray with Motion Health as our international spin-off.

It took me three years to round out a complete set of protections for our intellectual property in over 50 countries, covering most of Europe, Asia, the Middle East, South Africa and the Americas. I registered our web domains, social media handles, business names, and word and image trademarks in multiple classes. We were thorough, even if a little late to the party in some instances.

As we identified countries for a likely launch, I factored the cultural and competitive landscape in each jurisdiction, the way different healthcare systems operated, likely acceptance and adoptability of our franchise model in context, and even the economic stability and legal rigour of each geography.

The UK seemed the right place to start.

CHLOE, AN ENGLISH-TRAINED physiotherapist, honed her skills during the early 2000s working in Australia and New Zealand, where she first encountered Back In Motion. On returning home to the UK in early 2004, she set up her own practice and – presumably as a nod to the inspiration she found abroad – unimaginatively named it *Back In Motion* also.

Seven years later, using her married name – seemingly to conceal her prior known identity – Chloe reached out to me. Her request was for a detailed rundown of our franchising opportunity, citing plans to immigrate to Australia and start a business with us here. Nothing eventuated from her inquiry, but I soon later discovered Chloe had launched her own franchise model in the UK, under our shared moniker.

It was 2014 when I received her Opposition Notice to our trademark application in the UK. Recognising I had no legal entitlements in her country, I figured the best way to overcome an "enemy" was to make them a friend. I offered a creative collaboration. With the transferrable learnings and replicable system proven by our extensive footprint in Australia, combined with her startup in northern England, the mutual benefits were potentially numerous.

By Christmas we were locked in two-way due diligence and detailed negotiations. The total operating revenue of her fledgling network was comparable in financial performance to only one of our smallest franchised practices in Australia. Chloe was heavily dependent on part-time and casual clinical staff, rendering an unstable workforce. Her practices operated entirely out of co-located facilities that limited her brand exposure, but she appeared values-driven, congruent with our clinical and business philosophy, and appropriately ambitious to grow. It also seemed the industry and market forces in the UK at the time could be ethically exploited by our mutual strengths, providing a first mover advantage over other would-be operators.

I proposed a joint venture to franchise 80 practices throughout England – a single presence in each county – and then extend to the rest of the UK after establishing our beachhead. Chloe brought local knowledge, six locations and, most importantly, the registered Back In Motion trademark to the partnership. I brought scalable systems and technology with an industry team experienced in marketing, HR, finance, network development, practice performance, training and professional development, and clinical practice. I also had the capital to fund our growth. We agreed to share the equity in the initiative – 50% ownership each – a fair exchange on most assessments.

From February to May of 2015, our respective advisors went hard pulling together the multi-layered legal documentation. The complexity put the deal at risk a few times, but eventually Chloe settled her buy-in fee and was installed as my UK Director, carrying the front-line responsibility to manage and support our emerging network, reporting to me as Group Director.

I flew to London for ten days in June to finalise the last of our checks and balances, meeting Chloe and her husband in person. I worked with the team for a few days, visited all their premises, assessed new location possibilities, and gained a better understanding of the feel and flow of the physiotherapy profession in the UK. I connected with representatives of the National Health Service (NHS), Primary Care Trusts, Commissioning Groups, insurers, and likely referrers. I also made time to meet with Athletics UK, Unified Health, and various private practitioner groups that might one day form a coalition with us.

Two weeks later, Chloe arrived in Melbourne to complete her training with us, meet the NSO team, visit our flagship practices, and run through a fast-tracked curriculum of Iceberg Leadership. As she boarded her flight home, I feared her A380 may have been so overloaded with documentation, manuals, and promotional materials, it might be unable to take-off.

I should have feared her mental load. Upon arriving home, Chloe was overcome with doubt in her capacity to pull off the scale, sophistication, and responsibility of our planned network in the UK. She worried about the legal ramifications of underperformance and wanted to minimise her financial exposure. In a surprise turnaround, after seven months of planning, Chloe proposed a deal where I would buy her out for $1million, granting me full ownership of the venture. She suggested remaining on the payroll for two years to kick start our expansion, but because of her change in heart, my confidence in her was shot.

As quickly as our collaboration had begun, it was over. I wondered quietly if I had been played for a second time by the same person. *Fool me once, shame on you. Fool me twice, shame on me.*

Chloe gained enormous amounts of commercially sensitive information from our training programs and legal disclosures. As my hopes for a launch in the UK evaporated, it was hard to ignore Chloe's improved website and promotional literature featured many similarities to our Australian brand positioning and, in some cases, verbatim language. Whilst it's said, "imitation is the highest form of flattery", I felt hoodwinked.

Paulina mustered sympathetic and supportive encouragements, but I'm sure she was quietly rejoicing that, at least for the moment, we were not only an Australian-owned business, but we remained in Australia *only*.

WITHIN DAYS OF ceasing discussions with Chloe, a French-Canadian physiotherapist of a large sports medicine chain wanted to explore a partnership together. Arnaud operated a network of sixteen multidisciplinary rehabilitation centres in Quebec. Founded in 1987, and with close links to professional sporting teams across the country, Arnaud had chosen to franchise his brand with the help of two other physio partners. However, they each still owned (and somewhat financially relied upon) their own single, independent practices. None of them were putting much effort into the parent franchisor, which was necessary to make it a success. They also faced a slowing in their franchise enquiry rates due to competitors starting to build scale of their own, fracturing their relative control of the market.

Arnaud wanted to learn how we managed to grow so quickly, control the quality of our clinical care, and built scalable systems that supported an expansive network. By October 2015, he landed in Melbourne with his two business partners to explore a venture together, with our NSO team hosting their second international delegation within four months.

We wined and dined, exchanged gifts of Vegemite for genuine Canadian maple syrup, and then quickly got down to business. They eagerly observed our team at work, trying to glean everything they could about what we did, why it worked, and how it might transfer into their context. In reverse, we examined every aspect of their business model, corporate structure, shareholder agreements, financial performance, business plans, growth projections, trademark protections, franchise documentation, compliance processes, and marketing strategies. Our team did a deep dive into their client analytics including demographics, core services, pricing, and clinical outcomes. We showed them *ours*, and they showed us *theirs*.

By the end of the week, we had a formal proposal on the table to launch 50 Back In Motion locations in Quebec, and up to 100 practices in all of Canada. The new in-country parent entity was to be co-owned by the three Canadians and myself – each holding a 25% stake. We planned to publish a press release and host an industry launch in Montreal before April 2016.

To build confidence in our approach, I commissioned extensive financial modelling and site mapping to compare revenue buildups, costs, earnings, and productivity ratios across six different growth scenarios. Drinking my own Cool Aide, I choked. In the end, overcooking the analysis, I gave everyone – including myself – ample reasons to doubt the possibility of our likely success.

By January 2016, we agreed it was better to remain friends in the industry at large rather than overreach for a trans-continental partnership. We retreated to our separate businesses, me exhausted and now wary of my second near-miss of an international expansion in the same year.

Paulina breathed another sigh of relief.

AS THESE TWO doors closed, nine more opened. Over the next eighteen months, I was approached by interests in India, the Middle East, Philippines, South Africa, Vietnam, and New Zealand. I was ensnared in my own international wild goose chase, possibly for no good reason other than ego.

Ashutosh, owner of central India's largest physiotherapy and rehabilitation centre in Nagpur, sought my help to develop systems to improve their quality of patient care and business operations. Around the same time, but unrelated, Davesh applied for a master franchise licence to operate Back In Motion in Mumbai and Delhi, convincing himself that he could be the first to scale physiotherapy across his country.

Ritika from FranGlobal pressed me to work with her on expansion into Vietnam. Her firm had successfully done so with other major brands, including Cheesecake Shop, GAP, Max Brenner, Coffee Club, Boost Juice, and others across the Asia Pacific region. Their research showed Vietnam was enjoying incredible growth, owing to the rapid increase of the aging population, rise in consumer awareness to western medicine, favourable government policies, modernization of healthcare infrastructure, and growing medical tourism industry. She believed the timing was perfect for Back In Motion's uptake, and introduced me to many of her contacts. For months I batted away numerous approaches from various entrepreneurs who wanted to grab the advantage through a licensing arrangement with us, but few met my expectations.

And there was Gurvan, a management consultant based in Dubai, UAE, who pitched me with a mandate from one of his investor clients to collaborate on the feasibility of developing a sports-physiotherapy clinic in Kuwait. His country demonstrated strong demand for our services given the high-income levels, large expatriate community living abroad there, and their rapid increase in sports participation. The client was from a prominent family in the country and had direct access to sufficient capital to fund the project. Because of our successful track record, Gurvan wanted me to set up the prototype clinic, teach his management team how to operate it, and then expand into neighbouring countries where they perceived sufficient demand.

Many of the offers that came my way were attractive at first – if not, at least flattering – but during all this I was also preoccupied with resolving Spencer's exit, reeling from the failed launch in the UK, and opening 15 new practices in Australia. I slowly recognised the myriad of offshore opportunities as unwanted distraction and, in a rare insight to my limitations, closed most conversations not long after they begun. Timing was wrong; strategy was flawed; or quite simply, I was not ready.

After spending nearly two years in late night and early morning video conferences trying to build partnerships with people around the world, I had nothing to show for it. Well, not entirely. I had bags under my eyes, an exhausted team, and a frustrated wife who wished I had just concentrated on our domestic business. Paulina's foresight had eclipsed my impatience again.

77
civil uprising

WHILE SAILING TO conquer distant shores, dissent emerged on my home soil. A civil uprising within our franchise network was gathering early momentum, challenging the methodology behind our royalty calculations.

Aligned with industry norms, our established approach had always tethered royalties to local practice revenue; the more you billed, the more you paid. However, in 2015, a fervent faction of disaffected franchisees agitated for royalties to be calibrated to profits instead – a divergence fraught with complexities.

Central to my objection to this proposal was that royalties were a "cost of business", subsidising a raft of shared services that would need to be bought if the NSO didn't provide them. These included marketing, software, bookkeeping, human resources and professional development. Furthermore, I didn't dictate to franchisees most of their costs – they chose the hours they worked, what equipment they bought, who to employ, and their personal wages. If royalties were based on profits alone, it would be too convenient for them to enjoy the support services of the NSO and obfuscate their earnings through inflated self-payments, obliterating any royalty at all. Their confusion over these salient points of control left many with a misplaced sense of unfairness in their outspoken campaign.

Sales, profitability, and cash flow stand tall as the triumvirate which shapes the destiny of any business's economic success. Amidst the daily hustle, these metrics can often become confused in the minds of business owners, so grasping their distinct attributes is pivotal.

Sales embody the influx of revenue, portraying a venture's market traction. Profitability transcends income, revealing the true earnings after all expenses, showcasing operational efficiency. Lastly, cash flow –

the heartbeat of liquidity – charts the movement of funds, underscoring the capability to meet immediate financial obligations. Unravelling the nuances between these three fiscal pillars was paramount to me successfully defending the war that raged against our royalty model. However, it didn't come easily.

For numerous franchisees, the puzzle of prioritising sales or profit was a confounding dilemma. The relationship between the two eluded them, despite both holding significant importance. It was akin to asking whether food or water was more crucial for nutrition? The answer, of course, is "both"; but for different reasons, and possibly, at different times.

Every business owner wants to enjoy large sustainable profits from their business – top line being *vanity*, and bottom-line being *sanity*. However, I taught in Back U that all start-up practices should focus on building a loyal client base in their first two years to establish sales momentum if they hoped for enduring profitability. With revenue, profits would come; one had to walk before they ran.

My simple strategy was to increase sales, decrease costs, and better utilise fixed assets (such as our premises and equipment) to create a more profitable margin for every franchisee. Our case studies proved the model, our mature practices earning substantial profits on their million-dollar-plus billables – the top performers making more money than me.

Despite my educational campaign, the franchisee onslaught eventually reached fever-pitch. A vocal minority staged semi-public protests with me at our conferences, sabotaged the GAP meetings, wrote to board members, used smear campaigns and other guerilla tactics in social media, boycotted marketing campaigns and other NSO initiatives to stonewall our growth plans, used internal Facebook groups to spread anti-royalty propaganda, and even threatened to involve sympathetic stakeholders such as the FCA if I didn't acquiesce. It was a multifaceted barrage characterised by strategic manoeuvring, ideological clashes, and intense battles for control and autonomy within our franchise system. It may have only been led by a handful of antagonists, but nobody was spared.

After months of recurring tension, I felt the teeth marks left by the irrefutable discontent. I needed to broker a peace solution, otherwise the distraction risked undermining the substance of everything we had achieved through 7/50/100.

After careful consideration, and to acknowledge and reward the franchisees who genuinely merited concessions, I implemented a progressive system of royalty reductions. The calculation remained an assessment of practice revenue as the least ambiguous means of measuring business performance, but the overall cost of royalties was designed to reduce with time. As practices achieved higher revenue milestones, their royalty percentage decreased proportionately, eventually reaching a mere 2% down from the initial 7%. (It's amazing to recall that my first two franchisees signed agreements for 11% royalties – oh, how far I had succumbed to the civil siege!)

Although this measure might not have ever satisfied my most staunch detractors, it was warmly embraced by the majority, dousing the flames of our civil strife after a protracted period of unrest. And like with most of these tornados of trouble, the peaceful quiet returned amongst the people almost as quickly as it had been stirred up.

BY THE CLOSE of 2015, I was cooked.

My schedule was over-subscribed in 15-minute increments, a chaotic tapestry woven with discordant threads of appointments, obligations, and commitments begging for attention. The online calendar managed by my assistant, once a pristine white canvas, had every square teeming with an intricate mosaic of colour-coded engagements.

Management meetings, interstate flights, videoconferences with remote teams, new practice launches, SOS outreach missions, Iceberg Leadership masterclasses, and crisis management with troublesome franchisees. I even worked that year alongside the senior minister at our local church, helping him and the eldership consider weighty matters of leadership transition and spiritual governance.

If all this wasn't enough, we were sleeping in a cramped rental property as Paulina project-managed the design and build of our new family home with all four children still in primary school.

Each day unfurled like a frantic symphony, a cacophony of urgent emails and high stakes decisions, blurring the lines between the urgent and important. Each block of time, a battleground for competing priorities, seemed to shrink under the weight of unyielding expectations, leaving little room for spontaneity or respite.

My ambitious push for 7/50/100 had almost debilitated me. Big visions are like Hollywood movie plots – they are accompanied by drama and the mundane, love and heartache, adventure and mystery, heroes and villains, miracles and disappointments. Our story over the three-year span was no different.

I completed due diligence on more than 160 practices to buy or start during that epoch, closing out with 110 locations. We billed $115m in aggregate services, treated 108,000 new patients, delivered 1.6 million discreet services, and recruited 180 new team members. We trialled a diversified service mix encompassing podiatry, clinical psychology, osteopathy, and nutrition – a deliberate strategy for a more holistic offering. We blazed new trails in Queensland and Western Australia, consolidating our footprint in all other states. We nearly even expanded into the UK and Canada. We launched our new generation, hybrid cloud practice management system, and deployed over 220 volunteers through the SOS Health Foundation.

ONEteam had been successful but, amidst our triumphs, the toll was palpable. The handful of legal disputes and financial strain I suffered in the business were all likely symptoms of my single-mindedness for growth.

I found myself at the brink of exhaustion, feeling like I had stretched every limit again. Despite Paulina's remarkable resilience and patience, even she felt pushed to her utmost capacity. We both were overwhelmed by the increasing pressure to harmonise business, church, and home within the orbit of each other and our children.

Our marriage was the stable bedrock on which everything else rested, and yet it felt vulnerable to the erosive forces swirling around us. Caught in a relentless tug-of-war, the weight of our different obligations pulled us often in divergent directions. Each passing day felt like a precarious dance on a fragile tightrope, a performance I knew I couldn't sustain, and from which I would inevitably fall.

In rare quiet moments, I secretly prayed for God to replace me at Back In Motion. I wanted out, *again*. I couldn't see how it was going to happen, but I lived in desperate hope. I didn't know if what I was facing was a cliché mid-life crisis, or just the looming unease of having worked too hard for too long.

I allowed myself to dream with Paulina about the possibility of living abroad for a year in Chile or Spain. We fantasised about putting the kids in school there, learning the local language by immersion, working remotely at a much-reduced capacity, refreshed by the cool change of a foreign culture. The decision to go loomed like a heavy fog, the path forward obscured by the myriad of responsibilities we both carried.

I longed for a circuit breaker in the octane-fuelled arrhythmia my life had become. I was teetering on the edge of burnout. Back In Motion was a mountain weighing down my shoulders, threatening to crush me.

I longed for a breath – a moment to exhale, to sit idle and unburdened. A quiet whisper with God in the solace of introspection. I craved the chance to nourish the neglected garden of my own well-being. I didn't want to just endure; I needed restored conviction in my divine purpose and calling that had dimmed in the blinding chaos of boardrooms and bottom lines.

The confluence of those destabilising months created a crescendo of new conversations and prayers. I felt tingling urgency and a relentless questioning of my choices, rattling my comfort of familiarity. As the tempest howled through my exhausted soul, I groped for answers. Introspection and aspiration danced an unlikely tango, beckoning courage and curiosity with each new beat, lifting my eyes to the future.

With the board's awareness and Paulina's cautious support, I embarked on a new initiative to pivot my destiny. I committed to a meticulously structured and exhaustive quest for the elusive Holy Grail – my successor as CEO.

CRESCENDO

2016-2022

*the climax after a progressive increase
of intensity, force, or magnitude*

Joshua:
*"Not one of God's good promises has failed. God promised to give
us a [new, bountiful] land and we got the Promised Land."*
Joshua 23:14

CRESCENDO

78	second-in-charge	373
79	halftime	377
80	bad leaver	379
81	UK, take two	383
82	crossing the ditch	386
83	cents in the dollar	388
84	injustice	392
85	razor gang	397
86	super supreme	401
87	the big apple	404
88	windfall	406
89	deal or no deal	409
90	reset	413
91	frenemies	416
92	bike-and-hike	419
93	10x	421
94	facing my accusers	424
95	the Joseph plan	431
96	harley heaven	437
97	downside up	441
98	erosion	443
99	winners again	446
100	now boarding	448
101	ACCC encore	450
102	orthotic-gate	454
103	kangaroo court	462
104	mergers and acquisitions	464

105	corporate espionage	469
106	a sporting chance	473
107	natural conclusions	475
108	little things, big wins	480
109	contagion	485
110	old nemesis	495
111	new blueprint	501
112	coke versus pepsi	506
113	spoiled for choice	509
114	future of franchising	514
115	wish list	517
116	let's go shopping	520
117	project locomotive	522
118	timely leak	526
119	cracking the valuation code	532
120	the shortlist	535
121	central station	539
122	yes-no-maybe	545
123	panic-deletions	550
124	miracles	552
125	the long goodbye	556
126	closure	560

78

second-in-charge

I WADED INTO a torrent of mixed emotions as I contemplated a new CEO taking over the business; a potent blend of excitement and apprehension swirled daily. Handing over my life's work to a stranger felt unnatural and irresponsible. Intertwined with optimism for eventual freedom were irrepressible tinges of anxiety as I imagined releasing control, trusting another with the culture I had nurtured over the years, and the uncertainty of them staying aligned to the calling God had given us. It was like forfeiting my beloved ship to a new captain, knowing that while the destination may remain unchanged, their preferred route and leadership style may differ from what I (and everybody else) was accustomed to. Every prospect of change felt like hesitant ripples in unchartered waters.

Before I recruited a CEO, I needed to recruit a *recruiter*. After months of meeting with various talent-specialists, I chose someone with extensive industry experience who was crucially aligned with my commercial and spiritual purposes.

Together, we went on the hunt for someone aged 30-55 years with a compatible values-driven ethos. My ideal candidate exuded energy and charm, possessing a knack for forging enduring connections. A steadfast dedication to healthcare was also essential. When it came to leadership, I sought an individual with exemplary emotional intelligence, adept at both strategic planning and on-the-ground, tactical execution. And I envisioned someone who could empower and guide others rather than micromanage. I admit it all seemed like a tall order, but I nervously hoped I would find the perfect match.

I slowly trawled through a long list of candidates who seemed a good fit, at least on paper. We considered executives from other franchise systems and not-for-profit organisations, successful entrepreneurs who had started and since sold their own companies, management accountants and lawyers who had switched to executive portfolios, and numerous experienced managers looking for their next hill to climb.

It was a treasure hunt, looking for a rare gem amongst diverse stones. The quest included a small handful of existing staff who applied for the role, Philip being chief amongst them. At the time, he was my most senior finance executive, and disappointed not to make the short list of candidates. This decision of mine laid the groundwork for the biggest showdown of my career, but the climax wouldn't unfold for at least another year.

It was a gruelling six months. Endless interviews, reference checking, board debates, psychometric profiling, and dinners with candidates and their families. It felt more like an Olympic decathlon than a recruitment process. I wanted to exhaust every possibility – leaving no stone unturned – fully aware that selecting the new CEO would arguably be the most critical decision of my tenure.

ASHTON HUNTER ROSE to the top, high above anyone else. His application was strong, even if not flawless. The board had reservations about his appointment, yet this was true of every candidate, each foreboding their own uncertainties.

Ashton and I laughed for months after his start at just how exhausting and comprehensive the recruitment process had been. We counted more than eight formal interviews and hundreds of emails, phone calls, and ad hoc discussions that lead to the eventual decision.

With good-nature, I occasionally reminded him when he shed tears during one of the interviews; I asked questions delving into his values, unearthing painful stories of his past. Feeling empathy for his situation, Paulina handed him a tissue to blot the tears and blow his dribbling nose. Ashton went home that afternoon, convinced he'd blown all his chances at being offered the job. We obviously didn't share that belief – his honesty was heartfelt.

Despite Paulina and I having spent an evening at dinner with Ashton and his wife, we designed one more hurdle to test his compatibility. I invited the Hunters, with their four school-aged children, to spend the day with us at our beach house on Phillip Island. We enjoyed meat and seafood on the barbeque, paddled kayaks at the beach, and engaged in genuine conversation on the deck amidst the light sea breeze.

That was, until disaster struck. One of Ashton's sons tripped on the asphalt driveway while playing basketball in his bare feet. He tore skin and nails off his forefoot. In a sudden flurry of action, I jumped in the back of the car with the wailing child while directing Ashton to the nearby emergency centre. Fortunately, there were no amputations, surgeries or even injections, but the day finished differently to how we all expected.

Many of Ashton and my earliest interactions resembled clumsy, catastrophic scenes from a catalogue of epic Chevy Chase films. We laugh now, but it's a wonder we ever got around to signing an employment agreement. Yet, by mid-December 2015, our commitment to each other was solidified.

YET ANOTHER CHRISTMAS holiday period was consumed with work. In between trips to the beach, I was attempting to master the game of corporate chess. I needed more executive firepower and strategic advantage, onboarding five new colleagues to the NSO – including the white knight I hoped Ashton would become. It was sensitive and nuanced as I reallocated responsibilities across the broad portfolios of our existing team, making room for the newcomers.

Night after night throughout January, I mapped out amendments to our strategic plan and business model, projecting the new year's financial performance, and seeking to adjust the team structure and leadership philosophy to suit.

Ashton commenced at Back In Motion in February 2016. The board collectively agreed there was no rush to put Ashton in the top job; initially, he joined second-in-charge to me as the Group Director so he could learn the ropes before accepting full responsibility for the business. His starting remuneration was more than what I had ever paid another employee, and 50% larger than the drawings I took for myself. I felt Ashton was a worthy investment – both now and for the future.

Ashton swiftly absorbed the huge changes we had experienced due to our growth following 7/50/100 and caught up quickly on the leadership revolution of ONEteam. In his first weeks, I handed him responsibility for the international trademarking project that was midway complete and the mandate for our 2/20 Taskforce. He also rode shotgun with me on the legal dispute that was lingering with Spencer, getting a front row seat to the aftershocks of its disruption on the culture and commercial confidence within the ranks of some of our fragile franchisees. It was a baptism of fire rather than gradual acclimation.

It was a lot for the new guy to take in, but I revelled in having a highly intelligent, big-hearted, God-centred, strategically motivated, tireless Energizer Bunny in my corner. For the first time, perhaps since the earliest bootstrapping years, the weighty responsibility of leading our business didn't feel as heavy or isolating.

79
halftime

FUELED WITH ENTHUSIASM – and desperate hope – that Ashton's arrival in early 2016 would release me from my weekly 70-hour work commitments, I took the opportunity to enrol in the *Halftime* executive coaching program.

Inspired by the book of the same title, which had left a profound impact on me years before when Michael handed it to me as I set off on a holiday to Europe, the year-long program promised a spiritual journey. The facilitator urged me to delve into something beyond the goals and triumphs I ardently pursued in business – in the vernacular of their program, a shift from *success* to *significance*. Through readings, thought exercises, personal coaching, and collective networking, the program offered intense collaboration and accountability as I dug deeper into the clarity of my continuously emerging life purpose.

I was already in the habit of meeting monthly with a group of incredible business leaders from my local church. We opened the Bible together, shared our high and low points in daily life, and prayed with one another. I was the youngest of the cohort, and felt privileged to be amongst a room full of successful businessmen devoted to the purposes of God. As it worked out, our entire group decided to complete the Halftime program together.

The process compelled us to research our strengths, identify our passions, and define our personal missions. It was fascinating as we candidly unpacked our secret aspirations for the future. Most men around the table were at the threshold of significant changes in their businesses or personal lives, and so the program's timing was perfect for them. By the end of the year, or shortly thereafter, almost everyone had transitioned their role, sold a business, started a new initiative, or significantly changed their responsibilities. Everyone, but me.

My plan that year was to elevate Ashton to CEO of Back In Motion by January 2017, giving him 11 months to shadow my role. I then intended to become Executive Chairman three days a week, releasing me one day to invest into SOS, and another day for mentoring young leaders through the Iceberg Leadership Institute.

With great excitement, Paulina and I also made plans for our long-awaited year abroad, set for 2018 in Chile. It would serve as a rare family opportunity for a cross-cultural adventure, accelerating the kids' mastery of Spanish, and allowing us all to immerse ourselves in Paulina's heritage.

The perfect plan entailed my return to a thriving business in 2019, with Ashton capably leading the NSO, and my role shifting to a supportive non-executive Chairman at a more sustainable and balanced pace.

It was a solid strategy, yet, as they say, most plans don't survive their first encounter with reality.

80
bad leaver

MY HALFTIME INTENTIONS quickly unravelled almost as soon as I had declared them.

As I hosted our 2016 Director's Conference in the picturesque Barossa Valley of South Australia, one of our country's premier grape growing and wine-making regions, we celebrated nearly $43million in revenues across 106 locations. I had launched eight new practices in the last year alone and welcomed 14 new franchisees. An independent staff survey revealed 95% of our 600 staff believed in the future of our vision and 99% voiced alignment with our values, endorsing us as one of the best places to work in our industry.

But there was one who stood apart from the masses in stark defiance.

Philip and I first met in high school during my VCE years. He was a giant, standing a head taller than me, but gentle in nature and softly spoken. Philip possessed an extraordinarily high IQ, loved his cricket and football, and our friendship was sealed when we both learned of our mutual faith in God. Whilst I was shooting for medicine, Philip's aspirations initially lay with aeronautical engineering. Falling short of his expectations, he settled for a career in management accounting, going on to accept a patchwork of roles in finance teams across a diverse range of organisations.

Friendship with Philip was an absolute joy but, when he begged me for a job, our relationship dynamic changed entirely. He had recently been fired and feared his ex-boss would provide a negative reference to every prospective new employer. He had missed out on multiple roles already, convinced his career had stalled, and in panic turned to me.

Paulina was adamant that employing Philip was the wrong decision. I foolishly ignored her wise intuition, *again*. (I am a very slow learner.)

In late September 2013, I hesitantly invited Philip into the senior finance role. My prayer with him that day was that the opportunity would signify a new beginning for him and that our friendship would be stronger as a result. For two-and-a-half years, both were true.

THINGS CHANGED IN early 2016.

Philip was under immense pressure and not keeping up with expectations. We had acquired two new practices with a long history of losing money and, after six months of progressive investment, reported significant losses of over $1million. The trend didn't look like it was turning in our favour, and I had to sell our family home to meet loan covenants and to keep our business solvent. The board was anxious and looked to Philip for a financial strategy to navigate out of the predicament, yet he could provide little insights or clarity.

However, what escalated into an unavoidable confrontation, was a letter I received from one of my staff in early May. The allegations were serious, and I felt nauseous reading the four-page incident report.

Amongst some of the more troubling behaviours, Philip was accused of having covered up his failure to follow a board directive to place a copy of our source code for the Evo software in our lawyer's vault. He was also found signing off false timesheets for contractors, approving hours they hadn't worked as a misplaced gesture of friendship and to accrue favours for future redemption. Furthermore, Philip reportedly spent copious hours of office time on the phone soliciting votes and raising funds for his upcoming electoral pre-selection with a national political party, neglecting his executive responsibilities in the business.

All this information was new and shocking to me. The board believed the concerns were worthy of their highest attention, charging me with the unenviable role of confronting Philip.

Distressed that his character had been questioned, Philip was quick to defend his poor performance, which he said was due to juggling multiple balls amidst fast-paced growth. I was professional and direct, but not unfriendly, when I put the matter to rest with a formal warning. Even if my love for a friend had not dimmed, my confidence and trust in his competencies had been battered by the episode.

Less than a month later, Ashton raised further concerns about slippage in Philip's performance. A chartered accountant himself, Ashton brought fresh eyes and a high standard for financial accuracy and agreed deliverables in his new capacity. He believed Philip was lagging well behind industry expectations. Incorrect financial reports, poor staff management, weak commercial judgment, cost overruns, and significant delays in the rollout of our new online time sheeting provided mounting evidence of Philip's unsuitability for the role.

I wrote Philip a note amidst some of our hardest days: "My heart is for you… our friendship transcends these difficulties… I want to help."

Shortly after, Philip confided in me that perhaps his tenure at Back In Motion was drawing to a close. It seemed to me an ideal time for Philip to depart with dignity, and I proposed a transition period of up to six months to assist him while he sought a new opportunity. Two days later, he politely declined my offer, announcing his intentions to stay in the role indefinitely, creating an ambiguous predicament.

IF THE TYRES were showing wear in May, the wheels spun right off the axle in June 2016.

We had been working feverishly on securing an alternative software developer to continue the build of our new Evo practice management program. At the beginning of the year, the board gave Philip the responsibility to lead the search.

I sat with Philip, Ashton, and a small team on the first of June for a status report on the short list of viable candidates. Expecting to be near a decision from a well-considered short-list, Philip's pitch was over in three minutes. He emphatically recommended we remain with the incumbent inadequate supplier as the path of ease, presenting no alternatives for consideration.

The room was flummoxed. Over numerous meetings in the preceding months, Philip had masterfully weaved tales of exciting new prospects, and yet when it counted, his contributions were conspicuously absent. It was a jarring realisation how unprepared he was in such a critical moment. Philip's cavalier attitude worried everyone in the room. His stark indifference to the business risks left us stunned and scrambling to fill a strategic and operational void.

Philip's failure to lead punctuated with indelible ink all the previous concerns raised about his underperformance. I could barely contain my frustration and immediately left the room to cool off.

I slept poorly that night and woke to pen what would become a pivotal email in my relationship with Philip – and, as it turns out, the next five years of my career. I didn't sugarcoat my feelings. I reiterated to him what he must have already known – how extremely disappointed, frustrated, and concerned I felt over his lack of progress in a board-mandated, time-critical project. I made clear to him that his poor commercial judgement and reluctance to take responsibility for the outcomes we entrusted to him, put the organisation at risk, leaving me with little confidence in his leadership and execution. As a matter of high priority, I requested by close of business that day, an updated project management plan, copies of his email correspondence with prospective developers, and scoping documents for the further stages of Evo development, complete with costing estimates, risk matrices, and transition timelines. These things should have all been within arm's reach if his previous representations to me were truthful. And to extend him some benefit of the doubt, I invited a concise business case, supported with evidence, why he believed the status quo was a superior strategic option to all the other alternatives.

I did not hear from Philip all day, except to receive an email at 6:05pm disclosing he was taking up a new role in a construction company in Brisbane. He tended his resignation immediately and advised he was taking personal leave for the rest of the week.

A mixed feeling of relief and dread washed over me. I was grateful for closure to what had been a tortuous few months of strained relationship, but also fearful of how I would recover momentum in our key finance and technology initiatives at such a critical time in our business.

Little did I know how much more I should have feared Philip.

81
UK, take two

AMONGST THE HARDSHIP of losing Philip – or more accurately, the gap he left behind – I was again tempted by the possibilities of expansion abroad. Despite my repeated failures, I couldn't resist the insatiable drive of the Napoleonic conquest still surging within me. The irony being, the world I ruled at home brimmed with enough excitement and challenge to consume all my attention.

I entertained a master franchise agreement with English physiotherapist Mark, and his brother-in-law, Roger. With eight practices in key locations around London, after operating for 20 years they felt like they had reached a bottleneck in their growth. Primarily, they were seeking a technology breakthrough that our proprietary system could resolve. They were congruent with our clinical philosophy, committed to systemisation within their businesses, had an appetite for expansion, and were great guys to work with. It seemed all green lights.

Our shared plan was a rapid expansion of 30 new locations across key counties in England. I worked for eight weeks refining the strategic plan, modelling the financials, and building a Gantt chart of our progressive rollout. Mark and Roger, in like form, shared their local insights and provided feedback on my proposals, enthusiastic about a complementary partnership. Ashton rode shotgun with me in most of these meetings, taking an active role in the formative strategy.

By May 2016, just as the stitching began to fray with Philip, my two newest English friends arrived in Melbourne for an intensive, five-day visit, where we showcased our operations and hammered out the detailed terms of an agreement. I appointed Roger as the CEO of the UK venture on a full-time salary, Mark continued as the principal UK clinician, and I remained committed to the ever-increasing responsibilities of the group at large.

The stage was set to finally break ground in the UK for early 2017.

I FLEW TO London one month later to meet the larger team, assess their operational rhythms, and scope the intended footprint of the first tranche of new sites. Roger and I toured their locations, meeting the key stakeholders, assessing their technology challenges and marketing opportunities, and building more layers of trust and intelligence into our relationship.

Given many of their practices were within a ten-kilometre radius in busy central London, it was quicker to ride bicycles everywhere. Clad in a suit with a laptop satchel slung over my shoulder, I darted past iconic landmarks like Big Ben and the London Eye, weaving through the chaotic traffic, dodging black cabs and vibrant red double-decker buses, en route to my next stop.

After a full schedule of promising discussions and spirited agreement – ignoring the many near-misses with impatient drivers in the bustling streets – I flew home 12 days later, convinced our foothold in London was a certain launching pad.

Conversations continued right through 2016 into another disrupted Christmas period, during which I invested countless hours working with my team to fine tune the details for the new year start in the UK.

Mark especially loved our clinical model, and Roger was excited to integrate our Evo software as the panacea to all their technology issues created by numerous disjointed and incompatible third-party vendors. But, as time went on, they desperately did not want to lose their home brand, nor did they think our trademarked derivative, Motion Health, would fly well in the UK market. They pointed out to us that the word "motion" resembled a bowel movement more than it reflected athletic activity – an inescapable embarrassment that had never crossed my mind until they made this connection. And whilst other brand variations were contemplated together, the indecision gave rise to other hurdles.

In the end, Mark and Roger were reluctant to give personal guarantees to underwrite the obligations of the UK plan, given the balance of power sat in my favour. They were also wedded to some operational processes of their own that I felt compromised the newly minted partnership.

In their exact words, they warned me: "We think Back In Motion is changing the shape of physiotherapy around the world in profound ways, but we might become the rebellious teenagers in the family. We love what you do, your systems are great, the growth is impressive, and the people are remarkable, but we are strong willed and might buck the system when we don't like being told what to do."

Their ominous predictions made me cautious, and their feet grew colder with every passing month. By April 2017, the campaign was over.

I wrote to Mark and Roger on behalf of our team, expressing that meeting great people like them was what made the journey so much fun. We agreed to remain close friends in the adventure of building like-minded business in different hemispheres. True to our mutual commitments, we have continued infrequent contact over the years since, taking the opportunity to compare notes on experiences and congratulate one another whenever our respective achievements hit the public domain.

For me, it was two bites at the same cherry, and still no result.

82

crossing the ditch

IT SEEMS OBVIOUS to me now, despite the persistent comments from my wife and the board over many years, that cutting our teeth in nearby New Zealand was a wiser expansion strategy than over-reaching for the UK or North America.

In Australia, we call it *crossing the ditch* when we fly to New Zealand across the Tasman Sea. I had done it many times to speak at industry conferences and mentor other practice owners. My Network Development team, over many years, curated a healthy database of potential employees, franchisee prospects, Back In Motion alumni, and friends in the industry. And given our proximity, we regularly enjoyed an influx of Kiwi graduates every year, as they savoured the opportunity to work in our network.

Despite the close geography, I had already struck out many times attempting to build our brand in New Zealand, hindered mostly by a small business in the South Island town of Dunedin, which traded under our exact name. Realising my expansion opportunities were limited while they held legal rights to our shared name, I spent the first half of 2016 trying to convince the three owners to an outright sale of their trademark. I toiled for four months, flying back and forth, trying to agree on terms. However, their demands were unreasonably high, leading to my adoption of the US foreign policy stance of refusing to negotiate with *terrorists*. I disappointingly conceded that any expansion into New Zealand would need to be under our substitute brand, Motion Health.

Still reverberating in my ears was Roger's crude observation about how easily the word "motion" could conjure thoughts of bowel movements. Nervously, I hoped for a more discerning perspective from the Kiwis, our name embodying a respected brand dedicated to optimal human physical movement rather than any unintentional links to gastrointestinal activities or awkward bathroom references.

One could only hope.

BY MID 2016 my Network Development Manager introduced me to her leading candidate for partnership in Auckland. Andy was the owner of Physio One, five small locations generating over $1 million in aggregate revenue, and eager to grow.

Andy heard me speak many times at various conferences over the years, most recently one hosted by Physiotherapy New Zealand (PNZ). During my keynote I shared some of the high- and low-lights of my growth journey, Andy reflecting soon thereafter that franchising was an option he should explore further.

I was scheduled to be back in Auckland in August 2016 to host an Iceberg Leadership masterclass on behalf of PNZ. Whilst there, I made plans to meet up with Andy and his wife. I visited his flagship practice in Albany, which was a beautiful large open space with six consulting rooms and a well-equipped rehabilitation space. We also road-tripped to a few of his satellite locations, giving me an opportunity to observe the interactions with his team, taking special note of how he led through the various operational challenges common to all businesses.

We quickly sensed a kindred spirit. Andy expressed enthusiasm in the same master franchise arrangement I had unsuccessfully negotiated three times in the UK and Canada. With proposals and templates already created from my recent past attempts, I was able to give Andy a swift insight into the costs, obligations, and opportunities.

Whilst there were numerous hurdles moving outside of Australia, by November I officially galvanised our first international expansion, announcing five new locations in Auckland and surrounds.

What had taken me years in deliberations and false starts with others, took less than five months with what proved to the be the *right* person.

83
cents in the dollar

WHILE I HAD gained confidence from my dealings with Andy in New Zealand, I couldn't say the same of other recent franchisees.

Robert, a 63-year-old physiotherapist, had self-reportedly built from scratch the largest practice in Western Australia during the 1990s. Forced to sell it in a divorce settlement, Robert now set himself the new goal of running a million-dollar practice by 2020.

He was generating minimal revenues in substandard premises when I first met him, but had already scoped a new premium double-storey location and pre-negotiated with the landlord preferential terms for six consulting rooms, a large rehabilitation studio, and ample parking to support the volume of clients he anticipated. Given the rent was disproportionately high, and thus unsustainable for a physiotherapy practice, Robert intended on subletting the first floor as serviced offices. His hope was that Back In Motion was going to help convert all this potential into new fortunes.

I scheduled commencement of his franchise for March 2015 but, due to unexpected financial problems at the time, Robert couldn't secure the capital, and our offer lapsed. This should have been a red flag to me at the time, but his personal balance sheet revealed he had sufficient accessible assets to meet his financial obligations for both a franchise licence and practice fit out. He was also very compelling in his reasons for the inconvenient delays.

Based on his assurances, in July 2015 I granted Robert a new franchise licence with the caveat that it would not officially commence until March 2016, at which point he would supposedly have access to all his monies, and our fees would fall due and payable.

In a comedy of errors that hindsight says I should have predicted, Robert commenced in the intervening months to work with the landlord on his new practice design and committed to leasehold improvements outside our purview. His premature actions burned up his limited cash reserves – which frankly, were spent on the wrong things.

By December, Robert was in significant financial distress again, and he hadn't even made it to the starting line of his franchise commencement date. Our head of Fit Out and Compliance at the time was determined to cut him loose and avoid any further fallout for Robert or us.

Robert and his wife remained adamant they wanted to forge ahead, appealing to my goodwill to not give up on them. Their story, draped in despair, resonated with my compassionate nature, drawing me in like a moth to the flame. Robert was confident that with a $200,000 lump sum they would soon access from his superannuation nest egg, he would be able to settle all their commitments – among them, a high interest-bearing loan they had taken out without our knowledge for a fit out we hadn't approved.

In equal measures of grace and stupidity, I supported his intentions. Empathy betrayed me, unknowingly wielding against my better judgement. I let Robert defer payment of his initial franchise fee for another few months to give him the best opportunity to regather financial momentum and get in front of his debts. For the most part, I left the situation in the hands of our field team, happily hearing regular reports of Robert's steady growth over the months that followed.

That was, until September 2016. Ashton and I received an emotionally charged email from Robert confessing he would not be able to settle his weighty debt with us. Ashamed of the situation he now faced, Robert pleaded for another 12-month extension on his loan so that he could use his small remaining capital to cover the exorbitant rent he was carrying.

Reluctantly, I reported all this to the board. Understandably, they felt like I had been taken for a ride based on fanciful promises and endless goodwill. I had invested in someone who wasn't telling the truth, embarrassed again by my naïveté and infantile gullibility, both mocking me in the stark light of reality.

WITH A FIRM mandate from the board, I sent a formal Notice of Default for the unpaid franchisee fees to be settled by the end of September 2016.

Robert argued that nobody could have foreseen his series of bad luck and financial challenges. Citing his practice's recent record performance of 23% annual growth (and 109% increase on their seasonal low in January of that year), he felt confident he could repay the entire debt by November if I called off the dogs.

I should have known better, but the illusion of trust and hope was a relentless force, tempting me to believe in the inherent goodness of people.

I commissioned the team to put in place a full-scale campaign to help save Robert's practice. They considered new low-cost local area marketing initiatives; attempted to sublease unused space on the top floor of his premises to lighten the cost burden; worked on deferring supplier costs; and even met with Robert and his accountants, mortgage broker, and a lawyer to consider alternative funding pathways, including accessing his wife's superannuation funds prematurely, and securing loans from family members.

Inevitably, Robert ran out of options. He was penniless. He did not qualify for any institutional loan and, tellingly, his family was not prepared to lend him money either.

I was out of options also. I formalised our position with an official termination notice of his franchise agreement, immediately instigating procedures to protect our brand and clientele. I also issued him a creditor's statutory demand for the substantial money Robert owed our company, along with a letter of demand to Robert and his wife as personal guarantors.

Sadly, Robert declared bankruptcy in November, and I didn't hear from him again.

Robert went silent on all matters regarding his post-termination obligations. His lease was not transferred; the client list was not on-sold; and of course, we didn't receive payment for any of the money he owed us. The experience became another lesson etched into my memory; a harsh, but necessary awakening, a beacon guiding me toward a more guarded path, where wisdom and caution walk hand-in-hand with empathy.

Back In Motion proved to be Robert's largest creditor in an unsecured pool of substantial debts. I waited nearly four years for closure, eagerly anticipating payment after liquidators sought to recover value from his spread of assets. When the funds transfer eventually came through, it totalled a meagre two cents on the dollar. Our CFO joked that the pittance was barely enough to buy us a celebratory lunch for having concluded the matter.

He quickly forgave me for not laughing.

84
injustice

ROBERT'S FIASCO WOULD have been easier to accept if it had been an isolated experience. Typically, though, these tragedies ran in pairs or triplets, and sometimes, like in 2016, I scored the quadrella. If I had been a betting man, I would have made a windfall.

Derya and Emir Zeynip were a pleasant middle-aged couple who emigrated to Australia from the Middle East in their early childhood. I studied physiotherapy with Derya at the University of Melbourne, but it wasn't until after she heard me speak at an event hosted by the APA that she expressed interest in joining Back In Motion. Her application letter explained that whilst we had not spent much time together as undergraduates, she admired from a distance the success of our business.

Shortly thereafter, I welcomed the Zeynips into the group, granting them a franchise licence for their existing location.

For the most part, their first five years in our group were unremarkable. Our fit out transformed their tired, outdated premises into a state-of-the-art facility. They tracked through most of the key milestones we hoped for our franchisees, setting record sales year after year, tripling the size of their practice, fast approaching the million-dollar-club. Derya and Emir were a quiet, conservative and compliant couple who beavered their way to steady growth with rewarding financial returns, creating little disruption.

For all these reasons, I was surprised that, at their five-year anniversary, the Zeynips had no intentions of renewing their franchise for another term. In a sit-down with Derya, she disclosed they had committed to leasing their premises to another tenant, and implied they were going to travel for six months in the second half of the year before resuming independent clinical practice elsewhere.

I reluctantly accepted their decision, agreeing it was a straightforward process to wind up their licence when there was no default or dispute to remedy.

By June of that year, the Zeynip's attorney wrote to me with a combative undertone, asserting a different story. The couple had changed their minds. Rather than travel or sublease their premises, they had decided to keep trading from their same practice location under a new brand immediately. They challenged their post-termination obligations and restraints of trade, refusing to assign their tenancy lease to us as the franchisor. It was the first shot over the bow, and experience told me they were loading the canons for more.

CHRIS SWIFTLY ASSESSED the legal situation without any hesitation. The case had all the hallmarks of pre-meditated default. The Zeynips had used street-savvy advisors to set up their corporate structure and personal affairs well in advance to avoid being caught by the relevant, and normally robust, provisions of our franchise agreement.

My only protective mechanism against this couple taking the client list and continuing to trade our goodwill was to enforce a three-kilometre restraint of trade radius for the minimum 12-month duration, and ensure Derya complied with the anti-solicitation requirements in our agreement - a standard that is extremely hard to enforce. Chris wasn't optimistic, making me unsure whether it was worth the fight. I had to remind myself, *people matter* more than money!

I agreed to accept their withdrawal from the group without a contest, and simply hold them to account for their nominal end-of-term obligations to de-fit the practice of all distinct Back In Motion branding and technology. My team led the wind-up process, and I hoped this would be an amicable conclusion.

INSTEAD, DERYA CHOSE to launch a series of derogatory social media posts, colluding with former franchisee Spencer, from whom I had not heard from since late 2015. Proving misery likes company, the provocations were incessant and damaging, creating alarm within the NSO.

To compound my woes, the Zeynip's lawyer wrote to me again in early August, claiming his client's decision to join Back In Motion was based on blatant misrepresentations. He accused me of misleading and deceptive conduct – a charge that Spencer had attempted to build a case around previously. Their only evidence to support the accusation was a six-year-old, outdated copy of a Franchise Disclosure Document that cited old joining fees that were correct at the time, but naturally, no longer applicable. The lawyer demanded an immediate refund of all their fees, threatening to issue proceedings to recover the Zeynip's investment.

It was a comical assertion at best, based on selective documents that were entirely irrelevant to either Derya's and Emir's reason for joining our group. It would be like them complaining to a supermarket chain that their bread cost $0.80 less, six years ago, and despite the updated pricing clearly displayed on the shelf ticket today, arguing that they had been deceived.

The Zeynip's franchise licence officially expired in September 2016. They refused to comply with their end-of-franchise obligations. An audit log on our software system showed that they had exported a copy of the client database the night before their access was locked. They also failed to divert the phone lines as per our agreement, and would not cooperate with the decommissioning of our proprietary technology. Our undercover mystery shoppers confirmed Derya still introduced herself as being part of the Back In Motion Health Group long after her voluntary exit.

In a case of astute corporate manoeuvring, investigation by our legal team revealed that Derya had set up a new shelf company, making her 21-year-old daughter the sole director and beneficiary. As part of this cunning tactical move, she transferred all of the practice assets and leasehold to this entity, avoiding an actionable claim by us for violating her franchise obligations. Chris recommended we sue for loss and damage due to their misuse of our confidential information and copyright infringement, issuing a letter of demand for immediate remedy. I'd been through these legal gymnastics too many times before, and wanted to de-escalate the matter, if possible. Rather than counter with the threat of our own proceedings, I offered a compromise in the form of a mutual settlement on all matters, thus hoping to avoid the outrageous costs and massive distraction of litigation.

I offered to let the Zeynips retain the full client base and enjoy an unencumbered legal right to continue to trade their business from their current premises, in exchange for their return of our software data and other confidential information, and the final payment of the fees still due under the franchise agreement. I gave them seven days to respond; it took less than one. They rejected everything.

I gave our legal minds the green light to write to the Zeynip family, including the young daughter now innocently caught up in the centre of her parent's wrongdoing, advising our intentions to seek an injunction prohibiting them using our confidential information while we appealed to the Supreme Court for payment of all costs and damages associated with our claim.

With bold confidence, the Zeynips remained silent.

The ball was still in my court. *Should I slam it back, or let the ball fall to the back of the fence?* The legal cost to lodge our claim with the Supreme Court was heady; necessitating a private investigator, affidavits, filing fees, witness statements, and hearings. All told, I was looking at several hundred thousand dollars to see this matter through to completion. The money and time to run the case was weighed against what possible upside I'd gain if I was successful; the Zeypnip's capacity to pay; and the enormous distraction this matter created to an otherwise exciting and fast-growing business that demanded all my attention. Regardless of the injustice I felt, the legal system wasn't a sure bet – especially given that even if I won, I might only recover a portion of my costs.

I tried to be emotion-less and walked away.

NOT SATISFIED WITH her pseudo-win, in February 2017 Derya reported me to FCA for alleged false representation in our disclosure documents – a re-mount of her original case. After submitting a formal letter of defence in which I outlined the full history, provided sensitive legal advice, and showed evidence of the actual disclosure documents that Derya relied upon when first joining our group, investigators absolved me of all wrongdoing. But mud thrown still leaves a mess, even when it doesn't stick.

Derya was unhappy to learn how short her punch landed, and reminded the world often of this when she posted her frequent social media jabs against my integrity and our brand.

The irony is, the Zeynip's practice grew threefold after joining us. To this day, they have been able to continue momentum in their business with our intellectual property and confidential information, without paying royalties. And this is all possible because of mischievous corporate structures, crafty avoidance of moral obligations, and the burdensome cost to enforce one's legal rights.

I am regularly reminded, we are governed by a *legal* system, not one of *justice*.

85
razor gang

THERE WAS AMPLE evidence in seditious email trails and defamatory social media posts to confirm Spencer, Robert, and now the Zeynips, were in cahoots. It wasn't paranoia, they quoted each other's verbatim comments in their combative emails to me, shared legal strategy amongst their various advisors, and pushed one another's specific agendas in their individual statements of claim. What united them was a shared animosity towards a common foe, feeding their raging dissent and nudging the most outspoken amongst them to avenge justice on behalf of the collective.

Like a 1930s razor gang, they clumsily attacked me with a dis-articulated class action, carelessly hurling accusations in every direction, devoid of precision and evidence. Given their arguments lacked coherence, and because each situation differed significantly, all their efforts eventually proved entirely ineffective.

Caleb's folly was to join them.

I had shaken hands and swapped anecdotes with Caleb over the years as we orbited in the same physiotherapy universe, but our relationship never extended beyond pleasantries until the latter part of 2014. One of my Network Development colleagues put together a proposal for him to join Back In Motion that Christmas Eve, his launch scheduled to commence February 2015.

Caleb was fun-loving, passionate, opinionated, excitable, and a visionary thinker. He cared deeply about clinical care and building a name for himself in the profession – the two ideals entirely compatible. What I failed to realise in our early days together was, with his interests in education and research, he struggled to lead a team and operate a profitable local business on his own. He was obviously drawn to our franchise system to substitute for these vulnerabilities.

Whilst Back In Motion provided strategy, systems, technology, know-how, and support, the franchisee still needed to apply the elbow grease. As I repeated ad nauseum for 20-plus years, the local owner had to assume primary responsibility for the following three attributes in our model:

1. Ensure every patient is thrilled with every experience;
2. Lead the local team effectively; and, otherwise,
3. Follow our proven systems.

I thought it was simple, but Caleb never quite understood these principles.

A year after joining our group, he was frustrated that I wasn't running *his* practice *for* him while he travelled extensively, facilitating external courses around the globe. Feeling exasperated with each other, a dissolution of the partnership seemed likely.

Rather than engage in constructive exit options, by mid-2016 Caleb set himself on a collision course with our group as he sought every possible angle to detract from our model to vindicate his poor performance. He provoked several of our best performing franchisees with personal accusations, and mocked those who sat on the GAP for being clinically inept. He was disruptive at Director Symposiums, where he was unashamed to trash-talk our strategic approaches, despite being unwilling (or unable) to offer any compelling alternatives. And he relentlessly attacked me for lack of effective leadership.

Caleb's cornerstone assault was a series of intimidating emails brimming with threats of lodging formal complaints to the industry competition regulator, APA, and FCA. His lawyers apparently begged to be "let off the leash" to bring an action against me for several hundred thousand dollars – on what basis, nobody was clear – which he promised would result in public disgrace and irreparable reputational damage to me personally, and our group at large.

Having just observed what must have looked like a rollover on the Zeynips, it seems Caleb thought that if he agitated me enough, his squeaky wheel might get oiled.

Recognising the unfair advantage he sought to gain from this misjudged precedence, I resolved to withstand him. I didn't want franchisees thinking I was a pushover just because I chose not to pursue Derya and Emir. Finding the right balance between strength and mercy proved incredibly delicate, but I readied myself to vigorously defend another legal contest. Rightly or wrongly, I dug in, pleased to make an example of Caleb (and his baseless claims) to the rest of the group.

CALEB RESPONDED WITH vitriol and scaremongering.

To break the deadlock between us, I moved swiftly to formal mediation. Having experienced the rigours of this process a few times already, I was ready for the opening joint session, facilitated by the independent Queen's Council.

I had prepared written comments and was able to move through my various points expeditiously, outlining in order of preference the five compromises I was prepared to consider resolving our dispute – all of them resulting in us parting ways. Caleb, speaking extemporaneously, became combative and agitated before the negotiating even began. Both his legal counsel and the mediator intervened to calm him down, reminding Caleb of our shared objectives.

Throughout the day's proceedings I convincingly proved Caleb had overstated the financial performance of his practice in his disclosures prior to joining our brand in December 2014. I also discovered a previously undisclosed formal workplace health audit, commissioned by industry authorities, citing concerns about Caleb's adverse behaviour and dealings with staff, negative workplace culture, and high staff turnover, resulting in loss of client goodwill and deterioration in financial performance. These two significant pieces of evidence went a long way to dispelling any liability on my part for Caleb's practice's underperformance, given they both pre-dated him joining our franchise.

As the day progressed, Caleb's defences shifted from desperate to absurd. His intricate lies of mishap and disadvantage resembled the erratic seizures of a dying man's final twitches and lame kicks. When the last flickers of resistance faded, victory was ours, securing a formal dissolution of our partnership and rescindment of the franchise agreement.

Things didn't go as smoothly as the mediator foreshadowed, as it took us well into January 2017 to eventually secure Caleb's signature to all the necessary paperwork to affect our legal separation. He chiselled away at every clause, wanting to renege on various provisions.

When the commercial complexities and legal technicalities were eventually sorted, I turned my attentions to smoothing the ripples Caleb's defamatory comments had created in the wider industry circles.

I had secured victory in the legal case but, within the social context and public square, there lingered some uncomfortable doubts about my soft underbelly.

86
super supreme

DESPITE LEAVING OUR group years ago, and supposedly contending with a struggling practice and family in need, Spencer seemed unusually fixated on both me and Back In Motion. He considered it sport to hurl rocks in the digital space, making himself a nuisance to our online brand. He was a social media mischief maker, posting cryptic remarks that cast me and our group in negative light whenever the opportunity arose.

Even with offering Spencer a generous 70% discount to settle his past debts, a gesture in line with what God had prompted me to do, he failed to honour his commitment and make any payment. With accrued interest, his outstanding balance was substantial.

To neutralise Spencer's persistent efforts to undermine our brand goodwill, and to stall his relentless efforts to stir up other bad faith actors within our group, I initiated proceedings against him in early November 2016 for the debt he owed. I submitted my affidavit, verifying the amounts payable, and waited for his return fire.

A month later, Spencer's lawyers offered me progressive deals in exchange for me dropping the action. Our number was too high for them to reach, and their meagre offers were too low for me to accept. It was a lost cause – all counter-bidding soon thereafter stopping, with a date in the Supreme Court booked for a final determination.

Ashton, acting as my right hand, supported me during this extended legal battle, scouring the raft of requisite documents, attending legal briefings, and giving his observations and input on strategy. With commercial and spiritual rigour, Ashton shared my conviction that we should not fold.

At an estimated cost of hundreds of thousands, depending on whether the matter went to full trial, the board agreed in the strategic benefit of breaking up the posse that was acting against us. The decision to fight was not based on the legal costs or merits of this isolated case, but winning the war in general against franchisees who chose to ignore their obligations.

IF SPENCER'S INTENTIONS to settle before trial were genuine, he had a funny way of showing it. On the 17th of December he reported me to the Australian Competition and Consumer Commission (ACCC), APA, FCA, and the health regulator (AHPRA) for a litany of petty matters he could barely defend, fabricating much of the context to sensationalise his claims. Our lawyers were quick to draw up counteractions for defamation, breaches of confidentiality, and active disparagement, adding to our debt collection undertaking. It was a heavy-handed response, sending a message not just to Spencer, but his motley band of merry miscreants – including Caleb, Philip, and the Zeynips.

Spencer magnanimously offered to drop all his complaints to the various authorities if I forgave him the entire debt and let him walk away unencumbered. I held firm.

Spencer turned once again to social media in scathing attacks on my integrity. The online comments lit up with an outpouring of sympathy toward him, and vicarious anger directed at me. Our crisis consultant believed that Spencer's posts were professionally orchestrated, as they were well timed, expertly scripted, appropriately succinct, and fiercely impactful. We later learned that Spencer had recruited a personal brand strategist and digital management expert to proactively position him as the squeaky-clean victim.

Court was scheduled for 30th January 2017 – so I hunkered down for another busy and disruptive Christmas as I prepared to stand up and fight. We sifted through Spencer's affidavit, cross-referencing the chronological sequence of correspondence shared between us over our three-year dispute, concluding his version of events were hearsay at best, blatant perjury at worst. My team was ready.

On the morning of our Supreme Court hearing, I spent most of my idle time praying for God's favour in the proceedings. Pleasingly, it was the same day we launched a new franchise in a nearby location, only three kilometres from Spencer's original practice. The irony was as thick as the queue through security to enter the courthouse.

I hoped for a summary judgement in our favour and a quick return flight home. It wasn't to be. Spencer's 100-plus-paged affidavit served its intended purpose: distract, confuse, and obfuscate the court. It was an effective tactic at first, as the judge called a recess at 1pm to read through the copious information. When he returned, he conceded there were too many complexities for resolution that day and referred the case for trial in the Magistrates Court.

I left for the airport feeling exhausted by yet another drawn-out chapter in the saga of our business.

IT WAS OBVIOUS neither Spencer nor I wanted a full trial. As I prepared to board my flight home that evening, we exchanged some good-natured texts in the spirit of some hopeful reconciliation.

Four months later, after going around in repetitive circles, nauseated by the futile activity, but avoiding trial, the marathon dispute ended. Given the emotionally charged events that had characterised our furore, the finale was anti-climactic and underwhelming. One day, Spencer simply did what he had promised many times over, and paid the heavily reduced debt. I, in return, released the securities I held over his company, and breathed a sigh of immense relief that there was nothing further to fight about.

Of course, with Spencer, it was never really the end. Half a year later, he texted me a link to an online article, with no accompanying explanation: *How to spot a psychopath*. He continued to post disparaging comments in social media for years to follow. He tried to stir up trouble for me whenever he could, especially with prospective franchisees. But Spencer became increasingly irrelevant to our group, and impotent in his impact within the industry. Eventually, I just stopped caring about his antics, seemingly along with the rest of the world.

87
the big apple

DURING THE YEAR of my legal maelstrom, Paulina celebrated a milestone birthday – 40 orbits of the Sun. We had missed each other like two shooting stars in different skies for a couple of consecutive months, Paulina making a solo trip to Chile to spend time with her aging grandfather, and me with my hectic domestic travel schedule. My birthday gift to her was a two-week trip to New York City, without the kids.

It was a welcomed exchange – trading in the hustle of home for that of the Big Apple. Flying to the east coast of the US together in October 2016 was an opportunity to fit our puzzle pieces together again, refocusing on the big picture that often was blurred and obscured by our constant motion on separate paths. And what city could teach us better that the world was bigger than Back In Motion?

We packed a lot into our short stay. Staying at a midtown Manhattan hotel, we clambered aboard trains, ferries, and pushbikes. We reached our obligatory ten thousand steps by morning tea most days.

An Indian summer blanketed the city that month, painting the streets with hues of warmth and vibrancy, the air a delicate messenger of a season in flux. Central Park was adorned with shades of amber and gold, inviting lingering strolls and lazy stops at park benches, buzzing with locals savouring the last whispers of their cherished NYC summer.

We hit four of the five boroughs, never making it to Staten Island. We toured the predictable attractions, including the UN Headquarters, Carnegie Hall, Empire State Building, Time Warner Centre, Trump Tower, Grand Central Station, Times Square, Rockefeller Centre, Yankee Stadium, and the 9/11 Memorial. Of course, we kissed the feet of the Statue of Liberty, picnicked in Central Park, rode the bull on Wall Street, and filled a few shopping bags at Macy's.

Paulina especially loved being spoiled for choice with museums, marvelling at the installations on show at the MET, MoMA, and the Museum of Natural History, sometimes returning multiple times to her favourite exhibits.

And it's not a trip to New York if it doesn't pivot on food! Our days were often coordinated around amazing meals in local diners, cafés, and restaurants, many pre-determined before we even landed because friends had loaded us with hot tips of their favourite spots. We officially celebrated Paulina's belated birthday with a cake at the Loeb Boathouse in Central Park, made famous by many Hollywood films, but none more so that Meg Ryan's infamous scene in the movie, *When Harry Met Sally*.

It was especially fun cycling over the Brooklyn Bridge, through DUMBO (a well-known neighbourhood – *Down Under the Manhattan Bridge Overpass*), and then back through The Battery. And our nights were filled with trips to Broadway to watch a few shows, and taking in the night views and sounds from key vantage points.

We even took our seats rinkside to a confusing game of ice hockey at Madison Square Garden. I still feel bad for the Canadian tourist plonked next to us, who politely fielded my numerous questions about interchange, penalties, and the difference between the offence and defence strategies. He was gracious, but surprisingly didn't return after excusing himself to go the restroom between periods. I'm sure I spotted him on the other side of the arena in his red cap, thoroughly enjoying his newfound quiet.

But all good visits abroad must end; otherwise, they don't qualify as holidays. Besides, there was too much waiting for us at home, not the least were our four children, and their extended cousins - the growing cohort of needy franchisees.

We flew home just in time to watch the demolition team swing their wrecking ball into the old house we had purchased on the school boundary in Wantirna South. The excavators moved in next, with the concrete trucks booked to follow a month or so later. All Paulina's plans to build our second family home were coming together, even if it was going to take another year until we moved in.

88
windfall

ACTIF WAS OUR speciality occupational health brand, and endured various changes in ownership over its short life. At different times, six partners had come and gone, with me being the only constant. As the founder and largest shareholder, I tolerated these changes despite the disruption to operations and growth, because I had little choice.

Alastair, whilst a senior team member for seven years, only took up a minority equity stake in the organisation three years earlier. Based in Adelaide, he was responsible for the integration of the acquisition of ROSH, something that became an overwhelming role. Alastair had made more than a few inferences that, if I wanted to replace him, he would step aside for the overall good of the company (and the accretive value of his shareholdings).

I didn't have the bandwidth to oversee another critical transition, putting time and capital at risk, when I already had too many spinning plates inside the circus tent of Back In Motion. The constant turnover of owners within Actif over the previous five years signalled this wasn't my primary focus, hinting that a strategic divestment might be a better alternative.

ACTIF WAS AN award-winning business that employed physiotherapists and ergonomists to deliver return-to-work services, ergonomic assessments, and corporate wellness. We had teams in Melbourne and Adelaide, but enjoyed the loyalty of many blue-chip clients and specialist boutique businesses all over Australia.

Our revenue was modest, but the OHS sector was brimming with possibility if I could harness the right partners. Just before I disembarked at JFK airport for our whirlwind tour of NYC, I sent a confidential invitation to a handful of would-be suitors to explore these opportunities further.

More than five competitors swallowed the bait and were quickly hooked into a structured review process. I engaged in early discussions with these companies, but it was one bidder, backed by Quadrant Private Equity, that asserted their position as frontrunner. By mid-November, they presented a compelling offer in cash for the outright purchase of Actif.

Throughout January, during our annual vacation at Phillip Island, I was constantly interrupted by phone calls from accountants, lawyers, analysts, and staff. I also scrambled to respond to detailed queries from the purchaser's advisors. Alastair was excited to go with the business, giving a one-year commitment to the new owner as part of the transition terms. I agreed to a comprehensive non-compete and non-solicitation clause for five years, giving everyone confidence that the goodwill of the business wouldn't erode over time.

Final binding contracts were signed and exchanged on the 6th of February 2017, with settlement occurring one month later. With an adjustment for extraneous costs and leave entitlements, and a fair estimate of working capital to run the business, the final cash payment to us was the single biggest cheque I had ever been handed in the business' history to date.

Running your own business toughens you in ways unimaginable. We had spent 18 years navigating through financial straits, scraping to make ends meet, and mastering the art of stretching every penny. Whilst many perceived a flourishing business, and assumed Paulina and I were wealthy, they failed to grasp the disparity between assets and available cash. It was a constant challenge to find two cents to rub together, perpetually reinvesting, and living in a world where success didn't always translate into immediate financial comfort. We were always precariously strung between the lure of expansion and the necessity of liquidity. This cheque was our first windfall.

I shamelessly admit to taking a photo of the bank account the day the funds cleared, sending it to Paulina as co-heir, and putting up a prayer of thanks to God. He sovereignly provided a way for me to pay down all my business debts, extinguish our remaining mortgage on the land for our new home and, most importantly, make good on the pledges we had previously given to various charitable causes.

In one miraculous transaction, God pivoted us from being financially vulnerable – especially due to the mounting legal costs of the battles I waged on many fronts – to being debt-free. From that day, our balance sheet remained positive, without ever having to rely on a single dollar of debt to operate and grow our business ever again.

89
deal or no deal

MY ADVISORY BOARD members, Michael and John, provided invaluable support, encouragement, and commercial direction in the seven years we worked together. I counted them as special friends, wise mentors, and Godly exemplars. I needed no convincing that they were wholly vested in my success, which is why, in early 2016, I was flattered to receive a proposal from John to buy shareholdings in our parent company.

Back In Motion was a business committed to serving God's purposes. As a reflection of this organisational imperative, despite being the statutory shareholders, Paulina and I felt more like stewards than sovereign owners. For this reason, we considered the opportunity of selling equity to be a matter of important prayerful consideration. Conceptually, the business was not *ours* to sell without clear direction from God.

This said, I was attracted to the proposition of partnering with other God-centred advisors to strengthen my missional intent, and invited Michael to join the opportunity too. The challenge was to agree on an arrangement that didn't put our relationships in jeopardy.

THE CORPORATE STRUCTURE of Back In Motion was complex. Like most things, it began simple and grew into an entangled bowl of spaghetti over time.

The intellectual property of the franchise system – the *Golden Goose* – was held within our discretionary family trust. A head trading company operated the NSO and received the perpetual royalties that flowed up through the franchise network. I took my various equity positions in many of the practices through layers of subsidiary companies and unit trusts, totalling over 50 entities at the time. Sitting as an annexure, I owned 70% holdings in a small end-to-end technology business, Tech This Out, that had been started by my IT Manager, Dan. And my revenue from book sales and speaking engagements flowed through a separate company that ran the Iceberg Leadership Institute. All these structures sat aside from personal property and other diversified investments, only making the overall picture even more confusing.

John and Michael believed that, for a partnership to work, shares needed to be distributed at an umbrella level to align our interests with all the activities of the group. That necessitated a major restructure of assets to form one top entity in which all three of us could hold shares; a difficult, but not impossible undertaking.

As with most business transactions, valuation was the difficult part. Regardless of what some might infer, putting a price on a business is not an empirical science. Rarely do counterparties concur on the assessment of value, often relying on industry norms as some form of impersonal referee.

It was even more difficult in my case, as I had a complicated set of non-homogeneous assets, a mix of both mature and undeveloped (loss-making) ventures across different sectors (franchising, health, technology), and a long history of "sweat" investment on my part that was not fairly represented on the balance sheet. I also had Actif under offer of sale, and was in early discussions around the future of Revita.

According to our tax advisor, the biggest barrier to partnership was that our top entity in the structure was a family trust, and therefore had no shares to sell. We could restructure it into a unit trust or company, but that would trigger capital gains tax implications that might undo the value of the whole proposal.

Whilst many of these challenges could be overcome, there was a longer list of daunting questions: *Who pays the transaction costs? How do we raise funds for future investment? Will future board members expect the same equity opportunities? What short- and long-term incentives might we put to Ashton as the CEO-elect? How will we treat the personal loans I had taken from the business? Can my personal guarantees with landlords and lenders be swapped out? What dividend policies should we adopt? What salary would I be paid, given to date I had only received director fees at my discretion?*

What first appealed as a wonderful way to consolidate our relationship, quickly became a spider's web of unwanted complexity for all three of us. John, ever so careful to not bring any undue influence on my decision, introduced a proxy advisor to act on his behalf. We eventually engaged an industry expert to formalise the valuation of the business, adopting a sum-of-the-parts approach. Assigning a nominal value to our proprietary software, the supported valuation of the whole business was pegged to an eight-figure sum on a walk-in-walk-out basis.

This number created some awkwardness, the price discussions being high stakes and complex. I desperately didn't want to offend my two board advisors, nor did I want to slash the value of my company.

To land in fairer middle ground, I gestured to John and Michael a 20% discount on the Enterprise Value, making a minority stake a little more affordable.

IN THE LATTER stages of these sensitive considerations, Michael preferred to remain a personal mentor and board advisor without the commercial discussions and financial implications risking our relationship. John was initially still keen to proceed, but shortly thereafter also chose to set the deal aside.

I am grateful to both men for their gracious forfeit of an opportunity to invest into a business they had helped build. Michael remained on the board until the very end, and John continued to serve our cause faithfully for another two years through some of our most difficult decisions.

John continues to this day to be a wonderful source of wisdom and encouragement in my life. I value his commercial experience and financial insights, but mostly his love for God, the people around him, and an unwavering commitment to personal integrity. John does not compromise his convictions, acting with the careful balance of courage and grace, seeking to always bring truth in love. I am a better businessman, husband, and follower of Jesus, for the eight years John gave me on our advisory board, and I highly value every hour I get to enjoy with him.

Nonetheless, I remained a sole director and sole shareholder of the growing house of cards that was Back In Motion. It was a lonely experience at the top – with no business partner - surrounded by vast expanses of obligations and expectations. I had the weight of the world resting on my shoulders, a burden I didn't always enjoy carrying alone.

The weight of leadership was a constant companion, and I wanted nothing more than to share this with a true partner. I had this with Paulina in some dimensions of life, but the office felt like a desolate field, void of true empathy for the internal pressures I carried. Despite having Ashton in my corner and being surrounded by a team of advisors and staff, there was a palpable sense of detachment, as if there was an invisible barrier separating me from those I worked alongside. Vulnerability seemed a luxury I couldn't afford, having to always maintain a façade of strength. The journey would have been richer to have John and Michael join me in the cockpit, but it was not to be.

90
reset

I EAGERLY BID farewell to 2016, voting to pretend it never happened. Whilst there were always simultaneous highs and lows during my experience in business, plotting traversing curves on the graph of my emotions, those 12 months reflected a prevailing theme of hardship. The end of the year could not arrive quickly enough.

I secured the source code of our Evo software after hard-fought negotiations with the original development house. I won and lost in different franchisee disputes. I had travelled to the UK chasing a pot of gold at the end of the rainbow, only to realise my folly too late. The Iceberg Leadership Institute and the SOS Health Foundation were drawing on more of my time as they matured. Ashton had been recruited as my emerging CEO, but it had been anything than a normal year to onboard and train him in the routine operations. Moreover, I had also lost my key finance man and long-time friend, Philip.

Throughout the challenges, Paulina and I grappled with conflicting tensions, working hard to steer our marriage and family in the right direction. Like a ship's captain wrestling the helm amidst turbulent seas and high winds, our success fluctuated, tested by the changing seasons of life.

Our children were growing up and needed more of me. Lachlan, our eldest, graduated his final year of primary school and, as sports captain and athlete-of-the-year, was excited to pursue a career in elite sport. Fanatical for soccer, he trained five times a week, drawing all of us into his passion.

Lachlan's two younger brothers needed little encouragement. Sebastian won the first of three consecutive years as "Best and Fairest" in his age group, and Morgan scored 46 goals in soccer that season, decisively winning the "Golden Boot".

I celebrated Lachlan becoming a teenager with a rite of passage, inviting a handful of his friends and their fathers to a planned weekend. After surfing and go-karting, I gathered them in the evening to recognise Lachlan's coming of age. The fathers spoke words of encouragement and life advice to the young boys around us. We prayed and commissioned them into their next decade of development, knowing critical decisions lay ahead for each of them. It was a moving time, and laid a pattern for the tradition that I followed with all our children when they first became teenagers.

It was clear, I needed to make family a higher priority.

AS THE HOLIDAY season approached, it was obvious my break-neck pace was dangerous. Something – *many* things – needed to change. Paulina and I deliberated on how we should approach the upcoming year of 2017 differently.

We had previously talked in a NYC diner, only two months earlier, about being careful to not let the business drive a wedge between us. Back In Motion was a jealous companion, able to consume every waking moment of my life if I wasn't disciplined to guard against it. Family was also more demanding as the kids got older and faced new and different challenges in their approaching adolescence. I needed to be home more and, frankly, Paulina wanted to exercise some of her talent and gifts outside the home.

One strategy we revisited was Paulina joining me in the advisory board. She had carried multiple responsibilities in the practice during our first five years of startup, and again at the NSO during different times between pregnancies. Now, her potential involvement as a board member sparked an exhilarating chance to synchronise more of our time and integrate her valuable wisdom into our commercial decision-making. Whilst initially reluctant, Paulina eventually agreed, becoming a long-overdue voice in the boardroom in the January that followed.

At the same time, I transitioned from Group Director to Executive Chairman, paving the way for Ashton to step up to the top job of CEO. Whilst he was nervous when the time came – and wondered aloud to me whether he needed more time – my impatience to step away from the daily grind of the operations of the business blinded me to his hesitations. I intentionally weight-shifted away from Back In Motion and toward my wife and children, hoping for a more sustainable rhythm and order in my life. It was like pressing the "reset" button – believing for the new year to birth fresh unity and fulfillment at home, with the business under the care of a capable team.

My plan felt robust.

91
frenemies

SOMETIMES, THINGS GET worse before they get better. And the best laid plans fail!

After Philip's resignation in June 2016, he continued for a short time as a board member of SOS, and we met at cafés on numerous occasions, where he sought advice on how to excel in his new job in Queensland. Whilst his employment with me had ended, our friendship appeared to survive.

One month after Philip's resignation, final votes confirmed he failed to win a senate seat in the federal election. Possibly triggered by this disappointment, he spiralled into a mental health tailspin, abandoning his new role without as much as a phone call to his frustrated employer.

Unemployed again, likely gripped by fear and desperation, Philip unleashed a barrage of aggressive and abusive text messages, accusing me of being a "vicious, unreasonable, and relentless" bully. In a contradictory turn, he simultaneously demanded I reinstate him to his former position at the NSO. He rang me one morning, describing how cruel I was to put him through such unimaginable difficulty, and then later the same day, wrote back and apologised for his harsh dishonesty. This back-and-forth pattern continued, demonstrating his deteriorating health and apparent instability.

Philip's change of heart and colourful expletives blindsided me. My persistent refusals to re-hire him fuelled his disdain, leading him to bad-mouth me amongst existing staff and franchisees, with whom he was still digitally connected. He even reached out to my board members, creating a general nuisance of himself as he sought someone to advocate on his behalf.

AFTER ENDURING SIX months of this mayhem, in August 2017 Paulina and I made a sincere effort towards reconciliation by inviting Philip and his wife to our home. The first hour was filled with uneasy small talk and updates on family matters before Philip leaned in, his expression turning more serious.

He embarked on a fervent monologue, asserting that I was under the sway of malevolent forces and needed to be stopped. Philip boasted he had rallied over 20 individuals within the Back In Motion network to support his cause, seeking justice for perceived wrongs. Philip went as far as labelling me a verifiable criminal psychopath, declaring a moral crusade to take me down by any means necessary. His impassioned speech, akin to a courtroom closing argument, ended with him mentioning he'd discussed these matters with the senior pastor of his church. Supposedly, his clergy planned to oversee a hearing of the maligned claimants, insisting that I submit to this process.

Understandably, the evening ended abruptly. As I waved Philip out the front door, Paulina embraced his tearful and distraught wife in a slightly longer hold than usual, reluctantly accepting their friendship was over.

I wrote to Philip one week later, regretting the deep hurts we both suffered from the way things finished with his employment, and acknowledging his financial hardship, limited job opportunities, and mental strain. I also shared my desperate hope for reconciliation one day.

But I couldn't stop there.

I also challenged his serious allegations against me, noting that however strongly he may believe them, merely expressing them didn't make them true. I informed Philip that I had formally invited the members of my advisory board, a spiritual mentor, Philip's clergy, and my own senior pastor to thoroughly investigate his claims and determine if there was any basis for concern. I confirmed my willingness to come under their collective authority to determine what improper actions I was guilty of and, if any, the consequences that should follow.

Suspicious of the witch hunt Philip was conducting, I offered to hear the concerns of the alleged 20 people who stood in waiting to indict me. I promised to make available all my emails, texts, and other correspondence relating to any party in question, and welcomed honourable and independent people to judge the merit of their claims.

Philip didn't respond to my letter, although it was obvious he was agitating the waters within our franchise network over the consecutive months that followed. With little apparent ecclesiastical support for his campaign against me, Philip stepped up his assault with an accusatory letter to the ACCC, our nation's regulatory watchdog. In doing so, Philip pulled the pin on a deadly grenade, blindly hurling it into a public area, seemingly indifferent to the collateral damage that was to come of his actions.

92
bike-and-hike

IN MARCH OF 2017, Ashton had the privilege of welcoming 120 franchisees and their partners to our ninth consecutive annual Directors Conference, hosted in the seaport of Hobart, Tasmania. The theme: *Smarter, Better, Stronger*. It was the first time I hadn't given the opening or closing address, yielding the honour to Ashton and his team. It was a strange experience for Paulina and I to watch from the pews, as someone else stood in our pulpit. However, we recognised it as a crucial adjustment, essential for breaking Back In Motion's reliance on both of us.

My succession plan was still only in its formative stages, but I was impatient for the benefits I expected from the change. I immediately carved out two days a week to invest more time in the growing work of SOS. I also used my newfound freedom to develop the leaders both within and outside our group, as the Iceberg Leadership Institute enlarged its sphere of influence.

Amidst these unfolding events, I embarked on a four-day motorcycle solo-adventure – or, what I called, a *bike-and-hike*. For my 40th birthday, Paulina gifted me a travel pass for a solitary road trip amidst the stunning landscapes of Tasmania's remote wilderness.

It had taken me 18 months to carve out the space to enjoy the getaway. Laden with over-stuffed paniers, I boarded the Spirit of Tasmania on my 400cc Honda Shadow, bound for camping in some of the most breathtaking corners of Australia's southern island state.

I walked The Nut in the northwestern corner of Stanley soon after disembarking the boat. I circumnavigated Dove Lake and summited Cradle Mountain the next day. I then biked 400 kilometres across the face of Tasmania to Freycinet National Park, taking in the views of

Wineglass Bay and The Hazards. And I finished with a lap of Cataract Gorge on my way through Launceston, back to the boat harbor.

It was one of my favourite birthday presents, a chance to recharge in the quiet strength that lies in the unspoiled beauty of the world. The solitude of those four days was a sanctuary – an escape from the incessant demands that tethered me to the desk most days at home. The rhythm of my own thoughts replaced the cacophony of people's needs, abandoning my role of problem-solver and perpetual helper to those on my team. Far away from the constant buzz of phones and the weight of other's expectations, I breathed in the untainted air and let the vastness of the outdoors fill my spirit.

There was a serene liberation in the drone of my bike, the pummelling of my cheeks in my open-faced helmet, water streaming from the corners of my sand-blasted eyes. In the heart of nature, amidst the untamed wilderness, I heard God's voice clearly again. His whispers were almost audible: *The business existed to serve His purposes. People mattered. I was to help the poor.*

The open road in front of my bike became a canvas on which I painted new possibilities for work and family. My boyhood dream of becoming a devoted medical missionary felt within reach again.

93
10x

MY SMALL TASTE of victory with the sale of Actif whet my appetite for more strategic divestments. During various board and executive team meetings, I wondered aloud the fate for Revita – a much larger specialist aged care business that represented similar challenges to that of Actif. The sub-brand relied on a niche workforce with a corporatised client base of aged care service providers, and was a distraction to my franchise strategy.

I sensed the aged care landscape was changing. Providers were consolidating. Services were increasingly being centralised and corporatised to respond to the sophistication of the market. The aging population was accelerating in numbers. Policy and industry regulations were susceptible to the whims of change from federal government. Other parties, like insurers and offshore healthcare intermediaries, were exerting increasingly large influence on the sector.

Despite the forces of change swirling around us, Revita emerged as one of Australia's leading providers of aged care physiotherapy services. The business shone as a bright light in a crowded space, offering quality care at an affordable price to enable seniors to age with dignity. We enjoyed long-term contracts with residential aged care specialists Regis, Opal, Arcare, Bluecross, Anglicare, and others, in four of the big states of Australia.

Founded six years earlier, Revita employed over 100 therapists in 2017. We were beautifully protected in an industry sweet spot, even if I doubted the bubble would last forever. Our revenue doubled from $3.1 million in 2014 to $6.8 million three years later. In addition, industry pollsters were predicting that residential aged care facilities were estimated to grow another 35% in the following five years.

The two primary shareholders of the franchised business were Jeremy and Bao. Other team members shared in the balance of ownership, all stakeholders having owned or worked in other Back In Motion practices at some time prior to making the switch to Revita.

Throughout 2015, Jeremy had explored with me the possibilities of Revita breaking away from Back In Motion and doing their own thing. I owned the trademark, licensed them the aged-care systems, and provided back-of-house operational support – earning me a substantial royalty every year in return. It was not a surprise to me that, at some point, the commercial sustainability of our arrangement might be questioned.

I entertained several ways to sensibly separate the businesses, including amending the royalty structure, selling my trademark and technology in exchange for direct shareholding in the subsequent independent business, or putting the brand up for corporate sale on the open market, sharing the spoils. All the suggestions held promise, leading to non-adversarial conversations packed with good faith.

The winning strategy in the contest of ideas was to test the value of Revita in a competitive market. Early indicators were overwhelmingly positive, suggesting buyers might pay up to $6 million for our business; a price all parties deemed to be on the upside of fair. We moved forward with confidence.

After publishing a comprehensive prospectus in May 2017, and shopping it around to some selective interests, we were approached by three enthusiastic parties, building sufficient competitive tension in our favour.

By November, a specialist healthcare workforce management company, backed by a UK equity firm, became the leading prospect. They arrested our attention with a knockout bid 18 times our historical earnings, and 10 times our two-year projected profit.

ON THE FIRST of December 2017, I sent a memo to our executive team. It was titled, *Ring the Damn Bell*, celebrating the unprecedented result. After seven years of brand and business development, eight months of negotiation with four franchisees, 17 drafts of completion agreements, 11 legitimate offers for purchase, three sets of legal firms acting across two hemispheres, three different accounting firms, 72 hours of last-minute heated negotiations over restraints and warranties, and nearly $1 million in transaction fees, we sold Revita.

Ticket price: an eye-watering $18 million in cash and modest earnouts.

From that December announcement, it took until August 2018 to realise our full payment due to performance obligations that needed to be met; but at no point was I worried. Revita was a thoroughbred racehorse – poised for ongoing success and equipped to outpace its competitors in the market.

Revita's four primary shareholders, who previously considered their earning capacity to be generously capped at $150,000 per year, received a proportionate share of the full proceeds, setting up their families with millions of dollars for a lifetime of financial freedom.

Revita was my second accidental success in as many years. I seemed better at the things I didn't plan, thankful for another unexpected windfall.

94
facing my accusers

IT WAS JUST as well I sold Revita, as it put the money in my war chest to defend against the next assault from usual suspects.

Philip and Spencer had submitted a list of recycled complaints against Back In Motion, and me personally, to the ACCC back in December 2016. As an independent commonwealth statutory authority, the regulator's primary mandate was to promote competition and fair trading, making free commercial markets work for everyone. The ACCC took a particular interest in franchising which, at the time of writing, represented $173.8 billion, or 4% of the Australian economy.

The Director of Small Business and Industry Codes was obliged to follow up the allegations made against us, initially concerned we were not complying with our obligations under the Franchising Code of Conduct. In particular, the issues raised by Philip and Spencer related to the disclosures I made to prospective franchisees before they joined the group.

My accusers alleged I did not provide a complete list of the current and former franchisees, failed to outline all rebates and financial benefits I obtained from my relationship with suppliers, and did not satisfactorily describe the payments required to be made by franchisees. If found guilty, the penalties included fines of up to $51,000 per infraction, as well as court-ordered injunctions, compensation, and disqualification orders that could prevent me from managing a corporation again.

I responded to the formal ACCC investigators with overwhelming evidence that Back In Motion had always been, and would continue to be, fully compliant with the Franchising Code. After months of nervous waiting as they deliberated their findings, all allegations were dismissed, and the matter ended.

Or so I believed.

DUE TO PHILIP'S unsuccessful attempts to discredit me through church arbitration, he persisted a year later in raising further doubts about Back In Motion with the ACCC again. They were a bear easily poked, and I must have appeared a soft target. With seemingly nobody better to pursue, and indifferent to the cost to taxpayers, the ACCC heeded Philip's persistent agitations and opened a second investigation into my affairs.

In late November 2017, Ashton received an official ACCC notice indicating their intention to conduct a wide-scoping audit of our compliance with industry codes. We were given three weeks to produce comprehensive records showing our full history of disclosure documents, franchise agreements, occupancy leases, software licences, and financial statements.

Our administration team worked double-time to compile an electronic copy of every document requested. I submitted our hefty audit file with days to spare, assuming our response would resolve the issue once and for all.

Six months later, the ACCC wrote back advising their concerns that some of our contract clauses were potentially problematic under their *Unfair Contract Terms*, but had not formed a view on whether we had breached any codes. Their purpose in writing was to compel me to take prescribed steps to ensure future compliance. It was corporate double-speak and legalese to exert pressure on me to do things the way they wanted them done – despite not having clear authority under the law to demand it.

In a mischievous move – as the ACCC had made no adverse finding against us – a lazy journalist for the *Australian Financial Review* chastised Back In Motion in a nationally syndicated article for being a non-compliant franchisor. The employment scandals of fuel retailers 7-Eleven and Caltex, and the horror stories coming out of the Retail Food Group and Dominos, had placed the franchising sector in the crosshairs of the media's target and a Senate Inquiry into potential reform. I had unwittingly found myself in their unpleasant company.

Whilst I welcomed reasonable scrutiny, integrity checks, and appropriate legislative safeguards, I was wary of being labelled as a non-conformer, or worse, bundled in with the brands that were shown to take unfair advantage of their people. I had modelled our franchising and business systems on the best in the world and, in some cases, had become the market leader. We were far from perfect, but always sought to adapt and comply to changing laws to reflect the best standards of the marketplace. We did not deserve to have our name smeared in the public arena by uninformed reporters, where idle consumers wouldn't (or couldn't) make up their own minds through independent review.

I responded to the ACCC's concerns in mid-July 2018, explaining our contracts had been carefully scrutinised by our legal counsel at the time of their execution, and deemed to be in full compliance of the law. For the time being, the authorities seemed satisfied.

CONFIDENT IN MY submission, Paulina and I flew to Fiji for a family holiday in August 2018. Things didn't start well.

Unbeknownst at the time, our middle son, Sebastian, contracted gastroenteritis the night before we left. He felt unwell on the plane, but we put it down to a combination of nerves and excitement, accentuated by the tiredness due to our early morning departure. He convinced us otherwise when he vomited repeatedly throughout the first night in our transit hotel.

After one day of malaise, his appetite returned, as did our optimism for the remainder of the holiday. However, by the time we reached Plantation Island, each member of our family progressively caught the bug on consecutive days, such that a different person was sick with violent vomiting and nausea for the entire first week. It was a conga line of the worst kind as we all queued for the toilet, thankful that no one suffered intensely for longer than 24 hours.

By the second week, we had all recovered and were seeking to redeem lost time at one of our favourite resorts. And yet, on the morning of 21st August, my world stopped turning on its axis.

As I described in the opening pages of this book, I returned from a scuba dive to the distressing urgency to ring the office immediately. Paulina cautioned me to remain calm until all the details were known. As the phone rang at the other end, echoing like a distant bell tolling in an empty canyon, the eerie resonance seemed to amplify my sickening worry. I felt paralysed by the weight of the unknown.

When Ashton picked up the call I was abruptly thrust into a nightmare, the tranquillity of the Fijian islands shattered as unthinkable news unfurled. My business back home was under threat, entangled in a web of conspiracies and legal technicalities. Shock quickly gave way to a surge of anger and despair, as an overwhelming sense of dread knotted my stomach.

I was convinced I was about to lose the business. 19 years of toil for nothing!

IN MY ABSENCE, Philip had made a personal submission to a highly publicised Senate Inquiry, throwing me, our brand, and anybody who stood by us, under the bus in spectacular fashion.

The Parliamentary Joint Committee on Corporate and Financial Services commissioned the inquiry, delving into concerns regarding fairness, transparency, and power imbalances within franchise relationships. It aimed to investigate the effectiveness of existing regulations, express instances of exploitation or mistreatment of franchisees, and propose potential reforms to ensure better protection and fairness for all parties involved.

Philip's four-page letter was an all-out assault on me to ensure I never worked again. He described me as a "predator" with a "weak business model" who used "bullying tactics" to get my way. He blamed me for causing "mental health problems, multiple miscarriages, extreme financial distress" and even "suicidal tendencies".

Ashton wasn't spared either, labelled as a "heavy handed" manager accused of bullying staff. Philip even went to lengths to discredit Michael and John from my advisory board, citing alleged negligence in their duties, and linking them to other infamous franchised brands that had recently fallen into some disrepute.

If these accusations on parliamentary record weren't bad enough, Philip went to the free press with his allegations. A syndicated journalist, with an axe to grind against any vulnerable franchisor, quickly reported Philip's claims as facts. Ugly headlines like *Franchisees suffer Motion sickness, Hell on earth*, and *Franchisees bullied and trapped*, blasted in print and over the internet. The truth didn't matter. Mere statements under reputable media mastheads made them believable in the only places that counted – people's minds.

Ashton organised a conference call for a collective legal briefing. The caucus that day included Michael and John in their respective home offices, Ashton at his desk, a team of lawyers saddled in their boardroom chairs, and our crisis consultant in Queensland. Paulina and I were literally kneeling on the sandy floor of our Fijian bure, resting our heads on the bed, listening to the kids playing outside our open window. I was too shaky to stand, and figured we had to fight this battle on our knees in prayer anyway.

After an hour of discussion about the legal and reputational risks, and a lesson on the process and likely reach of the Senate Inquiry, we agreed on an internal and external communication script with a full legal strategy to match. As the call concluded, I felt the nausea of Sebastian's gastro bug returning. All I could manage was to recline in a hammock, gazing at the clear waters gently lapping against the reef before me, offering silent prayers.

I tossed up the idea of flying home early so I could be on hand as the situation escalated, but reason caught up with me a few hours later. I realised there was nothing further to do, regardless of where I was. It made sense to remain with the family and salvage what little rest we could in our disrupted paradise.

I did, however, write to the franchisees from my beachfront location. My heart bled in streaks of Back In Motion burgundy as I shared with them the unfair portrayal of our brand in the media. I assured them our NSO team and expert advisors had developed a comprehensive strategy in response, and that I believed we would endure through this challenge as the truth prevailed. I committed to doing everything within my influence to help each of them and their local practices flourish, despite our accusers trying to bring us down.

MESSAGES OF ENCOURAGEMENT and commiseration flooded in by email and text for the next three days. The gravity of the adverse media was felt amongst friends, family, colleagues, and suppliers. It was comforting that not everyone believed what they read, even if it was only a fraction of the audience with whom my name had now become mud.

By webcast, I tuned into the public hearing of Philip's witness statement to the Senate Inquiry. It was little more than an in-person reading of his written submission; no further allegations or information were presented. An objective assessment of his performance by others around me suggested he did a very poor job of passing off as a credible witness. Philip's noticeable lack of eye contact, melancholic demeanour, mumbling monotone words, and apparent look of disinterest wreaked of dishonesty. I worried it may have been a strategic attempt on his part to appear defeated by the hardships, seeking a sympathy vote for the beleaguered underdog.

My self-preservation instincts kicked into overdrive. I penned a lengthy, formal response to the allegations made against us to Liberal MP Michael Sukkar, Chair of the Parliamentary Joint Committee. I effectively countered most of Philip's malicious trumped-up claims in a candid assessment of our franchise agreements, an overview of our internal policies, and endorsements from multiple independent stakeholders. I closed the letter by reassuring the committee of my firm belief that our success as a franchisor was determined by the success of our franchisees. The long-standing and active members of our network continued to grow because of the advantages we gave them.

Sadly, I didn't get to present my views at the Inquiry, nor could I plead my case in the public square, as the media wasn't prepared to publish our side. All I could rest on was that I had put our position on official record, and hoped most people remembered there were always two sides to every story.

My version was simple: Philip was a disgruntled ex-employee who canvassed ex-franchisees to support claims that were blatantly untrue. My only recourse at this point was to let both stories play out in what was, hopefully, a short news cycle.

IN THE ULITMATE show of solidarity for our shared brand and my leadership, over 34 franchisees wrote their own submissions directly to Senator Deborah O-Neill, Deputy Chair of the Senate Inquiry, sharing their personal stories of gratitude toward me and the Back In Motion franchise system. They praised the characteristic fairness I had shown each one in helping them achieve their individual success, freely admitting that without our franchise model they would not have otherwise enjoyed the same commercial upside. Their endorsement buoyed me during a time when I could have easily forgotten all the good we had achieved together.

For the next few months, I patiently waited as the Joint Parliamentary Committee deliberated. In anticipation of a report they expected to publish in early November, I prepared a detailed risk matrix of six possible scenarios, ranging from the benign and incidental mentions of our name through to showcasing our brand as a major culprit of everything they thought was wrong about the franchise industry. I was very aware that, depending on where we landed on the possible spectrum of judgement, the clickbait-hungry media may well revive the bad blood of Philip's mid-year allegations. I was briefed on how to respond to journalists, and our PR team were scripted with multiple versions of different press releases ready to go depending on what landed.

As it happened, the report did not get published until March of 2019. Back In Motion did not appear in any of the citations and case examples provided, not even as a footnote. Philip's vitriolic allegations couldn't be found on the official record anywhere, seemingly having evaporated into the thick ether that hovered above the bureaucratic corridors of the federal committee. Philip had torched me, but we rolled out of the fire unburned, not even smelling of smoke. If I tried hard, I could almost take offence at our apparent lack of significance to even warrant notice.

In a dramatic show of pleasing irony, all 34 of our franchisees' letters of endorsement were included as official appendices to the final report. I interpreted this to be the Senate's way of giving us a subtle nod, softly inferring our business was worthy of commendation. At the very least, maybe they were sympathetic to the mistreatment we suffered by the crass narrative peddled through the mainstream press. It was a notable career victory to be vindicated in such unequivocal fashion, not ignoring that the last nine months had aged me about the same in years.

95
the Joseph plan

ASHTON'S FIRST YEAR in the big chair was anything but easy. He helped facilitate the sale of Actif and Revita. He sat through two different formal mediations, Caleb and Spencer. He backfilled the senior finance position after Philip's departure, until we recruited a new CFO. And, of course, Ashton rode shotgun with me on the ACCC submissions and response to the Senate Inquiry

On top of all this, our franchise model was showing signs of strain with some of the established franchisees now demanding a different model of support and reward from the Back In Motion brand. Whilst these agitations are not uncommon in a maturing franchise system, Ashton took over as CEO at a time when I was mandating a step change from some of these historically successful methods of support to new and evolving approaches. This dynamic proved difficult for some of the long standing NSO colleagues to accept – a game clearly stacked against Ashton when he was trying to fill the nuanced shoes of a founder-owner.

Throughout all this chaos, we onboarded numerous practices across Australia and New Zealand, racking up the frequent flyer points like a squirrel gathers nuts for winter. In a bittersweet irony, there was little time to dwell on the madness.

TWO LEGACY PRACTICES that Ashton inherited from our 7/50/100 growth season were small underperforming businesses. We didn't have a franchisee to take them on, and our NSO team found them difficult to manage from a distance. We had physiotherapists working in the practices on our behalf, but the lack of local leadership lead to high turnover and relative instability, all which hurt the revenue line, and made cost control near impossible. It was Ashton's unenviable responsibility to present the bleak board report on these two struggling businesses every month.

For a long time, I was determined to keep the failing practices, expecting to trade our way out of the difficulty. To close them would be to concede defeat, and that wasn't in my DNA. I remember lamenting to a fellow entrepreneur about losing more than a million dollars on them both, naïvely pleading we just needed a little more time to turn them around. The only crack in my bravado was an admission that, if God gave me a clear sign to sell them off or shut them down, I wouldn't hesitate. My friend flipped the scenario on its head and challenged me: "If they are losing money, why don't you shut the practices down now unless God gives you a clear sign *not* to?"

I shared with Paulina the possibility of disposing of the businesses, and she quickly agreed with the sentiment. At the next board meeting there was a unanimous decision to cut off the weak toes to save the limb, and we prayed for God to direct us otherwise if we were missing His divine plan.

It was an expensive and embarrassing undertaking to wind down the worst two practices in our network. We couldn't sell them for the same reasons we couldn't operate them profitability. They were in poor locations, with even worse facilities, and it was difficult to attract quality staff. A prospective owner could smell the risks a mile away. We salvaged what little plant and equipment we could, distributing some electrotherapy and exercise rehabilitation equipment across the rest of our practice network. I ran down the leases to their expiry, negotiating early payout figures on one site, and we offered relocation opportunities to the few team members who were still employed there, otherwise giving them generous redundancy packages.

The pain we carried on these businesses was not inherently Ashton's fault, even though it was his job to turn them around. If anything, they were legacy purchases of Philip's era – one of his last projects before resigning from the top finance role 18 months earlier. Ashton pulled out all stops to do whatever was humanly possible to redeem the subpar trading performance of those two remote locations, and it was disappointing for everyone that it finished up the way it did.

My learning in all this was success in one business doesn't guarantee success in the next. The hundred moving parts that make up the complex activity of launching a brand in a new community, building a team, and keeping costs lean, is fraught with danger and risk. A lot must go your way to eventually succeed. The size and strong trading record of our network, with its deep resources, had created a dangerous mix of complacency and hubris to think everything we touched would work.

The reality check was healthy for everyone, especially me.

THE GREATEST CHALLENGE Ashton faced amidst all these swirling priorities was keeping his national executive and management team aligned. Most of them had worked for me a long time – in some cases, more than ten years – and the differences in leadership style between Ashton and myself was as distinct as night and day.

It's hard for me to be objective on Ashton's effectiveness as a leader, as any assessment implies commentary on my own approach (about which I may be entirely deluded). Also, because Ashton worked *for* me, I can't be sure what it was like to sit *under* his authority. In my close observations though, I felt Ashton carried himself with equal measures of strategic thought, tactical detail, and accountability. Apparently, others didn't share my view.

What some failed to acknowledge was that I had asked Ashton to raise the standard of performance and accountability in the NSO. Our business needed to grow up and not everyone responded well to the enthusiastic rigour that Ashton applied with my encouragement. Despite his best efforts, Ashton couldn't inspire the team to a new way of working, with the prevailing criticism from some that he couldn't see the big picture, micro-managed every project, and frustrated people with his precision and exactness. Undoubtedly, my lingering proximity and availability also made it hard for Ashton to establish trust and new patterns of leadership with the team.

One franchisee wrote to me that Ashton had only one gear and, if the situation fitted the pace and level of detail he was equipped with, then he would undoubtedly succeed. But for all the other times, when he needed to be flexible and vary his approach, he couldn't adapt. I thought it was an unfair assessment at the time, but couldn't deny the clear trend in team perception.

Inevitably, people voted with their feet. I lost some of my most valuable and favoured colleagues during Ashton's transition. My champion for People and Culture moved on to become CEO of a smaller franchise system. My lead of Operations, one who had become like a brother to me, took up the number three job inside one of Australia's largest franchising networks, the Jim's Group. We lost our singularly most successful operative in Network Development to a national chain of pharmacies. And the resignations just kept coming. Our Marketing Manager exited next, then his number two guy, and eventually another one of our senior accountants.

Inevitably, I lost some of my most valuable and favoured colleagues during Ashton's transition – admittedly, not an uncommon phenomenon in any attempted leadership succession. My champion for People and Culture moved on to become CEO of a smaller franchise system. My lead of Operations, who had become like a brother to me, took up the number three job inside one of Australia's largest franchising networks, the Jim's Group. We lost our singularly most successful operative in Network Development to a national chain of pharmacies. Our Marketing Manager exited next, then his number two guy, and eventually another one of our senior accountants.

The list went on, one painful loss after another. At our lowest ebb I said goodbye to eight national team members in eight months, and many others before or shortly after that period. Some were terminations for which Ashton's decisions had my full support; others were disappointing resignations, collateral damage in an extremely challenging time of change. In most of these instances, though, the common theme in their feedback was their difficulty working with, for, and under Ashton.

I even lost my longtime Executive Assistant through this season. Jodie and I worked well together, but that synergy didn't translate to Ashton. Compatibility between an executive and their assistant is a delicate fit, and over the years I got it right as often as I failed. But Jodie had been one of the best, and it was a sad day when she was moved on. There was little I could do to protect her future if I truly believed in empowering Ashton with the operational decisions of the business.

Whilst the blame for the disturbingly high turnover of staff couldn't all be placed at the feet of Ashton, he was the face of change. This disruptive pattern became so obvious that he and I talked about it month after month in our regular catchups. The board was concerned, especially Paulina. I grieved over the many friendships we had built in our national team that seemed frayed and frustrated by my decision to sidestep the top leadership role. Frankly, with such an emphasis on the cultural disruption, Ashton was losing confidence in himself.

I was feeling growing pressure to return to the business in an executive role – but I didn't want to do it. As with the two failing practices, my instinct was to push through, not concede defeat, and give the transition a little more time.

That was, at least, until God reminded me what He had spoken a year earlier. I felt he had promised to give me a *Joseph* in the business, the same man famed for his technicolour dreamcoat in the Broadway show. Joseph of the Old Testament was a man who had always been second in charge – in Potiphar's house, in prison, and eventually in pharaoh's court. At the climax of this epic Biblical story, Joseph carried all authority in Egypt, second only to the king. He was able to bring about great prosperity to the land when he obeyed what God spoke to him.

It had always seemed to me that Ashton was my *Joseph*, but somewhere along the line I confused this narrative with that of *Joshua* – an equally epic Biblical hero – who became Moses' successor, leading the Israelites into the Promised Land. The similarities between the two men went only as far as their names - both starting with the letter "J" - and being recent descendants of Abraham. Other than that, I had completely distorted God's intentions, mixing up my Bible stories.

God's promise to me was a right-hand man to run alongside and support my mission – an associate, not a successor. I had mistaken Ashton's arrival as an opportunity to back out of my responsibility, leaving the burden for him to shoulder. I overreached for a sheriff when God had only provided me a deputy.

I needed to recover the "Joseph plan" quickly before there was nobody left to lead.

I BROUGHT MATTERS to a head in June 2018, inviting Ashton to what turned into a four-hour lunch so we could openly discuss what was plainly obvious. Neither of us could ignore the entrenched vote of no-confidence in his ability to continue as CEO, even if he had enormous contributions to still make as part of the executive team. I admitted my huge error in pushing him further than he initially wanted to go, remembering the cautions he raised after his first-year induction. I accepted full responsibility for having deviated from the "Joseph plan" - because of my impatience to become less operational in the business - which meant the mess that resulted was mine to clean up.

I explained to Ashton that it was my intention to resume the CEO role at Back In Motion. The board not only approved the decision, but begged me to do so. I asked Ashton his preference – step back to the number two role or take the opportunity for a new job elsewhere.

Ashton was open-hearted, humble, and receptive to the option of resuming an associate role, expressing some relief at the transference of responsibilities. He reluctantly agreed it was not working with him as CEO, with the physical toll and emotional strain of the last year clearly etched in his wry smile.

At Paulina's suggestion, I invited Ashton and his wife to our home for supper the next evening, knowing it would be difficult for them both to accept my unconventional proposal without feeling cheated or jaded. I took the opportunity to speak plainly about the change-up I was offering, so the four of us could process the likely impact together and avoid any mis-communication.

Ashton's wife was gracious that night as she listened to the rationale behind my decision to resume leadership of the business, effectively demoting her husband. She gave her understanding for the reverse transition, recognising it was better for Ashton in the long run and, by extension, a win for their family at home too. Our closing remarks, as we stood to depart that night, were ones of mutual gratitude, wanting to remain genuine friends.

Ashton took two weeks overseas to let his heart and mind settle with the unusual changes ahead, and then returned later that month as my second-in-charge. I should have done something similar to calm my nerves, but the very next day Paulina got me dressed, packed my lunch, and sent me off to work for the first day of my old job again. I dragged my feet and grabbed her skirt like a five-year-old reluctant to leave their mother's side on the first day of school.

By eight o'clock that morning, I was sitting behind my familiar desk of nearly two decades, wondering if this disappointing setback was a divine set-up for a glorious comeback!

96
harley heaven

PAULINA WAS UNFLAPPABLE during my years of failed succession, encouraging me to resume control of the business, composed in the face of inevitably high workloads soon to impact our family again. And, if not more patient and resilient than me, she was at least more realistic.

As a result of Ashton's removal from the CEO role, we never made it to Chile or Spain for the year abroad we had planned. No time with extended family for Paulina. No sabbatical for me. No international school for the kids. No European soccer for Lachlan. No learning the beautiful Spanish language by immersion in a foreign culture. Instead, we stayed home. I put my shoulder to the Back In Motion wheel once again, reluctantly accepting the opportunity to live overseas had passed us by.

But the year in Australia was by no means wasted. All three boys trialled for, and were accepted into, the junior National Premier League as starting eleven players in their respective age groups. Because of their different schedules and demanding routines, we had at least one child training literally every night of the school week, and multiple games on both Saturday and Sunday, making us a seven-day-a-week soccer family.

We added another member to the family, Monique. She was a gorgeous white Labrador puppy who needed carers as she trained to become a guide dog. Paulina took the reins (literally) with this project. She attended the various classes to get Monique ready for a life of service to a vision-impaired person. Monique travelled with us to the supermarket, into the classrooms at school, and even sat quietly by our feet during 90-minute church services, where we believe she found God and made a commitment to the Golden Rule in her own way.

We also took the kids to Thailand that year, visiting our friends who worked at the anti-trafficking organisation, stationed in Chiang Mai. We met with many of the children rescued from modern slavery, including sexual trafficking, bonded labour, and other forms of oppressive servitude. We toured through the safe house that we had helped support financially, seeing firsthand the difference our donations had made.

While travelling through the region, one highlight was a visit to an animal sanctuary where we fed and washed a small family of protected elephants. Morgan especially loved the wet spray and sloppy kisses from the 600-kilogram baby, Dumbo. I smile, even now as I write this, at the elation of a small boy riding bareback through the rainforest, high on the neck of his new pet elephant, like a scene out of *Jungle Book*.

On our return home, I lobbied Paulina for her blessing to purchase a new motorcycle. I had been riding trail and road bikes from our earliest years of married life, but was especially enamoured with Harley Davidson cruisers after hiring one in Queensland some years earlier, cornering through the Hinterland for an exhilarating weekend.

I garnered the support of Clive, a great friend and tax advisor, coming on ten years. An avid biker himself, Clive prepared, at my request, a formal letter of advice on official firm letterhead, outlining to Paulina the financial benefits of investing some of our Revita sale proceeds into a two-wheeled "appreciating asset". Of course, Paulina was not about to be hoodwinked by such cheap parlour tricks, but she laughed at the effort, giving me her nod of support.

After months of research, by the end of that year I proudly straddled a limited edition 2013 Harley Davidson Night Rod Special – with a fully blacked-out 60-degree, v-twin, 1250cc liquid cooled, four-stroke, four-valve Revolution engine that was built in collaboration with Porsche. It came complete with anti-skid braking, electronic fuel injection, 90 kilowatts of power, and 111 nanometres of torque.

The bike rode like a rocket, reaching 100 kilometres per hour in 3.2 seconds – if you knew how to ride it – one of the fastest street-legal drag bikes at the time. The rear tyre had been upgraded to a custom 160mm width, resembling Batman's bike more than the Marlboro Man. Pimped out with LED lights, slimline mirrors, hydraulic lift kit, mini ape handlebars, and a custom back rest matching the leather stitching in the seat, the hog was an enviable sight.

I registered the custom vehicle plate VXROD, nicknamed it *El Torito* (Spanish for "Little Bull"), and mounted it for my first ride home. Each twist of the throttle echoed my heartbeat. With the wind whipping against my skin, and the iconic rumble of the v-twin engine beneath me, every turn felt like a dance between man and machine. The distinct growl of the exhaust made me smile so widely I became a human bug catcher as I hit the Westgate Bridge eastbound.

As I repeat often to those who have never ridden a motorcycle, the Harley Davidson experience is more than just a ride; it is a symphony of sights, sounds, and a deep sense of liberation as you cruise through open roads.

It has been a lot of fun using the bike as a prop for some of my public speaking events at men's health seminars, business breakfasts, and even school assemblies. I often choose to ride the bike into conference rooms, churches, and school gymnasiums, giving the throttle a few squeezes on my arrival, letting the audience feel the reverberations of the thumping cylinders. I love watching the audience cover their ears and open their mouths at the spectacle.

The motorcycle, a compelling metaphor for life and business, embodies a high-performance vehicle demanding meticulous care. Like our personal endeavours, it thrives on the precise balance of the right fuel and well-suited tyres, operated at optimal speeds while navigating the corners and straights. This was true in my own career, recognising that every year, with its unforeseen twists – be they triumphs or tragedies – all becoming an integral part of the odyssey forming my character and sculpting my soul.

Returning to a full-time leadership role at Back In Motion, my priority was to quickly rebuild culture, trust, and value within the network again. I travelled to every state, listening to and learning from our franchisees and their staff on the ground. I openly shared the reasons for my leadership reset, with no spin, secrets, or mystery. I gave everyone a candid appraisal of my failed succession plan, taking responsibility for the cultural vacuum I had unintentionally created, and promising a renewed personal effort.

My return came with a warning, though. I had no intention of repeating the unhealthy habits I had succumbed to in my former years. 200 emails a day, 45 hours of meetings each week, less than five hours sleep per night, and dousing spot fires as they sparked and flickered across the group, was not my best contribution. I didn't want to bounce *back*; I expected to lunge *forward*. I was committed to finding new ways to do my job, innovate our processes, preserve relationships, redefine leadership, and set fresh direction.

I embraced the surging adrenaline and unfathomable risk of the business as a necessary part of my new quest, pretending sometimes it was like a high-octane ride on my Harley through the unpredictable backroads of our great country. Sometimes these mind games were exactly what I needed to stay upright and keep the throttle on.

97
Downside up

A HIGH POINT of 2018 was the October launch of my second book, *Outside In Downside Up Leadership*. Detailing the story of our 7/50/100 campaign, and the introduction of the ONEteam model, I extracted 50 leadership insights about organisational change. It was a warts-and-all confession of what went wrong and how we eventually exceeded all expectations.

Writing books is fun, publishing them is not. I undertook the assignment during a period when I hadn't anticipated returning to full-time work within the business. The project initially begun a year earlier as a collaboration with Beth, my lead for People and Culture, and the venerable poster girl for the ONEteam shared values. I ended up continuing the initiative on my own after Beth left to take on a new role. It wasn't long before I was liaising with potential publishers, wrestling the text with editors, getting custom diagrams drawn to explain my leadership concepts, finalising the cover design, and getting the intellectual properties, copyrights, domain names, and ISBN registered. Amidst this flurry of activity, along came Scott – my personal promoter of the title – and his success in the role demanded hours from my schedule I could barely afford.

Scott secured me maximum exposure in all the big newspapers, radio stations, and television programs, including with some of the media that had crucified me only months earlier as the franchisor "... from hell". Funny how fickle these journalists and their outlets can be, depending on who is pitching the story, and what they think their readership wants to hear.

I was interviewed for, or profiled in, a variety of print and online newspapers and magazines, including the *Weekend Australian*, *Australian Financial Review*, and *Smart Company*. I engaged in lots of professional and amateur podcasts, such as *Team Guru*, *Subtle Disruptors*, and the *CEO Institute*. I even flew to Sydney to do my second radio interview with ABC Finance Analyst Alan Kohler for his program, *Talking Business*, which was later aired on Qantas radio and scheduled with Channel 7's *Kochie's Business Builders* the same month.

Adding to the momentum, my mug shot was plastered on point-of-sale materials at train stations and airports in Melbourne, Adelaide, and Sydney, with most major book retailers agreeing to a prominent shelf display for the first month following the book's release. Friends and colleagues texted me all through November with their random spotting of my advertisements as they stumbled across them.

Someone gleefully tweeted their experience – spotting my face on a poster at Melbourne airport, then subsequently listening to my interview on their Qantas in-flight entertainment, and feeling so intrigued that they bought the book immediately on their arrival at Sydney airport before rushing off to their first appointment for the day. Scott was extremely pleased with his efforts.

The effective promotion of the new book led to a bevy of invitations to speak at various events. The mix was wide and varied, including CEO groups, industry conferences, churches, management seminars, local government initiatives, healthcare events, and franchise networking forums. Some of the engagements offered substantial sums for a keynote, where all I had to do was share a succinct version of my story and illuminate half a dozen of the key insights from the book. Many of these occasions led to further engagements, as enthusiastic attendees invited me to the next event they were hosting. I leap-frogged from one public address to another speaking gig, almost every week in some form or another, for the next 12 months. And, of course, off the back of every presentation, I sold more books and promoted the Back In Motion brand, building further opportunities.

Paulina regularly cautioned me not to accept every invitation, as I often had to travel interstate for the speaking engagements. Quite apart from the pressure it added at home, the travel also diminished my renewed commitment to lead the Back In Motion Health Group. There was a natural limit to what I could fit into an ordinary week, and I resolved to never go back to working an eighth day to get it all done. Finding balance was an elusive and delicate task, one I still hadn't properly mastered.

98
erosion

PARTLY TRIGGERED BY the unwelcomed ACCC scrutiny on our business and the sordid media coverage linked to the Senate Inquiry, two franchisees made the decision to exit our group in late 2018.

The first was reasonably uncomplicated, agreeing to sensible terms without much legal agitation. Having built one of the fastest growing practices in Victoria, landing convincingly in the million-dollar club before his second anniversary, and being awarded our Most Inspiring Practice Director in 2011, I missed Kane.

The second practice exit didn't resolve quite as smoothly. Newcomer to our group in 2017, Ethan was a lovable larrikin, enthusiastic about the things that mattered to him, and completely disengaged with everything else. Ethan had almost no understanding of the franchising concept and Ashton had been wrong to approve his application. The relationship was set up for failure from the beginning.

By November of his first year as a franchisee, Ethan earned himself not one, but two letters of default from Ashton's desk. The first was for failure to pay his security deposit, royalties and lease costs. The second was for failure to provide duly executed employment contracts to meet our compliance standards.

Things dramatically worsened in June 2018, when we enlisted the firepower of Warren - our new commercial law partner appointed by Ashton - to lodge a Notice of Dispute against Ethan's intention to relocate the practice to unapproved premises. Ethan was a law unto himself, giving little regard to process and authority. So much so, he ignored our concerns completely, until Warren wrote to him again in August requesting formal mediation.

Without remedying any of the breaches, Ethan approached me directly in October to buyout his practice. Frankly, I was relieved at the thought of not having him around. Except, shortly thereafter, he became uncontactable, seemingly abandoning his business.

After caretaking his practice during his extended and unexplainable absence, I wrote to him seeking clarity on his intentions. After insufferable waiting, we simply allowed his franchise agreement to expire.

Of course, this meant nothing to Ethan. Seemingly alive and well again, he continued to trade the practice, indifferent to the fact he no longer had a valid franchise agreement. Furthermore, I received second-hand reports that Ethan and his staff were colluding with a competitor in a neighbouring suburb, pilfering our client list by stealth referral. I received copies of emails, minutes of staff meetings, and client testimonies that confirmed the underhanded strategy.

I had all but given up on Ethan, figuring the fight wasn't worth it, especially with the ACCC keeping me on my toes, except Warren felt differently. He wrote a final letter of demand relating to breaches of privacy law and confidentiality, unauthorised use of our licensed software, breach of our restrictive covenants, client and staff solicitation, and sought recovery of our unpaid invoices. The estimated loss to us was in the hundreds of thousands of dollars. I doubted Ethan would take any notice, but Warren wanted the letter on record if matters escalated further.

They didn't, and I wrote off the losses as a small speedbump. So often caught in a relentless battle between ideals and pragmatism, my heart yearned for justice while my mind accepted the daunting practicalities of the legal realm – exorbitant costs, labyrinthine complexities, and the draining allocation of time and energy. I laid down the moral injustice in favour of other commercial priorities.

ETHAN HAD BEEN a thorn in Ashton's side from the beginning – an embarrassing decision resulting in a disappointing end. In addition, awkward relationships with some of the NSO team, lingering after his short tenure as CEO, made Ashton realise that things could never go back to the way they were in his first year working alongside me. Ashton resigned his associate role in November, only five months after his step-down.

On reflection, Ashton had been the *right* man put in the *wrong* position at a critical time, and not set up to succeed. A "brother from another mother", I lost much more than a CEO the day he understandably left for new and less complicated opportunities. Ashton helped move our business forward through a difficult but necessary time of upheaval, and even though his time with us was short, I am grateful for his contribution and personal loyalty.

Ashton's departure created a void in the NSO, paving the way for a new figure to step on the stage. Dan carried the DNA of Back In Motion deeply in his soul, having been part of our story for over 15 years, and arguably one of the most loved and trusted individuals within the group. From selling me my first computer when he was still a high school student, to overseeing the build of our entire technology platform, Dan had seen just about everything that had gone on under our roof. He was an intuitive man who knew where every skeleton was buried, and yet remained infallibly loyal to me.

As the winds of leadership shifted, it became Dan's time to be recognised. I promoted him into the Executive Team with the responsibility of Group Operations, fast becoming one of my closest confidantes – the *real* "Joseph".

The culmination of the year brought a sense of accomplishment. A new dynamic emerged within the NSO; relief coupled with burgeoning optimism. I was convinced God had me standing at the threshold of something remarkable.

99
winners again

2019 POPPED WITH a predictable bang as the premier event on our annual calendar was to invite our franchisees to sunny Sea World on the Gold Coast, celebrating our eleventh Back In Motion Directors Conference. Marie-Anne "Rusty" Rustichelli, Ashton's executive assistant that I gratefully inherited after he let mine go, did a superb job pulling the event together. This was clearly one of her greatest contributions to our team, as she took incredible pride in ensuring the smallest of details were executed to perfection.

I resumed my familiar post with an opening keynote, delving into the theme of unity, emphasising the strength of our competitive edge when we worked together. The sentiments of collaboration and alignment, fighting *for* each other and not *with* each other, reverberated around the walls of the plenary theatre as different ones acknowledged our bright opportunities.

In beckoning a new era for our brand, I commissioned a comprehensive market research project. The findings revealed how Back In Motion specifically, and physiotherapy in general, were perceived in the market, and what strategies we could harness to better position ourselves for greatest impact.

Off the back of these learnings, I launched our new brand position, *Movement for Life*. This was a huge step forward in simplifying our message to our clientele and aligning our people with one voice. I assembled a special taskforce of franchisees to weigh in on the strategy, ratifying the various elements of our brand-building campaign.

In the same weekend, Dan released long-overdue technology advancements, including a staff smartphone application to log their hours, manage leave entitlements, track professional development, and communicate directly with peers. We also deployed a unique clinical module that allowed therapists to plot and analyse a standardised range of empirical and subjective measures for every treatment session we delivered, ensuring patients received clear evidence of their progress, and researchers could substantiate our unique protocols.

Practice growth was running high. We welcomed new locations in Australia and New Zealand, with a steady pipeline of further interest. More franchisees had broken the $2 million revenue threshold, proving that barriers had previously been mindsets rather than realities.

Only months prior to hosting our conference, and less than a year since returning to my executive role, I was formally ranked the second highest Franchise Executive in Australia by *Franchise Business Review*, runner-up to CEO Natalie Brennan of Muffin Break. Many of our NSO team attended the awards night with Paulina and I. It was a pleasant surprise, after our bashing by the media, to still come out near the top amongst such a competitive and ambitious group of peers. The positive press releases and articles that flowed off that single award seemed to dilute the Google rankings of the more damaging reports from 2018, helping to give a more balanced account of our story.

The most anticipated part of our Directors' Conference is always the Gala Ball, where the Most Inspiring Practice Director is awarded. Delegates were bussed to Movie World and ushered into the Scooby-Doo Castle for a spooky take on a black-tie affair. The most coveted award was presented to Justin for outstanding performance in his two locations, giving him the honour of the first back-to-back win in our two-decade history, cementing his achievements into physio folklore. Kyle, a franchisee newcomer who had started a thriving greenfield practice in Tasmania, took out the Rising Star Award for nearly hitting the magical million-dollar-threshold before his first birthday.

It was great to feel like winners again.

100
now boarding

I WAS GRATEFUL Paulina joined our board at the start of 2017. Traversing the sensitivities of the Revita sale, the fallout with Philip and the associated Senate Inquiry, and my decision to return to the CEO role, were much more bearable with Paulina involved in the detail. Whilst discussions across the boardroom table still inevitably made their way to the kitchen table, it was more valuable to receive Paulina's insights at the beginning of our considerations rather than lament her recommendations after it was too late to change.

Having waded to safety through what had been our most treacherous waters, and given eight years of incredible support, John resigned from the board in December 2018. I felt I shouldn't continue as chairman either. Whilst it was appropriate when Ashton was CEO, since my resumption of executive duties, it was ineffective for me to carry both mantles in the boardroom.

These changes presented the opportunity for me to refresh the board, seeking at least two new candidates to round out our composition. I wanted an experienced chairperson who brought close attention to risk management and legal compliance, and a separate independent advisor strong in financial analysis and economic strategy.

I first met Jame a decade earlier, when I was invited to a networking group facilitated by Christian Management Australia. A lawyer of some 40 years, Jame was the founding partner of a successful Melbourne firm specialising in commercial, dispute resolution, and not-for-profit matters. In his semi-retirement phase, he chose to concentrate mostly on personal estate planning and governance training for NGOs and charitable enterprises. Jame's experience in legal structures and negotiating small and large business transactions were valuable insights for where I wanted to head, and his ability to chair the board with excellence and objectivity ultimately won him the job.

Neil was also invited into the fold. In the twilight years of his successful career, and still managing partner in a large accounting firm, Neil was a taxation specialist. Having worked with numerous international consulting firms, he was experienced in advising a broad range of publicly listed and private companies and trusts, professional partnerships, high wealth individuals, and not-for-profit organisations. Neil fitted the bill perfectly.

Above all, Jame and Neil were both men of deep faith, appreciating that my business mission transcended simple economics and commercial strategy. They quickly recognised the heart of our brand lay embedded in the conviction that we were to serve the poor. Back In Motion aligned with divine intentions, not merely pursuing profit or market dominance, but compelled to do work that resonated with our shared spiritual values. They were entirely comfortable with my prayer-centred model of decision making, having run their own endeavours with a similar mindset.

I commissioned the first meeting of our new board in February 2019 with Jame as chair, just in time to include them both in our Directors' Conference on the Gold Coast. I knew we had appointed the right people when I witnessed them both impeccably dressed for our Gala Ball, standing out as the two oldest guests in the room, but eagerly engaging with our youthful franchisees as they boarded the Scooby-Doo rollercoaster without any hesitation. Their roles were to become instrumental in the exciting crescendo that awaited us in the coming years of my story.

101
ACCC encore

NO SOONER HAD Jame and Neil rested their feet under the boardroom table, the ACCC came knocking again – seemingly hungry for a scalp they could hold up to the public in recognition of their fine work. Under scrutiny for glaring oversights in different sectors, the regulatory body was striving for redemption, and revisited our case file for a third time.

Their unprovoked concern during round three zeroed in on the historical and sensationalised media reports in the *Australian Financial Review*. The journalist's sloppy reporting six months earlier, falsely alleged I required franchisees to pay significant fees, as high as $600,000, to terminate their franchise agreement early. Despite it not being true, the ACCC built a case that this obligation – and other restraint clauses like it – were unfair, however seemed unwilling to make a definitive ruling on it.

The regulator seemed to be randomly trawling for a catch, and we were baited. In many ways, Back In Motion was an easy target now that others had publicly maligned us. If I managed to escape their net though, the ACCC risked looking weak and incompetent, so the stakes were high for both sides. Jame, with an acute legal mind, was astounded how far the ACCC were seemingly prepared to take matters.

The unusual wording in the ACCC's complaint letter coerced me to "volunteer" with an investigation that appeared beyond their scope; otherwise, they threatened to pursue me under different legislation that might afford them greater powers. Of course, I took it seriously and cooperated, delivering a detailed 14-page response in April 2019.

I repeated much of what I had tried to explain already to the Senate Inquiry, given the accusations were similarly vague and unsubstantiated. I characterised Back In Motion as a group with a united culture, high franchisee and staff retention, and relatively low disputation. Our track record of nurturing successful physiotherapists over two decades spoke volumes for the credibility of our model.

To support my case, I again referenced testimonials from franchisees, many now in the public domain and on official parliamentary record. I noted our proud legacy of being the largest, and still fastest growing, physiotherapy employer and provider of private physiotherapy services in Australia because of the qualities celebrated in the letters of endorsement. And without appearing spiteful, I gently reminded them of our numerous healthcare, entrepreneur, and franchise awards, including accolades for corporate social responsibility where, for the last decade, we had been working tirelessly on a pro bono basis amongst Indigenous communities to help close the healthcare gap.

To my knowledge, we were the only franchised physiotherapy business in Australia at the time. For this reason, I required bespoke commercial terms in our agreements to address the unique nature of professional health services. For instance, patient confidentiality, professional standards, and clinical compliance, were high priorities for me, but less relevant in other franchise systems. Despite these anomalies, I could demonstrate that our agreements consistently exceeded the high bar of industry standards and regulatory compliance.

Regarding the restrictive covenants that had attracted so much attention during the Senate Inquiry, I explained that the two biggest drivers of our success were (1) sourcing and training therapists, and (2) attracting and retaining clientele. Franchisees wanted covenants in their employment agreements to prevent staff from leaving with their clients. As the franchisor, I expected similar protections against franchisees who might try the same.

As for the recurring accusation of exorbitant exit fees, with some exasperation I repeated no such obligation has ever existed in our business. I explained our optional buyout fees, available to those franchisees who wanted to keep the franchised business without paying royalties, was not something I ever imposed, nor could trigger. Buyout provisions were special conditions crafted for the sole benefit of, and execution by, the franchisee as a safety net when their licence expired – a rip cord only they could pull – if and when they wanted to. It was akin to a tenant having an option to buy the house they lived in from the landlord, not a penalty I could wield at my discretion.

My legal team was convinced that the specialised counsel in the ACCC couldn't grasp our nuanced approach, and would come unstuck if they hoped to apply a generic regulatory standard to an unprecedented, innovative business unfamiliar to them.

SENSING BLOOD IN the water again, Philip finned the surface for another bite.

Three years after his resignation, I was still ducking and weaving his random punches. I had spent hundreds of thousands of dollars in legal defence and crisis brand management directly because of the Senate Inquiry he had instigated. We lost numerous new practice deals as a result, with a handful of prospective franchisees being spooked by the media. I had unruly cultural fallout to manage inside my network as a result, and now, with further ACCC investigations afoot, Philip sought to ride their unflattering coattails a little further.

Philip took to the public arena again to discredit me further, making unfounded allegations about Back In Motion in social media. My legal team were confident they had compelling evidence to indict him for slander, defamation, libel, and injurious falsehood. In sympathy for his wife and children whom we dearly loved, Paulina urged me not to issue proceedings.

Philip didn't stop at pursuing me. He aggressed Ashton many times in their various crossovers, and was especially vitriolic toward Dan, blaming him for the reasons he was "forced" to resign.

Philip's first assault against Dan appeared in November 2017 when Philip accused Dan of illegally disposing of obsolete political election materials. Dan had been doing him a personal favour, storing them in our Tech This Out warehouse, when he received written permission from the party office to destroy them. Philip threatened legal action, promising to "bankrupt" Dan out of spite.

Little came of the issue at the time but, on Christmas Eve of 2018, Philip issued proceedings against Dan and Tech This Out, demanding payment for the alleged unauthorised disposals. In many ways, it felt like Dan was taking the fall for Philip's jihad against me. Philip knew I was co-owner of Tech This Out, as he had helped facilitate the sale when he worked for me in early 2016.

In a comedic twist, Philip engaged the law firm co-founded by our new chairman, Jame, with whom Jame was still on friendship terms with the senior partners. As it happened, I had recently connected personally with his preferred solicitor at a networking event, adding to the layers of relational complexity and off-record disclosures. Suffice to say, Philip was left unrepresented shortly thereafter.

Dan decided not to retain legal counsel on the matter, and I wrote him a killer rebuttal to Philip's ludicrous claim. It wasn't the end of our bitter battle, but it won us an eight-month reprieve.

102
orthotic-gate

ONE OF PHILIP'S co-conspirators was a foundational franchisee, Malcolm. He was successful in many regards, having owned at different times five Back In Motion practices over a 15-year period. I thought Malcolm would have been grateful for his achievements, not aggrieved, but I was often warned by industry stalwarts that early franchisees are rarely loyal, as they eventually become jealous of the success of the brand (and its owners) they believe they had helped build.

Whilst Malcolm's business had under-performed in recent years, having fallen away from previous peaks, I would characterise his rhythm as slow and steady. He had originally invested approximately $400,000 in fit out and, over his aggregate term, conservatively generated $12 million in gross revenues, profiting an average 11.5%. Malcolm enjoyed a sustainable lifestyle, travelling overseas frequently, living in a beautiful home, and only having to work in "third gear", as he described it.

Despite all this, I think Malcolm lost his confidence as he watched younger franchisees enter the group, eclipsing his success and de-throning him as the pace leader. It seemed easier for Malcolm to throw stones, than pick them up and fortify his perimeter.

Malcolm and I endured a love-hate relationship from the beginning; our personalities in regular conflict, but genuinely grateful for one another's collegiate support. However, a lightning strike of personal attack came from him in September 2017 after I released updated franchise agreements with more generous terms to new members of the group.

Malcolm was scalding in his assessment, lamenting my gestures were too little and too late. In particular, he took issue with me offering our conversion franchisees a subsidised royalty via the Preserved Revenue

Threshold (PRT), something he was never afforded at his joining more than a decade earlier. He demanded reimbursement for 13 years of backdated royalties, oblivious that he wouldn't have qualified for PRT concessions at that time, even if they were available.

Unaccepting of my rebuttals, Malcolm extolled upon me, as a self-appointed spokesman of the group, all the reasons why he and the "rest of the franchisees" were unhappy with my leadership. He wrote me a detailed email outlining the issues percolating in his heart.

Curiously, Malcolm prophesied that within 12-24 months, the group would be decimated by mass exits of influential franchisees who would leave because of the "tidal wave" of disillusion, dislike, and distrust felt toward the NSO. He vaguely referenced "20 people" who apparently shared his sentiments, in much the same way Philip had thrown out that number under the guise it would scare me.

Maybe he did have the numbers behind him, maybe he didn't; I will never know. But Malcolm had one overriding motivation for unloading on me: self-interest. When pressed on what he thought would restore good standing within our group, he recommended all franchisees who had been with the group for ten years or more be exempt from future royalties. He argued that a show of such generosity would encourage long-term franchisees to remain with the brand and promote the opportunity amongst their industry peers.

Despite the commercial absurdity of Malcolm's proposal, nobody in my team believed his suggestion would solve the alleged cultural unrest. More than likely, it would only exacerbate inequality amongst our franchise cohort, creating an undesirable caste system of disparate earnings. The wealthiest franchisees would be the only ones to benefit from the policy, alienating the great majority. Royalties from the new and smaller practices would effectively subsidise the larger ones – the irony being they could least afford to do so.

Malcolm's lengthy one-sided tirade continued for two months over email, becoming increasingly personal. He assumed the noble stance of the truth-sayer, believing I needed to "hear it for my own good", and hoping I wouldn't "hate him for it". The self-righteous pomp was nauseating, a thinly veiled posture of egomania and personal gain.

His words cut deep though. Paulina and I realised how little our personal journey was truly known within the network. Few understood the immense risks we'd shouldered and the continuous investments we made into Back In Motion, because these people weren't present at the beginning and couldn't imagine what drama played out behind the curtain of our daily fascade. We bore disproportionate financial burden in the first ten years, risking everything multiple times over. I often extended loans, sometimes losing hundreds of thousands of dollars, to those Malcolm hinted were now opposing me – acts driven by friendship and empathy. Countless midnight hours were spent counselling franchisees through business and personal challenges, offering support unseen by the masses.

I had bled for my people, not getting it right all the time, but never from lack of commitment. I absorbed countless blows in silence over the years, unseen sacrifices Malcolm could never comprehend. I wasn't seeking his pity, but I hoped for a reality check. I definitely wasn't going to concede to his fabricated controversaries as a pretext for reducing franchise royalties; I had grown increasingly immune to negative rumours and hurtful hearsay as a method of manipulating my many insecurities.

A full year passed with occasional grumblings and rants from Malcolm, on much the same topics. In September 2018, after our brush with the Senate Inquiry, Malcolm re-engaged to discuss his future options.

At a quaint café in a hipster inner city suburb, I laid out a smorgasbord of options for Malcolm's consideration. He could renew his franchise agreement for a fourth time, enjoying staged royalty discounts as he pushed into higher revenue brackets; sell his practice back to the NSO, or bring in some partners on a one- or two-year succession plan; continue his practice independently of our brand, exercising his buyout option; or he could sell the business outright as a going concern. So many choices, but few to Malcolm's liking.

The one I encouraged most, was to bide his time until I could engineer a corporate transition of some sort – maybe an IPO, private equity sale, industry merge – whereby he, along with all stakeholders, would enjoy a leveraged payout for the unique business we had built together. This was starting to form as my favoured exit strategy for *everyone*, about which I talked openly at our frequent franchise conferences and summits. Malcolm didn't believe it was possible.

In desperation to find a way forward, I floated to Malcolm the possibility of a royalty-for-equity swap, where I forfeited all my perpetual royalties from his practice (as he had requested only a year earlier) in exchange for minority shareholdings in his practice. This would align us both to profit performance rather than sales growth, and substantially boost his bottom line by an additional seven percent. It was my first flirtation with quasi-de-franchising, as the suggestion was akin to a corporatisation of Malcolm's flagship practice, giving me an entitlement to dividends rather than franchisee fees. Malcolm and I did some math together at the table that morning on the latter strategy, with him quickly dismissing the option because he intuited the trade-off was more in my favour.

Crediting whatever achievements he had enjoyed to his own effort, rather than any support the franchise system had provided, Malcolm decided signing up for another five-year term would be unbearable. By December, his clear preference was obvious: he chose to exercise his buyout option before his franchise expiry date.

Reminiscent of the challenges Spencer had in extricating from his self-created web of complexity, Malcolm's biggest hurdle to jump would be convincing his business partner, who had equity only in a smaller, second location, to exit with him – something she did not want to do.

Like a consigliere negotiating with a rival mafia boss, Malcolm offered me a paltry sum to allow him to "go quietly". The number fell a long way short of the buyout figure stipulated in his franchise agreement. To up the ante in negotiations, Malcolm lawyered-up, insinuating it would be less painful for me to concede to his demands that endure another spat int the public domain.

Never one to respond well to threats, I refused to negotiate.

At this point, I was comfortable to let Malcolm run down the clock on his near-complete franchise term, terminate the licence, and reclaim our client list, practice phone number, occupancy lease, and social media handles for re-assignment to another operator. Malcolm bristled at this inevitable scenario, determined to broker an alternative.

Five months of hostile horse trading eventually concluded with agreement to a reasonable buyout figure, subject to him divesting his shares in the second practice to his business partner – who wanted to continue with us. It was a fair commercial outcome, avoiding further bloodshed.

The problem was Malcolm's partner couldn't afford his asking price.

RELYING ON THE only strategy he knew, Malcolm initiated a full-scale assault against me and the brand, under the guise of "clinical morality".

Our network developed protocols to use advanced gait scanning and 3D foot-modelling technology to prescribe, fabricate, and sell custom orthotics to patients. Malcolm exaggerated concerns that specific franchisees were defrauding medical insurers, misappropriating Medicare-approved billing codes set up precisely for this purpose. He trumpeted his claims as moral outrage, scaremongering that I had put the livelihood of every franchisee in peril by risking brand disrepute. Malcolm grandstanded on every platform available to discredit us. He wrote emails to the franchisees, got noisy at our state-based meetings, and even reported our alleged impropriety to the APA.

The scandal became known internally as *Orthotic-GATE*.

Stepping outside of a restaurant in Dunedin on the South Island of New Zealand – where I had just celebrated the signing for a new practice launch – I took a call from Malcolm. He unashamedly admitted his intention to "nail me on the cross" as his memorable legacy, crucifying me with public shame and legal indictments.

The seriousness escalated quickly. I launched a detailed internal investigation into the affair, scrambling to catch up and contain the matter before things went nuclear.

The heart of the concern was whether it was appropriate (clinically, ethically and legally) for a physiotherapist to complete a biomechanical assessment of a patient's foot and ankle, and prescribe custom orthotics under the Medicare regime – a service historically the exclusive purview of a podiatrist. It was a question layered with sensitive nuances, made more complex given we employed podiatrists also. The debate was fraught with conjecture and disagreement amongst insurers, clinicians, and administrators – a perfect scenario for Malcolm to cast sufficient dispersions and exploit his revenge.

I personally trawled through 87 related email threads to piece together the disparate claims made against us. I interviewed franchisees, consulted with professional advisors, and debriefed with board members. I spoke with account representatives and policy advisors of major health insurers Medibank, BUPA, HCF and NIB. I inquired of CEOs and executive branches of the APA, Australian Podiatry Council, and the Physiotherapy Registration Board (AHPRA). I schooled myself in the accepted best practice of podiatrists, podiatry service providers, and organisations who manufactured and supplied custom orthotics. Finally, I conducted my own desktop review of the laws and regulations around billing codes in physiotherapy and podiatry.

These conversations and discoveries were not linear or straight forward. Most people were open-minded, humble, and cooperative in the process, but in some instances, I was repelled by uncharacteristically hostile aggression and hurtful accusations. The stakes were high, and I was surprised how emotionally charged some became on what deceptively appeared to be little more than a bureaucratic puzzle to solve.

There were "variations of perspective" – as I wrote in one formal report – influenced by each one's point of reference, understanding of events, personal agenda, subjective judgment, or technical arguments. Some insurers showed an openness to the approach, while others quickly condemned our practice unacceptable. Many said it was "grey" and "untested", some conceding it a "technical loophole" in the regulations. Few perceived that what we were doing was any serious breach of conduct.

Different advice from the same insurer was not uncommon, depending on whom I spoke to, and which day I rang. These were not new challenges when seeking clarity from a multi-stakeholder healthcare system, but they did add to the confusion, frustration, and delays. In the myriad of views converging, I placed most weight on health insurers – as they were ultimately the purchasers of our services through private health insurance rebates paid to clients. I also wanted to be led by the APA, as they were the guardians of safe industry practice.

Fully cognisant of Malcolm's intent to incriminate me, I freely accepted responsibility for everything that happened under my roof at Back In Motion. I knew investigations moved slowly, and recognised I had to be better prepared for matters like this in the future, given we had become a target to be made an example of – the ACCC witch hunt having proved as much.

I concluded, despite Malcolm's agitation on the issue, there was no conspiracy or cover up as he continued to assert. I did not believe any of our clinical staff or franchisees acted with any malicious or fraudulent intent, or sought to hide their procedures. On the contrary, the hysteria erupted only because people were openly sharing their approaches in peer forums, celebrating the innovation. No patients were harmed, nor was the public put at any risk, as the matter related more to billing policy than clinical practice. Specifically, with regards to our new practice of orthotic prescription, there was no judgement against us or recourse from any external third parties. The industry-at-large seemed satisfied that we were exploring new boundaries of clinical practice in an ethical way, and benefited from the wide consultation that resulted during our probe.

Being unequivocal with our internal policy, I erred on the side of caution, instructing a revised procedure that ensured physiotherapists only delivered services to insured patients within currently confirmed scope of individual insurer protocols, determined on a case basis if needed. I believed this would ensure we remained beyond reproach, impervious to those who sought to exploit any hairline crack in our fragile brand shell.

Unsurprisingly, Malcolm did not accept my findings. He went to great lengths, at risk of defamation, forcing the issue for many weeks that fellow franchisees had acted with malicious intent to defraud insurers. He insisted I was personally guilty of gross misconduct, declaring he had lost faith in our group, the brand, and my leadership. He demanded I release him of all his franchise obligations to distance himself from any professional stain stemming from the collective reputation he had tarnished.

And there it was, the motivation behind his sabotage: a premature exit.

He threatened to continue agitating his peers with divisive views unless I cut him loose, waiving his buyout fee, and resolving the deadlock with his business partner. By this point in my career, I had learned to starve the wolves. I ignored his perceived upper hand, making Malcolm bide his time until September 2019, when he finally conceded to a more reasonable price for his shares in the second practice – making it a happy day for both of us.

The complexity of my relationship with Malcolm lay in the intertwining of our stories. He was one of the earlier franchisees – a bold leap where I took a significant risk, extending trust to someone who, in return, placed their faith in me. Working together became a mosaic of contradictions – marked by moments of genuine connection juxtaposed against periods of deep discord. I never viewed Malcolm as evil; rather, I saw him as emotionally unskilled – a difficult person to navigate due to the prickliness lurking beneath the surface. And undoubtedly, I brought my own set of flaws into our dysfunctional dynamic, adding to our troubles. Despite an undeniable relief in the finality of it all, my heart ached with twinges of melancholy given our long history together. I wished I had finished on better terms with Malcolm, the lesson that *people matter*, still something I was learning.

103
kangaroo court

COMPOUNDING MY DISTRACTIONS, Dan informed me in November 2019 that he been subpoenaed by the Victorian Civil Administrative Tribunal (VCAT). Philip was at it again, officially issuing proceedings against Dan and our tech company for the alleged illegal disposal of his campaign election materials – his third attempt in as many years.

Feeling entirely responsible for the real motivation behind Philip's attack, I apologised to Dan for becoming collateral damage. Whilst it was a nonsense nuisance claim, I chose to knock it on the head with legal firepower this time. Our lawyer not only knew Philip by association, but also was an active member of the Liberal Party, and so had intimate knowledge of how these delicate election matters worked.

He framed Philip's claims as "frivolous, vexatious, misconceived, lacking in substance and bound to fail", seeking an order from VCAT to have the matter dismissed, with full compensation for incurred costs. Our lawyer superbly defeated Philip's baseless claim by intricately outlining, with evidence, that the election materials in question were owned by the political party, not Philip himself. As such, Philip could not make any claim as the bailor.

A day before the directions hearing – presumably in a rare moment of rationality – Philip withdrew his claims against us. We were once again, momentarily, free of his pursuit.

I didn't have to wait long. In September 2020, Dan was issued a second notice from VCAT with a refreshed action submitted by Philip for the same matter. It confounded me what could possibly compel Philip to have a fourth bite at the cherry. His points of claim were materially the same as the last. It seemed his primary strategy was annoyance rather than legal substance.

Once again, I assembled a comprehensive defence for the Principal Registrar ahead of the hearing, requesting that the proceeding be withdrawn. Given Philip provided no new evidence in his latest application, and the tribunal had struck the former submission with no right of reinstatement, wisdom prevailed in the courts, and the matter was summarily dismissed.

Another year passed and, in October 2022, Dan was contacted by the state and federal branches of the political party that were allegedly represented by Philip. Our hearts sank as we anticipated a fifth round in the ring, an event we could almost calibrate our annual calendar to.

The party officials reaching out had only recently learned of Philip's historical claims made against us. They were apologetic for what Philip had accused us of doing in the name of their party, and offered a statement of support in writing should the matter ever resurface. They went on to advise they had their own difficulties with Philip, and his days as a representative of their party were numbered.

So ended another vignette in the horror film noir of Philip. The whole episode reminded me of a modern leadership parable. The crow is the only bird audacious enough to challenge an eagle. It perches boldly upon the eagle's back, persistently pecking at its neck. The eagle remains unperturbed, refusing to engage in futile conflict. Instead, the eagle extends its magnificent wings and ascends to loftier heights. As it soars ever higher into the sky, the crow, unable to endure the thinning air, is forced to relinquish its grasp and falls away, exhausted and defeated by its own limitations. Whilst I'm certainly not describing myself as a majestic eagle, I was pleased I had not let Philip distract me from my purpose, even though at times he was hard to shake.

It was comforting to have one less adversary prowling around, even if the resolution took more than five years to achieve. I hoped this was the end, but knew better than to expect Philip to give up easily.

104
mergers and acquisitions

GOD WAS PLACING bright lights on my horizon. The first of these was a speculative healthcare roll up, where I was pitched the opportunity to float our network on the Singapore stock exchange with the promise of 18 multiples of our annual earnings. It sounded too good to be true, and was soon confirmed as much, the initiative folding after a couple of attempts. However, the idea prompted me to genuinely consider partnership with another brand.

Then I met Barry in 2017 at a conference where I was a keynote speaker and mentor to some of the delegates we knew in common. Barry was the co-founder and CEO of Healthforce – an exciting up-and-coming physiotherapy brand with a network of 17 practices, where he owned 50% of each practice with a local partner. We swiftly recognised kindred spirits in each other, both driven by a desire to serve God's purposes in our shared profession.

I wrote to Barry in late 2018, aware that private equity firms were curious about our model, and suggesting we might be stronger together. After some preliminary discussions, our board supported a proposal-in-principle for Back In Motion to partner with HealthForce. Barry - a man with Godly values and commercial aspiration – was picked to become the CEO of the new larger group, offering me a way out of the operational role I had already tried to vacate in my failed succession to Ashton.

My only caution at the time was getting a Queen's Council opinion on whether the business model, operated by HealthForce, was deemed a franchise under law. We had some doubts that Barry's approach would hold up under scrutiny and, with the unwanted attention from the ACCC and the Senate Inquiry, I couldn't afford to inherit any associated liabilities.

As it happened, there were other obstacles I couldn't have known. Over the next month, Barry disclosed to me in commercial confidence that, prior to my approach, he had signed exclusive agreements to acquire two other small physio groups in the industry. Post the merge of these brands, he expected to have 40 locations in three states, approximating a revenue of $30 million. He was still under due diligence provisions and expected to settle in March 2019 if everything went to plan.

Further to this – and probably because of it – Barry's private equity investors were not keen to sell their stake to me. They wanted to ride the upside of the promise in the two planned acquisitions. Even if they chose to sell, Barry warned they would not be reasonable on price, expecting to be paid the anticipated future value of their holdings before the synergies of the acquisitions were realised.

Barry offered a different approach. In return for me stumping up the money for him to acquire the new businesses, I would be granted a substantial holding in the HealthForce Group, albeit the investment would stand alone from Back In Motion. A merge of the two brands could then be considered at a later stage, but without obligation. It was an attractive quid pro quo and, at the very least, would unite both of our brands into a strategic alliance – a useful fortification as new competitors were soon to be cashed up and looking to compete strongly for first place in our previously uncontested space.

I received the first draft of a term sheet from Barry in November 2019. I was undecided, and things moved slowly for Barry too – his due diligence on the new purchases taking longer than expected, eventually opting out on the second planned acquisition.

While Barry was negotiating with his five shareholders the agreeable equity splits in the new world we were envisioning, I got busy looking to acquire a separate fledgling network of 12 practices in New South Wales, and a small group of five locations in New Zealand. I figured the more I built our network, the more attractive we would become as an acquisition target for the public markets, private health insurers, and other institutional aggregators. The projected arbitrage being suggested to us at the time by independent advisors was that every dollar I invested would likely earn eight to ten dollars in consolidated valuation.

When Barry and I reconvened, the negative press evoked by Philip had spooked the horses in the HealthForce stable. Some of the investors got cold feet about entering what was, perceived then, as the murky world of franchising – the irony being that our subsequent advice was that HealthForce would likely be captured under franchise regulations anyway for the model of shared equity they had already adopted. Nonetheless, the cultural and PR risks for them overshadowed the expected commercial gains, especially with rumours in the media of a Royal Commission into franchising as a follow up to the Senate Inquiry.

Rather than outright refusing to partner, Barry's board downward varied the valuation of our contributing assets, slashing the benefits to me – possibly a diplomatic way of them saying: "No thank you". I respectfully rejected the offer, and rightly, HealthForce rescinded their term sheet.

It was an amicable dissolution of intentions, Barry an absolute gentleman throughout the entire process. I enjoyed dreaming with him the possibilities of working together, mutually grateful for the kindness, grace, and patience we each contributed – a rare and refreshing experience in the otherwise cold and callous corporate context.

THE DISAPPOINTING CONCLUSION with HealthForce was quickly replaced by a preoccupation with a new opportunity: a compelling offer from another emerging partner to acquire a stake in the royalty stream of the Back In Motion franchisor.

We were a unique franchise business in the otherwise wider landscape of retail and hospitality traders. Despite our unfortunate negative press 18 months earlier, we traded our best year with revenues over $45 million. Both client and workforce sentiments were high, as was our pipeline of new practice launches. I slated five new locations to open in Australia and four in New Zealand within the next six months, and industry investors were noticing all this.

The royalties and other annuities of the franchise business were low risk given we had minimum five-year terms, a 92% renewal rate, more than half of our group in their second or third franchise terms with million-dollar-plus revenues, and we boasted a consistent organic growth rate of over 10% year-on-year for two decades. Accordingly, our business was unlikely to experience much disruption to future earnings and presented high rates of underlying profitability.

All these attributes made us the prime target of Advent Health – an untested, emerging corporate aggregator, looking for a platform business to launch their own network. They supposedly had funding but no assets, and securing Back In Motion would create for them a positive domino effect, allowing them to knock over smaller deals with progressively less effort, one after another.

The original CEO of Advent Health, a friend and ex-president of the APA, had first approached me about the opportunity in August 2018. They were modelling their launch after the initial success of Healthia, a combined physiotherapy and podiatry business cobbled together by Glen Richards, the celebrity entrepreneur who starred on the Australian TV show, *Shark Tank*. Glen's credibility came from the success of a similar rollup and public listing of veterinary practices called Greencross, first debuting on the ASX in March 2007. The new team at Advent were seeking to mirror their strategy, acquiring a cohort of physiotherapy businesses that totalled somewhere between $60-80 million in turnover, and approximately $10 million of collective annual profit. They wanted to list on the ASX in the first quarter of 2019 at a discount, hoping all early shareholders and participating vendors would enjoy a minimum 20% price rise shortly after.

Whilst our board liked and trusted the Advent Health CEO, we were cautious about the moneyman who sat behind the enterprise. The key financial advisor had reportedly been embroiled in controversy at the Automotive Solutions Group, a similarly styled rollup. This situation involved four-wheel drive and SUV accessories businesses under the ASX ticker 4WD. In less than a year, the share price languished at $0.22, compared with the issue price of $1.00. The *Australian Financial Review*, and other publications, were also reporting extraordinary boardroom stoushes, warring factions, and leadership spills within management. Of course, my own experience with sensationalised and biased media reports gave me sympathy for what might be misinformation or distorted facts, but it nonetheless made us wary.

It didn't matter. By March 2019, my trusted friend resigned as CEO due to unfulfilled grandiose promises, causing a predictable fall-out and a loss of momentum in the venture. My interest went from cool to non-existent, willing to let the Advent Health offer pass me by. That was, until six months later, when another colleague I trusted (coincidentally, also a past-president of the APA), took up the reins to resurrect the potential in Advent Health. With his involvement, my interest to become the anchor brand was inevitably renewed.

The Advent dealmakers presented an optimistic picture, confident their nonbinding commitments from 16 vendor groups, representing

85 practice locations, could collectively generate a turnover of $51 million. The settlement of these options agreements was dependent on several factors, not the least of which was a technology system to integrate them all, and raising sufficient capital to complete the purchases. To lock Back In Motion in, and with it secure our coveted Evo practice management system as their operating platform, Advent Health offered me more money than the original offer – including a generous upside on the growth that was likely to be realised over the three-year estimate and a substantial bonus payment for every franchisee who joined the rollup.

Paulina and I prayed over the opportunity with earnest, the timing and headline terms of the offer incredibly attractive. But we never felt peace to proceed. I phoned the CEO in March 2020 to break the difficult news, which he graciously accepted.

As it turns out, I dodged a bullet. Two months later the *Australian Financial Review* reported that Advent Health was set to walk onto the ASX via a back door listing but, for lots of reasons, including the disruption to financial markets caused by the coronavirus, never made it. I was glad I hadn't been seduced by fanciful overtures, stalling my business for a promised sale that never would have eventuated.

105
corporate espionage

AS I SAT at my desk early one morning in August 2019, entrenched in my work, an unexpected interruption came in the form of a suspiciously titled email: *Urgent – Sensitive Information enclosed*. It was from a familiar, but infrequent, contact in a reputable professional firm that had been advising me on the HealthForce and Advent Health proposals. Curiosity piqued as I opened the email, intrigue unnerving me. My day went from the mundane to a plotline of a Tom Clancy novel.

Attached to the email was a sensitive document forwarded by a whistle-blower inside the Brisbane office of an accounting firm that was acting for our competition, Healthia. It was purportedly a leaked board memo with a scandalous outline of a hostile strategy to destabilise Back In Motion, and me personally, in order to gain leverage over our network. In this way, they sought to acquire our brand at a low price or at least eliminate me from the competition.

Someone had done their research. They knew of our financial performance, my directorships in other companies, and focussed very heavily on the bad press resulting from Philip's baseless accusations against us. The advice letter outlined three possible Machiavellian strategies to achieve their end.

The first was to acquire me with a low-ball offer, then oust me as CEO whilst they appeared like a "white knight" to disgruntled franchisees. Predicting I couldn't be easily bought, they admitted their tactics would need to be augmented with threats of further action from the ACCC, or other regulators, progressively reducing the value in my business with each new inquiry.

Strategy two was to propose a merger that preserved my role as leader of Back In Motion, and harness our footprint as the largest physiotherapy provider in Australia for referrals into their proprietary podiatry chain.

Their third strategy was to obtain copies of our existing franchise agreements to get legal opinion on whether the terms of our restraints were enforceable. If they were found to be robust, their approach was to stir up cultural unrest amongst the network, forcing me to the negotiating table. If the restraints were in doubt, they recommended poaching franchisees directly from us, luring them with more attractive terms.

Regardless of whether any of the strategies held merit for likely success, the clandestine communication left me feeling apprehensive. Clive, my tax advisor at KPMG, once a former partner at the Melbourne office of the accounting firm that issued the advice, was horrified at what he read. Neil and Jame, our newest board members, were equally appalled, admitting they had never witnessed anything like it all their careers.

I doubted Philip was directly behind any of the espionage, but he was still at large, stirring up trouble around the margins of our group, seeking to exploit any leaks in my hull. I took the disheartening discovery as a clear warning shot across my bow, people were trying to sink me.

I felt as if the ground gave way beneath my feet, tectonic plates colliding, causing an upheaval in the very foundations I relied upon. The subtle covert manoeuvrers felt like an invasion of the trust I placed in every advisor up to this point, threatening to isolate and undermine me, now fearful of everyone's secret agendas. My closely knit labyrinth of industry colleagues felt booby-trapped, rigged with hidden trip wires and dangerous landmines, each step threatening unforeseen catastrophe. Momentarily, I felt suffocated, not knowing who to trust, with the early stages of paranoia settling in.

I immediately went to prayer, asking God to protect our brand, safeguard our internal culture, and keep me beyond reproach in all matters.

I SWIFTLY CONFRONTED the Managing Director of the accounting firm whose official letterhead bore the evidence of underhanded corporate tactics. Despite initial reluctance to engage, after several attempts, he agreed to a conversation. He denied any knowledge of the memo, expressing his apology and commitment to investigate its source.

In parallel, I spoke with Glen Richards, letting *him* know that *I* knew what *they* had been told. I expected this would likely prompt internal inquiries of his own, potentially sowing seeds of distrust within their organisation and advisory group akin to what I now felt within mine.

At Clive's insistence, I also reported the issue to the Institute of Chartered Accountants, formally documenting the incident in case of further escalation. Beyond these actions, I found myself in a state of preparedness, forewarned about a potential forthcoming attack.

WITHIN DAYS OF this unsettling distraction, our family boarded a flight to India to work with a mission agency we supported, and to hike the foothills of the Himalayas. As the plane ascended, the burdens of work gradually faded away, shrinking into insignificance, much like the miniature cars and buildings below, allowing me to fully embrace the adventure ahead.

We arrived in Delhi and visited the usual historical sites and highlights, before taking a mid-morning flight to Dharamsala. There, we enjoyed a guided tour of the Dalai Lama's monastery, and enjoyed an evening in the street bazaar amidst the colourful saris, dazzling jewellery, and fresh spices, pickles, and books.

We then started our trek from Kareri Village, five days of walking some of the most pristine ridgelines, enjoying the views of the valleys below, traversing dense forests of bamboo, oak, and pine, passing through ancient villages, and camping in meadows beneath snow-capped peaks alongside rushing rivers. Each night we arrived to tents set up by our sherpas, warm cooked curries, and cups of sweet chai. It was a magical experience.

From the mountains of the Himalayas, we flew to Varanasi to meet with the staff of an English school we supported and to observe the water sanitation projects we had contributed to. We also took an evening boat ride on the sacred Ganges River, where we witnessed the ceremonial fire burials of the dead. The next morning, we rose early, took the train to the "city of love", Agra, where the Taj Mahal stood as the jewel of Muslim art, and one of the universally admired masterpieces of the world's heritage. We took a family photo re-enacting Princess Diana's famous pose before preparing for our return home.

As I carefully folded away memories of our incredible trip alongside neatly stacked shirts and shorts in my well-travelled suitcase, a familiar apprehension crept in – the return to an industry where trust had been strained and individuals sought to take advantage of me. I scrambled for hope, remembering Churchill's axiom: "Kites fly highest against the wind". I yearned to believe in the goodness of people, but the wounds ran deep. It was a conscious effort to suppress my looming fear, nurturing a tentative optimism that things might be different on my return.

106
a sporting chance

WITH AN EYE always on our future opportunities, I was determined to align Back In Motion with elite national sport. We considered a range of possibilities, including Australian Rules football, basketball, netball, and hockey, before deciding on the international game of soccer. My boys endorsed the choice, given all three were playing for National Premier League clubs.

In October 2019, Back In Motion became the Principal Partner of the Melbourne Victory W-League, one of the highest performing franchises in the A-League soccer tables. Melbourne Victory had over 26,000 members which, at the time, was 50% more than the next largest soccer club in Australia. They also had a social media following of more than 400,000 individuals, 61% of them in Victoria.

It was hard to side with a single team in a national competition, as state rivalry extended well beyond the pitch and into the classrooms, boardrooms, and lounge rooms of every school, business, and home. It certainly pervaded our network, creating real tension between franchisees, delineating divisions along lines of state allegiance. But we couldn't sponsor a team in every geography, and so I went with the option that promised the best outcomes for the whole, despite the persistent criticisms of a few hooligans within.

It was clear women's sport was a celebrated success, getting vast media attention, making it a great time to partner with such a progressive football code. Whilst the initial sponsorship ask was a significant six-figure sum, we managed to negotiate a more reasonable entry level for the first of a three-year partnership.

When the first game of the season kicked off, as the women's number one sponsor, our brand was front and centre on their jerseys, and boldly visible on the logo backdrop for all their media interviews. We were also showered with tickets to every home game and official event to share with franchisees and their staff. Most importantly, we had access to the Melbourne Victory membership database – every active and historical supporter for both the men's and women's teams – to promote ourselves through social media posts, digital mail campaigns, and special offers.

The first year was a modest success, at least until the coronavirus shut down the playing season in mid-2020. We achieved five times our sponsorship investment in direct media value, calculated using number of seconds our logo was on screen by the number of people seated in the stadium for any given match. The total online and live audience for the W-League games was over 250,000 people, Back In Motion enjoying a higher impression rate than even the major A-League partner AGL received, and nearly as much as Metricon, whose sponsorships were both seven-figures large. We also ran activation events in the A-League Victory Village to more than 5,000 fans every game, occasionally coordinating similar pop-up installations at interstate events, helping to appease our non-Victorian franchisees.

Despite intending to renew our partnership for successive years and build on this early traction, the pandemic, and its unprecedented uncertainty, meant this never eventuated. But our first foray into professional sport sponsorship was a lot of fun and made commercial sense.

During our short ride we got to know so many great personalities and players who thrilled the crowds with their epic through balls, long bombs, and strikes. I received a box-framed signed jersey of the girls that year as a fond reminder of the small part we played in their moderately successful season, ultimately placing fourth on the league table. To this day, I enjoy casual support of the W-League, keeping tabs on the remarkable journeys of key players like Tash Dowie, Lisa de Vanna, and Laura Brock, as they travel the world enriching the game they love, giving their fans something special to cheer for.

107
natural conclusions

GROWING IN PARALLEL with the scale and reach of Back In Motion, the SOS Health Foundation matured over its decade. Our First Nation people mattered. In the "lucky country" we knew Australia to be, it was unacceptable to me that Indigenous people didn't enjoy the same health of their white counterparts. We were determined to help close that gap. In 2019 alone, we deployed 38 volunteer health professionals into the field, providing services to 900 people.

Supporting the health of Indigenous communities was a complex mission. The issues were long standing and intertwined, noting Aboriginal people lost control over many of their determinants of health more than 200 years ago. Dispossession of land, stolen generations, stolen wages, discriminatory policies of segregation, racism, and disadvantages in education, housing and employment were just some of the underlying challenges we were up against as we sought to empower Indigenous communities in optimal lifelong physical health.

Systemic change was essential. These people needed more than allied health services for sustainable, generational improvement in holistic wellbeing and life expectancy. The goal could only be achieved through culturally sensitive education and genuine empowerment.

THE FOUNDATION'S GROWTH inspired me to look more closely at our theory of change, determined to ensure our impact was sustainable. After Lynda had capably managed the charity for more than nine years, Nikki, previously a board member of SOS, was appointed CEO in early 2018. To assess whether our efforts in the field were effective, we partnered with Swinburne University and the Centre for Social Impact, evaluating the measurable changes achieved through the different interventions we trialled. Indicative results revealed a substantial benefit to many of the communities we supported, in particular the Yolngu people of the Laynhapuy homelands in North East Arnhem Land and the Manbarra and Bwgcolman people of Palm Island.

In response, Nikki extended our fly-in-fly-out (FIFO) services in partnership with various Aboriginal community-controlled organisations across the Top End of Australia. She doubled-down on the permanent allied health centre operated on Palm Island, believing that a live-in presence, integrated with community activities, would allow our therapists to have far more meaningful and lasting impact. This enabled us to host regular Kids & Culture programmes within the schools, employ school-based trainees in the practice to complete a Certificate III in practice administration, and host Indigenous physiotherapy students from the mainland.

Because we didn't want to be "white people" imposing *our* solutions on these communities, we launched an initiative to identify emerging local high schoolers who wanted to be trained in allied health, funding scholarships for them to train at university to become registered health professionals. We also began putting wrap-around supports in place to ensure these trained professionals could return to Palm Island and contribute to the long-term health of their own people. Whilst strategically inspiring, these were, at best, five- to ten-year plans fraught with risk of attrition and failure.

To underwrite the expanding outreach programmes, our fundraising activities had to scale accordingly. Our annual marquis event was a Charity Day at Huntingdale Golf Course, peaking with 82 paid-up players and dozens of returning sponsors every year, supplementing the Back In Motion donations with substantial contributions. Whilst the event was a great success year after year, my golf game didn't improve much. Some players lost an occasional ball across 18 holes, but on one round I lost my seven iron, losing grip of the club as I pitched the ball across a water hazard, splashing into the middle of the lake. Understandably, as host of the event, I was the butt of most jokes in the afternoon speeches, where we celebrated that day's fundraising achievements.

Our practices continued to advocate for the cause too, September entrenched as the month where we promoted Work4Significance. The workforce across Australia got behind the foundation with their local fundraising and advocacy efforts. Our typical burgundy Back In Motion uniforms were swapped for royal blue SOS t-shirts for 30 days.

Our ordinary point-of-sale materials in the waiting and consultation rooms were exchanged for posters heralding the Indigenous cause. There were exercise challenges, BBQ lunches, and movie nights – all dubbed with congruent themes, Sweat4Significance, Sizzle4Signficance and Screen4Significance, respectively.

Nikki created the SOS Dream Team, acknowledging supporters who made a three-year commitment of $1,000 per annum. The donation "bought" a piece of a jigsaw puzzle, hand-painted by one of our Indigenous elders at Palm Island, titled *Mala* (meaning "hands"). In the artist's own words, the hands represented the "livelihood of [his] people, who could keep working after injury and pain, because the hands of SOS that helped them". It was a touching sentiment.

Our inaugural Dream Team sponsor was Sebastien, an 11-year-old who heard about the cause through his dad – an executive recruiter for Back In Motion – and gave $1,000 from his savings. Quickly thereafter, our Volunteer and Engagement Manager jumped on board, a huge sacrifice given she relied on a part-time wage at the time with a household of children to feed. Other donors joined slowly afterwards; Nikki determined to generate $50,000 in recurrent funding for three consecutive years, shoring up more in-field programmes.

OVER THE COURSE of three board meetings in 2019, I facilitated a strategic review of the mission, scalability, funding, sustainability, and impact of SOS. It was Paulina who first proposed the possibility of winding up our practice on Palm Island in favour of redistributing our funds and efforts where they could be more effective. Slowly, other board members opened their minds to this possibility, Nikki and I the only two staunch resistors.

To better assess our future direction, I suggested Nikki and Paulina meet with the Palm Island council to engage them in the planning exercise. Their report on return was not encouraging. Whilst the elders appreciated the role SOS played in their community, they did not rate healthcare amongst their top needs or concerns. Of far higher importance to them was youth delinquency, truancy, housing, and domestic violence. The goodwill that took five years to build with the local mayor was also at risk. He was facing charges of corruption and, irrespective of the outcome of the investigation on foot, had lost trust within the community. A change in leadership was inevitable and, with that, a likely disruption to the established services we provided.

Paulina and I sought direction from God on the best path forward. We set three conditions for continuing – a small funding contribution from the Palm Island council, safe accommodation for our staff, and a two-year commitment from a resident physio to oversee the work.

Sadly, none of these threshold criteria were met by the necessary deadlines.

By October, our role on Palm Island looked untenable. The Australian Federal Police had arrested the Palm Island Finance Director on charges of fraud, and most of the local elders and counsellors were implicated. The HR Director, Facilities Director, and Acting CEO all resigned, meaning everyone with whom we had any relationship and good standing, was gone. A government administrator was appointed to clean up and make sense of the suspected embezzlement, and our mission on the island was lost in the confusion and their preoccupation with higher stakes matters.

After a night of careful discussion and prayerful contemplation, Paulina and I decided, in our personal capacity as benefactors – not as chairman or director – to cease all future funding commitments from our family trust to Palm Island, beyond the budgeted year. It was an excruciating decision, and one that I would not have reached if Paulina had not led with her own convictions. We both held fast to our compassion for the plight of our Indigenous family, and believed there could be other ways we might play a role in God's mission to these beautiful people.

Nikki was unsurprisingly disappointed with our stance, despite being stoic about the implications. She had invested so much of herself in the two years leading to this point, inspiring many with her leadership, passion, and courage. Our decision to withdraw funding was in no way a reflection on her capabilities, and to a large degree, only made our final assessment more difficult for her to accept.

In a twist of divine Providence, as all these weighty matters were being considered, we received bittersweet news from Laynhapuy Health Services in North East Arnhem Land. On a monthly basis for eight years, costing us as estimated $2 million, we mobilised physiotherapists, podiatrists, and an occupational therapist, from around Australia, to join local medical and nursing teams serving more than 30 homeland communities. Federal and territory governments had finally recognised the sustainable impact of our work, and accepted our case for change. They approved a fully funded, permanent allied health service to continue what we started, bringing our partnership with Laynhapuy to a natural conclusion at the end of 2019.

In a matter of weeks, I accepted that our two largest initiatives – the pro bono service on Palm Island and our FIFO service in Arnhem Land – would not continue in 2020, offering an almost perfect exit strategy for our small charity. Both unexpected outcomes felt like the sign from God we had previously sought.

At our November AGM, the SOS Directors passed a series of resolutions to wind up all our partnerships and programmes in an orderly fashion by 31st March 2020. Surplus funds were to be transferred to another charity with similar objectives to those of SOS, in accordance with our constitutional obligations.

We offered our employees three months' notice of their termination, with ex gratia payments to help them transition to new employment. We de-listed from the Australian Charities and Not-for-profits Commission (ACNC), surrendered our eligible tax exemptions, cancelled our fundraising licences and permits in every state, and closed our bank accounts. It took an entire year to shut down what had taken ten years to build, officially de-registering the charity in November 2020.

I grieved over our decision to close the foundation for many months, even though I knew it to be right in my heart. As it would happen, the coronavirus pandemic hit our Australian shores three months after our final board meeting, and a full six months before we formally de-registered. Had we lingered in our decisions, or worse still, committed to pressing forward on Palm Island, almost certainly our donor base would have shrunk, our volunteer workforce would have been locked down, and our projects would have stalled anyway. Timing proved to be optimal – only God (and Paulina) knew.

108
little things, big wins

THE NEW DECADE opened with a literal bang. We celebrated 20 years as a Health Group with fireworks on a late February evening of 2020 at our White-dress Gala Ball. Franchisees and NSO team gathered in the Beachfront Garden, with the stunning backdrop of the Hilton Bali cliff top resort in Nusa Dua, Indonesia. It was our 12th Director's Conference, an incredible night to remember.

The birthday celebration theme was *Little Things, Big Wins*. In some ancient texts, including the Bible, the number 20 is often associated with a trial or period of waiting; after successful completion, it attracts a generous reward. In Hebrew numerology, 20 signals the conclusion of a great undertaking. It all seemed appropriate, as in many respects, 2020 brought Back In Motion to the completion of an era.

The adventure of my first two decades had been fraught with trials and breakthroughs, ups and downs, triumphs and failures. I attributed the first ten years to establishing foundations. The second ten were known for their explosive growth. To stand on the high side of the 20-year threshold was a great achievement for all of us who called Back In Motion "home". It was the end of a chapter – and, of course, simultaneously, the beginning of a new one.

(Incidentally, 20-year anniversaries are typically celebrated with items made of *China* porcelain - not wood, silver, gold, or platinum, like other memorable milestones. Fortunately, we chose Bali as our conference destination, and not China – despite the fitting gesture – which is just as well, given the global pandemic that was beginning to unfold. Outbound planes from the Wuhan province were uncharacteristically full that month.)

When thinking about progress, we often imagine how good it feels to achieve a long-term goal, or to experience a major breakthrough. Big wins are great, but they are relatively rare. Notable achievements usually don't require one monumental effort in a single moment. It's the series of smaller, everyday decisions and incremental steps – the little things done well – that afford the big wins.

Every measured step, unnoticed deed, and deliberate action, leads us in specific directions and builds momentum towards achieving results. Seemingly insignificant decisions and benign behaviours can be dismissed or deferred because they aren't perceived to deliver immediate value. But a hundred worthless pennies make up a dollar. Your life becomes the sum of your daily actions. Little commitments bring you closer to your goals and achieving greater wins. Conversely, the steps you don't take could rob you of greatness.

The most common question asked by physios, friends, and the media was: "What is Back In Motion's secret to success?" People presumably hoped for a profound insight or a single compelling advantage. But true to our birthday theme in Bali that week, our success came by doing a lot of small things well.

Much like Colonel Sanders' legendary fried chicken recipe of 11 secret herbs and spices, Back In Motion had its own essential ingredients. We promoted five core values. We automated six operational imperatives in our business model (internally referred to as *DNA Switches*). We delivered four core services – physiotherapy, massage, Pilates, and personal training. We created six proprietary stages of Results4Life. We focused on two priority goals in every strategic plan. And we had one brand position: *movement for life*.

There was no single answer to how we got here, but a series of small, albeit intentional choices that came together and eventually amounted to something worthwhile.

THERE WERE OTHER *little* things I reflected on during the 2020 conference that I believe contributed to our enduring success.

Firstly, my belief that *people mattered*, above all else. Not emails. Not projects. Not practices. Not money. *People*! I recognised the power of relationships for good and evil. I understood that my authority and influence came from the strength of my relationships, not from my perceived position. As a guy who is hardwired for tasks, deadlines, structure, and process, it was a lesson I needed to keep learning and leaning into, ignoring at my peril.

Then there was anti-complacency. In the same way anti-fragility is a helpful perspective on resilience, anti-complacency is about not letting laziness, boredom, hubris, or confidence cause us to fall short of our best. I wanted to remain diligent, persistent, and hardworking – take nothing for granted – even when I was winning. An old Nike poster from my university days challenged athletes: "The way you stay number *one*, is train like you are number *two*".

Sharing freely was another of our *little* things. Like paying it forward, we promoted the value of being a giver, not a taker. I wanted to live a life of generosity with an abundance mentality, sowing wisely today in order to reap the rewards tomorrow. I used to be so cautious about protecting the intellectual property of our business model, worried people would copy, steal, or ruin it. As time passed, I made my peace with the truth that it was more impactful to share what we had with the industry-at-large, understanding the value of holding onto that which is most precious with an open hand.

A fourth realisation was that pride is the first chapter in the book on failure. The American Puritan preacher, Cotton Mather, invited a young Benjamin Franklin to his home for dinner one night and showed him his library. As they walked through a narrow passage, Mather cautioned to Franklin, "Stoop! Stoop!". Franklin didn't understand the warning until it was too late, bumping his head on a low beam. Mather turned the situation into a sermon. "Let this be a caution to not always hold your head so high. Stoop, young man, *stoop* – as you go through this world – and you'll miss many hard thumps." Apparently, many years later, Franklin told Mather's son that he never forgot that moment. "This advice, thus beat into my head, has frequently been of use to me," reflected Franklin. "And I often think of it when I see pride mortified and misfortunes brought upon people by carrying their heads too high." With such a striking example to model, I have sought to stoop more often. That is, live with genuine humility, remain teachable, be open minded, and resist hubris. The more I practiced these life choices, the more my franchisees felt safe and comfortable to behave the same. I wanted to make it normal to ask for help, more often; give less demands and, instead, share my failures; and look for the learning in every situation.

And finally, a *small* thing that has led to many big wins is faithfulness – that is, being *full* of *faith*. Everyone entertains their own worldviews and spiritual perspectives, and I don't care to judge another person's beliefs. But power comes from whatever you base your convictions on. I couldn't live with self-reliance, doubt, or be driven by fear. I wanted to serve God's purposes in everything I put my hand to. Faith isn't complete until it's all you're holding onto, and God is the only one worthy of my absolute trust. The Bible compares faith to a mustard seed, something so small you can barely perceive it in your hand, but grows into a robust and towering shade. Just a hint of genuine belief can propel your further than almost anything else.

Life inside Back In Motion often felt like a blacksmith's forging fire. It got hot at times, and my sharp and stubborn edges were forcefully rounded and pummelled by the hammer against the anvil. My experiences during the 20 years in business, especially the disappointing ones I wished were not part of my story, have shaped me more than almost anything else.

Michael, my longstanding board advisor, made a similar comparison in our final board meeting of 2019. He described the ancient process of crafting an arrow – stripping a piece of acacia wood of all its debris, soaking it in water, making it straight by applying tension and force, shaving and refining it further. Eventually, the artisan attaches a stone tip to drive the arrow with purpose and intent. Michael lamented, we might not always enjoy or appreciate the shaping process, but the result is powerful.

The words we say, the habits we form, the food we eat, the thoughts we entertain, the shows we watch, the people we hang around, the errors we fix, the strangers we help, the behaviours we train, and the results we celebrate – all make a difference, whether we acknowledge them or not. These are the *little* things I'm still learning to value, driving me ever closer to the next big win.

OUR BALI CELEBRATION not only marked our 20th anniversary, but also the close of our three-year strategic plan, dubbed *Fortify and Build*. My two priority goals had been to optimise franchisee rewards and drive greater patient loyalty. I was confident that achieving greater rewards for and loyalty from these two primary "customers", I could create a new flow of measurable value to all other people in our relationship chain, including staff, suppliers, and referrers.

That year, we celebrated 21% increase in practice revenue, 28% increase in client spend, and 26% increase in new clients. More than

15 practices were welcomed into the million-dollar club, with a generous handful reaching the high bar of the previously elusive $2 million threshold.

Our core services expanded with pilots in exercise physiology, podiatry, and dietetics, driving an increased uptake in appointments that hit like a shockwave in our local practices. We celebrated a 17% increase in group-wide staff and a 10% improvement in their engagement scores. As a result of all this, I was thrilled to enjoy a big jump of 22% in franchisee loyalty – a far cry from the Armageddon Malcolm had prophesied only a year earlier.

Seven new practices launched in New Zealand, we secured eight trademarks in other countries, acquired a podiatry and orthotic group to merge with our core business, and completed the preliminary business plan for a mobile health care business. I was even contemplating the integration of chiropractic services – a shriek of optimism not everyone was ready for, considering the longstanding industry rivalry between physiotherapists and chiropractors.

Best of all, we managed to achieve all this growth while maintaining happy clients. Our client satisfaction score was 98% and, as a result, we enjoyed a group-wide uptick in referrals from GPs, families, and friends.

Our business had come a long way from the low ebb of cultural sentiment and practice performance during 2017 and 2018, when I had stepped away from the operational leadership. We had substantially driven greater rewards for our franchisees, which perked up the internal mood just in time for the next hill we were to climb together: COVID-19.

109
Contagion

RUSTY HAD A worried look on her face as she slouched over her desk in early February of 2020, a few weeks before our planned departure to Bali for our 20-year birthday bash. We had just finished relocating the NSO to a stylish co-working space, and our desks now sat adjacent to each other in the bullpen alongside everyone else.

Our new offices were the fourth location in two decades, having now come full circle. The original administration team – Paulina and her mother – worked out of the side carport of our home in Scoresby, and we had just returned to the same suburb, albeit in somewhat more upmarket facilities. Our new co-working space boasted three levels of offices, contemporary board rooms, training lecturettes, break out spaces, an indoor mini basketball court, and a popular barista. Little did I know that the frown on Rusty's face signalled that it all might soon become obsolete.

"We need to cancel the Director's Conference in Bali", Rusty said in total defeat. She had spent nearly a year in planning, and prided herself on finessing every detail with meticulous attention. I figured she was joking – she was more excited about the Gala Ball than I was.

"Okay" I said with little conviction, presuming she couldn't be serious, and was baiting me into one of her regular setups.

"I don't think we should travel outside Australia. The coronavirus is spreading," she said in an anxious tone. It was my turn to frown.

"There has only been one reported case in Australia, Rusty. I doubt this will turn into anything. Of course, we are going to Bali."

ON THE 25th of January 2020, authorities confirmed the first case of COVID-19 on Australian soil. By March, there were so many unemployed workers registering online for welfare support (more than a million in a single morning) that some mistook it for a cyber-attack.

It all started for us in late February as we concluded our celebrations for our much-anticipated Director's Conference. By the time we were boarding flights home to Australia, airport officials in Bali were handing us health declaration cards, where we needed to volunteer if we had a fever, sore throat, or dry cough.

COVID-19, a highly infectious respiratory illness caused by the novel coronavirus, is obviously now a well-documented phenomenon encountered around the world. The impact was significant and far-reaching, affecting nearly every corner of the globe. Different countries fared better or worse, depending on a range of factors, such as population density, healthcare system capacity, government response, and international cooperation. The United States was hit particularly hard, with more than 46 million confirmed cases and 750,000 deaths by late 2021.

By mid-March, following what seemed best practice as led by corporate Australia, we set up our own COVID-19 Taskforce, appointing Justin as the lead – the best man for the job because of his expertise in law, workplace relations, and business systems, delicately balanced with a genuinely caring disposition.

On a frantic Sunday afternoon, the 22nd of March, Justin, Dan and I huddled in my home office as we desperately drafted a coordinated response to the first set of government restrictions announced earlier that day. Later than evening, I called an emergency video conference with all franchisees, recording unanimous attendance with less than a day's notice, a testament to the urgency felt by everyone.

PRIME MINISTER SCOTT Morrison announced that afternoon that Australia was moving into stage one of a national shutdown as of noon the following day. The provisions were to be reviewed regularly, but were expected to last at least six months.

Schools remained open at this stage, although parents could keep their children at home if they preferred. Following the $17 billion already promised earlier in the month, Morrison announced a second economic response package nearly four times larger - a further $66 billion expected to support businesses and individuals.

Our group's strategic response needed to adapt to the daily new information coming to light, relying on predictive indicators to assess each stage of escalation. Our three pillars were *Protect, Prepare* and *Recover*. Protect yourself, family, team, clients, business, and the community from adverse impact. Prepare your practice and people for likely worsening conditions to come. Recover your team confidence, client loyalty, and practice momentum with intentional strategies and actions.

We carefully assessed the scope of escalation, spanning from negligible practice impact to total annihilation. We considered appropriate strategies for every imaginable scenario, Justin leaving nothing to chance.

I worked closely with the President of the APA, fighting for telehealth subsidies, special shutdown exemptions, employment safeguards, and cashflow provisions for practices across the industry.

Hot debate raged within the profession on every social media platform, contesting whether physiotherapy should be deemed an "essential" health care service. Both sides were passionate to save lives and protect businesses, yet seemingly at odds with each other. Unsurprisingly, given the febrile emotions boiling over, I had to contend with divergent views within our own executive team and amongst franchisees, many arguing a different ethical stance.

In the event of a drastic scaling-down of services, I recommended a "franchsiee + 1" response, where the practice owner and one other employee remained on staff to deal with inbound patient inquiries and provide urgent medical care to those in high need, even if only by telehealth. We encouraged all our franchisees to seek tenancy relief from their landlords, and, where appropriate, negotiate agreeable concessions according to government recommendations. We radically changed the shape of the NSO operations, reducing all network development activities, recruitment services, and most of our marketing initiatives. In record time, I commissioned new technology enhancements for telehealth, local area communication toolkits, and COVID-19 safety protocols relevant to each state and territory.

I pledged our refusal to lose a single practice during this ordeal, swiftly announcing our own $1.5 million support package to franchisees, distributed over two stages. In addition to discounting our royalties, I immediately and indefinitely suspended all marketing and professional development levies, saving the practices up to 4% of their revenue. I refunded their February levies to boost available cashflows and returned software contributions and cash bonds which we held in trust on behalf of local practices, rendering another $13,000 per location. I removed all minimum payment thresholds for franchise royalties and offered royalty relief and interest free cashflow loans to distressed practices on a triage basis. Furthermore, to help our team members work through the personal impact of these unprecedented challenges, I subsidised an Employee Assistance Program to give access to confidential counsellors and psychologists.

People demonstrated solidarity with our brand. It could have easily gone the other way, given the same boiling water that softens a potato, also hardens an egg. It was what we were made of that defined us, not our circumstances. I loved their tenacity, endurance, unity, and energy. Amongst gratitude for our support and instruction in the pre-emptive strategies, almost immediately we were inundated with requests from franchisees for rent relief, temporary liquidation of their security deposits, staffing advice, clarification on hygiene and infection control initiatives, and access to sanitation supplies.

And all this was just day one.

THE NEXT NIGHT, Justin and I hosted an online webinar for the broader industry to encourage and equip them with the same strategies we had developed to protect our own practices. We had more than 600 independent practice owners from Australia and New Zealand dial in and participate in our 90-minute debrief. The APA endorsed the event, building further goodwill and comradery across the sector for our willingness to share Back In Motion's approach to the crisis.

My best guess was that the COVID-19 trading restrictions would cause a 20-40% overall plunge in our group revenues. The NSO income was projected to plummet to as low as 20%, due to the franchise royalty concessions we were making to keep our practices afloat. Between March and December, I hunkered down for a $1.4 million shortfall in our central operating budget alone. At the time, I expected it may take up to two years to recover with modest rebound activity.

I wrote to my NSO team in early April with an austerity manifesto, describing how I planned to aggressively reduce costs to ensure our survival. I suspended all financial delegations of authority so I could control the rate and quantum of spending. I announced a small handful of redundancies, including my own executive assistant, Rusty, welling up in tears as I announced this to the team on a videoconference call. I asked everyone to make sacrifices – my family, theirs, and the board.

Nobody's pay rates were reduced, but people's contracted hours were adjusted such that everybody officially became part time. I valued their high work ethic, loyalty, and willingness to serve our franchisees, even when the demand pushed them beyond their set hours. With everyone working from home at this point, despite having just moved into a beautifully appointed new office suite only months before, we made Tuesdays and Thursdays our collective meeting days on videoconference.

Our People and Culture team worked with Paulina, putting together personal care packages for the staff. The hand-delivered pack included couverture chocolates, handmade face masks, lip balm, hand creams, jigsaws, quiz books, and a cash voucher for $1,000 to buy themselves something they could personally benefit from or enjoy during lockdown. One team member bought a treadmill the very next day, and showed off how they could walk and talk at the next videoconference.

Shortly after, the Australian government announced the JobKeeper program, which was aimed to help businesses affected by the pandemic keep their employees in jobs and to provide financial support for workers who had lost their jobs. Despite the economic support, at our lowest ebb during the pandemic, in April and May 2020, I stood down more than 250 staff across our network – many of them clinicians. Our sales dropped to 27% of normal trading volumes before experiencing a strong rebound in June, when lockdowns eased. The government recognised physiotherapy as one of the four primary reasons someone could leave home, and we reinstated not only all the staff we had put on furlough, but began actively recruiting as many more we could find.

Whilst our business seemed to have bounced off its low point, by mid-2020 Australia was still in the thick of it. A surge in cases led to further strict lockdown measures to contain the numbers. By September 2021, Australia had more than 75,000 confirmed cases, with more than 1,100 deaths. Our economy, hugely impacted by the pandemic, fell into its first recession in nearly three decades. The tourism industry was particularly hard hit, with the closing of international borders and burdensome domestic travel restrictions in place.

New Zealand initially fared much better, with only 4,800 confirmed cases and 28 attributed deaths by about the same time in September 2021. The country in general, and especially their internationally adored left-leaning PM, Jacinta Ardern, was praised for their early and aggressive response to visitors, forcing a wide sweeping lockdown in March 2020.

Melbourne, where I lived, experienced some of the strictest lockdown measures in the world, with the first one lasting 69 days between March and May 2020. We eventually suffered five more of them, totalling 262 days in all. The last of the six lockdowns finished in October 2021, after the state of Victoria reported a double-vaccination rate reaching 64%. At our worst, we had a curfew that restricted people from being outside their home between 9pm and 5am, except for special circumstances.

During lockdowns, people were generally only allowed to leave their homes for essential reasons such as grocery shopping, medical appointments, and exercise. Masks were mandatory in public and private indoor spaces. Schools were closed, and students had to study from home. Restaurants, bars, and cafés were closed for dine-in service, but allowed take-away and delivery. Non-essential businesses, such as gyms and hair salons, were closed. Weddings and funerals were restricted to a limited number of attendees – Paulina and I attending my sister's second wedding in her home by pixelated videoconference only – this all becoming our way of life for the foreseeable future.

THESE WERE ESPECIALLY challenging times for most families, ours included. Lachlan, our eldest son, completed a crucial year of his VCE in and out of lockdown, while our two other boys adjusted to their early years of secondary school by videoconference.

To add to our losses, we had given back Monique, the beautiful companion Labrador we had been training for Guide Dogs Victoria. The whole Smith family was heartbroken by her departure, even though we knew she was going on to serve someone who needed her more. After some months considering if we might get another dog, I compiled a master spreadsheet of everyone's wish lists – a Border Collie, Portuguese Water Dog, Poodle crossed with just about anything, and another Labrador.

I cross referenced the necessary criteria. For instance, I wanted to know whether the breeds would shed fur all year 'round, bark at night, dig holes, be good with children, and were easily trainable. As I researched each breed with the kids, we crossed and ticked the attributes in the matrix, building something of a score-based ranking system of the likely best pick for our family. As we slowly eliminated options, it was clear we weren't getting a Collie or another Labrador. The Portuguese Water Dog – Paulina's preference – was a strong contender and looking likely to come out on top. With only three breeds left in the running, I crossed out the Dachshund as being an unlikely friendly dog with children, causing Morgan to burst into uncontrollable tears. He had set his heart on a sausage dog for some time and couldn't hide his disappointment when it was struck from the list.

The moment I saw his reaction, the three hours of debating which breed would be best for our family was thrown out the door. I immediately declared the snag had won. All I wanted to do in that moment was comfort Morgan's distress and give him what he wanted. It was a father's heart, at its best... or *worst*. The rest of the family sat there with a gaping mouth because I had blatantly twisted the rules based on emotional weakness. They weren't wrong, and yet it was decided.

Slinky, a two-month-old silky black Dachshund with tan socks and snout, joined our family shortly afterwards. Whilst we had arranged to pick her up in late March 2020, due to the impending lockdowns, the breeder encouraged us to pick her up early or potentially miss out altogether. This little puppy became the highlight of our months in lockdown, where all six of us formed a special bond with her.

The predictable downside of Slinky – like so many wieners – was her particularly unsociable traits with guests and other dogs, barking incessantly at the doorbell and other unfamiliar noises. These annoying habits were exacerbated by the fact that she spent the first two years of her life in the COVID-19 bubble, barely seeing another soul outside our family – a similar problem for countless people around the world.

DESPITE ALL THE legal and cultural challenges we had faced in our 20-year story to date, COVID-19 presented a once-in-a-lifetime threat to everything I knew and learned about business. Our already complex organisation, across two countries, became infinitely more nuanced as each state and territory we operated in had premiers and health ministers who led with different economic and health and safety edicts. Each practice was subjected to different and specific laws and regulations unique to their geography. Our national team suffered split personality at least eight different ways, given every inbound inquiry from the field required different advice and strategies to overcome their local challenge, depending on where they were based.

Whilst all practices were in the same *storm*, they were not in the same *boat*; some fared better than others. Those in Queensland and Tasmania continued to grow at record rates, while practices in Western Australia and Victoria suffered from harsher and more extended lockdowns. Practices in the central business districts, like one in Melbourne, experienced extreme and sustained hardship, given the city was a ghost town for well over a year. Yet, new locations launched in the suburbs went on to have a bumper first year, indifferent to the apocalyptic conditions elsewhere.

Unique to this season of relative isolation, I hosted from my study at home a monthly series of online workshops for the broader industry, called *Practice Impact*. These events were not like the usual webinars, where you logged in and passively listened to someone else talk, occasionally asking an anonymous question through a moderated chat function. These workshops were interactive, on-camera, intense debates around relatable and specific situations in practice. I hit topics like the ethics of sales in healthcare, growth in crisis, and how to mobilise difficult people. I attracted practice owners, clinicians, and support staff of all ages and experiences, across many countries. I purposely tried not to repeat content that could be easily learned elsewhere in industry blogs and traditional sources of education. Instead, I favoured focusing on the mysterious, cryptic and sometimes, elusive secrets that are rarely shared. I asked lots of tough questions and didn't hide from the inconvenient answers. I opened Pandora's box and shared the sometimes-conflicting priorities between clinical excellence, commercial realities, and ethical responsibilities. The feedback was positive as the audience grew each month.

Despite the abrupt halt that COVID-19 restrictions put on my Iceberg Leadership program, I still managed to deliver six face-to-face masterclasses at opportune times through the year, graduating 95 delegates, in addition to the 260 I put through a single-day event at Melbourne Airport one weekend.

In true entrepreneurial spirit, I was determined not to waste a good crisis. As the national and state governments started to de-escalate restrictions in their respective jurisdictions at different speeds, I didn't want to go back to where we started. Rather, I aimed at thriving in our new normal and bouncing forward.

Justin and the Taskforce designed their own *Roadmap to Recovery*, a mirror image of our initial Crisis Response Plan, whereby we mapped the pathway out of the pandemic crisis with three strategic pillars: *Restore; Relaunch*; and *Reimagine*. Each level of de-escalation had predictive indicators we could track in the individual practices, our four focus areas being patients, people, practice and programs. The key initiatives included developing a COVID-safe policy and training curriculum, retraining our team members through new online professional development courses we had developed, gradually increasing staff hours in any practice where they hadn't yet been fully restored, and embarking on a national television advertising campaign advocating we were open for business as usual.

Just as we did at the start of the crisis, I shared this recovery plan with the broader industry in another publicly accessible webinar attended by over 1,000 private practitioners.

The mental health of our team undoubtedly ranked amongst some of our greatest concerns, especially as the pandemic dragged into 2021. As part of our recovery planning, I ran a groupwide pulse check on the wellbeing of our people, pleased to learn than 90% felt they were in a strong position to bounce forward from the impacts of COVID-19. Similarly high numbers reported they felt genuinely cared for by their franchisees, that we had communicated well and kept them updated regularly, and expressed confidence in my national leadership.

THE PANDEMIC WAS a rollercoaster for most of us but, amidst the uncertainty and fear, there were moments of hope and positivity that lifted my spirits. One of the most heartwarming impacts was it brought our people closer together, despite physical distancing measures. In times of crisis, I saw the best of humanity shine through our group. Individuals went out of their way to support one another. From sharing experiences late at night with those who needed encouragement, to loaning staff to nearby practices when others were off sick, and even giving financial support to those who needed it most. I witnessed countless acts of kindness, compassion, and generosity from within the peer group of franchisees, restoring my faith in why Paulina and I toiled so hard to keep our group aligned.

The pandemic also allowed many of us – me included – to take a step back and reflect on what truly mattered in life. I appreciated the simple joys of spending time with loved ones, taking walks in nature, and pursuing other passions than just work alone – and sometimes to even find the funny side of it all. To sit back and laugh at ourselves, or at least the flurry of YouTube comics who satirised everything there was about the absurdity of our times, including 15,000 different video memes paying homage to global toilet paper shortage. To think, at one time it was common practice, even if never admitted, to hide an irrepressible fart with a well-timed cough. Who would have thought that COVID-19 would turn this social norm on its head, making it more socially acceptable to fart politely to hide a COVID-suspicious cough. Some of us even developed a sixth sense for gauging who might not be vaccinated, and a personal radar alert when someone encroaches your invisible social distancing permitter.

In my case, the pandemic forced me to slow down, be present in the moment, and cherish the little things in life. In times of hardship, I saw the beauty of human resilience and our adaptability to change, experiencing afresh the wonderful grace and provision of God to overcome all that is set before us. I learned to be grateful for what I had, and was determined to find the joy amid difficulty.

It was uncanny that, whilst a few short years before, I wanted out from Back In Motion, and yet it was the most straining months of COVID-19 that gave me a second wind. As it turned out, it was exactly what I needed for one big last push to the finish line.

110
old nemesis

NOT EVEN CORONAVIRUS could not stop the ACCC from harassing us. At the peak of the pandemic in mid-2020, the anti-competitive regulator pressed me again on potential unfair contract terms, despite the unprecedented lengths we had gone to in providing financial relief and other support measures to our franchise network.

My last contact with the ACCC had been our detailed defence to their overstated concerns in April 2019. It took them six months to acknowledge our submission, proving either we weren't a priority in their minds, or they just needed more time to find something to pin on us. Either way, I had moved onward and upwards. I had continued to grow our group, issuing standard-form franchise contracts based on our convictions and detailed legal advice that I was well within the law, and according to best practice by world franchising standards.

The ACCC response in September 2019 was overall a positive one. They were satisfied by most of my explanations, and had narrowed their concerns to only a very specific area. They accepted I can, and should, be able to restrain physiotherapists from using our confidential information and unique systems, but were concerned that I should not restrain them from being able to work as physiotherapists in non-competing roles. I wasn't opposed to this variation, although obviously I was interested to learn what the ACCC might define as "non-competing". For instance, I was very happy for ex-franchisees to work in public and private hospitals, community healthcare, neurological and cardiothoracic physio, and even occupational health consultancy. I took issue, however, with a terminated franchisee working in private practice and potentially competing against the Back In Motion brand in the same local postcode, seeking out existing clientele using the competitive advantage we had trained them in.

My lawyer cited numerous case examples in the medical sector where the courts had upheld identical restraints for similar reasons, and some even in franchising. We were also able to demonstrate that I had strong support from most of our franchisees, who could see how these restraints provided protection to them as individual investors in the same brand. It was only the recalcitrant few who might want to commercially exploit the loopholes or take advantage of lesser restraints. On these arguments, I thought we had overcome the exaggerated concerns of the ACCC and rested our case.

In June 2020, when I was rebounding from the first of many lockdowns, the ACCC wanted me to submit to them the five most recent franchise agreements I had signed during the pandemic, to run another set of eyes over our latest documentation. With a yawn and a sigh, I cooperated.

If the ACCC were not going to leave me alone until they achieved some sort of win – allowing them to beat their chests in front of the media – it was my objective to make sure I offered them the most legally benign and commercially irrelevant concession. My legal team and I met with the ACCC by video conference to discuss what would qualify as a reasonable compromise to all parties to end their three-year witch hunt.

The ACCC wanted to remove all restrictions whatsoever on a franchisee working in the geographical vicinity of another franchisee's location. Our lawyers attacked this position as being unconscionable to the other franchisees who relied on these commercial protections. I was inclined to agree with the ACCC, however, only for new franchisees going forward, grandfathering the existing restraints for those currently in the group. The ACCC accepted that as a fair compromise.

In a rare tone of reasonableness, the senior advisor for the ACCC also confirmed that they would recommend to the Commissioner not to litigate the matter, but rather issue Enforceable Undertakings against me to ensure I complied with the agreed concessions. Regardless of whatever they called it, the likelihood of adverse media from however the ACCC spun the story, remained high. I put the PR and crisis management consultants on alert again.

To extend the gesture to the ACCC as far as I could without it materially impacting our commercial risk, I also offered to reduce our restraint of trade for terminating or expired franchisees to only nine months (down from 12), and limited the restraint area to only three kilometres around an existing Back In Motion practice. All new agreements would have no geographical restraints, a highly unusual situation for any franchise, but something I was willing to concede to appease the unruly powers above.

The ACCC took everything we offered, and then, like an insatiable animal, greedily overreached. They wanted to downgrade all our anti-solicitation clauses that restricted ex-franchisees from contacting prior clients to what they described as "active solicitation" only. How one differentiated between passive and active solicitation was a mystery to me. With no legal distinction, this clause added grey hues to what our agreements permitted and what was enforceable, when the law is best handled in black and white. The intentional ambiguity was reckless and punitive, but given the ACCC were never required to rule on a matter if challenged, I would have to rely on the courts to untangle the convoluted interpretations.

A specialist "restraint of trade" team inside our law firm joined the fray. They were confident the weight of precedence was on my side. If any court was to find our provisions unfair on the basis of what the ACCC put forth, it would undo most of Corporate Australia. Every business, from using basic employment templates to common commercial contracts, relied on similar protections that the ACCC was now labelling, in our situation, as unfair.

I bristled at the heavy-handed bully tactics forcing me into an uncommercial position, threatened by paralysing litigation and weighty penalties. I wrote to the ACCC that its unfavourable views mattered little in the context of law. Just because they perceived provisions in our franchise agreement to be potentially unfair, did not make them so. I believed our restrictive covenants were in place to protect the network as a whole; all franchisees relied on them, so it was a disservice to the upstanding members of our group to strike them out. These protections were neither unreasonable nor excessive according to our legal representatives. In fact, they did not go as far as those seen in many other well-known larger franchise systems.

The ACCC's aggressive and relentless pursuit of myself and Back In Motion, and their threats to bring proceedings against me, were a constant haunting distraction from which I could not see imminent relief. I could call their bluff and hope they'd acquiesce. Or I could have my day in court and presumably win the case based on the many that had been fought and won before me on similar arguments. Alternatively, I could save time, money, and emotional energy for things that mattered more – and simply give the ACCC what they wanted.

My legal team believed the ACCC were trying to build test cases to cement a common law position around their latest interpretations of the unfair contract's legislation. Precedence was everything and, to date, they had none. I didn't want Back In Motion to become the first – an exemplar, win or lose – for undergraduate legal students to examine and debate for the next decade. More importantly, I didn't want the unsolicited negative press that the ACCC would inevitably stir up against us to help build their case. I knew from experience the destabilising impact of hate-filled media on our brand.

The ACCC had a bee in its bonnet, and if I didn't want to get stung with a sizable court action, all advice from the legal team and my board, was to roll over. So reluctantly, muttering under my breath, I conceded. The bully won their fight.

In September 2020, to address the ACCC's persistent concerns, and as part of my ongoing commitment to ensure our agreements exceeded industry standards, I signed a binding voluntary undertaking to limit our restraints of trade and to remove the franchisee buyout option - eliminating the two sources of confusion and media angst against me. I made sure our lawyers drafted the agreement to avoid any admission of unfair dealings. Our language simply observed that the terms were *deemed* unfair by the ACCC which, on principle, I felt was an important point, given nobody on our side felt we were acting immorally or illegally. Despite the changes only having applicability in Australia, I decided to extend the amendments throughout our agreements in New Zealand also, reflecting best practice and preserving commercial alignment within our network.

The new terms took effect for all existing and new agreements from the 7th of September 2020.

I PREPARED FOR some industry fallout after sensationalised media headlines from a gloating ACCC press release. I even rehearsed canned responses in case I was called upon by hostile journalists without notice, but it was angst for nothing. By God's grace, a rarely understated announcement was made on the day of our signing. The ACCC made its customary website update and published the undertaking on the public register. A reporter from *Inside Franchise Business* reached out to me for a comment before publishing a short, benign piece but, unless you were looking for it, the news blip wouldn't have hit your radar.

There were just a few who tried to make more of it – Spencer, Philip and Malcolm - jumping all over the news. They made a few noises on social media, but I had long become calloused to their barbs.

One of the requirements of our undertaking was to send a notice to all potentially "disaffected" people. Ironically, the only person who potentially qualified under this strict legal definition was Malcolm. He had recently opted to exercise his right to pay a buyout fee to be released from his restraints and continue to trade his practice independently. It was inevitable that, upon sending Malcolm the official statutory notice prescribed by the ACCC notifying him of our recent change in stance with regards to restraints, that another face-off with my old nemesis was likely.

Surprisingly, the bomb didn't detonate immediately. Malcolm no longer retained his usual legal counsel - despite her having been the syndicated lawyer of many of our troubled franchisees - slowing down his predictable antagonism. Instead, Malcolm switched advisors to the same legal firm used by Spencer, further evidence of their collusion in all matters that were meant to be confidential and non-disparaging.

In October 2020, Malcolm's new legal team mounted a feeble argument that our franchise agreements had been unfair regarding his client's exit provisions – a simplistic repeat of the ACCC rhetoric. It was literally a cut-and-paste from whatever press release or article they had read on our Enforceable Undertaking, attempting to use a perceived admission against us. They demanded half of the buyout fee as restitution for my "unjust enrichment" at their client's expense.

Frankly, I was tired of fighting; it was death by a thousand cuts. Every alleged wrongdoing, unfounded accusation, hearsay, and inuendo had worn me down. I just handed the letter off to Warren, my legal counsel, and asked him to manage it however he thought best.

Fortunately for me, Warren was outraged. He refuted all the shallow allegations with sound rationale, concluding that Malcolm had no entitlement to any reduction in fee. Not the least of his arguments was that Malcolm had retained legal representation through the entirety of his exit negotiations – so, if there was any claim to be made, it should be against the negligence of his advisors and not us.

Adding to this, I had already reduced Malcolm's original buyout fee by about 50% in a show of goodwill at the time of settlement. Even if our Enforceable Undertaking was in full effect prior to Malcolm leaving – which clearly it wasn't – he would have been obliged to transfer his lease to me, assign the phone number, not trade in the area for up to nine months, hand over all our rightful copyright and confidential information, and in no way be permitted to actively solicit any of the clientele. In effect, he would have walked away from a $1.5 million practice – something I would have been pleased to inherit.

Warren laboured for five pages, burying Malcolm's lawyer in his own circular arguments, pounding him with fact and precedent in every paragraph. He cited the benefits Malcolm had obtained at a discount, and checkmated him that our Enforceable Undertaking gives his client none of the rights he wrongly assumed or argued under false pretence.

Malcolm instructed his lawyer to fight. We held our position, but the battle kept going through December and into the new year. Whilst everyone was struggling to keep their heads above COVID-19 waters, Malcolm was hoping whatever cash payment he might weasel out of us would help alleviate the losses he was feeling in lockdown. It was a classic shakedown – I had seen a few of these in my time.

Because of exciting offers that soon emerged to purchase our business (which I will come to shortly), Warren was in a hurry to settle the matter. I reluctantly conceded to a one-time nominal payment as *go-away* money to settle the nuisance Malcolm was creating. This avoided me making any admission of liability, side-stepping costly litigation, and most importantly, leaving nothing disastrous to declare to my potential suitors.

I inked a settlement with Malcolm in March 2021, but had long stopped being fooled these matters were final; experience taught me that some people kept coming back for more. With the likes of Malcolm, Spencer and Philip, I could never be sure.

111
new blueprint

THE SHOW MUST go on. In July 2020, with an ambitious forecast despite COVID-19, I launched Back In Motion's new strategic plan, *#IMPACT2030*. Strategic planning has often been described as a dark art, useful only for making astrology look respectable. Fraught with endless assumptions, speculation, and personal biases, I accept that every planning activity has its limitations. That said, I loved to plot a strategy.

From the rudimentary business ideas I first scribbled down in the back of the campervan half way around Australia, to the more polished and considered documents I was more used to presenting, I always placed high value on the importance of a roadmap to guide the investment of our time, money and effort. Even if most plans did not survive first contact with the enemy, at the very least the process of planning was important to consider strategic imperatives, debate alternatives, ponder opportunities, manage the threats, and gather people around a common purpose. The journey was far more important than the destination.

#IMPACT2030 outlined what we could achieve over the next ten years. It was a blueprint for our greatest achievements yet. Whilst I was sure the plan would adapt and morph with every passing year, it represented our combined best thinking at the time.

Having sold Actif and Revita a few years earlier, the Back In Motion Health Group was principally made up of two core brands at this stage: *Back In Motion* in Australia; and *Motion Health* in New Zealand. Collectively, these two brands formed the largest physiotherapy network in the Southern Hemisphere. In 2021, we hosted more than 60 flagship practices and an additional 84 satellite locations. My national team was made up of approximately 22 professionals, in partnership with just under 80 franchisees, employing nearly 700 staff, engaging 92,000 concurrent active clients, delivering over 600,000 consultations a year, and earning $58 million in revenue on a pro-rata annual basis. We were a resilient business, proved by our emergence from the unprecedented social disruption and commercial downturn of COVID-19, and were stronger than ever, boasting record sales performances across the network.

As I stood on the threshold of our third decade, my attention galvanised to converting all our energy, size, scale, experience, footprint, goodwill, and financial resources to create sustainable positive change – optimal impact for the local practice and franchisee, the health industry, the communities we serve, and the nations we loved. With enduring impact, I was determined to achieve our God-commissioned purpose.

BACK IN MOTION had been created to make a difference in the lives of others; I wanted to invest into those who needed it most. In my language, this is how we defined our *significance*.

The challenge at this point in our growth was to live this intention with conviction and stamina. To do so, I had to be committed to the disciplines of continued innovation, prototyping our changes, scaling what worked, and consolidating the successful ideas into repeatable systems. There were no shortcuts.

Whilst Back In Motion was still the largest physiotherapy network on record, we had recently been pushed to the number two position of integrated allied health providers. Recent ASX-entrant, Healthia – the same company which had been sent a scandalous memo to pick apart our group one practice at a time – held the top spot nationally. An aggregate of more than a dozen local brands – most notably 81 podiatry practices and 42 physiotherapy centres – Healthia boasted $88 million in revenue and $12 million in profits.

Of real interest to me were the macro trends emerging within our industry in allied and primary health, both domestically and abroad, and in public and private sectors. Back In Motion has experienced many different seasons, but a new era in allied health care was approaching. Our commercial and professional landscape was changing rapidly in ways not seen before. It was becoming more client-driven, technology-based, and clinically integrative. Funding was being invested into new care models, and legislation was adapting to provide greater freedoms and innovations in the way people received their services.

The allied health market seemed likely to continue to aggregate and synergise more intentionally. The coordination of allied health services needed to become more sophisticated to fully realise the emerging opportunities, abandoning the cottage mindset of treating patients as sick dependents and recognising them as discretionary consumers, often funded by hefty instructional third parties. Few people seemed to recognise the changes on the horizon, and of those who did, even less had the means to capitalise on it.

As a visionary group, Back In Motion was ready to embrace the promises of the future. We had invested 20 years establishing and growing an extensive practice network with people who shared a courageous paradigm of industry thinking. We had come so far, and yet in some ways, it felt like everything to this point had just been preparation for a much more significant impact yet to be made.

THE GROWTH PICTURE I envisioned for 2030 began with us delivering multiple new services. Whilst Back In Motion would continue as a premium physiotherapy brand, I wanted to initiate a range of innovative services that offered more progressive and truly holistic outcomes to clients.

I envisioned becoming synonymous with broader services including podiatry, osteopathy, chiropractic, occupational therapy, dietetics and nutrition, and possibly psychology. I presumed many of these services needed to be provided under a variety of brands for commercial and pragmatic reasons; however, they were to function under an umbrella of aligned leadership and governance with the benefit of shared support services.

Through this more complete group model, Back In Motion was to play a greater role in acute, sub-acute, and chronic disease management, aged care and disability services, and home-based healthcare. Wellness and preventative services would also become fully integrated as a cost-effective solution for workplaces and individuals.

The next thing I expected to achieve was a world-first integrated and managed service model catering to "packaged care" – the bundling of adjunctive services for a single treatment episode – anticipated to become the preferred future service model for institutional clients such as health insurers, private hospital groups, compensable bodies, corporates, and other large privatised third-party purchasers. I wanted Back In Motion to be the innovative leader in both business models and clinical outcomes to satisfy these new expectations.

Without doubt, opportunities for expanded roles in service planning and managed care were expected to also become increasingly apparent, especially as the National Disability Insurance Scheme (NDIS) cemented its permanency into the Australian healthcare outlook. Whether or not Back In Motion played a formal role in administrative case management, our best opportunity was to position ourselves as the leading service provider for the delivery of necessary care. We could then advocate that bundled or packaged funding contracts should be, in part at least, assessed on health and other performance outcomes. We were committed to providing rigorous clinical outcome data as an essential determinant for exclusive client leads and preferred provider status with key health influencers and referral hubs, separating us from the competition by a large margin.

Ultimately, I wanted to become a "commissioned" service provider. As state and federal governments sought to reduce the cost burden for preventative and medical services, I expected they would look to outsource, contract, and decentralise peripheral, high-cost and non-core services to community providers. I believed the allied health sector was already fulfilling many of these criteria and Back In Motion was well-positioned for a private-public sector partnership model, having a significant impact on chronic care and long-term rehabilitation, in- and out-patient hospital care, and community-based services.

Digital health technology also captured my imagination. Through COVID-19 I discovered the value of advanced virtual services. A progressive digital healthcare platform (building on the early iterations of tele-rehabilitation that became essential during lockdown) would permit the delivery of superior online consultations for those who either couldn't, or preferred the convenience of not having to, visit our practices. This was to be designed for selective services and even entire episodes of care that we were soon to build out.

Technology promised the holy grail of genuine 24/7 access: providing unlimited availability to practitioners for individual and corporate clients; access for regional, rural and remote populations; catering to the preference of the tech-smart generation; and permitting a limitless virtual reach of our brand and services internationally. As part of this advanced technology, I was determined to progressively incorporate the Internet of Things (IoT) to further enhance clinical diagnostics; biometric, anthropometric, and biomechanical assessment; a variety of clinical interventions; and the reportability of the patient experience in real time.

All these objectives amounted to no small undertaking. An ancient Japanese proverb warns that vision without action is a *dream*; but action without vision is a *nightmare*. I needed both in equal portions.

At the NSO, we committed ourselves to an outrageous objective, *Footprint400*. The vision was to enlarge the group's footprint to increase its leverage within the health system, and drive new and better opportunities through scale, spread, and diversity. I estimated four hundred access points was achievable through 300 practice locations, a supportive network of 50 partner brands (in which I owned a partial stake), and another 50 affiliated service providers. Achieving this goal would extend our reach to include clients in low saturation regions where we didn't need, or couldn't sustain, a permanent presence.

I was also committed to building deep "value wells" with our franchisees. Neil, our board advisor, encouraged me to continuously look at ways to keep our people engaged. Like cows in a paddock, you can either fence them in or attract them to the centre of the fields with a deep well of water that never runs dry. Limiting my franchisees with restraints of trade and other onerous legal obligations made exiting difficult, or at least unpalatable, but attracting people to stay because of an abundance of commercial and operational benefits was a far superior strategy.

To be successful in the changing health space, I felt ready to courageously step up once more, giving Healthia a run for its money on top of the dais. In the next ten years I was determined to pioneer new opportunities for expansion and truly realise our impact. We were an entrepreneurial brand after all – I couldn't stop taking risks after everything I had learned.

112
coke versus pepsi

WITH ALL THIS bubbling ambition, I launched *Project 10 Toes* in partnership with Alex and his wife – both Kiwis who had owned their own podiatry and orthotic company in New Zealand. Established in January 2004, the company had grown to 17 clinics, boasting a team of 38 staff, including 18 podiatrists, before they sold to big corporate.

Limited only to video conferences due to the pandemic's travel restrictions, in September 2020 we established a joint venture to provide podiatry services as a complementary and, eventually, integrated service of Back In Motion. The intention was to expand the delivery of services beyond traditional bricks-and-mortar practices and to innovate with online digital formats and through homecare visiting services. We focused initially on Australia and, once prototyped, planned to follow in New Zealand. I swiftly began to develop exclusive arrangements with third-party payers and insurers for the new services on offer, building centralised referral streams, attractive career pathways for podiatrists, and exploiting emerging technologies.

Despite the rising numbers of COVID-19 cases making them nervous, Alex and his family agreed to relocate to Australia to take up the opportunity, with their preference initially to be based in Sydney where the lockdown restrictions were not as severe. Alex became the Managing Director of our new footcare venture, investing some of his own capital to secure a 10% equity in the partnership vehicle that led the initiative.

Flying across the ditch in early February 2021, at the peak of the pandemic, Alex roared off with a great start. By June, only four months later, we had 18 practices with a resident podiatrist. We had another seven in the recruitment pipeline, and were about to attend the national podiatry conference to hopefully encourage more into the funnel. Furthermore, we contacted almost 1,900 owners of independent podiatry practices to initiate conversations around buying or merging their businesses, quickly forging partnership negotiations with four of the early responders.

Around the same time, I launched *Project Alignment*, the controversial exploration in converging osteopathy and chiropractic services into our group. I first met Martin through another attempted rollup of health care practices called Escencia, which didn't get very far because of its chequered history of false starts, eventually rotting on the vine like so many which had been attempted previously.

Martin was an entrepreneurial chiropractor who spent numerous years trying to integrate multi-site, multi-practitioner chiropractic services into a multi-disciplinary network focused on integrated care with high profitability margins. He had promising success in his pilot practices but was yet to secure sufficient capital to pull off anything on scale.

Martin believed he could bring ten vendors to the table, each locked into a minimum three-year agreement at an average purchase price of just over five times their profit. We proposed payment terms of 60% cash and 40% shares in the new parent entity I established. Basing the numbers on 2019 performance, before the pandemic's dip inevitably eroded the sales lines, the opportunity represented about $21 million in revenue with $5.5 million in aggregate profit.

My board showed cautious interest in the elaborate plan I presented. Chief amongst their concerns was the readiness in the market for a scaled integration of chiropractic services with physiotherapy – often pitched against each other with the same vitriol Coca-Cola and Pepsi are compared or, closer to home, Ford and Holden. They were more supportive of integrations with osteopathy and podiatry as our first move, believing these services faced lower barriers of opposition, both inside and external to our established business.

Martin went to work on furnishing evidence to support the proposed integration. He provided clinical evidence of the efficacy of chiropractic services working alongside and in synergy with other manual therapy modalities, and case studies of integration he was aware of in the USA and Australia. He worked on demonstrating detailed pre-COVID financial performance of many of these exemplars and introduced me personally to some of the vendors he hoped might become the early adopters to our new channel.

Martin was convincing. The board liked what they saw and, with this confidence, I was given the green light to sign a parentship agreement with Martin, where we both contributed seed capital to a new entity dedicated to the purchase of a selective cohort of chiropractic businesses. For the work he was doing in curating the right mix of partnering businesses, Martin was appointed the executive in charge of driving growth and further acquisitions within the chiropractic sector. He was also passionate about integrating psychology services, a mobile health fleet, and bringing in Medicare-funded diagnostic imaging. Early discussions about scaling the investment were already underway with an Australian-born billionaire, investor, and philanthropist who was looking for innovative pathways to imprint her legacy.

For the time being, I ensured the new group sat parallel to Back In Motion, and not within it. I needed to feel comfortable that integrating the two entities would not bring our core brand into any disrepute and, most importantly, would help to achieve our larger goals of #IMPACT2030. In the meantime, it was little more than a promising side hustle.

I spent a good part of the next six months travelling the country to meet with the vendor groups – verifying their performance, negotiating non-binding offers, preparing transaction paperwork, and building a queue of settlements ready for completion as soon as I could secure the right funding model.

I was genuinely excited to be at the helm of Back In Motion again after such a long time of reluctant leadership. The course we were charting inspired me, unable to deny my attraction to heady growth rather than mundane management. As I stood at the foothills of another steep ascent, my palms got sweaty and the adrenaline surged. I was eager for the gruelling climb.

113
Spoiled for choice

ONLY ONE THING caused me to consider slowing the likely purchase of a swathe of new podiatry and chiropractic practices. Back in April 2018 I was casually pitched a partnership opportunity with one of Australia's most successful multinational healthcare providers and hospital networks. They operated more than 500 locations in Australia, Europe, the UK, and Asia, earning a market capitation of $8 billion at the time. Despite making our business look miniscule, Back In Motion had a substantially larger physiotherapy footprint, and represented to them a strategic acquisition.

I met with the Australian CEO and executive team in their Sydney-based boardroom, aware that they needed to increase revenues through the rehabilitation care being driven by their inpatient orthopaedic surgeries. Hospital trends, especially in the US, were shifting towards the cost-effective services of high-quality outpatient providers to discharge people from hospital and back to their homes as quickly as possible. We represented one of the best ways to help them achieve this goal.

The health conglomerate already owned a string of pharmacies and felt they had the requisite skills to complement their retail health footprint with an expanded network of physiotherapy centres. I ran the gauntlet for an hour, batting away a barrage of questions about industry economics, international healthcare trends, and expected synergies from integrated operations. I felt outnumbered and outclassed by the heavyweights sitting on the other side of the mahogany table in their tailored suits, writing on company notepads with elegant Mont Blancs. But when asked to defend Back In Motion's cornering of the market, I held my own. I was supremely confident in our business model and buoyed by our two decades of record annual performance.

Their Head of Strategy, globally second in charge, later confirmed their commitment to an allied health rollout over the next two years, promising physiotherapy to be a major pillar of their plan. Ironically, NSW was the geographic priority for the hospital group. They had failed to penetrate that market in any meaningful way, mirroring our disappointing attempts also, leaving us both underweight in the same region.

I immediately started working with their corporate advisory team and management on what a scaling up of services would look like to meet the orthopaedic demand that could result from a joint venture. It was going to be costly to fast-track coverage in NSW, and I needed financial backing. A boutique private equity buccaneer confirmed they could provide $25 million of debt for our expansion plans on a three-year, low-interest loan, earning themselves an additional $5 million cash bonus if I successfully listed our group on the ASX any time before the close of 2019. Alternatively, I could raise an immediate $5 million of equity from institutional capital in Sydney and Melbourne if I wanted to move quickly, with the promise of follow-on rounds as needed.

I felt anxious about too many unknowns, trying to solve a complex puzzle with pieces that didn't perfectly match. I wasn't sure how this new corporate partnership would benefit our franchisees, if at all. I also was not confident my advisors had my best interests at heart, likely motivated by their own upside in a windfall. And, with the passing of time, COVID-19 became a cautious threat on the horizon, cooling the proposition entirely.

IN PARALLEL TO these conversations, advisors also introduced to the mix a possible liaison with Fitness First, Goodlife Health Clubs, and 24-hour fitness chain, Jetts. Collectively owned by Quadrant Private Equity, which acquired the brands in 2016 under their Fitness and Lifestyle Group, boasting over a thousand locations in total, I was offered to take up a small tenancy in each of their centres, enhancing the valuation ahead of their planned IPO or trade sale in the following year.

Dubbed (by somebody else) the unfortunate name *Project Krakenback* (a purposeful misspelling of "cracking-the-back") – which always got a few laughs from stuffy men and women in suits and ties hearing it for the first time – the initiative was a lot to consider. I felt like the prom queen with a swarm of suitors vying for a chance to dance, but unsure who to pick.

Seeing a strategy for a one-two punch, aligning the joint venture with Quadrant as a possible stepping stone to shoring up available NSW footprint for the previous hospital group venture, I negotiated with Quadrant's general counsel and CEO the terms of a master franchisee for a scaled rollout of Back In Motion centres across their Sydney footprint only. As a means of testing the mutual benefit of any suspected horizontal integration, I committed to recruiting, training, and deploying the workforce of physiotherapists in the shared Fitness First locations, leaving them to carry the operational costs of set up and trade. I refused to carry the risk of an expensive fit out, long-term leasehold, or to be responsible for driving the membership bump they hoped to achieve by the co-branding exercise. These latter deliverables were all to be within the control, effort, and remit of Fitness First executives and, like with most initiatives, required capital to be invested before any likely value would drop to their bottom lines.

After some elongated discussions, it was clear Quadrant were after quick wins, and I couldn't promise that. As a services-based model, our strength was in building steady long-term revenue streams through loyal clientele – not pop-up sensations that could artificially boost their sales for a month or two to impress shareholders. The disparity in expectations gave both parties good reasons to not proceed.

ALMOST TWO YEARS later, in August 2020 as Project 10Toes and Project Alignment were starting to hit their stride, my Sydney-based advisors confirmed the multi-billion-dollar hospital juggernaut was ready to talk again. The company had recently raised $1.3 billion to support its growth, and wanted to move swiftly into physiotherapy and the broader allied health sector through a scaled acquisition.

The corporate executives had been frustrated with their dawdling pharmacy expansion, the result of the over-regulation in the sector. In essence, they could only buy one pharmacy location at a time, which was painfully slow for their ambitious objectives. Back In Motion offered rapid scale and critical mass in one step, which was very attractive to a large company that was capitalised to expand further.

The deal-makers were non-negotiable on the structure of their purchase. They wanted me to corporatise my network, buying back all the franchised practices, and consolidating the assets into one entity. Their initial proposal was to fund these buy-backs as part of their acquisition of our group, a mind-boggling concept from a legal and technical perspective. The possibilities of how to approach this opportunity were endless as my mind wandered through the nuances of future structure and expansion, the difficulty of the transaction rising to nauseating levels.

To continue negotiations, I needed certainty around several issues – exclusivity, valuation, pricing, franchisee terms, employee retention, and timeframes. I needed to undertake extensive modelling, engage third-party advisory firms, and consider a range of complexities I was only just starting to uncover, not the least of which was whether my franchisees would even be willing to divest their interests as part of this strategy. And, if so, I anticipated each franchisee would understandably want to assert their own interests on pricing and terms that were specific to them.

Whilst in our franchise agreements I retained a call-option to buy back franchisees at my election (on a selective or network basis), the thought of forcing someone to do this against their will did not sit well with me. I promised myself that any deal I presented to the franchisees had to be commercially compelling to them, making my right to impose the decision a moot point.

One thing was clear; the hospital group was committed to an all-or-nothing proposition, determined for maximum footprint. I had to get everyone involved, or the deal was a non-starter.

SERENDIPITOUSLY, IN SEPTEMBER 2020, Barry from HealthForce probed my interest in another round of sale discussions. He had refinanced his business after the onset of COVID-19 and paid down a vast sum of previously held debt. This effort markedly changed their financial situation from when we spoke at the end of the prior year, affording them the means to offer a higher valuation for Back In Motion. Within two weeks, Barry provided a detailed terms sheet at a slightly higher multiple than previous and pitched at twice the general market based on the public records of Healthia's recent transactions. For added measure, it was a walk-in-walk-out deal in full cash with no claw backs. The simplicity was attractive compared with the complexity of the hospital group's undertaking, even though a year earlier I had refused something similar.

Allied health dealings are a small world – the advisor engaged to represent Barry was well known to me, having acted on my behalf in our record sale of Revita in 2017. After a short reminisce on the great experience we shared together, the two of us quickly re-postured on opposite sides of the net, acknowledging the different teams we now played on.

It was clear for all prospective transactions – be it with Fitness First, the hospital corporate, or HealthForce – that COVID-19 was going to overlay any assessment of performance with inconvenient complexity. Back In Motion enjoyed record profit during 2020 and 2021 – in some part due to unprecedented sales, and in some part due to government subsidies – and valuers were conservative in how they treated bottom line multiples given the uncertainties of forward estimates. I pressed all suitors to share with me their perceptions of commercial risk as we emerged from severe lockdowns, and the likely effect this might have on price and terms. I also needed a full declaration of their intentions with how they would treat my franchisees in any new future model – financially on transaction, and operationally in a newly integrated business format.

With two birds in the hand, and both vastly different offers in their respective appeal, I called a board meeting in early 2021 to clarify my intentions. I didn't want to spin my wheels again with dead-end, futile opportunities, distracting me from the self-imposed mandate of #IMPACT2030. I had an attractive line-up of chiropractic and podiatry practices sitting idle, waiting not-so-patiently, for me to put my money where my mouth was. They eagerly wanted to begin their new life under our group banner, but any purchases would undoubtedly preclude me doing a sale with either the hospital group or HealthForce, as it would materially change the economics and logistics of the deal mechanics.

It seemed ironic. I was considering dismantling and selling off my existing group in one hand, whilst simultaneously forming a new group to buy in the other. I couldn't be half-pregnant; I was either "in" or "out". I needed to ramp up my own growth plans for 2030, or look for the nearest exit.

114
future of franchising

WITH SOME OF these percolating opportunities, I submitted a provocative white paper in the board packet of February 2019, the first meeting of my recomposed board. I intended to fast track them in a range of high stakes considerations I had been contemplating over the prior couple of years, titling my paper, *The Future of Franchising*.

I provoked candid discussions about whether we should remain committed to the shared equity model that had served me well for nearly two decades, or whether it was time to consider alternative commercial frameworks that may better suit us in the changing climate.

Franchising in Australia was amongst the most dynamic and progressive business sectors in the economy. It had been recognised as a reputable way of trading for a long time. Franchise systems were present in most industry sectors, with its positive economic impact substantial and growing. Fast food, petrol, sporting teams, movies and television shows, and even churches had followed the franchising model with scalable benefits. Franchising had revolutionised retailing in Australia and provided small business proprietors with the competitive resources to compete against the large corporations that otherwise dominated the sector.

Back In Motion was deemed both innovative and disruptive 15 years ago when I first introduced franchising to the physiotherapy profession. Whilst we now stood as the largest physiotherapy provider in our cottage sector, we were no longer the *only* franchise. In the last five years, several other physiotherapy brands emerged in both Australia and New Zealand, attempting to franchise their unique approach, as were alternative formats arising in the UK, Canada, and USA. Furthermore, there were multiple other corporate physiotherapy business models that relied heavily on "local business partners" – in essence, acting as pseudo-franchisees, holding an equity stake in a single practice underneath a consolidated parent company controlling a common brand and systems.

Franchising was an undisputed success – in our sector, and the world at large – but expectations were changing. Vocal doubters and franchise naysayers were getting louder. "Haters", as my kids would call them, started to naïvely degrade franchising as a corrupt and unfair model. In the last two years, the franchising sector in Australia eroded much of its credibility, undoubtedly accelerated by the negativity and criticism in the media of the alleged mis-dealings of some major brands, such as 7-Eleven and the Retail Food Group. The Senate Inquiry that followed only fuelled the fire of negative sentiment.

I had obviously not sidestepped my own negative media cycle, albeit relatively short lasting. The mischievous jabs by disgruntled franchisees and ex-staff lingered in social media and, as you are now aware, the ACCC's repeated investigation into us dragged on well into 2020 before I conceded to changes. Without doubt, the combined impact of bad press and heightened industry scrutiny raised questions around the future of franchising in physiotherapy.

All this unwelcomed and undeserved attention created significant brand damage for us amongst many of our prospective franchisees at the time. Conservative estimates are that more than three dozen practice owners cooled off and fell out of our business development pipelines between 2018 and 2019 because of the perceived reputational risk of being associated with a media target. And then, of course, there are the ones who can't be counted, as they were scared off before we even met them.

It was a timely board consideration. Despite, on balance, franchising remaining a viable commercial option, my purpose behind the provocation was to probe the board's mind toward attractive alternatives to franchising – however hard it might seem to swap out mid-stream.

With all the possibilities swirling in my mind, I took to the podium at our Franchisee Summit in October 2018, a single day gathering of our national leaders. I welcomed the conversation around potential different business models and corporate expansion opportunities with everybody in the room, explaining the differences between IPOs, roll-ups and aggregations, joint ventures with health insurers, corporate ownership models, de-franchising with corporate buybacks, and so forth. I ran a live survey on the day that polled people's preferences, inviting them to imagine their preferred future.

I was relieved that day to learn that many were open to numerous possibilities that might see us wind out of franchising in favour of alternative models, if the conditions were right. These findings buoyed me at the time, giving me assurance that, if the right opportunity were ever to present, our people may be up for change.

It was premature to form any conclusions at that first board meeting for 2019, or even make recommendations. Still, I set the scene for robust discussions every month thereafter, right through to the moment where I found myself, with a compelling cash proposal from HealthForce in the right hand, and an infinitely more complex deconstruction strategy with one of Australia's largest hospital providers in the left.

115
wish list

WITH THE CONSOLIDATION occurring in our small sector, and the number of approaches I had entertained to buy, sell, or merge in the previous two years, I sensed the allied health bubble was soon going to burst. Despite the hospital group and HealthForce being tangible options on the table, it was naïve to think other choices didn't exist. I conceded to the probability that a transaction of some sort was inevitable in our near future, and it made sense to approach the market with a more intentional strategy than just jumping at unsolicited offers.

I felt excruciating conflict throughout September 2021 – emotionally torn between the freedom of letting our business go and the responsibility to hang on for another strategic season. Paulina and I found ourselves consumed by the choice every day, yearning to break free from the torment of indecision.

I rang a good friend to pray with me for wisdom, inviting any insights he felt God impress on him to share. Steve asked four questions, none of them simple.

The first was: "Is the mission God gave you at Back In Motion complete, or have you just been offered an opportunity seemingly too good to refuse?"

The mission was always the *people*, never the money or the business. I often confided in my friends that I believed God cared less about a chain of physiotherapy practices, and more about what He could do in and through them to impact me and others. My posture to serve God through Back In Motion was premised on the ideal: *Do what I can, with what I have, where He places me, for as long as He keeps me there.*

Owning the business was "accidental" – just a matter of obedience to what God had asked me to do. I was genuinely prepared to remain with Back In Motion for as long as it was where God wanted me, even though I looked forward to the day I might be released to new adventures. In my heart, from long before Back In Motion was even conceived, I had nurtured a dream to serve God's purposes by working amongst the poorest of the poor, and especially cross-culturally. He knew that. Only God held the key to open and close my doors of vocation and calling, and I was comfortable leaning on this one to see if He unlocked it.

Steve's second question: "What is motivating and driving the consideration of change?"

It was undeniable that the responsibility to operate the business was all-consuming, and a role with less pressure carried appeal. I knew this was likely a mirage - as whatever assignment I took on next would likely be high stakes in other ways too - but I hated being a slave to the machine. Selling the business seemed an elegant way to create more room in my life for everything else that was important to me.

He then probed further: "If you feel Back In Motion might be coming to an end, do you have any thoughts about what is next?"

In all honesty, I didn't. It was as though, for as long as Back In Motion was still my responsibility, I didn't have enough brain space or bandwidth to conceive much else. My hands were full, and I couldn't pick up something new until I put this one down. The best answers I could muster on the day were roles in leadership development and helping to relieve extreme poverty. Other than this, I drew blanks – and I was comfortable with my reasons doing so.

Then Steve landed his last question without any apology: *"Are you and Paulina in total agreement with the present and future possibilities?"*

It was a potent reminder that Paulina and I were in this together. I often ran ahead or lagged, creating unnecessary tension in our marriage. I had learned the hard way that God was unlikely to signal one of us about important changes in our family or business, leaving the other in the dark. If I felt prompted to go left, and Paulina was inclined to move right, then it was a sign for me to slow down, wait, and reconsider our options. Timing was everything, and all the big decisions waited until we both caught up.

On this occasion, we felt unusually aligned to inch forward.

MICHAEL PRESSED PAULINA and I in our September board meeting to reflect deeply on the personal non-negotiables of any future transaction. He wanted us to discover God's ideal framework for our decision before we got sucked into the vortex of possible greed or confusion, common accompaniments with grandiose corporate offers.

Our list of absolutes included fair market value for the NSO in cash on settlement, with any premium above this value taken in scrip for future upside. We wanted commercial and lifestyle benefits for our franchisees, evidenced by their support and engagement in whatever deal we presented them. Franchisees also needed to be preserved a choice to opt in, or go their own way without any legal or financial penalty if they didn't like the new direction.

Among my other wish list items for this negotiation, I wanted to provide our franchisees with an option to sell their practices at an above-market valuation. If they chose to stay with the group on the other side of the transaction, I hoped they would enjoy operational synergies that lowered their costs, improved their margins, and increased their client referrals. Whatever deal I agreed to had to also compensate for the large and profitable franchisees just as much as it adapted fairly to the new or less profitable performers. The network of more than 70 individual franchisees represented owners at different ages and stages; flexibility was a key attribute of whatever terms we negotiated.

In addition, an equitable agreement demanded a congruent alignment of personal values between the new purchaser and our senior management team, and for me to be released from all day-to-day operational responsibilities (other than for a reasonable transition period). I expected to make myself available for strategic consultation one or two days per week – but beyond that, I favoured the freedom for new beginnings.

Paulina and I presented our reflections to the board in a subsequent meeting. They smiled, gently cautioning us to be "reasonable" and "realistic". It seemed at first that our list was outrageous and unlikely to be fulfilled in the real world. Undeterred, Paulina and I agreed it would become a clear signal of God's intentions to proceed if we secured an offer that satisfied our demanding criteria.

That wish list became our prayer point at home for the next 12 months. We secretly held it as an acid test, that we might know whether God was orchestrating opportunities with His unseen hand rather than us forcing things to happen out of selfish intent or natural desire.

116
let's go shopping

WHEN WE SOLD Revita, I discovered the exorbitant fees of great advisors can bring a previously unknown buyer's universe into your atmosphere, worthy of the hefty price. Warren, our legal partner, lined up PricewaterhouseCoopers (PwC) to run a structured process for the sale.

In mid-September 2020, I was first introduced by video conference to Andrew, Partner of Mergers and Acquisitions (M&A) in the Melbourne office of PwC. I had been given the friendly warning that "he likes to talk" but, with the intelligence of a genius and the energy of a large army, this guy was a powerhouse of insights and activity. After my first meeting, if he were paid per word spoken, no matter how wealthy our deal made him, it would be cents in the dollar to what he was due. A 30-minute meeting took over an hour, because Andrew had an uncanny habit of summarising his immediately previous paragraphs multiple times throughout the conversation, unable to conclude without taking one more victory lap of his high points.

My kids called Andrew the "Running Man", because of the number of times I'd be ferrying them to soccer training while talking with him on loudspeaker in the car. They listened in on our detailed discussions about deal parameters, Andrew huffing and puffing his way around the dark suburban streets near his home, completing his habitual five-kilometre jog before putting in another three hours work that evening.

I gave Andrew and his team the various purchase and sale proposals we had considered over the years, and the most recent developments with the two offers on the table from the hospital group and HealthForce. Having managed some large health-related transactions in the last few years, Andrew's team began curating a list of potential buyers they were confident would be interested in our growth story. The list featured companies within the healthcare trade and financial sector, pitching us as a unicorn opportunity – a rare breed only seen in fairytales.

The financial buyers, mostly credible private equity firms, were experienced in providing growth funding and promised rapid expansion. This group had a flexible approach to structure, but were unlikely to offer the high valuations typical of synergistic trade buyers. However, the financial buyers could invest for three to five years, and then orchestrate a lucrative exit event for all parties.

I was upfront early that the right offer must include options for franchisees to either remain status quo or roll up into the parent entity. Andrew remained firm that the way to maximise network value and reach the higher multiples of profit was going to be through exercising my legal right to call-in franchisees under our buy back clauses. This action would compel them all to participate in the transaction, even if they didn't want to. I was adamant that such a forceful move was a last resort, and would only be considered if the far majority of our franchisees wanted the deal on the table but were being held ransom by a handful of resistors – as I couldn't allow a few reluctant participants to cost the entire group the pay day everyone else had worked for. Otherwise, I urged PwC to be more creative in their discussions with potential buyers, pursuing the elusive dream of keeping everyone happy.

PwC projected an achievable sale price of $45 million based on prior market performance and my minimum price threshold. We agreed to a six-week schedule of pre-marketing, another month of buyer engagement, with likely execution happening two months after we shortlisted whatever final offers in hand. I signed the mandate letter, and so began the high stakes game of corporate chess.

Nobody was prepared for what unfolded next - least of all, me.

117
project locomotive

FROM MY EARLIEST days conducting staff inductions for new physiotherapists, I used the metaphor of a train journey to illustrate our path. The tracks were laid, our destination clear. I emphasised that, if at any point, they felt their jobs weren't taking them where they wanted to go, they could pull the signal cord and disembark at the next station. I pledged to celebrate their contributions as they moved on, assisting them in catching a different train heading in their preferred direction. I also cautioned against expecting our tracks to bend to individual preferences – as accommodating personal detours wasn't a feasible plan on trainlines.

In keeping with this metaphor, I dubbed our sale mandate *Project Locomotive*.

Paulina and I, along with the NSO, served as the driving force - the *locomotive* - pulling the group forward. However, like a steam engine purposed by its carriages, our leadership was nothing without the individuals we guided and served. My mission was to bring everyone on our journey, making every effort to be all-inclusive unless someone chose otherwise. The most junior or newest team member, who might have felt like they were riding in the last seat of the little red caboose, was still hitched to my train. In this project I was determined to provide for them as much as anybody else.

The kick-off meeting in the first week of October 2020 involved the full PwC M&A team. We reviewed the transaction timetable and key tasks, took a shallow dive into our business and franchise structure, and looked at our past performance and future outlook. I received a cautionary heads-up about the impending flood of Requests for Information (RFIs) that were about to inundate me – a relentless stream of demanding inquiries resembling a food order catering to an insatiable crowd. I received numerous RFIs a day for more than three months as the team scurried to learn every aspect of our business, triangulate the unknowns, and respond to buyer queries. Meanwhile, I was left scrambling from spreadsheet to email, late into most evenings.

I brought Clive into the picture early. More than a tax expert in large and complex transactions, he was a trusted friend whom I relied upon deeply. I was confident in his ability to craft diverse tax and transactional structures optimal to the different appetites of each possible sale model.

At this point, everything was happening under the cover of darkness. I had not disclosed to any of my management team or franchise network that a silent auction for our business was underway. All my meetings were held by video conference from my home office, conducting the biggest deal of my life while in pyjama pants and Ugg boots hiding just below the screen shot of my laptop camera.

My secrecy meant I also had to field most of the initial queries myself, despite having long moved past being responsible for administrative and financial controls of our business. Shortly into the process, I realised I needed to bring my most senior executive, Dan, and a few other key members of my leadership team, into a limited scope of Project Locomotive – as they held the keys to the information banks I was needing to access daily. I also contracted Peter, an external financial analyst, to ride shotgun with me, removing a huge weight off my shoulders early in the piece.

It was just as well I had Peter in the second chair as, by early December, I fired my resident CFO for failing to heed his own internal financial controls, authorising an unrecoverable $75,000 payment to a bogus supplier invoice. Whilst the fraud was somewhat sophisticated, it was a completely preventable error if he had only followed the very process to which he held others accountable. By no means his first misstep, this latest gaffe was too big to go unnoticed by the swarm of forensic accountants pouring over our numbers and wanting explanations for every jot and tittle in our spreadsheets.

My corporate finance team put together an executive overview of the business for potential investors – a presentation covering all aspects of our services, franchise analytics, contractual terms, and financial performance. The pressure was on me, however, not just to deliver robust financial information on the NSO, but on every practice location. This was especially problematic because half of our franchisees had opted over the years to do their own bookkeeping rather than rely on our centralised accounting function. Their choice of bookkeeping systems presented varying degrees of compliance and order - some so unkept and disorganised that their balance sheets represented a negative value despite enjoying healthy businesses with strong asset registers and year-on-year profits.

Because of this, franchisees were at risk of missing out on enormous value if they couldn't get their numbers in shape. Many of them didn't know how to properly show the impact of the COVID-19 government subsidies, such as JobKeeper and Cashflow Boost incentives, skewing their figures in hideous ways. They also hadn't normalised their accounts for other irregularities or personal expenses, reducing their overall profit numbers and likely valuation. Expediency to fix all this was a priority, and I put as many resources as possible to assist franchisees to get their houses in order.

We eventually integrated all this information into a digital visualisation tool and interactive dashboard containing every practice within the network. This was an extensive undertaking, complete with financial performance, operational indicators, and geographical attributes allowing bidders to curate our information in a dynamic and meaningful way.

The data packs and financial models continued to grow as we developed five-year projections and populated an online data room that eventually held thousands of individual documents. I could track users in and out, and how many times various files were accessed, revealing a pattern of who was interested in what information, tipping me off to what else I might need to provide to strengthen our proposition to eager suitors. Owning our own proprietary software proved to be a huge advantage to me, tailoring hundreds of reports needed to dissect our business analytics across every imaginable permutation for the different buyer requests.

HEALTHFORCE DIDN'T WANT to get embroiled in a sealed-bid auction where competitive tension would pressure them to improve their offer, but they also feared bowing out early and foregoing the potential prize. Complicating matters, HealthForce's co-founder, Barry, was running his own parallel market process, looking for an investment partner to allow him and his shareholders to take some cash off the table. They were further along their timeline than me, already accepting offers before we officially went on the market. It seemed a conflicted space for both of us to be posturing a merger while we had representations within the same universe of possible buyers.

Both Barry's and my advisors kept their respective strategies guarded, obscuring any helpful collaboration. It felt like either of us could have ended up on the buy or sell side of a deal with the other, but in fairness to the formal and unbiased process we had both initiated in the open marketplace, we agreed to pause all discussions, parting ways unless circumstances naturally brought us back together.

JUST BEFORE CLOSING out for Christmas, at a cost of $250,000 and adding another six weeks to our bidding timeline, I commissioned an exhaustive Vendor's Due Diligence (VDD) report. This required an independent forensic auditor to test the veracity and accuracy of our data ensuring I was not guilty of any false representations.

My last communication received from the PwC team before flying the family to Tasmania for some remote wilderness hiking, was the first glance at the confirmed list of interested buyers. There was an exciting mix of predictable trade and financial bidders, and many new and surprising prospects I never had expected might harbour an appetite for a business like ours.

My emotions swirled in a kaleidoscope of excitement, pride, and a touch of apprehension. For the first time ever, I conceded to the certainty of a sale – and couldn't resolve exactly how I felt about that.

118
timely leak

WALKING THE WILD and inspiring alpine park of the Walls of Jerusalem in the world heritage Tasmanian wilderness, was a welcome break from the M&A blood sport I had been playing for the last three months at home. Its labyrinth of highland lakes, craggy mountains, and elegant strands of pure pencil pine forests took my mind off the turmoil... *mostly*.

As I returned into the range of cellular signal, my phone buzzed like SOS messages coming from the front line. The list of interest in our business had grown substantially, especially with our commercial materials now in wide, albeit secretive, circulation. I returned to an inexhaustible onslaught of emails from PwC advisors, whilst still juggling over 140 practice locations dropping in and out of lockdowns, contending with varying state legalisations as they complied with safe COVID-19 procedures. I couldn't afford to let our business suffer a downturn when we were grooming it for optimal profitability ahead of a promising sale.

By February, I had almost forgotten what the family looked like, except for their friendly faces poking around the corner of my study door as I hosted what seemed an endless loop of video conferences.

Fortunately, the kids were thriving at school and with their sport despite the COVID-19 disruptions. Lachlan continued playing soccer in the National Premier League and coaching one age group lower, as best he could in between forced lockdowns. He landed a job at Bunnings, and soon received his learner's permit to drive the family car.

Sebastian, at fourteen years of age, had launched a short modelling career, appearing in a few television commercials and print campaigns. He also worked part-time at our small technology company, getting an early appreciation for the value of a dollar earned.

Not to be outdone, Morgan kept up his soccer momentum with the National Premier League, became sports captain in grade six, and graduated primary school as Athlete-of-the-Year, like his older brother had done before him.

Paulina excelled, as always, in her various volunteer roles and keeping our family together as I kept tooting the horn of Project Locomotive.

PWC COMMISSIONED SOFT market soundings with nine hand-picked leading bidders to ascertain the value range and offer parameters they were thinking. It was a fishing expedition, intended to get early indications about the structure and terms each was contemplating. General consensus from the handful of sophisticated buyers sampled was they favoured a corporatisation involving some or all of the franchisees, not unlike the model put forward originally by the large hospital group.

Shortly after receiving this feedback, still under the cover of darkness, the speed dating began. I fielded questions from dozens of interested parties. Their chairmen, CEOs, chief investment officers, and all their counterparty advisors, trawled through our information and wanted a first jump at possible deal terms. They wanted to know my story: *Why was I selling? How did we perform through COVID-19 disruptions? What corporate structures was I considering in the new era moving forwards? How did we differentiate ourselves from other allied health groups? What is the basis of our sustainable growth over 20 years with better-than-average profitability?* I was in the hot seat with new scrutineers every hour for weeks on end, showcasing our best attributes but trying not to look too desperate or needy.

Enterprise valuations being offered at the time exceeded my early expectations, although they were far from being substantiated in the formative stages. There was a lot of chest-beating and ego posturing going on amongst the movers and shakers, who seemed to know each other better than I knew any of them.

Excluding unsuitable candidates was more important than pinpointing the "right" one at this early juncture. It was going to be impossible to pick a winner from such a diverse range of interested parties unless I could de-thatch the field and narrow my options. Fortunately, I had a precise profile for exactly what Paulina and I sought, compelling me to regularly cross-reference our predetermined wish list with the diverse array of prospects.

THE BIDDER INTEREST in early February was frantic, and the clandestine activity made me feel increasingly uneasy - as I hadn't properly disclosed to my team or franchisees any of the developments. I was also juggling negotiations to acquire several small independent podiatry and chiropractic practices, of which none were aware of Project Locomotive.

As industry activity heated up, I became more nervous that an inevitable leak was going to blow my cover and create unwanted suspicions in our network. I urged my board and advisors to allow me to disclose to my stakeholders the overview of Project Locomotive, preserving trust and transparency. The PwC team was especially hesitant about this, as I had signed confidentiality agreements with all bidding parties, and over-disclosure could be very damaging to the process they were running.

Franchisees had proven they were not all equal. Some, in fact, had shown extreme naïvete in how commercial and legal matters worked, and could say the wrong thing. And then, of course, there were our obvious adversaries, who would stop at nothing to sabotage or undermine our efforts if they knew of our pending transaction. The strong and consistent message from PwC was "say nothing" but, with the board's support, I couldn't remain silent.

I pulled the NSO team into the board room to give them a heads up on what was coming. In strict confidence I outlined my commitment to #IMPACT2030, showing the different projects I was working on in osteopathy, podiatry, and chiropractic, and how they all fitted like jigsaw puzzle pieces into the big picture. I recapped what they already knew about recent flattering offers from Advent Health, HealthForce, and the international hospital group, before then carefully introducing them to the language and objectives of Project Locomotive. I provided high-level market feedback that affirmed our brand was respected in the sector, being the only true national network. The public opinion clearly showed we were outperforming competitors on most KPIs, had superior technology, and proven resilience in the face of COVID-19. Without disclosing any of the bidders, I mapped out the spectrum of possible deal models, assuring everyone I was still a long way from a decision-point.

Some admittedly felt confused by the volume of information, but most expressed overwhelming excitement and intrigue for the possibilities. I fielded an hour of questions from my NSO team, encouraging them not to be distracted from their daily workflow as I continued to explore and probe the underbelly of opportunity. The team were united and brimmed with confidence that the franchisees would respond similarly.

Just as I was preparing to share a similar script with our franchisees, my worst fear was realised. A story about our pending sale broke in the *Australian Financial Review*, a reputable and credible masthead that caught the attention of commercially-minded observers. Fortunately, it was a positive piece, and probably gave us a little more promotion in some corners of the finance world, but timing with these things is everything. Titled, *Physio group Back In Motion pitches PE for leg up*, the article named Quadrant Private Equity, the Riverside Company, Crescent Capital Partners, and Adamantem Capital as likely contenders. The reporters didn't reach out to me for a comment on the article, which meant I wasn't guilty of breaching any non-disclosures. However, the news travelled the grapevine to the franchisees in record time.

I wrote to the network the same day to nip rumours in the bud. I confessed my disappointment that I had not been consulted on the piece, as I felt there were some corrections required to obvious misrepresentations. That said, it wasn't a crisis, and I simply pivoted it into a segue for an upcoming special meeting I had already called, planning to reveal to them more details. In hindsight, the leak probably helped my messaging as, with the secret out, I had more freedom to share the context around our project with no risk of being liable for breaking commercial confidence.

Unsurprisingly, I got close to total attendance the following week for the all-franchisee Zoom meeting. I had invited spouses and life partners to attend, being only the second time I had called an out-of-hours gathering in 20 years – the first during the initial outbreak of COVID-19. I opened with the observation that, whilst 2021 had been heralded to become the most *unpredictable* year for many business operators in successive generations, our ability as a group to bounce forward out of the pandemic promised some incredible upsides.

I reminded them of their feedback to me back at the 2018 Franchisee Summit, where 72% of the 67 franchisees at the time had pressed me to move into broader allied health services, including podiatry, chiropractic, digital health, and home care. A little over half had also expressed specific interest in our possible merge with another health group or private equity investor to accelerate our growth, and maybe even an IPO. Most notably, 40% wanted to consider selling their practice into a corporatised parent entity to realise their premium value. It was a solid starting point for our conversation, noting the tribe had spoken so clearly years earlier.

I laid out the tracks that Project Locomotive was running along; explaining we were picking up steam, but still had many stations to pass through. Keeping with the metaphor, I cautioned there were going to be turntables and central hubs at various points where I would need to align the group and consider the collective direction. But I reiterated my objective: bring everyone on the journey for as far as they wanted to come.

I encouraged the franchisees to dream the impossible and remain focused on the outcome. I talked through the various iterations of a deal, including a simple minority divestment of part of the NSO to raise capital to invest into our group, through to a full sale of the NSO which would imply a new franchisor. As practice owners, they could also consider selling a minority stake in their local business or roll up their ownership into a corporatised entity. We could remain a franchise under some offers already received, or de-franchise our group under others. Payment for their value could be in either cash or scrip of a parent entity, and likely some combination of both. I assured them all that the final deal matrix, if there was even one to present, would be an iterative process requiring multi-stakeholder input before any decisions could be made.

To assure stability, I presumed our brand wouldn't change; I would continue as their Group Director during any likely transition; the NSO team would grow; Evo would remain in situ; and our day-to-day operations would continue on plan. I acknowledged the different ages and stages of each franchisee, the spectrum of risk profiles they each represented, and varying group tenure and vintage to consider. I explained the scope of valuations that each of their practices might attract, and the importance of cooperating with our specialist team of accountants for site-specific reconstruction of their accounts for due diligence.

I closed out the session with another live poll, collating their preferences toward Project Locomotive. The first snapshot showed only about a dozen franchisees being reluctant to get on the train at all, the balance equally split between their desire to divest a minority or majority interest in their practices.

It seemed inevitable to me after that first night, my people were *on board*. This was going to happen! It was just a matter of when and with whom… and, of course, for how much.

119
cracking the valuation code

MARCH WAS A blur with PwC scrambling to build a three-dimensional data cube for second stage buyer due diligence and the VDD report growing in scope and complexity. It soon included an exhaustive analysis of customer buying behaviour insights, these in-depth details defending our business case for future maintainable earnings over coming years. The rabbit holes were long, deep, and convoluted, and I got lost in them from time to time, sometimes not surfacing for days.

It was like a game of Whack-a-Mole, constantly addressing new requests from bidders and their experts, alongside fielding questions from our franchisees who now knew just enough information to be dangerous and anxious. All this complexity unfolded over video conference and telephone calls as COVID-19 restrictions made face-to-face interactions impossible.

With every new balance sheet that was cleansed at the local practice level, our network analytics became clearer, as did the enthusiasm within the buyer's universe. At the evening meal, when Paulina would ask which prospects were still on the short list, I could barely keep track of the different investment firms or healthcare competitors I had spoken to that day. To avoid any embarrassment during upcoming video conferences, I meticulously updated a spreadsheet with key names and their corresponding roles and companies. This preparation was vital to me giving the impression during each conversation that it was the most crucial meeting of my day.

Fortunately, despite the growing preoccupation with numbers, dashboards, and analytics, our network continued to grow, posting a record sales performance in March 2021 of nearly $60 million pro rata. All credit went to Dan for his operational leadership, keeping the NSO team aligned and motivated for in-practice sales, and Justin who continued to keep us safe and compliant while trading under the different COVID-19 permutations. With only a few exceptions, all practices exceeded their prior year performance, and most exceeded February's sales. This result was pleasing given how large a chunk of the rolling 12 months was negatively impacted by hard, extended, and snap lockdowns across the two countries. It was helpful trajectory, and one I took enormous delight in sharing during the buyer update meetings.

I ARRANGED A second formal meeting of franchisees in early April to introduce to them my PwC advisors and give an update on our progress.

Jame, my board chairman, who had managed many large mergers and investment transactions in his time, opened the forum with comments about the level of difficulty and complexity we were facing. He encouraged franchisees to be patient and measured in their expectations around both timelines and price. I spent the second half of the night acknowledging that, with more than 90 prospective buyers, and in excess of 20 written formal expressions of interests, the likelihood of completing a deal that year was probable. Like a suburban auctioneer, I proudly announced: "The reserve price has been met, the business is on the market, and it will sell today".

I also explained that we had narrowed the preferred transaction structure down from over eight variations to two serious considerations. The first was a corporatisation event, whereby the franchisees and NSO would merge into a new aggregated entity, effectively de-franchising. The alternative option was that we sold the NSO only, and the network continued to function as a franchise system with individual local equity holders continuing in their respective practices, much the same way they currently were.

Of most importance to everyone was how buyers were valuing the network – individually and collectively – and how that methodology affected what they would be paid. In the Back In Motion online chat rooms we established, franchisees had been venting extensively about this issue. One franchisee was creating unrealistic expectations, citing that unless he received 15 to 17 multiples of his profit, he would not be participating – an outrageous benchmark to be targeting.

The unprecedented success I achieved with the sale of Revita and Actif were both atypical and unhelpful to rationalising people's expectations now. The underlying business models of those two sub brands relied on very different attributes, and I cautioned the group to be more realistic in what could be achieved. I shared publicly available data PwC had analysed, demonstrating the market was trading between two to four multiples of ordinary profit. Whilst I explained we should do better than this, because we were the largest and strongest performing group in the sector, I didn't want the bar set unreasonably high such that people missed a premium valuation when it was offered. Nonetheless, furore exploded over the valuation process that night, and understandably continued for some weeks.

I have learned over the years that profit multiples are not always a good basis for accepting fairness in a valuation. A high multiple of a low profit might equate to the same payload generated from a low multiple of a high profit. So, multiples alone are unhelpful unless you also secure the right profit threshold. And "profit" is an ambiguous term – taunting markets since the dawn of trade, masquerading in whatever form the beholder wishes to believe. I encouraged franchisees to be more focused on the actual dollar price they were hoping to achieve for their business and be relatively indifferent to the algorithm we used to generate their end number. I argued to them that the process shouldn't matter if I could secure them a price equal to, or better than, what they felt they deserved.

I inherently understood the difference between balance sheet value and strategic value in any business. The former reflects the net worth of the assets after removing the liabilities, approximating what is commonly known as "book value". Strategic value is the amount someone is prepared to pay for your distinct commercial advantage – be it speed to market, intangible benefits of brand and culture, a springboard for accelerated growth, or other factors that are uniquely attractive to selective buyers. The bottom line: the higher the perceived upside to the buyer, the more they might be prepared to pay above balance sheet value.

I diligently positioned our franchisees for optimal strategic value, emphasising to them the importance of collective participation. I made it clear that the more franchisees involved in the transaction, the higher the eventual payout for each of them. Fortunately, most grasped the logic of my simple math.

120
the shortlist

MOMENTUM WITH PROJECT Alignment was building month on month. In addition to six completed acquisitions during the first year of the pandemic, I was concurrently assessing with Martin five new separate targets, predominantly with integrated physiotherapy and chiropractic service offerings, showcasing their homogeneity on scale. Collectively, the practices represented another $11 million in annual revenue with more than a 25% drop to the profit line – further driving my perceived valuation in the active bidding war at play.

By early May, our team efforts were vindicated. The first non-binding offers rolled in from the most interested bidders like perfect waves for the patient surfer who had paddled hard to wait behind the breakers. I was elated with the substance of both price and terms, and believed a conclusion was imminent.

Our VDD report – all 87 pages of detailed financial disclosure – was distributed to the dozen leading bidders to progress to final stages of negotiation. Despite the "friendly fire" from PwC analysts, and the exasperating rigour I had endured to defend our numbers, the outcome was spectacular.

The difficult tension I struck was when many of the leading bidders wanted exclusivity on the deal. Naturally, I wasn't prepared to offer this right to any single party until I had full visibility to the complete suite of offers and could choose my preferred candidate. The best I could do was offer buyers a non-exclusive "favoured nation" undertaking, agreeing not to provide any other party unique or special concessions that would amount to a competitive advantage in the bidding process. Most were appeased with this, confident the business would not be sold out from under them before given a fair opportunity to put forward their knockout bid.

Through a structured process of elimination, I had whittled the complete list of potential partners from more than 90 candidates to 21 of the most credible and appealing offers. By late June, only three remained on my shortlist.

Paramount amongst the critical terms of our final deal was the flexibility I could offer my franchisees to either participate in full, opt for a partial sale in their local practice, or remain as a franchisee and not be disrupted in any way.

Further to this, I had spent 20 years promising that as we built scale together, the reward one day would be an above-average valuation. I wanted to make sure the strike price for each of the individual practices was a premium on whatever any single location or independent practice owner might achieve on the open market.

Thirdly, I stressed that unprofitable practices needed a unique valuation methodology to recognise their tangible assets and to garner a deferred payment on future performance at agreed milestones of their first, second, and third anniversaries, depending on the specific circumstance of each business. I could not allow those franchisees who had just launched their business, or fallen on hard times in the recent pandemic, to be penalised for the unfortunate timing of a deal that might otherwise suit everyone else. They needed an offer that motivated them to trade out of their slump, and be rewarded commensurately when they do so.

All three offers still on the table assured these terms, and so much more.

In fact, when Paulina and I compared the available terms against the wish list we had constructed nearly a year prior, all of the buyers qualified. That is, every expectation, as unrealistic as it seemed at the time of its conception, were met or exceeded in the term sheets of the three surviving options, confirming for me God's clear endorsement to proceed.

Of course, the only downside to having three compelling opportunities is making what seems an impossible choice. As I went to the weekend, Andrew urged me to return on Monday having decided the leading candidate - our Chosen One.

BEFORE I COULD decide, we hit a small bump. Warren, my cornerstone advisor – a genuine Harvey Specter – and the technical architect of the deal, fell out with his law firm. Whilst he did everything he could to shield me and our transaction from the possible fallout, the internal politics resembled an episode from *Suits*, distracting him and putting us at risk.

Not wanting to swap out legal counsel in the 11th hour, and counting Warren as a friend, I stuck by him as he continued to oversee the complexities of our negotiations while managing his own stresses. Fortunately, after a mediation session with his firm, Warren and his partners agreed to a swift and confidential resolution, enabling Warren to see Project Locomotive through to the end under the banner of another firm.

AS PAULINA AND I sat together on the Friday evening perusing the three outrageous offers scattered in front of us, we were perplexed. There was one superior proposal in terms of price alone, and another one that ranked better in terms of the flexibility it offered our franchisees. The third bid was a contender because it was a competitive blend of the other two, but slightly inferior on both attributes. The decision was daunting, each option carrying its own advantages and nuances. Distinguishing the top candidate solely through a logical decision matrix proved to be as challenging as choosing between your three favourite ice cream flavours – an agonising task of equal allure and difficulty.

I prayed for clarity and guidance.

God was merciful that weekend. By Saturday evening, I received a call from Andrew informing me that the Australian CEO of one of the bidders had convened with his German parent board on the Friday night, and their global chairman was concerned that the timing was wrong to bring another brand into their portfolio. They rescinded their offer.

So, then there were two. *Thank you, Lord.*

By Sunday afternoon, I received an updated term sheet via email from one of the remaining bidders. The revisions were minor, a nuanced adjustment in the language concerning the opt-in requirements for franchisees interested in joining the deal. Although these changes didn't affect the commercial price, they subtly hinted at the bidder's likely intent to preserve their rights regarding the unilateral call option in our franchise agreement. This suggested a possibility that franchisees not complying with the new owner's directives might face the risk of being bought out at later stage, conceivably against their will.

As I closed my laptop after reading the email, I looked up at Paulina with a ridiculous boyish grin. God had just nudged me in the direction of the single leading offer; I jumped on it as the confirmation I had prayed for. Later that evening, having chosen one bidder out of 90 options, I forwarded Andrew a signed binding agreement to sell our business on terms that made me a little bit giddy.

The next morning, I called the same PR and crisis management consultant who had guided me through the delicate Senate Inquiry, our arduous ACCC investigation, and had helped manage the long list of trolling franchisees. It was a pure delight to be reaching out on this occasion with a brighter, more hopeful theme. I briefed him in confidence on the developments of Project Locomotive and commissioned a content and communication strategy soon to be released to our network.

It was time to let the genie out of the bottle.

121
central station

THE LOCOMOTIVE PULLED into central station on the evening of the 12th of July 2021, marking it our third franchisee meeting of this project. It was by no means the end of the line, but an important junction with a significant turntable that might disorientate some people if I wasn't careful.

Paulina and I had met with my executive team that morning to bring them up to speed on the status of the deal. For the first time, I disclosed the successful candidate in our silent bidding contest. Their unreserved enthusiasm for the chosen buyer buoyed me as a I prepared for the tougher audience awaiting me that evening - our franchisees with more to gain, and arguably greater amounts to lose, if I picked the wrong winner.

As was habit throughout this transaction, I put out an email to a small group of trusted friends and family who were committed to praying on my behalf. With no details, I simply shared with them the significance of the meeting I was about to host. I believed God had faithfully led me through the process, albeit the journey was full of extreme and mixed emotions. Equally, I knew there was spiritual opposition that might try to undo me. I asked my friends to stand with me in prayer, believing God would keep Paulina and me aligned, connected, and healthy at home as we took the courageous and irreversible step of affirming the sale intentions with our network. I especially wanted to cement trust, unity, and enthusiasm with our franchisees, ensuring naysayers, dissenters, and objectors were marginalised. I sought supernatural physical stamina to not buckle under the workload, anticipating the final phase and eventual completion of our transaction had a long road still to travel.

I LAID OUT all the details for our franchisees and their spouses on my most important video conference yet. Because of market sensitivities, and the risk of people trading with inside information, I had to take a register of attendees on the night and give a verbatim legal disclaimer as prepared by our lawyers. After eight months of wading through countless hypothetical scenarios and fielding daily questions from persistent franchisees in our online chat platform, it was a relief to finally give them unfiltered clarity and certainty of my decision.

I warned the franchisees it was a complex consideration. The legal, commercial, financial, tax, operational, and even emotional layers would likely reveal huge differences of opinions, and were high stakes for everyone. I humoured with them that if this was an Olympic diving event, my routine would carry a nine out of ten level of difficulty – something akin to a reverse four-and-a-half somersault tuck, transitioning through the pike position, with a half-twist, and silly salmon tacked on the end just for laughs. I wasn't looking for their sympathy, but more so their patience and understanding as I stepped through the detail with them.

My objectives were clear: I wanted to identify the best partner for our long game and present an opportunity that everyone was excited for. I considered our values, cultural history, and strategic intentions as I negotiated optimal value for every franchisee, especially given they weren't at the table speaking for themselves. I traded off the delicate balance between price and other terms, to secure a deal that I could look at them square in the eye and believe was in their best interests – both now and in five years' time.

To many, my decision felt like an arranged marriage. Certain franchisees may have favoured the allure of stumbling upon love organically, opting to select their own local partner through serendipitous encounters. Problem is, it couldn't have happened that way for a group of over 80 individuals. I took some encouragement from the fact that arranged marriages, still common in many cultures around the world, have a higher statistical likelihood of not ending in divorce than those who make individual free choices. In fact, marriages that really thrive are those that involve both the parents and the couple in their decisions around compatibility and future direction, as it brings objectivity to the vital emotions, creating a potent alloy of perspectives and feelings.

Regardless of how this arrangement was perceived, Back In Motion was *engaged* to its future *partner* the moment I signed a binding term sheet. The *wedding date* was set for the 1st of October 2021, and the *invitations* were starting to go out. The apprehension on the call was natural, given most of the *extended family* hadn't met the *groom* yet.

With suspended breath, I dropped the bombshell and advised that we had chosen Healthia Limited as our new business partner. Healthia, trading on the ASX, represented more than 30 respected health brands, most of them local and small. They had launched into the marketplace only three years prior, in 2018, with an initial public offering that simultaneously acquired 104 practices in podiatry and physiotherapy predominantly. Approximately a year earlier, they had added a boutique optometry network. As of December 2020, Healthia boasted a strong shareholder base with a market capitalisation of $185 million and an enterprise value of $235 million.

Healthia was a choice partner because they represented the best overall fit, including providing alignment to our existing operational model and a shared commitment to (and therefore the greatest accelerator for) our #IMPACT2030 growth objectives. They were equally committed to both our Australian and New Zealand teams, where many of the bidders wanted to leave New Zealand behind. Healthia also offered one of the highest valuations in price, whilst preserving the greatest amount of flexibility for individual franchisees (including our small or underperforming practices), allowing each one to opt into the deal according to their level of comfort.

I didn't hide that my decision was a cost-effective way of launching Back In Motion onto the ASX through a legitimate back door, a feat that otherwise might have taken me a few more years to accomplish. In one seamless step, we enabled immediate shareholdings for anyone who wished to invest in the parent company, allowing staff, clients, friends, and families to participate fully in the growth story as they wished.

It was quickly obvious to me, through the pixelated images of hundreds of faces, that my announcement landed well on the night – many people visibly animated by the news, giving shout outs and thumbs up, accompanied by irrepressible grins that made their whole faces smile. I slumped in relief as I watched the wave of acceptance sweep across my screen.

Together with Healthia, we represented more than 350 locations. Our services would include everything we currently provided – physiotherapy, podiatry, Pilates, and chiropractic services – plus the additions of hand therapy, speech therapy, optometry, audiology, and occupational therapy. We were also to be immediately vertically integrated with an orthotics laboratory in the US and an allied health wholesaler of core products and consumables. Back In Motion and Motion Health brands were to be preserved as cornerstone businesses in the new integrated network, and our Evo software was to become the uniting platform for all disparate technologies. Together, we would make up about 3% of the $9.8 billion market in allied health – the largest by a huge margin – with enormous head room for further growth.

All the staff across our network were offered full continuity of employment under the same terms they were currently engaged. The NSO management team were to remain fully in place. My role was to pivot into an advisory capacity to the Healthia board, overseeing a small strategic portfolio of further business development. And best of all, every franchisee could choose their own adventure; they could stay as a franchisee, sell their practice, or pick a point along the sliding continuum between these bookends that best suited their circumstances.

There was an upside in the deal for everyone.

HEALTHIA OPERATED A partnership model rather than a franchise system. When acquiring businesses, they paid for part of the consideration in the form of Clinic Class Shares (CCS). This methodology provided the founders and vendors both capital rights on any further sale and dividend rights to a proportionate share of the profit performance of their local practice. For example, a franchisee of Back In Motion who previously owned half of their business in partnership with the NSO, would now own 50% of the clinic shares of the same location under Healthia, and receive a proportionate payment of the profits every quarter. If the local practice was ever transferred to another operator, they would also enjoy half of the proceeds on sale. It was a successful alternative to the extremes of pure franchising and mainstream corporate ownership, striking a favourable balance to most parties.

Founding chairman of Healthia, Glen Richards, was known to some of our group from his appearances on television. Lesser known was CEO, Wes Coote, with whom I had been engaged in most of the horse trading over the last few months. I was hopeful my people would like the new executive team and recognise them as sensible, relatable, passionate, and ambitious – qualities we found in ourselves.

The total value of the deal was a staggering nine-digit number if everyone participated, including deferred payments for high performances over a three-year time horizon and potential acquisition of the assets I lined up under Project Alignment and Project 10Toes. The sum far exceeded all previous independent assessments and was a significant margin above my personal expectations. Franchisees could elect to hold up to 48% ownership in their local practice if they wished and be paid a multiple of six times their normalised profit for the balance. This was the highest valuation Healthia had paid for any practice, and the highest I had observed anybody pay in the 20 years of trading community physiotherapy businesses. The offer was met with the appropriate gasp from most of my franchisees on the night, a fitting gesture to what had been a hard-fought and won battle at the negotiating table.

The final price was to be based on earnings up to and including June 2021, allowing each practice to bank the upside of an additional two months of growth trajectory coming out of COVID-19 lockdowns. If this wasn't enough to excite people, I also ensured the current royalty and marketing levies ordinarily paid under our franchise model, be added back to profit for the valuation on local practices, with a reduced management fee substituted in its place. The extra 4% that dropped to the bottom line equated to a 24% kicker in the final price because of the six times multiple that was then applied to it. Even those who were unprofitable had the rare privilege of banking the offer of six times their profit for up to three years, until they had earned their way out of a loss-making position, deferring the payment until it worked in their favour.

After trawling through nearly a hundred offers, I doubted anyone could find a better deal in the market. Nor did I think one this good would exist again in the next five years given the projected earnings of our sector and the general economic headwinds that were being forecast. The power of our group had afforded us a unique opportunity that was unlikely to be matched anytime soon, hitting the apex of the cycle.

As franchisor and partner in various local practices within our network, Paulina and I agreed to divest 75% of our personal ownership in exchange for a cash payment, transferring the balance of equity into shares in the listed parent entity, and clinical class shares into ongoing practices. Nobody could doubt my intentions – I put my money where my mouth was, the first stakeholder within our group to declare my commitment, regardless of who followed.

Having only scratched the surface on the detail with our franchisees that night, I provided a link to a comprehensive deal pack that included an outline of the commercial terms on offer, local practice valuation methodology, ongoing employment terms, tax and corporate structure implications, FAQs and proposed deal milestones and timelines. Ahead of the call, I also set up an automated calendar booking platform to allow franchisees to log in and reserve 20-minute appointments with me to work through their personal options and implications. I encouraged them to seek their own independent legal and accounting advice, and to bring their preferred advisors to the upcoming meetings to prepare for the mechanics of deal completion.

My final warning, at the close of the meeting, was to refrain from spending all the cash they thought they had just made, as there was a lot of work still to be done. Deals this complex can't be considered confirmed until the day after the cooling-off period has passed, and the sale proceeds have cleared in the bank accounts. There were a lot of steps to complete before pay day.

I slept well that night, a weighty burden ever so subtly lifting off my chest. The cat was out of the bag and, if I had read the room correctly, it seemed most of them loved the cute furball I had adopted.

122
yes-no-maybe

I ANTICIPATED A rush following my internal sale announcement, but I wasn't physically and emotionally prepared for the onslaught that hijacked my meeting schedule. I hosted 567 individual meetings over that six-week period – averaging 23 appointments a day, from as early as 6:30am through to 9pm, in twenty-minute intervals. Sometimes I hosted the same franchisee and their spouse, accountant, lawyer, or even parent or uncle, on consecutive days, up to seven times. I quickly became exhausted, waking up most mornings with a Locomotive hangover from the meeting bender the day before.

I was still limited to video conferencing as the only means of engaging with franchisees, courtesy of the stringent COVID-19 lockdowns in Melbourne. It saved me time by not travelling, but I had to contend with the impersonal, and often ineffective, channel of two-dimensional, granular laptop monitors to convey my sincerity that this deal was overall the best alternative for my people.

I developed a master spreadsheet with every franchisee's name and practice valuation, adding notes during each meeting on the questions they asked, unique deal anomalies, special considerations and, importantly, concerns and objections. To keep my assessment of group trends simple, I assigned an iconic traffic light colour to each file name as a reflection of their interest in taking the deal – green was *yes*, amber was *maybe*, and red was *no*.

In the first two weeks, as I met with every franchisee for the first time, the spreadsheet was awash with colours, like fairy lights on a Christmas tree. There was far more amber than I expected, and a few reds that caught me by surprise. As I tried to work patiently through each person's concerns and individual circumstances, call by call, every twenty-minutes, the filenames became greener. It was a major education campaign more than a negotiation. People were confronted for the first time with commercial terms and principles they had not yet learned about or understood the relevance of.

For example, I discussed the difference between an asset and share sale; I talked through the nuances of how to ethically normalise their financial statements and define what's in and what's out of profit calculations; I explained the deferred payment option for those who were not optimally profitable and might otherwise be selling prematurely if they took the deal; I had to factor capital gains tax into estimates of free cash post-transaction, and the differences in how a family trust might be treated in the transaction compared with that of a private company or partnership; and I mitigated concerns about the effective control Healthia might wield as the majority corporate partner. The complexity was numbing.

Endless consecutive sessions felt like scenes out of *Groundhog Day*, replaying the same conversation over and over. Each day carried immense weight, the discussions vital and consequential, yet the routine monotonous and taxing. Thankfully, within that initial month, it became clear to me I would succeed in bringing most people on the journey. With more than 80% of our group on board to do the deal, a sea of green lights flickered across my screen as I turned in for the night, prepped for a repeat of it all, starting early the next day.

WITH COVID RESTRICTIONS easing, I arranged a comprehensive road trip to visit all our operating franchisees over a two-week bonanza. In late July and early August, I planned to call on more than 50 locations in Melbourne, Adelaide, Perth, Gold Coast, Newcastle, and Brisbane, before a trip across the ditch, to Auckland, Wellington, and Dunedin in New Zealand. Wes originally planned to join me, but his partner had just given birth to their third son. He was spread thinly between completing the biggest transaction of his career and being present for those irreplaceable moments at home.

As it happened, Victoria went into another snap lockdown on the eve of my trip, the sixth of its kind, and so my travel plans were kyboshed. Instead of eyeballing people face to face like I had hoped, I was restricted to more video conferences all that fortnight, doing all I could to ensure important points were not lost in the pixelation and disrupted audio of the myriad of devices at the other end.

July through September were a blur. After having already met every franchisee and their advisors privately, together Wes and I did it all over again. With each meeting, we transitioned from the conceptual deal into the specifics of every unique case. Eventually, I was able to present the individual valuations to every franchisee, highlighting terms specific to their circumstances, and making small concessions when needed to ensure franchisees were comfortable. I ended up playing both sides of the fence at different times, sometimes advocating for my people, and other times acting as peacemaker and educator when I felt they were asking Wes for unreasonable demands.

Attempting to integrate Project 10Toes and Project Alignment into the deal flow pushed me beyond sanity. Whilst Wes tentatively agreed to incorporate as many new podiatry and chiropractic acquisitions as possible, the process felt like assembling a jigsaw puzzle with missing pieces and no reference image on the box. Every meeting with a prospective vendor seemed to distort the picture, leaving me perplexed about the end goal. Despite rallying a sizable group in Geelong, and a few new practices in Canberra, regional Victoria, and Christchurch, I realised in retrospect, that I had been distracted by the numerous possibilities. Only a handful of this tranche eventually managed to pass the rigorous due diligence, leaving many of the hopeful participators behind at the central station, never making it on the train after all.

Given our network comprised so many locations under different entities – the final architecture of the deal necessitated 64 standalone commercial contracts, each with their own anomalies and commercial idiosyncrasies. Accordingly, my inbox overflowed with multiple versions of different valuations spreadsheets, heads of agreements, salary reconciliations, normalisation schedules, inventory stock takes, draft business sale agreements, questions from advisors, and incessant requests to meet with franchisees multiple times over, after hours, on weekends, and late into the night.

The in-house counsel for Healthia was incredible, as she spun plates and juggled multiple balls in the air – a veritable circus act. She almost single-handedly coordinated the flow of paperwork between all parties when I didn't know which way was up. When Paulina poked her head into my home study to offer me food and drink, I was lost as to whether it was breakfast, lunch, or dinner. I had become one with my desk chair. The only times I seemed to have left the house was for a sanity walk with Slinky on those welcomed occasions when someone cancelled their appointment.

If all this wasn't complex enough, it soon became apparent that I needed to restructure my parent entities to transfer our proprietary software code and other intellectual properties, including trademarks and copyright materials. This required substantive work on everyone's part to create the right corporate vehicles to be established in readiness for the anticipated settlement.

As the closure on the Healthia deal lingered in waiting, each franchisee meticulously examined the details, increasing the likelihood that a few would grow hesitant. Just as anticipated, the initial and collective excitement for the opportunity began to wane, resembling pre-wedding jitters. Small groups of franchisees conversed, compounding their reservations. Some sought higher valuations, while others grew anxious about affiliating with Healthia's array of brands. Most were simply perplexed, grappling with the uncertainty of the future in contrast to the familiarity of their current situation.

Getting all my people to the starting line, and keeping them there, was like pushing a wheelbarrow of frogs around in circles. As I turned my attention to the one or two who jumped to the left, others hopped to the right. Herding cats would have been easier.

In late July, I was ambushed one evening by a somewhat friendly and good-spirited group – a syndicate of some of my largest practice owners. They had seemingly received joint legal advice and did not want to participate in Project Locomotive. The collective started down the familiar, well-trodden path of making thinly veiled threats about the ACCC unfair dealings and their rights to exit. I felt the temperature go up in the room immediately, wondering anxiously if this was going to be the undoing of everything I had worked so far to achieve. I silently prayed for wisdom and peace.

I promised to reflect on their requests and explore alternative pathways with my legal and deals team on their behalf. As it happened, without much intervention on my part, as quickly as the rebellion rose, it was snuffed out by its own means. I suspect the handful of franchisees who instigated the gambit took another look at their valuations and concluded they were unlikely to get an offer as good in the near future, if ever again. Some of their practices ended up selling for many millions of dollars, putting them near the top of the league table for industry records.

On reflection, it seems my most effective strategy for handling the varied objections levelled against the deal was simply to sit back and wait for reason to triumph.

In the end, only three franchisees unexpectedly hit the emergency stop, opting to disembark from the train. Each made an informed decision not to proceed with the deal, requiring me to devise special arrangements to honour their individual preferences. Despite the setback of losing these three, I managed to supplement our numbers by securing last-minute acquisitions and side deals, expanding our cohort for settlement beyond the initial count. The locomotive grew longer, the value soared higher, and momentum unmistakably swayed in our favour.

The end of the line was fast approaching.

123
panic-deletions

THE TRAIN ALMOST derailed in the final weeks with an unnecessary accounting scandal.

Our practice software kept an account of all prepaid and unused client services, including account credit and gift vouchers. The balance reflected the total value owed to the client – either in money or services – that had already been paid in advance. In accounting terms, these amounts were defined as a liability, not an asset. As a franchisor, I had chosen not to take a royalty on these payments until such time the services were rendered, thereby triggering the transfer of amounts from the liabilities of the balance sheet to income on the profit statement. This approach helped franchisees manage their cashflow in line with their cost base, but also encouraged some to leave as many of their account credits in liabilities for as long as possible, even after a client ceased attending the practice or after pre-paid packages had expired, indefinitely delaying any recognition of a payable royalty.

The problem now was these exaggerated liabilities worked against a practice valuation for sale. This realisation caused several franchisees to panic-delete account balances from their software, like some physiotherapy version of Enron, shredding every bit of evidence that might go against them under scrutiny.

Their basic strategy was to convert all unwanted client liabilities to recognised revenue by raising a faux invoice, and then credit noting the invoice to reverse the income. This shifted the net liabilities off the balance sheet, but prevented the money in bank from ever hitting the profit statement. Ingenious, if it wasn't so devious. Whilst some of this activity may have been prudent cleansing of inaccurate data – giving generous benefit of the doubt to a select few – most of it appeared suspicious adjustments to improve their valuation, potentially defrauding the purchaser.

Having been tipped off from some troubled franchisees, I investigated the matter in detail. Our accounting team ran a report on every logged adjustment to unused service packages, gift vouchers, and account credit for every patient that occurred across our entire network back to 2009 – establishing a trend line for normal activity on a per-practice basis. The search unearthed the disturbing likelihood of foul play.

We discovered the average monthly credit note total between 2009 and 2020 for the entire group was a meagre $5,300. The average monthly credit note total for the group in 2020 and 2021 was only slightly higher, at $6,500. Yet the credit noting for the single month of concern, being August 2021, peaked at $231,000, a whopping 35 times prior averages. The smoking gun was still red hot!

The illegitimate deletions of liabilities and use of false credit notes had some potentially serious implications morally, financially, and legally. It artificially inflated the net assets being purchased by Healthia; any underreporting of income could attract investigations and penalties from the ATO; it could also rob our clients of legitimate entitlements to future services – creating possible dispute and brand damage if a patient attempted to redeem their unused package, gift voucher, or account credit in the future; and if all this wasn't enough, these mischievous actions also defrauded the NSO of royalties I never received.

Our team targeted the six offending practices in the days that followed, working with them to reconstruct accurate balance sheets and client records, restoring original credit balances and practice liabilities. For everybody else, my warning was clear: no devious deletions or creative offsetting of unused packages with dummy invoices. The risk was not worth it.

It was a low point in Project Locomotive, and a stumble I couldn't afford so close to the end. Fortunately, we recovered well, most franchisees applauding the swift action, grateful that the deal was not jeopardised by an opportunistic few.

As often said, it's darkest just before the dawn.

124
miracles

AFTER ANOTHER MONTH of endless email enquiries, the last RFIs for the confirmatory due diligence, and the collation of literally thousands of separate documents that related to all the moving parts of our deal, I was ready to settle.

With a crescendo of paperwork on the final day, and a cacophony of advisors shuffling contracts in all directions to achieve a common end, I signed and exchanged the last binding documents to complete the transaction just before 10pm on Friday the 17th of September. Our model of sale effectively de-franchised our network, forming a new corporatised entity in which all former franchisees were now holders of a special class of shares in a wholly owned subsidiary of the listed parent company, Healthia.

Despite moving us out of the highly complex – and often controversial – sector of franchising, the sale enabled all our practice partners to retain, by choice, partial ownership in the businesses they operated. The final combined enterprise value of the transaction exceeded $100 million, providing $89 million upfront, and the balance in deferred or contingent consideration over the three years that followed. The payment we received was closer to 7.2 multiples of our profit (rather than the official rate of six originally offered by Healthia) after we had normalised various expenses and legitimately removed non-operational costs to boost our underlying earnings – a premium value by any standard.

Our entire workforce – from senior management through to the local practices – was retained on continuous employment terms, better than or identical to what they previously enjoyed. I was retained as an advisory consultant to the board of the parent company, two days a week for 12 months, to assist in the transition and integration of our business. Following that, I had few restraints to move on to new interests.

Aside from all this, I retained majority ownership of the Evo software code that underpinned the operations of the group, securing an ongoing source of revenue on an annual subscription basis.

Whilst a public announcement wasn't scheduled for release to the press until the following Monday, institutional investors caught wind of our sale early. They started leaking disjointed information through back channels and formal networks. The Healthia board issued a trading halt pending a formal announcement to the market. The move placed me and my franchisees in a blackout period for a few days where we could neither buy nor sell Healthia stock while the retail capital raise took effect.

That Friday night, Healthia's share price bumped nearly 12% on news of our signing, a new record price of $2.12, up from their original listing of $1.00 three years earlier. This uptick mildly worked against me in the strike price for the shareholdings I was about to receive as scrip in my sale proceeds, but a promising sign, nonetheless.

PAULINA AND I stared at each other in disbelief. At 46 years of age, what had taken over 8,000 days to build, was gone. We reached over to close each other's jaws as they both lay slack from a combination of exhaustion, exhilaration, and gratitude. Sitting in the home office where I had laboured for over a year in brokering the most difficult deal of my career against all odds, we put up a heartfelt prayer of thanks to our God of miracles.

Selling a business after years of relentless dedication and hard work proved to be an emotional odyssey that words struggle to capture. The journey was an intricate tapestry woven with passion, sacrifice, and unyielding commitment. Each thread represented late nights, early mornings, and countless moments of perseverance in the face of challenges. The decision to sell Back In Motion after enduring all that evoked a swirl of emotions that I cannot fully articulate – a blend of pride for what our team accomplished, a touch of nostalgia for the good times we enjoyed, and a hint of uncertainty about what lay ahead. It was a profound moment, marked by a bittersweet symphony of feelings that remain with me to this day.

Whilst there were too many miracles to count, it's important to try, so the memories stand as a tribute to God's faithfulness.

Paulina and I were reluctant participants in Back In Motion from the very beginning, believing God had marked our lives for cross-cultural missionary work rather than the marketplace. From our small carport in September 1999 to operating more than 140 practices spanning two countries, is an unlikely success that only God could have achieved.

A year earlier our board consented to selling Back In Motion for an agreed price if God made it possible. Overwhelmed with humility and awe, He delivered more than double the number we had earmarked.

We had agreed internally that a minimum of 80% of our franchisees needed to take up the sale offer for us to comfortably proceed. I feared at times this was an extremely high bar given the sensitivities of the deal and the mixed personalities, business stages, and personal circumstances of those in our network. There were no guarantees I could even get half the vote. As it turned out, despite three franchisees opting out, we ended up with more people participating in the sale than what I started with because of new businesses I onboarded throughout the process.

Numerous frustrations, missteps, disputes, and inconveniences with different advisory groups occurred throughout this marathon event – which is probably to be somewhat expected – but God prevailed, bringing resolution to all the outstanding matters in a way that was fair and acceptable to everyone.

COVID-19 lockdowns indiscriminately sweeping the nation could have caused us to miss sales targets, or at least shake the confidence of our buyers. Instead, our business continued to trade strongly throughout the worst affected states, growing year-on-year, bearing testament to God's care of every detail.

Right down to our share offering, God was in control. The stock in the parent entity had been volatile in response to Healthia's 2021 year-end results, still our strike price landed in an extremely favourable position that only God could know.

To prove God can multi-task in ways I only dream about, in my unrelated role as a non-executive director of an Independent Board Committee for the publicly listed dental group 1300Smiles (Ticker ONT), we simultaneously concluded another large transaction that had eluded us for years. Dr Daryl Holmes, founder and Managing Director of 1300Smiles, built a network of 33 dental practices, mostly in regional Queensland, and was seeking opportunities to either expand or divest. After enduring numerous setbacks, not unlike my experience with Project Locomotive, as a board we agreed to a Scheme Implementation Agreement with the Abano Health Group that rendered shareholders a windfall $8.00 per share (less a special dividend), up from the $0.80 listing price in March 2005. The deal amounted to a whopping $165 million enterprise valuation, which was 13 times the profit performance in 2020.

It was miraculous timing that the two biggest deals of my career ran parallel courses for over a year, culminating in a successful settlement within a month of each other.

As the congratulations poured in from people far and near, Paulina and I marvelled at the miracles of God. He had truly done the impossible, filling me with hope of a plan He must have for the years to follow, even if they were completely unknown to me at the time.

125
the long goodbye

OUR FRANCHISEES GATHERED in late September for me to address them as their Group Director and Franchisor for the last time. It wasn't a training or education session, nor an opportunity to Q&A the detail of the steps yet to transpire in the completion of each practice transaction. It was a night of celebration. An opportunity to acknowledge our 22 years together, raising our glasses to their future, and closing Project Locomotive properly.

Every great story has an ending. Just as we find satisfaction and fulfilment in a well-rounded tale or movie, so too do our businesses need closure. We often convince ourselves that brands and organisations should continue indefinitely, draped in the false honour of becoming an everlasting legacy. But just as they begin, great businesses can find their rest in a conclusion too, without negating the worth of their contribution while they existed. Our decade leading the SOS Health Foundation taught me this.

The 1st of October 2021 – the official settlement date of Project Locomotive – marked the end of an era, both collectively and personally, whilst heralding the seed of a new adventure.

I reminded our people gathered that night about the three things they regularly told me they loved the most about Back In Motion – (1) the common brand loyalty, (2) our business support services, and (3) the comradery we nurtured together. I was confident that, in the waves of inevitable changes to follow, these three things would continue.

It also seemed fitting to touch briefly on the two things they despised most about Back In Motion – (1) expensive royalties and (2) the limited, cumbersome exit options stemming from inter-related dependencies on brand and systems. It was a delight to boldly proclaim that both deterrents evaporated under the new model. The pivot into the new hybrid clinic class shares under the corporatised umbrella of Healthia did away with traditional marketing levies and franchise royalties, and simultaneously provided people the ease with which they could divest their business and chase other dreams whenever they decided.

On my final video conference, with more than 100 people present, Paulina and I popped a cork of bubbly while each one grabbed for their own glass of something. I opened the microphone for people to reminisce on their favourite memories, express their own gratitude, and cast vision for the hopes of our collective future. What I had scheduled for ten minutes in the agenda, quickly blew out to more than 40 minutes of spontaneous sharing, rating as one of my most treasured memories of my time in business.

In closing, I thanked my board and the NSO team, giving special mention to Dan for his faithful service over 18 years. I was incredibly grateful to all the franchisees who personally represented our brand every day with pride and consistency. I reserved my last comments for Paulina – words failing me on the night to convey the depth of my appreciation for her full contribution. She was, at least, equally responsible for everything we had achieved. Having worked just about every job in our support office over the years, and in many of our early practices, Paulina was (and remains) the most outstanding partner I could have been gifted. Every person on the call that night was a beneficiary of her patience, strength, counsel, caution, and faithful prayer. She is a keen strategist, matched only by her fierce compassion to help people. An unsung hero for most of our journey, Paulina was completely deserving of the highest credit.

OUR BANK ACCOUNT balance exploded in October when the sale proceeds landed, with too many zeros for me to capture in one screen shot on my mobile phone as I tried to memorialise the moment. Warren and his legal team showed up on our doorstep in a clandestine undercover operation to not spook the neighbours, as the COVID-19 lockdown provisions were still in full force. As the small team who had made most of the magic happen, we drained two bottles of Bollinger champagne in celebration of the moment.

Expectedly, the sale triggered the winding down of my advisory board. After sending Michael, Jame, and Neil gift packs to honour their incredible contribution to our business and family, we formally closed out their responsibilities and released them to other ventures.

At a celebratory dinner with my NSO team, it was hard to say goodbye to the many people who had invested so much of themselves. As a small gesture to ensure they felt included in the next chapter, Paulina and I gave each person a bonus cheque from the sale proceeds to buy direct shareholdings in the Healthia parent company or, if they preferred, do something more precious for their family.

And so began a festival of sorts.

We could not easily invite crowds to a special occasion, as the pandemic still loomed large. Instead, Paulina designed an intense schedule of intimate events, hosting small groups and, sometimes, just couples, on alternate nights for weeks on end as we met in our home and thanked people personally for their decades of support. Our kids got to share in some of these experiences, often sitting through the same stories multiple times over consecutive nights, but always looking enthusiastic and proud of what we had achieved as a family.

I spent the next three months facilitating the completion of all 64 separate transactions, settling them in weekly tranches of five to ten at a time, distributing the spoils of the sale proceeds to the eager franchisees just in time for Christmas. It was a thrill each time one of our people crossed the line. The grins on their faces were emphatic, as was the relief that washed over the rest of them. Most of our franchisees became overnight millionaires – and not just in balance sheet value, but hard cold cash that made them giddy with gratitude. As the money landed in all their accounts, it was a joy to observe how they each chose to celebrate the moment. Many took off on holidays, some buying new caravans and cars to travel our great country, others going overseas. Some paid off their home mortgages and enjoyed being debt-free with money to spare. Others diversified into other franchised businesses, while more than a few chose to invest their money into property freeholds. Most former Back In Motion franchisees took the opportunity to work a little less, for at least a season, with *#semiretired* appearing frequently in different social media posts and text messages for months on end.

The uncharacteristic white space in my diary was filled with a groupwide whistle-stop tour. As travel opened again around the country, Paulina and I attempted to visit many of our franchisees in person – something we hadn't been able do for well over 12 months.

It was a long goodbye, flying all over Australia and New Zealand, eventually taking us from December 2021 until August of 2022 to complete the final visits. There were days where we had breakfast, lunch, and dinner with three different couples, as we tried to make the most of every personal connection when we flew into different cities. Whilst we didn't get to everyone, it was an important way for us to close our journey in the same way we started – remembering that *people mattered* above all else and that without them, none of what we achieved would be possible or worth it.

126
closure

OUR SUITCASES SNAKED around the carousel at Tullamarine Airport as Paulina and I wearily returned from our last round of practice-visits in Auckland. We had just met our New Zealand team, quite possibly for the last time, and were anxious to hug and hold our kids who waited patiently for us at home.

As I walked into the crisp August night air toward where our car was parked, an alert on my phone calendar reminded me of a special church meeting we had been invited to - an evening with a handful of guest ministers. Despite feeling physically exhausted and emotionally spent, we agreed to drop by the church, honouring our commitment with a token appearance. We promised each other it would be a short visit, followed by an early retreat home.

Sitting a few rows back from the front, we periodically bumped each other to stay awake. Our bodies carried the exhaustion of a week spent traveling, and the cumulative toll of 22 years devoted to building our business. I became more alert when two of the guest ministers – whom we had never met before or since, and to our knowledge knew nothing of our back story – zeroed in on us.

The first put his hand on my shoulder and recounted a vision where he saw me engaged in mergers, acquisitions, and crucial negotiations – making high stakes business decisions, all with the motivation of serving poor communities in need. He encouraged me that God was pleased with me and had more assignments to come.

The second minister chimed in, sensing that both of us had been navigating a tumultuous season, thriving despite the challenges we faced. Directing her attention toward me, she described me as a "rollercoaster" guy (despite my abject fear of them), depicting me as someone who thrived on the thrill of the ups and downs; scaling impossible peaks and overcoming insurmountable obstacles. With confidence, she affirmed my relentless ambition and adventurous spirit as part of the nature of God, even if at times it pushed Paulina out of her comfort zone. She emphasised that the two of us were a gift to each other, carving out opportunities together to bring life, hope, and the sincerity of God's love, like missionaries in the marketplace.

These strangers couldn't possibly fathom the impact of their words. How could they know the journey we'd just completed, let alone understand the unfulfilled dreams of a ten-year-old boy still nestled deep within the recesses of my heart? Who could imagine the nagging heartache of disappointment I still felt from my early adulthood, falling short of my aspiration to become a missionary doctor, feeling I didn't meet God's high standard? So many years of my two decades in business had felt like treading water, biding time, hoping one day I might pass His intangible test. Over countless nights I begged God through tear-filled eyes to release me from the obligations of Back In Motion and send me abroad.

Now, the reassurance I received from friendly strangers was a testament to the unfailing nature of God's purposes and promises. It dawned on me that, indeed, Paulina and I were commissioned to be medical missionaries all those years ago, but not exactly in the way I had imagined. Our calling was to serve within our respective professions, tend to the needs of our workforce and clients, and extend our contributions to the broader business and neighbourhood communities where we lived and worked. We had scaled an ethically profitable national business, creating an economic engine to feed, clothe, educate, and serve the poorest of the poor, impacting numerous people around the world, our funds and experience making a difference where it counted. It became clear that God's plans for us were beyond our comprehension; His ways transcended ours. Where I felt overlooked, God had simply redeployed me for a mission I was better suited.

It struck me that there are truths we can only grasp when we look back upon our story from its conclusion, and sometimes we must rely on the observations of others to help us see them more clearly.

THE MOST COMMON question Paulina and I were asked in the wake of our sale of Back In Motion was: "What are you going to do next?"

It was a fair question from well-intentioned people who sincerely cared for us. However, having just finished a gruelling marathon, crossing the finish line with a record-breaking performance, all I could imagine at that point was a cold shower, a fresh change of clothes, and a foot massage. The thought of starting another race was very uninspiring.

Knowing it was healthy to temper ambition with contentedness, Paulina's wise counsel to me was to politely refuse every alluring opportunity that presented for at least one year. As unnatural as it felt, when the invitations streamed in for me to invest in other businesses, join different boards, coach executive teams, speak at industry events, or even travel to various mission fields, I reluctantly stuttered the words "No" – or at least, "Not yet". Paulina and I benefited greatly from lingering for those 12 months in a virtual decompression bubble, healing and recovering in ways we didn't even know we needed.

Henry Wadsworth Longfellow penned the words, "Great is the art of the beginning, but greater is the art of the ending". It has taken me some time to learn the importance of the latter, but the rewards have been worth it.

The second most common question asked of us was: "Do I miss Back In Motion?".

Paulina and I conceived the business in our early twenties – during the second year of our marriage – so Back In Motion was like a first born child. We cleaned up its messes, attended to its whims in the night, and eventually helped train and discipline it through its adolescence to grow into a mature and independent brand.

Do I miss it? Yes, but possibly not in the way you might imagine.

Lachlan, our eldest son, won a two-year college scholarship to play soccer in the US. It was a day of mixed emotions when he moved overseas to pursue his dreams; deep sadness that he won't be at our dinner table every night, but elation watching him stepping out, taking risks, and becoming his own man. In the same way, it was time for Back In Motion – our figurative first born – to move out. I still love the brand and people deeply – just like a parent adores their adult children, and even more so when they start producing grandkids – but I no longer feel responsible for the decisions the new owners make as the business moves on with its next chapter in life.

Paulina and I want to see Back In Motion thrive, and we will always be available to support from a distance when invited. Otherwise, we trust in the foundations that have been laid to guide its way forward.

In short, I am grateful for the "empty nest", and to cheer from a distance with no regrets over the sale.

THERE IS NO doubt that some days I still feel like an imposter – that the life I have reflected on, and written about in this book, must be someone else's tale. When hosts introduce me at events to share my story, I often cringe at the generous compliments and descriptions they flatter me with. Inside, I feel like a serial human accident who just keeps bumping his way through most situations, getting it wrong more often than I get it right. I've spent my whole life feeling like the underdog, working from behind the starting line, always trying to run and catch up. Figuratively, standing on my tip toes at the back of the photo pack, convinced I wasn't tall enough and couldn't be seen.

Like David in his epic Biblical battle with Goliath, I was an unlikely success. I am more surprised than anybody about the story I have lived – and now told. I don't feel like an entrepreneur, high-capacity leader, or whatever else people advertise about me in their magazine headlines and conference brochures. Most of the time I feel overwhelmed and inadequate in the face of the obstacles before me. I have been afraid for years that if people only knew my *real* story – the mistakes, regrets, and setbacks – they would see behind the many masks my roles have demanded I wear.

For those who have made it to the end of this prolonged and self-indulgent tome, the truth is now out.

But I am also learning that God sees me differently – not as an imposter, but "fearfully and wonderfully made" in His image (Psalm 139:13-16, Genesis 1:27 NKJV). I was created by Him for purpose, uniquely chosen to play a distinct role in a small scene of history that was scripted specifically for me. Every day presents opportunities to discover new insights into the person God intends me to become, fortifying me with enduring promise, lasting hope, and unwavering confidence. Not because of who *I* am, but because of who *God* is.

It reminds me of the passage in Scripture where God says He "chose the foolish of the world to shame those who think they are wise" (1 Cor 1:25-29 NKJV). He deliberately promotes "nobodies" into "somebodies". This is my story – and that of Back In Motion - where God called me as an inexperienced, foolish, weak, and unwilling agent to become part of an epic story that brings Him glory. My place of greatest pain became part of His greatest purpose. He did so much more with my "less" than I could ever have imagined.

AS PAULINA AND I eventually stumbled through the front door after our final trip to New Zealand – much later than expected but grateful for making the inconvenient detour via church – our bodies were limp, but our spirits energised. We gave each other a little pinch, almost in disbelief; the assignment of spearheading Back In Motion was complete. God seemed pleased and, most of all, He was not finished with us yet. If the uplifting words and heartfelt blessing we received that evening at church were indications of God's intentions, it seemed that exciting new opportunities to serve Him, and those around us, were perched on the horizon. But all in good time – for now, we yearned for deep, restorative sleep.

As I rested my head on the pillow and drifted towards slumber, cradling Paulina's soft and familiar hands, a heavy burden lifted. In its place, a divine peace settled over me like a warm, soothing blanket. In that fleeting moment, I hovered between the earthly realm and something ethereal, feeling weightless and serene. I knew this tranquil interlude wouldn't extend forever, yet I felt assured that, as the Sun rose the next day, fresh opportunities would greet me. The red dawn would signal the birth of a new season, promising more thrilling adventures to come, however *unlikely* they may appear.

FLASH-BACK

29th November 2001

"I hate business. No, I hate *our* business."
"People just take, take, and *take*. It's exhausting."
"This isn't even what I'm meant to be doing. I should be overseas, working with the poor, not stuck in this run-down hellhole of a practice. God has got this *so* wrong."

I MUTTERED CAUSTIC criticisms with hot venom to nobody specific as I parked our new campervan underneath the carport of our first home. To punctuate my indignant feelings, I used the vehicle to block the entrance to the sliding door of what was our original makeshift physiotherapy room, but now served as a small administration office for Paulina and her mum. It was my childish way of signalling a defiant protest to anyone coming or going.

I was eager to start planning. My ideal itinerary was a coastal crawl from the southernmost beaches of Victoria's Gippsland region through to the uppermost reaches of far north Queensland. If time permitted, given our proximity, it made sense to drive across to the Top End of Australia also, and drop back down through the Red Centre, enroute to home. I planned to be absent from the practice for at least three months.

"Should be enough time to cover the eastern half of Australia," I reasoned with Paulina. "And if not, we just keep going. Who cares?"

Part of the appeal of this get-away was not planning *too much* – spontaneity and improvisation, both alluring qualities of any extended road trip. But the greatest attraction of all was not having to spend another hour thinking about, or working in, our fledging practice, Back In Motion. I was 26 years old and already burnt out. I'd have happily given the business away to anyone who showed interest, and practically did when I handed the keys of our run-down, three-room medical centre to a Kiwi, someone who was not only new to the job, but new to our country.

"If the practice goes under while I'm away, I can blame it on the new guy."

My devious tactic was an attempt at strong-arming God into agreeing with my terms: abandon the business strategy and put Paulina and my healthcare training to good use in the developing world. It was a cunning plan, or so I thought.

On the eve of our departure, I surprised Paulina with a drastic makeover. After heading across the street just before dinner for a haircut from our neighbour, an unexpected radical urge to break free from my lifelong conformity overtook me. I had always adhered to rules, maintained a clean-cut appearance, was a square at school, and acted professionally at work. I mostly denied myself the indulgences relished in youth, and was afraid now that I had grown up too quickly.

In a rush of impulsive rebellion, I chose to bleach my curls and shave my head, leaving only a faint tinge of orange fuzz. It looked as ugly as it sounds, and every time Paulina looked at me for the next six weeks her brow furrowed in disbelief. But my unconventional haircut screamed a newfound attitude: I was going to live free and cut loose.

As some friends gathered to farewell us, Michael – who would become my lifelong mentor in faith and business – warned me, "You can run, but you can't hide…".

What does he think I'm running from? I quietly pondered, interjecting his cryptic assertion.

"…from God's call on your life", Michael finished his sentence, as though he could intuit my thoughts.

As you now know, I never wanted to be a businessman. Quite the opposite. I always thought God had prepared me for medical missions – learning an unknown dialect, sleeping in a grass hut, and working amongst the poor. This was, I thought, God's highest calling on my life. And when the dream for that life seemingly evaporated, I found myself neck deep in bank debt and people problems, courtesy of a small but fast growing start-up physio practice in the suburbs.

Michael was right; all I wanted to do was *run*.

He predicted that morning that I would return from my Australian odyssey, and God would most likely keep me at Back In Motion for another 20 years. Not because He cared so much about a network of physiotherapy practices, but because God cared so much about *me*.

Michael drew from the evidence in his own life story to illustrate that God wouldn't forfeit the chance to use the trials of business to shape my character, refine my mission, impart humility, and prove His unwavering faithfulness. And when the time was right, and my preparation was complete, He might release me from Back In Motion for something new He had prepared.

I deeply regret not being more attentive to Michael that day given the unsettling accuracy of his words. As I pen these closing paragraphs, I find myself perched at a vantage point within my own narrative, now able to behold something of the expansive canvas upon which God has sketched His pencil strokes. And as I reflect, a bittersweet smile escapes across my lips – a faint wish to have approached many things differently if I had appreciated God's masterplan, yet an overwhelming sense of gratitude for His divine guidance, even when my understanding fell short.

In the three years since completing Project Locomotive, Paulina and I have deployed a large portion of our earnings to establish a charitable trust to support those who are less fortunate, contributing to our lifelong calling. We also established a diverse array of investments to generate a lasting, reliable income that releases me to give myself fully to the new endeavours God directs us in, without having to worry about financial means. And I was appointed chairman of Halftime Australia, the organisation that was birthed by Bob Buford in America after writing his New York Times bestseller. Driven by the profound guidance I received from his book, shaping many of my personal transitions amid the pivotal phases of family and business, my aspiration is to pay it forward, creating transformative moments for others seeking purpose and significance.

And, of course, I have spent many idle days in the aftermath of Back In Motion, composing this book – in part, a cathartic exercise to distil and reflect on the learnings I hope to take into the next season of my life and, in part, to share the experience with you. Some will think I have over-spiritualised my journey; those closest to me know that I've understated it.

Working the averages, I'm midway through life – enjoying a drink break in the metaphorical "locker-room" at halftime. As I contemplate who I want to still become and how I want to play the game in the second innings, it's obvious I still have much to learn.

One thing I know for certain: I carry within me the seed of the Divine. When trials and challenges seek to bury me, rather than suffocating under the dirt, that seed can instead be planted for God's higher purposes. He is infinitely capable of bringing forth abundant fruit from any of my hardships. As Joseph recounts in the first book of the Bible, after being sold into slavery by his brothers and rising to become Prime Minister of Egypt, "You intended to harm me, but God intended it for my good" (Genesis 50:20 NKJV).

Yale professor Carlos Eire frequently cites with a vivid illustration: if the entirety of Earth's history was compressed into a single day, humans would emerge just 0.7 seconds before midnight. It's a late arrival for a remarkably brief moment – less than the snap of a finger or the sigh of your breath. Whether or not you agree with Eire's calculations, our lives are almost too fleeting to quantify, often symbolised merely by an iconic dash between the dates of our birth and passing on forgotten tombstones.

Despite my obvious brevity in this life, I am compelled to find meaning within it. Brene Brown postulates, "When you have the courage to walk into your story and own it, you get to write the ending. And when you don't own your stories of failure, setbacks, and hurt – they own you."

This is *my* story – a collection of triumphs and tragedies that, at times, I wish belonged to someone else. Yet, like a puff of smoke, or wisp of cold air on a solemn morning, my days are here and gone in a moment, shaping the rest of my eternity.

I wonder about *your* story. Even if I never read it in the pages of a book, know that your life is precious and significant. Live each day with the conviction that it matters, and may God unveil to you some of the greatest secrets and truths about His life and yours – those in the past, and especially about that which is yet to come.

Apostle Paul:

"I pray that our God will make you fit for what he's called you to be, pray that he'll fill your good ideas and acts of faith with his own energy so that it all amounts to something. If your life honours the name of Jesus, he will honour you."

2 Thessalonians 1:11-12

FROM WHERE I SIT

Paulina's perspective

*U*NLIKELY IS PREDOMINANTLY Jason's story and, though as his partner in life I helped sharpen his memories in the writing of the book, you have read *his* perspective in the preceding pages. After considering the idea to co-author this work with him, we eventually decided I would simply add this short contribution at the tail end. My chapter is another perspective, a different voice in the narrative, that aims to give a brief insight into the lessons I have had to learn and am still learning. We expect this book will serve as the chronicle to close a chapter in our lives together, and so it feels a fitting gesture that I would at least share in it with a few thoughts from my own desk. In addition, I hope these few pages will reinforce that none of us do life alone and that we need to be intentional to welcome different opinions in the making of ideas and big decisions.

My early years began in beautiful, warm, and vibrant Brazil where I was born to two Chilean parents who bravely chose to immigrate to Australia when I was ten years of age. Jason and my paths first crossed at primary school, but at that point we could never have predicted the adventures that awaited us, and the challenges God would guide us through.

We married in January 1998, and although Jason may have had the dormant entrepreneurial tendencies and an essential degree in physiotherapy to kick start our business, I have always shared the highs and lows of growing it with him from the very beginning.

As common to many business owners, my roles were many and varied. I worked *more than* full-time as the practice manager in the early years, then part time or a silent partner while raising our four children. Unsurprisingly, though, I was very much the *un*silent partner most of the times in between, given I was the original "seed funder", using my early nursing salary to prop up the initial investments into our money-hungry start-up. Jason was the face and driver of the business, and I became the support both behind and on the scene.

From cleaner to receptionist, accounts payable to receivable, events manager to board member, and the original author of our first policies and procedural manual that was the precursor for our franchise system, I've experienced a lot firsthand, and witnessed even more. Below is a collection of some of my learnings during this period of my life.

Conviction and Timing need to align

In the final year of Jason's physiotherapy degree, he approached me ecstatically with a job offer he didn't think he could turn down: an opportunity to join the staff at our local church as their Youth Pastor. My heart was full of questions: *How was this going to work? Will you finish your degree first? Why can't the opportunity be deferred for six months? What about our dream to become medical missionaries?*

Jason has always been someone who seeks wisdom and advice on major decisions, and he was getting mixed messages and feeling pressure from every side. I needed to tread carefully, as we were only engaged at the time, but I could see Jason was torn between the views of his fiancée and the pressure from church leaders to take on this role. Supposedly, the position needed to be filled immediately. The senior leaders of the church pursued Jason relentlessly, which only compelled me to raise my opposition in equal measure.

"The timing seems wrong", I asserted. "I can't imagine God would open the doors for you to get into Physiotherapy and then take you to within six months of completing the course only for you to pull out."

As an inexperienced 19-year-old, it was difficult to be certain of my conviction, but at the same time I knew God's voice. I had experienced his directional leading previously in my life, and the timing didn't feel right. In hindsight, it was the first of many occasions where I would need to stand up for what was best for us.

Needless to say, Jason passed on the role, graduated from university, and after a few twists and turns went on to build a small hobby business called Back In Motion. I am forever grateful that Jason invited and valued my insights in that decision, which proved to be the early foundations for an honest and true partnership in both marriage and business.

Risk profiles shift in seasons

A year into our marriage, returning home from a gruelling 12-hour shift in the ICU, I found Jason looking forlorn at the kitchen table.

"I need to tell you something", he warily cautioned.

As a young bride it's hard for your mind not to escalate into some frightening directions. I put my car keys and bag down gently on the floor, and nervously sat at the table in a chair across from him.

Jason continued with a broken voice, "I walked out of my job today. I cannot keep working at that physiotherapy practice after what I have seen and heard. I will start looking for other work, and hopefully get a new job quickly. I know we have a mortgage, bills to pay…" His voice trailed off as the strain overwhelmed him.

"Oh, we will get through this", I immediately consoled him, somewhat relieved at the true nature of why he was looking so forlorn. "We will be fine. I have work, and I'm sure you will find something else. You made the right decision given the circumstances."

As a child I had seen hard times growing up, and whilst my family were well-to-do in Brazil, upon arriving in Australia my father's professional qualification was not initially recognised. My parents had to find creative ways to earn money to feed a young family of three kids. I had known seasons where I lived with plenty, and other times, with very little – and both experiences gave me confidence that we would find a way through our current challenge. It was these extremes of my childhood which prepared me for learning how to adapt, take risks, and step outside my comfort zone in the uncertainty.

I encouraged Jason, "Maybe, this is the time you give more effort to treating patients at home, as it will at least bring in some money until we discover what opportunities God has for us next." My father had always talked about the uncapped earning potential if we went into our own business. After weeks of indecision and some fretful push-back, Jason eventually took the first small steps in our garage start-up.

It's fascinating to me looking back from the vantage point of today, how much Jason and my risk profiles changed over time. Representing something of traversing curves, I started optimistic, hopeful, and willing to "bet the farm", while Jason was extremely conservative and risk averse in most of our decisions. Over time, as he grew in knowledge, confidence, and experience, Jason began to think bigger, take larger risks, believe in the "impossible", and trust God for miracles… and I grew somewhat more conservative to counter-balance the extremes in our partnership.

It was in this tension of being true to who we were meant to be, as we shifted in and out of different seasons, that we found a helpful and productive balance.

Every Lamborghini needs a good set of brakes

Jason quickly became the visionary; the serial entrepreneur; the big dreamer of both family and business. Back In Motion was growing exponentially and his emerging team did well to keep up with the speed, heights, and workload he strived for. They were great supporters, working together to make Jason's ideas and business opportunities a reality.

Everywhere Jason turned, people cheered him on. They loved his ambition, courage, and passion; wanted him on their advisory boards, sought his investment in their business startups, asked him to mentor them, and requested him to speak at their next conference, event, or function. The opportunities within the business and church world multiplied beyond the time available for one human being – quite apart from the demands of being a CEO of his own enterprise, leading a charitable organisation, and eventually becoming father to our four children.

The breakneck pace was unsustainable.

Most car enthusiasts (or motorcycle fanatics – as is the case for Jason) boast the power and capacity of their engines, and how quickly they hit top speeds of 100 kilometres per hour. All impressive specs (*I'm sure!*) but these attributes of the vehicles must be balanced with an equally strong and impressive braking system. Of course, the brakes are never revelled in or celebrated, but are essential nonetheless to help these machines come to a safe stop.

Over our 25 years of marriage, I have had the unenviable job of being those "brakes" at times. After seeing Jason fall ill in the early days from exhaustion, displaying severe symptoms of stress, and generally living perpetually sleep deprived, it was perplexing and frustrating that very little deterred him from saying "Yes" to the next opportunity. His body continually broke down under the load of his commitments and it seemingly became my unofficial, unpaid, and unpleasant role to help him set reasonable limits on himself – for his own protection and ours, as a family.

I am grateful for all the "No's" Jason reluctantly gave over the two decades - not because the opportunities in and of themselves were bad, or even because I didn't recognise or celebrate Jason's capabilities and gifts, but because it meant that he could say "Yes" more often to the things that really mattered. As a result, he was able to be more present for our kids, in our marriage, and with our family. He had more energy to be a leader to our executive team who were sacrificing so much for our shared vision. He created margin to have headspace and time to be available to our franchisees – in life, and not just business. It gave him more time and capacity to deal with the unplanned opportunities and unexpected problems that inevitably arose, without it pushing him (and us) into dangerous overload both in time and finances. By selectively agreeing to speak at less events, he could arrive having prepared, prayed, and believed God had something specific for him to share for that personal audience. When the opportunities to rest with family on holiday eventually came around, it was wonderful to know that he was not sick or distracted and could be at his best. It's clear to me that Jason's willingness to curtail some of his commitments created enough space and capacity, through God's enablement, to make it to the end of his Back In Motion season without burning out.

We learned together that new opportunities come around often, and that by saying "No" to the *less* important things reserved our "Yes" for the *more* important ones. Though I burned through some brake pads over the years – sometimes applying the pedal too early or too hard – with each year that passed, Jason and I found more alignment and equilibrium.

My encouragement to others in this familiar challenge is to remember effective braking allows safe drifting through the turns.

Wisdom is a path, not a door.

In a world where we have so much information at our fingertips, it is often common to mistake knowledge for wisdom. One does not equate to the other – the former being a simple understanding of information, and the latter being the confidence to make insightful judgements with this information in different situations.

Listening to the teachings of the late Timothy Keller – an American theologian and cultural commentator - it struck me that wisdom is not a simple *door* we pass through during a moment in time but rather a *pathway*, something occurring through the passage of time which we must journey along. Wisdom often bubbles up and out of the steady, repeated, mundane actions that are done daily over a lifetime through the habitual practices that bring life, hope, and insights from the many experiences that make up our story.

If you were expecting to have all the answers with "ready-to-go" wisdom after reading *Unlikely*, I am sorry to disappoint, but there are no shortcuts to this coveted attribute. Our fleeting streaks of wisdom came through repeated life experiences, knowing God and His love for us, and discovering our shortcomings through ruthless self-examination and reflection. I realised achieving wisdom was not a five-step technique, but a lifetime of continuous learning and change.

The greatest gift our business has given me is the opportunity to obtain wisdom that could not have come from any other experience. I could not have discovered this through reading books, counselling, living vicariously through another's experiences, or even the contemplation of the many "what if" scenarios that sometimes fill our minds, albeit these are all helpful. There is no substitute for first-hand experience – the wins and losses, the disappointments and triumphs, the countless daily decisions thrust upon us – as from every moment sprouts the seed of a lesson or heart-felt inspiration that makes us better and stronger next time.

Thank you Back In Motion for patiently setting me down the path of wisdom, however much I resisted at times in being the eager follower. And of course, with so much more to learn, I accept it's the journey that never ends.

Slow to RSVP, but not late for the party

When Project Locomotive – the proposed sale of Back In Motion – was first raised at the kitchen table (long before it made it to the boardroom table!), I was at first sceptical and nervous. The upfront financial investment and associated relational risks with our key people were massive, offering no certainty of any payoff. The probability of success was infinitesimally small and the pathway between the starting line and eventual transaction fraught with many complex obstacles. To expect we could get the right price for all, achieve agreement with more than 70 individual franchisees, and overcome all the obstacles to finalise the sale, required a faith beyond me. The mountain appeared unscalable and insurmountable, and I feared Jason would be found listless in the death zone if we didn't reach the summit.

Reasonable thoughts plagued me: *What if we get near to the finish line and at the last moment the sale falls through? How will I encourage*

Jason to keep working as CEO, when he has already "resigned" in his heart? Is God really behind this or are we trying to force a premature exit? Thankfully, as I sat through the board deliberations and witnessed each of our advisors slowly grow more comfortable with the shape of the deal and the various strategies to mitigate risks, it was clear God's hand was at work. The quantum of the first unsolicited offers was initially encouraging, but the avalanche of formal proposals that followed convinced me a sale was imminent.

On the other side of the 18-month ordeal, I am in awe of the timing and provision of a loving God who seems to have planned our exit from the beginning, just as I am grateful to the many people who helped Jason pull off the deal of his career – our board members, NSO team, legal and tax advisors, PwC partners, and the people who prayed for us. When the intense negotiations were finally concluded, I remember with such fondness and relief the anti-climax of being alone in our home office late on a Friday night, courtesy of the COVID-19 lockdown. We sat in our familiar chairs and looked at each other in disbelief, relief, and gratitude before turning to the kids to share the news. As pandemic restrictions lifted, it was equally wonderful to then celebrate with our loved ones and key advisors, creating moments that I hold dear in my heart - then, now, and always.

Nearly three years on, I am still deeply thankful. There are no regrets and I feel honoured to have been part of something that grew beyond our wildest imagination. I give all the glory to God for His faithfulness. I also recognise with privilege and blessing comes enormous responsibility, and we carry that forward as we begin to explore how we can make a significant difference for the purposes of God in our next steps.

Deep gratitude

It's hard to believe Back In Motion isn't a present part of our life now; figuratively speaking, no longer occupying a seat at our kitchen table every dinnertime. As Jason has written, in some ways Back in Motion was like our "first child", and this precious life has demanded from us a lot of energy, devotion, and discipline. It has birthed many surprising joys, scattered learnings, incredible experiences, and also filled many buckets full with tears. At different times, it has brought us to our feet in applause, and conversely, to our knees in prayer.

Jason led our family on this journey, and I chose to follow and contribute, tentatively giving up my nursing career because I saw glimpses of potential. He was relentless, diligent, and at times, stubborn in the pursuit of countless goals. I have always known him to be hard working, loving, one who seeks fairness for all, and who strives to be ethical in his business dealings. Even now I can see that many of his ideas have revolutionised aspects of the profession, and whilst I know this didn't come easily, the changes are having impact on the generations of physiotherapists that follow. Above all, he is my amazing friend and husband; I could not imagine being on this journey with anyone else.

I also want to honour our children who grew up always knowing Back In Motion as the unseen, unheard, *other member* of our family – in the car, in the kitchen, late at night, early in the morning. They have grown with us through the joy and sorrow, the highs and lows, forever marvelling at what God has been doing in and through our family. They have paid a high price for the privilege of a front row seat in this adventure, observing our failures and successes, but also equally experiencing first-hand the power of God and His miracles in ordinary lives such as our own. Jason and I always sought the delicate balance of sharing "just the right amount" with them about the business story, hoping the richness would deposit wisdom in them without too much scarring, preparing them in ways for the future we can never fully know.

To our close family and friends who stood by us along the way, thank you for your prayers, encouragement, watching over our kids when we travelled, inviting us for a meal when we didn't look like we were coping, and for being beautiful distractions when it was clear we needed escape from the pressures and burdens.

To our personal and business mentors, words fail us in showing appreciation for investing into two young "green, altruistic, and ambitious" kids who had no idea what they were doing but you saw enough potential to generously give your wisdom, time, love, and care.

To our suppliers who took chances in doing business with our younger selves, thank you for being patient with all our questions, doubts, and indecision - and for being flexible when we tried to do things unconventionally.

And of course, to all our staff, the thousands over 22 years, each individual (sorry we can't list you by name) who took a chance to work for a "family business" without any certainty. We are grateful you supported our vision, added to the strategy, and helped innovate and refine our model and services so we could provide for our clients in ways nobody had succeeded in yet. As a team, we overcame the objection that physiotherapy services could not be franchised and have spearheaded change in the profession for the better.

And finally, to our patients and clients - some of whom became friends - and the beautiful communities which welcomed us: Thank you for your loyalty, personal referrals, and for sticking with your rehabilitation exercises even when they were boring - your health is our reward. We received many thoughtful gifts from you over the years, learned about your lives and personal stories, enjoyed your family recipes, and were encouraged by the heart-felt cards and notes that spurred us on.

There is so much more I could write, but in conclusion, the "crazy" I experienced in this *unlikely* story has been worth it. From the beginning, God prepared Jason and I through our unique life experiences for the long and unexpected journey ahead. We always wanted to be medical missionaries – instead, this first half of our lives has been consumed with Back In Motion. It wasn't what we dreamed but it was beautiful, nonetheless. As we learned to surrender and give room for God to shape and guide our lives, it resulted in something totally different that only He could have envisaged. With that adventure now complete, I am hopeful for the new ones that await.

ACKNOWLEDGEMENTS
a sincere thank you

THIS BOOK BEGAN as a labour of love to give our children an inside perspective on the journey they missed while growing up. Paulina encouraged me: "Write the Back In Motion story so they could appreciate the early context for our life". What started as journal entries and short stories, eventually become over 1,000 pages of disconnected memories, reflections, and learnings. It was around this time it became apparent that, whilst the kids will be given the un-redacted version, a sanitised edition may be suitable for a wider audience. My commitment to a third book was born.

As I have acknowledged previously, writing books is generally fun, publishing them is not! In this case, writing the book was the more difficult part. In fact, at times, reliving some of the hardships in explicit detail was more traumatic than I recall going through them the first time. Perhaps the rush of adrenaline sustained me back then, while the intense focus on every experience stung more deeply on review.

The research for this book was extensive, taking nearly three years to compile. I have relied upon photo archives, published press releases, newspaper cuttings, magazine articles, 22 years of electronic files and stored emails, franchise agreements, court transcripts, legal contracts, conference programs, annual reports, tax returns, our family Christmas stars (on which we write the key events of every year), personal journals, and even notes I took in the margin of my Bible.

I reached out to past employees and franchisees, inviting them to share important milestones and memorable moments, or to simply fact-check the ones I remembered involving them. To this end, I'm grateful to Anthony Belcher, John Contreras, Natalie Evans, Vida Foo, Bao Hoang, Simon Holt, Dan Martin, Craig Pritchard, Beth Pocklington, Adrian Persi, Adrian Quinn, Jonathan Salib, Aman Singh, and Ann Smith.

And through all of this, Paulina sat beside me. This book is as much her story as it's mine. It's told from my perspective because she was not inclined to write an opus, but we lived through every experience together. She rarely is given the credit and accolade for what we have accomplished, because I was the front man. But, as they say, behind every half-decent man is an amazing woman. This is true over and again in our marriage. Paulina is the strength, endurance, compassion, and inspiration for so much of what we achieved. She has a truly noble heart that challenges me to think carefully about every decision. I'm grateful for her love and friendship, and am so glad we committed our lives to each other over 26 years ago.

I'm also thankful for Paulina's patience to work through each chapter in detail, one experience at a time. Almost a therapeutic exercise, it triggered lots of discussion, mutual reflection, and personal learning for us both. It seems that long after Back In Motion was sold, it is the business that "keeps on giving" – fodder from which we draw countless life lessons that continue to convict and shape our character every day, accepting we are still a work-in-progress.

And a heartfelt hug to our three boys - Lachlan, Sebastian, Morgan – as you are, and will always be, Mum and my greatest accomplishments.

To my parents and sister, who gave me an incredible start in life, and who continue to shower their love and support for my family, I am forever grateful and love you deeply. And to Paulina's family, who have likewise cheered us on when we were winning and consoled us in defeat, we love you fully.

I feel eternally indebted to Michael Magyar and David McCracken for having mentored me all my adult life. They have never given up on me when I slowed down, resisted, or pretended not to hear them. They have been a steadfast, unwavering source of love, encouragement, direction, counsel, and friendship, in both the fun and difficult times. And they have always pointed me back to the Bible as the ultimate source of truth.

To the thousands of physiotherapists and support team who invested themselves throughout the two decades of Back In Motion, may your expertise, loyalty, and commitment be rewarded. Thank you for co-creating the most loved and trusted brand in our industry – a legacy you carry forward in your careers.

Special thanks to Kristy Echeverria, Marion Magyar, Michael Magyar, Dan Martin, and Ben Stickland for being my "test dummies" – or, as the industry says, *Advanced Readers* – trawling through my rough manuscript before editors even set eyes on the draft. Their feedback and input were invaluable in shaping what you hold in your hands today.

And to Lachlan Smith especially, who literally marked up every comma, capital letter, and parenthesis on a line-by-line basis, giving

ACKNOWLEDGEMENTS

meaningful comments to how the text could be improved for everyday readers. While incredibly impressed at his command of written prose, I was especially impacted by his insights where he notated questions and commentary about what was happening in my inner world during various events, sensitive to learn what God might have been saying to me in the quiet and chaotic moments. (And for the record Lachs: I've always considered you our *real* first born, not Back In Motion.)

And lawyer Warren Scott – I'm so grateful for your willingness to proofread the risky chapters, ensuring I didn't over-disclose sensitive information or cross any legal lines. I wanted to tell the truth of my story as honestly as possible, without causing anybody else pain or embarrassment.

And then there is Sue Publicover - something of a word surrogate, author coach, and content specialist living in Florida, USA. She is my book whisperer. Having worked with Sue on another project, she was the first professional I contacted with my draft manuscript, knowing the magic of her pen in being able to shape the flow and length of each chapter to be more reader friendly. Thanks Sue for masking your gasp when my first roughout of the book was over 350,000 words and it appeared my spell-check was broken. And especially for helping me decongest the cast of characters, distilling the 243 names I originally included to just the few dozen necessary.

Naturally, the book would never have completed if it wasn't for the talented team of professionals at Arkhouse Publishing. Thank you to all your editors, proofreaders, typesetters, graphic designers, printing, and distribution teams. A special acknowledgement to Graham Pockett (a fellow motorcycle enthusiast) for doing the final read through – devouring the manuscript in record time – and reminding me about the rules of Grade 3 English grammar that I had apparently neglected. And to my dear friend Donna Olney, for your meticulous review after-the-fact, picking up the countless errors that still slipped through the net - thank for your eagle eyes and close attention to detail. You all make me look better than I really am.

All credit to Michelle Wallace from Wallace Creative for the original cover designs; and thank you for the years of creative genius you invested at Back In Motion.

May everything good I do bring honour to God, and for all my inevitable and countless shortcomings that clearly don't, may God's name still be praised because He loves me (and you!) the same regardless.

other titles

Available in paperback, eBook, and audio at jasontsmith.com.au

 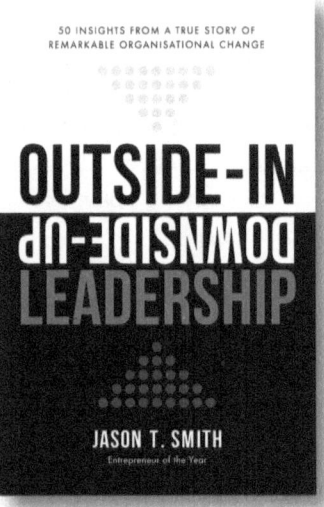

Follow Jason on social media

Clockwise from top left: Just hanging around in the kindergarten playground, wondering what my life would become (1979);

Me and my big sister. Looking at my scowl, I was obviously unhappy to be forced to hold her hand for the three minutes it took it take the photo (1981);

Terry (Dad), Ann (Mum), Leanne (sister) and me – posing as though we lived in Downtown Abbey. Nevertheless, a great start in life (1983).

Top: The "chickmobile" – my 1977 canary yellow Toyota Corolla - proving Paulina never loved me for my car! It did pay my way to my first mission trip to Cambodia, thanks to a rear end collision (1993);

Left: Working in Cambodia on the Princess Diana Limb Project, helping to rehabilitate Vithu – an amputee land mine victim (1997).

Left: Married young, at 22 and 21 years of age respectively, with no regrets and "no back doors". I am not allowed to repeat what Paulina whispered in that moment – Shhhh! (1998);

Below: The original carport practice, showcasing the bile-green gridiron logo "borrowed" from clipart that was never relatable to an Australian audience (1999).

Paulina and "Ollie" – our fully laden campervan enroute up the east coast of Australia, as I searched for purpose and meaning (2001).

Our inaugural Back In Motion team, excited to launch our first purpose-built practice in a burnt out pizza shop at Wantirna South (Jason far left, Paulina middle front, 2003).

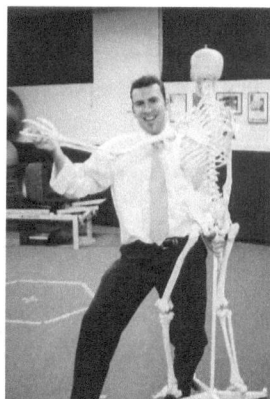

Doing the tango in our rehab studio with Max – my gutless physio aide (2004);

A debut cover model – I was the feature story of the APA magazine, *InMotion*, putting our franchise opportunity on the map for the first time (2007).

Our first Director's Conference - breaking a timber board in front of our franchisees with a hesitant karate chop (2008).

Despite still barely knowing how to wield a power tool, as part of an SOS outreach team, I managed to help renovate some dongas in outback NT to help with the housing shortages common to many indigenous communities (Jason right, 2010).

Paulina and I cut the ribbon on the opening of our third Network Support Office (NSO), with Lachlan (far right) and Sebastian (middle) looking on, wondering where we got such a big pair of scissors (2010).

Left: Cuddling some irresistible Indigenous children in the homelands of North East Arnhem, along with a three-week-old saltwater crocodile one of them had daringly stolen from the mother's nest (2011).

Below: Members of the NSO in full costume at our 4th Director's Conference – themed Valiance! (Jason left as Sparticus, 2011).

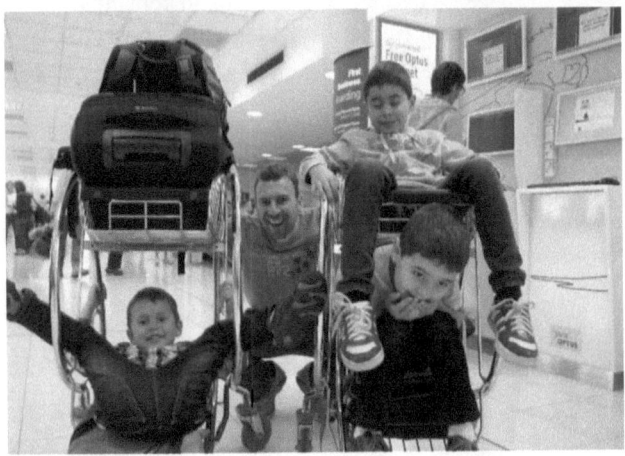

From top: Having a ball with some promo shots for the launch of my first book, *Get Yourself Back In Motion* (2012);

Disembarking in South America, I was overdue for a holiday. These three boys were also exhausted after the long-haul flight. (Morgan left, Jason middle, Lachlan above right, Sebastian below right, 2012);

The two wise men, John (left) and Michael (right) – our inaugural advisory board members posing at the awards dinner of our 5th Director's Conference (2012).

Left: Definitely a face for radio – being interviewed in the studio for one of many promotional programs (2012).

One of my media appearances, this being the Channel 10 breakfast show in Sydney (2012).

Clockwise from top left: Awarded by the publisher a box framing of my first book, *Get Yourself Back In Motion* – making the bestseller's list (2013);

Winners are grinners at the EY Entrepreneur of the Year awards ceremony in Sydney (2013);

Celebrating with our 25th and second-longest serving Australian Prime Minister, John Howard (2014).

Clockwise from top left: Learning to fish with Indigenous youth – eating healthy, living off the land and sea on a weekend walk-about with the SOS Health Foundation (2015);

Always up for an adventure, this time racing V8 supercars against other franchisor CEOs at Calder Raceway for a charity event (2016);

Speaking at one of many industry keynote events – often just telling my story and, with it, sharing unconventional clinical and commercial principles that not everyone could accept (2017).

Above: Paulina loved a formal family photo every two years, marking time as we watched our children grow (Left to right - Lachlan, Jason, Sebastian above, Morgan below, Paulina, 2017, Seedthree Photography);

Below: We flew physiotherapists and other health professionals into more than 30 homeland communities through northeastern Arnhem Land in the NT in partnership with MAF (2017).

Clockwise from top: The NSO bullpen –where all the action happened and magic was created (although apparently not that day!) (2017, Lavina Harte Photography);

Interviewed for QANTAS radio by Alan Kohler – economist and ABC business journalist – after my second book, *Outside In Downside Up Leadership* (2018);

Contemplating a contest of ideas with the team in our breakout room at the NSO (2017, Lavina Harte Photography).

Clockwise from top left: The bat-bike: Jason's beloved Harley Davidson Night Rod Special, nick-named 'el torito' (Little Bull) (2018, Lavina Harte Photography).

Taking a helicopter transfer to infamous Palm Island – where the SOS Health Foundation operated a permanent probono practice on the disused penal settlement, amongst the beautiful Bwgcolman people (2018);

Franchisees dressed in Gatsby theme for our 1920s annual awards dinner in Torquay, Victoria (Jason middle front, 2018).

Clockwise from top: After returning to the top job at Back In Motion in 2019, I was named second top Franchise CEO in Australia (2019);

Giving a speech at our 20-year birthday celebrations in the Bali Hilton, describing just how close we came to losing everything along the way (2020);

Whilst we didn't know it at the time, the final occasion (courtesy of COVID-19) all our franchisees celebrated together in person for a Gala Ball – our 12th Director's Conference in Bali (2020);

Standing on the beach at Qualia, Hamilton Island, celebrating the first $2m practice courtesy of Taskforce 2/20 (2019).

Clockwise from top: Packing down my office, getting ready for sale (2021, Lavina Harte Photography);

Two of our hard-working support team working the phones during the COVID-19 pandemic (2020);

Coffee anyone? I was always up for a marketing gimmick or branding opportunity (2020);

Our family at the time of the book going to print (From left to right, Lachlan, Jason, Sebastian, Paulina, Morgan, 2024, Seedthree Photography).

www.ingramcontent.com/pod-product-compliance
Lightning Source LLC
Chambersburg PA
CBHW030345240426
43661CB00052B/1752